to be even by a good life, or a series of good lives;
Nirvana, that is the cessation of thought, feeling & action,
through the absorption of personality into the impersonality of the
Universe — which is exactly what seems to happen at
the death of the individual, observer & subject of science.

Is why wish to escape from the fact of death
as we watch it happen, in the lives of the trees, the seasons,
& men into oblivion? What stands between us & this
simple & realistic outlook on death is the intolerable
egotism of the human being. Why should you wish to live for
ever? Perhaps it is the pain by usually accompanies
death, or the humiliation of one's ? Can then not anaesthetize
a narcotics, let offer an easy, even an agreeable
way out of life? One of the pleasantest sensations in
going to sleep: a sensation which is so agreeable
that it leads to the use of narcotics even when there is
entirely unpleasant — waking hours
to health. Our social aim should be to improve so
so as to bring about a fuller & creative
for all men, through serving their fellows & being
served by them, leisure to develop
individual tastes & new faculties. When decay of
body & mental health make this no longer
possible, why not a painless dissolution, leaving
happy memories in the minds of those whom you
have loved, the one fate to be avoided, and if
& those who have loved you?

The Diary
of
BEATRICE WEBB

Volume Four
1924–1943

"The Wheel of Life"

The Diary
of
BEATRICE WEBB

Volume Four

1924–1943

"The Wheel of Life"

Edited by
Norman and Jeanne MacKenzie

THE BELKNAP PRESS OF
HARVARD UNIVERSITY PRESS
CAMBRIDGE, MASSACHUSETTS
1985

Library of Congress Cataloging in Publication Data

Webb, Beatrice Potter, 1858–1943.
  "The wheel of life," 1924–1943.

  (The Diary of Beatrice Webb; v. 4)
  Bibliography: p.
  Includes index.
  1. Webb, Beatrice Potter, 1858–1943. 2. Socialists – Great Britain –
Biography. I. MacKenzie, Norman Ian. II. MacKenzie, Jeanne. III. Title.
IV. Series: Webb, Beatrice Potter, 1858–1943. Diary of Beatrice Webb;
v. 4.
HX244.7.W42A33   1982 vol. 4   335'.14'0924 [B]   85-7681
ISBN 0-674-20286-4

Contents

v

List of Illustrations

(Acknowledgements and thanks are due to the individuals
and institutions listed below)

Cover

Beatrice Webb 1941 (Radio Times Hulton Picture Library)
Sidney Webb date unknown (Nicholas Meinertzhagen)
Virginia Woolf, portrait by Lenare, 1926
Leon Trotsky as Commissar for War, 1924 (Radio Times Hulton
    Picture Library)
Ramsay MacDonald date unknown (Labour Party Photograph
    Library)

Between pages 240 and 241

The Labour Cabinet 1923 (Mansell Collection)
National Government 1931 (Labour Party Photograph Library)
Sidney Webb, Lord Passfield 1930 (Nicholas Meinertzhagen)
Kingsley Martin 1941 (Radio Times Hulton Picture Library)
Harold Laski 1927 (London School of Economics)
William Beveridge and Jessie Mair c. 1940 (London School of
    Economics)
Sir Stafford Cripps 1939 (Radio Times Hulton Picture Library)
Sir Oswald and Lady Mosley 1922 (Radio Times Hulton Picture
    Library)
Maynard Keynes and Lydia Lopokova 1945 (Radio Times Hulton
    Picture Library)
Philip and Ethel Snowden 1929 (Labour Party Photograph
    Library)

Lawrencina Heywor
1821–188

Catherine – Leonard
1847–1929   Courtney
            1832–1918

Georgina – Daniel
1850–1914   Meinertzhagen
          1842–1910

Blan
1851–1

Lawrencina – Robert Holt
1845–1906   1832–1908

Daniel
1875–1898

William
b.1878

Richard   – Eliza Wells
1868–1941   1868–1951

Barbara   – Bernard Drake
(Bardie)   n.d.
1876–1963

Blanche
(Julia)
1879–19

Catherine   – William
1871–1952   Dampier-Whetham
           1867–1952

Richard   – Annie Jackson
1878–1967   n.d.

Standish
1881–19

Robert   – Alice Graves
1872–1952   n.d.

Margaret   – George Booth
1880–1959   n.d.

Richard
1882–19

Elizabeth   – Edward Russell
(Betty)   d.1917
1875–1947

Frederick   – Florence
1881–1962   Maxwell Barnes
            n.d.

Rosie
1885–19

Philip   – Phyllis Palmer
1876–1958   n.d.

Lawrencina – Hubert
1883–1976   Warre-Cornish
            n.d.

Henry
b.1887

Edward   – Christabel
1878–1955   de Vere Allen
            n.d.

Katherine   – Robert Mayor
Beatrice   1869–1947
(Bobo)
1885–1977

Mary   – John Russell
(Molly)   d.1958
1880–1955

Louis   – Gwynedd
1887–1941   Llewellyn
            n.d.

Lawrence   – Evelyn Jacks
1882–1961   d.1978

Mary   – Alexander
1889–1943   Wollaston
            1875–1930

Georgina   – Ralph Neale
1890–1948   n.d

Mary – Arthur Playne
1849–1923   1845–1923

William   – Manuella
1870–1935   Meinertzhagen
            1871–1932

Richard Potter
1817–1892

William Cripps
1850–1923

Beatrice – Sidney Webb
1858–1943   1859–1947

Vera Pring
n.d.

Thomas Faulder
n.d.

Margaret – Henry Hobhouse
1854–1921 | 1854–1937

Rosalind – (1) Arthur
1865–1949 | Dyson Williams
1859–1896

Stephen – Rosa Waugh
1881–1964   1891–1970

Noel
1889–1918

Mary Ashley
n.d.

Rachel – Felix Clay
1883–1981   1871–1941

Beatrice Hart
n.d.

Eleanor
1884–1956

– (2) George
Dobbs
1869–1946

Arthur – Konradin
1886–1965   Huth Jackson
1896–1964

Patrick – Muriel Ware
1900–1981   n.d

Hilda Pring
n.d.

Esther
1891–1893

Leonard – Elaine
1901–1942   Cantaloube
n.d.

John – Catherine
1893–1961   Brown
n.d.

Kathleen – Malcolm
(Kitty)   Muggeridge
b.1903   b.1903

Paul
1894–1918

Richard – Phyllis Leon
1905–1980   n.d.

William – Ruth Dobbs
b.1906   n.d.

Theresa – Charles
1852–1893 | Alfred Cripps
1852–1941

Seddon
1882–1977

Ruth – Alfred Egerton
1884–1978   1886–1959

Frederick – Violet Nelson
1885–1977   n.d.

Leonard – Miriam Joyce
1887–1959   1892–1960

Stafford – Isobel
1889–1952   Swithenbank
1891–1979

Introduction

The End of a Pilgrimage

THIS IS the last of four volumes based on Beatrice Webb's manuscript diary, which she began in 1873 and wrote regularly until her death in 1943. In the course of those seventy years she lived through great changes, played some part in making them, and in the process changed herself from the handsome and privileged daughter of a railway promoter into the formidable reforming Mrs Webb.

The first volume described her troubled childhood and adolescence. As the last but one and least regarded of Richard Potter's nine daughters she found the mothering she craved backstairs among the servants, and there are obvious links between her early feelings of emotional deprivation and her adult sympathy for the socially deprived. There are also strong and conflicting traces of her upbringing in her later desire for command over persons and events. 'As life unfolded itself,' she wrote in *My Apprenticeship*, 'I became aware that I belonged to a class of persons who habitually gave orders, but who seldom, if ever, executed the orders of other people.' That paradox was only one of many attempts to reconcile private impulse and public order which made Beatrice speak of her 'duplex personality' – the struggles between self-indulgence and self-sacrifice, or between her sexual passion and her dominating intellectualism; the antithesis between her instinctive mysticism and her educated idea of a positive science of society; and the dialogue, which breaks out so often in the diary, between her vigorous and essentially individualist conscience and her growing belief in the collective regulation of behaviour. But it was the combination of social compunction with the imperious instincts of the governing class that was to provide the framework of her reforming enterprises. All of them were variants on the theme of a civilizing mission which was as relevant in Darkest London as it was in Darkest Africa.

It took Beatrice several years to settle to that mission — what she called her search for a craft and a creed — for she had grown up an earnest individualist, modelling herself on Herbert Spencer's theories of social science; and in the first volume of this diary she reveals very clearly how she translated her infatuation for Joseph Chamberlain into a philanthropic vocation suitable for a working spinster. Work was the great anodyne in those years of emotional distress, and it was also the means whereby she learnt to relate to Sidney Webb during their erratic and stressful courtship. Rejecting him as a lover, for marriage initially seemed to her an act of *felo de se*, she eventually accepted him as a husband and professional partner. 'We shared the same faith and practised the same craft,' she wrote forty years afterwards, insisting that 'living according to plan is a surer basis for happy marriage than the perpetual shifting desire for self-expression.'

For all the satisfactions of her marriage, which flowered into success and happiness in the second of these volumes, Beatrice never wholly curbed that impulse to self-expression. It was only in the diary that she let the Other Self speak, truly and frankly, as if it were the voice of the passionate and imaginative Beatrice Potter who had committed psychic suicide when she denied her love for Chamberlain and married instead the kindly, clever but workaday Sidney Webb.

By now she had moved on from individualism and philanthropy to socialism. She was nominally a Fabian when she married Sidney, although she took little direct interest in the Society until 1912, when the Webbs were politically isolated and she was casting about for allies and acolytes. They were members of what Sidney called *la nouvelle couche sociale* or, in Shaw's phrase, 'intellectual proletarians' — members of the enlightened élite that Auguste Comte expected to rule society in its Positivist phase; and both of them had a puritanical distaste for the lower depths of Victorian Britain. Beatrice often railed against the gross appetites of 'the average sensual man' and cried out for moral discipline, attitudes which played some part in her later attraction to the Soviet Union. Sidney was less prone to deride the class from which his parents' gentility and his own abilities had lifted him, but he had neither sentimental illusions about the proletariat nor any desire to see it take power. By education and reforms which would improve the condition of the working classes, the experts were to engineer a new, humane and hygienic society.

The Webbs were fascinated by the machinery of government. Beatrice was particularly given to such hydraulic metaphors as 'draining the swamp of poverty'. Seeing themselves as archetypes of the new breed of experts, they founded the London School of Economics — described in the second of these volumes — to train young men and women in the social sciences. High-minded bureaucrats, naturally inclined to collectivist principles because of the trend of social evolution (what Sidney was later to call 'the inevitability of gradualness'), were the most likely and best instruments of permeation, for they would offer soundly based advice to any party politicians who might be shopping for a policy. Indeed, Beatrice and Sidney made such a cult of non-partisan expertise, so played the game of *salon* politics and lobby intrigue, that they were both accepted and criticized as wire-pullers.

Their addiction to such a role, moreover, reflected the peculiar circumstances of their partnership. Beatrice had strong political ambitions and later showed her capacities as a remarkable organizer and a far from indifferent speaker in the Poor Law campaign. In another age she would have been an effective Cabinet Minister. But as a woman she was denied a direct role in politics, and after her marriage she fell back on the ways and wiles she had learned at her father's dinner table and the country houses of his family and friends. The manipulative style of the Webbs was also a matter of temperament. While Beatrice was born and bred a member of the governing class, Sidney was born and bred in the lower middle class, by training and temperament a civil servant and happy to defer to Beatrice in all the policies of the partnership. When she diverted him from parliamentary to municipal politics, enlisted him in the trade union history she already proposed to write, and set up their partnership in reform and research, she deprived the Liberals of a talented politician and provided herself with an untiringly loyal and immensely able instrument of her will. And that arrangement worked well for a dozen years.

Beatrice's work on the Royal Commission for the reform of the Poor Law, included in the third of these volumes, was a turning-point. The Minority Report, which was largely the work of the Webbs, and the campaign against poverty which followed it, took them away from the mainstream of reform. They were dropped by the Balfours, their influential contact with the Tory Party; they were out of sympathy with the Liberals, who were making headway with their own programme of social reform; they spurned Keir Hardie's I.L.P. and had no confidence in Ramsay MacDonald as leader of the emerging Labour Party.

The war made matters worse. Beatrice was miserable, neurotically unwell and lacking any compelling interest or activity to distract her from the slaughter in France. Sidney, too, lacked a satisfying occupation, and it was only when he was drawn, almost accidentally, into Labour politics that some kind of balance returned to their lives. Towards the end of the war Sidney began to work closely with Henderson and MacDonald to draft a constitution and a policy for Labour and to plan its bid for office after the war. Although this was the kind of behind-the-scenes work which Sidney liked best it was almost inevitable that he would assume more political responsibility. In 1922, when he was elected Labour M.P. for Seaham Harbour, the Webbs for the first time were thrust into the forefront of British politics, and this volume begins with the first Labour government and Sidney as a Cabinet Minister.

Although Beatrice never really felt that the House of Commons was the right place for Sidney and she was always critical of Labour in government, she responded to the new challenge. Her health and her spirits revived and she threw herself conscientiously into her public role. There were conferences and week-end gatherings, dinners and meetings; there was the monthly letter to the women of the constituency; and Beatrice formed the Half-Circle Club for the wives of the Labour M.P.s and other Labour women in London.

The end of the second Labour government in 1931 not only changed their style of life – they gave up a London home and settled permanently at Passfield – but it brought to a head their disillusionment with capitalist democracy and their lack of confidence in the Labour Party's capacity for reform. They turned instead to Soviet Communism as a better way of organizing society and this conversion provided them with fresh intellectual energy which kept them going through the discomforts of old age, ill health and the shadows of Fascism and war. Beatrice had been searching all her life for a faith to live by – for her, this had always been a stronger motive than the practical reforms which fascinated Sidney – and the whole cycle of her opinions, from individualism through philanthropy to collectivism, showed a progression from personal to public control. She moved through a phase when persuasion and voluntary agencies seemed the answer, when co-operatives and trade unions could be the means to collective self-improvement. But she soon concluded that some form of public regulation of behaviour was necessary, and she became a collectivist in a general sense.

In the second half of her life she was always trying to match a set of moral imperatives to the realities of politics, and the process made her increasingly critical of compromises and eager for more radical change. Beatrice never had much patience with the frustrations of democracy, nor with the opportunism of politicians.

Beatrice once said jokingly that some old people fall in love with their chauffeurs while she and Sidney fell in love with the Soviet Union. But their conversion was serious. Beatrice was not blind to what Lenin called the 'infantile disorders' of Communism in a backward country with a barbarous history. She believed that these shortcomings would fade as new values and new institutions were created; and this belief made her susceptible to many things which her judgement and principles told her she ought to condemn. She saw the Communist Party in Russia (she thought little of the Comintern and the British Communists) as a latter-day incarnation of Auguste Comte's social priesthood, and Communist ideology as the 'religion of humanity' which would combine a puritan morality with the application of science to politics.

It was a long pilgrimage that Beatrice described in this intensely personal diary which provides the background to her remarkable repertoire of achievements. Yet as each phase of her life reflected the changes in the world about her, the diary takes on a much broader significance. She was one of the foremost women of a whole generation which was struggling to reconcile political freedom and social equality as Britain emerged from the constraints of the Victorian age.

All four volumes have been based on the diary originally kept in fifty-seven exercise books and later transcribed either by Beatrice or a secretary. There has been silent correction of punctuation and other minor points of style, and where entries have been cut each brief ellipsis is indicated by three dots and longer excisions by four. In the last years of her life Beatrice had time to write at length, and most of the omitted entries simply summarize her reading, current events or outdated gossip with or about acquaintances. The full diary was published in a microfiche edition in 1978 by Chadwyck-Healey, Cambridge.

The editors wish to thank John Carswell, Dick Russell and Mr and Mrs Beyger, the present owners of Passfield, as well as all those named in previous volumes who have given information and other help. They are especially grateful to Professor Robert Webb, who read the whole text with great attention to detail, and Faith Evans, who prepared it for press with meticulous care. They also express their appreciation of the unremitting encouragement of Carmen Callil and her colleagues at Virago Press.

PART I

A Nine Days' Wonder

January 1924–March 1929

Introduction to Part I

'TODAY, 23 years ago dear Grandmama died. I wonder what she would have thought of a Labour government,' King George V wrote in his diary on 22 January 1924, the day when he asked James Ramsay MacDonald (1866–1937) to form a government. The idea of a Labour government was generally greeted with apprehension and anxiety. There was consternation among the more excitable members of the old parties and incredulity in the Labour movement. Many Labour M.P.s advised MacDonald against taking office without an absolute majority but he was increasingly convinced that it would be folly to turn down such an opportunity. By refusing, Labour would lose the parliamentary advantages it had gained when it became the official opposition in 1922. And H.H. Asquith (1852–1928) expressed the state of mind of the majority of the Tory and Liberal leaders when he said: 'If a Labour government were ever to be tried it could hardly be tried under safer conditions, given that it could easily be brought down by a combined Tory and Liberal vote.'

MacDonald had the difficult task of piecing together a government from supporters without experience of office, not only lacking knowledge of its traditional social rituals but, in many cases, actively hostile to them. He first selected the hard core of trade union M.P.s who had spent some years in the House of Commons. J.R. Clynes (1869–1949), the deputy leader, was appointed Lord Privy Seal and Leader of the House. Philip Snowden (1864–1937) became Chancellor of the Exchequer. J.H. Thomas (1874–1949) became Colonial Secretary. The party's outstanding organizer, Arthur Henderson (1863–1935), who had lost his seat at the general election, was returned at a by-election in March at Burnley and became Home Secretary. The left was, for the most part, passed over with the important exception of the appointment of

John Wheatley (1869–1930), a Clydesider, as Minister of Health. MacDonald turned instead to middle-class intellectuals such as Sidney Webb who, as President of the Board of Trade, had special responsibilities for unemployment, and C.P. Trevelyan (1870–1958), a rich radical and old friend of the Webbs, who was made President of the Board of Education. MacDonald decided to look after the Foreign Office himself. One difficulty was the House of Lords, where Labour was virtually unrepresented; he was forced to rely on non-partisan members such as the former Liberal Minister R.B. Haldane (1856–1928), who became Lord Chancellor and Chairman of the Committee of Imperial Defence. Haldane recruited Lord Chelmsford (1868–1933), an ex-Viceroy of India and a lifelong Conservative who, as F.J.N. Thesiger, had been a colleague of Sidney Webb's on the L.C.C. in 1904–05. Chelmsford was appointed First Lord of the Admiralty. Sydney Olivier (1859–1943) was given a baronetcy and appointed Secretary of State for India. Beatrice's brother-in-law, Alfred Cripps (1852–1941), now Lord Parmoor, was a distinguished lawyer who had become disillusioned with his Tory colleagues during the war and had soon afterwards joined the Labour Party; he became Lord President of the Council.

Parliament met on 8 January 1924 for the first time after the election, and that evening MacDonald addressed a great demonstration at the Albert Hall to the sounds of 'The Red Flag' and 'The Marseillaise'. Those Labour supporters who believed that this set the tone for great changes in British politics were quickly disappointed. In fact throughout this short-lived government many Labour back benchers behaved like an opposition – 'as hostile as though they were not of us', said MacDonald.

The main aim of MacDonald's political strategy was to allay fears and to gain the confidence of the country. He secured some continuity by retaining the Cabinet secretariat under Maurice Hankey (1877–1963) and Thomas Jones (1870–1955), and although his critics complained that he yielded too much to the pressure of authority and tradition, MacDonald's government was accepted and its stock rose during the first months of office. Snowden brought in a popular budget; Wheatley introduced an effective housing programme; Trevelyan made sensible changes in education; and MacDonald's skilful diplomacy resolved disagreements over war reparations with the introduction of the Dawes plan. Unemployment remained a recalcitrant problem and the

Labour government produced no distinctive economic or fiscal policies to solve it; but given the difficult circumstances, they had a number of achievements to their credit and seemed to be succeeding in driving the Liberals from the middle ground.

Then things began to go wrong. By the autumn confidence was undermined by a number of incidents. One had a hint of personal scandal. The head of McVitie and Price biscuit company, an old friend of MacDonald's, provided him with a Daimler car and an income to run it. Shortly after, the philanthropic biscuit-maker had been given a baronetcy. The others were more dramatically political – part of the 'Red Scare' that finally brought the government down. Anxiety had arisen over a proposed treaty with Russia. MacDonald had announced Britain's recognition of the Soviet government in February. After difficult negotiations two treaties were agreed and signed in August. Once these were completed, the government agreed to recommend to Parliament the guarantee of a loan to Russia, but the proposal was at once attacked by both the Liberals and the Conservatives. It seemed as if the government were now set on a socialist course and the Liberals threatened to withdraw their support.

The *coup de grâce*, however, was the Campbell case, which came to a head in September. Early in August the acting editor of the Communist *Workers' Weekly*, J.R. Campbell (1894–1969), had been arrested and charged, under the Incitement to Mutiny Act, as the author of a 'don't shoot' article urging soldiers not to fire on their fellow workers. When questions were asked about the incident in the House of Commons, Sir Patrick Hastings (1880–1952), the Attorney-General, found himself under severe attack from the left wing of his own party, and the prosecution was dropped. When Parliament re-convened in September, both the Tories and the Liberals accused the government of having acted improperly and on 8 October a Liberal vote of censure was carried. Since MacDonald had declared that he would treat the vote as one of confidence, Parliament was dissolved next day.

The atmosphere of Bolshevik menace which the Russian treaty and the Campbell case had created was confirmed towards the end of the election campaign, when the newspapers reported that revolutionary instructions signed by Grigori Zinoviev (1883–1936), the President of the Communist International in Moscow, had been sent to the Central Committee of the Communist Party in Britain.

The newspapers also printed a Foreign Office statement protesting against such interference in British affairs — a rash move which gave credibility to the damaging 'Zinoviev Letter', even though the Labour leaders denounced it as a forgery, an election stunt, and an attempt to jeopardize the improvement in Anglo-Soviet relations. The most recent explanations of this mysterious affair suggest that the letter was forged by White Russian *emigrés* and that Sidney Reilly, the well-known British agent, 'improved' the notorious letter and passed it off on the Conservative Party and the Foreign Office.

The result of the election which took place on 29 October was an overwhelming Conservative victory. The Tories carried 415 of the seats. Surprisingly, in view of the hostile Press campaign, the Labour Party emerged with 152 seats and an increase of over a million in its total vote. The Liberals were the real losers, being left with only 42 seats. Asquith himself was defeated and went to the House of Lords as Lord Oxford and Asquith.

The new government, with Stanley Baldwin as Prime Minister, took office on 7 November 1924. His plea for 'sane, common-sense government' and his slogan of 'Safety First' had a reassuring effect after the tragedies and anxieties of the previous decade. Winston Churchill (1874–1965), now back in the Conservative Party and Chancellor of the Exchequer in the new government, put the country back on the gold standard in his budget of 1925, a deflationary move which was in line with the general desire to return to the security of the past. Even so, new technological developments were bringing change. At the end of 1922 the British Broadcasting Company, under a manager named John Reith (1889–1971), was given an exclusive licence to send out wireless programmes. Its independence was strengthened in 1926 when the British Broadcasting Corporation was created by Royal Charter and was financed by an annual licence fee for receivers. The radio very soon replaced the piano as the main source of entertainment in British homes. Beatrice was affected as much as anyone by this novelty. In the quiet of her country home near Liphook she was an avid listener to news bulletins, and the wireless revived a musical interest which had largely lain dormant since her youth. She also now began to attend concerts in London.

This period of stability and optimism passed with one major interruption — the General Strike. The Tory government was no more successful than Labour had been in resolving the persistent problem of unemployment. The only apparent cure was to reduce the high cost of exports, and the simplest way to do that was to reduce wages. 'All the workers of this country have got to take reductions in wages to help put industry on its feet,' said Baldwin on 30 July 1925. This was a direct challenge to the unions, and as coal was by far the largest industry, with more than a million workers, it inevitably became the field of battle; there had, indeed, been a running struggle in the coal industry since the end of the war. On 30 June 1925 the coal-owners gave notice to end existing agreements with a new offer which sharply reduced wages. The miners refused to accept it and, to avoid a lock-out threatened for 31 July, the government agreed to subsidize wages for nine months, buying time with the appointment of a Royal Commission to investigate how to raise productivity in the industry.

The Commission sat under the chairmanship of Herbert Samuel (1870–1963), a lawyer and Liberal M.P. since 1902, with years of experience in government office. The Commission reported on 11 March 1926 with various reorganizational plans but with a recommendation for the immediate reduction of wages. The owners rejected the reorganization schemes and demanded longer hours instead. A.J. Cook (1883–1931), the militant general secretary of the Miners' Federation, expressed the reaction of his colleagues with the words, 'Not a penny off the pay, not a minute on the day'. On 1 May the miners were locked out and at a special conference they decided to let the General Council of the T.U.C. take command of the union side. The Council called for a general strike to begin at midnight on 3 May. There was an enthusiastic response from the rank and file but amongst the leaders there was pessimism and confusion. Though there were some riotous outbreaks, and London was alive with rumours as strike-breaking forces were moved in to deal with essential supplies, the strike was for the most part orderly and well controlled at the local level – the national leadership being uncertain and afraid the strike would lead to extremism. With the intransigent miners opposing any negotiation and Churchill taking a fire-eating line in the Cabinet, the T.U.C. found no way of reaching a compromise. It was not until Herbert Samuel recalled the members of the Royal Commission that negotiations were resumed. The Commission now drew up a memorandum which proposed to renew the subsidy and recommended

7

that there should be no revision of wages until the reorganization proposals had been adopted. The General Council accepted these temporizing proposals as a basis for discussion and the ending of the strike, but the Miners' executive refused to accept them.

The strike ended on 12 May but the coal dispute went on. The miners held out for six months but starvation finally drove them back to work on worse terms than those they had originally rejected. They had to accept lower wages and longer hours without any prospect of reorganization for the industry as a whole. Furthermore, the government strengthened its legal defences against trade union disruption. In May 1927 it brought in a Bill to amend the Trades Disputes Act of 1906 which made sympathetic strikes illegal and changed the basis of the political levy so that trade union members now had to contract 'in' to political funds instead of contracting 'out', thus reducing the income of the Labour Party by more than one third. The Labour Party nevertheless survived this attack and as the boom of the 20s began to crack the pendulum swung against the Baldwin government. At the general election of May 1929 Labour won 288 seats; the Conservatives gained 260, and the Liberals had to be content with 59. Labour, though still in a minority, was now the largest party in Parliament. On 5 June 1929 Ramsay MacDonald became Prime Minister for the second time.

VOLUME 38
∽ 1924 ∾

[?28] *January*. [41 Grosvenor Road]
Enter Labour government, January 1924. Exit November?

The Liberal and Labour M.P.s combined to defeat Stanley Baldwin (1867–1947) on Monday 21 January; he resigned next day and MacDonald went to the King at noon. Sir Henry Campbell-Bannerman (1836–1908) was the Liberal Prime Minister in 1905. Baron Erik Palmstierna (1877–1959) was the Swedish Minister in London 1920–37. Sir Hubert Llewellyn Smith (1864–1945) was a senior civil servant whom Beatrice had known when she was researching *The Co-operative Movement* before her marriage. J. R. Clynes, now Leader of the House, had been given the official residence at 11 Downing Street customarily occupied by the Chancellor of the Exchequer – in this case Philip Snowden. Stephen Walsh (1859–1929), an old-school trade unionist, had been a Labour M.P. since 1906. His small stature and plain appearance made him a favourite of news photographers. Beatrice had set up the Half-Circle Club in 1922 as a social focus for Labour women, particularly the wives of Labour leaders. Ethel Snowden (1880–1951), an ex-schoolteacher and suffragist, was a socialist lecturer noted for her social pretensions.

[?28] *January*. [41 Grosvenor Road]
I had hoped to have the time and the brains to give some account of the birth of the Labour Cabinet. There was a pre-natal scene – the embryo Cabinet – in J.R.M.'s room on Monday afternoon immediately after the defeat of the government, when the whole of the prospective Ministers were summoned to meet the future P.M. But the future P.M. did not arrive until half an hour after the time – so they all chatted and introduced themselves to each other. Lord Chelmsford, the one complete stranger, came up to Sidney and reminded him of the time when we stayed with them in Dorsetshire in old L.C.C. days, when Sidney was consorting with progressive L.C.C. Conservatives over the Education Bill of 1902–03. Whereupon Sidney introduced him to many of his future colleagues. Haldane meanwhile was beaming and telling anecdotes about the Campbell-Bannerman and Asquith and other Cabinets: our old friend is literally revelling in his Heavy Father's part! He carried off Walsh, the ex-miner and present War Minister, to dine with him in order to instruct him how to behave with his Generals, also

9

to see whether he could fit him out with a frock-coat for the ceremony at Buckingham Palace next day: but Walsh's figure proved impracticable even for Haldane's ample coat. On Tuesday J.R.M. submitted to the King the twenty members of the Cabinet and there was a formal meeting at 10 Downing Street that afternoon of the Ministers-designate. . . .

On Wednesday the twenty Ministers-designate, in their best suits (Sidney went in the frock-coat and tall hat he had brought from Japan and which had not been looked at since we returned in 1912 – fortunately it fitted and was not moth-eaten), went to Buckingham Palace to be sworn in; having been previously drilled by Hankey. Four of them came back to our weekly M.P.s' lunch to meet the Swedish Minister – a great pal of ours. Uncle Arthur was bursting with childish joy over his Home Office seals in the red leather box which he handed round the company; Sidney was chuckling over a hitch in the solemn ceremony in which he had been right and Hankey wrong; they were all laughing over Wheatley – the revolutionary – going down on both knees and actually kissing the King's hand; and C.P. Trevelyan was remarking that the King seemed quite incapable of saying two words to his new Ministers. 'He went through the ceremony like an automaton!' . . . .

On Sunday evening comes our old acquaintance Sir Hubert Llewellyn Smith, who has fought shy of the Webbs all these thirty years only to find himself at the end of his career Sidney Webb's 'economic adviser'. I welcomed him so affectionately as my lost son that he unbent and became quite sentimentally reminiscent of our rambles together on The Argoed hill before my marriage. He is a remarkably able man who was marooned by Lloyd George. 'You must rope him in,' I said to Sidney. 'He may like to return to the limelight as one of the big permanent officials who made the success of the Labour government and kept Lloyd George out in the cold.' A grain of malice to an ounce of public spirit and constructive zeal is not a bad mixture – if you *must* have mixed motives! So he becomes the economic adviser to Sidney's Committee on Unemployment.

Meanwhile I am living a distracted life which does not please me. I have taken over Sidney's unofficial correspondence and dictated forty letters yesterday in twice as many minutes. What is far more troublesome is acting as the 'doyenne' among Ministers' wives, in the organization of their social intercourse within the party and with outsiders like the Court. Just at present there are two questions – clothes and curtsys. A sort of underground communication is going on between Grosvenor Road and Buckingham Palace which is at once comic and tiresome. However, it is one job like any other and has to be gone through. I hope to get the whole business fixed up in a few weeks; it is clear that until all these outstanding trivialities are settled once and for all, I shall not have a free fraction of energy over for anything else. The very most I can do is to dictate my letters and write up my diary from day to day. But oh! for the cottage and the book! And will my strength stand this irritating tangle of issues, each insignificant in itself but important as one among many which make up the Web of Destiny! My latest job has been to help Mrs Clynes to get her establishment fixed up at 11 Downing Street. I have provided her with housekeeper, cook and butler – no, I forgot, the *very* latest task has been to soothe the feelings of Mrs Snowden, deeply offended at being excluded from occupying the usual residence of the Chancellor of the Exchequer in favour of the wife of the Leader of the House. But the whole of the Labour world would have revolted at the bare idea of 'Ethel' established in an official residence. She is a 'climber' of the worst description, refusing to associate with the rank-and-file and plebeian elements in the Labour Party. Hence every class-conscious Labour man or woman listens for the echoes of Ethel climbing, climbing, climbing, night and day! Out of the Labour world into that of plutocrats and aristocrats. There is so little climbing in the Labour Party that one climber stands out in morbid prominence. The only other climbers are Thomas and his wife and daughters; but Thomas drops his 'h's' defiantly; and Mrs Thomas is a retiring and discreet climber and has never pretended to be specifically Labour, and the daughters are so far removed from Labour circles that one of them, when asked by a partner at a Half-Circle Club dance whether she was a 'Fabian', retorted indignantly, 'No: I am a "Thomas"'!

One of the minor annoyances of my present existence is the sudden and effusive resurrection of the social acquaintances of former years . . . Every afternoon there appear cards reminding me of one or other 'revenant' of a former episode of 'being fashionable' – 1900–06, for instance. How to combine politeness and recognition of old ties . . . with keeping clear of Society folk is a delicate problem of manners. The plea of old age suffices for the more shadowy of these ghosts, but some bills on the past have to be honoured. When the newness of Labour Cabinet Ministers wears off, the mere lion-hunting will cease. But the persons who want places, mostly males, or the vaguer applicants for a chance 'to work for the Labour Party' – worldly women – means dozens of letters to be answered with courteous discouragement.

Harry Gosling (1861–1930), a former docker and President of the Transport Workers' Federation, became Minister of Transport in 1924. A.V. Alexander (1885–1965), a Baptist lay preacher and prominent Co-operator, had become an M.P. in 1922 and was now subordinate to Sidney as Parliamentary Secretary to the Board of Trade. Emmanuel Shinwell (b.1884) was one of the Clyde 'rebels', now appointed an Under-Secretary responsible for the mines. He survived to hold Cabinet office in the third Labour government, 1945–50.

8 February. [41 Grosvenor Road]
Sidney is liking his work at the Board of Trade – finds his officials polished instruments, waiting on him hand and foot, seemingly acquiescent in any practicable policy. Fabians who are in the office report that after the first meeting of the General Council of the Board of Trade, over which Sidney presided (and the subordinate Ministers, Gosling, Shinwell and Alexander attending), the permanent heads remarked to each other, 'These new men are very good – we have at last a business government – these men have trained minds.' A long and complicated agenda has been disposed of in a single sitting, and I think the old bureaucracy is inclined to be well content with the new democracy. And after all is said and done, the great majority of the new Ministers have been themselves officials, trade union, Co-operative, and in some cases, like Sidney, Olivier and Snowden, actually civil servants, accustomed to public business – which has not been the case with the members of the Liberal and Conservative governments. The peculiar characteristic of this government is, in fact, that every member, except perhaps Wheatley, has been a public servant and not a profiteer. . . . .

MacDonald's wife, Margaret, had died in 1911 and his eldest daughter, Ishbel, born in 1903, acted as her father's hostess at Downing Street. *Forward* was the weekly which spoke for the left-wing I.L.P. faction from the Clyde.

9 February. [41 Grosvenor Road]
At the suggestion of the Half-Circle Club executive, Ishbel MacDonald summoned a meeting at 10 Downing Street of Ministers'

wives (Cabinet and Under-Secretaries), to discuss whether or not there should be any organized effort to get acquainted with the wives of Labour M.P.s and to start a common room for the Parliamentary Party and their womenkind near the Half-Circle Club, pending the establishment of a permanent Labour Club. The stately formality of the Prime Minister's residence, with its messengers, menservants and private secretaries moving to and fro with an odd combination of secretiveness and solemnity, with its inhospitable hall where a dozen of us were kept waiting, and grand reception rooms, through which we were ushered like a deputation, is not a homely surrounding! But 10 Downing Street, and respect for the Prime Minister's daughter, attracted some twenty of the wives, including Mrs Snowden and Mrs Patrick Hastings, who are seldom seen in the homes of the humbler members of the Labour Party! Ishbel is an attractive creature; charming to look at, in a pretty new frock, simple and direct in speech and manner. Today she is a little puritan; how she will develop under the glare and glamour of official splendour and power remains to be seen. She herself is against anything that is 'organized'; she announced her intention of being 'At Home' one day a week, asking the Labour M.P.s' wives to visit her and have a 'homely cup of tea', and suggested that other Ministers' wives might do likewise. Mrs Snowden also thought that the matter could be left to individuals, and that 'tea on the terrace' [of the House of Commons] is what most women liked. The less important Ministers' wives were emphatically in favour of some common place for meeting; and urged that a determined effort to see Labour members' wives should be made, *at times which suited these women*; and that they should not merely be sent cards for 'At Homes' at big houses. . . .

Ishbel attracts me: one wonders what will be her fate – poor child. Will she have sufficient sturdiness of character to resist the moral erosion of attentions from London Society, the enervating atmosphere enveloping all those who enjoy the prestige of political power of the first magnitude? Throughout the proceeding, I myself was of two minds. I should like to keep clear of the whole business and get back to my book; but I do not want the Parliamentary Labour Party to become the play-thing of London Society and the despised of the more serious element in the Labour movement. It would mean ghastly disillusionment on the part of the active workers and the uprise of futile groups of exasperated revolutionaries.

13

The personal conduct of the Labour members and their wives will be just as important as the political policy of the Labour Cabinet, perhaps even more so. . . .

And this brings me to one of the most hotly disputed questions within the Labour Party – the question of the Ministers' salaries. Directly it became apparent that Labour was about to take office *Forward* opened hot fire on the 'extravagant salaries paid to Ministers', and the I.L.P. members passed a resolution asking the Labour Cabinet to reduce all Ministers' salaries to £1,000 a year. To the simple-minded Labour man or woman the £5,000 a year of the superior grade of Cabinet Ministers (not to mention the far larger remuneration of the legal officers) seems preposterous. He forgets that this £5,000 is reduced to £3,500 by income tax and supertax!, that in the case of the occupants of the official houses this latter sum does not pay for necessary outgoings unless there is rigid economy and far less than the customary 'entertaining'. Ramsay MacDonald and Clynes will not make ends meet on their £3,500, even if they stay in for the full year. . . . We may spend, owing to Sidney taking office, say £500 on extra entertaining and secretarial expenses – but unless we deliberately give it away, the remaining £3,000 is pure gain. (Do we not mean to pay for the new addition to the cottage out of this salary – if it lasts!) It is true that we have spent our lives in the public service without direct remuneration, but then we could hardly, as socialists, have justified accepting the thousand a year unearned income if we had not done so. . . .

However, I doubt whether the amount of the ministerial salaries will trouble us personally: no question of conscience will arise because I believe that we shall have a short run and I doubt whether the few weeks' or months' salary will cover the expenses of the coming election; whether this time next year we may not be actually out of pocket by Sidney's career on the Treasury Bench, if you take into consideration the expense of being a Labour M.P. from the first days of his candidature in Seaham. There may be a few hundreds to the good; but I doubt it. Politics for the Labour man who is not a trade union official is a losing game from a pecuniary point of view.

Jessie Norris served as a maid to the Webbs for many years. Leonard Courtney (1832–1918) had been a Liberal M.P. and the husband of Beatrice's sister Kate (1847–1929). Passfield Corner was the Webbs' country home at Liphook, Hampshire.

11 February. Passfield Corner
Came down here with Sidney and Jessie for two quiet week-ends for him, and nine days for myself; Jessie took to her bed with influenza, so on Sunday I stumbled through household work, and this morning was up at six o'clock to get Sidney his coffee and a fire before he left by the eight o'clock train. Now, having secured an excellent neighbour to do my work, I am sitting alone by the fire writing in my diary after an afternoon nap and a cup of tea. Cold dank weather, but absolute quiet; just a far-off hint that birds sing in the coldest and wettest February! How I should enjoy retiring here and getting on with my book! How I look forward to the time when I shall be able to do so — when Sidney is once again out of office or when the routine of a Cabinet Minister's wife is sufficiently fixed to permit me to spend half the year here. Clothes, curtsys, parties, dances and dramatic circles, all the detail of cultivating social intercourse within the Labour Party, Rebels versus Front Benchers, salaries and contributions out of salaries for collective purposes, are all absurd matters to trouble about when whole districts of Europe and some of the noblest individuals and promising races are dying of starvation and others are distorted with lust of power and greed of gain. How lacking in perspective seem most of my activities! But on looking back over a fairly intimate knowledge of the two great political parties who have hitherto ruled our national destiny, one remembers the careers of Joseph Chamberlain and Lloyd George, of Balfour and Asquith, not to mention the minor roles of my brothers-in-law. The root of their inefficiency as rulers was more often than not due to their absorption in a too aristocratic and pleasure-loving social intercourse. Leonard Courtney, for instance, a paragon of political rectitude, spent much of his energy and health on the amenities of luxurious and cultivated society. Some of my own lapses into the prevailing social and intellectual snobbishness of the nineteenth and early twentieth centuries were responsible for my failure to do the best for the community to whom I owed my livelihood. How different the world would have been now if the great and powerful personages in Europe had had better manners, had been what one sometimes calls 'Christian Gentlemen': unassuming and zealous in their service, and desiring only a warm-hearted and loyal understanding of all their fellow human beings, whatever might be their class, race or their outlook on life. . . . Unless we can maintain within the

Labour Party a far higher standard of manners, unless we can resist the scramble up the ladder, our terms of office and our wielding of power will leave the world no better than we found it. So I must go on taking my part in the social intercourse of the Labour Party until it has passed through the temptation of a party in office, with the prospect of becoming a party in power – I must do all that an old woman can do to keep its manners simple and unassuming and free from that ridiculous malady of social climbing. And the book must just wait, even if I risk being too old and tired to write it.

The Marquess of Londonderry (1878–1949) had been a Conservative M.P. and was Minister of Education in the new Ulster Parliament 1921–26. He was a landowner whose extensive estates included mines in the North-East coal-fields. Lady Londonderry, of Scottish descent, was a famous Conservative hostess and she befriended MacDonald from the time they met at a Buckingham Palace dinner in 1924.

3 March. [41 Grosvenor Road]
Definitely refused to go to Buckingham Palace to an afternoon party, which I imagine is to consist of Ministers' wives. The longer I watch the newspaper paragraphs about the Labour Ministers and their wives going to great houses to meet royalties – the Londonderrys for instance! – the greater seems to me the mistake that is being made from the standpoint of the morale of the party. It is right that Ministers should pay their respect to the King as the head of the government, whether at formal levées or in private audience. But there is not the remotest reason why the *wives* and *daughters* should be dragged into Smart Society, with the inevitable 'dressing up' and extravagant expenditure in returning hospitality. And once the wife has allowed herself to be presented and has made her curtsy she becomes part of the Court Circle and there is no way out of accepting invitations to meet royalties at the houses of the leaders of London Society. So I cut the knot by refusing – in the curiously ungracious accepted formula, 'Mrs Sidney Webb is unavoidably prevented from obeying Their Majesties' Command to, etc. etc.' – to take the first step into the charmed circle, and I shall not be troubled again!

What MacDonald can be thinking about in taking his daughter into this vortex of luxurious living and silly chatter, I cannot understand; it will make it impossible for Ishbel to do her duty to the party and it will undermine his influence with the left, and undermine it in the ugliest way. Altogether I am depressed about the Parliamentary Labour Party. It may be right to be wisely moderate, alike in action and in words; it cannot be right to be worldly. Personally I remain of the same opinion still – the Labour government, for the good of its own soul, *had better go out in the summer*. If we don't go out this year we shall go rotten: our virtue as a political party will not survive living on alternate doles of votes from the Conservatives or from the Liberals, taunted by friends and foes alike of not carrying out our declared principles. If we had a sterner leader, less susceptible to his social environment, we *might* have got good things done by playing Tory against Liberal, and Liberal against Tory. But that would need grim aloofness from both parties, and MacDonald is incapable of it. Deep down in his heart he prefers the company of Tory aristocrats and Liberal capitalists to that of the trade union officials and the I.L.P. agitators. It may be human nature but it is not good comradeship; it is not even successful politics.

Benjamin Spoor (1878–1928) was the government Chief Whip. Thomas Kennedy (1876–1954), M.P. for Kirkcaldy Burghs, was a whip in the 1924 Labour government. John Robertson (1867–1926), elected as a Labour M.P. in 1919, was now Junior Lord of the Treasury. George Lansbury (1859–1940) was editor of the *Daily Herald* until 1922 and he was one of the leaders of the pacifist left in the party. MacDonald's election as Leader of the Labour Party was due to the support of the I.L.P.

15 March. [41 Grosvenor Road]
The Parliamentary Labour Party is drifting badly in the House of Commons. Clynes is proving an incompetent and careless leader – curiously so. Is it the magnificence of 11 Downing Street that is overwhelming his energies? Ben Spoor, never a forceful personality, is weakened by recurrent malaria and has been absent most of the session; the dull-headed miners . . . who are subordinate to him, receive, but do not earn, over £1,000 a year as Household Officers: Haldane told me that the King had presented these men with their Court uniform. These Senior Whips – with the exception of Tom Kennedy, who is admirable – either do not attend to the business, or fumble it badly; Robertson, the Scottish Whip, is bitter: 'I may be a fool but I am not such a damned fool as to let anyone dress me,' he said to me, evidently referring to the royal gift. The relations between the leading Ministers on the Treasury Bench either do not exist or are far from cordial. The P.M. is unapproachable by

17

Henderson, who is responsible for the Labour Party organization in the country; and apparently by Clynes, the Leader of the House. 'No. 10 and No. 11 see no more of each other,' said Henderson to me, 'than if they slept and ate a hundred miles apart'. . . .

What interests me as a student of the British Constitution is the unlimited autocracy of the British P.M. – if he chooses to be autocratic or slips into it through inertia or dislike of discussion. It was MacDonald who alone determined who should be in his Cabinet; it is MacDonald who alone is determining what the Parliamentary Labour Party shall stand for in the country. So far as I gather from Sidney and other members of the Cabinet, they are not consulted about what shall be the attitude towards France: certainly no documents are circulated prior to despatch. So far as Henderson, Clynes and Sidney are concerned, the P.M. alone determines what line he takes towards other countries. And it is clear that the P.M. is playing up – without any kind of consultation with the majority of his colleagues or scruple or squeamishness about first pronouncements – towards the formation of a Centre Party, far less definitely socialist in home affairs, far less distinctly pacifist in foreign affairs, say, than Sidney would be if he were Prime Minister. MacDonald wants eight million voters behind him and means to get them even if this entails shedding the I.L.P., the idealistically revolutionary section who pushed him into power. That ladder will be kicked down! MacDonald is in fact returning to his policy of 1910–14, as we always foresaw he would. . . . I do not accuse him of treachery: for he was never a socialist, either revolutionary like Lansbury or administrative like the Webbs. He was always a believer in individualist political democracy tempered in its expression by utopian socialism. Where he has lacked integrity is in *posing* as a socialist, and occasionally using revolutionary jargon. If he succeeds in getting a majority of the electors into this revised version of reformist conservatism embodied in the Labour Party machine, things will move forward; the underlying assumptions will be changed by the rank-and-file workers, and the structure will necessarily adapt itself to the new outlook. It is another form of the famous policy of permeation, far more Machiavellian than that of the Webbs. . . . For after all, *we are and have always been socialists* and I doubt whether Sidney would take a salary to be anything else. One of the unpleasant features of this government has been the willingness of convinced and even fanatical pacifists to go back on their words when once they are on the Treasury Bench as Under-Secretaries for the War Services. Hot-air propaganda in mean streets and industrial slums combined with chill moderation on the Treasury Bench and courtly phrases at Society functions may be the last word of political efficiency but it is unsavoury, and leads, among the rank and file, to deep discouragement. Even Sidney is depressed. . . .

Lion Phillimore was the widow of R.C. Phillimore (1871–1919) who had been L.C.C. member for Deptford. Kendals was the name of the Phillimore house at Radlett, Herts. Arthur Greenwood (1880–1954), a lecturer in economics at Leeds University, had been a Labour M.P. since 1922. Lt. Col. Thomas Williams (1877–1927) had served in the Indian Medical Service and was elected M.P. for Kennington in 1923. George Bernard Shaw (1856–1950) and Charlotte Shaw (1857–1943) had been consistently loyal friends of the Webbs since the early days of the Fabians. Oswald Mosley (1896–1982) and his wife Cynthia were newcomers to Labour politics. He had been elected as a Coalition M.P. in 1918 but joined the Opposition in May 1920 in disagreement over Lloyd George's Irish policy. He joined the Labour Party on 27 March 1924, left it in 1931 and soon after founded the British Union of Fascists. His wife became a Labour M.P. in 1929. G.D.H. Cole (1889–1959), an Oxford don who taught politics, was a leader of the dissident Fabians before the war and an enthusiast for Guild Socialism. He had directed the Labour Research Department until 1924, resigning when it fell under the control of the Communist Party.

24 March. [41 Grosvenor Road]
A really useful and happy week-end with Lion Phillimore, who left me to select and invite the party – the result being that the Alexanders, Greenwoods, Colonel Williams and ourselves went down to Kendals on Saturday; Patrick Hastings and his wife motored down for lunch and tea on Sunday, the Bernard Shaws came over in the afternoon, and the Oswald Mosleys motored down to lunch and stayed the night on Sunday, taking Sidney and me up with them early Monday morning.

Now all these were not only pleasant-mannered but distinguished persons in character or intellect or both. The commonest and least attractive was Patrick Hastings and his wife – the man an unpleasant type of clever pleader and political *arriviste*, who jumped into the Labour Party just before the 1922 election, when it had become clear that the Labour Party was the alternative government and that it had not a single lawyer of position attached to it. His wife is like him, except that she has no intellectual gifts – just an ordinary little self-seeking soul so far as *public affairs* are concerned. Of course he had a horrid upbringing – his father, a wealthy solicitor and leading Wesleyan, having been convicted of gross embezzlement of clients' fortunes and sentenced to ten years' penal servitude just when Patrick Hastings was midway in a public school career. But whatever may be the cause, our Attorney-General is an unsavoury being; destitute of all the higher qualities of intellect, and without any sincerely held public purpose. He looks a little weazel of a man. Arthur Greenwood, with his gentle and intelligent wife, is one of the more attractive and useful of the younger Ministers – an old friend who has varied in his adhesion to Webbian philosophy from an early discipleship to a doubter of Webbian Collectivism and then led away by G.D.H. Cole into 'workers' control'. Today he belongs again to the Fabian centre and his creed is not far removed from ours in substance, but more romantic in expression. Alexander – Sidney's Parliamentary Under-Secretary – is a new discovery – a hard-headed administrative socialist, graduating in municipal service and recently identified with the Consumers' Co-operative Movement. He is a singularly good-tempered, sane-minded, direct-speaking person, alike in private and on the platform, with a strain of intellectual curiosity, of great value in social reconstruction. . . . Colonel Williams, who won Kennington at the last election, is a good-looking, well-bred, intelligent person; acted not only as medical but also as political officer in India. He would, I think, make an admirable Whip and was almost selected as such by MacDonald.

Finally, there were the Oswald Mosleys. He is applying for the Labour Whip directly he is in sight of a Labour seat. 'I have most sympathy with the Clyde people,' he told me. The rhetorical, picturesque and emotional aspect of Labour politics attract him and may become his snare. He is too clever at words and too inexperienced in affairs to be as yet a first-rate statesman. But he and his wife are delightful to look at and to listen to, and if Oswald Mosley develops the 'administrative sense', he has a great future before him as one of the leaders of the Parliamentary Labour Party. He is a Disraelian gentleman-democrat – tall, good-looking, courteous and deferential in manner, open-minded; with fervour for the people's cause rather than intellectual conviction. He is the most accomplished speaker in the House, and hated with a quite furious hatred by the Tories whom he has left. . . .

In 1923 Lady Frances Warwick (1861–1938) had offered the Labour Party the use of her home, Easton Lodge in Essex, as a conference centre. She had been one of the intimate companions of Edward VII.

7 April. Easton Lodge

We came down here for a fortnight, partly because I wanted some days' quiet in the country but mainly in order to observe this establishment so as to be able to give counsel about it, if I am asked. The Labour Party, under the influence of Henderson, has come to an arrangement with Lady Warwick for a year. The party is to pay £300, the rates on Easton Lodge and a little more, and, in return, they are to have the 'full and free' use of the house and grounds with a low tariff for food – £2 2s 0d for a week, £1 1s 0d from Friday to Monday week-end. The Countess continues to live here in her own apartments: a picturesque, floridly ornamented and lavishly equipped great barn adjoining the main structure of the house; and when she is in residence, she acts as hostess. After ten days' observation I *doubt* the feasibility or desirability of the arrangement. The house is far too gorgeous in its grandiose reception rooms and large and extravagantly furnished bedrooms. Owing to the devastation (by fire) of twenty-eight bedrooms during the war, there is an absurd disproportion between the *number* of the bedrooms (there can only be thirty guests and this entails a proportion of married couples occupying one room) to the plenitude and magnificence of the reception rooms. Then there is a grave disadvantage in having the Countess on the premises. She remains virtually in command of all the arrangements and has always to be considered and deferred to. I *like* the woman. She is human and handsome, vital and genuinely good-hearted. In spite of an abominable upbringing, she has lived *out* of her somewhat dissolute past, into a dignified, open-minded, and public-spirited old woman. And her socialist faith, uninformed and emotional, has proved to be deep-rooted and persistent. But at times she is a wayward child in her autocratic decisions, to which she gives immediate expression in words and acts without consideration for other people's standards of personal freedom and comfort. . . . The Labour Party is *supposed* to be in 'full and free' possession; but each individual is frequently made to feel that he or she is here 'on sufferance' – which, in spite of the comfort, even luxury, of the house, garden and grounds, makes the more sensitive or *individual* guest ill at ease. I have even been tacitly reproved for opening my 'north window'! . . . .

'The inevitability of gradualness' in abolishing poverty should not be combined with living in luxury or the *appearance* of luxury. The experiment must go on for this year but I am tempted to hope that it will fail financially by the overhead charges being altogether unwarranted by the use of it, and be terminated without soreness on either side before Xmas 1924. If the Countess does not part with the place, the grounds might continue to be used for galas and picnics. . . .

J.R. Clynes and his wife had lunched at Grosvenor Road on the previous Sunday, and Beatrice noted his 'depressed spirits' and the fact that 'the P.M. neither consults nor encourages him'. Frank Wise (1885–1933), a former civil servant now working as economic adviser to the Soviet Co-operatives, was an able and committed socialist who was M.P. for Leicester 1924–31.

12 April. 41 Grosvenor Road
. . . . The Labour government had better go out this summer. Three or four years' government by a Conservative Party reinforced by Churchill's liberalism would give the Labour Party time to organize itself under the leadership of the new generation of Labour M.Ps. – the Frank Wise–Wheatley–Greenwood–Shinwell–Alexander–Mosley generation – free alike from the cold timidities of the old trade unionists and the hot-air conditions of the I.L.P. leaders. There would be only one advantage in Labour remaining in, and that would be the more complete disillusionment of the left wing about the sincerity of J.R.M.'s socialism and proletarian sympathies. MacDonald has been useful to placate the ordinary man; I doubt his usefulness in the future. But the younger men will have a tussle to remove him. He will drop the I.L.P. and rely on the ordinary citizen who seeks an alternative to a Conservative government [that will be] just a shade more hard-working, public-spirited and progressive, and professing a more philanthropic and democratic creed than the old Liberal Party. And Sidney and I will watch with a smile this policy of inverted permeation – the permeation of the socialist party by the philosophy of the philistine citizen, instead of the permeation of the philistine citizen by the socialist creed.

Susan Lawrence (1871–1947), a Newnham graduate, was a member of the L.C.C. 1910–28, M.P. for East Ham North, and held minor office in the 1929 Labour government. She was an active Fabian, and for some time assisted

Mary MacArthur in organizing women workers. John Morley (1838–1923) had been a prominent politician in Gladstone's governments. Sidney had sat for the Durham mining constituency of Seaham Harbour since 1922.

Easter Week. 32 Maureen Terrace. [Seaham Harbour]
Five days here with Susan Lawrence: she and S. speaking twice a day, and I only twice during the time. I came here, weak from influenza, on the top of the distracted and noisy existence of London. I simply long to get out of it all, to lead again the life of 'learned leisure' – resting and writing according to my strength. I watch Susan with her wonderful health (she is only fifty-two, I remember) reading, writing and speaking, and I admire.

Susan Lawrence is a remarkable woman. More than 'well-to-do', with a forceful intelligence, presence and voice, more forceful than attractive, she is one of the best of souls. Brought up a Conservative and a churchwoman, she championed these creeds with capacity and courage for twelve years, first on the dying London School Board, and then on the County Council. 'Trying to carry social reforms by a Moderate party is like running temperance reform by a company of licensed victuallers,' said she. Susan and Sidney have always liked and respected each other. For so able a woman she is strangely emotional about persons and causes; but the way she expresses her love, pity or indignation is oddly irritating. She has read enormously, and gets up a case exactly like a lawyer, but her remarks are not original, and she lacks intellectual perspective. Above all, she is free from all the pettiness of personal vanity or jealousy. Is she lovable? I have never heard of anyone being in love with her; I am inclined to think this lack of the quality of lovableness accounts for a certain recklessness, a certain dare-devil attitude towards life, as if she cared not whether she lived or died. She is an enraged secularist and would be a revolutionary socialist if she had not a too carefully trained intellect to ignore facts, and far too courageous and honest a character to hide or disguise her knowledge. As a speaker she interests women more than men; her very masculinity and clearness of mind attracts women. Clever men appreciate her serviceable talent and lack of egotism, but she tires them. What I most envy is her capacity to digest any kind of food at any time of day, and to sleep for ten hours whenever she needs it, not to mention smoking all day long and strenuous exercise when she has a mind to it. Of her John Morley would certainly have said, as he did of me: 'Charming, no: able but not charming.' All the same, she is heroic:

23

as a woman chieftain she would have led her people into battle and died fighting.

Susan took away a melancholy impression of the state of mind and the state of things in Seaham, the lack of civilization in homes, streets, and surroundings. 'A town on a beautiful coast,' she said in effect, 'and all defiled with soot in the air, old boots, dirty paper and broken things on the ground; romantic ravines looking like newly made railway cuttings, no music, no public library, no hospital; the large unkempt picture palace in a back street, and a suspicious smell pervading back courts and closed-up corners — railway lines and coal trucks everywhere. . . . '

Throughout the Easter recess MacDonald has continued his remarkably successful 'word-spinning' (to use Lansbury's term of abuse). . . . His constant insistence that there is no need for an election, that no one wants it, and that the Labour government is quite prepared to carry on for two or three years, puzzles us. We are so completely outside his confidence that we do not know whether these sayings are said in order to get a longer term or merely in order to throw on to other parties the odium of all the insecurity and upset of the general election which he believes is imminent. We are inclined to think that he consciously and subconsciously desires continuance in office; from what his friends say, he is enjoying himself vastly, whether he is week-ending at Windsor Castle or receiving the homages, always paid to attractive persons in great positions, by the bulk of the inhabitants of Great Britain. It is amazing, the guileless, the stupid *worship of power* by the British people of all classes and all parties. Look at the relative position of Lloyd George and MacDonald today to what it was in 1918! It is a woeful ordeal to those subjected to it; equally demoralizing and disconcerting, whether it be the Up or the Down.

Philip Snowden, an itinerant socialist preacher and I.L.P. leader in Yorkshire until he became an M.P. in 1906, was a persuasive speaker. His budget speech of 29 April, a big success, was on orthodox lines; he reduced food taxes but there was no increase in unemployment benefit and no schemes of public works.

2 May. [41 Grosvenor Road]
'Snowden has had a great triumph,' Sidney reported to me on the Budget night. The Budget itself is extremely skilful and the explanation of it was Snowden's masterpiece. Altogether the Dark

Horse has turned out a winner. We were wrong about Snowden. In so far as a minority government is concerned, compelled to follow Liberal free trade lines, he has turned out to be the best available Chancellor. Thomas, too, is scoring success after success as a political 'performer'; he is disliked and distrusted as a 'bad colleague' but his cleverness as 'an old Parliamentary hand' and as an after-dinner speaker is incontestable. . . . The itch for recognition becomes, in fact, rather a horrid symptom, manifested in all sorts of ways by different persons, conscious and unconscious. Sidney is free from it to a quite unusual degree; he is too proud and too modest to resist or even resent being thrust into the background whenever it suits MacDonald or Thomas, or even an Under-Secretary. This instinctive dislike of any form of competition for place or power, this preference for working in the background of a movement and doing any job that needs to be done irrespective of prestige would, I think, have always disqualified him for any notable success in parliamentary life even if he had taken to it earlier in his career. I am glad that he has had a spell of Parliament, capped by becoming a Cabinet Minister, but I am not certain that I want that spell to last too long. Perhaps I am biased by my own dislike for the daily life of a Cabinet Minister's wife; but it seems to me that after this spell of office is over, his special gifts will be wasted in Parliament – he will be doing work which few men want to do and which no man *can* do with anything like the same real success. However, *he* must decide, not I.

Bryan's Ground, Presteigne, Radnorshire, was the home of Elizabeth Russell (1875–1947), the daughter of Beatrice's sister Lallie Holt. Her husband, Edward Russell, had been killed in 1917. She was suffering from Graves's disease. Margaret Bondfield (1873–1953) was a national officer of the General and Municipal Workers' Union and Parliamentary Secretary at the Ministry of Labour 1924. She became Minister of Labour in 1929. Margaret Cole (1893–1980) was the daughter of a Cambridge don and had worked with Cole in the Labour Research Department before their marriage in 1918. R.H. Tawney (1880–1962), the distinguished economic historian at L.S.E., was on the executive of the Workers' Educational Association. He had been a member of the Sankey Commission and was a valuable adviser to the Labour Party. C.M. Lloyd (1878–1946) was a Fabian journalist on the staff of the *New Statesman* and head of the social science department at the L.S.E. Beatrice had resumed the editing of her early diary for the volume of autobiography she published as *My Apprenticeship* in 1926. The T.U.C. and Labour Party offices were in Eccleston Square, Victoria. Beatrice had been trying to find club premises for the Half-Circle women and for Labour politicians generally; her old acquaintance Sir Arthur Acland (1847–1926), a wealthy Liberal and education reformer, had offered to pay the rent for three years, and other well-to-do members had agreed to help. Beatrice herself was willing to put up £500.

17 May. [41 Grosvenor Road]
Four months of continuous and distracting toil in London since Sidney took office (with only one interval of five days and that at Seaham) ends today with the opening of the Parliamentary Labour Club by the Prime Minister with a surging crowd of Half-Circle Club and Parliamentary Labour Party in and out of the premises. The Club owes its existence to my initiative and Arthur Acland's generosity. . . .

As a set-off to this success, I am left deadly tired with an ever-increasing longing for the peace and quiet of an author's life in a lovely countryside, alone with my thoughts and absorbed in the effort of expressing these thoughts – past and present – in an attractive literary form. I sometimes dream of making my tale sufficiently attractive to provide part of the endowment of the future Club! And now to Bryan's Ground for a month's rest and work on the book with Betty Russell, and her mysterious illness to observe and help. . . .

During these last days of London life I have had two miners' wives from the Seaham Division staying with me for the Women's Conference (a thousand delegates from all parts of Great Britain). What interested me was the moral refinement and perfect manners of these two women, who had never seen London before and never stayed in a house with servants. One of them was a delicate, excitable and intellectual woman – a bundle of nerves – the other a phlegmatic Scot. They were attractively clothed and their talk was mostly about public affairs, the one emotionally stirred by the socialist faith and familiar with all its shibboleths; the other shrewd, cautious and matter-of-fact in her political expectations. They were completely at their ease, and their attitude to their host and hostess was more that towards a class teacher and a minister of religion than to social superiors. I don't think they had any trace of feeling that they belonged to a different class, though they realized that we had greater knowledge and a wider experience of life. The conference was a real success; education, mothers' endowment, and birth control were the questions which really interested the assembly.

And there was a certain impatience at having to listen to Ministers or even to women officials; they wanted to talk themselves and hear from fellow delegates from the [Women's] Sections. At the Albert Hall meeting, they were of course enthusiastic about the P.M. and Margaret Bondfield and the other ministerial speakers – and with the singing of part-religious and part-revolutionary hymns, the great gathering likened a religious festival more than a political demonstration. What a strange blend of ancient tradition and modern outlook is the British Labour Party!

The day before we left London we had the Coles to lunch. . . . G.D.H. Cole continues to write Fabian articles for the *New Statesman* and to carry out his duties as staff officer to W.E.A. with exemplary regularity. But he has lost all touch with other people and has no spiritual home in or outside of the Labour movement. Politically he is a lost soul, the older men have ceased to fear him, the younger men no longer look up to him. . . . The waste of so brilliant an intelligence is pitiful. It is *he* who is strangled by stale doctrines, stale not because they are old but because they are not true and cannot be embodied in events. Also, in reputation he is suffering from the reaction against his bad comradeship in days gone by. Men like Tawney, Greenwood and C.M. Lloyd, who followed him or seemed to follow him out of Fabian socialism (though, unlike Cole, they remained in the Society), whatever pretty things they may say to him or about him, are not keen to work with him; whilst Eccleston Square does not want him back. He and his wife work on in the L.R.D., consort with the little knot of Communists who run that institution. . . . If there were a real revolutionary movement, I suppose the Coles would be somewhere in it, but they would be distrusted by revolutionaries and anti-revolutionaries alike. His best escape from this mental isolation would be to retire into an academic career, at any rate for a time. He is too much of the aristocrat and the anarchist, too childish in his likes and dislikes – he is not an artist – to succeed with an Anglo-Saxon democracy.

In the afternoon (it was Sunday) we had a bevy of men to see us. In the evening C.P. Trevelyan came in to supper. He talked with capacity about his department – he feels his foot firmly on the ladder of political advancement. He remains singularly unsympathetic and close-fisted. I wonder whether he is as self-regarding as he seems, or whether it is direct speaking, without any consideration for other people's moral conventions and susceptibilities, that colours, with an ugly egoism, his behaviour? . . .

As he left, I reflected that, on the whole, I had warmer feeling for G.D.H. Cole. Whatever may be Cole's defects of temper, he is personally disinterested – he is emphatically *not* out for his own advancement. All the same, C.P. Trevelyan is a wise and assiduous public servant, which Cole is not and never could be. And in resigning from the Liberal Ministry in August 1914, as a protest against going to war, Trevelyan proved that he believed in his principles – and in throwing in his lot with the pacifist section of the Labour Party and working, day in and day out, as one of the rank and file, he did more than prove that he had political principles; he showed that he held these principles with modesty, tenacity and courage. . . .

25 May. Bryan's Ground
Sidney came down here for forty-eight hours but had to return this (Sunday) afternoon by a slow train in order to be at the P.M. Monday lunch at which the inner circle (Henderson, Clynes, Thomas, Snowden, MacDonald, Sidney, and usually Ben Spoor) discuss the forthcoming week's business. . . . Sidney has had a strenuous week in and out of Parliament. He is still enjoying his work, and so far as his own department is concerned he succeeds in. and out of Parliament. In *general* debate on a *general* question he is not so good: he does not always seize the operative points or wind up triumphantly. But he has the satisfaction of feeling that Fabianism is justified – that slowly attained, incomplete and mixed communal control is all that is either practicable or desirable, and that the rival policies of revolutionary action or 'workers' control' or anti-socialism or fiscal 'Protection' are all on the downgrade and cannot be put in force. Unemployment is certainly the crux – and up to today the Labour Party has not succeeded in putting forward a practicable policy – probably because such a policy could only be developed slowly through a long course of years and with great deliberation and continuity of action. Where I think the Labour leaders have been at fault (and we among them) is in implying, if not asserting, that the prevention of unemployment was an easy and rapid task instead of being a difficult and slow business involving many complicated transactions and far more control of capitalist enterprise than any one has yet worked out.

Molly Holt (1880–1955) was Betty Russell's sister.

2 June. Bryan's Ground
Ten days alone in this enchanting countryside: living comfortably
according to my own habits in the gardener's cottage, working
quietly at the book in the mornings, long lonely rambles – five to
eight miles – in the evenings, and little visits to the nieces in
between, to cheer up poor Betty in her mysterious illness and
devoted Molly in her anxiety. So far as I am concerned, I have
thoroughly enjoyed the time – the peace and beauty – the only
breaks in the silence being the songs of the birds: robin, finch,
blackbird and thrush and the wilder calls of pewit, curlew and the
owl. Especially sweet is it to listen to the last song of the thrush or
blackbird or the first hooting of the owl in the gloaming just before
I go to bed; and to hear the distant lark of the hills in the morning
and then the sudden outburst of an uncounted orchestra of birds –
far and near, of every sort and kind, as if a conductor, invisible to
mortal men, had raised his wand and opened the overture for the
day. . . .

Herbert Morrison (1888–1965) had been secretary of the London Labour
Party since 1915, a member of the L.C.C. and a Labour M.P. since 1923. He
was a protégé and admirer of MacDonald's. Edouard Herriot (1872–1957) had
succeeded Raymond Poincaré (1860–1934) as Premier of France in May;
MacDonald, who was Foreign Secretary as well as Prime Minister, had invited
him to stay at Chequers, the Prime Minister's country residence, 22–23 June.
Charles Dawes (1865–1951), was the American banker who devised a plan for
revising war reparations to stabilize the shaky finances of Germany. The
government was preparing legislation for the nationalization of electricity and
feared that Morrison's doctrinaire questions about public ownership might
endanger it.

23 June. [41 Grosvenor Road]
Yesterday morning, being Sunday, as I was returning home from
the usual walk round St James's Palace, I thought I would look up
Haldane, whom I had not seen for many weeks. He was in his
dignified study – surrounded by the portraits of philosophers and
statesmen – two flights up, and welcomed me warmly. 'Are you
more satisfied with the Cabinet than you were when I last saw you?'
I asked. 'Yes,' said the beneficent one, who always reminds me
more of a French seventeenth-century abbé than of an English
politician, 'they are becoming more intelligent'. . . . Haldane's

one complaint was of the trade union element in the Cabinet; Henderson, Clynes and Shaw were 'frightened of their own people' and might refuse to make such terms with the capitalists as would mean a move-on with productivity – more especially with regard to electricity. Eventually I promised to arrange with Sidney that he, Haldane, should meet Herbert Morrison – now obstructing electricity proposals as non-democratic. Haldane was, as usual, busy manipulating civil servants and Ministers to his way of thinking – the only person, he said somewhat sarcastically, he did *not* see was the P.M. But then that is a common complaint among MacDonald's colleagues! Who knows what the P.M. is arranging with Herriot? Not one of his colleagues was with him at Chequers, and I very much doubt whether he has talked with any one of them about it. . . . It is one-man government, undiluted in so far as the P.M.'s work is concerned; and one-man government in each department until the department gets into a mess. If the mess is sufficiently serious, all the separate individuals combine, whether they agree or not, to save the group's life as a group, whether the attack is from within the party or from the acknowledged enemy, and the Minister concerned has to obey orders in return for his safety. But if all goes well, the individual Ministers are left uncontrolled. . . . What puzzles me – is MacDonald an able statesman as well as a clever parliamentarian and attractive popular preacher? My mind is literally a blank on this subject: I have not the remotest idea whether the P.M. is a genius, a mere spinner of words, or a sufficiently able man to make a good job of the country's business, on more or less Labour lines. This year, I assume, will show his calibre. He has certainly had good luck, up to now; and persistent good luck usually means a strain of unusual talent, if not genius. . . .

28 June. Passfield Corner
One week getting more furniture in, superintending builders and finishing operations, making provision for a drive to the house, seeing the Lady of the Manor about bridging the ditch, and our neighbour Anketell about an exchange of land; and at last I am again at work on the book, Sidney having departed yesterday after a happy week-end together. The cottage, with its comfortable study and delightful loggia, its woods and views and walks, is almost too good to be true! To make a new home when one is nearing seventy

seems, in some moods, a melancholy task: one is haunted by a vision of the funeral procession wending its way down the new drive, a few years hence, perhaps a few months hence, of one of us leaving the other one desolate and alone. . . . Also there is present in my mind that this new home must mean a certain separation from Sidney – at any rate, while he remains in Parliament. I comfort myself by remembering that for some years I always lived in the country during the spring and summer months whilst he was mostly in London on County Council business. But we were at work on the same book: he came back to me as a work-mate; we toiled together all the days he spared from administration; we talked about what we were both keen about. Now when he returns, we love each other, but he has interests about which I know little, and I am absorbed in creative writing in which he has no part but that of a kindly and helpful critic of style.

Gerald Gould (1885–1936) was an author and journalist and his wife Barbara Ayrton Gould (d. 1950) was on the Labour Party executive and later an M.P. Miss Dawson, for many years secretary of the Fabian Women's group, had taken a leading part in setting up the Parliamentary Labour Club. F.W. Galton (1867–1952) was research assistant to the Webbs in 1891. In 1920 he became secretary of the Fabian Society. The Duchess of Atholl (1874–1960) was a Conservative M.P. 1923–28 and Parliamentary Secretary to the Board of Education 1924–29. In the 1930s she became an outspoken protagonist of the Spanish Republican government. Noel Buxton (1869–1948) was a Liberal politician and philanthropist who became a Labour M.P. in 1922 and Minister of Agriculture in 1924. Beatrice received her LL.D. from Edinburgh University on 17 July.

8 July. [Passfield Corner]
Ran up to London for one night to complete furnishing, to dictate the answers to a pile of letters that had accumulated, to give a dinner at the Parliamentary Labour Club and take the guests on to the Gerald Goulds' reception at Hotel Victoria, to spend an hour or so talking to Labour Ministers and Labour journalists in a heated room, to walk back with Sidney and drop in at the House of Commons and await his arrival for a chat before bed. Then, the next morning, to begin shopping again, to see Miss Dawson about the P.L.C. and F.W. Galton about the Fabian Society between lunch and catching the 4.50 from Waterloo – and I am back, in the cool of the evening, sitting in the loggia and rejoicing in my new home! Five more days here, preparing a lecture for the Edinburgh

31

Fabians when I receive my LL.D. at Edinburgh next week; thinking about the garden; and then back again in the fray of a Minister's wife; journey to Edinburgh and three days' function, and twelve days in London entertaining Seaham folk, and seeing something of the Parliamentary Labour Party; and then at last, in the first days of August, settling down here for nine weeks' steady work at the book, varied by planning the drive and the garden, and entertaining Kate Courtney and others as guests. Always in the background the consciousness of amazing good fortune and a certain uneasiness of conscience as to whether one is justified in making oneself so comfortable in one's old age? Also a less personally responsible questioning about the soul of the Labour Cabinet. . . . How glad I am that I decided, at once and decisively, to cut myself off from London Society. So far as I can observe, the Society adventures of the P.M. have been his one big mistake as the leader of Labour, a mistake which has brought with it far more bitter blame than it deserves. It is a mere foible and it has been regarded as treachery. He and Ishbel have left, I gather, even such unexceptionally qualified wives of Cabinet Ministers as Mrs Noel Buxton gasping with astonishment at their obvious preference for the Duchess of Atholl and other Conservative aristocrats to the wives of colleagues!

Aldous Huxley (1894–1963) was a popular novelist whose first novel, *Crome Yellow*, had appeared in 1921. E.M. Forster (1879–1970) had just brought out *A Passage to India* after a long period of silence following his initial success as a novelist at the beginning of the century. Albert Einstein (1879–1955) received the Nobel Prize for physics in 1921; his *Relativity* was translated into English in 1920.

10 July. [Passfield Corner]
Assuredly some of the younger authors can write. Aldous Huxley is a brilliant *littérateur*, but at present a shallow-hearted thinker. E.M. Forster – a much older man, but one who has written fewer books, because he has thought and felt as well as searched after *le mot juste* – appears to me in his latest novel *A Passage to India* as a genius, and not merely a man with an exquisite gift for words. [Beatrice here quotes a passage from the novel about Mrs Moore.]

She had come to that state where the horror of the universe and its smallness are both visible at the same time – the twilight of the double vision in which so many elderly people are involved.

32

If this world is not to our taste, well, at all events there is Heaven, Hell, Annihilation — one or other of those large things, that huge scenic background of stars, fires, blue or black air. All heroic endeavour, and all that is known as art, assumes that there is such a background, just as all practical endeavour, when the world is to our taste, assumes that the world is all. But in the twilight of the double vision, a spiritual muddledom is set up for which no high-sounding words can be found; we can neither act nor refrain from action, we can neither ignore nor respect Infinity.

In this description of an old woman's mind, what appeals to me are the phrases 'the twilight of the double vision', 'a spiritual muddledom is set up'. Certainly with me there is the strange consciousness of standing on a bare and bleak watershed of thought and feeling — in itself a place without thoughts or feelings, but with countless thoughts and feelings streaming out of the past and into the future in directions so various and manifold that I can no longer estimate their relative value. And the concrete questions which I have investigated — trade unionism, local government, co-operation, political organization, no longer interest me: I dislike reading about them, thinking about them, talking about or writing about them. . . . Hence the aptness of the phrases 'double vision' and 'spiritual muddledom'. I am conscious of the past and I am conscious of the future; I am wholly indifferent to the present. It is my *duty* to be interested in the Labour Party and the Labour government, and I honestly try to show the symptoms of being interested. But I am not really interested, except in so far as Sidney's activity and happiness are concerned. Not that I think what happens to the Labour movement unimportant: all I feel is that I am personally no longer concerned with it. During the last few weeks I have been pressed to serve on two Royal Commissions and one government committee — London University, Lunacy and the Export Trade. The very sound of those words bored and irritated me. I should have loathed having to turn my mind on to all the maze of technical detail, and I am glad enough to plead 'old age' and to suggest some younger woman who would be proud to undertake the task. What rouses thought is: how can the human mind acclimatize itself to the insecurity and uncertainty of this terrible doctrine of relativity, latent in all modern science long

33

before Einstein applied it to the astronomical universe? It is a most disconcerting conclusion, that there is no absolute truth; and that the thoughts of the man are no more and no less valid than the analogous brain activities of the dog or the bee! What becomes of the existing standards of morality or capacity? They are obviously temporary, belonging to just the present state of things, here and now. Sooner or later they have got to be scrapped in order to invent standards more suited to another order of things? But *who* is to settle *when* these codes and tests are to be superseded, and *what* are to be the substitutes? Is morality a question of taste, and truth a question of relative standpoints? And are all tasks and all standpoints equally valid? What, in fact, is my own standpoint from which I survey the world of the past and the future? For it is exactly these questions which I shall have to answer in the last chapter of my book! And it is this point in space and time − the exact point at which I stand − that seems to me so singularly bleak and bare, so featureless.

21 July. [41 Grosvenor Road]
An exhausting forty-eight hours in Edinburgh receiving the LL.D. from the University. On the evening of arrival, a ceremonious dinner with speeches lasting four hours in the great hall of the University; the next day, lengthy process in the crowded MacEwan Hall of being 'capped' with sixteen other honorary graduates. . . . the walk through the town in cap and gown to the Cathedral, listening to an inaudible and dully read sermon by the Moderator; then another ceremonial meal, the lunch given by the Students' Union − at which I was one of the speakers − lasting another three hours; a reception at the Principal's; after that I struck work and refused to attend the evening function. On the following evening I lectured for 1½ hours to the Fabians, and then left by 10.50 night express for London. . . .

Tom Mann (1856–1941) was a trade union organizer who had played a leading part in the London dock strike in 1889, in the development of the I.L.P. and in the formation of the Communist Party in Great Britain. Clifford Allen (1889–1939), later Lord Allen of Hurtwood, had been a prominent pacifist and Labour journalist. He was chairman of the I.L.P. 1922–26 and was the energizing force behind the *Daily Herald* 1925–30. James Maxton (1885–1946) was a schoolteacher and persuasive orator. Elected in 1922, he was the leader of the Clyde 'rebels' in the House of Commons. Clifford Sharp

(1883–1935) was the first editor of the *New Statesman* in 1913. He had fallen out with the Webbs and was now part of the Asquith set. Lord Milner (1854–1925) had played a decisive role in imperial politics, especially in South Africa. On 21 August 1924 Snowden had criticized MacDonald's reparation concessions in favour of France in a *Manchester Guardian* interview, thus breaking constitutional convention.

30 August. Passfield Corner

Already one month of the recess past. In spite of the gloomiest August on record . . . we are more than satisfied with the Home of the Aged Webbs. The peacefulness of the place continues perfect; and the new room 'to work in' is already old in our affections and admired by all who come here . . .

Outwardly the session ended with a blaze of glory for the P.M. . . . . But within the charmed circle of the Cabinet there is disintegration going on; within the party disaffection is spreading . . . Then came Snowden's deliberately published criticism of the London pact, and his insinuation that British trade interests had been betrayed in the accepted French interpretation of the Dawes plan of reparations plus their freedom to remain in the Ruhr for another year – a criticism apparently designed to take the gilt off the gingerbread from J.R.M's reputation as a European peace-maker. Also Snowden has let it be understood that he is against the Russian loan and therefore the Russian agreement. The Snowdens lunched here the day after the interview and it is clear that the P.M. has no friend in the Chancellor of the Exchequer. All of which shows that the P.M. has not shown as much tact in the management of his Cabinet as he has in the European negotiations. I am inclined to think that one of his best friends is Sidney, still firmly of the opinion that J.R.M. is the very best available leader for the Labour Party and quite irreplaceable either in Parliament or in the country.

Meanwhile we do not know what is happening to the party in the country. The I.L.P. at its much-advertised summer school has been skilfully engineered by Clifford Allen, who is acting as J.R.M.'s hidden hand in keeping the left loyal to their former idol. Much depends on what happens at the Labour Party conference in October. The little band of Communists headed by the impossible Tom Mann are very active and much-advertised; Maxton and the Clyde brethren are restive; and the trade union world chaotic. We are not seeing any of them and are more ignorant of the internal currents than we should be if Sidney were outside the Cabinet or even out of Parliament. What with the stress and strain of Parliament and the Cabinet for a man of his age, and his rooted antipathy to leadership, Sidney is only too glad to spend the recess in blissful leisure, tempered by reading political biographies with a view to a book on the Cabinet as an institution when he retires. . . .

There was one odd remark of Philip Snowden's when he was here which struck me as indicative of a certain double-mindedness, which was not altogether creditable and which may be an index to his disaffection. Clifford Sharp is contributing articles to the *Evening Standard* generally pooh-poohing the Labour government and the labour movement. One of these articles was a clever piece of special pleading against there being any real conviction at the base of Labour's policy. There was practically no distinction between British parties, he sought to prove. Imperialism and socialism – the two rising forces in the last years of the nineteenth and early years of the twentieth centuries – were alike dead: J.H. Thomas was as much of an imperialist, or as little, as Lord Milner; MacDonald was no more of a socialist than Asquith or Lloyd George. Snowden referred to this article with manifest approval, and signified that he thought, with Sharp, that theoretical socialism was dead; and that we leaders of the Labour Party were no more socialist than the ordinary open-minded Liberal! And yet it was Philip Snowden who, a year ago, without consultation with the Parliamentary Party, and many thought to their detriment, brought forward the resolution in favour of socialism pure and simple as the only hope of the world, and backed it up by a fervent and uncompromising attack on capitalist civilization as doomed to die, and by the hand of the proletariat! I think his real opinion is revealed in his agreement with Clifford Sharp, and that his public insistence on the socialist creed, *sans phrase*, was merely in order to right himself with the left wing. I like Snowden far better than MacDonald; he is sympathetic to talk to, and has intellect. But I am afraid the war has killed his faith, and that if circumstances pointed the way – if the fortunes of Liberalism rose, and those of Labour declined – the Snowdens might be found in a Liberal Cabinet, and Mrs Snowden as one of the Liberal hostesses. Ethel loathes the I.L.P. and the left wing, is hysterical about the Communists, and dislikes all her husband's colleagues and their wives – in spite of her fair words to the one or two who, she considers, pass muster in Society.

2 September. [41 Grosvenor Road]

J.R.M., perhaps arising from his successful negotiation, seems latterly to have become even more aloof and autocratic towards his Ministers. For instance, Sidney saw announced the other day the appointment by MacDonald of a committee to advise the Foreign Office as to the effect of the Dawes scheme of reparations *on British Trade* – without a word of consultation with the President of the Board of Trade! . . . . Sidney, however, regards the whole matter of the Labour administration as so short-lived and exceptional that he is not concerned to criticize, except that he hopes it *will* be short-lived, or he fears trouble. . . . He is quite uncannily detached and personally unaffected – refuses to be ruffled at anything. 'Taking everything into consideration, MacDonald has done better than could be expected: all the same, the sooner we are out, the better for the party and also for MacDonald.'

On 13 September several London papers carried a statement by MacDonald in which he admitted that in March a boyhood friend, Sir Alexander Grant (1864–1937), had provided him with the use of a Daimler car and a chauffeur, and allowed him to draw the income on a small fortune in shares in Sir Alexander's biscuit company, McVitie and Price. The income, he said, met the cost of running the car and helped with the heavy expenses of living in Downing Street. Grant's subsequent baronetcy was awarded for more public benefactions, but the affair none the less revived the recent 'sale of honours' scandals, which had revealed that Lloyd George, when Prime Minister, had traded titles for donations to the private 'War Chest' he used to finance the causes and candidates he supported. It was soon clear that MacDonald had been foolishly naive rather than corrupt, and the matter was formally closed in December when he returned the car and the money. All the same, the affair tarnished his reputation.

13 September. [41 Grosvenor Road]

The Fall of MacDonald

(I write this heading early in the morning before I see the daily papers commenting on the extraordinary episode reported in the Stop Press in yesterday's *Evening Standard*.)

Has MacDonald killed the Labour Prime Minister by a blunder in personal conduct so grotesque that it almost disarms the criticism of his friends by its innocent crudeness? In March 1924 the P.M. accepts from his old friend Alexander Grant (the principal partner in McVitie's biscuit factory) £30,000 ordinary shares; in May his friend is made a baronet. Those are the bald facts. There are of course extenuating circumstances. Grant was not only a successful self-made man; he was a generous and wise public donor: he had given £100,000 to the public library in Edinburgh. He may be said to have 'deserved a baronetcy'. MacDonald is taking an income, not from a stranger, but from a lifelong friend. Further, other statesmen have done exactly the same thing; but have hidden it up. MacDonald did it in a way which was bound to be discovered, and therefore it may be assumed he saw no objection to it. For all that, the bald facts look as if he had 'sold a baronetcy', not for party funds but for his own pecuniary benefit. The blow is staggering: J.R.M. may not only have killed the Labour Prime Minister, he may have undermined, for a generation, the moral prestige of the Parliamentary Labour Party. Hitherto we have prided ourselves on being a party of incorruptibles. Shall we be so, even in our own sight, any longer? . . . Sidney and I are in a curious position. We are old enemies of MacDonald's; and Sidney voted against his becoming the leader of the Parliamentary Labour Party. We are therefore in no sense responsible for him. But Sidney is a member of his Cabinet, and MacDonald has behaved well to him, considering the past antagonism. Also Sidney has thought that, on the whole, he has done remarkably well – he has altogether surpassed our expectations as a brilliant politician and competent statesman. And then we are essentially observers and investigators – the event interests us – it is like an eclipse to an astronomer!

When MacDonald became Prime Minister he made an effort to end the seven-year isolation of Russia by recognizing the Soviet regime, and beginning talks to settle outstanding differences. The main issues were a trade treaty and compensation for British bond-holders whose pre-revolutionary claims had been repudiated. The Soviet price for agreement was a loan from Britain. There was disagreement in the Cabinet, where Snowden in particular objected to lending the money, and the negotiations broke down on 5 August. MacDonald persisted, despite strong Conservative opposition, presenting a general agreement and a more specific treaty relating the loan directly to satisfactory compensation. The Liberals now joined the Conservatives in denouncing these proposals – on 22 September, in a letter to *The Times*, Asquith called them 'crude experiments in nursery diplomacy'. By early autumn it began to look as though the government might be defeated on the Russian issue and obliged to face an election.

20 September. [41 Grosvenor Road]
The eve of the first Cabinet since the recess. The Irish question has disappeared – all parties apparently having agreed to pass the Bill,

and no sustained opposition being expected from the Lords. On the other hand, the Russian agreement may or may not bring about a dissolution – the issue lies exclusively with the Liberals and will be decided by the relative strength of Lloyd George, who is desperately anxious to end the episode of a Labour government, and the rank-and-file members who see no reason for a general election and dislike to go to the country on their rejection of peace with Russia. The Russian agreement is a muddle, and the loan is bad politics; but its rejection after the signature of a British P.M. is a nasty outlook for the succeeding government, who would have to begin all over again. Sidney thinks it is two to one that some compromise will be patched up between the P.M. and Asquith on the condition that this Parliament does not pledge itself to the loan but leaves the question open for further negotiation. The motor-car incident has had a far less serious result than we expected and the Press has come out of it with credit. But as Haldane says, it has taken the gilt off the gingerbread.

Lord Reading (1860–1935), now Viceroy of India, was facing civil disorders at a time when the government wished to pursue a policy of administrative reform.

24 September. [41 Grosvenor Road]
First Cabinet harmonious discussion exclusively about India, going through word by word the instructions sent to Reading with regard to demand for special powers. When they had finished and were about to break up, the P.M. said he wanted a general discussion about the state of affairs, and would they come back at three o'clock. When they reassembled, they talked at large about prospects; agreeing generally that there would not be an election over Russia, as no one wanted it except Lloyd George and Winston Churchill, but that they would play for an election on the King's Speech. J.R.M. – influenced no doubt by the motor-car incident – talked gloomily about his 'being sick of it', the party had behaved so badly, the parliamentary executive regarding themselves as a court martial and the *Daily Herald* queering his pitch perpetually. 'Supposing we did come back in a majority, would you welcome it?' he asked. And when most of them replied 'Yes', he said that he thought it would be a grave misfortune, as the party (not the Cabinet!) was 'not fit to govern'. All thought that they had improved

their position in the country and would gain seats, though nowhere near a majority. Poor Mac is suffering from mortified spiritual vanity. . . .

The Campbell case, which led to the fall of the government, was a farrago of blunders and equivocations. On 5 August the police raided the offices of the Communist *Workers' Weekly*, arrested J.R. Campbell, the acting editor and a war cripple, and charged him with an offence under the Incitement to Mutiny Act. He had published an article on 25 July urging soldiers not to shoot their fellow workers in either a class or international war. After a series of critical questions in the House of Commons the case was dropped, while Parliament was adjourned for the summer. There was then an outcry from the Conservative side, and when Parliament met again on 30 September the Conservatives tabled a motion of censure: the Liberals, swinging more strongly against the *rapprochement* with Russia, called for a committee of enquiry into the Campbell case, which by now had become linked to the Russian treaties. MacDonald decided to treat the Tory motion as a matter of confidence, and at the end of the debate on 8 October the Conservatives voted for the Liberal resolution. When this was carried by 364 votes to 198 MacDonald decided to dissolve Parliament the next day, and call for a general election on 29 October. The Labour Party conference, held in London in the first week of October, rejected the Communist Party's request for affiliation and resolved that Communists were not eligible for endorsement as Labour candidates.

1 October. [Passfield Corner]
General election decided on by the Liberals in spite of grave warnings of *Manchester Guardian*. It remains with the Liberals and the Labour Cabinet to decide whether they will have it on the silly little issue of the Campbell prosecution – or rather, the withdrawal of it – or on the Russian treaty. Anyway, that ends the episode of a Labour government, and by Xmas, at any rate, we shall be out of office. Meanwhile in the near future we personally will have to shift our home from London to the country as we cannot keep up both establishments for long without outrunning our ordinary income. The Cabinet Minister's salary has led us into expenditure for ourselves and for the party, and now we shall have to pull up sharp, and Grosvenor Road (directly I can find comfortable diggings for Sidney) will have to go. If he is still in office or likely to be soon again in office – which is almost inconceivable – we shall hold on; but if it looks like a Conservative government for three or four years, leave alone a débâcle of the Labour Party, quiet rooms where he could stay for the parliamentary week during the session would be amply sufficient. I should prefer to live permanently down here

and go up only occasionally, perhaps for a couple of months in the last weeks of autumn and the first weeks of winter.

10 October. [Passfield Corner]
The end of the tale of the Parliament of 1923–24, and of its Cabinet, is soon told. The two oppositions decided to kill the government on the Campbell issue. Some say they drifted into their decision; others that the Russian treaty proved unexpectedly popular and that the Liberals, in particular, would have lost not fourteen but fifty in the division lobbies if they had stuck to damning the treaty. Anyhow, the Conservatives ran away from their direct censure, and beat the government by the meaner Liberal way of the Court of Enquiry into the conduct of the Attorney-General – an enquiry which the Cabinet could not accept without lowering its prestige a few weeks before it was to be sent to the country on the Russian issue.

No one can accuse the Labour Party of any lack of swiftness in its call to battle. Before twelve hours had passed away, the P.M. met his colleagues with the King's consent for a dissolution that *very afternoon!* 'The King's Speech must be written and ready for him to see at one o'clock,' said he, looking round the table. 'Webb, you had better go and do it.' So Sidney and Tom Jones summoned the heads of the different departments, and a dozen men sat down at tables and drafted paragraphs, while Sidney strung them together and polished up the whole. At three o'clock the Council was held: and the Dissolution proclaimed.

Thus the Parliament of 1923–24 has followed, in its untimely end, the Parliament of 1922–23.

The following day Sidney was kept hard at it, drafting the manifesto for the party; in the intervals between the MSS's type-written and printed form, he struggled to get his own Seaham election campaign started. Yesterday he went off to Seaham, and I follow on Wednesday.

Meanwhile the Labour Party conference had given a most appropriate *mise en scène* for the fall of the Labour Cabinet – with its enthusiasm for the P.M. and its decisive rejection of the Communists' application for membership. So far as the party itself is concerned, no issue could have been better. The Russian treaty and the withdrawal of the prosecution of Campbell have made the party solid and enthusiastic, all the querulous criticism or serious

41

misgivings having vanished in a quite amazing way. Even the unsavoury Attorney-General stands out as a hero of social democracy; and as for the P.M., in spite of Court dress and the motor car, he has again become the idol of the left and the respected leader of the right of the labour movement respectively. But this unity and enthusiasm is confined to our own party. Heaven knows what is happening to the ordinary man who might, or might not, vote Labour, and on whom the result of the election depends. . . .

VOLUME 39
∽ 1924 ∾

The Campbell case and the proposed loan to Russia roused fears that Labour was secretly sympathetic to Communism. On 25 October, at the height of the election campaign, the *Daily Mail* intensified these fears by reporting the secret letter, actually forged by White Russians but allegedly signed by Grigori Zinoviev, the President of the Communist International, which was said to incite the British Communist Party to set up cells in military units and munitions factories and generally to foster seditious activity in Britain. Mac-Donald was taken in by the forgery at first and then mishandled the affair.

29 October. 32 Maureen Terrace, Seaham Harbour
All over except the count and the shouting! Sidney has been here about twenty days and has had about thirty meetings. I have been here thirteen days and taken fifteen meetings. . . . For us, in this remote corner of England, far away from reporters and other candidates, it has been the pleasantest of electoral ordeals . . . Especially gratifying to us has been the growing affection of these men and women for the Webbs: they and we are co-religionists, we have the same faith, but we hold the faith in a different and complementary way – through intellectual conviction with us, and through personal experience of the manual workers' life with them. From all appearance Sidney's majority will not be less than it was last year and may be more.

But in the country at large the Labour Party has had a bomb-shell thrown into its ranks in the Zinoviev letter, whether authentic or forged, and the inept Foreign Office reply – all due to Mac-Donald's shifty and bungling management, magnified by the loud shouters of the Press and the platform on the eve of the election.

The P.M. has shown signs throughout the contest of neurosis; he has lost his balance and floundered about badly. His task, be it said, has been intolerable, and made worse by wounded personal vanity over the motor-car episode and his prevarication about the Campbell prosecution. In this latest business of the Russian letter he has let his party, his Cabinet and the Foreign Office down – through carelessness or incapacity, a total inability to take counsel. . . . All the trouble over Russia may ultimately turn to the advantage of the Labour Party. The 'larger expediency' is that the Communist gang should be once more discredited, the blister pricked, even at the cost of risking loss of blood.

Polling took place on 29 October and the Conservatives won a decisive victory, capturing 419 of the 615 seats and gaining 48.3 per cent of the poll. The Labour Party came back with 151 seats. The Liberals had really been broken in 1916, when Lloyd George replaced Asquith to form a coalition with the Tories, and they had been smashed beyond repair by the Coalition's victory in 1918. Attempts to unify the factions, after Lloyd George himself was turned out, were too feeble and tardy. By 1924, the party which had been the epitome of progress for the past hundred years had become an ineffective rump. They now came back without Asquith, who went to the Lords, and with only 40 seats. Winston Churchill now returned to the Conservative Party. Arthur Ponsonby (1871–1946) was Parliamentary Under-Secretary at the Foreign Office.

[No date. Seaham Harbour]

The Fall of the Labour Government

Which of course was foreseen; but even we did not forecast the catastrophic character of the rout so far as the parliamentary representation of Labour is concerned, nor did we anticipate a two thousand drop in our majority. Poor Eccleston Square, obsessed by the unbroken enthusiasm of meetings and demonstrations, was in the depths of depression on the day of the declaration of the sweeping defeat, of the vast majority of 514 candidates, with a loss, on balance, of 40 seats.

A more careful consideration of the response of the huge electorate to the virulent anti-Communist propaganda carried on by Liberals and Conservatives alike makes us almost content with the verdict. . . . The Liberals come out of this battle of creeds a mere group, and a group divided among themselves, at least half of them supported by Tories and in effect adherents of the Baldwin government, whilst the other score are mostly moderates with a few energetic and progressive persons. . . . The assassin of the Liberal Party is Lloyd George; as unwilling assistant his poor dupe, the senile and alcoholic Asquith, who to save his own seat, sounded the fatal battle-cry of 'Labour the common foe of Liberalism as well as Conservative'. Incidentally, I note that it was to this much advertised call to all Liberals to vote Conservative that we owe the drop of two thousand in Sidney's majority — the three thousand Liberals who abstained last year in the absence of a Liberal candidate having this time voted solidly for Ronald Ross [Conservative].

Still, a majority of 10,700 is not contemptible.

The big joke of the general election is that the grave of anti-Communism, which the Liberal leaders dug so energetically for us, swallowed them up instead, whilst the Labour Party was left with a million increase on its total poll. . . . Now that the smoke of the battle has cleared away, all the Conservative leaders in the country are talking dolefully of the five and a half million 'avowed socialists'. 'Who are these new socialist voters?' asks a correspondent of the Conservative Press. 'They are the new voters — the young men who have got on to the register,' whispers back the more experienced of the Conservative wire-pullers. 'Who were the extra two million who voted Conservative?' 'The old women,' retorts the observant Labour election agent, who watched elderly wives, widows and spinsters trooping into the polling booths, clutching the Conservative polling card as a talisman of safety against the nationalization of women and the confiscation of all property from millionaires' millions to Post Office savings. . . .

Sidney reports that the last Cabinet, held yesterday afternoon, discussed the meaningless report of the committee appointed to go into the evidence about the Zinoviev letter. This *copy* of a letter came from the most trusted agent of the Foreign Office in Moscow on 10 October. It was communicated to the Secret Service department of the War Office, the Admiralty, Air Ministry and Scotland Yard for their observation: all these departments regarded it as a fake and merely added it to the pile of suchlike documents. The Foreign Office, however, after examination, came to the conclusion that it was genuine, and sent it on to the Prime Minister on the 16th. They did not show it to Ponsonby though he was at the office when it came, nor even to MacDonald himself, when he was there on the 13th — apparently because it was not the Foreign Office habit

44

to consider the Under-Secretary of any importance, and they wished to verify the letter before troubling MacDonald with it. From first to last they did not regard the letter as of any electoral significance. They sent with the letter a draft reply. Subsequent proceedings on the part of the P.M. and the Foreign Office are public property. . . .

6 November. [41 Grosvenor Road]
This morning Sidney said good-bye to his department. The Board of Trade is perhaps the least arduous and significant of any of the older and larger Cabinet departments . . . The President is kept occupied with interviews and deputations, a sort of buffer between pressure of outside interests on the Cabinet or the Prime Minister. The post has suited Sidney . . . and he was certainly popular with everyone concerned. I doubt whether he will be again in office unless he is compelled sooner or later to go to the Lords in default of other peers, which I trust is not likely as it would diminish our income and raise awkward questions. . . .

2 December. Passfield
At last in our dear new home and at the beginning of the last lap of life together − short or long. Surrounded at present with wage-slaves digging, planting, building and path-making, some dozen of them in all. Shocking sight, the aged Webbs adding acre to acre (the original eight has now grown to near twelve!), laying out these acres in park-like avenues, cutting down trees to make vistas, discussing with the expert from Kew (or rather bred at Kew) what trees and shrubs to plant − good to look at. We salve our conscience by assuring each other that we are preparing a country residence for the staff and students of the London School of Economics, but in our heart of hearts we see pictures of two old folk living in comfort, and amid some charm, writing endless works, and receiving the respectable attention of an ever larger public. But my greatest satisfaction is to get back to my particular work and to see before me a good year's work with few distractions. . . .

MacDonald handed back the shares on which the £1,500 endowment depended and gave up the motor car on 17 December. The Snowdens' country house, Eden Lodge, was not far from Passfield Corner.

19 December. [Passfield Corner]
We lunched with the Snowdens yesterday. Bitter about MacDonald and would have been more bitter if Sidney had encouraged it even to the extent that I did, out of a woman's curiosity! They are obsessed with the danger of Communism and playing with Communism on the electoral fortunes of the party . . . Snowden is an omnivorous reader of newspapers and periodicals: he is certainly no more than a collectivist radical and would be glad if the extremists broke away and there was a new opposition formed, including such radicals as survived and the original old gang of trade unionists, with himself as leader. The party is certainly in a bad state of mind – the fall of MacDonald from the real leadership, the secret contempt with which many of his Front Bench colleagues regard him, the anger of the majority of the rank and file, leaves the first place open to any big man, brilliant politician, clever intriguer or log-roller who comes along. . . . Poor MacDonald. What a mess he has made of it: all that is left of the glamour of nine months' premiership is the Daimler and the £1,500 a year clear of income tax. . . .

∽ 1925 ∾

12 February. [Passfield Corner]
It is a testimony to my industry that it is nine weeks since my last entry. It means that I have been too absorbed in the book to have energy left to write in the diary; also Sidney has been here and I never can write in his presence. . . .

Today after a racketty three days in London I am feeling desperately the worse for wear and I shall not get back to the book until the first week in March. But it is a comfort to have a real home to come to! . . .

We have had little political news . . . When I looked down from the Ladies' Gallery last Tuesday it was a shock to see no Liberal on the Front Opposition Bench; and to watch Lloyd George, almost a comic figure, gesticulating from under the gallery. Whatever else has happened, the Liberal Party as a force in the country is dead and gone. The only chance for the remnant is the possibility of a split in the Labour Party and the formation of an entirely new party by some of the Labour leaders. If the trade union levy were to disappear and the trade unions themselves develop serious rifts this *might* happen; but the British working class is conservative in its ways, and now that it has taken to a Labour Party it is not likely to turn back or break up into two hostile forces. . . .

In December the Webbs had made a three-month arrangement to share their London house with Susan Lawrence, who eventually took it over.

20 February. [Passfield Corner]
Ran up to London for two or three days to attend a Labour Party reception and make arrangements with Susan Lawrence to take over two floors of Grosvenor Road – drawing-room with study and two second-floor bedrooms, leaving us with dining-room, two attic bedrooms and box-room – for £200 a year unfurnished, a sum which will cover all our outgoings except service, lighting and heating. Now that we have the cottage with nine acres of grounds, a gardener and his wife, I am making it into my permanent home, and Sidney's too, except for House of Commons days during the six to nine months' session. It seems wasteful to have Grosvenor Road on our hands even if it were wise for us to afford it. But I felt that Sidney had a right to a comfortable abode close to the House of Commons, even if owing to the noises and distractions *I* could not live there. Also, he hates moving away from surroundings to which he is accustomed – the dining-room, with all his books and papers, and Emily to look after him, is all that he requires. And we both like Susan Lawrence. When I have to be in London for a few days I would rather have someone else in the house to talk to. I can't work there, so I like to gossip! It seems an ideal arrangement, especially after the solitude of this place. On both sides may it turn out to be as good as it looks!

Meanwhile I have altered the plan of my book. To my surprise I discovered that with Chapter IV finished I have written about 100,000 words and that with the next chapter, which brings the tale up to our marriage, I shall have done as much as can be contained in one volume. Why not publish the volume, say next winter, thought I. At my age the other may never get finished and I am beginning to feel that I need a break and a holiday. And yet it would be depressing to take a holiday without some sort of achievement to my credit; also the cash would be acceptable, with all our present outgoings! . . . What I want is the prospect of a good holiday next winter or spring. I am very very tired; I need a change of thought and scene.

My depression is, I think, probably a reflex of Sidney's lowered interest and lesser participation in the work of Parliament. He has not been well treated by the Tories – the more vulgar of the young bloods jeer at him. He has never got complete control of the House of Commons: he is too modest and feels his own limitations without having the personal ambition needed to put himself right. Also the ruck-up within the Parliamentary Labour Party against the ex-Cabinet and the old junta of MacDonald, Henderson, Clynes, Thomas, Snowden and Sidney has affected him at least as much, perhaps more, than it has the others, as he is a comparative newcomer in the parliamentary arena and has never quite got his footing in the party. He is so unegotistical and unselfconscious that he may not feel it as much as I think he does. . . .

Shaw had written *St Joan* in 1923 – it was first performed in London in March 1924 – and its success reaffirmed his position as Britain's foremost playwright. Charles Booth (1840–1916), the ship-owner and social statistician, had been responsible for Beatrice's participation in his great survey of the *Life and Labour of the People of London*. He had been a colleague of Beatrice's on the Poor Law Commission. His widow, Mary Booth (1847–1939), was Beatrice's cousin. Beatrice's niece, Margaret Meinertzhagen (1880–1959), had married the Booths' son George (1877–1971), a director of the Bank of England 1915–47, and the Webbs developed a close friendship with the couple.

19 March. [? 41 Grosvenor Road]
Spent three days, one with Lion at Radlett, two with the Shaws. GBS in excellent spirits, back from Madeira, feeling very successful and fully appreciated. His prestige since the publication of *St Joan* has bounded upwards, everywhere he is treated as a 'great man' and his income must be nearer thirty than twenty thousand a year! Charlotte purring audibly: these two are very happy together and both are full of kindness towards old friends and new.

The Booths were delighted with my account of Charlie and his work and very complimentary about the chapter generally. At Charlotte's request I am sending them the four chapters: I don't think GBS will find the time to read it all. I suppose I am tired, but I have become rather morbid about the book, far too anxious for its success and counting too much *on its being a success*. I don't think

Sidney quite likes it: he does his best to approve, still more to help me, but there is something about it that he not exactly resents, but to which he is unsympathetic. In his heart he fears I am over-valuing it, especially the extracts from the diaries; the whole thing is far too subjective, and all that part which deals with 'my creed' as distinguished from 'my craft' seems to him the sentimental scribblings of a woman, only interesting just because they are feminine. However, I have enjoyed writing it and the book as a whole will have some *value* as a description of 'Victorianism'. Old people ought to be *less* anxious for applause. Poor dears, I am afraid they are more affected by personal vanity than the young. It is now or never with them!

31 March. [Passfield Corner]
In better spirits. Sidney also is enjoying what he calls 'walking through his part' at the House of Commons. He likes the life. I know he would miss it if he settled down here to do nothing but write and read. This house and garden is getting settled. Grosvenor Road will be available after Easter to go up to. I have got a bicycle, and when the weather is warmer I shall go further afield instead of mooning over the common near by. The book gets on apace. . . .
If this book is successful I shall go on with another volume: *Our Partnership*. I await with some anxiety the opinion of the Shaws; they are sufficiently true friends to give an honest one.

Brian Hodgson (1800–94) was an Oriental scholar who had retired to Gloucestershire. He had been a neighbour of Beatrice's and for a time had some intellectual influence on her. Lord Parmoor had been married first to Beatrice's sister Theresa (1852–1893) and later, in 1919, to Marion Ellis. Formerly Conservative, in the 1924 Labour government he had served as leader of the House of Lords and had been a non-party member of MacDonald's Cabinet. Lord Birkenhead (1872–1930) was now Secretary of State for India.

1 May. [Passfield Corner]
Three successive weeks spent in eight days at Seaham, a week at Freshwater with Kate Courtney, recovering from the strain of public speaking, and five days in London having thirteen teeth out, on the likelihood that pyorrhea was responsible for my depression of spirits and general malaise of the last months. Now I have six months to complete the book and if possible to get it printed. It is time I did so, because the dragging on of this task and the

uncertainty as to whether I have been right to undertake it is becoming nerve-racking. GBS's letter is encouraging, though he is evidently puzzled as to what will be its fate, whether it will be a success or a failure on publication. Charlotte does not like it (I gather from her letter), in the main because her uncle, Brian Hodgson, is not sufficiently appreciated! Which balances the Booths' admiration because *their* great man *is* hero-ized. And then Charlotte does not really like me any more than I really like her: our continued friendly and mutually respectful relations and quite genuine loyalty and friendliness towards each other are a testimony to good manners in the widest sense – to tolerance and kindliness on both sides. . . .

Sidney dined alone with the Parmoors last night, I being too exhausted by teeth extraction to go. He reports that Alfred dislikes working with Haldane in the House of Lords and distrusts him and all his works. Says he is hand-in-glove with Baldwin and Birkenhead and very busy with the Imperial Defence Committee, all of which we knew. Haldane has one overpowering impulse: he likes to be and to feel himself to be behind the scenes at the seat of power. That is one reason he came over to Labour; that is why he has always been anxious to collaborate with any government – Tory, Coalition, as well as Liberal. Being himself in office was only a slightly superior form of being in power. It remains to be said he is personally loyal to old friends, even when they are not in power. With Alfred he has never been friends and for him he has a kindly contempt; regards him as an amateur in politics and without political capacity. Alfred is a deeply religious man and his political opinions and activities are merely the extension of orthodox Christian ethics to public affairs. . . .

9 June. 2 a.m. [Passfield Corner]
Indigestion and sleeplessness. The book drags on and I sometimes wonder whether I shall end it, or whether it will end me. . . .

What has upset me is growing uncertainty about the book, largely because the persons whose judgement I most value do not think much of it. GBS and Charlotte, for instance, have been staying here for two or three days. He asked me somewhat perfunctorily how it was getting on, but showed not the remotest desire to see any more of it; Charlotte has not even mentioned it, though she has been unusually affectionate and appreciative of the comfort and attraction of our new home. . . . Courage, old lady, courage.

GBS has been thirty days ill with a nasty attack of influenza. In spite of his amazing success with *St Joan* he is dispirited for he, too, has become involved in a book which he cannot end – a book on socialism, designed to explain matters to a stupid woman. It will be a marvel if it is not a bad book and I think he knows it is, and yet will not let go. He has spent too much time over it. We have had some talks together; it is clear he does not believe in the scientific method of observation, reasoning and verification. To him it is 'magic', used to amuse others. 'What we need is more thought, more new thought, *thoughts that will wake people up*'. . . . What he means by new thought is some hypothesis which will startle people because it is wildly at variance with their own experience. To him it is irrelevant whether it turns out to be in accordance with fact; so long as the idea has 'troubled the waters', that is sufficient justification. . . . To him the use of the intellect is limited to dialectical logic for the purpose of making men discard one idea for another so as at any rate to get the direction of man's activities *changed*. . . .

One change in GBS's mentality I note. He has lost his old habit of self-advertisement, of telling people that he is a great genius, that he is infallible. And this change is coincident with, even if it is not caused by, his late-won prestige. His self-esteem is fully satisfied. If he speaks of himself, which he seldom does, he suggests that he has lost his capacity, that he is 'finished'. And this is not by way of extracting a denial: it is unmistakably genuine. 'It is time we old people blew ourselves up,' he muttered in an undertone. Charlotte is intent on his starting another play instead of meandering on with this work on socialism. And I think she is right. He is a magnificent critic of life and consummate literary craftsman. He is absolutely futile as a constructive thinker. He has no sort or kind of intellectual or moral consistency. All his solutions of problems, whether the problem be theoretical or practical, fall to pieces directly you examine or try them.

11 June. [Passfield Corner]
GBS graciously asked to see that part of the chapters on Observation and Experiment that was finished and he was interested in it – and gave me some admirable criticisms which will be most useful. Consequently I am in better spirits about the book. . . .

Harold Laski (1893–1950) was professor of political science at the L.S.E. He was married to Frida Kerry (1888–1977). Robert Smillie (1857–1940) was the leader of the Miners' Federation, a pacifist and I.L.P. supporter. A.J. Cook became secretary of the Mineworkers' Federation in 1924 and he was to play a leading part in the General Strike of 1926, but he was more of an agitator than a negotiator.

22 June. [Passfield Corner]
Completely recovered my sanity about the book. The Shaws and the Laskis pricked the bubble which had blown up in my mind . . . I no longer think that it is going to be a literary success or add to my reputation, and some may say nasty things about it. . . . But today it is almost finished and it would be sheer cowardice to funk publishing it. Also it will be of value and interest to some persons – even helpful.

Sidney reports that the joint meeting of the General Council of the T.U.C. and the Labour Party executive was most disheartening. Robert Smillie, with his little bodyguard of pseudo-Communists, is trying his level best to damage the P.L.P. and cut off trade union support from MacDonald, and the General Council, which has always been restive, is now openly and defiantly so. . . . The plain truth is that J.R.M. has lost all his moral standing with the Parliamentary Labour Party as well as with the inner councils of the trade union movement, and his growing alienation from the I.L.P.ers is only symbolic of a general 'rotting' of his influence. . . . Certainly the Liberals must be smiling in very broad smiles over the revolutionary speeches of Smillie, Maxton, Lansbury and Cook on the one hand, and, on the other, the vision of J.H. Thomas in frock-coat and top hat at Ascot and J.R.M. taking tea with their Majesties at the Air Force pageant! Poor old Labour movement: you will get the power your leaders deserve, and I fear it will be a minus quantity. . . .

What puzzles me is the gross discrepancy between the alarmist views, held not only by left-wing Labour men but also by competent Conservative and Liberals, about the industrial decadence of Great Britain – confronted by the absence of all *signs* of extreme poverty among the people at large. Compared with the 80s, even the early years of the twentieth century, there is no outward manifestation of extreme destitution: no beggars, few vagrants, no great and spontaneous demonstration of the unemployed, no 'bitter outcries' or sensational description of sweaters' dens and poverty-stricken homes, no Lord Mayor's Fund or soup-kitchens. Also, even in one of the stricken trades – cotton – there is a bigger holiday exodus from Oldham this year than there has ever been, and £300,000 is being spent by Oldham folk on this year's 'wake'. In the mining area, again one of the black spots, there is no appearance of the poverty which we have been led to expect. The Communists are dwindling; socialism is certainly not making headway, and the more revolutionary the utterance of Labour men, the less inclined are the people of England to listen to them. . . . What is the explanation of this curious combination of the permanent unemployment of eleven per cent of the population with a general sense of comparative prosperity on the part of the bulk of the population, a prosperity which is reflected in the diminished death-rate and the general appearance of the children at school, the common people in the trams and the streets, and also in the absence of spontaneous revolutionary feeling? Are we living in a fool's paradise fostered by the Press, are we living in some abstruse way on credit, running up debts which some day we shall have to pay?

Arthur Purcell (1872–1935) was a left-wing organizer for the Furnishing Trades' Association and chairman of the T.U.C. in 1924. He won the Forest of Dean by-election with a 3,000 majority over his Unionist opponent. The coal-owners were trying to enforce a reduction of wages in the industry. By the end of July negotiations with the miners had broken down, and the General Council of the T.U.C. was given a mandate by the trade union executives to call a strike. The government intervened by offering a subsidy for nine months and setting up a committee to investigate the industry, under the chairmanship of Herbert Samuel. Lord de la Warr (1900–76) was an aristocratic convert to Labour, and Labour Whip in the House of Lords. Lord Thomson (1875–1930) was a regular soldier turned politician. He was Secretary of State for Air in the 1924 and 1929 Labour governments.

8 August. [Passfield Corner]
Henderson came down for the week-end. He is full of the decline of MacDonald's influence owing to his recent lapses of good sense – refusing to speak or even write a letter for Purcell in the Forest of Dean election, and his extraordinary speech after the débâcle of the government before the combined obstinacy of the miners and mine-owners, denouncing the subsidy on the grounds that Baldwin had given way to Communistic direct action! What Henderson says is that these incompetencies are the result of MacDonald's exclusive association with a 'smart set'; the only members of the Labour Party

he consorts with are the de la Warrs, Thomson and Mosley and J.H. Thomas and one or two smart ladies, whilst he is constantly in the company of the great who emphatically don't belong to the Labour Party. . . .

Sidney came down for good last week, with a heavy cold and considerably exhausted. He has quite made up his mind not to stand at the next election and has told Henderson so. It is clear he can be of little further use to the Labour Party; the turmoil within the party is too great; only a young and vigorous man can swim in those troubled waters and it is a waste of his remaining energies to walk through the lobbies and at best lead at standing committees – the younger men can do that. He is more use finishing up our books. We have got to settle into our last home before we cease to be able to adapt ourselves to new conditions.

The *Daily Herald* contained a two-column attack by Arthur Cook and James Maxton declaring that the workers, 'by the use of well-organized and industrial power, could bring capitalism to its knees'. On 'Black Friday' (15 April 1921), the railwaymen and transport workers failed to carry out their 'Triple Alliance' pledge to support the miners.

17 August. [Passfield Corner]
I have pasted in this page of today's *Daily Herald* because it expresses the 'headiness' of the leaders of the left wing brought about by Baldwin's surrender to direct action. The direct action was inevitable owing to the cynical arrogance of the coal-owners and non-redress of grievance by Parliament. . . . The turn of events means a tremendous accession of popularity and apparent power to the left wing of the Labour Party. The I.L.P. and their middle-class friends, fearing to be superseded, as the left wing, by the Communistic trade union leaders (Cook, Purcell and Co.), are plunging head-over-ears into grandiose schemes of immediate and revolutionary changes, in the interests of the workers. Most of their proposals – Mosley's state organization of credit, for instance, are as impracticable as they would be mischievous if carried out; whilst Maxton's notion – that if it came to a stand-up fight, by direct action, against the continuance of capital enterprise as an institution, the workers would win – is pathetically absurd. Of course all this talk may fizzle out. Red Friday may be succeeded by another Black Friday next year, the miners being left to fight alone. But if the General Council of the T.U.C. were really to put into

execution their threat of a general strike there would be a repetition of 1848 on a far more imposing scale. If I had to prophesy I should forecast some such catastrophe to the labour movement as the price of a return ticket to sanity. . . .

William Beveridge (1879–1963) was the Director of the London School of Economics, Jessie Mair (1876–1959) the Secretary. In 1897 she had married David Mair (1868–1942), a civil servant and a cousin of William Beveridge. K.B. Smellie (b. 1897) was also lecturing in political science at the L.S.E. The Webbs always made their own arrangements for the printing and binding of their books and met the bills from their receipts. Longman's distributed them for a commission.

18 August. [Passfield Corner]
With Miss Piercy away for a fortnight's holiday; with Beveridge, the Mairs, Laskis and Smellie (in the bungalow) round about us, driving, walking and picnicking, and above all with the proofs of my six chapters rolling in, I am in a thoroughly idle mood and inclined to be lazy, at any rate for ten days, before beginning my last chapter. . . Our usefulness to the Labour Party is exhausted; all that remains to be done is to retire gracefully and graciously without taking sides in the coming struggle between the discredited right and the inflated left. On balance, *my* sympathies are with the left – their leaders are sounder in character and more honest in their convictions; they won't have the opportunity to carry out their wild and chaotic schemes but they will put fear into the hearts of Conservatives (and Liberals) who will think out applications or alleviations and pass them into law and administrations. Permeation of the upper and middle classes will still be the main method of advance, fear taking the place of persuasion. . . .

Although the Mairs had four children their marriage was never very satisfactory. Beveridge became friendly with the family in 1906 and increasingly dependent on Jessie Mair. Although she was only three years his senior it was more of a mother-son than a sexual relationship. They began to work together in 1915 at the Ministry of Munitions, when she became his private secretary. Beveridge was appointed Director of the L.S.E. in 1919 and by the end of that year had brought in Mrs Mair as Secretary, and so head of the administration. Although they made an efficient team there was considerable criticism among the Faculty at the ambiguity of Mrs Mair's position and at her unofficial power in the affairs of the School through her influence on Beveridge. David Mair, reticent by nature, concealed his distress and resigned himself to the liaison with good grace. His family dispute Beatrice's suggestion that he took to drink.

Beatrice was probably unaware that he had suffered a blow to his career in 1922 when he failed to get an expected promotion in the Civil Service Commission. After his death in 1942 Beveridge married Mrs Mair.

20 August. [Passfield Corner]
There is today complete anarchy in opinion about sex relations. So far as I can make out from watching the behaviour of intelligent and well-intentioned men and women there is no objection to unfaithfulness to the marriage tie; no recognition that either husband or wife has any claim to the continued affection of the other, no insistence that legal marriage shall precede cohabitation. Some taboo is still maintained about homosexuality, as this is a criminal offence. Also the increasing freedom between men and women has, I think, weakened the hold of perverted sexuality. With this exception, no one insists on any code and there is little or no social ostracism. Whether this absence of disapproval means predominantly more irregularity or less hypocrisy and secrecy I do not know. But today men and women can have what relations they like and no sensible person will shun them. . . .

As an instance I take the relation of Beveridge, the Director of the School of Economics, to Mrs Mair, the Secretary. Whether they are, or have been, technically 'lovers' I really don't know. But they are inseparable and have all the appearance of being more than friends. He, at any rate, is obviously infatuated and everyone sees it. What upsets my equanimity is watching the unfortunate husband's reaction to this absorption of his wife's interest and devotion by another man. Mair is a distinguished civil servant and a cultivated and attractive man. He has accepted the position with benevolence and dignity. But anyone can see his misery and after two years' interval since I last watched this strange 'family party' day by day, it is clear that the unfortunate man has taken to drink as a silencer of his mental agony. We like both Beveridge and Mrs Mair and they have been charming to us; but from the standpoint of a large educational establishment, with three thousand students of both sexes and mostly young, this relationship of the Director and the Secretary is not a desirable 'example'. And yet we all turn away and say, 'It is their affair'. Doubtless there is some scandal, but it has never been raised among the Governors of the School and the relationship seems now to be taken for granted in a way that would have been inconceivable forty years ago.

I cannot believe that this lack of any fixed sexual code is a good thing. Of course it enables persons 'to live openly'; they need no longer dissemble. But it also leads others, who would have controlled themselves, to give way to new sexual attractions, and the change in public opinion must lead to increasing promiscuity. Is it or is it not a bad change in public opinion? My instinct is against it and my reason is silent. . . .

22 August. [Passfield Corner]
The Philip Snowdens spent a long afternoon with us, he in the best of forms and she looking exceedingly attractive in black. Every time we meet they seem to be more moderate in opinion, more satisfied with the *status quo*, more hostile to the I.L.P. and left-wing trade unionists. Snowden said that he had tried to 'convert' Wheatley, had chaffed him about his stunt that the capitalist system was falling to pieces and that there would be a socialist revolution in eight years. 'Not in eighty years,' said Snowden, 'but we are going on very nicely to a modified capitalist system.' Mrs Snowden was full of anger against the 'ca' canny' of the manual worker and wanted to preach 'harder work' and more sense of obligation. In opinion, Snowden is now collectivist Liberal; Mrs Snowden a liberal Conservative; neither are socialists and they are far more intolerant of revolutionary socialists than we are.

Meanwhile the expression of the revolutionary socialism becomes every day more conspicuous among the Communistic trade unionists on the one hand and the I.L.P. on the other – the two rival left wings try to outdo each other. Maxton, Wheatley, Lansbury and Cook are the four leaders of this revolutionary socialism, and judged by their public utterances they have really convinced themselves that the capitalist citadel is falling. In our opinion capitalism may be 'in decay' but it is only by the slow erosion of private enterprise and increment of collective control that it is changing into the socialist state. Any attempt to upset it suddenly and violently would mean its entrenchment against crumbling – and possibly a Fascist reaction, hampering trade union action and re-establishing the authority of the House of Lords. If it comes to anything like a fight, by which I mean an upheaval which would upset the comfort of the citizen, the capitalist will win hands down.

A legacy from a friend had made it possible for MacDonald to move to

Upper Frognal Lodge, an attractive old house in Hampstead. Sydney Arnold (1878–1945) was a Liberal M.P. who joined the Labour Party in 1922 and was Under-Secretary of State for the Colonies in the 1924 Labour government. C.G. Ammon (1873–1960) was a Labour M.P. and trade unionist who was Parliamentary Secretary to the Admiralty.

19 September. [Passfield Corner]
'A depressing party,' said I to Sidney as we travelled back from London late last evening from J.R.M.'s house-warming at Hampstead.

The surroundings were charming: an old Georgian twenty-roomed house stowed away in a romantic corner of old Hampstead, perched over a wide view of London. Inside, all was dignified and attractive, books everywhere, the home of a scholar and a gentleman. The company was sparse and heterogeneous: a few Hampstead friends; four of the late Cabinet – Henderson, Thomson, Thomas and Sidney; five of the Under-Secretaries – Lord Arnold, Margaret Bondfield, Ammon, Greenwood and Alexander; one or two Labour M.P.s, a few society dames and the Maurice Hankeys, who had stayed on out of curiosity. Our host looked very ill and was evidently depressed; Ben Spoor was there, smelling of whisky; Arthur Greenwood looked as if he were going the same way; Thomas has less bounce than when I last saw him, and no one was in good spirits. . . .

To sum up, being wise after the event, I think it was a mistake to have taken office as a minority government. MacDonald has too poor a character and was too casual and inexperienced. And the rest of the Cabinet were a scratch lot – they looked better than they were. They had too little faith – they were too accommodating to the manners and customs of a society they had always denounced. And it was MacDonald who led them astray. If Lloyd George were not discredited and intensely disliked by the best of his own following the Liberals would have a chance of regaining their foothold in the country. . . .

19 September. [Passfield Corner]
Baron Palmstierna motored down to lunch. He is an attractive and extremely intelligent man and likes us. We gather from him that the circle in which he moves – foreign diplomats and the British ruling class, political leaders of all parties and great industrialists and financiers – are *certain* that Great Britain is going down in

trade and wealth and that presently her credit will be severely imperilled. The brainworkers are inferior in training, the manual workers are ca' canny and all have too high a standard of leisure and pleasure; the nation as a whole is slipping down the slope of casual and sloppy thinking into a period of great hardship and poverty, possibly revolution. One heard it all before, just before the Great War. . . . It does not, however, follow that our foreign and home critics are wrong today because they were wrong in 1914. . . .

Sidney is optimistic in believing that the Conservative government will go forward in our direction; that exactly as the Labour government failed to go rapidly forward, so the Conservative government will find itself prevented from going backward. Public opinion in both cases will insist on the *middle way*, but it will be a collectivist middle way. In his heart of hearts I think he still believes in Fabian permeation of other parties as a more rapid way than the advent of a distinctly socialist government. . . .

Graham Wallas (1858–1932) was one of the early Fabians and a close friend of the Webbs. He was teaching at the London School of Economics and his book *The Art of Thought* was published in 1926. Ada (Audrey) Radford (1859–1934), a writer with a modest talent, had married Wallas in 1897. The Webbs were still working on their comprehensive history of local government, the first volume of which appeared in 1906 and the last – on the Poor Law – in 1929.

27 September. [Passfield Corner]
Graham and Audrey Wallas here for two or three days. A grand old man in the art of lecturing, more especially for American audiences. Much beloved, also at the London School of Economics, of which he may be said to be one of the Fathers if not Founders. He is a dear old friend and I find him interesting to listen to. If one is too tired to talk oneself one just sets him off, and he flows on continuously into reminiscences and reflections. Sidney, who does not appreciate unnecessary communications even from me, is apt to be bored or impatient. But this visit they and we had something to talk about together; we three spent the time we were not working in our separate sitting-rooms, in reading each other's manuscript books and criticizing what we read! Graham brought twelve chapters down, Sidney submitted his great description of the eighteenth-century Poor Law, whilst I contributed my proofs. Graham's psychological treatise is pleasant to read and full of suggestiveness, but it leaves no positive impression except that of

general distrust of democracy and of government action. I asked him why he launched off into psychology when we stuck to the study of social institutions. He answered that in 1898 he began to doubt his old faith in democracy . . . He found he did *not* believe in the democratic theory of life and his books are the result. . . .

In kindliness and honesty Audrey is a fit mate for Graham. I respect her, even admire her; but she irritates and bores me and I could live more easily with many an inferior woman. Her combination of literary pretensions, practical incapacity, and queer self-consciousness – she is always deprecating her lack of personal or social distinction – is tedious and ugly. She has suffered badly from an inferiority complex with Graham's friends. She revealed a quite unexpected bitterness about Charlotte Shaw who, it appears, had resolutely refused to endorse GBS's invitation to them to stay at Ayot. 'We are summoned to lunch once in two years, but that is all we see of them.' As Graham was, next to Sidney, GBS's nearest friend, it was not very kind of Charlotte to ignore Audrey. Audrey told me that when in the early years of her marriage she asked Shaw (who had come down to see them at their cottage at Radlett) to bring Charlotte next time, he said 'My dear Audrey, Charlotte likes people according to the size of their income,' a saying that remains branded deep in her memory. . . .

Graham and Audrey are delighted with my book, quite un-expectedly enthusiastic – a 'work of art', Graham calls it. Of course it describes the state of things they remember and therefore they are interested, but there are not many readers over sixty-five! . . .

Sidney first sat on the Labour executive as the Fabian representative: he did not cultivate either a popular vote or a power base and was content to remain a purely parliamentary figure.

2 October. 2 a.m. [Passfield Corner]
'The great surprise in the election of the Labour Party executive is the defeat of Mr Sidney Webb,' was announced in a clear tone of pleasant satisfaction over the wireless last night.

It was no surprise to me, though I confess to a slight shock when I heard it broadcast to millions of listeners! We both of us expected that he would be defeated and I had suggested last spring that he should not seek re-election. 'I prefer to be compulsorily retired,' he answered, 'then I shall feel quite free to devote myself to our books.'

Otherwise the [Labour Party] conference, from newspaper accounts and Sidney's letters, has gone unexpectedly well for the parliamentary leaders, more especially for J.R.M., who has done brilliantly and re-asserted his dominance. . . .

23 October. 1 a.m. [Passfield Corner]
Sleepless nights over these last few pages of the book on 'The Other One'. Can I dash in the portrait so as to make it attractive without the absurdity of over-appreciation by a loving wife? It must be lightly and swiftly done, without affectation or self-consciousness, indicated more than described. This last chapter is, I think, distinctly good if only I can give it a good end.

29 October. 5 a.m. [Passfield Corner]
Done it! and never before have I been so relieved to see the last words of a book, for never before have I been so utterly and painfully uncertain as to its value. . . . Added to this uncertainty is the unpleasantness of selling your personality as well as your professional skill. You are displaying yourself like an actress or an opera singer – you lose your privacy. But today the book is done and in spite of all opinion to the contrary, I believe it is well done! . . .

What troubles me is that before I die I should like to work out more completely than I have done in *My Apprenticeship* my conception of the place of religion in the life of man. All that is happening in the world today, whether it be the absence of any definite rule of conduct, as we have it here in England, or the positive preaching of violence, oppression and intolerance in Italy and Russia, or the cynicism of capitalist dictatorship in the U.S.A., confirms my faith in religion as I understand it – that is the communion of the soul of man with the spirit that makes for righteousness, in order to raise human values and ennoble behaviour. But can you get the habit of prayer without a church and a rite? And can you get good conduct without an agreed *rule* of conduct accepted by the faithful? . . .

10 November. [Passfield Corner]
Maurice Hankey, the permanent secretary of the Cabinet, and his wife spent a week-end with us. An attractive personality, trusted and liked by all Cabinets in succession, for the good reason that he likes them and is absolutely loyal and amazingly appreciative of the

different statesmen he serves. A simple-minded soldier of the conventional type, devout Christian, a puritan in habits, a perfect gentleman in manners. He assumes that the men he serves are public-spirited, however they may differ in opinion and capacity. He has plenty of shrewd intelligence, but no intellect; abundance of good temper but no wit. . . . 'Who would you pick out among all the distinguished men you have worked with as the most intellectually distinguished?' I asked. 'Lloyd George and Balfour,' he answered, which hardly shows discrimination, for whatever else Lloyd George may be he is not a distinguished intellect, still less a distinguished character! Which is only another way of saying that Hankey, like other simple-minded persons, mistakes power over other people for real distinction of thought and feeling. But this absence of censoriousness, this slightness of critical faculty, combined with absolute integrity, kindliness and loyalty and quick wittedness, make him an ideal secretary to Cabinets. . . .

13 November. [Passfield Corner]
The book is now at the printers. So I have nothing to do and spend my time reading, walking and chatting with Sidney, and listening to the wireless and giving Oliver instructions about the garden. The only disturbing thought is the fear that we are overspending – country life is turning out far more expensive than I looked forward to. The twelve acres are a drain; something has to be done with this land and very little can be got out of it! . . .

Elizabeth Haldane (1862–1937) was Haldane's sister. She was a Governor of the L.S.E. and the first woman magistrate in Scotland.

19 November. [41 Grosvenor Road]
Two days in London for reception – Susan Lawrence and ourselves to the Parliamentary Labour Party and candidates – most successful affair. . . .

Lunched today with Haldane. I wonder whether it is the last time! The hand of death seemed to be moulding his features. To me it was inexpressibly sad watching him eating, drinking and smoking away his life, though he looks so far gone that what he does matters little. In some ways the rapider these last stages the happier for him. He still goes to the House of Lords and speaks, and his mind seems clear enough, but there is a look of vacancy in his face which is new. In spite of this one weakness of a – to others – harmless physical self-indulgence, he is a dear soul. On other counts his conduct has been well-nigh irreproachable. There are few friends who have been so continually friendly to us as R.B. Haldane; there are few men who have been more absorbed in the public good, and more beneficent to other human beings, to all and sundry according to their need. He has been the very soul of kindness, and a model of disinterestedness. His one mental foible is a childish liking mingled with personal vanity, to be 'in the know', with, I will not say a finger, but a whole hand in the pie! But it is always a helpful hand he holds out. And his sense of humour, always good-natured humour, makes him a charmer. As I watched him, I wondered whether he knows the end is near? Elizabeth, who was there, showed no sign of anxiety. Perhaps we are wrong. 'A death's head,' said Sidney as we left the house. . . .

22 November. [Passfield Corner]
The Shaws have been here for three days. Charlotte has taken a fancy to this cottage; or rather, she now dislikes Ayot and is glad to get away for visits. They are both at the top of their form. And they are good enough to be complimentary about the two last chapters of the book, quite unexpectedly so, especially GBS, who declares that my style has become like his and that he finds nothing to alter! . . . Meanwhile he is putting in a great deal of work on *The Intelligent Woman's Guide to Socialism*, trying to reduce each thought to its simplest and most lucid expression, 'so that any fool can understand it'. He is also meditating another play on revolution or the coming of socialism. . . . What has always been disconcerting to me in GBS are the sudden revolutions in his ideas. For instance, two years ago he gave out that a child's thought should be left completely untrammelled by the authority or even by the influence of elders. Today he is praising the Soviet practice of teaching a rigid Communist gospel to all children in all schools, compelling them to accept the 'true word' – in this case the word of a militant minority. Of course he would be the first person to denounce such a policy if it actually happened. It is merely the outcome of his impatience with contemporary influences, all the more absurd because what he wants is some chance for the minority against the majority, and that could hardly be brought about by state autocracy in education, unless the minority seized power as they have done in Russia. GBS never tests or finishes his processes of reasoning – it is all brilliantly

expressed improvisations to meet new emergencies or carry out sudden impulses, usually dislikes and indignations. Bertrand Russell has the same characteristic.

At the beginning of January 1926 the Webbs left for a holiday in Sicily, stopping off in Rome on their way back to form an impression of Mussolini's regime. L.H. Myers (1881–1944), the well-to-do son of Frederic Myers, a founder of the Society of Psychical Research, was a writer of moderate distinction. His novel *The Clio*, a trivial piece deliberately in Aldous Huxley style, was published in 1925. He committed suicide. D.H. Lawrence (1885–1930) made his name with *Sons and Lovers* in 1913. His novel *The Rainbow* (1915) was suppressed as obscene. At this time he had just completed *The Plumed Serpent*, which appeared early in 1926. Aldous Huxley published *Antic Hay* in 1923 and *Those Barren Leaves*, a collection of stories, in 1925. Stephen Hobhouse (1881–1964) was the eldest son of Beatrice's sister Margaret Hobhouse (1854–1921). He had married Rosa Waugh (1891–1970) in 1915. A conscientious objector during the war, he served a severe sentence under penal discipline – 'an act of heroism', said Beatrice, 'which raises national standards of personal conduct.' His wife declared that he had been sexually incompetent since his imprisonment. Eleanor Hobhouse (1884–1956) was the third of Maggie's seven children. She never married.

5 December. [Passfield Corner]
In another month we shall be leaving for our five weeks' holiday, a sort of water-shed in our career. . . . These three years have been nerve-racking and unless I had retired to the country I should have broken down and I doubt whether even he [Sidney] would have weathered it.

I have not exactly enjoyed my association with the Parliamentary Labour Party. I have done my level best, but there remains the fact that I dislike MacDonald and do not really respect him, and it is disagreeable to try to help a person you neither find agreeable nor think admirable. . : . Also, I do not and never have liked political life – there is too big an element of intrigue, too continuous a conflict of personality, too little essential comradeship. . . .

The work on the book has exhausted health and strength and upset my state of mind. I have learnt a good deal from it. I have ruminated over my experience of life and the reflections have sometimes been pessimistic. Somewhere in my diary – 1890? – I wrote, 'I have staked all on the essential goodness of human nature.' I thought of putting the entry into the book. I did not do so because it was too near the truth! Looking back I realize how permanent are the evil impulses and instincts in man, how little you can count on changing some of these — for instance the greed of wealth and power — by any change in machinery. We must be continually asking for better things from our own and other persons' human nature. But shall we get sufficient response? And without this, how can we shift social institutions from off the basis of the brutal struggle for existence and power on to that of fellowship? No amount of knowledge or science will be of any avail unless we can curb the bad impulse and set free the good. Can this be done without the authoritative ethics associated with faith in a spirit of love at work in the universe?

One reason for my happiness with Sidney is that *he* does not seem to have any evil impulses; he does not want to get the best of every bargain; he has an instinctive liking for equality and a definite impulse towards inconspicuous and unrewarded service. But then, as he is always saying, he has got my love, and what does he want more?

Our life together is, in fact, ideal. In the dark days of winter I miss him for the four days a week. But the new home, besides giving me health and beauty and a growing pleasure in birds and plants, has introduced me to music! With the wireless I am gradually being taught to listen to music and I am beginning to go to concerts at Haslemere and in London. . . . Besides music, I have more time for miscellaneous reading than in London — about a volume a week, mostly light reading, the best-written novels. What interests and disturbs in the output of writers like Aldous Huxley and L.H. Myers, D.H. Lawrence and a host of others, is the utter absence of any kind of ethical code and of any fixed scale of values. Judging by the types of character they choose to portray, there is a preference for men and women who combine a clever intellect with unrestrained animal impulses (e.g. *Antic Hay* and *Barren Leaves, Clio*). Analytic descriptions of these lascivious and greedy creatures, with their wit and clever dialectics, creatures who are too low-toned for passionate vice, leave alone heroic virtue, abound in the modern novel. Reduce all human activities, whether of head or heart; the emergence and intellectualization of the instincts of self-preservation, or sex and the love of power, seems to be the recipe for novel writers, carried out with astonishing dexterity. There is no tragedy in this human nature — it is all too low comedy, fastidiously and artistically expressed. . . .

Stephen and Rosa Hobhouse staying here for a week. Neither the man nor his wife attract me but they both interest me, and he is the best loved son of my old chum and sister. 'If you are in trouble,' said Margaret as she lay dying, to Rosa, 'go to your Aunt Beatrice, and take her advice.'

Rosa has a tale to tell about that queer monkish man. . . . My own opinion is that he was never in love with Rosa, and that she trapped him into the matrimonial net by religious sentiment and a somewhat superficial comradeship. . . . They are both too genuinely ethical to separate from one another and there does seem to be a sort of affection between them. But both are egotists, Rosa of the exuberant type, Stephen the sanctimonious. And yet when all is said and done they are both of them public-spirited, honourable and benevolent citizens, woefully conscientious and courageous in the expression of unpopular opinions, and uncompromising in living the virtuous life according to their lights. Poor little Rosa is now suffering from living with Stephen in a cottage in the country, instead of inhabiting the tenement dwelling in Hoxton where she spent her life in good works among her poorer neighbours and in talking about these good works with her religious chums, gushing about her own philanthropy and the light and warmth due to her presence . . .

The moral of these two lives seems to be that the religious spirit without discipline, following the inner light wherever it leads, however much it may inconvenience other people and however inconsistent this conduct may be with current opinion, leads to states painful to the persons themselves and extremely annoying to those who do not share their views. Also it is dangerously encouraging to self-deception and spiritual pride. Submission to some external authority, deference to the will of *some* community, seem almost essential to a healthy state of mind.

Another weird character in our family circle for the week-end – Eleanor Hobhouse. A woman of forty years of age, with £300 a year to live on, she leads a lonely life in a Tyrolean valley, having broken with family ties and British society, spending her time among Austrian friends caring for Austrian children, housekeeping in a primitive village and doing her own work. She is more eccentric but less intellectually self-centred than Rosa and Stephen; she joined the Theosophists some years ago and has knocked about in an adventurous way among all sorts and kinds of foreigners. But she suffers, like Stephen, from self-pity and self-will, and is equally inconsiderate of other people's habits and ways of life. . . .

William Graham (1887–1932) was M.P. for Edinburgh 1918–31 and President of the Board of Trade 1929–31. The British Broadcasting Company was set up in 1922 and broadcasting began in London on 14 November 1922. J.F.S. Russell, 2nd Earl (1865–1931), was Parliamentary Under-Secretary, India Office, 1929–31.

23 December. [Passfield Corner]

This year ends on a note of happiness and encouragement. Sidney has been re-elected on to the Parliamentary executive and I have my book and all arrangements for publication in the U.K. and U.S.A. finished and done with. . . . We are well established in our new home and like it better and better every day.

The Labour Party itself is in a wholesomer condition than it has been since the Labour government went out of office. . . . The P.M. has recovered his position to a certain extent, sufficient for his leadership in the country, and the saner members of the Front Bench – Henderson, Clynes, Graham – are distinctly in the ascendant. Against this is the mess being made of the miners' case by A.J. Cook and the hardening of the Tory capitalist determination to put Labour in its 'right place'. We are going to have an infernal row next summer unless Labour is willing to take the attack on hours and wages – first among the miners – lying down. But living out of the way I hear little or nothing of what is happening in the country.

To my mind by far the most significant event of the last two years is the spread of wireless and the admirable way in which the B.B.C. is using this stupendous influence over the lives of the people, in some ways greater than the written word because it is so amazingly selective and under deliberate control, and on the whole of an eminently right control. This new power must necessarily be a monopoly and cannot be left to Gresham's law of the bad coin driving out the good. . . . Moreover there is at present no pecuniary self-interest involved; no one is the richer or the poorer because one programme is adopted rather than another. And the result is certainly remarkable. Every item in the day's programme is not to one's taste, but the ensemble is admirable . . . But what a terrible engine of compulsory conformity in opinion and culture wireless *might* become. . . .

Gradually we are making ourselves a neighbourhood round our home. There are a few members of the Labour Party within easy motoring distance – the Snowdens, Ponsonbys and Lord Russell . . .

Then there are various schoolteachers, a district nurse, a dissenting minister, friends of my gardener and his wife, more or less Labour in sympathy and with a good deal more to talk about than the ordinary *rentier*. I do not wish to live an isolated life. I accept the obligation of near neighbourhood, especially towards the intellectual proletariat, the minor professionals who are hard-worked and denied the pleasures of life while rendering fine service to the community, very scantily rewarded. But I see no reason for knowing the gentry of the neighbourhood, even if they cared to know us . . . they would only know us out of curiosity and because we were 'personages'.

∾ 1926 ∾

My Apprenticeship was published on 25 February. The Webbs went on holiday to Italy at the beginning of January, where they interviewed journalists and politicians about Mussolini's regime.

18 February. [Passfield Corner]
Back at Passfield again, refreshed in mind but exhausted in body by our Sicilian tour. . . . Except that I did not find Sicily a health resort, the tour was a success. . . .

The present regime is a ghastly tragedy for all the intellectuals who are definitely non-Fascist, more especially, of course, the politicians and the journalists who find themselves not only robbed of their livelihood and their liberties as citizens but also physically threatened. To the ordinary man, who in Italy is not in the least interested in public affairs, the Mussolini government is a relief from anxiety and bother: there is more efficiency and regularity and honesty in public and private affairs. Also, he feels that he is getting his own back in foreign affairs – Italy is, or appears to be, in the ascendant. Mussolini's bullying attitude towards Germany, Austria and France is an agreeable change from the old rule of 'poor relation'; and the Duce's bombastic utterances about the inheritance of the Roman Empire etc. are pleasant day-dreams, even if the citizen shrugs his shoulders and laughs. What is more seriously taken is the demand for colonies and room for expansion in view of the perpetually increasing population. Corsica, Savoy, Tunis and other French colonies – all these must fall into the lap of

Italy if justice is to be done. And Mussolini will insist on this justice. Mussolini is imposing on the mass of his countrymen grandiose views as to the national destiny, exactly as the German Emperor and his General Staff imposed these on the ordinary German before the war, the only difference being that the Italian citizen has not the remotest intention of either fighting or paying for the coming glory! It is to come to him without exertion or cost. . . .

On the eve of publication I am downcast! Courage, old woman, courage: be game to the end. And don't give way to the egotism of old age; live up to what old age *ought to be*, the impersonal beneficence of the Ancient unmoved by the opinion of a world he or she is about to leave. The book is done and cannot be undone; now I must forget the last bit of work so that I can get on with the next for while there is still strength to do so. The night will soon be here.

1 March. [Passfield Corner]
Reviews of the book are unexpectedly good and my self-esteem ought to be more than satisfied! I have now to turn my will to three separate tasks, and to rid my mind of the egotistical brooding over my own personality which has been induced by autobiographical writing; to concentrate on the history of the Poor Law so that we finish that work by this time next year, and to create a neighbourhood here of kindly sympathy and good will. . . .

Beatrice had been reading the recently published papers of Colonel House (1858–1938), the American representative at the Paris Peace conference. Austen Chamberlain (1863–1937) was Foreign Secretary. His crowning achievement was the Locarno Pact of October 1925 in which Germany, Belgium and France agreed not to make war. Germany was also admitted to the League of Nations but this was delayed for six months and caused the resignation of Brazil from the League. Aristide Briand (1862–1932), the French Foreign Minister and winner of the Nobel Peace Prize, was the chief advocate of reconciliation with Germany. Bertrand Russell (1872–1970) had married Dora Black (b. 1894) in September 1921. Their son John Conrad was born in November 1921 and a daughter, Katharine Jane, two years later. Russell bought a house at Porthcurno on the south coast of Cornwall. A new edition of *Principia Mathematica* was published in 1925.

15 March. 2 a.m. [Passfield Corner]
It is during sleepless hours in the night that I get things down in my diary; during the day I am either at work, or reading news-

papers and interesting books, or listening to the wireless or wandering about the country, or merely chatting or brooding – I have no inclination to write. But in the loneliness and silence of the night, impressions and thoughts fly through my brain and if I refuse to express them I begin to worry. Also, to begin to write is an excuse for a cup of tea!

From that master negotiator House to that bungler Austen Chamberlain! Why is it that the great majority of those who have watched Austen at one and the same time respect and despise him? It is not that they respect his character and despise his intellect – they despise his character and they are not without a certain respect for his intelligence. The answer is, I think, that he is undoubtedly a man experienced in affairs, with certain gifts and accomplishments, and he is personally disinterested. But he is dull and closed-minded, and in his outlook on public, as distinguished from private affairs, he is morally as well as intellectually dense, and equally unaware of the subtler nuances of right and wrong and of truth and untruth. . . . Chamberlain's behaviour to the Germans, in his intrigue with Briand to 'do' them out of the results of Locarno, showed a moral denseness, and his conduct gives the impression of meanness in public affairs as well as stupidity. The same moral denseness is seen in his attempt to dodge British public opinion, and even apparently the instructions of the Cabinet. There is even a suspicion that Brazil's veto – which he professes to deplore – has somehow or other been arranged for by Briand, with a view of delaying Germany's entry until a commission is appointed to narrow down the constitution of the League in the interests of France. . . . Behind that imposing monocle there is a whitewashed but empty chamber, said a sharp newspaper man.

Bertrand Russell and his wife have spent a week-end here this spring. He has settled down to happy domesticity and the agreeable task of earning his livelihood by brilliant thinking, brilliant writing and still more brilliant lectures. Half the year is spent in one of a row of tiny houses in a by-street of Chelsea; the other six months in a rough rambling abode at Land's End. Absorbed in the education of his boy and girl, and apparently still in love with his wife, with an entourage of old college friends and young disciples, his daily life is the last word of bourgeois regularity and respectability. Every two years he betakes himself to the U.S.A., gives some forty lectures in as many days, investing last time £1,500 as the net result. 'Just enough to pay for the education of one child,' he remarked. His wife suits him. She also has improved since I first saw her, softened by motherhood and admiration of her great man, and refined by intellectual companionship and hard work – for she lectures incessantly during the winter on birth control and maternity clinics. She retains her rather rasping short-range intelligence; she argued for at least thirty minutes that there was a *science of ethics* which would demonstrate the *truth* of her particular brand of anarchic liberalism. . . .

He told me that he had exhausted his interest in mathematical reasoning and found getting out a new edition of his great book intellectually boresome. He likes going from subject to subject. That's the worst of Bertie; he refuses to verify any of his conclusions. He has not the patience for observation, inference and verification. Each successive book contains a series of original and witty impressions or suggestions, flashed out as his mind comes into contact with some outstanding fact – usually these flashes are denunciations of what exists. Frequently these judgements or descriptions contradict each other; he seems to have no care for consistency; he does not care even if they do contradict each other. It amuses him to watch the bewilderment of disciples who have no sense of humour! And why should he trouble himself to produce a thought-tight philosophy of life? As a lecturer he commands a big price, especially in the U.S.A. and China. He is disintegrating prejudice and 'rattling' people out of old conventions. Upsetting people's thoughts is good fun; and it is very agreeable being brilliant in thought and expression. Of all forms of mental superiority it is quite the most agreeable for the possessor, the most soothing to his self-esteem.

J.L. Garvin (1868–1947) was the editor of the *Observer* 1908–42.

30 March. 5 a.m. [Passfield Corner]
Haldane's imposing review of my book, accorded the pride of place in the *Observer* of the 28th by the friendly Garvin, symbolizes by its friendly, critical attitude our longstanding and close association with this remarkable personality.

For more reasons than one, the book has roused some antagonism in his mind. Perhaps he had a right to expect more recognition of his spontaneous and useful friendship to Sidney and me during our engagement and on our marriage. But I doubt whether this slight subconscious grievance did more than release what is and has been a genuine and permanent judgement about us – the sort of judgement which we would give in conversation with an intimate friend. 'The Webbs are very able, whether as writers or organizers; they are honest and public-spirited; they are remarkably hard-working and purposeful. But alike in intellectual gifts, personal culture and social standing, they are restricted in range – they are in fact "little people" who have accomplished a useful but not outstanding important book.'

And of course in one sense he is right; we have, in fact, never claimed to be otherwise than useful citizens. How useful depends on the rightness of our particular scale of values.

Haldane's reaction is due in the main to a radical difference of opinion on three important questions. First, we have no personal respect or liking for certain centres of power – social circles or institutions which Haldane has not merely appreciated as a man of affairs but which he has approved and admired. 'The City', by which he means the dominant financial groups, used to be one of his idols, an idol by the way which has latterly been somewhat cast into the background, I know not why. The second idol has been 'good society', the tip-top circle which includes the Court (more especially the entourage of Edward VII), and the greater and more distinguished aristocrats, plutocrats and social charmers. His adoration of and subordination to Rosebery, in the days of that hero's glory, shocked us. . . .

The second point of difference is our total inability to sympathize with or even to understand his peculiar brand of metaphysics – Hegelianism. In his opinion this philosophy alone is the 'Pathway to Reality', and to him it has united science and religion – the good, the beautiful and the true.

Closely connected with what he would call our deficiency in culture is our prejudice against what he calls 'university education', the sort of diffuse and general culture about men and affairs, literature and philosophy which were characteristic of John Morley and the little set of politico-literary-philosophic personages who, in the last decades of the nineteenth century, were always breakfasting and dining with each other. These two latter criticisms give point to his objection to my denunciation of London Society. 'Have you a right to criticize a social institution which you have not known and which you are incapable of appreciating?' he asks. My answer is that we have been able to realize the effect of London Society better than he because we have looked at it from below and watched its effect, not on the few who have dominated it, but on the multitude who have accepted its scale of values in the conduct of their own lives. And here I come to the root difference between his scale of values and ours — the difference between the aristocrat caring for the free development of the select few and the democrat eager to raise the standard of the mass of men. In many ways these two aims can be pursued together, in others they can be harmonized by wise compromise. Whenever and wherever this has been the case, Haldane and we have worked together without enquiring too curiously about each other's instinctive aims. But now and again our diverse scale of values have obviously clashed, and then we have become for a time antagonistic or indifferent to each other. There has even been not a little mutual contempt. . . .

VOLUME 40

The Royal Commission to look into the mining industry, which had been appointed in September 1925 with Herbert Samuel as chairman, published its report on 11 March 1926. It called for a reduction in wages but rejected the mine-owners' request for longer hours. Negotiations between the Miners' Federation and the Mining Association were now resumed but came to a deadlock at a meeting on 13 April.

14 April. Passfield Corner
Back from our Easter visit to Seaham — a gloomy business, with the dark prospect of an embittered strike hanging over our little meetings of miners and their wives.

The beginning of another long spell of work coincides with the first page of another diary book, and the two together incline me to look inward and tell what I am thinking, when not at work on my subject. . . . I am perpetually brooding on my inability to make clear even to myself, let alone to others, why I believe in religious mysticism, why I hanker after a Church with its communion of the faithful, with its religious rites and its religious discipline and above all with its definite code of conduct. The arguments against religious mysticism, still more against a Church, with its rites and authoritative teaching, are formidable. . . . The possible validity of religious mysticism is not contradicted or denied by the latest findings of physical science. . . . Somehow or other we must have the habit of prayer, the opportunity for the confession of sin and for the worship of goodness, if we are to attain personal holiness. Otherwise we suffer from a chronic devitalization of the religious faculty. But how can we get a Church without a dogma, a dogma which will offend intellectual integrity and moral sincerity? No such Church seems within sight. Like so many other poor souls I have the consciousness of being a spiritual outcast. I have no home for my religious faculty, I wander about disconsolate – that is the root of my indifference to life. In spite of my unusually happy circumstances and keen intellectual interests, I am not at peace with myself. I have failed to solve the problem of life, of man's relation to the universe and therefore to his fellow man. But I have a growing faith that it will be solved by a combination of truth-seeking and personal holiness, of the scientific mind with the religious life. When will such a leader arise who will unite the intellect of an Aristotle, a Goethe or an Einstein with the moral genius of a Buddha, a Christ or a St Francis d'Assisi?

2 May. [Passfield Corner]
Not getting on with the Poor Law book and feel quite incapable of doing so. This time last year I was sleepless with worry about the book I was writing; today I am worrying again, this time about the increased expenditure of country life compared to London life and the hypothetical dishonesty of a little servant girl. The extra cigarette with which I try to dispel the worry increases the heart's irritation and so makes me worse than I need be! Meanwhile I have let myself in for a Labour gathering here to meet J.R.M. and other Labour men on 30 July, which is assuming larger proportions than I intended, in trouble and expense, and which is another source of worry! In the background is the fear, which will one day be justified, that I am not fit for further brainwork and shall have to lean back and content myself with an existence of harmless leisure – passive reading and playing about with gardening, pets and wireless! And I am inclined to think helping Sidney with this History of the Poor Law will be my last literary task. However we have done a good day's work and I ought to rest satisfied. Fortunately Sidney is more than content with life; he is actively grateful for his past and present happiness. His good health and continuous happiness is a

joy to me. We have had an amazingly delightful companionship —
never a shadow between us. . . .

The intervention of the T.U.C. and the government failed to resolve the
deadlock between the miners and the mine-owners. Several meetings between
the Prime Minister, the owners and the miners' representatives and the
Industrial Committee of the T.U.C. took place in the days before lock-out
notices took effect on Friday 30 April. Labour leaders failed in their attempt to
get the lock-out notices withdrawn so that negotiations could be resumed. At a
meeting of trade union executives at Memorial Hall they agreed on strike action
in support of the miners and to hand over the conduct of the dispute to the
T.U.C. General Council. Last-minute negotiations went on through the night
of Saturday 1 May but next day Baldwin precipitately broke off negotiations and
rejected a settlement with the T.U.C. General Council, thus forcing them into
strike action in support of the miners. On Monday 3 May the public learned
with little warning that it faced a general strike that very midnight.

3 May. 4 a.m. On the night of the great strike. [Passfield Corner]
'The Decay of the Capitalist System' has certainly begun in the
biggest and most characteristic of British industries and unless the
government ends the reign of the profit-maker it will end the
government — may indeed break up the country. Why the capitalists
of the coalfields are so dreary and incompetent a lot is a curious
question, but the verdict that they have been and are wholly unable
to run their business with decent efficiency has been given over and
over again and by all parties in the state. There is not a Conservative
politician or journalist of repute that dare advise that the colliery
owners be left to go on as they are doing at present. Each successive
court of enquiry, whatever its composition, has declared against
them. But alas! this conversion of those in power has been more
apparent than real. They have not any honest determination to do
the job; they want to *seem* to do it but to leave it undone. . . .

The General Strike will fail; the General Council may funk it
and may withdraw their instructions on some apparent concession
by the government, or the men may slink back to work in a few
days. We have always been against a General Strike. But the
problem of the collapse of capitalism in the coal industry will
remain — and woe to the governing class that refuses to solve it by
taking control, in one form or another, of the organization of the
industry.

Away here in the country I have not been able to watch the march
of events. The General Council of the T.U.C. has certainly

succeeded in giving an epic quality to their slow and reserved but decisive attitude towards the miners' dispute. There has been no tall talk and hot air during the negotiations; and the egregious A.J. Cook has been ignored. In fact when the announcement came on Friday evening that the railway workers and other key men would cease work tonight – it crept over the wireless – it did not appear in the newspapers until twenty-four hours later. . . . The one note of hysteria came on Saturday night from Baldwin, again over the wireless and again not appearing in the newspapers. 'Before giving the weather forecast and news bulletin,' said the announcer in a hurried voice, 'there is a message from the Prime Minister.' Then in a stentorian voice some other person gave this message, two or three times, each time with louder and more pompous emphasis: 'Be steady, Be steady' – pause – 'Remember that peace on earth comes to men of good will.' Perhaps if Baldwin himself, in his kindly and commonsense accent, had spoken his own words, the effect would have been different. But in the emissary's melodramatic shout it sounded not a little absurd. What is wanted is to face the facts with knowledge and determination. *Goodness*, i.e. diffused sympathy, is beside the mark. In a great crisis these sloppy emotions rouse irritation or contempt in the listeners to the wireless . . . you listen coldly and critically to all that comes, and bathos is easily detected in the silence of your own sitting-room.

4 May. [Passfield Corner]
When all is said and done we personally are against the use of the General Strike in order to compel the employers of a particular industry to yield to the men's demands, however well justified these claims may be. Such methods cannot be tolerated by any government – even a Labour government would have to take up the challenge. A General Strike aims at coercing the whole community and is only successful *if it does so* and in so far as it does so. Further, if it succeeded in coercing the community it would mean that a militant minority were starving the majority into submission to their will and would be the end of democracy, industrial as well as political. Sooner or later – in Great Britain, sooner rather than later – the community as a whole would organize to prevent such coercion by penal legislation. But there arise emergencies when it is better to fight even if you cannot win than to take oppression lying down. And this is especially so when the struggle is within a good-natured

community who will recognize that men who fight and lose must be generously treated by the victorious party: that a willingness to fight, with the certainty that you will lose, implies a big grievance. Whether these considerations hold good on this occasion I do not know. To us it was as clear as noonday that with the trade union movement in its present state of mind this weapon of a final strike would be used. When it has been tried and failed, as fail it will, the workers will be in a better frame of mind for steady and sensible political action. . . .

The net impression left on my mind is that the General Strike will turn out not to be a revolution of any sort or kind but a batch of compulsory Bank Holidays without any opportunities for recreation and a lot of dreary walking to and fro. When the million or so strikers have spent their money they will drift back to work and no one will be any the better and many will be a great deal poorer and everybody will be cross. It is a monstrous irrelevance in the sphere of social reform. If it be prolonged a week or ten days it may lead to reactionary legislation against trade unionism and possibly to a general election. But I doubt it. If the government keeps its head and goes persistently and skilfully to work in reconstructing services the General Strike will peter out; and the noxious futility of this mild edition of the 'dictatorship of the proletariat' will be apparent to everyone, not least to trade unionists who find their funds exhausted and many of their most able members victimized by being permanently displaced by patriotic blacklegs! There will be, not only an excuse but a justification of victimization on a considerable scale. . . .

For the British trade union movement I see a day of terrible disillusionment. The failure of the General Strike of 1926 will be one of the most significant landmarks in the history of the British working class. Future historians will, I think, regard it as the death gasp of that pernicious doctrine of 'workers' control' of public affairs through the trade unions, and by the method of direct action. This absurd doctrine was introduced into British working-class life by Tom Mann and the Guild Socialists and preached insistently, before the war, by the *Daily Herald* under George Lansbury. In Russia, it was quickly repudiated by Lenin and the Soviets, and the trade unions were reduced to complete subordination to the creed autocracy of the Communist Party. In Italy, the attempt to put this doctrine into practice by seizing the factories led to the Fascist revolution. In Great Britain, this belated and emasculated edition of the doctrine of workers' control will probably lead to a mild attempt to hamper trade union activities. Popular disgust with the loss and inconvenience of a General Strike will considerably check the growth of the Labour Party in the country, but will lead to a rehabilitation of political methods and strengthen J.R. MacDonald's leadership within the party itself.

On the whole, I think it was a proletarian distemper which had to run its course — and like other distempers, it is well to have it over and done with at the cost of a lengthy convalescence. Above all, as the Italian Fascist government has discovered, the subordination of the trade union entails an almost equal state control for the capitalist employer. In a word, the workers' control movement has led throughout the world to the extension and strengthening of state bureaucracy. . . .

7 May. 2 a.m. [Passfield Corner]
Russell brought Sidney down in his car, and came in for a pipe and a talk. They were both of them, particularly Russell, far more apprehensive of a long strike and of bloodshed in the streets before it ended than I had been. Sidney says the forty miners' members are obdurate about any reduction of wages or lengthening of hours and were furious with J.H. Thomas for suggesting that if the coal-owners' notices were withdrawn, the miners would consider the question of a temporary reduction of wages during the immediate re-organization of the industry. Also, reports show that the working class generally is far more anxious to strike than the General Council of T.U.C. and . . . reports Henderson as angry with the miners, and J.R.M. and Thomas as depressed at their powerlessness to bring about a settlement. Philip Snowden, being dead against the trade unions, is philosophical. The inner circle hates the General Strike and sees no good coming out of it. . . .

The General Strike was called off by the General Council of the T.U.C. on 12 May on the understanding that negotiations would be resumed. A second general strike began on 13 May, when men going back to work found themselves either refused or accepted only with a reduction of wages. Those who had gone out on strike to help the miners now found the miners deserted and themselves left to strike anew for their very livelihood. In the next few days, settlements were made in the industries concerned and the men returned to work. But the coal dispute continued, until it crumbled away at the end of

December with a loss to the miners on all counts. Royalty-owners were those who received payment from the mining companies for coal extracted from their land.

14 May. General Strike, 1926 [Passfield Corner]
Little more than a nine days' world wonder, costing Great Britain tens of millions, and leaving other nations asking whether it was a balked revolution or play-acting on a stupendous scale? In the first two or three days there was complete stoppage and paralysis of trade, but hosts of volunteers started skeleton services, and Hyde Park and Regent's Park became great camps of soldiers living in tents, with improvised shelters for the store of milk and other commodities. Not a shot has been fired, not a life is lost. In one town the police and strikers played cricket, and the victory of the strikers is published to ten million listeners by the government-controlled wireless! Slowly buses and trams begin to appear; the London taxi-cab drivers decide to 'come out', but the next morning the buses are seen in the London streets obviously driven by professionals!

On Monday, the seventh day of the strike, Sidney and I travel up by the milk-train to London – it is crowded but not a single remark did we hear about the strike; the third-class passengers at any rate were unusually silent, even for English passengers, more bored than alarmed – and the same silence is in the streets, more like a Sunday with the shops open, but with no one shopping. Just a very slight reminiscence of the first days of the Great War, the parking of innumerable motors in the squares and by-streets and here and there officers in khaki, even one or two armoured cars in attendance on strings of motor buses piled up with food. It is characteristic that government lorries, sometimes driven by army engineers, are labelled 'food only', as if to appeal to the strikers not to interfere with them. No strain or fear on the faces of the citizens, male or female, only a sort of amused boredom. Universal condemnation of the General Strike but widespread sympathy with the miners. . . .

On Tuesday morning I passed through the Fabian bookshop to see Galton. The hall was occupied by a score or so of men – the strike committee of the London branch of the Railway Clerks' Association (so I was afterwards told), and one of them was speaking through the phone. I caught the words, 'I recommend that we go in.' 'What's up?' I asked Galton. 'The usual thing,' said he in his cheery cynical voice. 'They've got cold feet. A week ago, that man who is the secretary of the committee told me that in three days' time the Cabinet would be on their knees, that the soldiers and police were on their side and a lot of other bunkum. Yesterday afternoon he came with tears in his eyes. 'Twenty of our men went in this morning. I saw my boss this morning', he added, 'and he says my place is still open but will be filled tomorrow. I can't afford to stay out – I am going in and I am going to advise the others to do so too.' In the afternoon of the same day Galton told me that at a meeting of about fifty the majority determined to stay out but fifteen, including the chairman and secretary, left the room for their respective offices.

The second episode filled me with dreary forebodings of terrible disillusionment. On Thursday morning, the very day of the 'call-off' of the strike, I motored with Susan [Lawrence] into her constituency [East Ham]. Just before we started, Laski phoned up and told me confidentially that the General Council was going to Downing Street at eleven o'clock and that the Strike would be settled. So I warned Susan to be careful what she said. All was quiet along those wide streets of the Poplar and East and West Ham constituencies. Our first meeting was about 1,000 railwaymen at Ilford, then we visited the Council of Action, and an open-air meeting in Susan's constituency, from where we went to the Poplar Council of Action. In all these gatherings the men seemed determined but depressed, and I gathered from Susan's manner that she also was disappointed – possibly my cold scepticism depressed her. But she worked herself up into a fine spirit of demagogic optimism. . . . A little before two o'clock we drove into Palace Yard, Westminster and she jumped out. 'The strike is settled,' said the constable in a non-committal and respectful tone. She hurried in and I walked off to lunch through a grinning crowd of sightseers and special constables, thinking mostly of the amazing change in Susan Lawrence's mentality – from a hard-sensed lawyer-like mind and conventional manner of the moderate member of the London School Board, whose acquaintance I had made five-and-twenty years ago, to the somewhat wild woman of demagogic speech, addressing her constituents as 'comrades' and abasing herself and her class before the *real* wealth producers. Today Susan is a victim to spasms of emotional excitement which drive her from one weird suggestion to another. She lives in an unreal world. In order to keep in touch with what she imagines to be the proletarian mind she has lost touch with facts as they are. And yet she is a real good soul, devoted and public-spirited. It is a bad case of the occupational disease so common among high-strung men and women who come out of a conservative environment into proletarian politics. By continuously talking to another class in the language they think that class speaks instead of in their own vernacular, they deceive themselves and create distrust in their audience.

What will those East End workers think who listened to Susan yesterday, coming straight from the centre of things, to tell them that they were winning hands down, when they heard the news a few hours later: General Strike called off unconditionally? What is the good of having professional brainworkers to represent you, if they refuse to give you the honest message of intelligence but treat you to a florid expression of the emotion which *they* think the working class are feeling or ought to be feeling? The next step is that the brainworkers deceive themselves and think that they *have* the emotion they are expressing. Which subtle insincerity destroys their usefulness. They are neither brainworkers using their intellects, nor exponents of the initiative decision of the unthinking multitude who, if left alone to feel their way for themselves, are by no means such fools as some people think. . . .

18 May. [Passfield Corner]
Churchill's announcement in the House today that the General Strike will have cost the government no more than three-quarters of a million — a sum which the death of a couple of millionaires will pay — puts the cap of ridicule on the heroics of the General Strike. The three million strikers will have spent some three million pounds of trade union money and lost another four or five in wages; they will have 'gone in', owing to Baldwin's wisdom, on the old conditions in wages and hours, but considerably shackled with regard to future strikes of a lightning character. If anti-trade union legislation does not follow it will be due to the utter failure of their movement to carry out its bombastic threat of paralysing the country's life. The government has gained immense prestige in the world and the British labour movement has made itself ridiculous. A strike which opens with a football match between the police and the strikers and ends in unconditional surrender after nine days, with densely packed reconciliation services at all the chapels and

churches of Great Britain, attended by the strikers and their families, will make the Continental socialists blaspheme. . . .

Let me add that the failure of the General Strike shows what a *sane* people the British are. If only our revolutionaries would realize the hopelessness of their attempt to turn the British workman into a Russian Red and the British businessman and country gentleman into an Italian Fascist! The British are hopelessly good-natured and [full of] common sense, to which the British workman adds pigheadedness, jealousy and stupidity. What oppresses me is the fear that these elements of crass stupidity and pigheaded obstinacy may prevent the revival of British trade, and that trade unionism may diminish and not increase efficiency. The miners in particular are plunging about without any idea in their heads except resistance to cuts in wages or lengthening hours – they don't care a damn about the reorganization of their industry and they are even hostile to nationalization of royalties because of their obsession about no compensation to royalty-owners. In their conduct towards the General Council they have been impossible, demanding a General Strike but refusing to consult about the settlement they would accept. The General Council has been equally impossible in their treatment of the Parliamentary Labour Party; they drifted into the General Strike, and suddenly closed it down, in both cases being swayed by the impulse of the moment without any consideration for the necessities and interests of those with whom they were co-operating. And yet they mean so well! They are so genuinely kindly in their outlook; they would gladly shake hands with anyone at any time, whether it be a Tory Prime Minister, a Russian emissary or their own employers. They play at revolution and they run away from the consequences with equal alacrity. The General Strike of 1926 is a grotesque tragedy. The Labour leaders and their immediate followers, whether political or individual, live in the atmosphere of alternating day-dreams and nightmares, day-dreams about social transformation brought about in the twinkling of an eye, and visions of treachery in their own ranks and malignancy on the other side – all equally fantastic and without foundation. We are all of us just good-natured stupid folk. The worst of it is that the governing class are as good-natured and stupid as the labour movement! Are we decadent – or is this growing alarm about the future only a reflection of my own old age? I have lost my day-dreams, I have only the nightmare left – the same sort of nightmare

I had during the Great War: that European civilization is in the course of dissolution. . . .

William Gillies (1859–1929) was a Labour M.P. and miners' leader. C.T. Cramp (1876–1933) became general secretary of the National Union of Railwaymen in 1920. Walter Citrine (1887–1983) was general secretary of the T.U.C. 1926–46. Herbert Smith (1862–1938) was President of the Miners' Federation 1922–29. The T.U.C. and the Labour Party occupied neighbouring offices in Eccleston Square, Victoria.

22 May. [Passfield Corner]
Gillies came down to lunch yesterday afternoon; he had been watching events at 33 from 32 Eccleston Square and he has been at the conference of executives on the Saturday at which it was decided to send out the notices for the General Strike. Cramp was in the chair; there was no discussion; before the vote was taken, a document reciting the result of the negotiation with Baldwin and his refusal to insist on the notices being withdrawn by the mine-owners had been circulated to the executives at twelve o'clock on Friday night, and at ten o'clock the following morning they were asked whether or not they agreed to the General Council's proposals to call out the first line of defence – railways, transport, etc. The roll of the unions was called and one by one their representatives gave their decision – the vast majority and all the great unions answering 'yes'; one or two of the little unions said they had not any authority to vote one way or the other. 'Pure fatalism,' whispered Cramp to Gillies. 'We can't win.' But neither he nor anyone else said this to the meeting. Gillies told me that he had never felt before, at any meeting, that the persons concerned were being carried away by the feeling *that they had to do it*, that the rank and file would expect it, and another Black Friday would be intolerable.

The calling off the strike was equally without discussion. All the members of the General Council were in favour of it, largely because they were indignant with the miners for not accepting the Samuel Memorandum. Here again was a fatal misunderstanding through lack of discussion and agreed decision. The General Council had imagined that when the miners asked them to call a General Strike, it was agreed to put the General Council in command of the negotiations with the government and the mine-owners. The miners declared that they had throughout said that they would not accept any reduction of wages. No records had been kept as the two secretaries – Cook and Citrine – had been sent out of the room when the General Council and the Miners' executive were in session! Gillies thinks that it was this revelation – that the miners intended the General Council to go on until the government and the mine-owners had accepted the *status quo ante* – that induced the General Council to call off the strike at once. They thought that Baldwin had accepted the Samuel proposals; but, as Gillies observed, the miners' stubborn refusal to accept the compromise relieved the Prime Minister from his private undertaking, even if he gave one, which seems uncertain. 'It is not a question of bad leadership,' summed up Gillies; 'there was no leadership at all – the General Council, including Thomas, seemed to drift backward and forward as if moved by some external force which had no relation to their own minds.' As for the Miners' executive, they knew their districts would not accept a reduction without a fight, however hopeless and disastrous the fight was. When the joint research department brought before them a table of figures showing that the *status quo ante* meant closing so many mines and another 300,000 unemployed, 'Let them be unemployed,' said Herbert Smith.

All the intellectuals who watched the General Council and Miners' executive during these days (Gillies, Laski, Tawney) made one observation. Those fifty or sixty men who were directing the General Council were living a thoroughly unwholesome life – smoking, drinking, eating wrong meals at wrong times, rushing about in motor cars, getting little or no sleep and talking aimlessly one with another. During the day before they called off the strike, the assembled executives were sitting in groups singing songs and telling stories, soothed and enlivened by a plentiful supply of tobacco and alcohol. At crucial meetings at which important decisions were taken there was no real discussion; the secretaries were usually sent out of the room and nothing was recorded. There were perpetual misunderstandings between the General Council and the miners; they were silent or 'rowed' each other according to their moods. After a Council meeting some of the members would adjourn to a neighbouring public house and discuss matters at the bar with reporters present. It is characteristic of Smillie that he left London for Scotland on the outbreak of war, the other miner representative on the General Council being absent on account of illness. So, as A.J. Cook complains, the miners were unrepresented on the General Council throughout the 'nine days'. Citrine, the able secretary of the General Council, was treated as a shorthand typist and was seldom allowed to attend the meetings, leave alone offer advice. . . .

31 May. [Passfield Corner]
There remains over from this sensational episode of the General Strike, the miners' lock-out – a far bigger challenge to capitalist enterprise. The million miners are obdurate and no one can take their place; they have a stranglehold on British industry and can paralyse it as effectually though not as suddenly as the railwaymen.

There are only two ways of beating them: sheer starvation, or a sufficient importation of coal to make them feel that the struggle was useless. But dare the government let them and their wives and children starve? At least the women and children are getting food at the ratepayers' expense, and the men must get some of that food, and, with the huge public subscription, must eke out the rest. If there were to be any sensational stoppage of food in the pit villages or if coal were to be freely imported, a drastic sympathetic strike would burst out again. . . .

12 June. [Passfield Corner]
At the back of my mind is a certain personal discomfort about the miners' lock-out. Ought we or ought we not to give, and ask others to give, to the fund for the miners' wives and children? Neither Sidney nor I would have given a penny to it if no one would have been the wiser. I gave my name to the Committee and sent a cheque for £10 simply because I conformed to the loudly expressed opinion of the world of labour – with which I secretly disagreed. 'Not a cent off the wages, not a second on the day' was *not* the best way to get the reorganization of the industry . . . I think the miners and the General Council could have got it if they had been skilful, if J.R. MacDonald, Henderson and Thomas had been allowed to negotiate. Assuming the government refuse to do it, is there the remotest chance of the miners compelling reorganization by holding out indefinitely for conditions which cannot be given without reorganization? Sidney thinks that by holding out they are *diminishing* the amount of reorganization which will be actually accomplished; that they are making it easier for the mine-owners to slither on without improvements, and that the probable outcome of a prolonged struggle will be to break down the dyke of the national wage and

generally to worsen conditions of employment throughout the industry. Hence that £10 was misgiven; the truth being that it was easier to give than to explain why we were against the fund. Also we were not *certain* that we were right: so we gave our £10, but refrained from asking anyone else to subscribe. A weak, perhaps a cowardly compromise! Perhaps we ought to have *not* given, but remained silent about our reasons, not feeling sufficiently confident of their rightness in opposition to the current public opinion of the movement. Moral pedantry? What does it matter? Disgruntled old folk we are.

18 June. [Passfield Corner]

The letters from the Seaham women reveal no distress and some light-hearted enjoyment of the excitement of the strike: the children, one mother tells me, regard the school feeding 'as a picnic that happens every day', the food being better than they get at home. The relief provided by the guardians is nicknamed 'Kind Joe', and some women, at any rate, are better off than they were before the lock-out. What I fear is a horrible time of disillusion and suffering when the men are back at work with some of them out of work and all the conditions worsened; with credit exhausted and outstanding debts. . . .

What will the labour movement be a year hence? The Labour Party will prosper; the Baldwin government is going to become hideously unpopular; but wages will fall and hours will lengthen and unemployment will be rife, and there will be a slump in the birth and marriage rate. When the next Labour Cabinet takes office Great Britain will be in a slow decline in population, trade and wealth *relatively* to other countries. We may not lessen the amenity of life – our working class may escape even temporary misery, through the decline of the birth-rate and emigration, though I doubt it. Our *rentiers* and professional class may even, through decrease in luxury and greater strenuousness, improve in character and intelligence. There will be no revolution, either Communist or Fascist. If the Labour Party comes in it will move to the right and not to the left, whilst the Tory Party will move to the left and not to the right. Both parties will be mildly collectivist and Great Britain will slither on to a spate of relative quiescence and powerlessness in the world's affairs. The one hopeful feature is the steady improvement in hygiene and manners and in the facilities for a comfortable and interested life. The consumption of wealth is far more intelligent than it has ever been before, and if the production of wealth keeps up, the inhabitants of Great Britain may become less powerful, and relatively to other races, poorer and less luxurious. So I end on a hopeful note . . .

Sir Almroth Wright (1861–1947) was a bacteriologist at St Mary's Hospital, London, who introduced anti-typhoid inoculation. Shaw admired Wright and it was a visit to him that inspired the theme of *The Doctor's Dilemma*. The political play Beatrice refers to emerged as *The Apple Cart* in 1929, which was written, Shaw told Beatrice in a letter of 5 September 1939, 'to your order'.

23 June. [Passfield Corner]
GBS and Charlotte here for the inside of a week. Since we were with them in April he has been seriously ill with kidney trouble and continuous temperatures – threatenings of organic disease. Now Almroth Wright tells him that he has apparently cured himself. It has been a depressing time; Charlotte says he has lost interest in everything, though he went on working at his book. This book on socialism is turning out to be a nuisance, a veritable bog of dialectics; also he is obsessed with his correspondence. Charlotte says he is jealous of his right to write letters! But ill or not ill, he is just the same dear friend and somewhat sobered but still brilliant sprite that used to stay with us at The Argoed over thirty years ago. He never changes; he never grows old; he has the same delightful personality; he is less vain than he used to be – indeed, he is not vain at all; he has lost all the old bitterness, and with it the capacity for invective. But that is perhaps due to his outstanding success. The wonder is, not that he has lost the spirit of revolt, but that he has retained the demand for equality and his consideration for the underdog. He is brooding over a new play – a political play. . . .

28 June. [Passfield Corner]
Herbert Samuel, ex-Cabinet Minister, back from the governorship of Palestine and the chairmanship of the Coal Commission and (within the last few weeks) from persuading the General Council to call off the General Strike, spent the week-end with us. He has changed little, either in appearance and manners or in outlook, from the rich young man, conscientiously and energetically entering public life, whom we first knew nearly forty years ago. He is just a trifle stouter and more debonair; he is even *more* economical in

personal expenditure, circumspect in behaviour and discreet in speech; these are tendencies which have grown on him. He is less conceited – indeed, he is not conceited at all. Considering his marked success as a Cabinet Minister, parliamentarian and pro-consul, he is, in fact, singularly modest. The exercise of power has softened, not hardened his heart, and industry and experience have extended and matured his faculties. He is an estimable citizen, an able public servant, a devoted husband and father. He is not exciting; his words leave no pictures either of events or persons; his arguments are restricted in scope and his conclusions, though sensible, are commonplace. His sense of humour takes the irritating form of tactless irony at the expense of the person he is talking to. All the same, I thoroughly appreciated an eight-mile walk with him and twenty-four hours' talk about the past, present and future. : . . Samuel's heart is centred in his family and his race and Palestine would be his home. He and his wife wanted to go on living there but the government objected to the presence of an ex-governor directly after his term of office. Our longstanding relation with Herbert Samuel, like the man himself, has worn well . . . and we parted with the kindliest feelings of mutual respect and friendship. . . .

30 June. [Passfield Corner]
. . . . the chasm between the Cabinet (who have now become parliamentary agents to the coal-owners) and the miners who, maintained by the rates and public subscription, herd after Cook and Herbert Smith, is widening past repair. I see no reason why the stoppage in Great Britain's basic industry should not continue almost indefinitely in a stalemate until one or other party goes under in disastrous collapse, with the other side almost as badly damaged by the process.

There is one outstanding new fact never seen before in our country. The two political parties, one of which *must* be in power, are today definitely and permanently pledged to carry out, in the political sphere, the demands of one or other of the combatants in the industrial world. And it is exactly this drastic drawing of the lines of conflict that has finally smashed the Liberal Party. Asquith, Grey and Simon found themselves fighting with the capitalists: Lloyd George and some others deliberately ranged themselves with the trade unionists. The Report of the Liberal Royal Commission has proved to be a rotten bridge. Why? Because whilst its diagnosis bore out the miners' contention that longer hours and lower wages could not save the industry from decline, its recommendations were rooted in permissive legislation which left the colliery-owners free to go on as before. 'He who is not whole-heartedly with us is against us,' is the today's cry on both sides. For the present at any rate, 'the inevitability of gradualness' and the desirability of compromise are at a discount. The diehards are in possession. . . .

Lloyd George announces his intention of going to Russia in the recess – and he will come back as a qualified admirer of the Soviet Republic. Austen Chamberlain, to whose lifeless voice and pompous intonation we listened over the wireless the other night, is booming Mussolini as the saviour of Italy and the originator of a 'great and successful experiment' in social reorganization. *We* regard Soviet Russia and Fascist Italy as belonging to one and the same species of government, the creed-autocracy insisting on the supremacy of one social philosophy bringing unity to the people over all conflicting creeds and sectional interests. Russian Communism and Italian Fascism are both alike a reaction from caste or syndicalist anarchy. The British people have a mild attack of this epidemic of self-will, and the identification of one political party with militant capitalism and the other with militant proletarianism is the form this epidemic takes. It will be interesting to observe which type of reaction will set in in our country, or whether we shall revert to a bran' new form of social democracy incorporating our tradition of liberty with an accepted social order? Are we declining? Or are we inventing a new rule of life?

18 July. 2 a.m. [Passfield Corner]
The last few nights have been so hot and sleepless that I have spent some hours on a portrait of Sidney for use in *Our Partnership*, assuming that volume ever gets itself written. I have honestly tried to describe him as I see him objectively with all his defects, not as I, in my weaker moments, should like my beloved to appear to the world. I know that what is true of other lovers is true of me – it is silly to touch up the photograph, to smooth out all the ugly lines and disproportions; the outcome is a meaningless human being in whose existence no one believes. If they believed, few would like so faultless a person. Pity and loyalty as well as admiration and dependence are among the ingredients of love. And how can one

pity or be loyal to an all-perfect being? Meanwhile my share of the Poor Law book does not get done — in the main because I am preoccupied with preparations for the Labour fête on the 31st — an annual undertaking for us; and expensive as well as troublesome. But I felt I must do something for the local Labour people; they are down-hearted, living as they do in a hostile environment. We shall pay for it out of the parliamentary salary.

Perhaps more distracting has been my worrying about Jessie and her influence on the young servant who has been brought in to help her from the village. Jessie Norris has been with me for fourteen years: she is, in many respects, an excellent servant and I have a real liking for her, and I think she was fond of me. But bottles of whisky disappeared at a greater rate than usual. I checked her entries by keeping an account myself and the result was unmistakable! Which raises doubts as to her trustworthiness in other matters, a horrid state of things. For the last two years I have been so absorbed in the book that I have been a careless housekeeper; also I am getting old and my memory fails me when I am working hard. The result has been an unwelcome rise in weekly expenditure which we cannot afford even if we ought to allow it. After consulting Sidney — who also is attached to Jessie as an old servant — we decided 'to wait and see'. We shall judge by the cost of housekeeping, and give her the benefit of the doubt for the doings of the last months.

24 July. 2 a.m. [Passfield Corner]
Thirty-four years ago, on 23 July, we were married, and yesterday we celebrated it by spending the whole day together like two young lovers, driving in the morning to Petersfield to redeem the land tax on this plot of land and going for a long walk in the afternoon, finishing up by listening to a symphony concert over the wireless in the evening. The Other One is extraordinarily well and happy; perhaps getting a wee bit restive at dissipating so much time at Westminster and thus not getting on with the book. . . . For my part, except for my chronic melancholy — perhaps *indifference to life* is the better phrase — due to declining vitality, I am content with this last year. The labour and worry spent on *My Apprenticeship* has been justified, so far as public appreciation is concerned. 'Original and distinguished' has been the general verdict. It is clear that the book will influence thought, and be read by students and thinkers

and quoted by future historians. From a pecuniary point of view the outcome is less flattering. Four months' sale in U.K. and U.S.A. (1,200 in U.K. and 500 in U.S.A.) has paid our printers' bill for nearly four thousand copies and yielded two or three hundred pounds profit. . . . My literary reputation has gone up considerably but our past income of £500 a year from books will not be *increased*. This masterpiece of my old age may just about keep this modest reward of all our labours past and present, intact for another ten years! Which means when Sidney retires from Parliament we shall have about £1,500 a year to spend, assuming of course that Great Britain retains its present production and goes on distributing the national income in the same way as heretofore. Fifteen hundred a year would enable us to live here comfortably, but we should have to cut down some of our social activities, like this Labour gathering on Saturday. . . .

31 July. 2 a.m. [Passfield Corner]
The Miners' delegate meeting has endorsed the Miners' executive resolution that they accept the memorandum of the bishops, signed by Herbert Smith and A.J. Cook – immediate resumption of work on April terms with a subsidy to inferior mines, awaiting the interpretation by the Royal Commission of their own report, and arbitration on all questions arising out of it, including wages, except hours. If they had agreed to this six months ago there would have been no General Strike and no miners' strike. Today the government and the owners think they are on the eve of victory and will refuse to negotiate on these lines; the employers, clearly, want a fight to the finish. But the miners are still in a strong position – a far stronger position than any considerable body of strikers have ever been. There is no possible substitute for their labours; if they don't hew coal, no one else can; and if British coal is not worked, British industry can hardly survive as a going concern. Hitherto the miners could be starved into submission: today humanitarian sentiment and working-class control of local authorities makes that impossible with regard to the miners' families and difficult in the case of the men themselves. . . .

I am inclined to think that this miners' strike is going to be by far the most momentous industrial struggle in my lifetime. Among other things, it may settle whether Great Britain is going to solve the problem of democratic government or not. . . .

2 August. [Passfield Corner]
Our gathering of near on two thousand members of the Labour parties of Hampshire, Surrey and Sussex, arriving in eighty charabancs, to listen to MacDonald and Margaret Bondfield, with Ponsonby, Russell, de la Warr and ourselves as minor performers, went off brilliantly, to the great satisfaction of Croft, the headquarters organizer, and to the amused astonishment of the neighbourhood. We did what we intended to do; we showed headquarters how to wake up these tracts of commons and residential parks, of small towns and seaside resorts, unprovided with halls for big meetings, at a low cost or at no cost at all. For if we had had a little more experience we could have made the occasion pay its way. The secret is that with charabancs and the increasing habit of jaunts of town workers into the country, combined with the difficulty experienced by ardent party workers of seeing their leaders in a homely sort of way, these garden-parties are bound to attract large numbers, and are also an advertisement of the existence of the Labour Party in an effective form. There is the risk of bad weather, but even here it can be almost overcome if you provide, as we did, a monster marquee. Our luck was a delightful warm grey day ending in a burst of sunshine when J.R.M. was giving his second speech and final farewell. All the same, the arrangements have cost me thought and anxiety and expense and I shall not do it again in a hurry.

The leader of the Labour Party was in his best form. He is an attractive creature, he has a certain beauty in colouring, figure and face, a delightful voice and an easy unpretentious manner, a youthful enjoyment of his prestige as a prime minister, all of which is amusing to watch. But his conversation is not entertaining or stimulating – it consists of pleasant anecdotes about political and Society personages, occasionally some episode in his own career, told with calculated discretion. When he and I walked round the garden together he talked exclusively about his weekly visits to Christie's and the pieces of old furniture he was picking up. Directly you turn the conversation off trivial personalities on to subjects, whether it be general questions or the domestic problems of the Labour Party, J.R.M. dries up and looks bored. Not once did we *discuss* anything whatsoever, and even the anecdotes led nowhere. . . . Ramsay MacDonald is a magnificent substitute for a leader. He has the ideal appearance. ('Every day he grows more distinguished-looking,' writes the *Nation*.) But he is shoddy in character and intellect. Our great one has yet to come. Shall I live to see him? Or will it be *she* who must be obeyed?

5 August. [Passfield Corner]
'Look for the man.' In poor Jessie's case a dissolute married man, who has already seduced a well-to-do woman, got married to her and is today living on an allowance she makes him to be rid of his claims. He is the son of our builder and has frequently worked here. This unfortunate affair which, unknown to me, was one of the scandals of the village, ended in the infatuated Jessie outrunning all discretion by letting him sleep with her in the scullery, in sight of the little girl from the village. Here is the explanation of all the rest of her misbehaviour – pilfering whisky and perhaps other things, underhand dealings of all sorts and general untrustfulness. She seemed dumbfounded when I said she must go; apparently she has counted on my affection for an old servant to cover all her sins – not a flattering estimate of my capacity as a mistress. . . .

The break-up of all the conventions about sexual relations makes the relation of mistress and servant far more difficult than it was in the good old times of recognized Christian ethics. How far has the mistress the *right* to demand chastity in the woman servant? In London the question does not necessarily arise. Who knows and who cares? In a village *everything* is known and talked about. . . .

J.M. Keynes (1883–1946) was an economist. As a Treasury official, he had attended the Versailles conference in 1919. Disillusioned, he attacked the treaty in *The Economic Consequences of the Peace*. He was closely associated with the Liberal Party and wrote regularly for the *Nation* and *Athenaeum*. In 1925 he married the ballet dancer Lydia Lopokova (1892–1981). He was one of the central figures in the Bloomsbury Group.

9 August. [Passfield Corner]
There must be scarcity of politically constructive minds if J.M. Keynes seems such a treasure! Hitherto he has not attracted me – brilliant, supercilious, and not sufficiently patient for sociological discovery even if he had the heart for it, I should have said. But then I had barely seen him; also I think his love marriage with the fascinating little Russian dancer has awakened his emotional sympathies with poverty and suffering. For when I look around I see no other man who might discover how to control the wealth of

nations in the public interest. He is not merely brilliant in expression and provocative in thought; he is a realist: he faces facts and he has persistency and courage in thought and action. By taste an administrator, by talent a man of science, with a remarkable literary gift, he has not the make-up of a political leader. Not that he lacks 'personality' – he is impressive and attractive, he could impose himself on an audience and gather round him a group of followers and disciples; if he could tolerate a political party as God makes it, he could lead it. But he is contemptuous of common men, especially when gathered together in herds. He dislikes the human herd and has no desire to enlist the herd instinct on his side. Hence his antipathy to trade unions, to proletarian culture, to nationalism and patriotism as distinguished from public spirit. The common interests and vulgar prejudices of aristocracies and plutocracies are equally displeasing to him – in fact he dislikes all the common-or-garden thoughts and emotions that bind men together in bundles. He would make a useful member of a Cabinet, but would he ever get there? Certainly not as a member of one of the present Front Benches. I do not know which one – Conservative or Labour – he would despise most. As for the rank and file! Heaven help them. What Keynes might achieve is a big scheme of social engineering; he might even be called in to carry it out, but as an expert and not as a representative.

As an ardent lover of the bewitching Lydia Lopokova this eminent thinker and political pamphleteer is charming to contemplate.

12 August. [Passfield Corner]
Haldane must have been considerably hurt by the sin of omission in *My Apprenticeship* for he has not sent me his book on *Human Experience*, a popular exposition of his philosophy. Which grieves me, as the omission was accidental and did not represent my lack of gratitude and appreciation; it was due to absent-mindedness in the hurry-scurry of a fagged brain to finish with the damn thing. Distinguished persons who outlive the publication of reminiscences of friends and colleagues, as Haldane has, must learn to put up with absent-mindedness – it is the least of the evils they may have to tolerate! And Haldane is exactly one of the personages who will come off unduly badly in memoirs: his personality is affectionate but he has excited jealousy by his social charm and apparent

influence with inner circles. Also, his brand of political thought and his capacity for intrigue are not liked or admired by Englishmen; he is too satirical and subtle, too contemptuous of the common man. He excites distrust in the public schoolboy type and fear in the good party member; they like to depreciate him and his influence. Thus he will find himself ignored or run down in the memoirs of his contemporaries because the authors either don't want to mention him or cannot place him satisfactorily to themselves. . . .

21 August. [Passfield Corner]
The agony of the miners' resistance to the owners' terms has begun; how long and how fierce it may be no one can say; I am inclined to think the end will come before the Trades Union Congress the first week in September; Sidney says 'the end of September'. . . . Taken with the failure of the General Strike it is a big catastrophe; it is the biggest defeat trade unionism has ever experienced, somewhat akin to the collapse of 1834. But, as in the Great War, it is very doubtful whether the victors will not lose as much as the vanquished. The capitalist owners have proved themselves as malicious as they are stupid; the government has shown itself as incompetent to end as to avert the most costly industrial dispute that has ever occurred; it has proved so partisan that it has turned many Conservative workmen into good Labour supporters. So far as I can see, the only organization that comes out the stronger for this disaster is the Parliamentary Labour Party – for the simple reason that the prestige of the General Council of the Trades Union Congress has been destroyed, and the strike as a weapon has been discredited. Indeed, the agony of the Miners' Federation *might* mean a Labour government after the General Election of 1928. . . .

The thought of all this needless misery, the burden of debt in the miners' homes, the disheartening unbelief in leaders and causes, is a nightmare made worse by a subconsciousness that Sidney and I, though associated with the miners, have not been able to give a helping hand. We have simply stood on one side. All we could have given is money and to give money has seemed to us at best throwing it away. . . .

All the same I feel horribly mean, living here in comfort and peace, whilst the battle rages and the lines of the workers' army begin to waver before the savage onslaught of the employers. It would have been easier to have sent £100 and – I will not say saved one's conscience – but saved one's reputation! 'We sent £100 to the Miners' Relief Fund,' one could have whispered sympathetically to our Seaham friends. 'We did not see what else we could do,' one could have added in deprecating tones, 'we are not open-air speakers!' And it is Heaven knows what we shall say when we get up to Seaham in October. It is clear we can't tell the truth even if the battle is over, which it may not be in Durham. In the first hour of defeat the truth would be far too cruel for human endurance.

VOLUME 41

1 September. [Passfield Corner]
Sidney came back from two days and one night in London exhausted and unusually depressed. He had spent six hours or more looking up references for the book at the British Museum and the House of Commons. During the rest of the working time, listening to the dreary debates on the Emergency Regulations and the miners' strike or at parliamentary meetings of one sort or another. 'The Miners' executive,' he said, 'had given out to the press that they were going to meet us in order to settle a joint policy; when they came at eight o'clock on Monday night, they had nothing to say but that they could say nothing before the delegates' meeting on Thursday!!!' J.R.M. tried to persuade them to make up their minds to ask the government for a meeting with the mine-owners with 'an open agenda'. A.J. Cook was frankly in favour, but Herbert Smith was obdurate. It is like watching a man committing suicide – it is worse because the leaders are killing not themselves but the men's organization. Six months ago they could have kept the seven-hour day and the national agreements; today they have lost both and are at the employers' mercy about wages. Meanwhile the Parliamentary Labour Party is left without a policy; they are tied to the tail of the miners without being consulted as to which way the tail should wag. A.J. Cook goes to tea with Lloyd George and is reported to have been much impressed; no doubt his present conciliatory policy is due to Lloyd George's tact. He does not come and consult (nor do any of the other members of the Miners' executive) with any members of the Labour Front Bench or even with the miners' M.P.s. These pitifully inarticulate trade union

officials dare not consult or confer with anyone who counts on terms of give-and-take. All they are willing to do is to state their terms, in a muddled way, and then leave the room. They run away from discussion. I very much doubt whether they really *discuss* the situation with each other. They repeat, repeat, repeat the old slogans and then take a vote, and the vote tends in favour of some other body making the decision! The miners' leaders are suffering from general paralysis of the will and have been for some time. Robert Smillie, in spite of his impressive personality and sombre eloquence, never had a policy, industrial or political. All he has are dogmas like 'no compensation for royalty-owners', the sort of dogma that actually prevents things getting done. . . .

5 September. [Passfield Corner]
G.D.H. Cole and his wife – always attractive because they are at once disinterested and brilliantly intellectual and, be it added, agreeable to look at – stayed a week-end with us and later came on to the T.U.C. Middle age finds them saner and more charitable in their outlook. Cole still dismisses this man or that with 'I hate him,' but it is the remnant of a mannerism, for he no longer means it. He is still a fanatic but he is a fanatic who has lost his peculiar faith. He is disillusioned about workers' control – the fumbling of the workers in their own limited affairs is too obvious. I doubt whether today his vision of the future development of society seriously differs from ours, except that he longs for *decisive landmarks*, something to startle the world, a new and bright idea that will serve as a revolutionary thought or crisis or anything which will enthuse the world. But he has failed to discover it: all he can think of is a sensational denunciation of inheritance and 'regionalism'! He writes, lectures and manipulates indefatigably, lives plainly; he is devoted to his wife, plays with his two little girls, but with nothing else. He has no silly pleasures, and for art or music he has only an intellectual comprehension. In his family life he is a model in self-control and reasonableness, and he is an excellent citizen; he is indefatigable in his public-spirited industry. What does he lack to make him a big influence? Humanity and sympathy, I think. He is not interested in men; he is not interested in the working of their minds or in the drama of their relationships; he is curiously abstract in his ideas about society. He neither admires nor pities human nature; he is contemptuous of his fellow men – at best he tolerates

and uses them. Margaret Cole is more human and more capable of affection and intimacy, but not so tenaciously clever or coldly incisive. But they are both distinguished and attractive. . . . Despite a desire to be rebels against all conventions, the Coles are the last of the puritans. G.D.H. Cole will end, I think, by being a scholarly historian; certainly his *Life of Cobbett* is his best bit of work. Why he remains so genuinely attached to the working class, so determined to help forward their organization, puzzles me. The desire *to raise the underdog and abuse the boss* is a religion with him, a deep-rooted emotion more than a conviction. Will it endure? It certainly has survived many disappointments. And yet he is essentially an aristocrat of the sophisticated, ascetic, priestly type, aloof from the common passions and low pleasures of the average social man, intent on impressing his own mentality on those with whom he associates. But what exactly is the content of that mentality? What *is* Cole's ideal? It is not universal benevolence! Is it freedom to do what you like?

W.R. Inge (1860–1954) was Dean of St Paul's 1911–34.

10 September. [Passfield Corner]
Two days at the Bournemouth Trades Union Congress. The same old crowd (mostly grey-headed, *not* bald-headed, for the British Labour Party keeps its hair on, actually as well as metaphorically!) of heavy solid men meeting punctually at 9.30 in the morning and adjourning five minutes before the time in the afternoon, a habit which amazes our Continental comrades. The same sensible procedure, strictly enforced, the same orderliness and unfailing good nature and, in spite of unemployment and empty trade union chests, the same jokes and laughter. Behind these persistent traits there was a difference . . . There is almost a note of panic in the talk of the delegates among themselves; there is bitterness about the national strike; there is anger against the miners among the boiler-makers and the shipwrights and the cotton workers; anger against the General Council among the miners, determination in the heart of each of the larger sections – Railway, Cotton, General Workers – that *never again* will they lose control of their own actions . . . 'Capitalism is not dead – it is not weakening,' was the burden of the speeches. The miners sat silent and depressed . . . They were not treated well by the General Council and if some of the delegates

gave Cook an enthusiastic reception, there was a marked coldness on the part of others. Apathy tempered by pessimism was the atmosphere of the Bournemouth Congress.

We were chatting with Ammon and Lansbury in our hotel on Monday when A.J. Cook came up, and, rather to our surprise, he stayed on to talk to us . . . He is obviously overwrought, almost to breaking-point; but even allowing for this it is clear that he has no intellect and not much intelligence. He is a quivering mass of emotions, a mediumistic magnetic sort of creature, not without personal attractiveness, an inspired idiot, drunk with his own words, dominated by his own slogans. I doubt whether he even knows what he is going to say or what he has just said. Today he is in a funk. . . . He has led his army of a million miners into a situation where they must surrender at discretion on any terms Winston can impose on the mine-owners. It is tragic to think that this inspired idiot, coupled with poor old Herbert Smith, with his senile obstinacy, are the dominant figures in so great and powerful an organization as the Miners' Federation. Neither one nor the other is intellectually articulate; they can neither comprehend nor express complicated facts and arguments. Relatively to the diffculty and magnitude of their job, A.J. Cook and Herbert Smith are mental defectives. An honest mule and an inspired goose, coupled together, make bad leadership for any herd. To think that these two men have controlled the industry and trade of Great Britain for six months! It is a caricature of trade unionism. . . .

As a dramatic contrast to A.J. Cook the proletarian leader, there was J.R. MacDonald, also staying at our hotel . . . He was particularly gracious to us, came to our table and took us into his private sitting-room. But he was evidently absorbed in the social prestige of his ex-premiership, enhanced by a romantic personality. Immaculately groomed and perfectly tailored – too deliberately so for artistic effect – it made him look commonplace. . . . His thoughts and his emotions are concentrated on his agreeable relations with the men and women, especially the women, of the enemy's camp. His mentality is approximating to that of Dean Inge – he is becoming impatient with the troublesomeness of the working class. He did not attend the Trades Union Congress gatherings at Bournemouth, he was not associated with any of the delegates except ourselves; he was motoring with members of the Rotary Club. Nor did he want to talk to us about politics – he wanted to talk about old furniture and 'Society' personalities. As I know little or nothing about either of these topics our conversation was always on the point of petering out. And yet, though he has lost his influence with the inner circle of the devout, J.R.M. is the inevitable leader of the Parliamentary Labour Party. There is no one else in the party who has anything like his prestige in the country at large, and it is the outer circle of the electorate that counts in gaining a Labour majority – the devout we have always with us.

It remains to be added that . . . the dominant impression left on my mind by the T.U.C. of 1926 was chaos among the rank and file, disheartened chaos and the absence of leadership. We ourselves felt like ghosts – 'Ancients' – coming back from the backwoods of historical research to our old haunts, there to discover other ghosts wandering among a gathering of bewildered and frightened children. . . . The British labour movement seemed passive and indeterminate – a no-man's-land between the more virile cultures of Russia and the U.S.A. respectively, between two militant autocracies each claiming to dominate the world, according to the dictates of rival economic creeds – one the creed of the Have-nots and the other the creed of the Haves. Shall we escape being devastated by a clash of creeds? Shall we come to rest as we did in the fifteenth century, during the Continental fight between the Pope and the Protestants, in a sort of Anglican compromise that will bring rest to our soul? . . .

Beatrice's mother, Lawrencina, died unexpectedly in 1882 at the age of sixty-one. Her father, Richard Potter (1817–92) suffered a stroke in 1885 and was incapacitated for the rest of his life. Lallie Holt (1845–1906) was Beatrice's eldest sister; she died of cocaine poisoning. Mary Playne (1849–1923) was the third of the nine Potter daughters; she died of cancer. Maggie Hobhouse was the seventh daughter and closest to Beatrice; she also died of cancer. Blanche Cripps (1851–1905), the fifth sister, strangled herself.

18 September. [Passfield Corner]
I imagine one of the refinements of the future hedonistic society will be that whilst the unwanted child will be prevented from coming into life, the Ancient, who is tired of life, will be allowed to leave it in a painless and dignified way. From the standpoint of personal and race happiness I am more doubtful about birth control than I am about the freedom to depart! The memory of poor little

Mother's death struggle and of Father's long-drawn-out senility, of Lallie Holt's slow self-poisoning, of Mary Playne's loss of memory, of Maggie's melancholy and neglected ending, of the unnecessary horror of Blanche's suicide – all point to an art of dying which will include a voluntary exit before life has become meaningless or troublesome. Whether this act would be able to adjust the individual's desire to live with the social inexpediency of his being alive is the crux of the question. I have always been haunted by the fear of life, and in old age one's fear becomes a more continuous state of mind. I have often wondered whether other old people have this fear of life. Many of them seem to cling to life and one hesitates to suggest to them that they would be better out of it . . . At present a voluntary departure, a refusal to outstay your welcome, is a slur on your own capacity for a useful and happy existence and a reflection on the kindness and generosity of your relations and friends. In the case of the voluntary death of an aged person, perhaps even of a person who is hopelessly sick or mentally defective, 'the tragic death of' ought to read 'the happy ending of'!

Alys Russell (1876–1951) was the first wife of Bertrand Russell. Although the marriage broke down in 1901 they were not divorced until May 1921.

20 September. [Passfield Corner]
Jessie Norris leaves us tomorrow after fifteen years' service. . . . Alys Russell was anxious to have her – she knew and liked her – and though I told her about the scandal she was willing to take her on trust . . . If we were going again to live in London I should certainly risk keeping her – so I suppose I am justified in allowing Alys to risk it. But it has been a horrid business and rather a disreputable one, with a young girl from the village to watch and report on the intrigue to all and sundry. And I, who have always prided myself on having no trouble about servants! . . .

Meanwhile our gardener Oliver and his wife are becoming confidential servants. Oliver I selected from a host of others – gardeners are a drug on the labour market – largely on account of his very respectable-looking wife and on his record. He is about thirty . . . energetic and intelligent, and she is tall and good-looking . . . He is keen in all that he does and immensely appreciates companionship in his work, delights in new schemes and wants to be helpful in all your undertakings. All the same a gardener and a garden — twelve acres of land — is a luxury and costs at least £200 (including the interest on capital expended on the bungalow); but then without a gardener it would be difficult to provide electricity, water, vegetables and protection for the house and its inmates when Sidney is away. It is the principal extra expense of living in the country . . . If our income from books (about £500 a year) were to fail us we could barely afford to live here. . . .

2 October. [Passfield Corner]
The last days of the spell of work on Volume I of English Poor Law History; yesterday we sent the last chapter to the printer and tomorrow we start off on our autumn tour — London, Margate (Labour Party conference) and Seaham. . . . Whether this ponderous tome will get itself read except by a few highly specialized students, is doubtful, but taken with Volume II we shall have written a definitive history of English Poor Law. As the work has proceeded I see that it will really sum up a good deal of our social philosophy. . . .

If it had not been for the dull ache of the miners' lock-out, which has called up the memory of the Great War, Sidney and I would have had a very happy summer together. But the miners' lock-out has been a horrid business, a catastrophic waste of material wealth and, what is infinitely worse, of human heroism. And it means the triumph of the baser type of capitalism — the undoing of the self-devoted labour and endurance of hundreds of devoted men and women . . . It is the men who will be beaten and humiliated; it is the nation at large who will bear the national loss. And the reorganization of the coal industry will be indefinitely put off. . . .

We go to Seaham with a £100 subscription to the relief fund in our pocket, but what shall we say?

The 1925 Labour Party conference had voted decisively (2,870,000 to 321,000) to exclude Communists from membership, and also to deny them the right to be delegates from affiliated trade unions. Successive attempts to reverse this decision were always crushed by the trade union 'block' vote. The miners, eager to restore their bargaining power and to find a means of staving off wage-cuts in their depressed industry, sought an embargo on imported coal and a levy on persons employed in other industries. Both demands were so unrealistic that the other unions were not prepared to support them. E.D. Simon (1879–1960), Manchester businessman and Liberal M.P., was one of the group of rich men who financed the *New Statesman*. Later Lord Simon of Wythenshawe, he became chairman of the B.B.C.

12 October. Margate Labour Party Conference

The swing to the right, especially among the trade unions, is even more emphatic at the Labour Party conference than at the Bournemouth T.U.C. The Communists were snowed under on the first day; on the second day the ragged remnant of the Miners' Federation (Cook and Smith did not appear) put up a fight for the embargo and the levy. But as this was virtually an appeal on purely industrial issues from the T.U.C. to the Labour Party conference it was easy for J.R.M. and J.H. Thomas to carry the conference overwhelmingly against them. . . .

J.R. MacDonald is, despite the I.L.P., completely in control of the rank and file of the political movement and I think of the trade unions. J.H. Thomas is under a cloud, Clynes is ignored and Arthur Henderson's absence is *felt*. There is no sign of any new leadership, either by individuals or groups. The predominant tone is chaotic. No one knows what to be at – intellectually the movement is drifting, the only direction apparent on the surface being away from direct action and workers' control in favour of all forms of communal control, and especially of expert and bureaucratic control. There is today no reason why Keynes, E.D. Simon and Herbert Samuel should not be among the leaders of the Labour Party – they are certainly more advanced than MacDonald and Thomas in their constructive proposals. . . . MacDonald would rejoice in having these Liberal intellectuals as possible Cabinet members. For the rest, the company at the Queen's Hotel was distinguished by its elegance and its aristocratic flavour – the Mosleys, de la Warrs and other lithe and beauteous forms – leaders of fashion or ladies of the stage attended by six-feet-tall and well-groomed men, J.R.M. is *not* a snob,' said that charming boy de la Warr to me, 'but he genuinely prefers the aristocratic to the proletarian as everyday associates' . . . .

Hugh Dalton (1887–1962) joined the Fabian Society as a Cambridge student and went on to become an academic economist, a Labour M.P. and Chancellor of the Exchequer in the 1945 Labour government.

15 October. [Passfield Corner]

Sidney was not elected to the Labour Party executive. I suggested that he should not attend but he said that he wished to offer his services once more and would prefer to be dismissed – a queer little spark of pride. This emphasizes the rightness of his decision not to stand for Seaham again. Hugh Dalton coming to the front, the most cautiously skilful of the younger men; he may overreach himself, for he is not quite a genuine article. However, the *will to power* seems a necessary but ugly attribute of the successful leader. This will to power, by manipulating masses of men, has to be exercised in devious ways which are ruled out by any high scale of moral values . . . Possibly there have been great statesmen who have been indifferent to personal power – they have usually been aristocrats or those who have been in possession of power without striving for it. But the possession of power without directly and constantly struggling for it is not possible in a proletarian democracy when all men start from the bottom and have to struggle upwards. The struggle upwards in competition with other persons struggling upwards, especially if pleasing the multitude is the road to success, is a bad preparation for disinterested service. . . .

19 October. [Passfield Corner]
The Miners' Federation has taken the last desperate step and declared war on the coal-owners and on the community; they revert to the slogan 'not a cent off the pay, not a minute on the day'; they call on the safety men to come out, they demand an embargo on coal and a levy on all trade unionists in work; and they openly base their last chance of success on withdrawing power and heat from the whole body of consumers at a time of year when all will feel it. Apparently they build on the decline of coal imports, on the approach of winter, and on the possibility of stopping the drift back to work by another promise of speedy victory, if the men stay out and heating becomes impossible. The coal-owners – who have plenty of coal for their own use, whether as companies or individuals – are equally cold-blooded, and the government is hoping that by withdrawing relief to the women and children in one area after another, they can starve the mining population of food before the miners deprive the rest of the community of heat and light. This immense industrial conflict is the last word of sectional egotism and class stupidity, leading, one might almost say, to the suicide of each and all of the three parties to the dispute – the nationalization of a ruined industry, the worst of both worlds. . . .

24 October. [Passfield Corner]
Back from autumn visit to Seaham. In the six days we had twelve

meetings – crowded-out meetings – and we saw many of our leading supporters. The surface facts show no exceptional distress; indeed the pit villages look clean and prosperous and the inhabitants healthy (death-rate unusually low). Various people told us that the men and boys had benefited by the rest, sun and open air and abstinence from alcohol and tobacco. And the women were freed from coal-dust and enjoying regular hours, whilst the school-children, through the ample supply of first-class food (eleven meals each week at a cost of 3s 6d per child at wholesale prices) were certainly improved in health and happiness. The one want was clothing and boots, and our gift of £100 to the Repair Fund was much appreciated. . . .

The state of mind of the miners and their wives was less easy to discover than the state of their health. I had a lunch of the thirty chairwomen and secretaries of the Women's Sections and a delegate conference of about four hundred representative members. They all seemed in good spirits, hard at work running relief funds and collecting money by whist drives, football matches (women players), dances and socials; they had raised, in the last two months, £1,700 for the central relief fund for pregnant and lying-in women and infants. Some of the lodges were paying a few shillings a week to the unmarried men; the Guardians were paying 12s a week to the wives and 4s a week (3s 6d deducted for school meals) to each child. But to return to the state of mind of the women. There was certainly no sign of strain. As I looked at the gathering of four hundred miners' wives and daughters in their best dresses, and the prettily decorated tea-tables with piles of cake and bread and butter, it might have been a gathering of prosperous lower middle-class women. . . .

The men and boys were more silent and sullen; some of the elder men were anxious and wistful. Sidney's speeches were not encouraging about the future; and though the audiences were respectful, even affectionate in their attitude towards him and his wife, it was clear that they were disappointed with his guarded and deprecatory attitude towards the strike, and some of them said so. . . . We came back gloomy about the future but we can do little or nothing to help to make it better. We gave our £100 not because it would help but out of gratitude to the miners for their generosity towards us – we were paying back some of our election expenses – that was all!

What is needed today in Great Britain is more discipline – even more compulsion – first on the capitalists to run their establishments in the public interest or clear out, and on the men to work on the terms deliberately fixed by the community. Now that lock-outs and strikes are on a scale that is meant to starve out either large masses of men on the one hand or, on the other, the community of consumers, to permit them is a tragic absurdity. If we cannot find a constitutional way of doing this we shall drift into compulsion without democracy or free speech, a Communist splutter leading to a Fascist government. The workers have far too much to lose, and the bourgeoisie and aristocracy are far too able, for a dictatorship of the proletariat à la Russia. Are we of the Labour Party going to spend the next decades in fighting a Fascist Conservative government, with a growing Communist minority hanging on to us, to hamper our movements and trip us up? It is a melancholy prospect. Plain speaking and constructive thought are, at present, lacking in the Labour Party owing to its dependence on the trade unions. . . .

T.E. Lawrence (1888–1935) was an Anglo-Irish scholar interested in Middle East archaeology. His friendship with the Arabs, described in his masterpiece *The Seven Pillars of Wisdom*, enabled him to raise Arab levies during the war which contributed substantially to the Turkish collapse. After the war he joined the R.A.F. and changed his name to Shaw in an effort to hide his identity. He met the Shaws in 1922 and Charlotte became particularly attached to him. He was killed on a motor cycle which the Shaws had given him. W.L. Mackenzie King (1874–1950) was Liberal Prime Minister of Canada 1921–30 and 1935–48.

8 November. [41 Grosvenor Road]
A hectic seven days in London. Took the chair for [Bertrand] Russell's lecture to the great Kingsway audience on the imminence of creed wars, a subject I had suggested to him but which quite naturally he did not treat in the way I should have done! A first-rate lecture, admirably delivered, though largely read from the MSS of a book. I had, in my opening remarks, asked him a leading question. Were not the creed autocracies of Italy and Russia, with their amazing intolerance of any opposition of the mildest sort, the reaction from the creedlessness that had overtaken those countries? Russian and Italian intellectuals had lost their religous creed, and they had never gained the western creed of democracy, tempered by free thought, with its pseudo-scientific ethics. With their loss of a

creed, they had lost all codes of morals, private and public; they had no rule of conduct to which all instinctively adhered. They needed some code of conduct in order to be effective. Communism and Fascism yielded a militant minority with a creed, and in both cases it had been imposed on a reluctant and apathetic people. But neither the Communist nor Fascist government felt secure with a world unconverted to their dogmas, so they became, like the Christian and Mohammedan empires of the middle ages, militant and fanatical autocracies in their own countries and vehement propagandists in other countries. Out of this state of affairs creed wars might arise. Russell parried my question by stating that he took a more 'Marxian attitude' towards this phenomenon; proceeded with wit and lucidity to foretell a supreme struggle between the two great powers of the world judged by material resources and the massing of men – the U.S.A. and Russia – the rival Capitalist and Communist civilizations. The U.S.A. would dominate Western Europe; Soviet Republics would dominate Asia and sooner or later they would get at each other and fight for world supremacy. It was brilliantly done but I thought it was one more of Russell's gambles with ideas . . . What interested me was his materialist assumption that material resources and masses of men were the all-powerful forces moulding the society of men, and that quality of thought and character counted for nothing in the scales of power. . . .

Sunday we spent with the Shaws. GBS is in good health and in the best of spirits, with an income of tens of thousands rolling in from all quarters of the world – the adored one of all companies and not in the least spoilt by it – the same kindly philosopher, witty raconteur, disillusioned but devoted idealist, daring inventor of ideas, above all faithful friend. Charlotte purring pleasure at her great man's success and looking after his health and happiness with great efficiency. . . .

At lunch Colonel Lawrence came in to bid the Shaws farewell before leaving for India; he was in private's uniform. He is short and stocky in build, high forehead, deep-set and close-together eyes, long powerful upper lip and chin and a magnetic glance; an attractive and arresting figure, obviously self-centred and self-conscious. He was more interesting to look at than to listen to; he had wonder-working eyes, the enquiring expression of half child, half genius. More than a bit of a poseur, vivid but shallow in thought, with wit and sensibility but without knowledge or reasoning power – a spoilt child of fortune delighting in cheap abuse of democracy and dogmatic assertions on matters about which he knew nothing. . . .

Last night Susan [Lawrence] and I entertained the Parliamentary Labour Party and today Sidney and I lunched with the Oswald Mosleys to meet Mackenzie King. So ends my week's dissipation, and I go back to the cottage to work – rather a wreck. . . . A week in London means talk, endless talk and unaccustomed food and hours, small doses of alcohol and too many cigarettes – consequent unhealthiness. In the country one works too hard. Don't fuss over the last years of life, a voice tells me. Take yourself lightly, for the world will do so! Self-importance and self-pity in Ancients, and too careful a husbanding of strength, is absurd. The Ancient should fade away from the sight of fellow mortals noiselessly leaving, like the Cheshire Cat, a smile, and then the memory of a smile. There is comedy in the way we old people – Shaws, Haldane, Graham Wallases, etc. etc. – gaze and listen to each other, watching for the signs of senility and wondering whether the symptoms are as apparent in ourselves as they are in all the others! While the younger folk class us all in the herd that are 'getting old' and must just be tolerated and humoured and sometimes 'honoured', GBS has indeed ascended above the herd of the 'getting old' and has become, in his lifetime, an Idol, enthroned in an international Temple, all by himself. The wonder is that with all this idolization GBS has gained the grace of humility and unselfconsciousness.

10 November [Passfield Corner]
I began today to work on the second volume of the Poor Law and find the prospect not alluring. There is a good deal of fresh research to be done for at least four chapters of the book. With Sidney's parliamentary preoccupations I very much doubt our finishing the volume by next autumn. . . . However the Relief of Destitution has become vividly topical owing to the gigantic expenditure on the locked-out miners and their families. It is comic to watch one capitalist after another waking up to the fact that the employing class have lost the Whip of Starvation! When we come to the last chapters there will be some revolutionary doctrine and some plain speaking. . . .

Agreements were reached between the miners and the owners in each district from the end of November to 23 December. The terms varied but in general the owners won on all counts. The miners lost the national agreement and had to work longer hours for lower wages. In the next few years unemployment in the industry reached tragic proportions. A.C. Benson (1862–1925), essayist, biographer and novelist, was master of Magdalen College, Cambridge from 1915 until his death.

15 November. [Passfield Corner]
The Miners' Federation delegate meeting surrendered yesterday to the government terms – the worst possible terms, barely better than unconditional district surrender to the employers – and they have surrendered in the worst possible way. They refuse responsibility but refer the terms to the districts with a recommendation that they be accepted, which means that some districts will accept and others will not. Hence the government will be able to repudiate its own proposals whilst the miners will stream back to work imagining that peace has been declared!

A.J. Cook has characteristically taken to his bed so as to be out of the fray whilst the army he has misled crumbles up and, in cold literalness, disappears underground! No critic or enemy of the trade union movement could have planned or even imagined so catastrophic a defeat. . . . The shock may disintegrate the present industrial order; but I cannot see how it can lay the foundation for a better one. . . .

Arthur Christopher Benson wrote fifty books and five million words in his diary; he spoke of his complaint as 'logorrhea'. That is what I think I suffer from in my old age – febrility of temperament and imagination. Some who suffer from logorrhea write interminable letters to friends, which I have never done. I prefer writing to myself because I can say exactly what I think without considering its effect on others and the chance of it being repeated. But it means energy running to waste, and after this scribbling in the early morning hours one is less capable of work.

2 December. [Passfield Corner]
. . . . The fact that a considerable number of articles have disappeared, under the domestic dispensation of Jessie and Alice during the last months of their service, has left me a prey to doubts about the honesty of everyone, and conscious of my own stupidity and helplessness in not preventing it. And under black skies and perpetual rain, with Sidney away all the week, I connect these

personal mishaps with a rising fear of a general decay of morals and manners, which I seem to see all around me – all of which may be subjective and due to the depression of old age – a general persecution mania. Meanwhile men and women, each one with his or her peculiar interests and troubles, come and go, claiming my sympathy and asking my advice; and I drudge on day by day with the book, varied these last two days by dictating the Seaham letter – a tiresome task – because what *can* we say to those sick-hearted and downtrodden folk? My brain whirls round quicker and quicker and I get more and more sleepless, and wonder whether life would be tolerable if Sidney were gone or I were to become incapable of writing books and getting them published. But then am I not supremely fortunate, at nearly seventy years of age, to have devoted mutual love and absorbing work which is recognized as useful? – recognized the other day by the University of Munich sending honorary doctorates to Sidney and Beatrice Webb – the *jointness* being a pleasing touch, a recognition not only of our work but of our love.

～ 1927 ～

1 January. [Passfield Corner]
So the year opens hopefully for the old Webbs. Good health in body and mind, an interesting and steady occupation, and our always continuing love for one another and joy in companionship – our relations with the outer world being peaceful and agreeable. Old age and a country home means that we see few people, but these more intimately than in London. We live in the inner circle of Labour Party intellectuals and of the London School of Economics, with occasional foreign visitors. Walks in this delightful country, wireless music with a few concerts thrown in, and new books from *The Times* Book Club are our main recreations. News of the labour movement reaches us through Seaham, Sidney's days at the House of Commons and the Labour Press: the Labour Party swells in volume but the cross-currents and general 'choppiness', at any rate of the surface, leave a bad impression. The Front Bench gets steadily less keen in its pursuit and more moderate in its ends. The rank and file are broken into groups, red flag waving, and

disputing among themselves as to which of them is furthest left.
A.J. Cook careers between London and Moscow and threatens
bombs and revolutions. But I imagine the direction below the
surface is strong and steady towards a better life for the common
people – towards solving this ugly problem of poverty in the midst
of riches that is the problem set to our generation. One's interest in
the business gets fainter; it is not declining faith but slackening
energy. We are nearing the end of our life's work and must leave it
to others to settle policy, contenting ourselves with finishing up one
or two jobs before the night overtakes us. Our day has been a long
and happy one, and we are grateful for our amazing good luck in
our journey through life.

22 January. [Passfield Corner]
Enter my seventieth year: I am well and happy and hard at work on
the second volume of the Poor Law. This book will be our last big
piece of research. . . .

Miss Piercy became Beatrice's secretary in 1924. Sidney thought the *Political
Quarterly*, proposed by a group of academic Fabians, was 'not likely to be a
success'. It was eventually launched with some subsidy from Shaw and it still
survives. W.A. Robson (1895–1980) was an active Fabian and specialist in
local government who became a professor of politics at L.S.E. Basil Kingsley
Martin (1897–1969), a conscientious objector during the war, was to leave his
lectureship in politics at L.S.E. to become leader-writer on the *Manchester
Guardian*. He became editor of the *New Statesman* in 1931. C. Delisle Burns
(1879–1942) was a Fabian intellectual. Leonard Woolf (1880–1969), a
Cambridge graduate, was a colonial administrator who returned to England in
1912, when he married Virginia Stephen (1882–1941). Together they set up
the Hogarth Press. He was an active Fabian.

29 January. [Passfield Corner]
Four busy days in London. Three long mornings at the British
Museum rushing through piles of volumes with Miss Piercy at my
side copying out extracts. Sidney, on the other side, at his own
researches; three 'dining-outs' – Haldane, Parmoor and a staff
dinner at the School of Economics; one lunch to discuss a new
political quarterly – Tawney, Robson, Lloyd, Kingsley Martin,
Delisle Burns, Leonard Woolf; and the last afternoon taking the
chair at a housing conference of the Labour Party. Result,
considerable exhaustion!
Haldane looks old and ill, but he is hard at work on his Privy

Council judgements – they are short of judges, and those they've got are aged – some over eighty and most over seventy! Elizabeth looks anxiously at him. He was beneficent but had little to say. I asked how he, an old Liberal, accounted for the collapse of Liberalism. 'The Liberal leaders lacked "the Spirit" – they had ceased to desire change, they were obsessed by old formulas.' 'And enveloped in luxurious and leisured London Society,' I added. 'Perhaps so,' he answered doubtfully. . . .

In her diary for 29 January Virginia Woolf also refers to this visit to Passfield Corner, where the Webbs lived 'in an emphatic lodging house with blue-books in the passages. . . . On a steely watery morning we swiftly tramped over a heathy common talking talking. In their efficiency and glibness one traces perfectly adjusted machinery; but talk by machinery does not charm or suggest: it cuts the grass of the mind close at the roots . . . Mrs W. is far less ornamental than of old: wispy, untidy, drab with a stain on her skirt and a key on her watch-chain; as if she had cleared the decks and rolled her sleeves and was waiting for the end, but working.' Clive Bell (1881–1964) was an art critic who married Virginia's sister, Vanessa, in 1907. Virginia Woolf attacked Arnold Bennett in an essay called 'Mr Bennett and Mrs Brown'. She was just completing *To the Lighthouse*: Beatrice had probably been reading *Mrs Dalloway*, which was published in May 1925.

6 February. [Passfield Corner]
The Leonard Woolfs spent the week-end here – we had lost sight of them and were glad to renew relations with this exceptionally gifted pair. A dozen years ago, when we first saw them, they were living under a cloud – she on the borderline of lunacy, he struggling desperately to keep her out of a mental home. For some years it seemed doubtful whether he would succeed. Now the cloud has passed away. Her appearance has altered: instead of a beautiful but loosely knit young woman, constantly flushing and with a queer, uncertain, almost hysterical manner, she is, though still beautiful, a spare, self-contained ascetic-looking creature, startlingly like her father, Leslie Stephen; the same tall, stooping figure, exquisite profile; refined, an almost narrow and hard intellectuality of expression. Woolf also is matured and has lost his nervous shyness. Wholly unconventional in their outlook on life and manners, belonging rather to a decadent set (Clive Bell is her brother-in-law) but themselves puritanical, they are singularly attractive to talk to. In one matter they are not up-to-date, for they are rigid secularists, regarding theology or even mysticism as *l'infâme*. Here his Jewish

blood comes in: he quite clearly is revolted by the Christian myth, the anger of a Jew at an apostate from the Judaic faith. (Considering the persecution of the Jews right up to the nineteenth century by the Christian Church, I wonder why they are not more obsessed by hatred of the author of Christianity.) He is an anti-imperialist fanatic but otherwise a moderate in Labour politics – always an opponent of 'workers' control' and 'proletarianism'. She is uninterested in politics – wholly literary – an accomplished critic of style and a clever artist in personal psychology, disliking the 'environmental' novel of late Victorian times, especially its latest exponent, Arnold Bennett. Like other works of the new school of novelists, I do not find her work interesting outside its craftsmanship, which is excellent but *précieuse*. Her men and women do not interest me – they don't seem worth describing in such detail; the mental climate in which they live seems strangely lacking in light, heat, visibility and variety; it is a dank mist of insignificant and monotonous thoughts and feelings, no predominant aims, no powerful reactions from their mental environment, a curious impression of automatic existence when one state of mind follows another without any particular reason. To the aged Victorian this soullessness is depressing. Doubtless our insistence on a purpose, whether for the individual or the universe, appears to them a delusion and a pernicious delusion.

The last hours with them were spent in a raging argument about denominational education and the validity of religious mysticism. They were against toleration. What was 'manifestly false' was *not* to be *taught* at the public expense and not to be *thought* by persons above a certain level of intelligence who claimed to be honest with themselves and other people. I pleaded for 'the endowment of error', and threatened them with fundamentalism, or Roman Catholicism, if they insisted on universal and compulsory sectarianism.

Ellen Wilkinson (1891–1947) made her début in politics as a non-militant suffragist. She became an active Fabian and after moving from the I.L.P. to the Communist Party she became a Labour M.P. for Middlesbrough East in 1924. She was Minister of Education in the 1945 Labour government. Her pertinacious manner at Question Time so irritated the Tory M.P. for Dulwich that, on 28 September 1926, he dubbed her 'little Miss Perky'; the nickname was taken up by the newspapers. Kingsley Martin married Olga Walters in July 1920; they separated in 1934 and were divorced in 1940. Beveridge had drafted the report of the Samuel Commission and was annoyed by Martin's gibes at it in *The British Public and the General Strike.*

7 February. [Passfield Corner]
Ellen Wilkinson reached here on Friday for lunch in a state of collapse from over-speaking at great mass meetings, mainly about China. I have known her slightly for ten or twelve years; she was one of the Guild Socialists and University Federation group of 1913–19. The daughter of a Lancashire cotton spinner of rebellious temper and religious outlook, she passed from the elementary school to the pupil teacher centre, from thence, on a scholarship, into Manchester University, where she took a good degree. After a year as a suffrage agitator, she became an organizer of the rapidly growing Co-operative Employees' Union [later the Union of Shop, Distributive and Allied Workers] and finally landed herself in the House of Commons in 1924 as M.P. for Middlesbrough. 'The mighty atom,' she was immediately nicknamed. For the first session she was the darling of the House; in the next session she became a formidable debater, and now, as 'Miss Perky', she is somewhat under a cloud of disparagement, suffering the penalty of immediate popularity and premature success. She is amazingly vital and a first-rate debater. She is not vain or self-conscious; with her tiny lithe figure, delicate pale face, brilliant red-brown hair and red-brown eyes, she is personally attractive, at times extremely pretty. But *feminine* she is not; I suppose it would now be said that she is 'under-sexed'. Her manner with men is straightforward and offhand, even a trifle hard. If she had been a man she would have been an excellent common-law pleader of the Patrick Hastings type. She has not a distinguished intellect; neither as a reasoner nor an observer is she subtle or artistic; perhaps her life, from a poor scholar in Manchester to a hard-worked organizer, has been too continuous a grind, too shrill a cry of revolt to result in the finer mental processes. But she is a real good sort – direct, devoted and public-spirited, free from malice, and, for so notorious a person, peculiarly lacking in personal vanity. Her opinions do not strike old people like ourselves as wise or particularly relevant; she is a left-winger who has altered her views to suit the fashion of the hour; she was in 1913 syndicalist, in 1917 Communist and is now 'agin MacDonald' and enthusiastic for 'Socialism in our Day'. 'Ellen Wilkinson, regarded as a practical politician, is a fool,' says

Sidney. But the House of Commons, and the amenities of social life it brings with it, are taming her spirit and she is becoming, unknown to herself, moulded for the Front Bench and eventually for office. . . .

Our other guests for the week-end were Kingsley Martin and his attractive young wife. K.M. was a Cambridge Fabian of the war period and has already written rather brilliant and thoughtful books. He has certainly literary talent and a quick and appreciative mind; he is today an assistant lecturer at the School of Economics, one of the Tawney–Laski group. Unkempt and with the appearance of being unwashed, with jerky ugly manners, but tall and dark with a certain picturesque impressiveness of the Maxton type, he is a fluent and striking conversationalist, intellectually ambitious, with a certain religious fervour for social reconstruction . . . Just at present he is in revolt against the Beveridge–Mair dictatorship and in the black books of those high and mighty personages because of his booklet on the General Strike. He was a brilliant Cambridge graduate, the son of a single-hearted, Nonconformist minister, an old and respected member of the Fabian Society, and he was offered a fellowship at his college. One of the promising younger members of the Fabian Society and thoroughly Fabian in his methods, he differs from Sidney in thinking that the Communist propaganda is likely to disintegrate the Labour Party and lead to revolutions and strikes and a Fascist government in Great Britain, though of course less pronounced than Italy. . . . We talked incessantly all our waking hours from 4.30 on Saturday afternoon, when the Kingsley Martins arrived, to nine o'clock on Monday morning, when the whole party, minus I, left for London. . . .

Lord George Hamilton (1845–1927) was chairman of the Royal Commission on the Poor Law 1905–09, on which Beatrice had served. She and Sidney wrote its famous and eventually influential Minority Report.

14 February. [Passfield Corner]
I am working well at the Poor Law book; having finished the chapter on the Royal Commission of 1834 I am now beginning the chapter on the Royal Commission 1905–09, rushing through the thirty-five volumes of evidence and reports, refreshing my memory of those troublous days. From my diary and the correspondence with Lord George Hamilton about my enquiries, I think I shall be

able to make a lively chapter which will excite interest. But we are getting nervous about the length of the book; each of us is inclined to over-elaborate, and the vice of one accentuates that of the other. With our over-punctuality, Sidney and I alone are always ten minutes early for a train or an appointment; when we go together we are twenty minutes early! We have become too comprehensive and meticulous in the writing of a book. These bad habits increase with old age. . . .

What troubles me about this volume is what exactly will be our recommendations? How can we devise some treatment of the unemployed which will be 'less eligible' than wage labour without being blatantly *inequitable* to the men and their families who are out of work through no fault of their own? There is little or no difficulty about the non-able-bodied – that is a mere question of how much the nation can afford to spend; there is no psychological problem, for the more you spend on the infant and child, within any conceivable practical limits, the better for the race. And that is also the case with nearly all sickness and the segregation of mental defectives, whilst expenditure on the aged and impotent is a harmless luxury. But the maintenance of the able-bodied in idleness is an ultra-dangerous business. And yet confronted with the idle rich man, how can you justify to a political democracy harsh treatment in the interests of the community? . . .

The L.S.E. ran special classes for army officers and also for young railway managers. William Wedgwood Benn, later Lord Stansgate (1877–1960) became Secretary of State for India in 1929, and Secretary of State for Air in 1945. The youngest of his three sons, Anthony Wedgwood Benn (b. 1925), renounced the inherited peerage and became the prominent Labour politician Tony Benn.

28 February. [Passfield Corner]
Another two days and nights in London lunching and dining out, back home to entertain Beveridge and the senior officer of the army class to lunch and tea, and then the Wedgwood Benns for the week-end – talking, talking, talking – by Monday morning totally unfit for work. Then at least five days off work. Resolve not to go to London again before we leave here at Easter.

Wedgwood Benn (son of Sidney's old L.C.C. colleague Sir John Benn, and brother of Ernest Benn, the publisher and noted individualist) is an acquisition for the Parliamentary Labour Party.

He is a neat little man, neat in person and precise in intellect, and a good fellow in every sense of the word. Considering his excessive 'moderation' in opinion, he is very popular even with the left wing of the Labour M.P.s. From the time he entered the House of Commons in 1906 he was devoted body and soul to mastering the technique of parliamentary procedure, and has become a real expert in 'opposition'. He knows every rope and keeps himself up to date in all the questions of the hour in so far as these crop up in the House of Commons. Apparently he spends three hours a day in reading *The Times* and *Hansard*, and aided by secretaries he has a wonderful plan of filing the information so that he is able to turn up what Ministers have *said*, or what has appeared in the newspapers and parliamentary papers. He has even a file for jokes and smart sayings. The result is that his questions, interjections and speeches are apt and amusing and he can put spokes into the wheels of the Front Bench. For the rest he is unpretentious and most agreeable, with no malice and a good streak of kindly wit. He is in fact a triumph of alertness, assiduity and good nature. But he has no awareness or understanding of the problems underlying political events and his coming over will not add to the constructive capacity of any future Labour government. Formerly a convinced economic individualist, he is now a Fabian socialist. . . . He came over to Labour in the best possible style, resigning his seat and leaving the Labour candidate to contest it at a by-election – a seat which he would certainly have won if he had chosen to re-contest it as a Labour candidate. He is fifty years of age and has a pleasant little woman as wife twenty years younger than himself, and two little boys. He is the last word of respectability and has a peculiarly pleasant manner and agreeable disposition and will be an excellent party man, always playing a straight game.

5 March. [Passfield Corner]
I think of Sidney as an optimist – and so he is, in the sense that he discounts fear and worry and believes in a brave attempt to see the best in men and affairs as one way of getting a better state of things. But when the other day I asked him whether he would accept another life – beginning afresh in the same sort of circumstances – if it were offered him, he answered that, on balance, he thought he would not care to risk it; the whole business was too meaningless, or rather too uncertain and unknowable in its meaning, to make the

risk of personal unhappiness worthwhile. That is *my* predominant feeling. . . .

Old age brings acquiescence in what is; questions cease; one goes on, so far as capacity still exists, at some particular job. In technical proficiency the output may be good, but the spirit – whether the scientific spirit or the reforming spirit – is lacking, and whether one dies before completing the task or lives to begin and complete yet another, seems of no particular importance to oneself or anyone else. This twilight of the mind is a curious sensation: hope and fear being alike absent, aspiration and therefore prayer seem no longer relevant. Intellectual curiosity and a certain grandmotherly kindliness linger on. . . .

The Revolt in the Desert was an abridged and public version of Lawrence's privately circulated *Seven Pillars of Wisdom*.

20 March. Ayot St Lawrence
Read most of *The Revolt in the Desert* staying here this week-end (the thirty-guineas edition had not reached the Shaws). Lawrence appears as the perfect A. – Aristocrat, Anarchist, Artist – to which must be added, according to this account, Ascetic. His book is an epic of courage, personal charm and sympathy, achieving leadership, in a great adventure, over men of inferior mentality. Certainly he is a distinguished artist in word and act – though curiously limited in scope and variety. He is a consummate egotist; his outlook at times seems petty and peevish, he has no settled purpose or faith, and as an intellectual he is not remarkable for knowledge or for reasoning power. Unless fate follows him with another great occasion he may not achieve another epic. But having attained a dizzy position of literary fame I cannot believe that he will sink into an eccentric nonentity as a private soldier in India. Without creativeness one would think he would find such a daily life unendurable. An artist must create, an aristocrat must dominate, an ascetic must deny himself, and an anarchist must do what he d___ pleases, or die by drink, drugs or depression. A call will come and he will disappear for a while into another desert, free from the presence of the common civilized man, more especially the bourgeois democrat whom he detests. He is contemptuous of his fellow men, especially of his fellow countrymen and more particularly those of his own class. He claims a pedestal from which he can survey the

118

world in order to lead, by personal magnetism, an alien herd of child-like dispositions. Among the complicated issues of western civilization, with its scientific tests and personal persuasion, Lawrence is a lost soul. In uniqueness, in the intensity of his personality, lies a large part of his distinction. A thousand Lawrences would be a public nuisance. With a thousand Sidney Webbs you could reorganize Great Britain, but no one could pick them out, at sight, from their fellow men.

27 March. 4 a.m. [Passfield Corner]
Struck work. For the last month I have been doing little at the book; every morning I have worked as best I could, reading and dictating, getting dizzier and dizzier and seeming to lose not to gain my grip of the subject. At night I cannot sleep and when I do drop off I awake in some sort of nightmare – all of which means that my reserve strength is exhausted. So I have decided to take five weeks' rest from any attempt to work, ending up with a week with Kate at Beachy Head. . . .

A Bill to change the law concerning strikes – the Trade Disputes Act – was then being debated. It declared sympathetic strikes illegal and abolished the political levy; in future, union members would 'contract in' to a political fund rather than, as previously, 'contract out' of paying the levy. It reduced the Labour Party's income from affiliation fees by over a quarter, but it increased working-class support for the Labour Party.

5 April. [Passfield Corner]
Henderson and his wife staying here. Was there ever a more sterling character than his, conduct more uniformly guided by public spirit and personal devotion and good comradeship? He is thick-headed – intellectually he is a clumsy instrument – but there is shrewdness in his judgement: the sort of realization of the facts which arises from long experience of men and affairs and an absence of self-deception. Further, he is never elated and never gloomy – he just plods on along the chosen way towards some dimly perceived social betterment. . . .

With the present state of mind of the Labour Party, Sidney and I feel singularly indifferent to their coming into power – so does Henderson – the Labour Party as at present constituted is not fit to govern. MacDonald is a fine façade, a platform performance; Snowden is no longer a socialist; Thomas has never been one and is a social climber, more blatantly so than Snowden's wife – see the wedding of Peggy Thomas, with Baldwin and Lloyd George signing the register and a host of Tory and Liberal notables, exactly at the time of the Trade Union Bill! Henderson is a first-rate general manager, but he is not a first-class statesman with a policy of his own to carry out. Wheatley and Maxton – in many ways the most attractive figures in the Labour Party – and their I.L.P. followers are Utopians and pseudo-revolutionaries, peddling phrases without understanding what is involved and without constructive capacity. Johnson, the editor of *Forward*, is the best of the Clyde lot and a good party man but he is slight in mental make-up.

Hugh Dalton is probably the ablest of the younger men but he is obviously playing the political game – some of the old hands discount his capacity whilst his contemporaries distrust his sincerity; Mosley, brilliant but without weight, deemed to be a political adventurer by many left- as well as right-wingers; C.P. Trevelyan worthy but dull; W. Graham weighty as well as worthy but if anything duller; Noel Buxton a charming gentleman, but mediocre in intellectual calibre and physical strength. As for Sidney, he has retired from any attempt to lead. He tries to be helpful but he is an aloof and slightly bored spectator with the historians – a subordination of current events to a past and a future. The rest of the Front Benchers and the rank and file of the back benchers are just nowhere. Deficient in brains and starved in money, it is a miracle that the Labour Party steadily grows in voting power. The impression left on the observer's mind is of a slow underground social upheaval, moving independently of leaders or organization, propelling a lower strata of society into a more dominant position. This soulless momentum gives a certain colour to the materialist conception of history. . . .

14 April. [Passfield Corner]
It is seventeen days since I struck work, and I am no better – the whizzing in my right ear and the buzzing in my head gets continuously more troublesome, and my capacity for either walking or reading grows less and less. It all reminds me of the spring of 1916 – though then it began with pains in the back, changing during the summer into dizziness and heart failure of a neurotic type and lasting well into the winter months. I have had these nervous breakdowns before. One of the worst was in the summer

and autumn of 1900. I used to go out on the Yorkshire moors and cry from depression. This I cured by starvation. Another spell in 1916, perhaps more severe, was accentuated by war neurosis, and our first experience of personal unpopularity and depreciation. Today we have no reason for discouragement except the coming of old age, which being inevitable and universal it is cowardly to resent. . . .

23 April. 41 Grosvenor Road
Back from Seaham. The miners and their wives are deep down in gloomy bewilderment, the responsible ones deploring the mess made by their leaders, despairing about the condition of the industry and furiously angry about the Trade Union Bill, the irresponsible ones talking vaguely about another strike. . . . The miners want to be loyal to their leaders but are utterly at sea as to who *are* their leaders. They will vote straight at the next general election – their herd instinct becomes stronger with their sense of weakness – but what they will be voting for other than the repeal of the Trade Union Bill and Eight-Hours Act they do not know.

Douglas Hogg, later Lord Hailsham (1872–1950), was a Conservative barrister who was Attorney-General between 1922 and 1928, then Lord Chancellor.

3 May. [? Grosvenor Road]
Heard the opening of the Trade Union Bill second reading. Hogg was nervous and made an obviously disingenuous speech; the Tories sat silent with the expression 'it's dogged that does it'; and the two rank and filers I heard repeated, apparently with conviction, the party slogans of personal freedom and emancipation from minority dictatorships. . . . The Labour Party was a ragged mob, shrieking irrelevant and vulgar interruptions, continuously repressed by the Speaker. . . . It was a depressing evening; there is unreality in the parliamentary debate. The Tories are determined to make hay of trade unions while the sun of their majority shines; the Labour Party is equally determined to use the Trade Union Bill as an election bogy. There is no interchange of thought and no desire to compromise or gain the largest measure of consent. Each party appeals to its own mob. The Liberals have been submerged by the tempest. . . .

Thomas Jones, sometime Fabian and professor of economics, became the confidant of Lloyd George and then assistant secretary to the War Cabinet.

8 May. [Passfield Corner]

Tom Jones, whom I have not seen to talk to since the Reconstruction ' Committee time — except for the Sankey Commission episode — spent a week-end here. . . From his account, Baldwin is stupider and weaker than we thought. He lives an isolated life, never reads or talks with experts and has a horror of clever brains 'like Keynes and the Webbs'!!!

Tom Jones has had a remarkable career. When first we knew him he was a raw Glasgow graduate, destined by his family to become a Methodist minister. Losing his faith, he took to philosophy and social economics, came to the London School of Economics as a Shaw scholar, became an assistant lecturer in Economics, first at Glasgow then in Wales, was taken up by Lloyd George and made secretary of the Welsh National Insurance Board; then when Lloyd George became P.M. he was transformed into one of his private secretaries, being finally landed, where he still is, assistant secretary to the Cabinet, second to Maurice Hankey. He is undistinguished-looking, short and stumpy, with badly fitting clothes, homely manners and speech, the very antithesis of the model civil servant . . . What amused me in talking to him was to note that his dozen years as a confidant of a succession of P.M.s and Cabinet Ministers from Lloyd George to Baldwin (excluding MacDonald, who refused to have anything to do with him, disliking his dowdiness and familiar ways and suspecting him of being Baldwin's spy) has not given him any insight into public affairs superior to that of the clever student or professor of public administration. Of course he can give you titbits of political gossip; but with regard to the problems themselves he knows less than many persons who are excluded from the inner circle. The Great Ones — those actually exercising power — have no time to solve the questions submitted to them; they have to depend on others who can concentrate on investigation. Their success or failure as governors of men will depend on whether they can acquire this knowledge second-hand — a knowledge which is often hid from them by the inaccessibility of high office and the absorption of Ministers in mere official routine and social ceremonial. Jones says that Lloyd George's great quality was his readiness to get this knowledge and to be intimate with anyone who could help him. Which I think is true. Winston had that gift of accessibility and eagerness to know. Haldane also, and – in a certain but much more limited fashion, because of his indolence and fastidious aloofness – A.J. Balfour. . . . 'He and Haldane are the only statesmen who really care for the advancement of science and learning,' was Jones's opinion. We three agreed that the chasm between the two parties and the way in which even the experts are divided from each other by party ties, does not make for mutual comprehension or the scientific study of conflicting questions. . . .

24 May. [Passfield Corner]
GBS and Charlotte staying here; Sidney and I reading proofs of *The Intelligent Woman's Guide to Socialism and Capitalism* and giving him our criticism. Sidney corrected innumerable small mistakes and argued with him all the morning about what he considers major fallacies and perverse mis-statements of financial problems. GBS's dogmatic conclusion is that socialism consists of two ends – equalization of incomes and compulsory labour – and he suggests as the proper slogan for the Labour Party 'The Redistribution of the National Income'. This morning, while he was eating his breakfast, I gave him the result of a midnight meditation on the book – not as criticism but merely as observations. . . . 'In stating the two ends of socialism, equality of income and compulsory labour, you have insisted on hammering in the thick edge of the wedge; neither equality nor compulsion are made to appear conceivable, practicable or desirable. Indeed, you contradict yourself more than once in the book, and you give the impression that you are advancing your conclusions not because you really believe in them but because they are startling.' It is amusing to note that artists like himself are to be allowed to keep their individual gains, however unequal! He was, I think, rather impressed, especially as I insisted that I did not want him to alter anything he has written. . . .

The Shaws are so happy here that they are returning for another week-end. But though I enjoy having them, and it is always useful to discuss with them, it means that I do not get on with the book! . . .

In our old age Charlotte and I have become affectionately intimate. She interests me because her present placidity (compared with her striving restlessness of earlier days) is due not only to the latter-day prestige and wealth of her husband, but also to her acceptance of one of the innumerable revivals of religious mysticism. By her bedside for continuous reading and meditation are two little books of some three thousand words each, one of which deals with righteousness, wisdom, goodness, and the other with power, holiness and faith, entitled *The Way of Silence* (studies in meditation published by the School of Silence, Kensington) by Adda M. Curtis. The thesis is that by continuous meditation, or self-hypnotism, you will rise above the self-conscious self and realize the 'God Power' within you – your *wholeness* with the reality which lies beneath an appearance. . . .

There is nothing original in these little books – the same sort of emotional meandering is appearing in dozens of contemporary publications in all countries, making use of all the modern terms such as *Subconscious Self*, *Holism* or *Wholeness*, etc., etc. Compared with the older mysticism it lacks charm and richness of experience. The relations between man and man are practically ignored. Indeed, this religious quietism has led Charlotte away from all efforts to make things better for those who are suffering from their heredity or environment. As all depends on the self-conscious self, why trouble about poverty – external conditions are powerless for good or for evil. Hence she wends her way through a luxurious existence, spending lavishly on clothes and self-beautifying, thinking of her own state of mind and of GBS's health, happiness and capacity for work . . .

All the same these daily meditations make Charlotte happy. However self-centred her activities may be, she has developed admirable manners and a pleasing and cheerful personality. Like a perfectly appointed house there is fascination in an exquisitely clothed and cared-for person, if those artifices are combined with personal dignity and graciousness. Certainly she holds fast GBS's respect and affection; he recognizes her value to him not merely as a devoted wife but as an appropriate complement to his own distinction, restful at home and more than creditable abroad.

Maud Keary was secretary-companion to Beatrice's sister, Kate Courtney.

3 June. [Passfield Corner]
One of the disadvantages of a small but comfortable country home is that if you happen to combine a hospitable temperament with old age or other form of delicacy you find yourself continually over-

taxing your strength. I am no longer fit for the friction of visitors staying in the house – the most I can bear is two nights, and I prefer one! This Whitsun I have Kate Courtney and Maud Keary staying ten days or more and various persons coming to tea or lunch during the week; consequently I am sleepless and worried, and long to see the last of my guests. Kate is a dear and generous old lady. The restlessness of old age takes the harmless form of dozens of little walks round the garden, and up and down the drive, in the intervals of ethical thoughts and sayings on public affairs – more especially, foreign affairs, interspersed with proportional representation propaganda. . . . Except for a little fussiness about her ailments and a chronic, rather aimless restlessness of body and mind, she is a model old person, actively interested and enthusiastically benevolent, intent on doing kind things and succeeding in doing them.

Fred Keeling (1886–1916) was one of the founders of the Cambridge Fabian Society. He became the Leeds manager of one of the newly-formed labour exchanges and assistant editor of the *New Statesman*. He was killed in France. Rupert Brooke (1887–1915) was a gifted poet who died in Greece on his way to Gallipoli. James Strachey (1887–1967) joined the Fabians in 1908. He was the brother of Lytton Strachey and the translator of the works of Sigmund Freud.

20 June. [41 Grosvenor Road]
Among the younger men – a member of the two executives, national and parliamentary – is an old acquaintance of ours, Hugh Dalton, who, with his wife, has been staying with us this week-end. Over six feet, large and loose-limbed, practically bald and somewhat pasty-faced, Dalton was meant to be athletic but has been sedentary; hence he is not, in early middle life, personally attractive. When we first knew him in 1907 he was a tall, slim and graceful Cambridge undergraduate, straight from Eton and a home in the outer Court circle (his father being Canon of Windsor and Court Chaplain). At that time Dalton belonged to the remarkable group of Cambridge Fabians – Fred Keeling, Rupert Brooke, Strachey, etc. – but in a few years he veered to Liberalism and became one of the promising young men who hung about the Asquith set. Perhaps for that reason we saw little of him between 1909 and 1914. In the war he served as a gunner in Italy. On his return in the autumn of 1918 he renewed our acquaintance and his membership of the Fabian Society; presently he became a lecturer at the L.S.E. and

then a Labour Party candidate at one or two elections, but he did not win a seat until the general election of 1924. He is not popular with his colleagues at the L.S.E. – they say that he is a careerist, considering all things by the light of his own security and promotion. He is inclined even to pose as such. In the Labour Party he *is* popular; the right wing trust his judgement and knowledge, the left believe in his fervour for 'Socialism in Our Time'. He gives *us* the impression that he believes in the 'inevitability of gradualness'. . . .

Henderson thinks him the most promising of the younger men; even suggests that when the old gang go off the stage, Dalton may be first favourite for the leadership of the party. And certainly he has knowledge, a good voice and admirable manner; he is a lucid and impressive speaker, and would, I think, prove to be an energetic and sane administrator. But he has no personal magnet-ism, and though an intellectual and moral man, he has neither intellectual nor moral uniqueness or distinction. . . .

Fred Bramley (1874–1925), previously secretary of the Foundry Trades Association, was secretary of the T.U.C. for two years before his early death. Citrine gives a full description of this visit in his autobiography *Men and Work* (London, 1964). 'I felt that they were looking at me in much the same way as an entomologist might peer at a new species of butterfly safely impaled on a pin!'

28 July. [Passfield Corner]
Walter Citrine – the general secretary of the T.U.C. – and his wife spent the week-end here. An electrical engineer by training, becoming in early manhood a national official of his union and secretary of the Liverpool Engineering Federation, he arrived four years ago as the assistant secretary at 32 Eccleston Square, succeeding Fred Bramley as general secretary last year. Under forty years of age, tall, broad-shouldered, with the manners and clothes and way of speaking of a superior bank clerk; black hair growing low on his forehead, large pointed ears, bright grey eyes set close together, big nose, long chin and tiny, rather 'pretty' mouth, it is difficult to say whether or not he is 'good-looking'. In profile he is, in full face he is not. When arguing, his features twist themselves up and he becomes positively ugly. By temperament and habit of life Citrine is an intellectual of the scientific type. He is sedentary, taking too little exercise for his health; he is assiduous, always improving himself by reading and writing and working at his job unremittingly. He has no 'silly pleasures': he is a non-smoker, non-drinker, small,

slow eater, takes a daily cold bath, sleeps with his windows open – altogether a hygienic puritan in his daily life. He is loquacious, naively vain and very disputatious, self-conscious and sensitive. Susan [Lawrence] says he is a goose. I think he is very ambitious – expects too much relatively to his faculties. . . .

Citrine is contemptuous, largely justifiably contemptuous, of the members of his General Council and the Trades Union Congress and, like all the other brainworkers who were in the inner circle of the trade union movement during 1926, he gives a picture of deplorable lack of grip, alike of intellect and character, among those who led the millions of trade unionists in and out of the General Strike, whilst the leaders of the miners approach, according to his estimate, mental deficiency. And yet he believes in the future of trade unions as a great controlling force through the weapon of the national or sympathetic strike, or rather the threat of it, and was indignant when we put forward the thesis that trade unionism as an organ of revolt was obsolete; that it would become during the next two generations a subordinate part of the machinery of government; and that this evolution would take place under British political democracy as well as under the creed autocracies of Russia and Italy and the industrial feudalism of the U.S.A. . . . .

Beatrice Ross had been companion to Beatrice's sister, Mary Playne. Mary Playne's son, Bill (1870–1935), was badly wounded during the war. He and his wife Manuella had created difficulties over Miss Ross's future after Mary's death. She lived at Box Cottage on the Playne estate at Longfords, near Stroud. Beatrice had lived at Box House before her marriage.

28 July. [Passfield Corner]
Two days with Bice Ross in her most attractive Cotswold cottage filled with the titbits of Longfords furniture bequeathed to her by the Playnes. Bill Playne's retort was to block the view by selling the plot opposite for building purposes! No intercourse between Longfords and Box Cottage.

Wandering over Minchinhampton Common, starting from a few yards from Box House, the whole intermediate time between unmarried life and today seemed blocked out. If I could have foreseen an old woman of seventy striding across the common with forty years of successful literary work and thirty-five years of a perfect marriage, and both work and love continuing, how high-spirited and happy I should have been. . . .

In the evening I strolled down to Longfords to see Bill. He and Mannie are physical and mental wrecks – he with his paralysing wound and habitual booze, she with a mysterious disease, a sort of creeping paralysis that completely disables her and grows worse year by year . . . Bill was cordial though confused. About the government, said he was going to 'vote Labour', asked after Sidney and generally tried to make himself pleasant.

17 August. [Passfield Corner]
In spite of horrid south-west storm of rain and cold grey skies Sidney and I have been happy at work on the book – he galloping on with the big central chapter, 'Sixty Years of Administration', and I crawling along with the 'Framework of Prevention', feeling distinctly old for so heavy a task, but still content to be doing it. In and out of our daily life, in an agreeable sort of way, come friends, mostly of Labour sympathies. Ellen Wilkinson and her sister settled for a fortnight in the bungalow . . . Ellen interests me with her hard-grained capacity and absence of emotional temperament – undersized, with her brilliant gold red hair and vivid talk, she is attractive to men, but not attracted *by* them and therefore not seductive . . . Ellen Wilkinson is becoming every day more of a labour *politician* and less of a labour missionary, but I think she will remain an honest politician.

How eminently respectable are those three women Labour M.P.s. – Susan Lawrence, Margaret Bondfield and Ellen Wilkinson – you can barely think of any one of them having an 'intrigue', even a flirtation. They all lack the temperament of the lover – they are distinctly celibates. Endless activities and continuous self-expression uses up all their energies, whether of body or mind; there is no energy left to go sour! . . . Rush and push – push in the House of Commons, rush in the constituencies; that is the order of their days. Margaret has her religion as relaxation; Susan and Ellen have their travels, their gossips and their smokes; not one of the three seem to need emotional companionship. . . .

The 'Clyde group' were the extremist I.L.P. representatives from the Glasgow area.

22 August. [Passfield Corner]
. . . . The Labour leaders who have been manual workers seldom have wives who are equal to their husbands, no status as brainwork-

ers (Mrs Clynes is a notable exception). By stimulating their social proclivities, their new opportunities make them more common than before. There was no harm in Mrs Citrine and Mrs Alexander – they were good little wives, but they were unredeemably common with their over-smart clothes, their tight, slight and pointed toes and high-heeled boots, their flattering words and their obvious pride and delight in the gatherings of the highly placed. In their formulas they were still on the side of the workers, but in their hearts they were rapidly veering round to the worship of Mammon; even their formulas were getting shaky. It was easy to see that a reactionary sentiment roused an echo in their little minds. This social subserviency of the Labour man's wife is one of the evil features of the Parliamentary Labour Party. I tried to counteract it by starting the Half-Circle Club, but I failed. Unfortunately MacDonald and, more blatantly, Ethel Snowden, have led the way into 'London Society'. I should rather say that they have escaped into the 'Upper Circles' and their escape has been observed by their followers; the herd wavered and quite a few men, and most of their wives and daughters, have timidly pressed forward into the breach made by the ex-Prime Minister and his leading colleague's wife and have entered the insiduously opening social paradise – in Great Britain open to all those who have, or are likely to have, political power. . . .

The inevitable reaction from the social climbers is the fanatical exclusiveness of the Clyde [group]; their refusal to meet for the purpose of discussion the better-off or more moderately minded intellectuals of their own party. Hence the disaster of divided counsels and competing manifestoes, and the use of revolutionary phraseology which is meaningless. Maxton, when he says, 'rather a few months of turmoil than a certainty of degradation', *seems* to mean by 'turmoil' civil war. But he doesn't; he means nothing but the *emotion* of revolt. His violent words are magic rite, not a call to action. It is all so futile and leaves on the mind of the ordinary Englishman an impression of self-seeking subserviency on the one hand and, on the other, of tall talk and tall talk only.

12 September. [Passfield Corner]
The T.U.C. of 1927 has come and gone. If Scarborough (1925) was the high water mark, Edinburgh (1927) is the low water mark of that tidal wave of revolutionary sentiment which sweeps the

British proletarian mind backwards and forwards, decade after decade, without effecting any substantial achievement to compensate for the disturbance of the nation's life. . . . Susan Lawrence, who was in May 1926 enthusiastic about the General Strike and indignant at its unconditional calling off, now writes from Edinburgh approving of the new tone of moderation . . . Even G.D.H. Cole, who has been staying here, is satisfied with the new spirit. He still clings to the notion that salvation will come with the establishment of *One Big Union* – but though he has faith he has little hope!

20 September. [Passfield Corner]
. . . . For the last eight weeks Sidney has been working continuously, from morning to night, whilst I have been putting in a regular morning's work every day of the week. We have been very happy honeymooning in our walks and our talks together, gossiping and discussing with friends and relatives. As recreation when [work is] done Sidney has relapsed into miscellaneous reading and I have listened to music on the wireless or enjoyed the rare intervals of sunshine in this most gloomy of summers. The book is a monstrous performance – one of the most monstrous, in its bulk and weight and elaborate and meticulous detail, that the Webbs have perpetrated during their thirty-five years of partnership! Sidney has excelled himself in hunting up lost links in the narrative and in completing the argument on each count.

Meanwhile we have started an investigation into the present administration of outdoor relief to the able-bodied up and down the country. Whether my strength will hold out to take part in this work, or, at any rate, to effectually supervise it, remains to be seen. Also I am not confident that either Sidney or I have the mental vigour and resilience to tackle new problems. We can still collect and marshal already known categories and facts, perhaps as skilfully as ever. But can we discover the *new* issues and gauge the new proportions of the problems involved, e.g. chronic unemployment? And is there any practical solution should this unemployment prove not only to be chronic but also progressive? . . . Where I think we went seriously wrong in the Minority Report was in suggesting that we knew *how to prevent unemployment*. We did not. All we knew was that it was high time to set about getting this knowledge, and that this could [not] and would not be done by six hundred local authorities whose one and only business was the relief of destitution. If in our last two chapters we manage to get this thesis over the footlights, we shall have done well. With this pious hope I end this volume of my diary covering almost exactly one year.

VOLUME 42

Friedrich Adler (1879–1960) was the Austrian secretary of the Second International. Jane Wells, whose marriage to H.G. Wells (1865–1945) had survived despite his notorious promiscuity, died of cancer on 6 October 1927, and was cremated four days later at Golder's Green. Charlotte Shaw was embarrassed by Wells's panegyric: 'It was hideous - terrible and frightful,' she wrote to T.E. Lawrence on 10 October.

1 October. Passfield
Our days at Roker were filled in with Sidney's seven meetings, and my usual lunch to the thirty officials of the Women's Sections and the Federation meeting in the afternoon – the mornings being taken up with Poor Law interviews and expeditions. Having settled that Sidney retires at the end of this Parliament, our visit was spiritually perfunctory, our chief interest being who will be his successor . . . Sidney intends to give notice early in the session, so if and when we next visit Seaham, it will be to chaperone the new candidate.

Meanwhile GBS has created a sensation; he has gone out of his way to testify to the excellence of Mussolini's dictatorship, to its superiority over political democracy as experienced in Great Britain and other countries. Hence an interchange of letters, public and private, between him and Friedrich Adler (the secretary of the Socialist International). This correspondence arose out of an episode last February: an interview with Shaw in the *Daily News*, a telegram from the Italian socialists objecting to the same, a reply by Shaw to Adler which the International office refused to publish on the ground that it would appear in the Italian Press without any rejoinder. There the matter was allowed to rest. But GBS fortified his admiration of Mussolini by spending eight weeks and £600 in a luxurious hotel at Stresa in continuous and flattering interviews with Fascist officials of charming personality and considerable attainments; [he] handed to the Italian Press, in the middle of October, a deliberately provocative answer to Adler's February letter, this letter being broadcast, considerably garbled, throughout

Italy. From the published correspondence in the English Press, and still more from a private correspondence with Adler, it appears that GBS puts forward the Mussolini regime as the New Model which all other countries ought to follow! His argument seems to be that either the Haves or the Have-Notes must seize power and *compel* all to come under the Fascist or the Communist plough. It is a crude and flippant attempt at reconstruction, bred of conceit, impatience and ignorance. It will injure GBS's reputation far more than it will the democratic institutions in Great Britain. But it reinforces the Italian tyranny. It is only fair to add that this naive faith in a superman, before whose energy and genius all must bow down, is not a new feature in the Shaw mentality. What is new and deplorable is the absence of any kind of sympathetic appreciation of the agony that the best and wisest Italians are today going through, any appreciation of the mental degradation as implied in the suppression of all liberty of act, of thought and of speech.

He and Charlotte lunched with us the day we passed through London . . . For the first time I noticed that he 'gabbled' as he told us, in a confused way, how the recent correspondence with Adler came about. He was very insistent that we should agree with him, and peculiarly exasperating in his dialectic. So we all got rather hot, but presently I turned away and talked to Charlotte about Jane Wells's death and funeral, and Sidney tried to turn the conversation with GBS on to other subjects. GBS alarmed us by saying that he had added three 'constructive' chapters to his book on socialism – as a retort to my criticism last spring that he suggested no alternative to capitalist enterprise plus political democracy. What his proposals will be we do not know; we imagine the same crazy combination, foolish thinking and brilliant expression, that so often nullifies his underlying wisdom. . . . He intends making a great pronouncement at the last Fabian lecture. It will be a nine days' wonder among socialists, will please one or two die-hard Tory politicians and West End club men, and then go the way of so many of GBS's passing aberrations – on to his own private dust-heap. . . .

I have a real affection, as well as admiration, for GBS, and he certainly is the only person, other than myself, whom Sidney would seriously miss from the world he lives in. If only GBS could get started on another play, the mood might pass from him. It is writing this d_____ socialist book whilst living a luxurious life in the midst of a worthless multitude of idle admirers that has upset him, a somewhat similar experience to that of a Nonconformist minister concocting his Sunday sermon in the intervals of gambling in a low public house! Charlotte's inveterate love of all that accompanies wealth and social prestige and her dislike of 'little people' is largely responsible for this vicious mental climate. For GBS, like all realistic artists, is dominated by his immediate environment. Imagine the hot indignation and withering wit with which the meagrely fed Irish journalist of the 80s, writing in his dark lodging, would have chastised the rich world-famous dramatist of 1927 defending the pitiless cruelties and bombastic militancy of the melodramatic Mussolini. The rack-renting landlord of *Widowers' Houses* would appear as the victim of circumstances beside the self-made and self-styled saviour of modern Italy. It is not wholly irrelevant to remember that it was after the first years of enjoying a large income that GBS turned the corner in the character of Undershaft in *Major Barbara*. For the first time he glorified the ruthless use of physical force in order to get efficient wealth production and abolish poverty. . . .

14 November. [Passfield Corner]
Sidney and I are both suffering from 'suppressed lecture'; he gives his Kingsway lecture on Wednesday – an explanation and defence of modern democracy – and I give my Sidney Ball Foundation lecture at Oxford on Monday – a somewhat elaborate pronouncement on the past, present and future development of the Poor Law. So work on the book stops and we are both feeling a little below our common task. . . .

Shaw's lecture, 'Democracy as a Delusion', was the last of the Fabian autumn lectures and was delivered at the Kingsway Hall on 23 November.

[?24 November ?41 Grosvenor Road]
Out of curiosity I attended the Shaw lecture on 'Democracy and Delusion'. An utter failure, evoking in the highbrow Kingsway audience of some two thousand persons no response except a polite attempt to appreciate the few levities he threw in to lighten up a dull and wandering dissertation of one hour and twenty minutes. He opened in a lively fashion by twitting the five preceding lecturers with their scepticism about the reality of democracy, even insisting that Sidney's elaborate description of the multiform character of modern democracy was only another way of saying that democracy

did not exist. Then he laid down his own definition of political democracy as 'government by the people' — which he interpreted as the referendum, the initiative and the recall and to which he added, oddly enough, proportional representation. As all of these devices were found to be mischievous and to lead to anarchy or absence of efficient government, democracy was proved to be a failure. From that point he proceeded to defend dictatorship and the Efficient Tyrant in an extraordinary rigmarole which was almost unintelligible. The capacity for successful violence was the only road to successful use of benevolent power . . . He hammered and hammered on absolute equality of income and compulsion to work as the be-all and end-all of social organization. This could only be brought about by a dictatorship. . . .

The audience became more and more bewildered and when he sat down at ten o'clock — in order, as he remarked, to avoid any questions — there was the feeblest clapping I have ever heard at Kingsway Fabian lectures, and a hurried and silent departure of depressed men and women. He himself seemed down-hearted, and observed that he must 'give the lecture a good many times' before he could make his points clear. If he does, he will not add to his reputation! Poor Charlotte looked gloomy and suggested that we should discuss the subject with him when we go to Ayot for next week-end. But it will be useless; he is too old and too spoilt by flattery and pecuniary success to listen to criticism. He has the illusion that he is and *must* be right, because *he* has genius and his critics are just ordinary men. He wants to *impose* himself as a political thinker as he feels he has imposed himself as a dramatist. What effect will it have on his self-complacency when he finds his ideas simply ignored? Fortunately there is the convention of courtesy and kindness to aged but distinguished persons.

Waldorf Astor (1879–1952) was Conservative M.P. for Plymouth from 1910 until the death of his father in1919, when he succeeded to the peerage. His American-born wife, Nancy (1879–1964), was elected to succeed him, becoming the first woman to take her seat in the House of Commons; she held it until she was persuaded to stand down in the 1945 election. She was an outspoken and provocative member, and the Astor home at Cliveden became a notorious political and social centre during the 30s. The close friendship with the Shaws, which lasted until their deaths, was just beginning at this time. Sir Philip Sassoon (1888–1939) was Under-Secretary of State for Air 1924–29. The Shaws were invited to lunch at his country house on 19 December.

5 December. A week-end at Ayot

GBS and Charlotte were in excellent spirits — just a wee bit apologetic and wistful about GBS's escapade. The lecture was a 'dead failure', he cheerily remarked. 'I ought to have rehearsed it. I lost the trend of the argument.' So I gave him a bit of our mind about it, put gently. . . . But he is still obsessed about Mussolini, and his obsession takes queer forms. Out walking on Sunday we got back to the subject and he suggested that, in the proposed Fascist law making adultery and fornication a *crime* to be prosecuted and punished, Mussolini was interpreting a desire of the Italian people to become *moral* and that he was a new John Knox intent on transforming Rome into a City of God! Almost, GBS implied that he *approved* of this new departure. That from GBS, who was always advocating freedom in sexual relations as something in *itself* desirable! is funny; but the vision of Mussolini as a puritan is still funnier. When we observed that such a law, if it were actually put into force, would transform Rome into a city of spies and black-mailers, and that it was a mere gesture of hypocritical respect for ecclesiastical tradition which would not even take in the Vatican, he somewhat retreated; but we had not convinced him. In talking with Sidney, Charlotte declared that where we differed from them was that they looked forward to a new world with a new race of men — or supermen (this, by the way, was her argument in favour of the feasibility of a complete pecuniary equality from birth upwards!). What with no political or personal freedom, with compulsory equality and compulsory work, it is a weird utopia. We are utterly baffled. There seems neither poetry nor reason nor common sense in GBS's state of mind. We suggested that it was a pity that they never saw the younger men of the socialist movement — Laski, Tawney, Dalton. 'They bore GBS,' said Charlotte. 'You are the only people with whom he cares to discuss political questions.' He is loyal and affectionate to his old friends the Webbs, but he does not really care to discuss with us . . . He no longer subscribes to the Fabian Society; he has never subscribed to the Labour Party. All that he gives is an annual lecture or speech, which is accepted, not on its merits, but because it brings men and money into the hall. There has set in a sort of mutual contempt between GBS and the labour movement; they make use of each other without mutual liking or respect. The sooner he gets back to his plays the better for all concerned. In his old age he is not fit for the criticism of public affairs. All the same, with his pleasant temper, philosophic wit and remarkably good looks, he is a charmer, a gay and irresponsible charmer. It is the note of *indignation* at cruelty and oppression that has vanished – he has lost his pity for suffering. He has become complacent with the world of wealth and leisure he lives in. Does he really want it changed here and now? I doubt it. He and Charlotte are spending Xmas with the Astors! They were recently at the Philip Sassoons. Alas! poor Shaw, you have succumbed to Charlotte!

↶ 1928 ↷

2 January. Passfield
A happy new year alone with Sidney (the Tawneys spent Christmas with us), working well at the book . . . But few will buy these ponderous volumes. Who today is interested in the question of 'Poverty in the midst of riches'? The rich seem to be more callous than of old; fear of Communism, of increased taxation and diminished privilege, has become their dominant emotion; pity for the misery of poverty is dead; indeed, there is a certain resentment at the rise in wages, following the rise in prices, and also at the 'dole' . . . Anyway we delight in this continued work together – one perpetual honeymoon – day after day, year after year . . . 'Ridiculous old souls,' we say to one another as I curl up on his knees in the firelight!

Sidney Arnold became a peer when he was appointed Under-Secretary at the Colonial Office in 1924. He was a close friend and travelling companion of MacDonald. Lord Kimberley (1848–1932) was another of the small group of peers who joined the Labour Party after the war; Lord Gorell (1884–1963) held minor office in the post-war Coalition.

12 January. [Passfield Corner]
Arnold spent the week-end with us. The Labour group in the House of Lords must be the oddest assortment of men that has figured in any country as the official Opposition or alternative government. The only outstanding and distinguished personality is Haldane, the ex-Lord Chancellor and therefore ostensible leader, who is certainly not Labour in opinion and is always dissociating

himself from the Labour Party's programme. . . . For his Labour colleagues in the House of Lords he has complete contempt and never hides it. Out of the nine, only three are aristocrats. Russell is eccentric, clever and poor, disqualified from office – not legally but by Court etiquette – by having been convicted and imprisoned for bigamy; de la Warr is a charming boy of no account; Kimberley aged and boozy and otherwise 'off colour'. The remaining six are all official peers or the sons of official peers. Why the well-bred, conventional and literary Gorell joined the group no one knows. Chelmsford was drawn in for Cabinet purposes, anxious to serve his country and earn a livelihood without committing himself to the policy of the Labour Party. Parmoor is a dear old sentimentalist . . . Of the three peers manufactured by J.R.M. – Thomson, Olivier and Arnold – Thomson is presentable, a typical man about town, Olivier, though a distinguished civil servant, has appeared in the House of Lords a rather dull nonentity, whilst Arnold, public-spirited, assiduous, keen, with considerable political experience, is hopelessly unpopular because of his unattractive combination of an insignificant and bourgeois personality with a fussy activity in and out of the House of Lords . . . Little Arnold is a real radical and convinced socialist, though he admits that the peers are well-mannered and 'make you feel at home' at the afternoon tea-table and in the smoking-room. 'You would like the place, Mrs Webb,' he added, I thought irrelevantly. . . .

21 January. 3 a.m. [Passfield Corner]
The eve of my seventieth birthday! If I thought I were fifty instead of knowing I am seventy should I feel aged, I wonder? I have my eyesight and my hearing intact, perhaps a wee bit hard of hearing when voices are low and words mumbled. I am seldom actually ill. I do not suffer from colds or headaches, from rheumatism or other of the usual ills of aged persons; such minor ailments as eczema, sleeplessness and bowel trouble I have always had and have now. I am just as keenly interested in rather a wider range of subjects . . . I have even added a new source of delight – music – mostly wireless, but I go to more concerts than ever before . . . All the same, I am conscious of failing strength; the hours I work, or *could* work, get shorter and shorter like the autumn days; the longer walks we took the first years we were here, when I was in bad health, have been given up. If I let myself worry over anything I

feel less able to cope with the trouble. And I think I notice the same slackening in Sidney's energies. There is not much to complain of in this slow and painless decline of energy. But it means that we must learn 'the habit of resignation' . . .

In the early hours of Saturday, 7 January, a combination of gales, flood water and high tide produced a surge which broke the parapet of the Thames by the Tate Gallery. Fourteen people were drowned, of whom six were in nearby houses in Grosvenor Road, where all the basements were flooded.

7 February. [Passfield Corner]
Raging south-west gales, torrential rain, alternating with days of dull, drizzly mists, have been our lot this winter. Never before have I heard the winds springing up on all sides, wailing and moaning round the cottage and through the trees insistingly, night after night, driving away sleep. An atmosphere of gloom: the disaster of the Thames tidal wave, six persons drowned in the basements of our span of Grosvenor Road, heard one evening over the wireless, seemed but the climax . . . The basement is to be virtually closed, and we are to clear out of the box-room to serve as Emily's bedroom and to give up the pantry as a kitchen for Susan [Lawrence]. Emily is to transfer her services to Susan and we are to pay for all the service we have with appropriate arrangements about lighting and heating in proportion to use. That means that we shall seldom go to Grosvenor Road; we mean to take a real holiday when we have finished and published these two volumes.

What with the extra work of the Sidney Ball lecture in the autumn and the writing of a highly paid chapter on 'Labour in Western Civilization' for an American publication, I have been working at too high pressure. To which tasks I recently added accepting an offer to broadcast: a quarter of an hour's talk on Herbert Spencer (for which I get ten guineas) on 27 February. It is absurd that I should put two or three days' work and considerable worry into this little piece of artistry. But it struck me that when I am no longer pressed with writing I might like occasionally to broadcast − *if I prove to have the knack of it.* I doubt the quality of my aged voice and my nerve before the microphone. However it will be an experience, like flying would be. Now and again Sidney and I prospect a trip to Russia by aeroplane; probably it won't come off, for there are limits, and rather narrow limits, to my physical endurance. . . .

29 February. [Passfield Corner]
I was in a devil of a funk as I walked along the Embankment to Savoy Hill – in fact my heart and brain were so queerly affected that I wondered whether I was going to be too ailing to get through the job. The extraordinarily restful atmosphere of the B.B.C. mansion set my mind and body at ease; I was comforted by a sense of my own unimportance. . . . I waited in the 'Artists Room' – one or two men with instruments and another with a photographic apparatus wandered through this passage apartment. About nine o'clock there entered a tall, fair-haired, clean-shaven gentleman, in evening dress . . . and he led the way along the silent passages. I tried to enter into some sort of relation with him, but he barely answered me. We entered the padded chamber . . . The announcer, without even looking at me, sat down at the table over which hung the microphone, and in a mechanical voice, read out the news, pausing between each item and keeping his eye on the clock. At 9.15 sharp he rose slowly out of his chair, remarked in the same impersonal tone to the microphone that 'this evening Mrs Sidney Webb, economist and social historian, will give the talk on Herbert Spencer,' made way for me, again without looking at me, and left the room. Once seated at the table and thinking myself alone I started off with little or no nervousness – indeed I rather enjoyed myself – it was like rehearsing in one's bedroom. I had hardly any consciousness of being listened to, so private and quiet was the place one was in. As I came to the last page of the MSS I was conscious of someone just behind me getting restless. I looked at the clock and saw that I was two minutes over my time. I refused to hasten and finished off on a good round note, with a pleasant sense of successful achievement. When the red light went out, I made some harmless observation to the attendant youth. 'Anyone could hear *you*; but what a terrible life the poor man must have had,' was his informal retort. The red light flared on again: 'London will take a little music while Daventry takes the shipping news.' Then he hurried out of the room, and I made my way through silent empty passages to the entrance and out into the Strand. . . .

I found the conditions most agreeable and attractive and I gather from friendly listeners that I did my job well and, compared to the ruck of talkers, in first-rate fashion. All the same, I doubt whether the value of my talk to the listeners equalled the cost to me in nervous exhaustion. I was horribly tired, not by the talk but by the long-drawn-out fear of it. How can one do justice to anyone's life and work in fifteen minutes? Poor old man; he would not have been satisfied.

The portrait of the Webbs was painted by Sir William Nicholson (1872–1949).

5 March. [Passfield Corner]
This morning Sidney and I started on the last lap of our English Poor Law history. I doubt whether it will be a well-finished book. Sidney is preoccupied with Parliament and I am not strong enough for sustained day-by-day drudgery. The most I can do is to add architectonics to his more massive knowledge. And to interrupt our few mornings' work together there comes a fashionable portrait painter to construct a picture of the Webbs for the Founders' Room at the L.S.E. Though flattered by Beveridge's insistence that we must be staged as the recognized Founders, I disliked the procedure of his 'dunning' people for their names and their guineas. It is against both my principles and my sense of good manners. But we both felt it would be ungracious to refuse, so we acquiesced. . . .

Barbara Drake (1876–1963), second child of Georgina Meinertzhagen, was Beatrice's favourite among her many nieces and nephews.

18 April. [Passfield Corner]
A gathering of nephews and nieces at 'Aunt Kate's'. A sort of gathering the dear old lady delights in. The hundred and fifty odd nephews and nieces, grand-nephews and nieces and now great-grand nephews and nieces are a mixed lot, of whom I only know, at all well, about a score . . . Very representative of English society, the older generation pre-eminently a company of businessmen and their wives, the younger generation being more professional – lawyers, medical men, civil servants, university dons. But among the lot there is an ex-chorus girl, an ex-duchess, half a dozen peers' sons, a baronet, an out-of-work actor, a shorthand typist, an old curiosity dealer. In so large a group, in which males predominate, it is odd that there should be only one minister of religion, and he only a Unitarian who gave up his ministry when he married our niece and who was killed in the war. There is one suicide and one lunatic in the first generation and one suicide and two mental defectives in the second. Otherwise the family group is distinctly

above the average in health and capacity. But there is no great personal distinction – not so much as in the group of parents, the nine Potter girls and their ten mates. Among the great-nephews and nieces there are one or two who *promise* distinction . . . The only *friend* we have is Barbara Drake – a Fabian, a writer on economic questions, a member of the Education Committee of the L.C.C., a lover of music and a charming woman. . . . My relation to all of them is 'dutiful', not affectionate, and unless they want to see us, or I think they do, I certainly don't want to see them. Kate is the real centre of the Richard Potter family life, in so far as it has a centre. She is herself fond of her sisters' children and very generous in her timely donations on all sorts and kinds of occasions. Kate is loved, I am liked and Rosy is tolerated. So fare the remnant of the Richard Potter sisters in the minds of their descendants.

Sir Sidney Chapman (1871–1951) was a career civil servant. Beveridge went to America in the autumn of 1928 on an L.S.E. fund-raising visit. Mrs Mair did not go with him. Her son Philip had emigrated to America in June 1927.

30 April. [Passfield Corner]
It is always interesting to bring up to date the career of any old acquaintance. Hubert Llewellyn Smith and his wife stayed with us for the week-end. He is now sixty-four; he has been 'retired' from the position of economic adviser to the government (salary of £3,000) in favour of Sir Sidney Chapman, late permanent head of the Board of Trade, so as to make way for a Protectionist chief officer; not altogether a culminating success of a successful career. He is the same secretive, self-complacent able man I have known, off and on, for forty years; but rather more expansive in conversation than when in office and certainly more friendly to us. . . . I think the couple enjoyed their stay here more than they expected. Beveridge joined us Saturday evening, and the two old colleagues were evidently very friendly but not, I think, intimate. . . .

Mrs Mair turned up to lunch; she took me aside and asked me whether I thought she might go to the U.S.A. with Beveridge, at any rate travel there in the same steamer, her excuse being that she wanted to visit her engineer son. 'Better not,' was my reply in guarded language. Whether she will abide by my advice I am not so sure. It is, I am pretty certain, a platonic relationship, but in spite of their mature age it is far too romantic to be comfortable for the institution over which they preside as Director and Secretary, or agreeable to her husband or children. But she is so wrapt up in Beveridge and he is so dependent on her that separation, one from the other, would be far harder to bear than in most marriages. . . .

Harley Granville-Barker (1877–1946) and Lillah McCarthy (1875–1960) had played a significant role in launching Shaw's plays at the Court Theatre in the 1900s. They went to America in 1915, where they were divorced. He fell in love with a rich American, Helen Huntington, and married her in 1918. After the war Lillah married Sir Frederick Keeble (1870–1952), who had been director of the Royal Horticultural Society's gardens at Wisley and now had a fellowship at Oxford. Desmond MacCarthy (1877–1952), a member of the Bloomsbury Group, was for many years dramatic critic of the *New Statesman*.

2 May. [Passfield Corner]
At the Russian Art Theatre performance with Barbara Drake last night, watching that amazing Russian acting, the effect heightened by the musical though unintelligible language. A few rows behind us, on the other side of the gangway, I noticed a short, commonplace, smiling, self-important man, well-groomed and in immaculate evening dress; at his side a pale, dark-eyed woman, also the last word in correct clothes for the occasion. They were looking at *me*. Their appearance roused no memory and my eye passed on, seeking out possible acquaintances. During the next interval the man crossed the gangway and I became conscious of an outstretched hand and a warmly intimate greeting. The fat, featureless face still puzzled me but I recognized the voice – a singularly attractive voice – it was an old friend, Granville-Barker. Clearly he was pleased with himself and prosperous. Lillah McCarthy, now Lady Keeble, is, I understand from the Shaws, as pleased with herself and as prosperous. The divorce seems justified, but they have both ceased to be artists. Lillah was never more than a competent performer with a handsome face and a fine figure. She is probably more useful as wife and hostess to a distinguished scientific worker and public servant than as a second-grade actress. But Harley had creative power, intellectual and artistic. The American wife has smothered this fine faculty in luxury and social pretension. Which is *Waste*, with a slightly different plot than that of his remarkable play, the waste of an artist-thinker instead of a politician. It is to be hoped that he will not become aware of the *Waste*. Fatty degenera-

tion has gone too far for recovery – why not be happy? Desmond MacCarthy says they are a 'sad little couple' in a luxurious house. I may add that this little group of men and women who have married and unmarried and remarried (the American wife has had three husbands) have had no children. It is a vision of sterility as well as waste.

There has been an event lurking in the background of our life – intensely interesting but unimportant to us personally – the break-up of the Christian Church in Great Britain. The rejection of the revised Prayer Book by Parliament and the consequent unseemly controversy which has raged among the ecclesiastics has awakened the English public to the fact that the English are no longer Christians in any real sense of the word . . . Dean Inge openly advises, in the pages of a profane journal, that no candidate for orders now believes in the supernatural element in the Christian faith, or in any of its specific doctrines; all that is needful is that he should be a mystic, that he should have a sort of an idea that there is a Force that makes for righteousness at work in the Universe. How long this queer state of mind, the Church with its creed and its rites, its pomps and its ceremonies, can continue part and parcel of the British Constitution is difficult to foretell! But the rotting away of this ancient structure, in sight of curious and contemptuous citizens, is ugly and distressing; Dean Inge acting as a cynical guide among the crumbling ruins adds a touch of ironic humour to the melancholy picture. . . .

5 May. [Passfield Corner]
Nicholson, the agreeable portrait painter, has been here three week-ends doing studies of us to be translated on to the large canvas, a pleasant waste of Sidney's time and my strength and other people's money. I doubt the result. It may be a clever picture ('especially of the brickwork,' GBS suggests), but it will be an insignificant portrait, the figures being too small relatively to the background and too insignificant for the Founders' Room. If it be desirable that the L.S.E. should have a Webb seal, this particular seal will do as well as any other. . . .

Ada Webb (1864–1946) and Charles Webb (1857–1954) were Sidney's sister and brother. Beatrice knew them for over half a century but they are scarcely mentioned in the diary.

28 May. 3 a.m. [Passfield Corner]

To the Lighthouse by Virginia Woolf represents the latest fashion in the technique of novel-writing. The story, so far as there is a story, is told by a running description of the 'stream of consciousness' in the principal person's mind. When this person dies, then another mind is taken as the medium; in this book both are women. To me this method is objectionable because it assumes that the author *can* see into and describe another's mind and record what happens, exactly as a person's behaviour can be watched and his words recorded, and his surroundings and what happens to him retailed. What one suspects is that Virginia is telling you of her *own* stream of consciousness, the only one she knows 'of her own view and knowledge'. And that brings me to the question: could I record my own consciousness? So often it seems too vague and diverse and disconnected – there are currents on currents, continuously rising or falling in relative vividness, sometimes pictorial, sometimes vocal, sometimes aloof or detached, sometimes part of a pattern made up of personal contacts and relative positions, sometimes intellectual, concrete or abstract or emotional, personal or impersonal. All in all even one's own consciousness defies description.

For the last few days I have been haunted by the shocking appearance of Ada Webb – she came here with the Charles Webbs for lunch and tea. She has always been plain, but this time she looked repulsive and Sidney perceived it as quickly as I did. 'Some drug on the top of loneliness, no occupation and the lack of any creed or purpose in life,' I ventured as an explanation. She has become immensely fat, especially the lower part of her face relatively to her forehead; and her body seemed swollen. She said she was 'quite well'. I remembered that poor old Lallie said the same when she was obviously dying of cocaine poisoning. Ada was sucking tablets, she said, for her cough. . . . It is the tragedy of a vacant heart and an unoccupied mind. Her condition raises the question, and Charlie writes anxiously to Sidney: can anything be done? Neither of her brothers are in a position to take charge of her, even if *she* would allow herself to be controlled; they have done all they can do in giving her a sufficient income to live in ease and comfort. And at sixty-five years of age, there is little chance of a change of conduct in the direction of deliberate self-control. But the thought of her sinking into a self-drugged senility (Charles says it is overeating without exercise) is painful. One feels guilty of neglect without exactly knowing why one should feel guilty, and without the remotest intention of accepting further responsibility. So that's that. . . .

The Aberavon constituency, for which MacDonald had sat since 1922, required too much of his time and money. He was elected for Seaham Harbour in 1929 and 1931 but in 1935, having broken with the Labour Party when he formed his National government four years earlier, he was defeated by the Labour candidate Emmanuel Shinwell.

28 May. Whit Sunday. [Passfield Corner]
The Snowdens lunched here to meet the Hendersons, who are staying a long week-end with us. Snowden was remarkably fit and self-complacent. Mrs Snowden looked out of sorts. I took her round the garden and she insisted on confiding to me, very deliberately I thought, that she *might* be suffering from an internal complaint. She is at the turn of life and obviously feared cancer, like nearly all women do at her age. And she added 'very confidentially' that she had never 'lived with' Philip and that as she was a 'normal woman' her lot had been very hard. Which I can well believe; it excuses a good deal of her search after social prestige and the agreeable excitements of the smart set. Henderson and Sidney agreed that if J.R.M. disappeared Snowden was the best man for the party leadership, better than good little Clynes, who seems the only alternative. Why not 'Uncle Arthur', said I? A conclusive *no* was the answer.

Henderson is convinced that Baldwin will lose his majority and that the Labour Party will be called to office, however short may be their tenure. Sidney still believes in, or hopes for, a small Conservative majority and the non-success of the Liberal campaign. Henderson, I was interested to note, assumed that if the Labour Party took office Sidney would go to the House of Lords. 'I shall obey orders,' Sidney remarked, 'but quite sincerely I should prefer not.' To which I added 'Amen'. . . .

Meanwhile Henderson and Sidney are conspiring to hand over the safe and cheap seat of Seaham Harbour to 'our leader'. Who would have thought that the embittered vendetta of former years would have terminated in such a model manner!

Neville Chamberlain (1869–1940), the son of Joseph Chamberlain, had been the Conservative Chancellor of the Exchequer in 1924. He was currently

Minister of Health and responsible for the Poor Law. In 1937 he became
Prime Minister.

30 May. [Passfield Corner]
Clear to us that the chapter we began on 5 March will not be
finished before we leave for our holiday. The portrait, a succession
of week-end guests, my fagged brain, have combined to prevent it.
However long it takes, this concluding chapter or chapters have got
to be as good as we can make them. What troubles me is that we do
not yet see our way to get off the horns of a dilemma. How can we
show up the disaster of unconditional outdoor relief to able-bodied
persons without seeming to justify Chamberlain's callous application
of the worn-out principles of 1834? His present policy means semi-
starvation to thousands of *bona fide* workers (and their children) for
whom no work is available within their reach, however willing
they are to do it. Here in the exquisite countryside, living in
comfort and ease, surrounded by friends and social consideration,
out of sight of poverty, are we not certain to fall into accepting a
morass of misery which is at once cruel and preventable? I am
arranging to go to South Wales on our return and see for myself
what exactly is happening to those derelict mining villages. Some
way out *has* got to be discovered and laid bare. What depresses me
is the probability that it needs more virile and more adventurous
brains than ours to discover the way out of this social jungle.

The Intelligent Woman's Guide to Socialism and Capitalism had just been
published.

9 June. [Passfield Corner]
GBS has had a good Press for his five-hundred-page socialist tract.
His acknowledged genius, his old age, the warmth and depth of his
earnestness and his amazing literary brilliance have paralysed his
would-be critics and opened the hearts of fellow socialists, especially
those on the left. He denounces society as it is, he gives no credit
and no quarter, and he preaches a curiously abstract utopia, which
eludes criticism because of its very unreality. To me the book is
boresome. Perhaps any other work on abstract capitalism or abstract
socialism would be, to me, unreadable; only Shaw's amazing
cleverness can make such a subject, here and there, entertaining
and thought-provoking. . . .

146

15 June. [Passfield Corner]
Watching a well-known portrait painter at work has been instructive. He has taken an incredible time over me, owing to the wrong scheming of the picture in the first instance. I have been painted in and painted out half a dozen times. Now at last the figure satisfies him and is quite good enough for me – rather too young and good-looking, but that fault is inevitable in a woman's portrait.

20 June. [Passfield Corner]
GBS and Charlotte were jolly with us and pleased with themselves; she is becoming more and more the accomplished Society woman, full of pleasant chat about books, art and people; he orates agreeably and is delightfully friendly. He spends many hours of the day answering letters of all and sundry arising out of his book. Charlotte complains that he is obsessed with the writing of letters, that if there are no letters or few letters he is obviously disappointed. He believes his book will influence the general election, win the votes of some of the have-nots and possibly lose the votes of some of the haves. We avoided discussion either of the book or of current politics. The Shaws and the Webbs love each other and flatter each other. Today he and we have not enough in common to argue or discuss. Bertrand Russell came to lunch and he and Bernard Shaw scintillated . . . It is comic to associate the Shaws, in their present state of being, with an ardent faith in equality of income and compulsory labour! But GBS remains the charmer I knew first thirty-six years ago and Charlotte is a fitting mate – they seem today better suited to each other than ever before. . . .

5 July. Val d'Isère, Savoy
Not for years have I enjoyed a holiday as I have this fortnight here; the long-houred walks up the villages by rushing glacier streams, resting among the rocks, larch and flowers, watching the glorious intimacy of mountain, cloud and sun – all the time honeymooning with my beloved! Also I am glad to discover that I can still walk for five hours or more and even climb three thousand feet in broiling heat without serious strain. . . .

Richard Meinertzhagen (1878–1967), soldier and anthropologist, was the son of Beatrice's sister Georgina. He was married to Annie Jackson. Robert Holt (1872–1952) was the son of Beatrice's sister Lallie. His son was Oliver (1907–60). He was suffering from polio, not sleeping sickness.

19 July. [Passfield Corner]
A hot four days at tiresome St Gervais, a still hotter twenty-four-hour journey across France, and we were stifling in the heat and noise of Grosvenor Road, smothered in papers, listening to Susan's account of her battles with Neville [Chamberlain] and pulling ourselves together to begin work again and pick up plans to see this person or that. A melancholy dinner with dear old Haldane and the devoted Elizabeth, Haldane looking desperately ill and feeling miserable; if I had not seen him looking almost equally bad before, I should imagine he was near his end: contemptuous of the Labour Party and all its works, and especially so of his little bunch of Labour peers. . . . An evening with dear old Kate, who has failed to find comfortable summer quarters and comes here for August. Two family tragedies – Dick Meinertzhagen's wife, an attractive and wholly desirable person, shot herself accidentally whilst revolver practising, and Bob Holt's boy down with the most ghastly of ills, sleeping sickness. That about sums up the situation – at least the foreground of our consciousness. The background is menacing: growing unemployment, the desperate condition of the miners, the terrible dilemma of demoralizing outdoor relief on the one hand, and, as the alternative, semi-starvation and slow demoralization, a hell of a mess which we have got to describe, if not prescribe for, during the next six months. Fortunately I *do* feel stronger in body and mind and the memories of that Val d'Isère are wonderfully refreshing.

Beatrice had now engaged Jean and Annie Smith, two Scots girls, who remained at Passfield for the rest of her life.

24 July. [Passfield Corner]
Not succeeded in getting back to work, partly owing to the heat, partly to visitors – Hugh Dalton, Arnold and Beveridge, partly to trouble about my little maids and their incredible carelessness about my belongings and their own reputation! What worries me is that I have neither the energy nor the habit of looking after young servants, and that's worse for their future than it is for my present convenience and safety . . . But the real difficulty is that I am desperately tired of the subject and that owing to age and infirmity I cannot enter into real contact with the facts of today. I have got to a time of life when mere drudgery is immensely distasteful, whilst

adventure in the search of raw material is too hard work for me. What I should like doing would be to browse among books and write or not write as I felt inclined – perhaps try some new style of thought and expression.

To go back to Virginia Woolf's method of novel-writing; the description of the streams of consciousness of one or other of her characters. Can I describe my own? There seem to be certain main currents, one or other becoming uppermost, leaving the others, for the time, more or less subconscious. There is always a groundswell of physical sensations, mostly unpleasant, in old age; tiredness is perhaps the dominant one. I have less pain and active discomfort but also less physical exhilaration than in youth or middle life. Intellectual interests, satisfied by current news and discussion, and by books and conversation with clever folk, are perhaps the most constant element in my consciousness. There are spells of enjoyment of music or natural beauty, but these are short-lived. The mental background throughout is religious, a merging of self in a mystically beneficent spirit alternating with complete scepticism as to there being any meaning in life other than we put into it by our own wayward imaginations. Here today, gone tomorrow. In old age the doubter overcomes the devotee – or rather, all conflict ceases. Why trouble? So far as my own conduct is concerned I accept the religious hypothesis; so far as other people's doings are involved I have ceased to sit in judgement. Each generation must find its own footing in the world. . . .

12 August. [Passfield Corner]
After an interval of six years Clifford Sharp came here for a short week-end. He had intimated that he would like to see us again and we had wished to close the episode of unfriendliness due to his anti-Labour policy during the three general elections. He has not changed except that he looked more physically shattered by drink; but he was sane, cynically able, and frank. He was contemptuous of the Labour Party; its leaders had no courage, it was based on the interests of one class, its only chance was coalition with the Liberals and that would mean an inward split. Politics were deadly dull. There were no issues of interest to the general public. There was a dearth of talent in public life and also literature. Altogether it was a sombre and unlovely world we lived in. He told us a good deal about Beaverbrook, who had made him various offers of highly

paid employment. He was tired of the *New Statesman* but hated the idea of anyone else controlling it. . . . I should not be surprised if Clifford Sharp ended by deliberately drinking himself past recovery; he seems to have lost hope either for himself or for the world. . . .

R.B. Haldane died on 19 August 1928.

21 August. [Passfield Corner]
Haldane's death was no shock. We saw it coming and no friend could regret it. He was not only powerless; he was wretched. But it is a sorrow to think that our oldest and most constant friend has passed away. It was Haldane who created and fostered the flattering 'Webb myth' that flowered so agreeably and advantageously for us and our schemes in the first decade of the twentieth century. Even when the idealized myth withered and was replaced by a caricature, Haldane was one of the few who, in spite of a certain disillusionment, remained faithful to an old friendship . . .

What bound us together as associates was our common faith in a deliberately organized society, our belief in the application of science to human relations with a view of betterment. Where we clashed was that *he* believed more than we did in the existing governing class – in big personages, whether of Cabinet, City or Court, whilst we held by the common people, served by an élite of unassuming experts, who would appear to be no different in status from the common man. But about his personal disinterestedness there can be no doubt. He loved power, especially the power of the hidden hand, or shall I say of the *recognized* hidden hand, but he frequently sacrificed his own prospects if he could thereby save a friend or promote a cause he believed in . . . About men and affairs Haldane was not only wise but also witty, full of curiosity about motives, or judgement about faculties. It was this human side of his that made him excellent company. . . If I had to write his epitaph it would be 'a powerful and beneficent personality, a great citizen, above all a loyal and generous friend.'

Beatrice spent ten days at the end of August touring the mining districts of South Wales to collect material for the conclusion of the Poor Law history.

1 September. [Passfield Corner]
. . . . My general impression is that the Welsh miners, though not starving – there are no soup kitchens and the homes look clean and

the people respectable – feel themselves to be 'down and out'. There is a grim silence in the streets, and the little knots of boys and men look apathetic and slink about as if ashamed of the shabbiness of their garments. The homes are getting barer and barer and the food deteriorating in quality – there is little drinking and smoking. . . . In fact the Rhondda valley reminded me of the streets of Hamburg when we were there in 1923; the people were respectable and quiet but they looked terribly depressed physically and mentally . . . The only ferment is political and economic, and the Labour Party dominates the situation in the Welsh coalfields alike in local and national politics. . . .

I returned to Passfield tired out. But I have stood the test well and the stuff I have collected and my general impressions ought to help us to write a better conclusion than we should have done without it. All the same I feel too old for the job; my memory frequently fails me and I get flustered in going from place to place, and muddle-headed from continuous talking. The buzzing in my right ear troubles me at night and I get dead tired in the day. Sometimes I wondered whether I could hold out until the end of my visit – but I did!

28 September. [Passfield Corner]
Sidney works steadily on at the book; for the last fortnight I have done little or nothing to help him except some suggestions as to arrangements etc. Not exactly ill, but hopelessly unfit – insomnia, bowel trouble, intermittent rheumatism and headache. And Mr Nicholson appears again on the scene and requires more sittings. He is a most agreeable and sympathetic person. But the long-drawn-out process annoys and irritates me, so far as my portrait is concerned. Neither the artist nor anyone else likes the result of all this effort. It seems all right to me. If only he would leave it alone and finish the picture and be gone! . . .

Point Counterpoint by Aldous Huxley was published in 1928. *The Magic Mountain* by Thomas Mann (1875–1955) was published in 1924 and translated in 1927. Mrs Humphry Ward (1851–1920) was a notable late-Victorian novelist. D.H. Lawrence had just completed, but not published, *Lady Chatterley's Lover*. Norman Douglas (1868–1932) made his reputation with *South Wind* in 1917 and wrote *In the Beginning* in 1927. David Garnett (1892–1981) was a Bloomsbury novelist and critic. Compton MacKenzie (1883–1972) had begun his long career as a novelist with *Carnival* in 1912 and *Sinister Street* in 1913.

151

26 October. Roker

Our last visit to this little seaside suburb of Sunderland – my last meeting with the miners' wives, daughters and menfolk, saying farewell and introducing Ishbel MacDonald. An upright good-looking girl, plain-speaking, puritan and public-spirited, without any particular gifts of personal charm, wit or intellect; proud of, but not intimate with her father; with an obvious appreciation of her delegated importance as an ex-Prime Minister's daughter who may any day again be hostess at 10 Downing Street. We did not interest each other, but we made pleasant conversation on our drives to and from the meetings, and in our walks along the sea front . . . It is good to feel that our relations to Sidney's constituency have been wholly friendly; we leave no enemies and many good friends.

While Sidney has been out at six meetings I have been reading Aldous Huxley's *Point Counterpoint*, and pondering over this strangely pathological writing, pathological without knowing it. The febrile futility of the particular clique he describes reminds me of that far more powerful book *The Magic Mountain*, by Thomas Mann. Far more powerful because Mann is describing a society of sick people, and the sick people are more varied and significant in character and life history than in *Point Counterpoint*. Huxley's group do not know that they are sick and are presented as a sample of normal human life. What with their continuous and promiscuous copulations, their shallow talk and chronic idleness, the impression left is one of simple disgust at their bodies and minds. . . . And the book, apart from arousing a morbid interest in morbidity, is dull, dull, dull. In a few years' time it will be unreadable – it represents a fashion. In this characteristic of fashionableness Aldous Huxley is like his maternal aunt, Mrs Humphry Ward; also in his tendency to preach.

'Your generation,' said a Cambridge undergraduate to his mother, 'lost faith in God. Our generation has lost faith in man.' The 'Religion of Humanity' and its successor, 'The coming of the Superman', alike mild reflections of the consciousness of God, have vanished from the public eye in my lifetime. The Great War disgusted everyman with its manifestation of human power, which appeared as the Will to Murder. Today there is a demand for the sub-human in art and literature and music. Clever novelists – Huxley, D.H. Lawrence, Norman Douglas, David Garnett,

Compton MacKenzie – are all depicting men and women as mere animals, and morbid at that. Except always that these bipeds practise birth control and commit suicide. So it looks as if the species would happily die out! It is an ugly and tiresome idol of the mind, but it lends itself to a certain type of fantastic wit and stylish irony.

Neville Chamberlain was now dismantling the Poor Law system that had lasted, in its essentials, since 1834.

15 November. [Passfield Corner]
I am still grinding at the last chapter of the book – 'The Recurrence of Able-bodied Destitution' – pruning each section in passing, sharpening the points, adding illustrations. Meanwhile the Poor Law guardians are being swept away, without anyone else paying the least attention to their fervent protests. . . . the guardians are thoroughly discredited and even clerks to guardians are saying confidentially, outside their board-rooms, that their boards are *not* fit to govern. Whether after the demise of the guardians anyone will care to read our elaborate two volumes of history, giving a detailed account of this particular form of government from start to finish, is seriously concerning us; how many copies to print, for instance? . . .

May Wallas (1891–1972) became a French lecturer at the London School of Economics.

21 November. [Passfield Corner]
Graham Wallas here for four nights and his daughter May for one night. I enjoyed his visit; he was not boresome as he has been of late, less obsessed with his own work, more ready to discuss at large, so we talked and talked . . . Certainly we old Fabians – GBS, Wallas and the Webbs, and for that matter many of our other Fabian contemporaries – are pleasantly self-complacent. We are a lot of happy old people, who think they have done well by the world and also had a good time of it.

May Wallas is an admirable spinster – admirable in all ways, and especially in her wonderful gift for self-subordinating herself to the life of her parents. She struck me as a woman one would gladly live with – unlike either parent in this respect. Poor Audrey has had an operation for cancer and is in a depressed and nervous state. She is popular with the greater part of Graham's friends and acquaintances; to me she is singularly unattractive in body and mind. For which I am remorseful, because Audrey is a virtuous woman, not only according to the ten commandments, but also in her determination to give her husband and her daughter a good time of it to her own detriment. Graham is encouraged to go to the U.S.A. and display himself in lectures and talks, which he loves doing – he brings back a few hundreds – but this extra income is usually spent on trips of Graham and May to Palestine or Italy or Austria, leaving Audrey to economize at home. Why is it that the good is so seldom combined with the beautiful? . . . It is so easy to win applause, luxury, power, by personal charm, whether of body or mind, but the ways of virtue are dull and the toil of thought is hard. Audrey has certainly had a duller life than she would have had if she had had less goodness and more charm.

29 November. [Passfield Corner]
I listened from the Ladies' Gallery to Sidney's 1½-hour speech on the Local Government Bill. To me it is a nerve-racking ordeal – I am far more agitated than if I were speaking myself. Any little imperfection in delivery or in the arrangement of his subject matter, any little slip in tact or unnecessary repetition of phrases, makes me wince as if my nerves were being cut one by one. But as it turned out, the speech was a great success; delighted his own party and was attentively listened to by the opposite benches. In its criticism alike of de-rating and of the abolition of the boards of guardians without providing for the break-up of the Poor Law it was masterly; what it lacked was a good delivery and a quick understanding of the effect produced by each successive sentence. He is not 'at home' in the House of Commons. . . . He is one of the 'characters' of the House and is always being caricatured as the enigmatic learned person, at once absurd and impressive, who, somehow or other, is trusted and followed by the party of the proletariat and who does not hide his boredom and contempt for the ignorance and indolence of the representatives of property and privilege. When the commoner type of Tory comes in after dinner, a little the worse for liquor, and finds Webb speaking, he jeers; in his sober moments he sees the sinister figure of an English Lenin who is bringing about Communism, not by force, but by underground manipulation of the democratic machine. Not an altogether

unpleasant reputation. Anyway, neither of us feel we have anything to complain of. Considering how low we have valued the interests and opinions of our own class, we have been kindly treated. . . .

Tom Shaw (1872–1938) was a textile trade union official who had been Minister of Labour in 1924.

24 December. [Passfield Corner]
Oswald Mosleys stayed here. We had seen little of them since a week-end at Lion's in the autumn of 1922, when he had just come over to the Labour Party and was about to lose his seat therefore. It struck us both that he and she had changed – partly from his long illness last autumn and winter, partly from the ups and downs of electoral failure and success; also from social boycott by their own set and an uneasy position in the Labour Party. He is disillusioned. Labour politics for an aristocrat are not attractive – current and cross-current from left and right and very little real comradeship. 'Labour people,' said Cynthia, 'especially the better sort and the intellectuals, are shy of us, except the few snobs among them who are subservient.' Sidney and I are recognized as genuine 'Ancients' in the labour movement, but even with us there has been the difficulty of becoming *intimate*, the sort of intimacy we have had with Haldane, with Beveridge, Wallas and GBS, with the professors and lecturers of the School of Economics. There is no *intimate* inner circle in the labour movement; every Labour leader (except perhaps Uncle Arthur) is a lonely figure, neither friendly nor unfriendly towards other leaders but merely unconcerned about them. J.R.M., of course, is incapable of intimacy within the movement. He is reputed to be intimate with Conservative dames; he told Sidney that he was on 'christian-name terms' with Lady Londonderry. He goes off travelling with Arnold, with the Buxtons, with the Mosleys or the de la Warrs. A significant selection! But these journeys are just rushes through sights and social functions, and don't seem to lead to any real consultations.

Mosley has his political career before him, and with his money, his personal charm and political gifts, his good-looking and agreeable wife, he is dead certain of Cabinet office, and possibly has a chance of eventual premiership. He, Dalton and C.P. Trevelyan seem today the most likely successors to J.R.M., assuming that the latter remains the leader for another ten years. . . . Sidney is good friends with all the party; constantly consulted, always willing to help or to stand on one side, as is most convenient. He, Willie Graham and Tom Shaw, at the request of the Parliamentary executive, are to meet at Philip Snowden's to draw up a programme of immediate legislation and administration, should the Labour Party find itself bound to take office after the June election. . . .

ᘯ 1929 ᘰ

Neville Chamberlain, the Minister of Health, had introduced a Local Government Bill on 27 November 1928. The Poor Law guardians were abolished and their powers transferred to the counties and county boroughs, whose responsibilities in other fields were extended.

4 January. [Passfield Corner]
Exactly twenty years ago — 1908 — we were putting the finishing touches to the Minority Report, I in a state of abject exhaustion. On New Year's Eve 1928, we were writing the last words of the epilogue of our lengthy history of the English Poor Law, recording the sentence of death passed by Parliament on the boards of guardians and the opening of a new era in the legal relations between the rich and poor. These two volumes will be the last big work of research. They will have cost over £1,000 in printing and some hundreds in out-of-pocket expenses of investigation and typing, not to mention all the previous researches for the Minority Report, without which this larger work could not have been undertaken. . . . A few days spent on pruning the last chapter and I, at least, will be done with the Poor Law . . .

There has been a certain exhilaration and self-complacency in the writing of the epilogue because it is clear that so far as the Chamberlain Bill goes it does *break up the Poor Law* in respect of the non-able-bodied. Further, it leaves the whole problem of unemployment in such a hopeless tangle that it is safe to predict that the second part of the Minority Report — a national authority for the able-bodied — is almost certain to be carried out. It is in fact in process of being formed in the Ministry of Labour. To be able to *make* history as well as to write it — or, to be modest, to have foreseen, twenty years ago, the exact stream of tendencies which would bring your proposal to fruition, is a pleasurable thought! So the old Webbs are chuckling over their chickens!

16 January. [Passfield Corner]
In the beautiful Founders' Room at the L.S.E. there was a reception to see the Webb portrait hung over the mantelpiece – a really lovely picture, as a picture, whatever criticism my friends may make about my portrait. And a most friendly little gathering – mostly Fabian – the other subscribers not turning up. Beveridge made a gracious little speech, far too impressive about us. He is a very faithful admirer. Altogether our stock is up, or rather, we have, through old age, ceased to have detractors; no one troubles about aged folk except those who respect and like them. Which adds to the pleasantness of life, though possibly also to its illusions. . . .

2 February. [Passfield Corner]
The winter months have slipped past at great speed, owing to the strenuous routine of our lives. Every morning our cup of coffee before eight o'clock, then the morning's work, Sidney at it continuously, I as long as I can stand it. Lunch at one or 12.30; the hour's rest, a cup of tea about three o'clock, a walk and back again at work until the 'News' on the wireless at 6.15; perhaps a little music, supper at 7.30, a little reading or wireless music, bed at ten o'clock. Each successive twenty-four hours is exactly like the past one. And this is the life I have been leading all our married life, except for the two years on our travels round the world, and during the years spent on the Royal Commission of 1905–09, or the Minority Report agitation of 1909–10 and the wartime committees of 1915–18. An extraordinarily peaceful and interested life, one long day of loving companionship and joint intellectual endeavour, no anxiety about ways and means, no serious illness or prolonged ill health, always free and able to do what we thought best. 'We *have* been fortunate,' Sidney often says. . . .

S.K. Ratcliffe (1868–1958) was a Fabian journalist and lecturer. The relativity theory of Albert Einstein was now publicly known, if not understood.

20 February. [Passfield Corner]
Uneasy about GBS's state of mind. At Galton's urgent request, he came to the social gathering of the Fabian Society the other night in a devil of a temper. He struck out here, there and everywhere. The Fabians were dull dogs, the new tracts were unreadable, the

reviews in *Fabian News* were contemptible – all of which led up to his real complaint. The most ignorant reviews of his book on socialism had been by Fabians. (This was a hit at Laski's review and also at Ratcliffe's.) He had just heard from Germany that Einstein, who, it appears, is a socialist, was absorbed in his book. Who were the Fabians compared to Einstein? All this was a repetition of what he and Charlotte had signified when last we lunched with them a few weeks ago. What irritated GBS is that his treatise has not been taken seriously, either by the labour movement, or by the opponents of the Labour Party. Winston Churchill, in his new book, has called him the 'Socialist Chatterbox', but that was in reference to his views about the war. In all the pre-election platform speaking, GBS's manifestoes have not once been noticed. And now comes the newspaper rumour that he might be, or ought to be, made a peer by MacDonald when Labour forms a government. 'A very sensible suggestion,' he is reported to have said, 'but I have not yet heard from MacDonald.' This may be one of his little jokes, but I am not sure that he does not fancy himself upsetting the world from the benches of the Lords. . . .

GBS has had in his later years an immensely successful career alike in prestige and riches; he has been adored and flattered by the smart set of intellectuals at home and by more substantial minds abroad. In his old age few and far between have been his outspoken detractors. But he is not satisfied with his reputation as an artist. He hungers after acceptance as a great thinker and social reconstructor. Which he is not, never has been, and never could be. But why should he expect to be a superman in social reconstruction? He does not claim to be a mathematician. 'Nancy' [Astor] is having a bad effect on him!

6 March. [Passfield Corner]
On the morning of Saturday 24 February Mary Anne, Kate's old servant, telephoned me that Kate was dangerously ill and begged me to come at once. I had just time to phone Sidney that I would join him in London and to catch the early train. When I reached Cheyne Walk it was clear that she was not dying, but near to death. She was glad to see me, and as the only nurse who could be got in this epidemic of influenza had been with her two nights and one day, I took her place for the rest of the day. Her medical man assured me that we would pull her through; it was influenza poison,

there was no pneumonia and the bronchitis was not severe. The poor dear did not like her nurses and there were three in succession during her week of illness. But she was happy in her mind and in no pain and would have liked to talk to me more than I dared let her. Reassured, I dashed down to Passfield on Sunday afternoon to finish packing, planning to return on Tuesday. But on Monday morning Mary Anne again telephoned for me and from that afternoon I stayed with her until she passed peacefully away on Tuesday the 27th at about three o'clock in the afternoon, choked by an accumulation of phlegm which she could not cough up. Apart from weariness and restlessness and all the discomfort of laboured breathing, I don't think she suffered. . . .

Kate was the most beneficent of my sisters and was the most beloved by nephews, nieces and friends. She was in a sense faultless – she had no malice, no envy, little egotism; she was in the best sense pious; she was always thinking good thoughts, repeating to herself beautiful poems which she had learnt from Leonard, arranging to do kind acts to all sorts of persons. Since Leonard's death she and I have seen much of each other . . . but we had never been intimate. I do not think she was really intimate with any of her sisters; the rest of us had a certain hardness or cynicism which was intensely repellent to her nature. Indeed, one of the curious facts about the Potter sisters was that though we were very good sisters to each other and never quarrelled, we were not intimate. And perhaps I was the least intimate, and so was most to blame for this lack of tenderness. For Margaret [Hobhouse] I had a real affection and her death was a direct sorrow. For Mary [Playne] too I had a tender heart. Kate's death, now that it has come, is also a sorrow, but the sorrow is more because I feel I *ought* to feel her loss more than I do, than because I *do* feel it. I sorrow because her beneficent presence meant so little in my life. . . .

The Liberals won two of the three by-elections in March. J. Blindell gained Holland-with-Boston from the Tories and defeating by 3,706 votes the Labour candidate G.R. Blanco White (1883–1966), a lawyer and sometime member of the Fabian Nursery, who had married Amber Reeves (1887–1981) after her liaison with H.G. Wells. R.J. Russell gained Eddisbury, and at East Toxteth the Tories held the seat in a three-cornered fight with little more than a third of the votes cast. Before the war Shaw had been infatuated with the actress Mrs Pat Campbell (1865–1940), for whom he wrote *Pygmalion*. The character of Orinthia in *The Apple Cart* was based on her. Shaw had refused her request to include their correspondence in her book *My Life and Some Letters*, not wishing them to be published until after Charlotte's death. Despite this refusal, they were eventually published in a separate volume.

25 March. Hastings

The sensational Liberal victory at Holland, following on the expected victory at Eddisbury and the increased Liberal poll at East Toxteth, may be the result of Lloyd George's grandiose 'cure for unemployment' (the expenditure of £200,000,000 in relief works – relief works they will be, whatever they choose to call them). To the pure party man in me, this turn towards Liberalism is annoying – I said 'damn' as I read the result of Holland. But from the standpoint of getting on with the job of social reorganization, I am not so down-hearted. Sooner or later, Labourites and Liberals will have to coalesce. Labour needs brains and money and Liberalism needs numbers and a sound working-class basis. . . . The worst of it is that Lloyd George's schemes, though brilliantly conceived and advocated, are always unsound and turn out terribly expensive. And I doubt whether Great Britain can afford any more expensive remedies – like insurance for health and unemployment – which neither alter the environment nor cure the patient. However, on the whole, I am glad he has set the pace. Among the Front Bench Labour leaders there is far too much dull acquiescence in continued unemployment. . . .

Sidney says that the Holland victory was largely due to local conditions and may not represent a swing towards Liberalism. I shrewdly suspect that Amber's personality and regrettable past experience were to some extent responsible for Blanco's abject failure. Very hard on both of them. But when a person is under scrutiny for five years by hostile eyes eager to discover flaws, sensational episodes like Amber's story will inevitably come out, in whispered if not in overt scandals, and may be all the more damaging because the channels are underground.

As we thought, the new Shaw play (*The Apple Cart*) is a savage burlesque of a Labour government. In 1962 the governing class has gone out of politics, and the Cabinet is made up of Labour men and two Labour women (caricatures of Susan Lawrence and Ellen Wilkinson, GBS told us) . . . The only redeeming feature is that it is very good fun – GBS at his cleverest and naughtiest, reflecting the outlook of the Astor set. The love scene, sandwiched in between the beginning and the end of the political crisis, is an obvious reminiscence of Mrs Pat Campbell and her overtures and GBS's refusal to comply; a very brutal portrait, a tit-for-tat, his belated retort to her publication of his love letters some fifteen years ago.

After her first broadcast Beatrice was asked to read poetry; she declined but suggested a series on 'How to study social facts', for which she asked £50 – 'a good deal more than the ordinary fee'. Her terms were agreed, but Sidney had to deliver the first, as it coincided with the death of Kate.

28 March. [? 41 Grosvenor Road]
I struggled through the three BBC talks, without failure but on a low level of achievement, the last talk especially poor quality; it had to be scrambled together after Kate's death, when I was on the brink of collapse. Meanwhile Sidney has been slaving at the last stages of getting the book through the Press and the special editions sent off to subscribers: about 350, not quite half of the number offered, which cannot be said to be a brilliant result for all our efforts, barely worth it. Altogether we are rather depressed and glad to get away. We need a complete change of scene before we start on the eighth decade of our lives, the fifth of our married life and in all probability the last of our partnership. When I was down at Passfield the other day surveying the building alterations I longed to be back in the quietude and peace of our little home. 'But we shall want a book to write,' Sidney observes.

Also, said Henderson, with whom we lunched . . . 'You will be wanted in a Labour government.' We don't believe it; we see no chance of a Labour majority and we doubt whether it would be practicable to come to terms with Lloyd George. It is just conceivable that J.R.M. would find himself called to office, but his tenure would be short. It might be long enough to send Sidney to the Lords. . . . If he is wanted in the Lords he will go and do his best, and on the whole, he will be glad to go – a new experience, just rounding off his experience of public life – civil servant, London County Councillor, M.P. Cabinet Office in the Commons, leadership in the Lords! If he is not called up, I shall be relieved of an unwelcome task of entertaining in that unpleasing circle of Labour M.P.s and their wives on the one hand, and the official connections of some government department on the other. I prefer our little circle of intimate friends at work on our own subjects, varied by a couple of months in the autumn in London, going to concerts and reading at the British Museum and seeing nephews and nieces and the lecturers and students of the London School of Economics. Making new acquaintances no longer attracts me. I've done so much of it, all my life, under pleasanter circumstances and at a time of life when one is keener on studying varied personalities. (So here ends the account of Our Partnership from October 1927 to April 1929.)

PART II

A Drift to Disaster
April 1929–December 1931

Introduction to Part II

IN APRIL 1929 the Webbs took a six-week holiday to Greece, Turkey, Germany and Austria. The outstanding episode of their stay in Constantinople, Beatrice said, was their 'romantic' interview with the exiled Soviet leader Leon Trotsky on the island of Prinkipo. Sidney had written a letter suggesting a meeting and it was quickly arranged.

In a ramshackle villa, with a secret service officer sitting in the garden, we found Trotsky and his wife and son. We were alone with the great revolutionary for a couple of hours. He is a charming and accomplished man; looks more like an intellectual musician than an organizer of war and revolution. He opened in polished French with a suave and deferential claim to being one of our disciples who had strayed away from our teaching! He refused to talk himself either about Russia or to let us talk about England; he led the conversation exclusively on to the inevitability of a world revolution – perhaps not the inevitability but the desirability? He admitted eventually that it might be that capitalism was finding a new equilibrium in the U.S.A. and Europe. In that case Soviet Communism would fail in Russia; that system could not stand against a hostile and vigorously successful capitalist organization in the rest of the world. He intimated that the only chance for Russian Communism was the approaching great war between the U.S.A. and Great Britain, which would wreck the *status quo* in both countries. We tried to explain that this war would not happen, that revolutionary propaganda of the kind carried on by Communists was doomed to ignominious failure in the U.S.A. and Great Britain. We suggested that if the Russians could make Soviet Communism successful so that the worker would gain a higher standard of life and more freedom and dignity in

165

Russia than elsewhere, then an enormous stride would have been made in converting other countries to Communism. And why should not this success be possible?

I don't think we impressed each other with our respective arguments – partly [because] we could not speak much French and he could not understand English well enough to come to grips with each other's outlook. Also I think beneath all his polished intellectualism he has the closed mind of a fanatic who refuses to face the fact of Western democratic organization.

His wife is a commonplace little person and his grown-up son, who had followed his father into exile, resembles his mother rather than his father.

The Webbs ended their holiday in Munich to receive honorary degrees from the University there, and they returned to England at the end of May to see the run-up to the general election which was to take place on 30 May. It was a dull campaign. Lloyd George was making a final bid for power but the Labour Party was optimistic about its own prospects; by-election results had indicated that the government would be defeated. There were a number of three-cornered contests which enabled Labour to emerge for the first time as the largest party in the House of Commons. They won 287 seats against 261 for the Conservatives and 59 for the Liberals. It was an ambiguous result, especially as Labour had only polled 8.3 million votes against a combined total of 14 million for its opponents, but Baldwin preferred a minority Labour government dependent on Liberal votes to a Tory–Liberal understanding which would have brought Lloyd George back into a leading role. He accordingly advised the King that MacDonald should succeed him.

The Cabinet that MacDonald formed on 3 June was little better and only a little more experienced than the government he had led in 1924. It was dominated by the same five men – himself, Snowden at the Treasury, Henderson at the Foreign Office, Clynes at the Home Office, and Thomas as Lord Privy Seal with a special responsibility for tackling the chronic unemployment (over one million) that had persisted since the end of the post-war boom. Margaret Bondfield at the Ministry of Labour became the first woman to enter the Cabinet; Sidney Webb, now Lord Passfield, combined the Dominions and Colonial Offices in one portfolio; the ageing Lord Parmoor was Lord President of the Council. The other appointments – with the exception of Lansbury (who was given the Board of Works as a sop to the left) and Sir Oswald Mosley, who became Chancellor of the Duchy of Lancaster and special assistant to Thomas on the unemployment issue – went to known moderates and right-wingers.

It was a government ill equipped for the serious troubles that lay ahead. Its leaders were not only at odds with the vociferous left-wingers in the party, who found it hard to bridge the gap between socialist rhetoric and the constraints of office; they were also so ignorant of economics that they could neither refute the Gladstonian notions which the Exchequer officials shared with Snowden nor discover any effective alternative to them. 'The Treasury mind and the Snowden mind', Churchill wrote after the 1931 crisis, 'embraced each other with the fervour of two long-separated kindred lizards.' As the economy faltered through the next two years, and unemployment rose dramatically towards a peak of three million, Snowden clung to the shibboleths of financial orthodoxy: he believed in clinging to free trade when one country after another was slipping into protective tariffs, in rigorously maintaining the gold standard which the City saw as the hallmark of its credit among world bankers, and in securing a balanced budget by cutting public spending rather than by raising taxes or stimulating the economy.

With such a penny-pincher as Snowden at the Treasury and the boozily incompetent Thomas in charge of unemployment, the Cabinet staggered into what MacDonald called 'an economic blizzard' that blew more strongly after the Wall Street crash on 23 October 1929. A year later, unemployment in the United States had risen to at least seven million; it was over five million in Germany, where the burden of war debts that the French refused to cancel added to the troubles of the Weimar Republic; and a wave of tariff wars, defaults, riots and revolutions rippled across the world. The slump was out of control and it would run its ruinous course all through the 30s until it ended in rearmament.

MacDonald and Henderson were more effective in foreign affairs. MacDonald was an unexpectedly effective negotiator, who genuinely wished to revise the harsher aspects of the Versailles Treaty; and in January 1931 the League of Nations accepted Henderson as chairman of the World Disarmament Conference that was to begin meeting in February 1932. But the Labour government ran into trouble in four countries for which Sidney Webb was responsible: in Kenya, where the white settlers wanted land from the native reserves; in Egypt, where nationalist feeling was rising against the British overlords; in India, where Mahatma Gandhi was moving towards a policy of civil disobedience; and in Palestine, where there was Arab rioting against Jewish immigration and land settlement. Labour's apparent hostility to Zionism, moreover, embarrassed its limited relationship with the United States.

It was, however, the government's failure to cope with the economy of Britain that led to its catastrophic downfall, and the issue on which it fell, in August 1931, was the fast-rising cost of unemployment benefit. On the one hand the City and Wall Street bankers were demanding cuts in the dole, which came from a fund that was requiring ever larger subsidies, and there were many in the Cabinet who could not agree to such cuts. On the other hand both the Liberals (advised among others by John Maynard Keynes) and the I.L.P. members were pressing for bolder and less deflationary policies. Mosley, with the help of John Strachey, drafted proposals which combined public and private stimulants to the economy — ideas similar to those of Keynes and the policies Roosevelt was to include in his New Deal. Yet the Labour leadership dismissed them as casually as it shrugged off I.L.P. demands for nationalization and redistributive taxation. Mosley resigned, letting his personal pique flare into a brief period of criticism before it guttered into the futility of his New Party and the later squalor of his British Union of Fascists.

MacDonald's response was to make some minor administrative changes. Sidney Webb surrendered the Dominions part of his portfolio to Thomas, while MacDonald himself became chairman of the committee of Ministers dealing with unemployment. It made no difference. As the structure of international and national credit collapsed and both City bankers and Treasury officials demanded solvency at almost any price, the government was driven into a corner. They could only avoid a crisis of confidence by accepting economic policies which they did not like and could not persuade their supporters to accept.

Although there were rumours of revolts and intrigues within the party throughout the spring of 1931, and a scheme by one group to make an agreement with the Liberals, the sudden collapse of the Labour government came as a surprise. It began as a technical crisis, when the failure of the Kredit-anstalt bank in Vienna put such stress on the chain of credit that it broke at several points. In the ensuing rush for liquidity the British banks found they could not recover their recent advances to Germany and they were forced to meet their obligations in gold. In the two months after 15 July, when the run on sterling began, Britain lost £33 millions in gold and £180 millions in foreign exchange – substantial sums at that time.

This technical crisis quickly escalated into a crisis of confidence in the Labour government. Snowden had set up a committee under Sir George May (1871–1940), chairman of the Prudential Insurance Company, who was asked to propose economies in government expenditure. In July they produced a sensational report, its two Labour members dissenting, which amalgamated all the public deficits to a total of £120 million and proposed that they should be met by severe cuts in the dole, in the pay of teachers, police and the armed services, and in the money allocated to public works. This report, coming when the run on the pound began, made matters worse for the government; now the two opposition parties began to demand the same trenchant economies as the City and foreign financiers.

MacDonald thereupon set himself up as chairman of an 'economic committee' which included Henderson, Snowden, Thomas and William Graham, who had become the President of the Board of Trade. He hoped to secure a compromise between the proposals of the May report and the demands of the T.U.C. and the Parliamentary Labour Party. This attempt failed and MacDonald was now faced with a political crisis. He met the General Council of the T.U.C., who stood firm against cuts in unemployment benefit; there were several Cabinet meetings and confidential contacts with Liberal and Conservative leaders, with the bankers and with the King. Finally the Cabinet was edged towards a package of emergency measures; the sticking point was the dole. Eight members of the Cabinet were prepared to resign rather than accept the ten per cent cut in unemployment benefit demanded by the American bankers as a condition of a loan to save the pound. On the Sunday night, after the whole Cabinet had put their resignations in MacDonald's hands – many believing that he was resigning with them – he saw Baldwin, Neville Chamberlain, Samuel and three bankers. Next day, after a second meeting with the King, he became Prime Minister of an emergency government with included the Conservative and Liberal leaders.

MacDonald's opaque eloquence mirrored his opacity of thought. He seems to have entered the last phase of the crisis with three conflicting possibilities in mind. He could try to save the pound, though that might mean splitting the party. He could try to preserve the party by resigning, though he seems to have thought the pound might collapse before Baldwin could form an alternative government. Or he could try to make some temporary arrangement with the Liberals and the Tories. He tried each of these solutions in turn. Late on Sunday night he told Baldwin and Samuel that he would not join a coalition government but would help to pass any emergency legislation that might be needed. Even when he returned for a last meeting with his Cabinet after he had seen the King on Monday morning, he merely said that some 'individuals' would carry on the government for the time being, putting through the crisis measures on which the outgoing Cabinet had agreed — plus the cut in the dole which was the condition of the American loan. Even then he seems to have thought he was sacrificing himself for the good of the country, and that he would cease to lead the stop-gap administration once Parliament had passed the necessary legislation. His former colleagues, however, assumed that he had deserted them and they were bewildered and outraged.

Whatever MacDonald's motives, the destruction of the Labour Party was certainly a consequence of his defection. At the election held on 27 October 1931 the Labour Party saved only 52 seats, while MacDonald's National government swept back with 566 supporters. It took the Labour Party years to recover from the shock of that defeat; and in those years it painfully sought to rebuild its organization and to remake its policies.

VOLUME 43

⌒ 1929 ⌒

Beatrice was staying at the house of her late sister, Kate.

30 May. 15 Cheyne Walk
The heat of the battle of today is not between His Majesty's Government and His Majesty's Opposition but between the two oppositions. And rightly so. It is comparatively unimportant either to Baldwin or to MacDonald, or to the causes they represent, whether the Tories remain in for another two or three years and get defeated at the next general election, or whether the Labour Party takes office this year and gets defeated in a subsequent election. What is at stake is the continued existence of the Liberal Party and the continued power of Lloyd George. If the Liberals fail to double their numbers at today's polls, they disappear as a political force; if they succeed in winning a hundred seats or more they become a possible alternative government to the Conservatives, and the demand for the equalitarian state ceases to be the main issue in politics. . . .

Considering how the result may affect us personally we feel singularly unconcerned and detached. A decisive Labour victory or even the advent of a minority Labour Cabinet would probably send Sidney to the House of Lords and into the Cabinet. My own impression is that Sidney would rather like to be in office again, and that I should dislike it. I certainly disliked it last time. But I doubt whether the remainder of our lives would be much affected. The spell of office would be brief and once over it won't be repeated. We shall go on living the same sort of life anyway; old people can't and don't change their habits, physical or mental. From the public point of view what counts is the *presence* of a powerful Labour Party, not its *taking office*! The rate of social progress depends on the amount of good will and knowledge among administrators and legislators. What is desirable is clear enough and not seriously disputed. What is lacking is the heart to desire it and the head to work the process out. . . .

1 June. [15 Cheyne Walk]
Sidney and I sat up with the Laskis till 2.30, listening to the flowing tide of Labour victories — almost hysterical at the prospect of Labour being in a majority in the House. Today the relative numbers of Labour and Tories has settled down near Sidney's forecast — its difference being that the Tories excel in votes and Labour in representatives, instead of vice versa, as he had predicted. What has been accomplished is the final collapse of the Liberal Party. Considering their money, their Press, their brilliant demagogic leader with his pledge 'to cure unemployment in one year', the failure to add even a score to their numbers is decisive. They will never again reach their present number in the House of Commons. . . . Baldwin will be smoking his pipe philosophically, enjoying the prospect of a rest from responsibility, certain in his own mind he will come back to office in a few years' time. J.R.M. will be enjoying the sensation of inflated prestige and weighing the advantages of taking or not taking office. But for Lloyd George the future is blank. . . .

4 June. [15 Cheyne Walk]
Baldwin resigns. Informed public opinion — *The Times*, the *Evening Standard* — insisted that the wisest course was dignified resignation and acquiescence in the advent of a Labour government. Also, Baldwin must have felt that this step gives the 'go by' to Lloyd George and the Liberal Party; it deprives them of their casting vote, or of any bargaining power. The idea that Lloyd George would intrigue with Austen and Winston to keep the Conservatives in office 'on terms' must have been supremely distasteful to Baldwin, who loathes Lloyd George. So Baldwin makes way for MacDonald and virtually agrees to support him so long as he does not introduce socialism by instalments . . .

During the next few days *we* shall be uncomfortable and unsettled — we are out of a home, and I am in the midst of an exhausting job, distributing the belongings of Kate Courtney among the nephews and nieces and friends. If Sidney gets caught up in the Labour Cabinet, I shall feel harried; if he is not invited, I suppose we shall both feel a bit flat! I am glad the decision is not with us, but with those who are better able to judge what is best for the party . . .

If I examine my thoughts and feelings about it, I find: entire approval of his absence of claim and willingness to serve; of his refusal to be a peer except as a condition of office; doubt of the new responsibility and new calls for a man of his age; and, on my own part, positive distaste for the social obligation involved, even a certain fear that my strength will give way under the strain. But in spite of these doubts and hesitations, there is the all-pervading *amour propre* – why is there no English word? If he were not asked he would feel, and I should feel for him, slightly humiliated and depressed; also he is still strong enough to enjoy the excitement as well as the enhanced prestige of high office. . . .

5 June. 10 a.m. 15 Cheyne Walk
Over the wireless we heard that the P.M. had submitted a list of his Cabinet to the King this morning, so that finished the uncertainties of these last few days. If it had not been for the curious assumption of Henderson, Arnold, and Parmoor that Sidney would be included in MacDonald's second Cabinet the idea would never have occurred to us. But anyway it has dispelled any fear that he should find himself willy-nilly in the House of Lords.

Midnight. A violent ringing of the front door bell. I thought it was Maud Keary locked out, but found her coming down to answer it. 'Must be a telegram,' she said. I followed on, opened the telegram – 'Phone me tonight, MacDonald.' I woke Sidney who came near swearing, trying to discover, still dazed with sleep, J.R.M.'s telephone number. He is to be up at Hampstead by nine. 'Wants to persuade you to accept a peerage without office,' said I. 'I shall not do it,' said he, and returned to his bed. I have asked him to telephone to Passfield, whither I go tomorrow at nine o'clock, what exactly is the meaning of the midnight call.

Sydney Olivier, an ennobled Secretary of State for India in the 1924 government, was passed over in 1929.

6 June. [15 Cheyne Walk]
The interview ended in Sidney accepting a peerage in order to take over the Colonial Office. The immediate reason for this very handsome offer was that J.R.M., anxious to complete his Cabinet at once, had not complied with the constitutional requirements that there must be two Secretaries of State in the Lords. He immediately thought of Sidney for the job. Sidney was delighted with the Colonial Office; it is his old office as a civil servant, one about which he knows a good deal more than about some others. Mean-

while I was at Passfield awaiting the news by telephone – amply disguised by code. An odd compound of satisfaction for him, of tiredness on my part and of a rather morbid awareness of old age in both of us, came over me for the rest of the day. When poor old Olivier called (quite obviously unfit in body and mind), quivering with anxiety and indignation at not having 'heard from MacDonald', I wondered whether there ought not to be a hard and fast retiring age for Cabinet office? Parmoor, for instance, is too aged and infirm for leadership of the House of Lords. What are other people saying of the old Webbs? . . .

And now I have to finish up this tiresome business of distribution, find servants, settle back into Passfield, before sitting down to consider how I can best fulfil my part of Sidney's job – entertaining his colleagues, colonials and the rank and file of the Parliamentary Labour Party. We must spend freely from the £3,500 net income, and if my strength holds, create some sort of social centre for the Labour Party. . . .

Leopold Amery (1873–1955), former Fabian and journalist, became an ardent imperialist and held office in several Conservative governments. W.A.G. Ormsby-Gore, later Lord Harlech (1885–1964), himself became Colonial Secretary in 1936.

9 June. 3 a.m. [15 Cheyne Walk]
It is characteristic of English political life that within an hour of the officials of the Colonial Office becoming aware that Sidney was to be their chief, Amery (the outgoing Secretary of State) followed him from Cheyne Walk to Grosvenor Road in order to put him *au fait* of the personalities of the office. Yesterday, the second day of his attendance at the Colonial Office, Amery and Ormsby-Gore (the Under-Secretary) paid him friendly visits, offering to give him any information, etc. Much the same procedure is going on at all the offices. The general atmosphere of friendliness is peculiarly present at this changeover . . . The British governing class have been taken aback by the solidness of Labour's advances: the absence of losses, and the way in which one industrial district after another is roped in by Labour propaganda. And their reaction is not bitterness or abuse, but 'let these fellows have their innings – let us show them that we are playing a fair game'. . . .

I have been so absorbed in my job [of the distribution of Kate's belongings] that I have not heard any Labour gossip about those who have been left out or not promoted. Arthur Ponsonby is in a melancholy mood – he very naturally expected to be promoted to the Cabinet. Instead, he is Sidney's Under-Secretary for the Dominions, a position of less interest and importance than his Under-Secretaryship for Foreign Affairs in the 1924 government. Ponsonby is an exceptionally attractive aristocrat – a charming *littérateur* with a scholarly temperament. But he is a sentimentalist and without horse sense, an amateur and dilettante in politics. And he stands aloof from the rest of the party – he is poor and can't afford to entertain, he is fastidious and does not care to associate with the trade union element. And his wife does not help him; she is sickly, critical and somewhat rude. They live in an old fourteenth-century priory [at Shulbrede] six miles from Passfield, enchanting to look at but deadly dank and dark to live in. Which accounts for their pale faces and lack of *bonhomie*. . . .

Round about all the new Ministers there is the agreeable buzz of congratulations, together with the political deference of the English towards 'men in power', or at any rate 'men in place'. Lloyd George alone is bitter and insulting; he orders the Labour Government to do what he knows they are about to do, and he tells them if they apply 'socialist theories' he will turn them out and they will have to depend on 'Tory votes'. Seeing that the programmes of all the three parties abound in the application of 'socialist theories' and that Tory votes are just as good as Liberal votes, Lloyd George's threats and taunts are silly . . . Lloyd George is, I think at the end of his tether and knows it. That accounts for his undignified and obviously futile rage.

20 June. 41 Grosvenor Road
When first it was mooted that Sidney should go to the Lords the question of becoming 'Lord' and 'Lady' was discussed between us. My instinct was against the use of a title, and Sidney, though feeling less strongly, acquiesced. But breaking a convention, which all accept, needs something more than mere dislike, which may arise from distorted pride, subconscious superiority, self-advertisement or other forms of egotism. The test is always: would it be desirable for all other people to do it? In breaking the convention are you making it easier to sweep away an evil thing or create a good one? Moreover, if the use of a title is not desirable, why should you put yourself in the position of having to refuse to use it? Why accept a peerage?

This last question is easily answered. The British Constitution being what it is, short of a physical force revolution, there have to be Labour peers in order to form and maintain a government. Whatever objection there may be to accepting a peerage, it is immeasurably less objectionable than the refusal to take over the responsibilities of governing the country. In short, the acceptance of peerages by a sufficient number of persons helps to sweep away what you believe to be bad, and to create what you believe to be good. So far as Sidney is concerned, assuming that he thought himself fit to be in the Cabinet, he was in duty bound to go to the House of Lords.

The second question, and one which is not so easy to answer: having accepted the position, why make a fuss about the title? And here it seems to me, and also to him, a question of manners and not of morals, and a question which was different for the peer and for the wife of a peer. We object to a caste of peers, and to all that honour and glamour that surrounds this social caste; we want to destroy the prestige enjoyed by the 'ennobled' in order to ease the way for destroying the constitution of an hereditary House of Lords as part and parcel of the British government. In particular, we do not want this liking for the institution of a nobility to spread in the Labour Party; we do not want members of the Labour Party to seek the social esteem at present belonging to this venerable institution. Now, one way of undermining the respect for the House of Lords is to give up the use of titles attached to peerage *as far as this is practicable*. It is clear that Sidney himself, having accepted a peerage, is bound to use the title in his official acts; he has accepted office on this condition and he might just as well refuse to call himself Secretary of State for the Colonies. But this obligation does not extend to his wife; nor, I think, to himself, when out of office or in an unofficial capacity. By refusing to become one of a social caste — honoured because it is a caste — I make it slightly more difficult for other Labour men to succumb to the temptation. By merely passing over my right to use a title I help to undermine the foundations of British snobbishness. There is far too much snobbishness, far too much regard for rank and social status, in the British labour movement. It is a good thing to set the example of not considering a title as honourable to the person legally entitled to it . . . An honour ignored is an honour deflated. What amuses me is that the only possible retort, as far as I am concerned, on the part

176

of the Court and London society generally, is social ostracism, and that, of course, is the one that will best suit me. I *want* to be dropped out of the Buckingham Palace list because it saves me from having to consider whether I am justified in refusing to attend Court functions. I respect our King and Queen and I acquiesce in a constitutional monarchy – the British monarchy is an anachronism but it is a useful anachronism, an institution for which it would be precious difficult to find an equally good substitute. But its social environment of aristocracy and plutocracy is wholly bad; and the less the Labour Party accepts this environment the more wholesome will be its internal life. The ideal I set before me is to refuse to accept what seems to me a false scale of values, without bad manners or discourtesy . . . I shan't be fussy or pedantic about it; if I find myself called 'Lady Passfield' on official occasions I shall not protest. Obviously anyone has a right to call me by that name. But I shall persistently call myself Mrs Sidney Webb and when once Sidney is out of office my intention will prevail . . .

21 June. [Passfield Corner]
Sidney is of course enjoying himself. It is agreeable to be treated with deference by a long procession of persons of importance, to have skilled assistance in every task and to give what seem to be your own decisions on innumerable questions, especially when you happen to have an outstanding capacity for swiftly mastering new issues and intricate situations. And his lack of all pretension and his genuine kindliness and courtesy towards his subordinates is bound to make his way easy in the office. Whether he will stand the unaccustomed strain of continuous responsibility, day after day, time will show. I dislike the inevitable separation which this office work will entail. Which means that we must have a comfortable abode in London – the getting of which will be my next job – and a full-time secretary. Fortunately the singularly helpful and attractive little woman I had at Passfield for a year, Miss Burr, is now in London and is willing to come for the period of Sidney's office, short or long. If I have not sufficient work for her I can lend her to one of the women Labour M.P.s. So that's that.

Sidney, in fact, continued to use the title until his death.

29 June. Ayot St Lawrence
The episode of 'Mrs Sidney Webb', wife of Lord Passfield, has

passed off quite happily. The Press have been quite pleasant about it . . . To get it published was not my intention. But the publication has been fortunate as everyone now calls me Mrs Webb. The Labour people I have seen are quite pleased. By the general public it has been accepted as 'an extreme feminist gesture'; not as a depreciation of titles, which might have caused resentment. No one has yet tumbled to the reason for Sidney's assumption of 'Passfield' instead of Webb as his ennobled name. But now that I have got my name accepted, he will gradually drop the title in private life, whilst using it punctiliously in public life. And when he retires from office we shall manage to get the second step accepted – his resumption of the name and status of plain 'Sidney Webb'.

The Bernard Shaws are in high spirits. He wanted to persuade us that the Labour Party must do some 'window-dressing', and he was to be the dresser. The shows provided to amuse the people were: first, a Press law prohibiting, under heavy penalties, any glorification of war or any instigation of racial hatred; secondly, the creation of a Ministry of Fine Arts (incidentally, a post for Olivier); thirdly, the creation of a Senate to replace the House of Lords. Also the need for the equalitarian state was to be taught in all the schools. Banks were to be nationalized, and smallholders and small mastermen to be given extensive credits. Above all, the Labour government was to put forward arresting policies – seeing, as he said, they would do nothing! Then they were to go to the country. Impatience, impatience and again impatience is GBS's frame of mind. He told us, by the way, that his gross receipts for royalties etc. in 1928 were £40,000.

What strikes me in watching Sidney at the Colonial Office is the perfect smoothness of the British administrative machine in the changing from a Conservative to a Socialist government. The permanent heads and the corps of discreet private secretaries see to that. I walked with Sidney to the Colonial Office yesterday morning. . . . When the Secretary of State passes through the door, a bell rings throughout the passages and silent and attentive messengers spring up at intervals, ushering him into the large ugly room in which he sits. . . . It is all very funny, very unlike the informal camaraderie of the labour movement. At the National Labour Club where I usually lunch there are to be found, sitting side by side, short-haired typists from the trade union offices, M.P.s, Cabinet Ministers, all being served in strict order of their coming, and all chatting together indiscriminately. 'Well, Mrs Webb,' said a porter to me at King's Cross, 'I really don't think a live Lord ought to travel third-class. I see you are not using the title,' he added in a tone of approval. So we stood and chatted, one or two other porters joining in. A taxi-driver jumped down from his seat in Downing Street and grasped Sidney's hand. This consciousness of social equality among all ranks of the labour movement is a great asset to a political party, a precious possession which we must keep intact and foster as the party grows larger. Of course, at the extreme ends, left and right, there is conscious or unselfconscious exclusiveness. The Clyde group keep to themselves and never attend party receptions and the aristocrats, less ostentatiously, do not associate privately with the proletarian or lower-middle-class M.P.s and candidates, except on public platforms, victory gatherings or possibly in their own constituencies. . . .

Lt.Col. Sir Humphrey de Satge (1874–1964) was ceremonial secretary at the Colonial Office 1925–31. Margot Asquith (1864–1945) was the second wife of H.H. Asquith, who had been ennobled in 1925. The Duke of Connaught (1850–1942) was the brother of Edward VII and uncle of the reigning George V.

6 July. [41 Grosvenor Road]
I have won on the name and lost on the curtsy! At the Colonial Office there is a cleverly tactful official, Colonel de Satge, who acts as Master of Ceremonies and organizer of social gatherings . . . In the first days of Sidney's official life, de Satge informed him of all the social functions already arranged and pressed for my participation. 'Could Mrs Webb be induced to present some dozen colonial ladies at the forthcoming Court?' 'No,' said Sidney. 'A woman of over seventy ought not to be expected to attend evening Courts. But my wife will gladly meet any colonial ladies who wish to see her,' he added. 'Then Mrs Webb will no doubt be present at your reception of the Canadian Clubs on July 3rd; there are many women members who would like to see her,' blandly enquired the wily de Satge. Of course I agreed, all the more readily as Sidney not being yet a peer, the invitation went out as from 'the Secretary of State for the Dominions and Mrs Sidney Webb', a fact which was greeted by the Press a few days later (Sidney having meanwhile become Lord Passfield) as a defiant announcement that I intended to keep my commoner's name. What de Satge had not told us was that the

Duke of Connaught and Princess Patricia would be present at a certain stage in the proceedings. This was suddenly sprung upon us when we were halfway through the reception. Sidney was hurried away to receive the Royalties at the entrance of the University, while I was left to await their entry, with two or three hundred loyal Canadians standing behind me. Without a grave breach of courtesy there was no way out of the curtsy. The Duke is a kindly old man and as he hobbled up to me I had not the heart to disappoint him. 'She curtsyed,' recorded the Press correspondents in some of next morning's papers. I am told that this world-moving event was duly broadcasted that very evening. So that's that, and curtsy I must on all future occasions. . . .

An odd parallel between two careers in which I have been specially interested. Joseph Chamberlain first entered the Cabinet in 1880 as President of the Board of Trade; he finally retired from Cabinet rank in 1903 as Secretary of State for the Colonies. Sidney Webb first entered the Cabinet in 1924 as President of the Board of Trade; he is again a member of the Cabinet in 1929 as Secretary of State for the Dominions and Colonies. When Mary Booth came to congratulate me yesterday and embraced me with emotional enthusiasm I could not help suspecting that this dramatic coincidence, with the long time-lag between the twin events, was in her mind as it had been in mine. A few days ago, Sidney met Austen Chamberlain at a dinner to the Prime Minister of Egypt. After compliments to the new Secretary of State Austen lent over the table and observed in a confidential tone: 'I wonder whether Mrs Webb remembers my coming with my father to stay with Mr Potter when she was acting as hostess? I was a boy at Cambridge. I fell desperately in love with one of her nieces,' he added, by way of explaining this reminiscence. It was during the winter of 1883 that Austen narrowly missed becoming the stepson of the lady who is today the wife of one who has succeeded his father at two Cabinet offices. A curio in the play of destiny.

We attended the Thanksgiving Service in Westminster Abbey . . . a survival of a dead ritual, meaningless to the majority of those present. The King and Queen were formal figures, not impressive or attractive. The last touch of ugliness and unrest was given by the figure and expression of the Countess of Oxford in a prominent corner seat of the front row – over-dressed, haggard, rouged and seemingly desperately miserable. As we filed out behind the Royal cortège Margot [Asquith], followed by a child, pushed past me, fighting her way out with the ugly intentness of a spirit escaping out of Hell. The fall from prestige, power, meant to her boredom tempered by misery. Which brings me to a reflection of these last days.

What J.R.M. called, at the zenith of his first premiership, before the motor-car incident and Russian episode had dimmed his outlook, 'the exhilaration of high office', seems a morbid state of inflated self-esteem due to the abject deference and subtle flattery which every P.M. in office gets so long as he remains in office. This inflated personality is passed on to his wife if she happens to be a notable figure in Society, as Margot was . . . Poor Margot enjoyed this inflation for the crucial ten years of her husband's premiership, after a whole youth of another kind of inflation due to beauty, wit and wealth. After ten bitter years of political failure, her husband died. In spite of her new rank as Countess, she has become an unattractive nobody, ignored by those who dominate the gay world. What has happened to Margot tends to happen, to a less degree, to everyone who has enjoyed the prestige of high office, except perhaps to aristocrats like the Cecils, who start and remain great personages irrespective of whether or not they are in office . . . So I must beware of the old Satan of personal vanity, a devil not laid by old age. Indeed old age, because of the decay of mental faculties, seems peculiarly susceptible to flattery, to alternate waves of inflation and depression in self-esteem, a most painful process. In Margot's case it seems to have become a veritable agony, which caricatures her former self.

12 July. Passfield Corner
My first night spent in our little home since I left it to hurry back to Kate's deathbed – over four months ago.

It is exactly five years since I settled down here after we had made the small cottage fit for our everyday home by building on our study, two bedrooms and a servant's bedroom. Sidney was then in office, and I was down here a good deal, working at *My Apprenticeship*. Today we settle down again to a far more attractive abode – no longer a cottage but a rather perfect little house, fit for a peer to live in!

I have no book on hand, and I look forward with a certain nervous dislike to this spell of official life. Our plan to write a

Manual of Social Study is clearly impracticable. It may be that after six months of social life, mainly in London, I shall begin to collect the material for *Our Partnership*. Whether I could be as frank about our married life and joint career as I was about my girlhood is doubtful; the narrative might have to be far more objective and less personal. It would depend on whether I write for publication during our lifetime or merely prepare the separate episodes for our editors' use. Also I should have to consider Sidney's susceptibilities. What I yearn to do is to sum up my experience of life. Have I come to any conclusions? What troubles me is our own good fortune – a superlative good luck, a good luck which is almost ridiculous in its completeness, contrasted with the daily grind of human life, as it is lived by the vast majority of men. . . .

If we were really single-minded about the equalitarian state, ought we to be living a life of relative luxury and social prestige? Ought we to have a flat in Whitehall Court? Ought we to buy expensive clothes? and participate in extravagant entertainments? Puzzling over these questions gives me a kind of mental nausea which is very upsetting. One longs to get back to the peaceful student's life, and yet one has moments of sly enjoyment of the other, leading in its turn to tiredness and depression. Is it wrong to spend far more than would, under any equalitarian regime, be practicable for one married couple, in making a home for oneself and one's friends? Or is it a question of compromise between two desirabilities – the desirability of an equal sharing of the available service and commodities on the one hand, and on the other the desirability of charming homes, especially for those who are doing important work? . . . We have tried to compromise, leaning heavily towards the simple life, and since Sidney has been in politics, refusing to associate with the other camp. But then we are old and blasé – it is easy to resist temptation with these disabilities. . . .

27 July. [Passfield Corner]
I am quits with the Court! Ethel Snowden told me that the King and Queen were seriously annoyed – she said 'hurt', which was meant to be appealing – at my refusal, in spite of seven years of invitations, to present myself at Buckingham Palace. I replied that it never occurred to me that my absence would be noticed. But that if it were resented I would, of course, go whenever I received

another command. I had already settled in my own mind that a Secretary of State's wife had Court obligations unknown to an M.P.'s wife, or even to the wife of a President of the Board of Trade. The invitation came to 'Lord and Lady Passfield' and we attended the Garden Party. The organization of this super-fête seemed defective. The refreshments for the ten thousand were heaped up in one marquee and no one without an active person in attendance ready to push through the crowd could get service. The dense semi-circle of gazers at Royalty, seated or standing round the Royal enclosure as if it were a show, was ugly. The manners of the crowd, mostly upper-class, were not kindly, leave alone courtly . . . Sidney had to present colonials, whilst I wandered about in the crowd, quite amused by this private view of Buckingham Palace gardens, chatting with old and new acquaintances. At the end of Sidney's presentations the Queen asked, 'Is your wife here?' 'Yes, Ma'am, she is in the crowd out there. I am afraid I could not easily find her,' he added. 'That's a pity,' said the Queen, 'I should like to talk to her.' 'Thank you, Ma'am,' said Sidney, and retired. It was past six o'clock and the Queen and her cortège passed into the Palace. Seeing that I was not told that I was to be presented or invited into the Royal enclosure it was not my fault that I came away from Buckingham Palace without being presented to Her Majesty. But in deliberately going there I have done my duty and need do no more!

H.B. Lees-Smith (1878–1941) was an L.S.E. lecturer who had been a Liberal M.P. before the war; he joined the Labour Party and became President of the Board of Education. Thomas was appointed Lord Privy Seal in charge of employment. Lansbury was First Commissioner of Works with a seat in the Cabinet. He and Mosley were to assist Thomas. Beatrice had crossed swords with Sir Horace Wilson (1882–1972) in the pre-war days of the Poor Law Commission; he became Chamberlain's chief adviser at the time of the Munich crisis, and head of the civil service in 1942. The Webbs had met Sir John Hope Simpson (1868–1961) on their 1911 visit to India, and again on their recent visit to Greece. Susan Lawrence was Under-Secretary at the Ministry of Health and was threatening to resign because of her dissatisfaction with the programme of her department.

28 July. [Passfield Corner]
Arnold and Lees-Smith dined here to meet Olivier who is staying the week-end. Arnold is in a great state of discontent with J.H. Thomas's incapacity as organizer of employment. Oswald Mosley

and Lansbury, his lieutenants, report that Thomas does not see them, but that he is in the hands of that arch-reactionary, Horace Wilson – my old enemy – whom he calls "Orace' and obeys implicitly; that he refuses to sit down and study the plans proposed and therefore cannot champion them in the House. Then he gets 'rattled', and when not under the influence of drink or flattery is in an abject state of panic about his job. Arnold thinks he might any day break down in health as he has done in temper . . . The Prime Minister, oddly enough, is attached to J.H. Thomas, who amuses him, and accepts the position of inferiority and spices it with affectionate familiarity and wit. Also, Thomas is popular with the other side. In spite of his bad language, his coarse wit and his more than doubtful City transactions, no word of scandal or disparagement appears in the capitalist Press. To the suburban conservative, 'Jimmy' seems the one redeeming personality in the Labour government. He is undoubtedly *labour* because he drops his h's and is common to look at, which panders to their sense of social superiority. And yet he disowns socialism in public and scoffs at the programme of the Labour Party over his cups. Snowden appeals to the banking world. The P.M. is popular in refined aristocratic circles and at the Court. Certainly Susan is justified in beginning to sniff! But the resignation of keen reformers who have also brains would not improve matters. They have got to stick it and fight *within* the party and within the Cabinet for all that is practicable. The trouble is that the Cabinet is so taken up with day-to-day routine, and the Ministers are so absorbed in departmental work, that unless the P.M. were to make a point of conferring with groups of Cabinet Ministers, there will be no consultations. But the P.M. prefers to spend his spare hours otherwise; he does not *like* his colleagues. There is something wrong with the British Cabinet as a supreme organ of government – the Cabinet does not govern. It broke down during the war and had to be superseded by the 'War Cabinet'. Some such inner circle is needed for carrying out the War against Poverty.

Ponsonby came over to meet the Hope Simpsons . . . He reports that the Conservatives are furious with my refusal of the title and regard it as a mischievous attack on the prestige of titles or an insult to the 'fountain of honour'. Which is borne out by Mrs Baldwin's rudeness at the Garden Party, when she literally shouted at me, '"Lady Passfield" we shall call you whether you like it or not.' He thinks my example will be followed – I am not quite so optimistic!! He said that the question whether I had any moral right to frequent the Peeresses' gallery had already been raised. So it is fortunate that I have already decided not to do so, and had gone to the Strangers' gallery when I went to the House of Lords the other day. . . .

2 August. [Passfield Corner]
One reason for liking the student's and author's life over that of hostess, guest and general manager is that the content of one's consciousness becomes so far more agreeable and wholesome – more peaceful and more stimulating than the thoughts and feelings of what the Americans call 'the good mixer'. Leonard and Kate Courtney could always fall back on reciting to themselves their favourite poetry; other people enjoy re-reading classics. Neither of these ways of filling up my consciousness with good stimulating stuff is open to me; I have no rote memory and re-reading something I have read before bores me. I must have something new to discover or digest, or I must myself be engaged in the art of expression. That is why I write a diary. Without this invigorating food, I go on chewing the cud of some past episode or imaginary happening that panders to my personal vanity or to my sense of personal grievance or desire to justify myself to myself – and I repeat, repeat and repeat the same thought or feeling, the same phrase or argument over and over again, until that part of my brain becomes painfully weary and I am incapacitated for other forms of mental activity. How well I remember, at different crises of my life, the peaceful contentment of working on documents or the welcome distraction of interviewing experts on their own technique, after weeks or months of morbid brooding over this or that relationship, this or that castle in the air in which I was heroine or martyr. On the other hand, by merely describing my pleasant or unpleasant adventures I can often rid my mind of them and start free of morbid imaginings, hopes or regrets. All of which points to getting, as soon as I have the strength, something outside the daily life to think about, some state of being to be discovered, described, analysed or summed up. . . .

In a letter of 31 July MacDonald told Sidney that 'you are getting me into hot water.' The King had apparently objected to an official invitation which read:

'Lord Passfield and Mrs Webb will receive . . .' MacDonald plaintively suggested that 'no principle is involved. In this matter poor Mrs W. is pinned on to you and you drag her up automatically.' Sandy was Beatrice's dog.

4 August. [Passfield Corner]
In response to J.R.M.'s very courteous remonstrance Sidney instructed de Satge to omit my name from the card of invitation to the Canadian and American undergraduates next Thursday, and it will be so in all future invitations. Sidney suggests that I might appear notwithstanding, but I thought that would look like an evasion of the objection to the presence of 'Mrs Sidney Webb'. The only way out of defiance or surrender is for me to efface myself as the wife of the Secretary of State for the Dominions and Colonies – which means, in effect, limiting my entertainments to the Labour world plus old friends, and such of the colonials as I can ask privately to come and see 'the Webbs'. All of which looks promising for literary work next spring.

I love this little house in sunshine and rain: the absolute quietude during the night, the distant sounds now and again in the day, the long rambles in Woolmer Forest and Ludshott Common, honeymooning with my beloved or brooding alone with Sandy as my companion. And I enjoy the visits of friends, listening to the music and talks on the wireless. On the other hand, social functions in London weary me past endurance in body and mind; and if, by chance, the people I meet excite and interest me, they excite and interest the wrong part of me and I feel the worse for it. The one pleasure of this episode is watching Sidney enjoying himself in the Colonial Office work. He is conscious of doing it well. What troubles me is the offchance that my recalcitrance might make matters less easy for him, might prejudice the smooth working of his official life. . . .

Lord Lugard (1858–1945) had a long career in African administration and had successfully promoted indirect rule in Nigeria and in his book *The Dual Mandate in British Tropical Africa.* Joseph Oldham, a former missionary, was on the Advisory Committee on Education in the Colonies 1925–36. St John Philby (1885–1960) was a noted and eccentric Arabist whose son, Kim, became a notorious Soviet intelligence agent. In the new colony of Kenya three million Africans and little more than twenty thousand Asians lived under the ascendancy of ten thousand white settlers, many of them ex-officers who had gone to Africa after the war.

13 August. [Passfield Corner]
On Friday we stayed the night with Lord Lugard to meet Oldham and his wife and talked Kenya. When we stayed with him in Hong Kong in 1911 we singled him out as the wisest and most human governor we had known. He is a Conservative in politics, but sympathetic to the Labour Party's beneficent intentions with regard to 'natives'. He is pressing Sidney to do something to curb the naively barbaric capitalism of the white settlers in Kenya and elsewhere. The policy these settlers are carrying out is to deprive the natives of land ownership and subject them to taxation in order that they should be at their mercy as wage-earners. The wrong turn was taken when the white settlers were given self-government and freed from the control of Whitehall. The sympathies of the British Labour Party, far from the scene of the racial conflict, have been and are overwhelmingly on the side of the exploited coloured wage-earner. . . . But it is not easy to turn back and withdraw the self-government of the Kenyan white settlers. The apparent alternative is to supersede or curb that power by other machinery of government dependent on Whitehall without rousing too overwhelming a reaction, or without involving too long a delay. 'You won't have a Labour government in power for long,' says Sidney. 'Get the most you can now, even if it is not all that you want, before the South African Dominion joins up with a reactionary British government.'

The same question of how to apply the principles of self-government to mixed populations is the question arising in Palestine and Cyprus – countries in which two races of more or less equal status are struggling for the control of a particular area. Lugard suggests the traditional policy of the Colonial Office of finding some section of the inhabitants to whom to grant self-government is wrong; that wherever the inhabitants are broken up into communities whose economic interests, religious faith or manners and customs are irreconcilable, there should be no self-government granted; but the ultimate control should be retained by the pro-consul representing the far distant and disinterested empire, supplemented by strong advisory committees representing the rival races or communities.

Of course there is the alternative of withdrawing and leaving the inhabitants to fight it out among themselves with or without the help of some other far or near, interested or disinterested empire. Sidney keeps an open mind in regard to the relative advantages of partial self-government or bureaucracy, tempered by advisory councils, but altogether objects to Great Britain withdrawing and letting things rip. I am not so sure. . . .

I pick up all these disjointed thoughts from Sidney as he sits in his armchair and tells me about his day's work at the Colonial Office. I wonder what they think of him there? A super-civil servant added to the Colonial Office staff? His main activity is to pick the brains of all and sundry, selecting from or harmonizing conflicting or divergent policies. Not quite all and sundry, by the way! His would-be visitors are censored. 'Not desirable that you should see Philby. He has been most troublesome to the Office, fomenting discontent over there,' said his official adviser. And Sidney did not see him. 'Why not meet him casually in the Fabian office,' said I, on behalf of the rebel, who happens to be a Fabian approved by Galton. 'Perhaps,' replied Sidney, doubtfully.

(2 October. He did.)

Gerald Balfour (1853–1945), his wife Betty (d. 1942) and his brother, the Tory leader A.J. Balfour (1848–1930), had all been on close terms with the Webbs in the first years of the century. Eleanor Sidgwick (1845–1936) was the Balfours' sister; she was Principal of Newnham College, Cambridge, 1892–1900. Sir Horace Plunkett (1854–1932) was an Irish statesman who had done much to promote rural co-operatives. He was an old friend of the Webbs.

30 August. [Passfield Corner]
The day of unusual excitement: our first flight in the air, and a visit of reconciliation to the Gerald Balfours.

The flight, each one alone, in a Moth, off the Brooklands aerodrome, was arranged and provided by our old friend Horace Plunkett, at whose house we stayed last night. This fragile and, we always thought, hypochondriacal old man, four years my senior, has suddenly found salvation from insomnia in becoming a pilot of his own machine. He is actually applying for his certificate, which he will not get. Having failed to persuade the Shaws to fly, he tried it with us. I did not need any pressing, as I wanted to break down any hesitancy by experience, so as to be willing to fly whenever this was the best way to get to and fro the world. Sidney, with some reluctance, agreed to follow suit. A very delightful jaunt it was. I suffered neither from nerves, noise or sickliness. Sidney said he had 'quakings', but was satisfied that he could stand the ordeal of a journey through the air if required.

The other ordeal was less welcome, though I am glad to be

through with it. The strange breach of my friendship with Betty Balfour and the break in our friendliness with the Balfour brothers I have never understood and always regretted. This spring, when I heard that Arthur Balfour had retired to Fisher's Hill — it was thought, to die — and that my old friend was leading a troubled life with three or four aged relatives of the Balfour clan, my heart softened. The publication of our Poor Law book with the chapters on the Royal Commission of 1905–09 — an episode so closely connected with our friendship with the Balfours — seemed to offer an occasion for some sort of reconciliation. So I sent them an initialled copy of the special edition. The warmth of her reply drew from me a letter in the old style of intimacy . . . Last night Horace Plunkett, who is a very old friend of both parties, told me that Betty Balfour wanted me to lunch there on my way back from Brooklands; he would send me in his motor car that way to Passfield. So I found myself once more at Fisher's Hill after an interval of fifteen years. At sixty years of age Betty Balfour has become an old woman, though she retains much of her charm of voice and manner. She embraced me, but in what she said and in the way she said it, there was not the ring of friendship. Indeed, her attitude was effusive more than frankly intimate; it was, I think, an attitude rather than a feeling. 'In her cold effusiveness she reminded me of Mary Booth,' I told Sidney. A.J.B., she told me, was slightly better; he kept to his room. She implied that he would never again be able to move out of his present abode.

Horace Plunkett told us that his condition was pathetic; he had spells of a wandering mind, alternating with a clear mind, coupled with a painful inability to swallow. She told me about her daughters and their pursuits and we chatted about the 'title' question . . . At lunch Gerald and Mrs Sidgwick joined us. Gerald was friendly; he looks obsessed. Apparently he and his sister and another elderly man are absorbed in an endless study of 'cross-correspondence', a form of spiritualism. Mrs Sidgwick is, to my mind, an ugly and embittered old woman, a blight on the Fisher's Hill *ménage*. Altogether I am inclined to agree with Horace Plunkett's verdict that poor Betty Balfour has a heavy load to bear and has borne it with singular courage and self-devotedness. So if my visit interested or pleased her I am glad I paid it. But whether she likes me . . . today, I really don't know! Any overt friendliness is, however, now at an end, and if she cares for my friendship she can have it.

Sidney's term as Colonial Secretary was bedevilled by the problem of white land tenure in Kenya and Jewish land tenure in Palestine. Under Zionist pressure the British government in 1929 agreed to the establishment of a Jewish Agency as a quasi-governmental organization; and the indigenous Arabs had shown their opposition to Jewish immigration and land settlement in a series of riots, which began at the 'Wailing Wall' in August, 1929 – 133 Jews and 116 Arabs were killed. Josiah Wedgwood (1872–1943), was a former Liberal who became a Labour Minister with strong anti-imperialist views and an equally fervid commitment to the Jewish National Home promised by the Balfour Declaration in 1917. It was to be said later that Sidney's acquiescent temperament made him vulnerable to the anti-Zionist bias of his officials.

2 September. [Passfield Corner]
One of the few advantages of old age is that having no future before you, you have nothing to gain and nothing to lose and therefore tend to be detached and disinterested. Otherwise Sidney's life at the Colonial Office might be harassing.

Roused by the tragic happenings in Palestine, there have buzzed around him Jews and the admirers of Jews, great and small, in a state of violent grief and agitation demanding revenge and compensation. It is noteworthy that no representative of the Arabs – not even a casual admirer of the Arabs – has appeared on the scene. What one gathers from these excited persons is that the British officials on the spot are held to be perniciously pro-Arab, not because they love the Arab but because, for one reason or another, they hate the Jew.

Is there any principle relating to the rights of peoples to the territory in which they happen to live? I admire Jews and dislike Arabs. But the Zionist movement seems to me a gross violation of the right of the native to remain where he was born and his father and grandfather were born – if there is such a right. To talk about the return of the Jew to the land of his inheritance after an absence of two thousand years seems to me sheer nonsense, and hypocritical nonsense. From whom were descended those Russian and Polish Jews? The principle which is really being asserted is the principle of selecting races for particular territories according to some peculiar needs or particular fitness. Or it may be some ideal of communal life to be realized by subsidized migration. But this process of artificially creating new communities of immigrants, brought from any part of the world, is rather hard on indigenous natives! The white settlers in Kenya would seem to have as much right, on this assumption, to be where they are, as the Russian Jews in Jerusalem! And yet exactly the same people – for instance Josiah Wedgwood – who denounce the white settlers of Kenya as unwarranted intruders, are hotly in favour of the bran' new Jewish colonies in Palestine! But I wander from my original remark. Sidney annoys the agitated ones by remaining in both cases rather cold. Obviously order must be maintained in Judea; and the responsibility for the looting and murdering must be fixed and proper action taken to prevent recurrence. But the case for the Arab has not yet been heard; whilst the case for the Jew has been vehemently and powerfully pressed on the government. The Zionist movement and the Mandate for a National Home for the Jews in Palestine seems to have originated in some such unequal pressure exercised by the wealthy and ubiquitous Jew on the one hand and the poor and absent Arab on the other.

Sooner or later the League of Nations ought to work out some principle of conduct with regard to the relative rights of the native and the would-be immigrant, and as to the type of emigration to be promoted. Whether this new code would recognize the 'two thousand years ago' inhabitance by some mythical ancestors as a valid plea, on either count, I very much doubt. If it were recognized it would be because there was also Superior Fitness. But how does this high-sounding principle differ from the old Whig doctrine of free migration throughout the world and devil take the hindmost, whether he takes them by slaughter, or imported drugs, or civilized disease? Shall we come, in the last resort, to a scientifically planned distribution of this planet's surface among different races according to relative fitness, standardized by a controlled birth-rate and a national minimum of civilized life for each race, coupled with anaesthesia for all unwanted infants? Then, perhaps we could afford to be benevolent to all living humans; we might even encourage variation of species, and experiment in breeding the human race.

At present, our colonial administration seems a queer hotch-potch of conflicting aims and competing aspirations.

Our life here, these last six weeks of delightful sunshine, would have been restful if it had not been for Sidney's off-and-on visits to London, varied by telephone messages when here, and a stream of welcome and unwelcome visitors during the week-end. . . . Every now and again I get nervous about Sidney's strength holding out . . . With him, advancing old age takes a pleasant form. He has lost all his old irritability and aggressiveness; he is the most pleasant person to live with and to work with; he has become complacent towards the world, minimizing all present trouble, optimistic about the future. . . . All this means that he has lost his arresting, challenging quality: he gives the impression of acquiescing in the world as it is. Intellectually he is still quick at the uptake – he can consider new problems, master new facts, answer new arguments, with ease. But emotionally he is quiescent. All his desires are satisfied; he has no discontent. And he is too honest to pretend to have hot indignation about particular grievances. 'The world is full of dark places,' is his reply to the denouncers of other people's wickedness.

In August 1929 Snowden, Henderson and Graham were British delegates to the Hague Conference on reparations. Snowden made a sensational, unexpected stand against the Young plan, standing out for an increase in the British share. He returned a national hero and was invited by the King to Sandringham. In the event only one instalment was paid by Germany.

9 September. [Passfield Corner]
Tom Jones and his little wife (intelligent but unattractive) here for the week-end. He has, at last, made friends with Ramsay. He is the most homely and informal of officials – a sort of confidential brainworking servant to successive Prime Ministers– accumulating experience about the smooth working of the Cabinet machine . . .

T.J. described vividly the scenes at 10 Downing Street during the night of the declaration of the poll. There were the Baldwin family, Winston Churchill, the private secretaries, sitting in an adjoining room, with the results coming through on the tape. All the company expected, not victory, but the maintenance of a small Tory majority. The Baldwins were cast down by the news, the wife indignant. Winston Churchill got wildly excited and would not listen to the tape, thought it was being tampered with, drank whisky continuously and was left scowling at the tape at three o'clock. . . .

On Sunday we went to see the Snowdens . . . He talked mostly about the visit to Sandringham. He and Ethel are intrinsically loyal, personal admirers and political supporters of our worthy sovereign and his consort. The King is still a King, in the old sense, to the Snowdens, and every detail of their visit was retailed in a deferential tone, as if the information were likely to be eagerly listened to. Which sounded strange from an old and experienced socialist propagandist. One can hardly imagine this attitude towards royalty from Arthur Balfour or Lloyd George! There would be respect and consideration, but slight boredom at having to go to Sandringham and certainly no pride in having been there. This romancing about the royal family is, I fear, only a minor symptom of the softening of the brain of socialists, enervated by affluence, social prestige and political power. We are all suffering from it; though in other Ministers it takes other and less amusingly naive forms. Whether Philip will show as much courage and obstinacy with the nation's millions on equalizing conditions at home as he has done in saving them from the foreigner will test the depth of this softening power. When and where shall we find a leader who will be fervent in faith, scientific in method and really equalitarian in manners and aims? Perhaps he was killed in the Great War?

Malcolm Muggeridge (b.1903), a journalist with a Fabian background, was married in 1927 to Kitty (b.1903), the daughter of Beatrice's sister Rosy. His play *The Three Flats*, which Beatrice sent to GBS for comment, was performed at the Prince of Wales Theatre in February 1931. Jacob Epstein (1880–1959) was a controversial modernist sculptor.

12 September. [Passfield Corner]
. . . . Malcolm Muggeridge, Kitty's husband, is an extremely clever young Cambridge graduate about thirty years old, now a professor of English in Cairo University contributing articles on Egyptian affairs to the *Manchester Guardian* and *New Statesman.* They were in lodgings near us and, hearing that he had written a play, I asked him to come and read it. The company consisted of ourselves, two young elementary teachers engaged to each other, and a young Anglo-Catholic priest, a Cambridge friend of Malcolm's. *The Three Flats* was unexpectedly brilliant. But it was grossly coarse in incident and language – so indecent that I went hot all over and wondered whether I ought not to stop it, seeing that there was a young girl present and a priest. But I listened to the end without interrupting. 'How true to life,' exclaimed the girl. The man of God, when I tentatively disapproved, remarked, 'It is what they are all thinking and feeling and doing, Mrs Webb'. . . .

On analysing my objections I find that they consist of two – dislike of unaccustomed frankness and literalness in sex questions, which may be unreasonable; and disagreement with the picturing of the ordinary man and woman as embodiments of casual sexual impulse, of evil and petty motives without any code of morality, personal dignity or public spirit, or even kindliness. These young people's mania for the sub-human in art, literature, music and manners – Epstein, D.H. Lawrence, Aldous Huxley, Jazz music – is disturbing to aged Victorians. The priest would observe that if you deny the super-human you will inevitably fall into sub-human! There is bound to be some reaction from the super-human craze, but this concentration on the sub-human is ugly and joyless – at any rate for the white man. I was never a hero-worshipper or a believer in the superman, but the sub-human seems to be a far worse idol of the mind because it points downward.

29 September. [41 Grosvenor Road]
Our last twenty-four hours in the little house overlooking the Thames, where Sidney and I have spent, off and on, near forty years of married life – an amazingly happy and full life.

I, certainly, feel relieved to be rid of it, or rather of the small part of the house which was still our possession. The untidy, dingy dining-room, the long tramp up three flights of stairs – fifty-nine in all – to the two little garret bedrooms, and the dreadful noise, back and front, made the old home an unpleasant lodging for me on my occasional visits to London. For Sidney, with his preference for the habitual, it has served well. Incidentally we part company with Susan Lawrence on the best of friendly terms, but without intimacy, given or taken. I respect and admire her, but I do not like her – a mixed reaction which I recognize that not a few persons have towards me! . . . More regretful am I in parting from my old servant Emily Wordley, who transfers her allegiance to Susan rather than follow me into the country.

Good-bye little house on the Thames. I doubt whether you will outlive the Webbs!

The Shaws also had their London home in Whitehall Court, a large, much turreted block standing between Whitehall and the Thames Embankment. The National Liberal Club is housed in it. Philip Noel-Baker (1889–1982), a Labour politician much concerned with disarmament, was in the 1945 Labour government and won the Nobel Peace Prize in 1959. H.B. Usher (1892–1969), a civil servant who had twice run as a Labour candidate, was Ramsay MacDonald's private secretary 1929–35. F.W. Pethick-Lawrence (1871–1961) had been, with his wife, one of the leaders of the constitutional suffragists; he became Secretary of State for India 1945–47. Louise Creighton (1850–1930) was the widow of Dr Mandell Creighton, late Bishop of London, who had been an old friend of Beatrice's and had helped in the launching of the L.S.E. Mrs Thompson had nursed Beatrice's father in his last years.

2 October. [2 Whitehall Court]
Settled in our costly furnished flat in Whitehall Court (fourteen guineas a week including service!), which we have taken for six months to enable us to entertain (in return for our salary) the Parliamentary Labour Party and colonials. Whether we should not have chosen better if we had paid the thousand pounds we shall spend during the year in that way into the party funds, and saved my health and strength, is a moot question – perhaps we shall do so the second year of office if there be one. Meanwhile, whilst Sidney will spend five days a week in London, I shall still live mainly in the country.

We spent the week-end at Brighton at the headquarters of the Labour executive and attended one day of the conference. The Parliamentary Labour Party has the air of being thoroughly established; all the Ministers are self-possessed and self-confident and just at present purring over the popularity of their government – not quite all, I imagine, as the absent Margaret Bondfield was much more abused than she was defended, and J.H. Thomas has not yet established his parity in popularity with Snowden, Henderson and the P.M. There will be ructions during the next few months between Snowden, representing the Treasury, and Thomas, egged on by Mosley and supported by Henderson, representing a forward policy on unemployment.

What interested me was the submerging of the trade unionist and the growing prominence of the old nineteenth-century government class – Dalton, Mosley, Noel-Baker, Usher, the Lawrences, Susan and Pethick – in the Parliamentary Labour Party. The left was not in evidence. The Communists have been effectually excluded and the I.L.P. discredited as an impracticable faction without constructive force. . . .

The evening before our Brighton visit we saw *The Apple Cart*, that amusing and annoying satire on democracy. Magnus and his sayings are a d____d clever invention of GBS's skittish political philosophy, or pretence of philosophy, for I don't believe that he seriously believes in a dictatorship as an alternative to the political democracy of Great Britain. What struck me as odd was the very minor note of sex, even in the interlude. Magnus's relation to

195

Orinthia is that of a prudish philanderer, clearly incapable of sexual passion in the sense it is now exploited by the Aldous Huxley–D.H. Lawrence school of novelist. No wonder our brilliant nephew Malcolm dismisses GBS as 'early Victorian'.

The smugly bourgeois audience received the new tidings of loyalty to the royal family with fat satisfaction and swarmed out with beaming smiles to the strains of 'God Save the King'. The wonder is that GBS and Charlotte have not been invited to Sandringham, but Baldwin refused to recommend him for the 'O.M.' on the ground (so Tom Jones told us) that GBS might 'guy' this still revered honour. So little do we now know about GBS's mind that we have not the remotest idea of what line he would take about consorting with the Court or accepting the Order of Merit. He would, I think, accept a peerage as a new type of platform for political orations. We have never liked to discuss these delicate questions of personal behaviour with him – for the very good reason that Sidney thinks his presence in the House of Lords would be bad for the Parliamentary Labour Party but does not wish to say so, either to GBS himself or to anyone else. Fortunately the present P.M. has not asked Sidney's advice on this matter.

Meanwhile I am suffering from cold feet physical and mental – sleeplessness by night and dizziness by day, and I wonder whether I shall escape without some severe breakdown during Sidney's period of office. I have got to concentrate my strength on helping him – his health and peace of mind are all important; everything else is relatively of no consequence. Amen.

5 October. [Passfield Corner]
Rosy here for a week. Whether because we are the only sisters left or because she is particularly well and pleasant, I have really enjoyed her stay, and the gossips, mostly about her own family affairs. Her five children are all now settled in the world, two married with babies, and all rather impecunious. She has the disposal of £1,500 a year – certainly she does not spend it on herself – her husband makes his own small salary of £500 and keep in the hotel, so she is free to subsidize her children's earnings . . . She loves them all and is perpetually thinking about them and slaving for them. . . . As her recreation she travels adventurously, far and wide, at an incredibly cheap rate. She has decided artistic talent, but not enough to be a professional. Altogether, at sixty-five years

of age, Rosy Dobbs is a remarkable woman who has weathered well . . . She shocked us with her free ways during her widowhood. Today her free ways are *à la mode*. . . . Meanwhile I have been compelled to shift my position and to tolerate and accept conduct in the younger generation which twenty years ago I should have boycotted. The decay of religion, whilst not affecting the current code on many matters, has completely undermined sexual morality. There is no common opinion today about the right use of the sexual impulse – we live in a state of anarchy – we have even lost the very notion of normality – anything is permissible – not, indeed, according to the law, but according to the public opinion of the intellectuals who are not definitely religious. . . .

7 October. [Passfield Corner]
A sense of sadness in old age is watching one's contemporaries tumbling into senility – pity being intensified by self-pity. 'There, in a few months or years, shall I be,' is one's reflection. Two old friends, alike in their nobility of character – Louise Creighton and Mrs Thompson (Father's old nurse) – have I visited lately and tried to help and encourage. Louise has had a stroke which disables her from further activity. Few people come to see her and she greeted me warmly when I journeyed down to Oxford to arrange about the copy of her portrait of her great man for the School of Economics. . . .

Ramsay MacDonald left England on 28 September for America – it was the first visit of a British Prime Minister – to discuss naval disarmament. He arrived back on 1 November after two weeks in Canada. A Five-Power Conference had been arranged for January 1930. His visit was a milestone in British foreign policy, marking the end of Britain's supremacy at sea and America's emergence as a naval power.

15 October. [Passfield Corner]
A feat of endurance and a triumph in political activities has been J.R.M's visit to U.S.A. Whatever other defect the second Labour administration may have, its doings have not been dull! Whether Henderson will be able to follow up the P.M.'s magnificent rendering of a friendly neighbour and uplifting statesman by a practical success in limiting expenditure on navies at the Five-Power Conference remains to be seen. But I am inclined to think that Sidney was right when he replied to Thomson's pessimism that

any binding together of Great Britain and the U.S.A. was better than the continuance of the covert hostility of the Chamberlain regime. The U.S.A. and Great Britain have *got* to develop a common international policy if the peace of the world is to be maintained . . .

Between the Imperial Conference of 1926 and the drafting of the Statute of Westminster in 1931 there was much discussion about the changing and ambiguous status of the 'autonomous communities' which were to form the British Commonwealth.

20 October. [Passfield Corner]
Sidney has for the moment settled the affairs of Palestine and Iraq; his daily preoccupation is now Kenya, and the conference of experts on the constitution of the British Commonwealth. About Kenya . . . he has to pick his way warily to some compromise which would safeguard native interests as far as they can be safeguarded with the white settlers in possession of land and capital. In any case he will be denounced by idealists and no one will be satisfied.

The other task, guiding the conference of legal experts through the mazes of law, agreements, nationalist aspirations and Buckingham Palace fears, with the aid of the Attorney-General and Colonial Office officials, is more to his liking. The Irish Free State and the South African Commonwealth want independence, and the Canadian and Australian Dominions want the best of both worlds. He seems to be doing the job well. . . . My general impression is that . . . the British Commonwealth of Nations is likely gradually to dissolve into vague ties of sentiments which will have very little governmental meaning. The British Empire is suffering from a sort of senile hypertrophy, which has been quickened by the exhaustion of the Great War, and the increased responsibilities of the mandates for Palestine, Iraq and African territories. 'Free trade within the Empire' and other stunts are pre-doomed attempts to galvanize the evaporating tie of sentiment into something substantial. How long will the ghost of the British Empire survive? Fifty years?

The Woolfs dined with the Webbs on 22 October. Virginia reported: 'We sit in two lodging-house rooms (the dining-room had a brass bedstead behind a screen), eat hunks of red beef; and are offered whisky. It is the same enlightened, impersonal, perfectly aware of itself atmosphere.' Leonard Woolf, secretary of the Labour Party Advisory Committee on Imperial Affairs, was urging Sidney to finance education and roads for the native population of Kenya. Beatrice does not refer to the visit in the diary.

27 October. [Passfield Corner]
'Tell Oldham,' said I to Tawney, 'it is useless to wire-pull an old hand wire-puller; it arouses derision.' Ever since the Wilson report about Kenya came out, Sidney has been receiving letters from men of eminence and good will, frequently forwarded by other Cabinet Ministers which, to his experienced eye, all come from one source. He has done the same so often himself, but I trust with more skill. But watching a Cabinet Minister at work makes one realize how situations are prepared for them by those who manipulate public opinion, so that they feel impelled to this way or that. Thus when Virginia Woolf exclaimed, 'How thrilling it must be to watch actual decisions being made, decisions which alter the life of nations,' I retorted that it is 'outsiders representing interests or enthusiasms who make the decisions' or 'permanent civil servants; Cabinet Ministers are relatively unimportant.' Which of course is a paradox, only partially true.

Which brings me to an analysis of the working of democracy. Personally I see no objection to what is called 'wire-pulling' – it cannot and should not be avoided. The great mass of citizens are uninterested in some or other – many of them in all – these current political issues. Wire-pulling is only the way in which those who *are* interested and have a certain knowledge of particular questions bring their experience and will into the common pool. Perhaps we ought to invent more direct and acknowledged channels for that influence – but, so far, that has not been done. All GBS's railing at democratic government comes from some naive notion that democratic theory involves the equal participation of all citizens in every act of government, and that anything short of that is a sham. . . .

Herbert Hoover (1874–1964) was Republican President of the United States 1928–32. Lady Cynthia Mosley, who was the wife of Oswald Mosley, was a Labour M.P. 1929–31. The Wall Street crash had taken place in October, but Beatrice does not refer to it. At the time its repercussions were not fully appreciated. Unemployment was then about 1,300,000.

2 November. [Passfield Corner]
Sidney reports J.R.M., who summoned his Cabinet Ministers to meet him on his arrival at 10 Downing Street yesterday, is

immensely pleased with himself and says that he has done more for Hoover than for Great Britain. The Labour Cabinet is still in its honeymoon. But dark, thunderous clouds are arising among our own people – coal and unemployment; for the public at large, increased expenditure. Mosley, whom I met at lunch, is contemptuous of Thomas's incapacity, of the infirmity of manual working Cabinet Ministers generally and very complacent about his own qualification for the leadership of the Labour Party. That young man has too much aristocratic insolence in his make-up. Meanwhile E.F. Wise has made a brilliant début. Cynthia has charmed the house. The Labour Party is no longer as dull and ugly as it was in 1924 – on the contrary, its appearance to the outside world is brilliant. It is not the window-dressing, it is the stock behind that is in question! Baldwin and Lloyd George, neither of them have control of their followers, and their followers have no desire for a general election. There will be a tacit conspiracy to keep the Labour government in until it has become unpopular with its own people, and with the man in the street. The old governing class has lost faith in itself – it has no creed. When Neville Chamberlain objected to increased pensions and allowances as 'giving something for nothing' and therefore demoralizing to character, the charming Cynthia retorted, in her maiden speech, that she herself and most of the Honourable Members opposite had been brought up 'on something for nothing'; were they all demoralized? There was no answer. 'No Liberals and few Tories will dare to vote against the Widows' Pension Bill,' sums up Sidney. And yet pensions for young and able-bodied widows during their widowhood seems to me about the worst form of public provision, whether in the effect on wages or on sexual morality.

4 November. [Passfield Corner]
Wedgwood Benn, his wife and Elizabeth Haldane for the weekend. If it were not for an unusual alertness of manner, an almost brilliant rapidity of response, which would make an outsider wonder who the devil the man was, the Secretary of State for India would appear an insignificant little person; a city clerk perhaps? He is short and slight in figure, going bald and grey, clear-skinned, clean-shaven, small-featured, and *very* gently clad; he is gifted with a sunny smile often breaking into a pleasant laugh. Markedly unpretentious, puritan in habit, but open-minded and tolerant

200

towards other people's self-indulgences and vanities, he is universally liked by the party he has joined, and respected by the party he has left. But no one could say that Benn was a great statesman or a distinguished thinker. His opinions – one can hardly call them convictions – sit lightly on him. Always a democrat, he changed over from economic individualism to political collectivism without any more reasoning or searchings of heart than detestation of Lloyd George and a shrewd idea that the Liberal Party was doomed to extinction. In spite of this slightness of texture he is a thoroughly successful politician and so far as one knows, a good administrator, not likely to be rattled either by reactionary panics or revolutionary threats, which is what the Secretary of State for India is going to get from the right and left during the next few months.

For Dominion status has been promised to India over and over again during and after the Great War. But in how near or distant a future? Next year or fifty years hence? And how can any one kind of uniform status be given to the whole of India, broken up, as it is, into native states and British India, with different races, languages, castes and religions. . . .

28 November. [Passfield Corner]
. . . . About Kenya, Sidney had prepared an elaborate memorandum for the Cabinet, setting forth in detail what he believed to be a wise compromise between the Hilton Young and Wilson Reports, a report which he suggested should be submitted to a joint committee of both houses as the Cabinet proposals. But the left wing is in revolt, determined to have the blood of the settlers, to make them *feel* that they are beaten. . . . Josiah Wedgwood, of course, is the prime mover in the revolt of the left, partly because he is a fanatical believer in crude political democracy on strictly numerical basis, and partly from a desire to upset MacDonald's government. Wedgwood does not suggest that the Arabs in Palestine shall be allowed to vote down the Jewish settlers. He is just as angry at Sidney's lack of unqualified enthusiasm for the case of the Jewish settlers as he is at Sidney's lack of unqualified hostility to the English settlers in Kenya. What Wedgwood demands is *fervent partisanship.* Unless you are a *partisan* you must be a scoundrel.

Sidney, on the other hand, seems to have no likes or dislikes for a particular person or communities; about every project he asks, 'How will it work, what state of affairs will it actually bring about?

How will all the persons concerned – for after all they are all God's creatures – like it and benefit or lose by it?' And he is singularly indifferent whether or not *his way* prevails. If the Cabinet decides to listen to other voices, then he will carry out their wishes to the best of his ability. When he is acting in a responsible administration he is, in fact, an excellent civil servant; his instinct is to obey the orders of his chief and make the best of the business.

J.C. Smuts (1870–1950) was an influential Boer military commander and statesman in South Africa. He was Prime Minister 1919–24 and stood for co-operation with the British Empire.

2 December. [Passfield Corner]
The Hendersons and General Smuts stayed here, the Snowdens, Ponsonby and Arnold looking in for lunch, tea or dinner.

Henderson is enjoying his work at the Foreign Office – far more, he says, than any work he has ever done. But he is also supervising the Labour Party office and preparing for the next general election, and trying to lend a helping hand to the P.M. in Cabinet business. Outside the difficulties of his own job, he is most concerned about the collapse of Thomas, who is completely rattled, and in such a state of panic that he is bordering on lunacy. Henderson reported that the P.M. feared suicidal mania. The joy-ride to Canada has brought no result except discredit. Meanwhile Thomas is too neurotic to take counsel, won't even listen to it, regards all suggestions as accusations of failure. Henderson is now suggesting to the P.M. that he himself must take the subject in hand, that there must be a committee of home defence against poverty, that Cole must be engaged if possible, and a proper department started, and that Jimmy, who is drinking heavily, must be sent away for a rest and Oswald Mosley installed, under the Council, to carry out agreed plans. . . . What worries Henderson is the lack of any organization of Cabinet business, especially with regard to finance. Ministers come, one by one, with demands for money to successive Cabinet meetings. There is no kind of survey of their respective demands with a view of discovering which of the proposals are most important! He blames the P.M. for meddling in the details of the Foreign Office instead of keeping himself for general management of the whole business of the government. He says that MacDonald sends for the officials of the Foreign Office, even for his private secretary, and discusses affairs with them without communicating with the Foreign Secretary. However, Henderson considers that MacDonald is absolutely irreplaceable. 'I could not work under Snowden and Snowden could not work under me.' So that's that.

General Smuts is a delightful man with whom one becomes intimate at once – a real charmer with a gift for subtle flattery, half serious, half comic. He is deeply concerned about the Dominion Conference – would like Sidney to play for time, whatever that may mean. Fears the breakdown of all the ties. What puzzles me is what will remain of the need for a British Empire when disarmament, international law courts and international machinery for international legislation are established . . . The British navy is really the only tie and that will no longer rule the sea; the U.S.A. is becoming the strongest world power whilst even Japan will be stronger than we can be in the Pacific Ocean. . . . Anyway there does not seem much reason for the present congeries of Dominions and Colonies which is called the British Empire. It is depressing to administer a concern which is in process of dissolution. However, neither Sidney nor Henderson share my pessimism – they believe in God's Englishman. And oddly enough, so does General Smuts, and in a sense he is justified. When he or any other leading South African comes to London they are tactfully looked after, they see anyone they wish to see from the King to GBS or the P.M. . . . Again one notes the capacity of the governing class of Great Britain to assimilate would-be hostile elements by courtesy and open-mindedness. . . .

Henry Devenish Harben (1874–1967) was a wealthy left-winger who had helped to finance the suffragette movement, the syndicalist *Daily Herald* and the *New Statesman*.

10 December. [Passfield Corner]
GBS and Charlotte staying here with our old friend Harben down for the night. Harben is exactly his old self, minus the neurotic anarchism brought about by the war. . . .

GBS is very lovable, he is always so gay and kind. No longer stimulating on general principles or events, he is always entertaining about people and personal episodes. Charlotte is the perfect hedonist. Taken together, they are the last word of agreeable self-complacency. They live in an atmosphere of admiration, not to say adulation; they are continuously flattered by friends and honoured by foreigners. Who troubles to run down an old man in his eighth decade? The younger generation of thinkers and authors are busy boosting or damning their own contemporaries, who may be comrades or rivals. As I watched the handsome 'Ancient' talking and laughing with Harben I realized that I should miss him more than anyone else in our intimate circle: he is the one most closely associated with our long married life, most continuously our friend. And Charlotte is a fit mate. Enthroned in the world's esteem and enrobed in wealth, they smile at each other and gaze with an amused good nature on the rest of the world. It is a pleasant sight to look on! 'We never think or talk of old age, we try to forget we are old,' said Charlotte; and GBS acquiesced.

Snowden had been crippled by a spinal infection since 1891. Thomas was broken by his failure to cure unemployment. Beatrice gave a weekly lunch to persons in public life; these were often held at the L.S.E.

21 December. [Passfield Corner]
Along with other Cabinet Ministers and their wives we attended the Guildhall ornate ceremony – the Mansion House lunch in honour of the P.M. and the Chancellor of the Exchequer. No Conservative Front Benchers and only Lord Reading on behalf of the Liberals; no Labour left-wingers. Otherwise it was a triumphant social event for our two great men. J.R.M. is, I think, the great political *artist* (as distinguished from orator or statesman) in British political history. His figure, features, colouring, gestures and voice 'make up' splendidly; his phrasing, his metaphors and literary allusions, his romantic sentiments and moral axioms, are all admirably adapted to an audience of British citizens . . . To some of those present Philip Snowden appeared a more distinguished *character*, though less of a charmer; his diction is less flowing and there is greater personal dignity and sincerity in his appeal. The deeply lined pale face of intellectual effort, in spite of apparent physical suffering, the two sticks and the slow drag of his disabled leg, is in picturesque contrast with his blunt insistence on England's rights and other countries' obligations – an insistence which might otherwise seem patriotic prejudice. Both these men were at the top of their form. J.R.M.'s handsome features literally glowed with an emotional acceptance of this just recognition of his great public service by the citizens of London. . . .

In pitiful contrast to these supremely successful ones sat Jimmy Thomas in the front row gazing at the ceremony; his ugly and rather mean face and figure made meaner and uglier by an altogether exaggerated sense of personal failure. While we were waiting for lunch at the Mansion House I went up and shook him warmly by the hand and reproached him for not having answered my invitation to a Wednesday lunch. We sat down for a chat together. The poor man was almost hysterical in his outburst of self-pity; everyone had been against him and the 'damns' flowed on indiscriminately. Margaret Bondfield and her d_____ Insurance Bill, the d_____ floods, the d_____ conspiracy between restless Lloyd George and weathercock Winston Churchill to turn out the Labour government and the d_____ windbags of the Clyde, who were responsible for not fulfilling the d_____ pledge, which he had never made, to stop this d_____ unemployment. There is honesty and shrewdness in his depreciations of the facile remedies of doles and relief work for the unemployed. But he took no counsel, not even with Mosley and Lansbury who had been appointed to help him, either about the appointment of his staff or about remedial measures. Then he lost his nerve; with it his strength. Poor Jimmy is egregiously vain and therefore subject to panic when flattery ceases and abuse begins. For years he has looked on himself as the future Prime Minister; today the question is whether he will drink himself into helpless disablement, whether he will be fit for any position at all in a future Labour Cabinet . . . Jimmy is a boozer, his language is foul, he is a Stock Exchange gambler; he is also a social climber. He is, in fact, *our* Birkenhead. If J.H. Thomas were typical of the Labour Cabinet, *The Apple Cart* would be justified as a gibe! . . .

Margaret Harkness (1854–1923) was Beatrice's second cousin, an active socialist and feminist who wrote novels and articles under the pseudonym 'John Law'.

27 December. [Passfield Corner]
Preparing a broadcast on 'Changes in the World of Politics' during the half-century I look back on, and cursing myself for having engaged to do it. I am no longer fit for any public engagements!

This autumn has been less trying than I feared. It is clear that owing to the dropping of the title I shall escape from the dissipation of my dwindling strength in Court and other social functions. . . .

Why, I do not know, but my mind goes back forty years to the
Xmas of 1889, spent at Box House with the Courtneys and the
Playnes. Father we had thought was dying, but he was slowly
recovering consciousness and I was getting back to my writing of
the first chapter of my book on the Co-operative Movement. The
weather was dark and gloomy, as it is this week, and I was feeling
discouraged by not having the material I wanted and living without
companionship, struggling on day by day alone in the world. 'Why
not go back with Leonard for a week's change,' Kate had suggested.
'There is Browning's funeral at the Abbey on Saturday the 2nd —
you can go with Leonard.' Rather a grim diversion, thought I, but
I could go to the British Museum and get what I want. I will get
Margaret Harkness to introduce me to someone there who will put
me on the track. And it was in her little lodging opposite the British
Museum that Sidney and I met in that first week of January 1890.
And now, at the very tag-end of our joint life together, he is again
at work in the Colonial Office, not as a clerk but as Secretary of
State and a peer. So far as we are concerned it has certainly been a
topsy-turvy world, but the top has come last. Yet just because it has
come last, it does not seem a top at all, only a step on one side from
our own way in life, which has been the way of research and the
writing of books. If I did not feel that I have very little capacity left
I should long to get back to our own way of life and the writing of
more books. But I am content to give the leavings of my energy to
keeping his home going and looking after his health, helped by the
memory of those forty years of blessed companionship, a companionship in love and in work without a flaw. And we are still on our
honeymoon! Lucky mortals!

But personal content is not the sum total of consciousness. And
1929 ends in gloom, so far as I realize the condition of my country.
Is Great Britain suffering from a sort of sleepy sickness? Sidney
says so.

A letter from my clever nephew-in-law, Malcolm Muggeridge,
describing the present state of chaos in ethics among his generation
and justifying his portrayal of it in his play *The Three Flats*. Which
of course raises the question whether you do not extend a type of
bad behaviour by describing it. Human beings, especially young
human beings, are so imitative, so open to suggestion. What he is
justifying is the act of deliberately providing a low mental environment. For his play is not science; it is art. It does not offer food for

the intellect but food for the emotions. It impresses on the listener a state of mind, a state of mind I happen to think a bad state of mind, and he agrees that it is so. Why not choose a good state of mind for your example?

So ends 1929.

VOLUME 44

౿ 1930 ౭

23 January. [Passfield Corner]
The broadcast went off happily on the eve of my seventy-second birthday. The B.B.C. young man cheered an old woman's heart by telling her she has a perfect voice and is a born broadcaster. But in spite of these blandishments, broadcasting is a doubtful venture compared with the effort I put into composing the talk and the nervous strain of these infrequent interviews with the microphone . . .

5 February. [Passfield Corner]
I sat next to Baldwin at the Smuts dinner and we had a free and easy talk together. He is an engaging personality with no side or solemnity, but not without vanity; who is? An easygoing temperament, essential refinement and rather extensive literary tastes. He glories in having no expertise in political and economic questions and no cut-and-dried theories. He is a big man and an ugly-featured man, but he has a most attractive voice and the pleasantest of smiles . . . He loathes Lloyd George and likes Ramsay. I should prefer to go round the world in his company rather than carry out a difficult job as his partner. I doubt whether he could do a good day's brainwork. He is a man of leisure, not of learning, or even of outstanding business capacity. He broadcasts well. . . .

Since the New Year we have had, for week-ends, the Tawneys and Coles and Citrines, all of whom have been described in these diaries. Citrine is, as before said, a self-centred man but an accomplished and an assiduous brainworker. He is too contemptuous of his political leaders and never doubts his own hasty criticism of what he chooses to think their incapacity for getting through business. In a somewhat heated argument I gave him a bit of my mind about his intellectual arrogance, assuming always that he knew best what was practicable, as well as what was desirable, in legislation and governmental administration. He was quite astonished and rather offended at my reaction to his summary condemnations, and answered back in style that he knew better than I, in all these questions. But I laughed and smoothed him down with the remark that I was an old woman and liked him much, admired his zeal and brain, but that I reserved my right to say things 'for his good'. We parted excellent friends and there will be a record of my impertinence in his diary. He has of course a slightly swelled head, through his dominance of the T.U.C. and its general council. Also he is disillusioned with the Labour world and thinks he has discovered that the other side 'is far abler'; even the late Conservative government is superior man for man to the present government. . . .

14 February. [Passfield Corner]
John Wheatley came to my Wednesday lunch. He has deteriorated mentally and physically since I knew him as a member of MacDonald's 1924 Cabinet. As a Cabinet Minister he was a brilliant success, alike in his department and in the House. As a rebel in the party he has been a failure. His expression is sullen, his words are bitter, his lips are blue and his complexion is patchy – and he closes his eyes at you. He says that he has lost his faith in political democracy; the common people have no will of their own; they are swayed backwards and forwards. He would be a Communist if he were not a pious Catholic. As it is he has no consistent position and will, I imagine, drop out of politics. . . .

Grigory Sokolnikov (1888–1939), a Bolshevik since 1905, had been editor of *Pravda* and Commissar for Finance 1921–26 before his appointment as Soviet Ambassador in London 1929–32. He was to die in prison, a victim of the great purges of the 30s. Beatrice was much influenced by him and his wife.

20 February. [Passfield Corner]
. . . . The Russian Ambassador and the lady who is acting as his wife (it is said there is no legal tie between them) dined with us in our little flat and met the Shaws, Ponsonby and Noel-Baker. Neither of them could talk fluent English, but owing to GBS's wit and Noel-Baker's French, we had a successful evening. A young man, with a naive faith in Communism as the last word of science,

studious and ascetic, a veritable puritan – a non-smoker and did not drink his wine. One would say he belonged to the best type of young workman of good character in quest of knowledge. He may develop personality; his expression and behaviour give an impression of sincerity and honesty. His attractive little wife is an author, was correspondent of *Izvestia* in China and has published a book on Women of the French Revolution. They spend most of their leisure in the British Museum Reading Room. Certainly they are strange members of the diplomatic circle. The Ambassador would be more at home as tutor in the W.E.A. As Ambassador I should imagine he would be, at first at any rate, a nonentity. Probably some other members of his staff are sent to look after him. But in their simplicity and unpretentiousness the two were an attractive couple and we shall see more of them. The only embassies who have hitherto noticed them are the German and the Turkish. Will she be presented at Court, I wonder?

Woodrow Wilson (1856–1924) was President of the United States 1916–20 and the chief architect of the Versailles peace treaty with Germany.

25 February. [?2 Whitehall Court]
The life I lead is displeasing in its restlessness. Always week-end visitors chosen for political reasons, which means talk, talk and again talk – often interesting, but always exhausting. Then two or three nights in London: lunches, dinners, afternoon parties, Press interviews and occasional social functions of a more pretentious sort. These I avoid like the devil; they have to me a ghostly flavour. Last night at the Foreign Office reception, where I went from a dinner at 10 Downing Street, as the wife of the Secretary of State for the Colonies, there arose a memory of my first Foreign Office reception. I had come from the dinner at which I first met Joseph Chamberlain – forty-seven years ago! At Admiralty House a funny picture emerged of a flirtation in a corner of the great reception room with an Admiralty clerk in 1876 – the year I 'came out' – over half a century ago. It is uncanny, this looking backwards through vistas of bygone figures, great personages or interesting but little-known individuals, all dead and gone. Then I turn and gaze at the new crowd, more especially at the younger men and women, still in the stage of hopefuls struggling to the front; not more than one or two will arrive, the others will recede further and

further and be lost among the multitude of 'might-have-beens' who no longer count. When Lloyd George came and shook hands, after an interval of eleven years, he seemed a ghost from the middle period of my life. Thirty years ago he and his wife used to dine with us at Grosvenor Road: he a bright young M.P. 'on the make', his wife a homely little body in a high black silk dress with curls. In another fifteen years he had become the central political personality, not only in his own country but in Europe, his only rival as a world celebrity being President Wilson. Now Wilson is dead and largely discredited, whilst Lloyd George hovers uneasily in the wings of the British political stage, unable to come to the front but unwilling to step out of the way of MacDonald and Baldwin. As I watched these three men, within a few yards of each other, Lloyd George seemed to be saying to himself, 'One or other of those two must be tripped up, and that before long,' and he looked at Baldwin. These shifting scenes, actual or imagined, would be amusing if the background were not lowering with a sense of national decadence – mistaken pessimism perhaps, but there it is sure enough, not only in my ageing mind, but also in other observers and these not the least experienced. . . .

If a general election were to come tomorrow – and it may come any day – all the three parties are so rattled that no one could predict what would happen: which party would suffer most from the lethargy induced by general disillusionment? I would gladly ascribe my own depression to senility – old people so often rail at imaginary contemporary disasters. But the young and the middle-aged seem even more disgruntled with the world than some old people. Indeed, Sidney remains unperturbed and says that most of the pessimism is 'calculated'. It may be that the 'decay of capitalist civilization', which we prophesied and described ten years ago, is actually taking place, and that some new and better forms of social life are struggling through in ways we fail to recognize. . . .

22 March. [Passfield Corner]
Arnold here last night. 'I have only seen MacDonald twice since Christmas,' he complained. 'Can you explain why Jimmy has such a hold on him; after all the P.M. is a man of distinguished intellect and great refinement. How can he like associating with that coarse and common-minded Thomas?' 'Neither distinguished intellect nor great moral refinement,' thought I, but did not say it. 'MacDonald

suffers badly from personal vanity,' I suggested. 'Thomas grovels to him. Also, Thomas has his good side: he is honest, he says exactly what he thinks, he is witty, he is shrewd and he is emotional, and thus breaks through J.R.M.'s reserve. The P.M.'s other principal colleagues – Henderson, Snowden, Clynes,' I added, 'do not really like or respect him. I doubt whether Snowden even admires him. He puts up with him because he can't get rid of him.' As for all the other members of the Cabinet they are absorbed in the daily work of their departments; they never see him except at Cabinet meetings . . . All the three leading figures in the Labour world have been completely gobbled up by the society of great personages – whether of the Court (Snowden), the City (Thomas) or Smart London Society dames (the P.M.). It is very deplorable. Meanwhile poor little Arnold feels left on the doorstep. It is an amusing scene. What strikes me about the Cabinet is that as an organ of consultation – as a way of arriving at a policy, of coordinating all the departments of government – it does not exist.

Ethel Snowden had given a lunch, without consultation with MacDonald, to Lloyd George and other Liberals to discuss government action on free trade.

23 March. [Passfield Corner]
Lord Thomson with the Keynes couple here for the week-end. He is as violently critical of the Naval conference now that it has happened as he was of its prospects before J.R.M. went to U.S.A. . . . So far as I can make out from Thomson's incoherent abuse, without any personal knowledge of the issues involved, the root of his violent discontent is that the Air Force is stunted in its development compared with the two other services. He implies that under the circumstances he does not care to be responsible for the safety of the Empire. All the same Thomson is an agreeable guest.

Keynes grows on one as an intellectual and his wife is a charmer of the first order. Whether all Keynes's deductive reasonings about wages and the control of investments are verifiable by facts I do not know. But he has a fine intellect and an attractive personality. From all we heard from Thomson and from Keynes there have been 'conversations' between Lloyd George and the P.M. over and above Mrs Snowden's far-famed luncheon party, pointing to an arrangement with the Liberals for some months of next year.

A special commission led by Sir Walter Shaw (1863–1937), a well-known colonial judge, had gone beyond his brief to report on the recent riots in Palestine and declared that a national home for the Jews was inconsistent with the League of Nations Mandate under which Britain governed the country. MacDonald's first idea was to ask Smuts to review the Mandate, but on reconsideration Sir John Hope Simpson was sent to study land settlement and immigration. Sir John Campbell (1874–1944) had been in the Indian civil service before becoming economic adviser to the Colonial office 1930–42. Harry Snell (1865–1944), a strong ethical socialist, was a Labour M.P. on the Shaw commission.

30 March. [Passfield Corner]

For the second time Sidney has found crucial questions referred, not to the Cabinet for consultation and decision, but to a suddenly called meeting of the two ex-Prime Ministers, the P.M. and himself. The first was the Dominion status question which will dominate the autumn Imperial conference. Today it is the Palestine Report, which turns out to be far too pro-Arab for the P.M.'s taste. The commissioners, with a demurrer from Snell, after adjudicating on the immediate occasion of disorder in August deliver *obiter dicta* on the impracticability of a National Home for the Jews without ousting the Arabs, which of course they deprecate as inconsistent with pledges under the Mandate. The Mandate, they imply, is self-contradictory and ought to be revised. The P.M. was much perturbed. What was to be done before the Report was published? The first step was a lunch given by Sidney, at the P.M.'s request, at which the P.M. met the leading Zionists, then, in the afternoon, a private meeting between Baldwin, Lloyd George, Herbert Samuel and Sidney. The decision was to employ General Smuts, accompanied by Sir J. Campbell of the Colonial Office, to report on the Mandate. So straight away the P.M. wires Smuts and arrangements are made with Baldwin to ask the appropriate questions in the House of Commons.

The P.M., after further thought, decided against Smuts as too Zionist, and allowed Sidney to engage Hope Simpson to enquire into the land question. Meanwhile the Cabinet has not seen the Report, leave alone considered Sidney's memo! As for the Parliamentary Party and the House of Commons as a whole, neither one nor the other comes into the picture. . . . Of course, there is a Cabinet meeting every week, which confers and decides about all issues likely to divide the Parliamentary Party, but the main business of these meetings seems to be telling the Ministers, as a body, decisions already arrived at by other means, in order that thus they may all tell the same story to Lords and Commons and party meetings. . . .

3 April. [Whitehall Court]
The last evening at 2 Whitehall Court. 'A rich man's slum,' as it has been nicknamed by contemptuous millionaires. Our little furnished flat, at the extravagant rent of fourteen guineas a week including service, on the gloomy but quiet side of the building, has served us well . . . But it is unpleasant living economically in an expensive establishment and we shall be glad to get into Artillery Mansions, where everyone has modest means or wishes to live modestly.

I have finished up entertaining the Parliamentary Labour Party for this first year of salaried office. I have invited all the 292 M.P.s to lunch (over 200 came) and given a reception to them and their wives, and Dominion and Colonial personages, at Admiralty House, all being successful. . . . And now I am going to rest from this distressful pursuit of social life for the Labour Party and try to concentrate on working out some practicable scheme of parliamentary devolution. Having broken up the Poor Law, why not break up the British Constitution?

Churt was Lloyd George's country home in Surrey. The writer G.K. Chesterton (1874–1936) was notably rotund.

5 April. [Passfield Corner]
H.G. Wells, whom we had not seen for some seven years, turned up for lunch on his way to Churt to collogue with Lloyd George. 'He uses me as a super-press man,' he jovially remarked. H.G. has grown super-fat and wheezy, almost rivals Chesterton. This fatness accentuates the piglikeness of his features. (The pig face is uncommon in England – English are mostly dogs and birds – less often horses, cats and apes, but still fewer pigs.) Wells has acquired the habit of monologue – badly. In old days part of his charm was his intellectual curiosity and the rapidity of give and take in conversation. Today he was wholly uninterested in what we were thinking. Probably he thought he knew it all. But he was curious to see how the old Webbs were wearing and what sort of home they had made for themselves. 'This is a charming room,' he remarked,

as if surprised. I was glad to see the genial old sinner, a *revenant* from the middle period of our life when we were all pals together. He has the poorest opinion of parliamentary institutions in general and of the late and present government in particular. In his forthcoming novel he is said to have caricatured the lot of us. There is something likeable in his frankness and lack of solemnity about his own life, his bubbling egotism, his comradeship with the younger scientists, his insistent determination to educate his fellow men on all aspects of life – from the organization of industry to the relation of Man to the Universe. How he and Lloyd George will enjoy themselves abusing the Labour government, inventing slogans for the next general election . . . Apparently of all contemporary politicians Lloyd George is the only one with whom H.G. has any dealings. They are two old buccaneers, out of joint with the world as it is, and impatient to see it altered to their likes, with themselves as the principal actors. But like ourselves and GBS they are voices from the past. Wherefrom will come the voices telling the future? They may be calling and we may be deaf to them. Are they from Russia? From the U.S.A? Or from the Far East or India? They are not from Great Britain nor from Western Europe.

16 April. [Passfield Corner]
. . . . Why did Trotsky become a revolutionary at seventeen years of age, risk death and incur imprisonment and exile? He was not oppressed; he was the son of well-to-do parents, he was a model boy at school, and though he disliked his masters there was no reason to suppose that they would have been more likeable under any other system of society. The love of adventure, and that strange conversion to an idea charged with emotion – religious fanaticism, in fact – seems to have been the compelling motive in Trotsky's life. And this fanaticism is shown in his faith in what he calls the *permanence of the revolution*; that is, its inevitable spread to all other countries. If it does not do so, so he holds, it will fail in Russia. It is on this issue that he quarrelled with his party, refused to abide by their decision, became a rebel and was exiled. He is in fact an absolutist. And yet he is a man of great intelligence. His autobiography, which he sent me, is a badly planned and badly written work, but it is fascinating not only as a description of the origin of that great and tragic drama, the Russian revolution, but also as a study of

religious fanaticism of a high order. And yet Trotsky probably believes that he is a free-thinker! practising the scientific method. . . . How exceptional and frail is the nineteenth-century deliberate tolerance of other faiths than your own.

M.K. Gandhi (1869–1948), the leader of the Indian nationalist movement, had just made his 'salt march' to the sea; he was among the 54,000 arrested for 'civil disobedience' offences in 1930.

4 May. [Passfield Corner]
Gandhi arrested; and now we shall see how deep-rooted is the following of the Indian saint, whether faith will move mountains of Indian disunity and inexperience and upset the British Raj! 'The only way of compelling the Englishman to get off the back of the Elephant is for the Elephant to make it damned unpleasant for him,' the nationalist Indian would answer. It is not prejudice in favour of autocratic British rule in the mind of the Labour Cabinet and the Viceroy that blocks the way to granting immediate Dominion status, but sheer perplexity as to how on earth to do it without tumbling India into a state of civil war. We did it in Ireland by separating off the Ulster Protestants from the Free State Catholics and securing Ulster from any interference from the new Dominion. But how to keep the hostile races, communities and castes of India from trying to dominate one another seems to pass the wit of man! Whether it would be better for the people of India to be left to fight it out among themselves is another matter. But would the other white races and Japan leave India to fall into the state of China?

On 23 January 1930 Mosley, who had been asked to help J.H. Thomas combat unemployment, bypassed him and sent MacDonald a memorandum proposing reform in the machinery of government, a large-scale programme of public works, and the mobilization of national resources to combat unemployment. A Cabinet committee chaired by Snowden rejected the proposals, which would have meant abandoning free trade and the gold standard. Before a third discussion on 19 May, Mosley saw MacDonald and said he proposed to resign; after a powerful resignation speech in Parliament on 28 May he began to organize a breakaway party.

19 May. [Passfield Corner]
Oswald and Cynthia Mosley here for the night, at a critical moment of his career. After the turning down by Cabinet etc.,

under Snowden's influence, of his plan for coping with unemployment, is he or is he not going to resign? Cynthia complains that since the advent of the Labour government they have seen little or nothing of J.R.M. and the latter has refused to discuss unemployment with her husband. Mosley says that the party is breaking up in the country, that there will be a débâcle at the next election and that the party will be so disintegrated that it will not revive for a generation. It is fair to add that, except in the case of Thomas, Mosley does not abuse the leaders. About Thomas he is contemptuous; Jimmy began by being arrogant and has ended by giving way to maudlin despair. The scenes at the meetings of officials to discuss plans with the Ministers concerned are more discreditably comic than any in *The Apple Cart.* 'I've an 'ell of an 'ead,' Thomas was wailing at the last meeting, the quite obvious explanation being a night of boozing. And capacity to understand plans put before him is as lacking as decent manners. Mosley respects and likes Snowden but says that he has become conservative and anti-socialist without knowing it, largely owing to the 'classy' adventures into which Mrs Snowden has dragged him. She is reported to have said that she needs no friends because she is so intimate with the royal family. About J.R.M. the Mosleys and we were equally reticent; we agreed that he was a great artist, and left it at that. About the participation of the Cabinet Ministers and their wives in Court and London Society functions, the Mosleys are far more acidly emphatic than I am; Cynthia told me that they were humiliated by the jeers of their relations and friends in the smart set at the social climbers in the Labour Party. . . .

Certainly the two Mosleys struck us as sincere and assiduous in their public aims. Whether Mosley has sufficient judgement and knowledge to lead the Labour Party in home affairs I have no means of judging. Sidney thinks not. If he resigns, he intends to lead a new group who will vote solidly to keep the Labour government in office, but will be continually critical in the House and propagandists in the country. . . . Looking to the future, he foresees a growing cleavage between the constituency parties led by left-wing enthusiasts and the trade unions led by rather dull-witted and conventional trade union officials. The keenest of the young trade unionists are in revolt against the block vote and the dictatorship of the well-established officers of the big trade unions. Sidney observed afterwards that the constituency parties were frequently little unrepresentative groups of nonentities dominated by fanatics and cranks and extremists, and that *if* the block vote of the trade unions were eliminated it would be impracticable to continue to vest the control of policy in Labour Party conferences. . . .

John Strachey (1901–63), son of the famous editor of the *Spectator*, was a left-wing intellectual who first supported Mosley's New Party, then became an influential Marxist propagandist. He finally returned to hold high office in the Labour governments of 1945–51. At this time he was Mosley's parliamentary private secretary.

29 May. [Passfield Corner]
Mosley's speech in the second attack on Thomas is acclaimed as that of a distinguished parliamentary orator, wholly admirable in manner and style; however, opinions may differ about the practicability and desirability of his plan. The P.M. promises to place himself at the head of the Cabinet committee for dealing with unemployment. It is interesting to note that he has never once mentioned the question to Sidney. Who is he consulting? The question has not been referred to the new research department – on the contrary, it has been expressly warned off, on the ground that it is the specific job of Thomas's department. And yet we all thought that this new departure in the machinery of government was devised because of the breakdown over unemployment. Has MacDonald found his superseder in Oswald Mosley? MacDonald owes his pre-eminence largely to the fact that he is the only artist, the only aristocrat by temperament and talent, in a party of plebeians and plain men. Hitherto he has had no competitor in personal charm and good looks, delightful voice and the gift of oratory. But Mosley has all these with the *élan* of youth, wealth and social position added to them. Like Mosley, MacDonald began as a utopian, but today he is a disillusioned utopian, whilst Mosley has still a young man's zeal – and is more able to use other men's brains. Whether Mosley has Mac's toughness of texture, whether he will not break down in health or in character, I have doubts. He lacks MacDonald's strongest point – genuine puritanism. He is entangled in the smart set and luxurious habits; he is reputed to be loose with women; he rouses suspicion, he knows little or nothing about trade unionism or Co-operation, he cannot get on terms of intimacy with working men or with the lower middle-class brainworker. He is, in fact, an intruder, a foreign substance in the labour movement, not easily assimilated. Mosley will be a great success at public meetings,

but will he get round him the Arthur Hendersons, the Herbert Morrisons, the Alexanders, the Citrines and the Bevins, who are the natural leaders of the great organized communities of the proletariat? Hitherto these men have had little use for Oswald Mosley, and it is they who will decide who shall succeed or supersede Ramsay MacDonald – not the John Stracheys and Fenner Brockways and Wises, all of whom, like Mosley, are intruders into the world of manual workers.

Thomas was moved to the Dominions Office on 5 June among other government changes. The unemployment problem was now taken over by a panel of Ministers under the Prime Minister.

31 May. [? Guernsey]
On the night of our departure for the Channel Isles Sidney reported an interview with MacDonald, who is struggling out of the depths of difficulties with the party. Sixty members had signed a demand for the dismissal of Thomas and the P.M. was considering how to find a way out for his old friend and colleague. Sidney played up and offered to clear out of either of one or of both his offices as Secretary of State for Dominions and Colonies. The P.M. expressed his appreciation, but two Secretaries of State would still be needed in the House of Lords. There was, however, the possibility of appointing a new Secretary of State for the Dominions leaving Sidney as Secretary of State for the Colonies, giving Thomas the Dominions. Indeed this division has always been contemplated. Sidney acquiesced, told Wilson and Harding to prepare for the division of the office as best they could and came off for our fortnight's holiday in excellent spirits. He reports MacDonald as 'disgusted with the party and professing indifference to continued office' and very angry with Mosley. Whether Thomas will agree to this confession of failure and whether the King and the Dominions will approve of this way of shelving a discredited politician we shall see during the next week. But 'Jimmy' is a favourite in the higher circles of society. If he drops his h's and is frequently on the booze, he is sound on the sanctity of property and the free initiative of capitalist enterprise. Also he panders by his illiteracy and gross language to the superiority complex of men of rank and men of property. So in spite of his failure he has had an excellent Press. And MacDonald has a real affection for him – told Sidney that sooner than accept Thomas's resignation he, MacDonald,

would resign himself. One up for Jimmy. There must be something lovable in this ugly and low-down specimen of humanity – he has a sort of genius, a pungent and appealing personality, and above all a gift of intimacy so insistent that it overcomes MacDonald's intensely secretive mind.

But saving Jimmy's face will not save the situation.

A socialist government cannot take up the attitude of *non possumus* to all schemes for making the lot of the workers secure against the ravages of unemployment – either remunerative work must be found or maintenance on tolerable conditions alike of mind or body must be given. Such an aim may, for lack of inventiveness, be unfulfilled for a generation, but it must be attempted, and again and again attempted with undaunted courage until this intolerable state of affairs has become exceptional – like typhus is today in the big cities of the world. It is absurd to assume that with the present enormous power of production we cannot so distribute the services and commodities available so as to insure to all men a sufficient livelihood. If the requisite services and commodities *could not be produced* with the existing means of production, we might have to starve some in order to supply others. But the ironic fact is that in Great Britain and Germany, in Italy and U.S.A. and Japan, the immediate cause of workless and wealthless persons is an *over-production* of commodities and services. The Soviet government, by killing capitalist enterprise, has not abolished poverty – all it has done is to distribute poverty, due to *under-production*, equally over the whole population. That at least makes the burden of poverty less demoralizing. But it does not lift it off the life of the people. . . .

What no party and no country as yet realizes, except perhaps Russian Communists, is that the state cannot *guarantee* livelihood except under the conditions of a *managed* population, and that this management must start with a complete register of every individual within the community, so as to insure that the principle 'from every one according to their capacity' in return 'to every one according to their need' will be enforced. Knowledge here or elsewhere is the beginning of wisdom. And it is the passion for knowledge and faith in applying it that has become the obsession of the governing class of Russia.

16 June. [Passfield Corner]
A satisfactory holiday in the Channel Islands, wandering to and fro

Guernsey, Sark and Jersey as 'Mr and Mrs Sidney Webb'. In both the hotels not recognized as 'personages' until the end of our stay – in each case there were guests who spotted us and at the end of each visit a letter or telegram giving Sidney's official name away, a blunder on the part of correspondents . . .

Now I have to prepare the B.B.C. talk and then read up for the larger exposition of the scheme in the autumn and winter. If strength permits I shall go forward with *Our Partnership*, though I see little or no chance of either writing all of it or publishing any part of it during this last decade of my life. So long as Sidney is in office my brainwork will be scrappy and incompetent. Whether under more restful conditions it could be of any decent quality? But one must keep occupied or grow senile prematurely.

Before I left London I was 'vetted' by an accomplished woman doctor. Her report was that lungs, heart, kidneys, were all A.1. – and the arteries those of a young woman. But excessive whizzing in the ear and sleeplessness are chronic; she suggested specialists for each, including a psychologist for sleeplessness! Whether I shall take her advice I have not yet determined; each specialist will probably assure me that there is nothing the matter with me, except old age. 'Why do you want to work at your age?' the last medical man I saw asked me.

Sir Edmund Ovey (1879–1963) was British Ambassador in Moscow 1929–33.

30 June. [Passfield Corner]
Sidney showed me a remarkable report from Ovey, the British Ambassador at Moscow. The gist is that Soviet Communism is firmly established and increasing its hold day by day in the medley of peoples making up the Russian Empire. Communism, he holds, is analogous to Mohammedanism of medieval times; it is a potent religion which is sweeping through continents, and like Mohammedanism and all other religions will sweep on until it finds its margin of cultivation. And he believes the Communist Party will succeed in destroying the capitalist system within its territories and will bring into practice a way of life based on common property, equality of income and the supremacy of the workers' interests. Autocracy is indigenous in Russia and will survive in the Soviet Republic as a political institution. What has been revolutionized is

the *purpose* of government, which is, under Communism, to bring about a millennium through the transformation of the motives of man – in *this* world and not in a mystical afterlife. . . .

1 July. [Passfield Corner]
Astors, Sassoons, Snowdens, with Royalties and Dean Inge intervening, and a circle of celebrated printers and publishers, actors, actresses, stage managers and artists of all sorts, from prize-fighters to lady photographers, is my impression of the social environment of the Bernard Shaws. They 'process' through life – and every now and again they visit this cottage home of the Webbs as their last resting-place within the labour movement . . . . Meanwhile discontent and disillusionment grow within the Parliamentary Labour Party and throughout the movement in the country. The Front Bench is strangled by the multitudinous and complicated issues raised in government departments, and by the alarming gravity of the two major problems – India's upheaval and the continuous and increasing unemployment. The Labour government will be kept in office by the two other parties, because neither Baldwin or Lloyd George want an immediate general election; and the instructed public think that for both India and unemployment it is best to have a government of the left – *The Times* actually said so. But it is rather a humiliating position for the genuine socialist of the movement. . . .

India House, along with Bush House and Australia House, formed part of the scheme to rebuild the Aldwych as an imperial quadrant.

9 July. [Artillery Mansions]
. . . . A most tiresome and rather odious ten days in London entertaining and being entertained during the Colonial Office conference. My four lunches of about twenty-four persons each, at the London School of Economics – governors and their wives to meet distinguished strangers – were most successful. But going to official dinners and other people's gatherings, though it satisfies curiosity, is, in this hot weather, almost unendurable. Also I detest the social atmosphere, especially when Royalties are present – the cringe before these admirable automatons and the self-importance of everyone concerned. At the opening of India House, by the King and Queen, there was added the ironic background, in everyone's consciousness, of the grim upheaval in India – the elaborately

decked-out native rulers and the picturesquely clothed Indian ladies seemed to make them traitors to Indian nationalism. . . .

What is as clear as noonday is that though the Indians may not be able to govern themselves they may make it wholly impracticable for Great Britain to govern them – if the non-resistance movement persists and spreads. Neither Great Britain's means, nor her public opinion, would permit any government to reconquer India by force of arms. We failed to maintain law and order in Southern Ireland, with three million people, and close at hand; with three hundred million people far away the idea is tragically absurd! And we are up against a saint with his *soul force* – a force which seems potent to destroy the existing order but impotent to create the new. Rather like Tolstoy in pre-war Russia.

York House was the London residence of Edward, Prince of Wales (1894–1972) who became Edward VIII for eleven months before he abdicated in December 1936. Lady Minto was the widow of Lord Minto (1845–1914), a pre-war Viceroy of India. Lady Abercorn was the wife of the third Duke of Abercorn. This was one of the rare occasions on which Beatrice answered publicly to her title.

13 July. [Artillery Mansions]
. . . . an informal dinner at York House – my first introduction into the Court circle. The Prince, having devoted himself at dinner to the young Countess (Minto) and the middle-aged Duchess (Abercorn), settled down afterwards by the aged Baroness (Passfield) and opened out into an oddly intimate talk about his religious difficulties.

'What do you really believe, Mrs Webb?' he asked in an agitated tone. (I was there as Lady Passfield.) He is a neurotic and takes too much alcohol for health of body or mind. If I were his mother or grandmother I should be very nervous about his future. He clearly dislikes having to go to the Anglican Church, but whether he has leanings to Catholicism or is becoming an unbeliever there was not time to explore. 'The Duchess wants to take leave,' the equerry presently announced, and the half-hour's tête-à-tête ceased. I felt sorry for the man; his expression was unhappy – there was a horrid dissipated look as if he had no settled home either for his intellect or his emotions. In his study there were two pictures of the Queen, one over the mantelpiece and the other on his desk, but no symbol of the King. On one side of the wall hung a huge map of the world;

on another side there were shelves filled with expensively bound library editions, obviously never read – there were no books in general use. Like all those royal suites of apartments, there was no homeliness or privacy – the rooms and their trappings were all designed for company and not for home life.

But it was the unhappiness of the Prince's expression, the uneasy restlessness of his manner, the odd combination of unbelief and hankering after sacerdotal religion, the reactionary prejudice about India and the morbid curiosity about Russia revealed in his talk that interested me. The Anglican Church, whose services he said he 'had to attend', he clearly resented. He must be a problem to the conventional courtiers who surround him! Will he stay put in his present role of the most popular heir-apparent in British history? As I talked to him he seemed like a hero of one of Shaw's plays; he was certainly very unconventional in his conversation with a perfect stranger. Was it the Dauphin in *St Joan* or King Magnus in *The Apple Cart* that ran in my head? Not so mean as the first, not so accomplished as the second of GBS's incarnations of kingship!

But how I loathe London Society in all its aspects. The last fortnight has made me more than ever content with bourgeois status and absence from social functions. What I detest most of all are my own reactions to it – the stimulus it gives to latent personal vanity, contemptible in an old lady of seventy odd! . . . I have tried to compromise: I have declined to go to the evening Courts and I have not been presented to the Queen. But can I avoid dining at Buckingham Palace if I am now invited, when I have dined at York House?

When once Sidney is out of office I shall be quit of the whole business – in any case I intend to give up entertaining at Christmas and save the remainder of our official salary lest worse befall old England and our own little income. Again the desire to be 'thoroughly comfortable' in one's old age! Personal vanity curbed by greed! Alas! for human nature, I am of the old opinion still: I do not *like* human beings.

20 July. [Passfield Corner]
Laskis down here, Harold full of gossip . . . He had dined at the Coles and met Mosley, with whom Cole is coalescing[?]. He mentioned incidentally that cocktails, wines and liqueurs abounded, presumably in Mosley's honour! . . . Laski was very critical of the

Mosleys. They lived a luxurious and fast life. They had no well-thought-out constructive programme. Mosley was ignorant and Cole was gambling with one proposal after another. But then Laski has always disliked Cole and Mosley had largely ignored Laski; they had not been to the Mosley's house for four or five years, Mrs Laski let out. Both the Laskis denounce the snobbishness of the wives of the Cabinet Ministers, and the aloofness of the leaders from the rank and file. . . .

2 August. [Passfield Corner]
Sidney always checks me when I denigrate his colleagues, whether it be the P.M., Thomas or Margaret Bondfield. Even when J.H. Thomas left him out of the British delegates to the Imperial conference (an absurdity which was rectified by the Cabinet) Sidney made no remark and seemed not to resent it. Whether it is old age or the absence of personal ambition he is ready to retire whenever J.R.M. no longer requires him, and certainly will not join another Cabinet if by any chance Labour comes back to office after the next general election. Personally I think the Tories will romp back; the rot within the Labour Party is serious and there is panic among the well-to-do, not about the unemployed, but about the maintenance of the unemployed. At the back of the mind of the middle classes there is a settled conviction that if a man cannot be given work he ought not to be given food, at any rate not more than is necessary to prevent the scandal of deaths by starvation. The propertied classes are not yet prepared to accept the third alternative of maintenance under training or disciplined occupation. As this solution is also objected to by the uninstructed proletarian it is not likely to be adopted by either of the alternative Cabinets. Meagre unconditional outdoor relief is still the one and only device. Enlightened public opinion seems paralysed; both Front Benches refuse to think – they just drift between putting men on the dole or striking them off. The Labour government has put men on, the Conservative government will throw them off and try to solve unemployment by fiscal protection.

3 August. [Passfield Corner]
The Soviet Ambassador and his wife here for a day and night, a singularly sympathetic man and woman. . . . They are refined and admirably mannered, quiet, dignified, straightforward and pleasant,

not aggressive but very staunch in their upholding of Bolshevism in a hostile world. Of the two, she is the most outspoken. They had been in Glasgow and she observed the dull depressed attitude of the people in the streets. In Moscow everyone was excited and neurotic. England was healthier to live in but not so interesting. Certainly the tone and the temper of these two, their outlook on life, seemed to be calm reason and goodwill; doubtless there is a strain of fanaticism, an undue certainty in their opinions compared to the cultured scepticism of Western Europe about all things human and divine. But can there be organized movement without faith? Philip Snowden lunched here to meet them . . . He impressed Snowden favourably. Sitting after lunch in the loggia and discussing the Five Year Plan, Sokolnikov described the enthusiasm with which the Communist workers were accepting low wages and a relatively hard life in order to save money for capital improvements. 'That's sound,' said the British Chancellor of the Exchequer. 'I sometimes despair about the working class. Next week I have to meet the General Council of the T.U.C. They want more wages, shorter hours, greater expenditure on social services, here and now, when we, as a community, ought to be saving in order to bring our old-fashioned plant up to date.' 'Ah, Mr Snowden,' said I. 'You will never get the British workman to work harder on less wages when he sees the employing class enjoying leisure and large expenditure. It is the equality of income that enables the Soviet government to ask and obtain increased energy and sacrifice from the manual working citizen. The workers know they are working not for other people's children but for their *own* children.'

7 August. [Passfield Corner]
Charlotte is presenting me with the complete edition of GBS's works and I am reading the volumes one by one . . . GBS has never understood that in the world of affairs, a mere actor of parts (that is, a *poseur*) will fail to dominate his fellow men. What is false within him will find him out. On all crucial occasions he is discovered to be not a real man, with whom you can have consecutive dealings, but the appearance of a man — worse still, of a series of different men with conflicting motives and varying ends. Secondly Shaw is wrong in imagining that he understands science — he has never had the remotest inkling of the scientific method and even if he could be made to understand it, he has neither the

225

patience nor the intellectual conscience to seek truth for its own sake. . . . To some of the most accomplished intellects of his time he seems little more than a clever buffoon, a brilliant but unstable intellect, whose thoughts, when they are his own, are mostly flippant and perverse. Mandell Creighton, Haldane, Courtney, thought him absurdly overrated; Arthur Balfour admired him as a *littérateur* but never thought of taking either his arguments or statements seriously. GBS himself thinks that the elect of all times will read and reverence Bernard Shaw as they continue to do Plato, Dante, Shakespeare and Goethe. Not even his admirers take him at that valuation. But in sheer vitality of brain, other able persons – Sidney and I, for instance – are dwarfs beside him. . . .

W.T. Cosgrave (1880–1965) was the moderate Premier of Ireland 1922–32. The Black and Tans were the para-military force of ex-soldiers sent to reinforce the Royal Irish constabulary in the 1920 guerrilla campaign.

6 September. [?Passfield Corner]
A week-end at the Viceregal Lodge [in Dublin] and three days with Lion Phillimore, a visit arranged when Sidney was Secretary of State for the Dominions. Should I or should I not curtsy? intrigued my mind as we drove with the A.D.C. from Kingstown to the very royal residence of the titular head of this very little kingdom. I gathered during my stay that the smart folk curtsy, somewhat derisively, and the humble folk do not curtsy, somewhat bashfully. I compromised, curtsied on arrival and at the 'state' dinner party, but not otherwise. 'Their Excellencies' and the splendour of the Viceregal establishment (twenty-seven indoor servants, fifteen gardeners) seems an expensive anachronism for so small a community and will, I imagine, be dropped – the institution is clearly not popular with the citizens of Dublin. Republicans and Labourites refuse to recognize the Governor-General, and Belfast boycotts and is boycotted. . . .

At the Viceregal Lodge we met the leading politicians, judges and foreign Ministers. At Lion's we saw the Cosgraves more intimately. The able group of young men now governing the Free State struck me as similar in speech and personal conduct to the Viennese municipal administrators: they certainly had much zeal and no 'side'. The quiet efficiency of their administrators made me ashamed of the long struggle for Home Rule, culminating in the disgraceful episode of the Black and Tans. The most notable impression left on my mind was the heavy hand of the Roman Catholic Church. In no other country have I become aware of the spiritual oppression of the common people by the fear of Hell. One almost began to feel this fear oneself. . . .

There is much bitterness about the separation of Ulster. 'The Irish will never forgive, until that is put right,' one Cabinet Minister said to me. 'Sooner or later we shall fight for it,' he added. They feel that they have been 'done' by wily Englishmen . . . Throughout our visit we were accompanied by an armed escort – an armed guard slept in the house with us when staying with Lion. Cosgrave's house was heavily guarded and everywhere he went he was attended by armed detectives.

The Imperial conference had opened on 1 October with a series of receptions. Mrs Lunn was the wife of William Lunn (1872–1942) who was Parliamentary Under-Secretary to Sidney at the Colonial Office. James Scullin (1876–1953) was the Labour Prime Minister of Australia. George Forbes (1869–1947), leader of the United Party, was Prime Minister of New Zealand. Patrick McGilligan (1881–1960) was Irish Minister of External Affairs. Richard Bennett (1870–1947) was Conservative Prime Minister of Canada. James Hertzog (1866–1942) was the Nationalist Prime Minister of South Africa.

4 October. [Passfield Corner]
A spate of high-class social functions this week – I avoided two dinners and reception at Lancaster Gate, but got through two lunches and an afternoon gathering in a little over twenty-four hours, and a Buckingham Palace state dinner on Friday, returning here for the middle of the week to rest and write letters. . . .

The Buckingham Palace dinner centred round the delegates from the Dominions and their wives; it was part of the web of imperial destiny, and well wrought. The ceremony and its settings combined dull dignity with refined magnificence: there was almost a religious atmosphere as the 120 guests trooped up the stairs into the sumptuous range of reception rooms, each guest bending over the hands of the two Idols on the way to the inner temple of the banqueting hall – with the golden plate and crimson-clothed attendants. What spoilt the pageant was the dowdyism of the women guests, in marked contrast with the superb garments and jewels of the Queen and her aristocratic Court ladies. I, for instance, though I appeared as The Lady Passfield, wore a high-necked long-sleeved grey chiffon velvet which I have been wearing for six months at every dinner I have attended; Mrs Lunn, the Under-Secretary's wife, had donned a conventional black satin, obviously bought for the occasion from the local Co-op. Ethel Snowden, with a paste tiara and a cheap fashionable frock, was the intermediate link between we humble folk and the Court circle. At the table, the royalties sat in a heap opposite each other; close beside them the Dominion representatives, each man or woman being tenderly looked after by some great lady or nobleman attached to the Court. It was amusing to watch these charming women sparkling their eyes and softening their voices to fascinate Scullin, Forbes, McGilligan and Bennett (if I remember right, Bennett's sister being placed on the other side of the Prince of Wales). Hertzog was honoured by a minor Princess whilst their male counterparts bent over the Dominion ladies with a like solicitude. . . .

After dinner the Queen [Mary] stood in one of the large reception rooms and we ladies grouped ourselves round the walls, a few being picked out and led up to the Queen by the Duchess of Devonshire for two or three minutes' perfunctory talk, I being one of them. The Queen is a fine figure of a woman: she holds herself well and is magnificently apparelled and bejewelled, the lines of her face extensively 'made up'; she is stiff in manner, curt in words and lifeless in expression, and really looks like an exquisitely executed automaton – a royal robot. I gather she is an honest and kindly soul, but curiously shy – she was painfully at a loss of what to say to me. To avoid silence I told her about our visit to Ireland and mentioned that we were having General Hertzog and the Scullins to stay with us. 'Where do you live?' was her only contribution. 'In a cottage near Liphook, Ma'am.' 'Liphook!' she said in a puzzled tone, and seeing another lady being prepared for an audience I back away. . . . About 10.30 o'clock the King and Queen and other royalties walked through the gallery and the King, who is far more homely and gracious than his royal mate, stopped in front of me and hoped 'that you are not too tired', to which I mumbled some amiable reply. So ends my first and last appearance at the Court of St James's!

On 5 October the airship R101 crashed at Beauvais in France. The forty-nine dead included Lord Thomson, Secretary of State for Air, who was flying on this maiden voyage to India.

6 October. [Passfield Corner]
A bare week ago Thomson was here for the week-end, and only a week today and tomorrow I met him at successive lunches. Oddly enough it flashed through my mind, 'Shall I meet you again?' In the few words he said to me, and in his expression there was something that made one uneasy – probably the awful event has magnified this dimly remembered presentiment. His death is a real loss to the Labour Cabinet and I feel it more than I should have foreseen. He was an attractive colleague and friend; antagonized no one, and amused and interested all of us; the one trait I did *not* like, and which still puzzles me, was his apparent intimacy with the P.M. and yet his constant depreciation of him . . . The inner circle has lost one of its very few charmers – indeed, barring the P.M., is there any other charmer in government circles? The forty odd Ministers are a drab company!

There was a rapid and fierce Zionist reaction to Sir John Hope Simpson's report on land settlement and the Passfield White Paper. 'It is really the work of the Office,' Sidney had written to Beatrice on 10 October when the draft was completed, but he had to take responsibility. He believed that, apart from reflecting the idea of a 'Jewish State' (as distinct from a 'National Home'), the government had done nothing to give the Jews ground for complaint; there was to be no limit on continued colonization and no change in the existing limit on non-racial immigration. Sidney, moreover, had kept in private touch with Chaim Weizmann (1874–1952), secretary of the World Zionist Organization. But the Zionist 'hurricane' raged so furiously that Weizmann was obliged to resign at the ensuing Zionist congress for failing to take a sufficiently strong stand against Webb's policy. In March 1931 MacDonald made some concessions to Zionist pressure.

26 October. [Passfield Corner]
Sidney, by the publication of the Hope Simpson paper, and the *Statement of Policy* accompanying it, has involved himself and the Labour government in a storm of anger from Jewry all over the world. What interests me about all this ferment over Palestine is the absence, from first to last, of any consideration of Palestine as the cradle of the Christian creed, as the Holy Land of Christendom. I have never felt the lure of the Holy Land, but then I am not a Christian. But imagine the awful shock to the medieval Crusaders if they had foreseen the Christian Kingdoms of England, France and Italy withdrawing Jerusalem from Islam in order to hand it over to the representatives of those who crucified Jesus of Nazareth

and have continued, down all the ages, to deny that He is the Son of God! Has the glorified romance of Jesus of Nazareth, of his birth, of his life message, of his death and his resurrection from the dead, vanished from the mind of man? Is the promised land, for the Jewish Home, yet another sign of the rapid decay of Christendom? Lloyd George, in his speech denouncing the *Statement of Policy*, ends his peroration by urging the claim of the Jews to 'the land which their ancestors made famous for all time'. The Christian tradition of the infamy of the Crucifixion is ignored. An additional touch of irony to this ill-doomed episode lies in the fact that the Jewish immigrants are mongols and not semites, and the vast majority are not followers of Moses and the prophets but of Karl Marx and the Soviet Republic.

But this, after all, is a mere sidelight and has nothing to do with the bargain between Balfour and the Zionists. At the time of the Balfour declaration, the one and only consideration was the relative power (to help us to win the war) of the international Jewish financiers on the one hand and on the other the Arabs in revolt against the Turkish empire. The man on the spot gave promises to the Arabs; the British Cabinet gave promises to the Jews – always qualifying the promise of a Jewish Home by the perfunctory condition of the well-being of the Arab inhabitants. After ten years it is clear to all who study the question that these promises were and are incompatible – either the Jew or the Arab, or partly one and partly the other, will have to be deterred from getting the full value of those promises. Owing to the superior wealth and capacity of the Jews, it is the Arab who has suffered damage during the last ten years. The Jews would answer that the Arab has not been forcibly driven out of the land and that *in buying him out*, or rather in buying his landlord out, they have been acting in the normal way, in the way that any man might have acted under the laws of civilized peoples.

Today they are furious with the expressed intention of the British government to protect the Arab cultivator from being expropriated and becoming a landless proletariat. This protection of the Arab is not only justified on grounds of justice but on the ground of expediency. Unless Great Britain is prepared to keep an army of occupation in Palestine indefinitely, she cannot prevent the old and new Jewish settlements from being periodically raided by the neighbouring Arab states as well as by the resident Arabs. The

British Cabinet have also to consider the feelings of the Mohammedans of India, not to mention Egypt. The responsibility for this débâcle lies with the fatuous promise of a Palestine Jewish Home which, if it meant anything worth having for the Jews, meant a Jewish Palestine from which the Arabs would be gradually extruded by economic pressure.

Meanwhile Sidney remains unperturbed. He has done his best to hold an even balance. . . . The *Statement of Policy*, by the way, is a badly drafted, a tactless document – he ought to have done it himself. But so far as the Jews are concerned, that betterment of form would not have made it more acceptable. Probably future governments will be only too glad to have had the ice broken and the Jews forced to be more considerate and reasonable. . . .

30 October. [Passfield Corner]
Why is it that everyone who has dealings with Jewry ends by being prejudiced against the Jews? Sidney started with a great admiration for the Jew and a contempt for the Arab, but he reports that all the officials, at home and in Palestine, find the Jews, even many accomplished and cultivated Jews, intolerable as negotiators and colleagues. Weizmann Sidney admires as a remarkable and, in a way, attractive personality. I remember thinking him so when Dick Meinertzhagen brought him to see us in 1919. He is a disinterested idealist, a clever administrator, an accomplished intellectual, all rolled into one. But he is a champion manipulator, and uses arguments and devices regardless of accuracy, straight-forwardness or respect for confidence, or other honourable under-takings. 'If you show Weizmann any document, in the strictest confidence, you become aware that he has communicated it to others. A clever devil; I take my hat off to him,' Sidney told me. 'It was not the *Statement of Policy* but the facts revealed by Hope Simpson's report that he was up against – it was these facts that were so damning. Weizmann is in the difficult position of a company promoter confronted with an adverse expert's report, damaging to his prospective enterprise. So he turns the attention away from the Report and on to the *Statement of Policy*, to an assumed breach of the Balfour promise and the terms of the Mandate, in order to excite the indignation of the Jews and make them forget the adverse report. In that way he hopes to keep up the flow of subscriptions. Also he has to counter the detraction of his left wing, the cry of the

revisionist. Revision, he knows, is impracticable, and would set the world against Zionism. But he has overplayed the part and reaction will set in.'

Meanwhile Hope Simpson has asked impossible conditions for undertaking the job of land development – so Sidney, if the Labour government remains in office, will have to find someone else to carry out the Hope Simpson propositions. But little Palestine with its troubles, insignificant to the rest of the world, is likely to be forgotten in concern over the revolution which some say is going on in India. For the next six weeks the P.M. and other Cabinet Ministers, having finished with the Dominions, will be absorbed in the Round Table conference to settle the fate of India, or rather of the British in India. Here in old England, dissolution is in the air in more sense than one.

Is it a further cause for pessimism, or a consolation tinged with malice, that other powerful races are rolling in tempestuous waters? The U.S.A., with its cancerous growth of crime and uncounted but destitute unemployed; Germany hanging over the precipice of a nationalist dictatorship; Italy boasting of its military preparedness; France, in dread of a new combination of Italy, Germany and Austria against her; Spain on the brink of revolution; the Balkan States snarling at each other; the Far East in a state of anarchic ferment; the African continent uncertain whether its 'paramount interest' and cultural power will be black or white; South American states forcibly replacing pseudo-democracies by military dictator-ships; and, finally – acutely hostile to the rest of the world, engulfed in a fabulous effort, the success of which would shake capitalist civilization in its very foundations – Soviet Russia, struggling with fanatic fervour to bring about, for the first time in the history of the world, an equalitarian state, based on an uncompromising scientific materialism.

What a world has been opened up by the Great War!

12 November. [Passfield Corner]
We lunched on Thursday at the Soviet Embassy – a princely mansion in Kensington Palace Gardens with great reception rooms and large garden, its occupants looking, according to ordinary diplomatic standards of style and expression, strangely out of place. Indeed it was impossible to distinguish the Ambassador, his wife and staff from those serving them in what is here called a 'menial'

capacity — ideas, manners and mutual relations being the same all through. This expression of the equalitarian state was unique and to me pleasing. . . .

The Sokolnikovs encouraged us to go to Russia, altogether denied that we should find it expensive if we arranged the trip through their Tourist Agency . . . We are the only 'Cabinet' members who have consorted with them. The Hendersons do not 'know them' socially, nor the P.M. . . .

19 November. [Passfield Corner]
. . . How I should revel (if I were thirty years younger) in a year spent in the U.S.A. and also in Russia, just to see what is actually happening in those two stupendous social experiments; in uncontrolled capitalism on the one hand, and on the other despotically controlled Communism. Which will win in the race for maximum output? And what will be the relative quality of the human nature produced? Will the American or the Russian turn out to be the more civilized being, the more gifted in intellect, art and manners? Or will old Europe keep her supremacy in science, literature, music and the art of life?

23 November. [Passfield Corner]
The Hendersons here for three nights. We always enjoy our talks with him — he is so direct and honest, so keen to 'make good', whether as party manager or as Foreign Secretary . . . Henderson does not know what may be the P.M.'s intentions, whether he is going to make terms with the Liberals; if so, whether he is going to remodel his Cabinet, whether he desires to give up the leadership and go to the House of Lords as Foreign Secretary, leaving Henderson in his place as P.M., or whether he wants Henderson to go to the Lords; whether he wants a general election or not, and if he were beaten, whether he would retire from leading the party; or whether he is going to sit tight and leave others to turn him out. Altogether J.R.M. either hides his real intentions or alters them from day to day — the latter seems to Henderson the more probable. . . .

14 December. [Passfield Corner]
Sidney came back from London depressed. 'People will say', he sadly observed, 'that your husband has not been a success as a

233

Minister.' The P.M. is cross about Palestine: the Shaw Commission and Hope Simpson, with his Report, both nominees of Sidney's, have been too pro-Arab. A White Paper, which the P.M. saw and approved, was 'tactless' – indeed he allowed Lloyd George, in his virulent attack on the White Paper, to assert that 'the P.M. has not seen it', which was mean of MacDonald. . . . Sidney would like to retire, but as there must be two Secretaries of State in the Lords that would put MacDonald in a difficulty, and it would be taken as a victory for the Jews over the Arabs and might lead to trouble in Palestine. . . .

VOLUME 45

1931

Stafford Cripps (1889–1952), the son of Alfred and Theresa Cripps, was an outstandingly successful barrister. In the 30s he was expelled from the Labour Party for persistently supporting left-wing causes. His wartime missions to the Soviet Union and India were followed by his appointment as Chancellor of the Exchequer in 1947.

19 January. [Passfield Corner]
A bevy of nephews and nieces during the Xmas holidays. . . . Malcolm Muggeridge, Kitty's husband, stayed two days. He is the most intellectually stimulating and pleasant-mannered of all my 'in-laws'; under thirty years of age, ex-teacher in India and Egypt, now leader writer on the *Manchester Guardian* and playwright. His first play, *The Three Flats*, is to be acted by the Stage Society in February. An ugly, but attractive and expressive face, a clever and sympathetic talker, ultra-modern in his views on sex, theoretically more than practically I think. A great admirer of D.H. Lawrence and his 'return to nature' – 'animal emotion overflowing into the human brain and arousing the sense of beauty and abandonment to pure sexual delight'. Yet I think Malcolm is a mystic and even a puritan in his awareness of loyalties and human relationships. What is attractive about him . . . is the total absence of intellectual arrogance; partly because he has a keen sense of humour and an understanding of his own ignorance, also a knowledge of the world and a sense of proportion.

And now Stafford Cripps enters the political arena as Solicitor-General and the winner, by a huge majority, of the Bristol seat. Stafford is a convinced Christian of the Sankey brand: tall, good-looking, pleasant voice, an essentially modest and well-mannered man; but a first-rate advocate, in receipt of a large income. He is the only one of the 155 nephews and nieces who might become a big figure in public life. His one handicap is poor health.

22 January. [Passfield Corner]
My seventy-third birthday: a basket of flowers from the Soviet Ambassadress, a bunch of carnations and lilies from the Countess of Warwick, a few telegrams – one from Cynthia and Oswald Mosley. The trend of my reputation is clearly to the left and not to the right . . .

Sidney and I had an evening in our little flat with Laski; he is bubbling over with delight at his own importance, which takes the form of graphic and amusing stories, some true and others invented, about his dealings with the Zionists, especially the American Zionists, and with the Indians, in order to smooth the way of the Labour government. He is a devotee of Sankey's and has been used by the great man as an assistant negotiator running between various groups of Indians, Mohammedan and Hindu. The intimate talks he reports with 'Mac' (so he says he addresses him) about appointments and policy are, I think, 'imaginary conversations'; there was a curious hesitation as to whether they were at Downing Street or Chequers. But it is all very good fun; he is never malicious or mischievous, but the tales he tells, if they are not all true, are vivid anticipations of what might have happened. What I fear is that he is dissipating his power of thought in all these personal comings and goings, among personages of all sort and kinds so stimulating to his great fault – personal vanity. His appearance is just a trifle too smart for a professor of socialist opinions.

23 January. [Passfield Corner]
Considering how I had best use the few more weeks or months of loneliness. I had hoped to brood over the material for *Our Partnership* and deliver my soul of paragraphs or pages of the future work. But my Scheme of Reform has had sufficient *réclame* to bring requests for other contributions, and I am today at work on an article for the *Spectator*; also a suggestion from the B.B.C. that I

should give another broadcast. Clearly if the call comes I must continue work on the reorganization of our machinery of government – to be completed, when Sidney is free, in the form of a book. I want an eloquent and convincing introduction, a confession of faith in democracy, at any rate in Great Britain. I am not going to accept without protest the swing of the pendulum against personal freedom, more especially in its most essential aspect of freedom to think and to express your thoughts. The odd feature is that it is exactly the most anarchic minds, persons who have vehemently objected to any censorship of their own opinions or any interference with their own freedom of action . . . who are now advocating creed dictatorship as the only way out of our difficulties. Their argument – and it is a strong one – is that assuming you desire, as I certainly do, to sweep away the evil of class inequality in social well-being between man and man, or rather between a minority of wealthy men and multitudes of poor ones, you will never do this through a political democracy but only through a dictatorship of fanatical believers in equality who will tolerate no resistance to complete conformity with their creed. I do not as yet believe that counsel of despair. . . .

2 February. [Passfield Corner]
I started today on the first page of *Our Partnership*. I shall not take this venture so seriously as I did *My Apprenticeship*. That was a terrific labour, an agony of mind . . . Sometimes I cursed myself for becoming entangled in the self-conscious 'scribblings of a woman' (as Sidney once called the diary), and wondered how I could get out of printing it after letting it be known that I had been working on it for some time. The event proved, as it usually does, that neither inflated expectations nor neurotic forebodings are justified; the book had a *succès d'estime* but not a popular success, and my profit on the publication of these two years' effort, deducting the cost of the secretary, was a few hundred pounds – certainly not a livelihood for the author. . . .

Snowden, now faced with a Budget deficit, was in the impossible position of trying to solve the problem in such a way as to pass the House of Commons and please his own party. The Conservatives had tabled a motion censuring the government for its 'policy of continuous addition to the public expenditure', and the Liberals called for an independent committee of inquiry. After a dramatic speech by Snowden on 11 February the House agreed to such a committee, to be

236

headed by Sir George May (1871–1946), the former secretary of the Prudential Assurance Company.

4 February. [Passfield Corner]

'I should not like to say it to anyone else,' Sidney observed last Thursday morning, 'but I wish we had been defeated last night.' This is partly due to being tired of his job, but it also arises from the lack of any kind of plan in the Labour government's treatment of the unemployed – just a drift towards more doles in the autumn of 1929, and then a reaction against this liberality in 1931. The proposed curtailment of unemployed benefit, which Sidney says is contemplated by the Prime Minister and the Chancellor of the Exchequer, will complete the disintegration of the Labour Party. The time seems to me to be coming very near when Great Britain, Germany, Australia and any other capitalized country will be compelled to repudiate a large part of its debts, internal or external, or to lower its standard of civilization for the whole of the people; governments will also have to decide which discipline is to be enforced – the whip of starvation for the manual workers or the communistic discipline applied to all sections of the inhabitants equally. We in Great Britain are trying to do without either form of discipline; the U.S.A. is verging on starving and terrorizing the poor; and Soviet Russia is enforcing with great brutality the subordination of all to the common will, expressed in a general plan for the enrichment of the whole country . . . Ramsay MacDonald and Snowden and many other Labour Front Bench men, in their heart of hearts, do not wish a *change in policy.* It is an absurdity that the Labour Party, as at present constituted, should be in power . . . In home affairs the Labour Party has no policy; it has completely lost its bearings.

What I am beginning to doubt is the 'inevitability of gradualness' – or even the practicability of gradualness, in the transition from a capitalist to an equalitarian civilization. Anyway, no leader in our country has thought out *how to make the transition* without upsetting the apple cart. Sidney says 'it will make itself', without an acknowledged plan accepted by one party in the state and denounced by the other. We shall slip into the equalitarian state as we did into political democracy – by each party (whether nominally socialist or anti-socialist) taking steps in the direction of curtailing the tribute of rent and interest and increasing the amount and security of

237

revenue of labour. But this cannot be done without transferring the *control* of the savings of the country, and I don't see how that is to be done gradually, or without a terrific struggle on clearly thought out lines. And no one is doing the thinking. So we shall just drift on into some sort of disaster, as we did into the Great War. . . .

12 February. [Passfield Corner]
Snowden's speech in answer to the Conservative vote of censure bore out the previous description of his attitude – the end of it was cheered by the Tories and received in deadly silence by the Labour back benchers. The long continued conversations of the Prime Minister and other Labour leaders with Lloyd George and his group of followers, in and out of the House of Commons, looks like a definite concordat against the Left. The likelihood of the government being turned out by their own followers, supported by the Tories, is growing greater every day. When we visited the Snowdens the other afternoon, Ethel said they did not intend to fight another election and intimated that Philip would go to the Lords, which Sidney welcomed as enabling him to drop out, if the government goes on. But Sidney still thinks they will be out before the end of the session . . .

Another 'Hungry 30s and 40s' will not end in a fiasco for the working class as it did in the last century; it will end in a social revolution, and I think eventually in the Communist direction . . . If we were twenty years younger we should be drawing up a constitution for the rebels – more likely our ashes will be buried under the roots of the ash tree which I love to look at in its winter leafless tracing out of our study window.

What troubles me is not the impoverishment of the minority of property owners, but how far liberty and equality are compatible with each other? Under the capitalistic system the property owner has liberty to do what he likes and the workers have not – even the amount of personal freedom given by what is called the dole is not practicable for long periods. Under Russian Communism everyone has to obey orders, and yet with increase in productivity it ought to be possible to give to all complete personal freedom over the larger part of their time and their energy, as well as plenty of opportunities to enjoy the nobler pleasures of life. The present dilemma – the more produced, the poorer the community becomes – is a tragic absurdity, as absurd, though not quite so tragic, as the Great War. . . .

Only Russia is hopeful. But even here the hopefulness seems hysterical, and based on a fanatical faith in a coming salvation. The present state of things in Russia is at best purgatory – some would say Hell. Compared with the outlook of the 90s, how sad and how exciting. We seem to be living through a social earthquake out here, there and everywhere.

Only four Labour M.P.s followed Mosley into his New Party, which was soon transformed into the British Union of Fascists. Lord Beaverbrook (1879–1964), owner of the *Daily Express*, and Lord Rothermere (1868–1940), owner of the *Daily Mail*, had started a scheme for 'Empire Free Trade', which was a remodelled version of Joseph Chamberlain's notion of Imperial Preference. They ran candidates against official Conservatives with little success.

25 February. [Passfield Corner]
An amazing act of arrogance, Oswald Mosley's melodramatic defection from the Labour Party, slamming the door with a bang to resound throughout the political world. His one remaining chance is to become the He-man of the newspaper lords in their campaign against Baldwin's leadership of the Conservative Party. But Mosley's egotism would presently clash with Beaverbrook's and they would part company. As an orator, as a platform performer in a political circus, he would be pre-eminent. A foreign journalist at the Labour Party conference nicknamed him 'the English Hitler'. But the British electorate would not stand a Hitler. Mosley has bad health, a slight intelligence and an unstable character. I doubt whether he has the tenacity of a Hitler. He also lacks genuine fanaticism. Deep down in his heart he is a cynic. He will be beaten and retire. In the chaos of our political life today, there will be many meteors passing through the firmament. There is still Winston Churchill to be accounted for. Have there ever been so many political personages on the loose? Mosley's sensational exit will matter supremely to himself and his half-dozen followers but very little to the Labour Party . . .

A National Policy was an enlarged version of the Mosley memorandum on unemployment which had been rejected by the Cabinet. Dr Forgan was Labour M.P. for West Renfrew; Oliver Baldwin (1876–1947), son of the Tory leader, was also a Labour M.P.; unlike Forgan and Baldwin, W.J. Brown (1894–1960) did not rejoin the Labour Party when Mosley's drift towards fascism drove his left-wing supporters to leave him.

1 March. [Passfield Corner]

The Mosley manifesto is an able document; its argument in favour of a general plan, and there is much reason for it, is well done. But its proposals are as grandiose as they are vague. From the standpoint of propaganda it is a failure; it falls dead in the no-man's-land between those who wish to keep and those who wish to change the existing order. . . . The Mosley episode is another instance of a little knot of *clever* and inexperienced young men talking themselves into an impossible project – exactly like Mellor, Cole and Co. did about Guild Socialism. The 'New Party' is another bubble on the surface of political life . . . I regret the loss of Mosley – he was the only orator in the labour movement, except MacDonald. But I am afraid he has slammed the door behind him, and not even Uncle Arthur will be able to let him in again, not even as a prodigal son! Except that it means the loss of five seats, the other resignations – John Strachey, Dr Forgan, Oliver Baldwin, W.J. Brown and Cynthia [Mosley] – are of no importance to the labour movement. The New Party will never get born alive; it will be a political abortion. . . .

The resignation of C.P. Trevelyan on 2 March was the herald of a more far-reaching split which led the I.L.P. to disaffiliate from the Labour Party in July 1932 and become a dwindling party of pacifist and anti-Communist leftists. In 1930 MacDonald resigned his membership of the I.L.P., which he had held since 1894.

5 March. [Passfield Corner]

C.P. Trevelyan's resignation – timed to do the maximum damage to the leadership of the Labour Party – is otherwise of little account. He and his wife, owing to a certain meanness, financial and otherwise, are very unpopular politically and socially in the Labour Party. To me Molly Trevelyan is an odious woman, but I feel that to be a biased opinion, for she has always disliked me – long before I disliked her. The Trevelyans, now that they have great wealth and a big estate to manage, are no longer interested in politics . . . C.P. Trevelyan, it is stated, will take his seat with the I.L.P. group; he is a bitter critic of the Prime Minister and his entourage and was at one time a runner-up for the leadership against J.R.M.

D.N. Pritt (1887–1972) was a prominent barrister who defended the Soviet

Above: Labour Government, 1924. *From left, standing:* C.P. Trevelyan, Stephen Walsh, Thomson, Chelmsford, Sidney Webb, Sydney Olivier, John Wheatley, Noel Buxton, F.W. Jowett, Josiah Wedgwood, Vernon Hartshorn, Tom Shaw; *seated:* Willie Anderson, Parmoor, Philip Snowden, Haldane, Ramsay MacDonald, J.R. Clynes, J.H. Thomas, Arthur Henderson. *Below:* National Government Cabinet, 1931. *From left, standing:* Sir P. Cunliffe-Lister, J.H. Thomas, Reading, Neville Chamberlain, Samuel Hoare; *seated:* Philip Snowden, Stanley Baldwin, Ramsay MacDonald, Herbert Samuel, Sankey.

Left: Lord Passfield at 10 Downing Street, Budget Day, 14th April, 1930. *Below:* Kingsley Martin, 1940. *Bottom left:* Harold Laski, centre, 1927. *Bottom right:* William Beveridge and Jessie Mair, c. 1940

Facing page. Above left: Sir Oswald and Lady Cynthia Mosley, 1922. *Above right:* Sir Stafford Cripps and his wife, Isobel, 1939. *Below left:* Maynard Keynes and Lydia Lopokova. *Below right:* Philip and Ethel Snowden, 1929

Above left: Ellen Wilkinson, left, and Marion Phillips

Above: Margaret Bondfield and Ramsay MacDonald, 1929

Left: Susan Lawrence campaigning

Below: Herbert Morrison, 1922

Above: Grigori Sokolnikov, 1940

Above right: Ivan Maisky at the Russian Embassy, 1940

Right: Malcolm Muggeridge in Red Square

Below: Sidney Webb and Barbara Drake in Russia, 1934

Above left: Dora Russell

Above: Bertrand Russell and his third wife, Peter, 1945

Left: H.G. Wells and Moura Budberg at the Gargoyle Club, 1939

Below left: Odette Keun at Lou Pidou, Grasse

Below: Bernard and Charlotte Shaw, 1934

Beatrice
and her
sisters,
Kate, left,
and Rosie

PASSFIELD CORNER,
LIPHOOK,
HANTS.

ON THE THRESHOLD OF THEIR NINTH DECADE:

SIDNEY AND BEATRICE WEBB

AT HOME

SATURDAY, 12TH JUNE, 1937.   3 TO 7 P.M.

TO ALL THE DESCENDANTS OF RICHARD AND LAURENCINA POTTER,
TO THE THIRD AND FOURTH GENERATIONS, AND THEIR SPOUSES.

CARS COMING SOUTHWARD BY THE PORTSMOUTH ROAD, TURN SHARP RIGHT AT LIPHOOK
VILLAGE, BEFORE REACHING THE ANCHOR HOTEL; TAKING ROAD B 3004 FOR 2 MILES TO
PASSFIELD OAK HOTEL, WHERE TURN RIGHT, DOWN WINDING LANE FOR 200 YARDS TO
FIRST GATE ON RIGHT.

Above: Invitation
to the Potter
family party

Right: Beatrice and
Sidney with Sandy

Above right: The
Webbs and
Bernard Shaw at
Passfield

Sir William Nicholson's portrait of the Webbs, painted in 1928, which hangs in the Founders' Room at the L.S.E.

Photographs of Sidney and Beatrice Webb taken in 1941. The contemporary caption read 'Two Friends of the Soviet Union'

purge trials and was eventually expelled from the Labour Party as a Soviet apologist. The Fabian Research Department, led by the Coles, eventually fused with the Fabian Society proper to create an organization strong enough to survive and prosper through the Second World War.

8 March. [Passfield Corner]
. . . Sidney and I took part on 2 March in a House of Commons dinner given by Henderson (who was in bed and did not appear) but organized by G.D.H. Cole, to restart the Fabian Research Department with the help of Stafford Cripps and Pritt K.C., the two new lawyer arrivals in the Labour Party – 'loyal grousers', Cole called the new body, as distinguished from the seditious seceders. It was a very pleasant family party, and may lead to something. . . .

12 March. Hastings
Sidney went to see Philip Snowden, who is rather seriously ill with inflamed prostate, but who expects to recover in time to bring in the Budget. Snowden repeated that he was not going to fight another election and expected to go to the Lords before the end of the Labour government – an expectation which Sidney warmly encouraged, suggesting that Snowden should become Secretary of State for the Colonies, which would enable him (Sidney) to retire from office. Snowden acquiesced and they discussed together the time and manner of the reconstruction of the Cabinet which, if the government survives, would take place in June, July or August. For which I shall be honestly grateful. The episode has been an honourable and lucrative one, but we are both of us weary of our continued separation. There is one fear that haunts me: that Sidney may find the continuous monotony of studious life in the country, one day after another, deadening after all the varied interests and self-importance of high office, but he says not . . . Anyway, it is going to happen one way or the other – he still thinks by the Labour government going out of office this spring. Against this is the increasing friendliness of Lloyd George (Sidney met him calling on Snowden) with the Prime Minister and the Chancellor of the Exchequer, and the fractious state of the Conservative party. The internal dissension in the three parties, each party finding its bitterest enemies among its own members or *ci-devant* members, would be ludicrous if it were not a sinister symptom of the decadent disrupture of British public opinion, owing to lack of faith either in

the present order or in any consistent and comprehensive principles of reconstruction.

Joseph Stalin (1879–1953) had just launched the first Five Year Plan. It was a major factor in winning support from socialists disillusioned by the failure of social democracy to cope with economic collapse.

15 March. [Hastings]
. . . . If the Russian General Plan succeeds in proving to the world that production can be carried on successfully *without* the incentive of profit to the capitalist and the lash of starvation for the wage-earner, the lines will be drawn for either a great war against the dictatorship of the proletariat or the spread of Communist civilization by peaceful penetration throughout the political democracies of the world. That the barbaric Russia should lead the way to a new civilization is the most humiliating prospect for the cultured Frenchman, the scientific German and above all for 'God's English-man'.

19 March. [Passfield Corner]
My week at Hastings, whither I had taken the older of my two servants to recover from an illness, was spoilt by a domestic brawl at Passfield between the Olivers and the younger sister, due to Mrs Oliver's overbearing temper and Jean's neurotic temperament . . .

I have had, in my long career as mistress – before marriage, of many servants, since my marriage, of two – only three absolutely trustworthy servants, Neale and Mrs Thompson in Father's household, and Emily Wordley in my own. All these have earned, by their trustworthiness, annuities, and they richly deserved them! Skill and industry one can buy, but perfect honesty and absence of all deception is priceless, and should be rewarded long after the service is at an end. It is interesting but depressing how quite intelligent and otherwise well-conducted servants will carry on an illicit and gainful business – take a commission from a tradesman or send parcels home, for instance. They seem actually to enjoy the risks of it: it is a form of gambling, and they have no notion of the eventual loss of confidence and gratitude on the part of the mistress, not to mention their own peace of mind! However, there is a far higher level of honesty today than there was fifty years ago when I started housekeeping, largely because servants and mistresses are on far more equal terms. There is more friendship between them, and no decent person cheats a friend. Small deceptions and peculations are, like personal cleanliness, largely a question of class or degree of education. Petty theft is like having nits in the hair and leaving them there. . . .

27 March. Passfield Corner

I shall be glad when Sidney retires, as the lonely life down here, with the alternative of days and nights in London (equally lonely during the day, and with the discomforts of the little flat and the noise and bustle of the streets), are beginning to prey on my nerves, and might end in a bad breakdown. I am beginning to feel the *helplessness* of old age, which with me is masked by will-power and physical activity. To other people I seem in full possession of my faculties, but in my own consciousness I am depressed and dazed; memory fails me and I worry about this thing and that. . . .

Harold Nicolson (1886–1968) gave up his career in the diplomatic service and joined the *Evening Standard* in 1930. In March 1931 he joined Mosley's New Party and become editor of the party's journal, *Action*. He was married to the poet and novelist Vita Sackville-West (1892–1962). John Reith, later Lord Reith, was the founding Director General of the B.B.C.

1 April. [Passfield Corner]

Leonard and Virginia Woolf here for the week-end. Leonard a distinguished Jew — a saint with very considerable intelligence; a man without vanity or guile, wholly public-spirited, lacking perhaps in humour or brilliancy but original in thought and always interesting. She stands at the head of literary women, fastidiously intellectual with great literary artistry, a consummate craftsman. (She is beautiful to look at.) Coldly analytical, we felt she was observing us with a certain hostility; she is also extremely sensitive – apt, I think, to take offence at unintentional rudeness. Among their intimate friends are the Harold Nicolsons, the ex-diplomat and present broadcaster, to whose persiflage we always listen on Friday evenings. He is a convert to Mosley and one of his prospective candidates. Reith of the B.B.C. is another disciple. Apparently Mosley is convinced that he will sweep the constituencies and become Prime Minister in the near future, and is already choosing his Cabinet! Which argues megalomania. If he gets returned himself, he will be lucky. It is passing strange that so clever a man . . . should be so completely ignorant of British political democracy, of its loyalty and solid judgement, of its incurable dullness and slowness of apprehension of any new thought . . .

Virginia Woolf had met the Prime Minister at a small dinner of six persons, at which he seemed to be completely absorbed by Lady Londonderry. MacDonald's aloofness from his colleagues and open dislike and avoidance of all Labour M.P.s has become one of the standing jokes of British political life. It is he and not his sons and daughters who have banged the door of Downing Street and Chequers in the face of the Labour Party, which also largely accounts for the disgruntled state of the General Council of the T.U.C. and the bitter hostility of the I.L.P. They feel that J.R.M., after being raised by them to the position of Prime Minister – and it was the I.L.P. who made J.R.M. chairman of the Labour Party in 1923 and therefore Prime Minister in 1924 – has socially 'cut them' as well as betrayed the common faith. . . .

On 8 July 1930, Dora Russell gave birth to a daughter, Harriet. Although the father was a young American journalist, Griffin Barry, the child was registered in Russell's name, a subject of long legal controversy. Eventually the daughter changed her name by deed poll. Two years later Dora Russell had a son by Barry, and she was granted a divorce from Russell in 1935. He succeeded to the earldom in 1931 on the death of his brother, Frank.

21 April. [Passfield Corner]
Bertrand Russell, now an Earl, lunched here on Sunday to talk over his new role as a Labour peer. I had not asked his wife. But in the course of conversation he remarked, 'My wife was so sorry she could not come, but she has the infant to attend to.' I accepted the apology and turned the conversation. Now it was the advent of the baby, advertised by her to her friends as another man's child and accepted by him as not his own, which had decided me to withdraw as Dora's acquaintance . . . What interested me was the change in Bertrand; he looked wretched. I watched his expression and tried to describe it in words. Is it sheer disgust, a sort of savage resentment? He has lost the sardonic liveliness, the cheerful and witty cynicism of the first years of his marriage . . . Poor Bertie; he has made a miserable mess of his life and he knows it. He said drearily, when I asked him if he was going back to his old love – mathematical metaphysics – 'I am too old to write anything but pot-boilers'. . . .

The Olivers had been dismissed and a new resident gardener named Miles had been installed in the bungalow with his wife and daughters.

1 May. [Passfield Corner]
Finished the first chapter of *Our Partnership* on the trade union movement, and opened the second on municipal administration. Now that I have got over my domestic troubles and the beauty of the spring has arrived, with the birds singing from early morning to late in the evening, I am working better and enjoying life in my charming house. Also, I am looking forward to a happier autumn and winter, with Sidney by my side and a holiday abroad. . . .

Sidney had just written to MacDonald requesting permission to retire, certainly not later than October.

25 May. [Passfield Corner]
A happy Whitsun alone with Sidney, he helping me with the book – the part describing his administration of the Technical Education Board and the London School of Economics. He is quite pleased with my biography. The writing of this book I thoroughly enjoy; it is comparatively easy. . . . Finally, it interests and amuses me to look back over our life together; it heartens me to realize that we have had a jolly good time of it and turned out some useful work, and that, taken by and large, we have carried out our general plan of life, almost without being aware of it. . . . I think Sidney and I are as well as old persons can be – certainly Sidney is, and I am not far off that happy state. Every year or so I have to cut off a mile from the habitual walk . . . I feel less and less inclined to leave my home – but ill I am not, nor do I suffer pain. My one and only trouble is that I am always physically and mentally tired. Tiredness – irrespective of effort – is the specific disease of old age.

18 June. [Passfield Corner]
The Shaws here for a long week-end. GBS read us the first act of *Too True to be Good* – a fantasy or farce – on the thesis of the present chaotic state of morals and the futility of self-expression and self-indulgence. Amusing, suggestive, brilliant, but leading nowhere, a characteristic in itself representative of the present lack of purpose and consequent restless disgust with human nature. The Shaws continue to 'process' through life, enjoying their wealth and prestige. The one drawback – Charlotte dislikes Ayot and finds the servant

245

trouble 'intolerable'; has a permanent grudge against the lower orders for upsetting her plans and failing to consider her comfort. The Shaws suit each other and, like the Webbs, look as if they would go on indefinitely. . . .

Beveridge had bought a bungalow at Avebury in Wiltshire in August 1929. He was now completely absorbed in Jessie Mair's family.

1 July. [Passfield Corner]
Five crowded days in London, including a day and night with Beveridge and Mrs Mair, her daughter and two young medical men, in Beveridge's bungalow in Wiltshire. Beveridge has in fact annexed the Mair family, minus the husband and father; what has happened to this unhappy man no one cares or knows. Clearly the arrangement is to everyone's advantage so long as you ignore Mair's right to his wife's devotion; but has he any rights? That question ought to have been settled long ago; it is that ambiguity that is unpleasant.

13 July. [Beachy Head Hotel]
All Passion Spent, by Vita Sackville-West; an exquisite description of old age in the setting of the British governing class, a perfect piece of craftsmanship, a real literary gem.

Beachy Head — it must be twenty years since I stayed in this bungalow hotel. The last time, I remember, was when I had a serious breakdown over my squabbles with the majority of the Poor Law commissioners about my independent enquiries and the leakage in the Press as to the preparation and conclusions of the Minority Report. That was in 1907 or 1908, and Sidney went up to London to propitiate Lord George Hamilton, leaving me to recover my courage down here. Those peaceful days of peace and prosperity, when we looked forwards with confidence to the steady betterment of the people by establishing a national minimum of civilized life, a framework of prevention within which the capitalist organization of industry would be gradually transformed into collectivist ownership or control, and the grosser inequalities between one man and another would be gradually eliminated! Today we live on a crust that is perpetually breaking down, into what we do not know — Communism? Fascism? war? or economic chaos? Not only is there misery below but there is doubt and distrust in the upper circles, a lack of leadership . . .

The Italian-born Humbert Wolfe (1886–1940), poet, translator and civil servant, was well known for his tart witticisms. Ellen Wilkinson's relationship with the cartoonist and Labour M.P. J.F. Horrabin (1884–1962) ended with his marriage soon after this entry. She later had a complex attachment to Herbert Morrison. GBS went on a visit to Russia with Lord and Lady Astor on 18 July for two weeks. It provoked a sensation in the Press.

28 July. [Passfield Corner]
Ellen Wilkinson and Charlotte Shaw down here for the week-end. Ellen has been tamed politically by being the loyal parliamentary private secretary of Susan [Lawrence], and is full of affection and admiration for her chief. Humbert Wolfe, the reactionary official of the Labour Department, better known as a poet, is insolent in his remarks about the subserviency of his chief (Margaret Bondfield) to his influence and direction. About Susan Lawrence, he observed that she was a 'virago intacta', which was as witty as it was true. Susan and Margaret, I suggested, are the last of their class of celibate women in public life – a type of which there were many in my young days in the philanthropic world. . . .

On our long walk together Ellen asked me what I thought on these questions: was it reasonable to expect a woman in public life, who did not want to get married, to remain a celibate if she found a congenial friend who happened to have an uncongenial wife? I answered that I remained a puritan on such questions but that I was not dogmatically opposed to extra-matrimonial arrangements so long as they were not promiscuous, were founded on real companionship of heart and head, and also did not involve *cruelty* to others who had 'vested interests' of an emotional character. Ellen referred, I think, to her own relations with Horrabin. She is a strong, able and honest woman with a quick sense of humour and considerable intellectual power, and very self-sacrificing to her brothers and sister, who largely depend on her. I like her as a companion and respect her as a people's representative. But she has been hardened and a little coarsened by her life in Parliament, on the platform and in the Press. For good or for evil the political emancipation of women and their entry into public life has swept away the old requirement of chastity in the unmarried woman! The conventions (there is no code) are now the same for men and women.

Charlotte Shaw was in her usual beaming mood about the greatness of her great man; and brought batches of cuttings giving his paradoxical sayings and the universal homage of the Russian people. . . . Shaw's apparent wholesale approval of Russian Communism is a little discounted by his equally demonstrative admiration of Italian Fascism three years ago; their net conclusion being that what he admires is neither of their several social ideals (seeing that they are diametrically opposite, alike in economic principles and in metaphysical method), but their one common political constitution – the dictatorship of a creed oligarchy, a way of government that not only disfranchises but persecutes those who object, in Russia to Communism, in Italy to capitalism. However, as I am sympathetic to the social aim of Soviet Russia and hope that the General Plan will succeed, I shall listen to GBS's testimony after his ten days' inspection of show institutions, surrounded with admiring crowds, with interest, and a bias towards taking his account at its face value – very different from my intense irritation when listening to his praise of Fascism!

In mid-May the Kredit-anstalt Bank in Vienna failed and Germany's tottering credit was further shaken by the withdrawal of foreign funds; the German Chancellor and Foreign Minister, who visited London on 6 June, said they could not restore confidence unless they were relieved of the continuing burden of reparation payments. In the next few weeks MacDonald and Henderson were trying to get the French and Americans to agree, especially as the German crisis was having 'serious repercussions' in Britain, where the foreign reserves of the Bank of England were draining away. Sidney's report that MacDonald and Henderson were 'jolly and cordial' seems extraordinary, for there had been no agreement on helping Germany and Britain now faced a double crisis – of liquidity and confidence – which was intensified by the report of the committee that Snowden had set up in April, chaired by Sir George May, to propose economies in public expenditure. In July, the May Committee suggested a reduction of £96 million to be achieved by cuts in unemployment benefit, public works and payment of teachers, police and armed services. A Cabinet committee consisting of MacDonald, Henderson, Snowden, Thomas and Graham was set up to consider these proposals, to consider ways to reassure foreign investors and to ease the strain on sterling. A minority of the Cabinet resisted each suggested cut, and opposition to cuts in unemployment benefit began to grow in the labour movement. The situation worsened all through August.

4 August. [Passfield Corner]
Sidney reports that the Cabinet held immediately after the return of the P.M. and Foreign Secretary from Berlin was a very 'jolly and cordial' meeting. Henderson and Mac were well pleased with themselves and satisfied with the results of the visits. The plain truth is that, like GBS in Russia, they have been the centre of

admiring crowds, respectful great personages and a good Press. But the Cabinet is really in a very tight place. The Report of the Economy Committee appointed by Snowden, made up of five clever hard-faced representatives of capitalism and two dull trade unionists, is a sensational demand for economy in public expenditure, not merely cutting down what they consider 'doles' but also health and education services. Luxury hotels and luxury flats, Bond Street shopping, racing and high living in all its forms is to go unchecked; but the babies are not to have milk and the very poor are not to have homes. The private luxury of the rich is apparently not *wasteful expenditure*. A Cabinet committee has been appointed to consider it, and the matter will have to be dealt with during the first weeks of the October session. The best thing that can happen to the Labour government is that it should be defeated in its refusal to carry out the Report. But Snowden is responsible for appointing the committee. And he is really in agreement with the Report! . . . Sidney would like to be out of the government, not only because he is tired but also because he does not like to accept responsibility for a reactionary policy; he is inclined to think that Henderson will stop it and that the outside members of the Cabinet will back Henderson up against Snowden . . .

8 August. [Passfield Corner]
GBS spent two nights here and gave his pleasant chatty address on Russia to the Fabian summer school. He was tired and excited by his visit to Russia; carried away by the newness and the violence of the changes wrought. Here is tragedy – comedy – melodrama, all magnificently staged on a huge scale. It *must* be right! The paradox of the speech: the Russian Revolution was pure Fabianism – Lenin and Stalin had recognized the 'inevitability of gradualness'! Also they had given up 'workers' control' for the Webbs' conception of the threefold state – citizens, consumers and producers' organization. What is not Webbism or Western is the welding together of all three by a *creed* oligarchy of two million faithful, dominating a population of 120 million indifferent, lukewarm or actively hostile. That is the crux of the controversy between those who approve and disapprove of Soviet Russia. It is odd that it is this domination by a creed that seems so attractive to GBS; he being that great destroyer of existing codes, creeds and conventions, seems in his old age to hanker for some credo to be *enforced* from birth onwards on the

whole population. GBS owes his immense vogue – perhaps the greatest in the world today – not to wisdom or wit, but to his fascinating personality. In his old age he is a supreme charmer; appearance, voice, manner, gesture, outlook on other human beings, build up a perfect old man to be adored by the multitude.

18 August. 3 a.m. [Passfield Corner]
The Snowdens, who lunched here yesterday [Sunday, 16th August], were full of GBS's speech . . . 'It was a wickedly mischievous speech,' Philip muttered, whereupon they and we had a hot dispute over Sovietism, they denouncing it as a cruel slave state and we upholding it as a beneficent experiment in organizing production and consumption for the common good. It was significant of our completely different outlook on life. Without being conscious of it Philip Snowden has completely changed his attitude towards the organization of society . . . From being a fervent apostle of utopian socialism, thirty years of parliamentary life and ten years of Front-Bench politics have made him the upholder of the banker, the landed aristocrat and the Crown. . . .

The special Economy Committee reported to the whole Cabinet on 19 August and the meeting lasted nearly twelve hours. It discussed the balance between taxes and cuts in meeting the expected deficit, but it could not reach agreement on the reduction in unemployment benefit, which was to prove the sticking-point for most of the Cabinet. Without some such cut MacDonald could not secure Liberal and Tory support for an emergency package, or placate the foreign bankers whose support was needed to stop the run on the pound. The financial crisis was turning into a political crisis as well. After MacDonald had met the General Council of the T.U.C. and the Labour Party executive on 20 August, it was clear that he had to choose. He could try to save the pound at the cost of splitting his party; or he could preserve party unity by resigning, though his resignation might lead to a financial collapse before the Liberals and Tories could form a government. On Friday 22 August he had a private meeting with Neville Chamberlain (Baldwin was on holiday) and Herbert Samuel, who offered to serve in a temporary administration if it would make the necessary economies. MacDonald told the Cabinet of this meeting when it met on Saturday morning. One of the proposals was to raise funds by a special import tariff, but some of the Cabinet were obdurately anti-Protectionist.

22 August. 4 a.m. [Passfield Corner]
Sidney came back from the Cabinet meeting on August 20th – which had sat all day and was still sitting at seven o'clock when he left to catch his train – tired and depressed. He goes up this

morning for another long day of critical meetings. The financial plight of Great Britain, whether because of the incompetence of the governing class, political and industrial, or because of the mischievous depreciation of its resources by its enemies in other countries, or because of the inherent weakness of its financial industrial situation in 1931, is very serious, and certainly does not do credit to the Labour government in general or to Philip Snowden in particular. At any rate, the Budget of last spring looks now a fatuous device to save the present taxpayer at the cost of the future solvency of the country. Snowden was very ill at the time. But to think that none of his colleagues knew what the Budget was to be, or the facts on which it was based, or the arguments which induced Snowden to make such a Budget, until the day before its introduction! The only excuse for the Labour Cabinet is that no other group of men, whether politicians, businessmen or academic economists, whether Tory, Liberal or Labour, seem to understand the problem. No one knows either what the situation is or, assuming it is bad, the way out of it to sound finance. Even the fundamental facts of the situation are unknown. . . .

Sidney observes, sadly, that he would have resented being excluded from the consultations of the inner Cabinet about the financial position, if it were not that he feels that he knows no more than other people about the real situation of the British people in the world welter and he has no clear idea of the way out.

At the Cabinet it was suggested that the 'transitional class' [50,000 of the unemployed] should be struck off the dole and simply transferred to the Poor Law. Sidney stopped that by a vigorous protest. The free traders were beaten over the revenue tariff on manufactured goods – a humiliation for Philip Snowden. Yesterday Sidney did not go up for the 8.30 p.m. meeting held after the conference with the Opposition leaders – the T.U.C. and Labour Party executive. He is deliberately swinging rather loose from the Cabinet, as he wishes it to be understood that he is retiring on the first opportunity. If there were to be any resignations he would be among them. But he does not want to give any useless trouble to his colleagues. It might end in a coalition government, which would break up the Labour Party for many a long year. Anyway, it is a sorry end to the second Labour Cabinet . . . they will leave the state of England worse than it was when they took office. . . .

22 August. [Passfield Corner]

Sidney came back from London yesterday, after five hours of Cabinet meetings to receive reports of the interviews with Opposition leaders, the Labour Party executive and the General Council of the T.U.C. 'The General Council are pigs,' he said. 'They won't agree to any "cuts" of unemployment insurance benefits or salaries or wages. They are referring their conclusions to the T.U.C. meeting on 7 September. The Conservative leaders refuse to consider more than twenty-five per cent increased taxation, if that. The Cabinet is now unanimous against tariff; they stand on 50/50 in "cuts" and taxes, representing "equality of sacrifice". Parliament is to be summoned on 14 September; and the government expects to be defeated; and the Conservatives will take office. "No resignations," urged J.R.M., "and no general election till the Budget is balanced."'

But just as Sidney had finished telling me this, the phone rang up to tell him that there was to be a Cabinet at 9.30 today, so off he went by the 8.12 train this morning. He is serious about the financial situation. The bankers have let us in for it by their £150 million long-term credits to Germany. Whilst accepting short-term deposits of £200 million from other countries, the German credit cannot be withdrawn whilst the other countries are withdrawing their deposits, because British finance is not solvent! And the British people are not solvent because of the dole!

He thinks J.R.M. has behaved in all good faith over the whole business. The discredit of Great Britain abroad is said by other Labour leaders to be absurdly overdone; it is the result of the sabotage of British credit by the yellow Press to bring down the Labour government. The so-called 'governing class' has been deliberately and insistently pessimistic about the 'water-logged' condition of British money owing to the dole. What with the sabotage by the capitalists of Labour Cabinet administration and the sabotage of British industry by trade union pigheadedness, the prospect is extremely disturbing to public-spirited citizens. We have reached a state of hidden class war, conducted with good manners and tolerance of each other's opinions, resulting in a disastrous stalemate in industrial and social reconstruction. Both parties refuse to 'play the game'. Anything may happen. . . .

23 August. [Passfield Corner]

Sidney reported that at the Cabinet meeting yesterday morning the

Prime Minister stated that the Conservative and Liberal leaders refused to accept the Labour Cabinet proposals and demanded seventy-five per cent cuts, mainly of the dole, and twenty-five per cent taxes. The Cabinet refused to compromise to that extent, and the King was informed by telephone and decided to return to London from Balmoral. J.R.M. raised the question of a Coalition government, with some of the Labour Cabinet Ministers remaining in office. This, he intimated, was what the King desired and might propose. This proposal Henderson and other members hotly rejected. The impression left on Sidney's mind was that J.R.M., Snowden and Jimmy *might consider it*. 'A good riddance for the Labour Party,' I said. They rose at twelve o'clock, under the impression that it was settled that the P.M. would resign and Baldwin would take office. However, in the luncheon hour J.R.M. and Snowden met the Opposition leaders again and suggested another compromise (Sidney said that J.R.M. was not authorized to do it), which Chamberlain accepted, *assuming that the City agreed*. It was left to the Bank of England (vice-chairman) to consult the Federal [Reserve] Bank of U.S.A. whether they would back such a governmental policy, and their decision will be reported today (Sunday) when the Cabinet meets at seven o'clock.

So it is the financiers, British and American, who will settle the personnel and the policy of the British government. Sidney hopes that they will decide against the Labour Cabinet remaining in office, and hand over the government to their friends the Conservative and Liberal leaders. It certainly is a tragically comic situation that the financiers who have landed the British people in this gigantic muddle should decide who should bear the burden. The dictatorship of the capitalist with a vengeance! Henderson blames the P.M. for spending so much time in negotiation; he thinks it would have been far better to have settled really what the Labour Cabinet would be prepared to do in economies, and resign if it were rejected by the Opposition, assuming that it was not possible – owing to the action of the international financiers – to await the decision of the House of Commons on the 14th [September]. It seems that owing to the run on the banks by foreign financiers (*which has not been reported in the Press*), the policy had to be settled straight away; otherwise there would have to be a moratorium on Wednesday. Graham thinks that the City is bluffing the government. The Labour Cabinet ought to have stood up to the financiers. Let the Tories come in and stand the racket; and that is Sidney's opinion. The plain truth is that the Labour Prime Minister and Chancellor of the Exchequer, together with the ineffable Jimmy, are converted to the capitalist creed and would be quite contented to carry it out if the party would agree to let them!

If the Cabinet decides to break off negotiations with the Opposition these three might decide to join a Conservative government, which would leave the Labour Party free to reorganize on sterner lines. It is fortunate that the King does not like Henderson, which is another way of saying that Henderson does not 'kow-tow' to the Court. The royal family are as good as good can be in fulfilling their dreary functions. From the purely political point of view, for a commonwealth of free nations made up of innumerable races with diversified civilizations or absence of civilization, our constitutional monarchy is irreplaceable. But owing to its social prestige and its envelopment in London society, the Court is a shocking – I use the term deliberately in its double meaning – atmosphere for Labour politicians. It stimulates the unutterable snobbishness of the lower type of Labour representatives like Jimmy [Thomas], it wiles away the integrity of aesthetes like J.R.M., while it gobbles up *arrivistes* like Ethel Snowden and it even deteriorates decent folk like the Alexanders and Clynes. . . .

The problem is how to prevent the subtle disease of mental enfeeblement in the next Labour government. Can we grow a socialist faith, entailing rules of personal conduct for the faithful, without developing a group of self-righteous and self-centred cranks like the I.L.P., reiterating shibboleths and refusing to face facts?

24 August. 6.30 p.m. [Passfield Corner]
The Fall of the Labour government 1929–31. Just heard over the wireless what I wished to hear, that the Cabinet as a whole has resigned, J.R.M. accepting office as Prime Minister in order to form a National Emergency government including Tories and Liberals; it being also stated that Snowden, Thomas and alas! Sankey will take office under him. I regret Sankey, but I am glad the other three will disappear from the Labour world; they were rotten stuff, each one of them for different reasons. A startling sensation it will be for those faithful followers throughout the country who were unaware of J.R.M.'s and Snowden's gradual

conversion to the outlook of the City and London society. Thomas has never been a socialist and will probably cease, like other *ci-devant* trade union leaders, to be even formally on the side of the labour movement. So ends, ingloriously, the Labour Cabinet of 1929–31. A victory for the American and British financiers – a dangerous one, because it is an open declaration, without any disguise, of capitalist dictatorship, and a brutal defiance of the labour movement. The Third International will gloat over the 'treachery' of MacDonald, Snowden and Thomas . . .

Sidney, who is staying in London overnight, is, I assume, consulting with the other dissenting ex-Ministers with regard to the statement they will issue to the Press or make to the Wednesday meeting of the joint executives as to their reasons for refusing to accept the terms of the U.S.A. and British financiers, and thus co-operate with the two capitalist parties of Great Britain in putting the cost of the sins of capitalism on to the manual workers' livelihood. British credit may be temporarily saved but internal peace is jeopardized for many a long year . . .

The danger in front of the labour movement is its deep-seated belief that any addition, under any condition, to the income of wage-earners is a good thing of itself. That was why it was so fatal to start state-subsidized insurance; it was bound to end by becoming unconditional outdoor relief, and that 'addition' to the livelihood of the poor was certain to increase the area of unemployment. It is a most demoralizing form of voluntary idleness. Under capitalism the wage-earner's life is often so hard, and the wage-earner is so irresponsible, that idleness with a regular pittance is comparatively attractive to large bodies of men. They won't accept and won't keep work they don't particularly like and are not accustomed to – and when they do accept it, they are not over-keen to bestir them-selves. . . . That is the danger of the Labour government, and always will be, as far as I can see. The sins of capitalism become excuses for the sins of labour, and the sins of labour become the justification for the sins of capitalism. Politics become a question of reprisals, each party or class trying to damage the other, to sabotage each other's institutions. . . .

25 August. [Passfield Corner]
Sidney came back early in the afternoon of our second Fabian Garden Party. He was exhausted, and rather upset by the queer end

of the Labour Cabinet – but delighted to be out of it all. At the seven o'clock Sunday night Cabinet meeting, J.R.M. brought back an inconclusive answer from the U.S.A. and British financiers to the revised Cabinet scheme of economies, indicating that more cuts in the insurance benefit would be required to satisfy the U.S.A. financiers. Whereupon nine members of the Cabinet, headed by Henderson, revolted and stated that they would not go so far in cutting the dole *even as J.R.M. had done on their behalf.* Whereupon the Prime Minister left for Buckingham Palace and adjourned the Cabinet for twelve o'clock on Monday. At that meeting he announced that he had accepted a commission to form a National government. His colleagues listened with the usual English composure, Henderson intimating that discussion would be out of place; after which the meeting proceeded to wind up the formal business about documents etc.; passed unanimously a vote of thanks to the P.M., proposed by Sankey, and without further leave-taking left the Cabinet room. Whereupon Sidney joined up with Henderson and Lansbury and some six others, and went off to lunch at the Office of Works to discuss the situation. There was a certain relief that their association with MacDonald was at an end, and a very distinct opinion that he had meant to come out as Premier of a 'National' government all through those latter days of panic and confusion.

Whether MacDonald had already arranged with Snowden and Thomas some days ago no one knew, but it is assumed so. What is in doubt is whether MacDonald himself, and the Conservatives and Liberals with whom he negotiated, expected a considerable group of Labour members to follow him. If he or they did, they will be grievously disappointed. One of the good results of the National government under Mac is that it unites, as no other event could, the whole of the labour movement under Henderson in determined opposition to the policy of making the working class pay for the mistakes of the financiers. . . .

MacDonald had written to Sidney a characteristically opaque letter about the weakness of Labour representation in the House of Lords. At first the Webbs took it as a hint that MacDonald would take a peerage and let Henderson become leader of the Labour Party; they later took the guarded phrase as the first hint of a coalition.

27 August. [Passfield Corner]
Arnold reports that Lansbury told him that J.R.M. spoke to him

casually at the end of July after the issue of the May Report as to the desirability of a National government if the financial position became serious. Lansbury rejected the notion as impossible and J.R.M. dropped the question. By the light of this incident the P.M.'s letter to Sidney on 14 July, which puzzled us, seems to indicate some such solution, put forward tentatively. 'You may think I have been doing nothing,' he wrote, 'but as a matter of fact I have been working at it for week-end after week-end and am at a complete dead end. We have not the material in our party that we ought to have. The solution will have to come, I am afraid, by moves which will surprise you all. I am still working at it, however!' I don't believe that Mac deliberately led the Cabinet into a trap, tried to get them into agreeing to economies in the process of bargaining with the U.S.A. financiers [whilst] all the time intending to throw his colleagues over and form a National government – but he drifted into doing it, largely because he is secretive (he never can be frank), yet will let the cat out of the bag, in a moment of queer indiscretions, to someone who is a comparative stranger, like Sidney, or even an enemy like Lansbury. I trust the Labour Party is quit of him finally and completely, and I wish him well among the dukes and duchesses. . . .

2 September. [Passfield Corner]
A shock to public opinion, at home and abroad, is the swift, cold and practically unanimous repudiation of MacDonald, Snowden and Thomas by the entire Labour world. . . . How different from Joseph Chamberlain's break with the Liberal Party in 1886, carrying with him not only a group of distinguished M.P.s and the majority of Liberal peers, but a solid block of nine Liberal constituencies in the Midlands, which he kept to the end of his life! The last touch was put by the contemptuously silent 'showing of the door' to Thomas by the N.U.R. The Labour Party emerges stronger, far stronger and more united than they were three weeks ago.

This spitting out by the Labour Party of those they hated with a gesture of getting rid of some poisonous substance is, of course, partly due to the dramatic issue – are the sins of the capitalists to be borne by the mass of the workers? – and partly to the class consciousness of a political party based on the trade union movement. But it is also intimately bound up with MacDonald's aloofness from the Labour world. . . .

257

19 September. Malvern

Here for five days with the Shaws, attending the Gloucester Festival. My own suggestion, partly because I wanted to renew my memories of fifty years ago, partly because I enjoy the Shaws' company, and finally and principally to hear music direct, and not over the ether. I *did* enjoy the music but my brain whizzed and I was preoccupied with the catastrophic politics of today and tomorrow. . . . In the course of a decade we shall know whether American capitalism or Russian Communism yields the better life for the bulk of the people; whichever of these 'cultures' wins, we in Great Britain will have to follow suit. The position seems to me very similar to the struggle from the twelfth to the sixteenth centuries between Christianity and Mohammedanism for the soul of Europe. There was no third creed open to the civilized world of those days; they had to follow Christ or Mahomet.

Now in view of this conclusion, how shall we spend our old age? Am I strong enough to go to Russia so as to give vividness to any line we take? Can we master the intricacies of capitalist finance sufficiently to be able to expose its futility? For without doubt we are on the side of Russia. . . .

Henderson was called back to London to receive an urgent letter from MacDonald.

20 September. 3.30 a.m. [Passfield Corner]

The Hendersons came down on Tuesday night – he depressed and tired, sad at leaving the Foreign Office and not enjoying the worry and toil of leading the Labour Party and explaining the ambiguous attitude of late Ministers to economies. But, as always, Henderson is not rattled; he is not thinking of himself or J.R.M.'s tortuous ways, but of the country first and the party second. He dislikes and intensely resents the way in which J.R.M. (all the time intending a National government) led his colleagues into a 'cul-de-sac'; into accepting, provisionally, some of the terms of the enemy without having gained any equivalent concession. They were, in fact, first compromised and then dismissed. . . .

Henderson says that J.R.M. expected to take a hundred members of the Parliamentary Labour Party with him; he only took eight, excluding Snowden and Jimmy and his own son . . . No wonder the P.M.'s Liberal and Tory colleagues think that he has 'done' them and are trying to make fresh terms; the Liberals wanting a period of steady government without a tariff, and the Tories demanding a tariff as the only way of preventing the fall of sterling and the drain of gold with or without a general election. It looks like a big smash-up.

The new government had been formed to save the pound from collapse; its first significant act was to devalue the pound by cutting its link to gold.

23 September. [Passfield Corner]
When, on the Sunday afternoon, two ex-Cabinet Ministers and two ex-Under-Secretaries were discussing the probable character of the P.M.'s summons to Henderson to return to London, not one of them had the remotest inkling that the decision was 'to go off the gold standard'. The silly old Snowden had broadcast the day after the formation of the National government the horrors – the bankruptcy of all business, and death by starvation of the working class – implied by the 'loss of the pound'; no suggestion of giving up parity had been even mooted at any Cabinet meetings. The saving of the parity of the pound had been the very purpose of the negotiations with U.S.A. and France, the reason for ousting the Labour government and forming the National government. At the meeting with the T.U.C. Thomas and Mac had slobbered over the agony of 'going off gold', had vividly described the sudden and simultaneous disappearance of all luxuries and most necessities from the homes of the workers. And now, having dismissed the Labour government and exacted the 'economy' Budget and thrown the unemployed back on to Poor Law, the bankers advise the government to repudiate gold and go back to the prosperous pre-parity days of 1918–26. The plaudits of the Press on Monday and poor Snowden's second broadcast explaining that the whole difference between disaster and a 'new start for industry' lay in the fact that 'the Budget had been balanced' – a 'scrap of paper' which the Labour Cabinet was quite willing to provide – was a comic and humiliating exposure of the consummate trickery of the financial world, when it feels itself menaced either in profits or power. It is also, alas, not a very complimentary sidelight on the financial acumen of the Labour Cabinet, that not one of them saw through the little conspiracy of the City. And at the cost to taxpayers of some £10 millions by the way of the fruitless loan. But one step forward

has been secured. We know now the depth of the delusion that the financial world has either the knowledge or goodwill to guard the safety of the country over whose pecuniary interests they preside. They first make an appalling mess of their own business, involving their country in loss of money and prestige, and then by the most bare-faced dissimulation and political intrigue they throw out one Cabinet and put in their own nominees in order to recover the cost of their miscalculation, by hook or by crook, from the community as a whole. . . .

It so happened that on Monday afternoon we were engaged to visit the Maynard Keyneses, their car coming to take us the sixty miles to their country home: a ramshackle old farmhouse under Firle Beacon, with an old-world garden overlooking the Vale of Lewes, and the joy of the bare Downs rising up behind the farm buildings. A delightful setting for that charmer, Lopokova. Keynes, accompanied by Citrine . . . joined us before dinner in a great state of inward satisfaction at the fulfilment of his policy of a measure of inflation. Apparently he either knew or suspected the outcome of the crisis, for he said he assumed the announcement of going off the gold standard would come over the Sunday wireless. Another intimation that the Labour Cabinet had been kept in the dark. He had lunched with Winston, who said that he had never been in favour of the return to the gold standard; he had resisted it in 1926 and had been overborne by the City, backed up by Treasury officials. Keynes, of course, is enjoying a febrile self-complacency over the fulfilment of his prophecy in *The Economic Consequence of the Peace* . . .

We stayed up till twelve o'clock and left at nine the next morning, Sidney going up by train and I accompanying Citrine in his car . . . In London, we lunched with Beveridge, who heartily dislikes Keynes and regards him as a quack in economics. These two men are equally aloof from the common man, but they have little appreciation of each other; Keynes, the imaginative forecaster of events and speculator in ideas, his mind flashing into the future; Beveridge bound down to the past, a bureaucratic statistician, intent on keeping intact the inequality between the few who can govern and the many who must be governed, and believing in the productivity of the acquisitive instinct. The contrast is carried out in the women of their choice – the perfect artist Lopokova, with her delightfully sympathetic ways, and the hard-faced administrator and intriguer Mrs Mair – the Russian prima donna dancer and the Scottish businesswoman and social *arriviste*. Beveridge is beginning to suspect that I am a Bolshevist at heart, and therefore 'out of the picture'; but he still believes in the good sense and experience of 'the Other One', with his comfortable slogan of 'the inevitability of gradualness'.

Ernest Bevin (1881–1951), secretary of the Transport Workers 1921–40, was becoming the dominant figure in the trade union movement. He was Minister of Labour in Churchill's wartime Coalition and Foreign Secretary in the 1945 Labour government. William Jowitt (1885–1957) was a lawyer who became Lord Chancellor in 1945. The Australian economist Colin Clark (b.1905) ran as Labour candidate in 1929, 1931 and 1935 before returning to a distinguished career in Australia.

10 October. Scarborough

Dull, drab, disillusioned but *not* disunited is the impression I got of the Labour Party conference of 1931. There are few women among the eight hundred delegates; there is a marked absence of wives; there are numbers of pale and listless men in the conference; there is an uncanny absence of laughter and mutual chaff; there is no anger and very little sympathy with rebels – the I.L.P. were steam-rollered by two million to 200,000 out of the party. The Communists and their absurd little paper the *Daily Worker* are ignored. Henderson got a great reception; there was singularly little attempt to call the late Ministers on the platform to account, and little more than a silent contempt for J.R.M., Snowden and Jimmy. These apostates seemed to have no following in the conference. There was, of course, an opposition, a very powerful though silent opposition, at the conference in the Citrine–Bevin–T.U. element, but it was an opposition that has no intention of overtly opposing. The General Council is intent on carrying on its own alternative policy in the outside world, of industrial co-operation with employers, together with determined resistance to any lowering of the money income of the working class by cuts in dole or by the means test or reduction of wages. Thus this crisis, with its indirect lowering of the people's income, has not converted Citrine from his policy of co-operating with leaders of industry.

At headquarters (Prince of Wales Hotel). The scene has completely changed from the last conferences I attended – Margate 1927 and Brighton 1929. The smart set that surrounded MacDonald and gave the tone to headquarters — Thomson, the Mosleys, de la Warr, Jowitt, Usher, etc., have disappeared. Henderson's body-guard of intellectuals (Dalton, Noel-Baker, Laski, Colin Clark), together with the younger Labour Ministers (Morrison, Johnston and Susan Lawrence), are very much in evidence. The most notable newcomer — one who is already acclaimed *the future leader* — is Stafford Cripps. He moved among the younger men with ease and modesty, he is able and virtuous without personal vanity or airs of superiority, uncontaminated by 'society', a homely person, a distinguished intellectual and first-rate advocate, but not yet an artist like J.R.M. or Mosley. He is not to me, though he is my nephew, *personally* attractive. He has neither wit nor humour, neither subtlety nor artistry. But if he has sufficient physical vigour he will go far, because he has character as well as intellect; he is pious in the best sense. Isobel Cripps is a good sort, and they are a devoted couple, the very essence of good bourgeois virtues, un-worldliness and personal refinement. With all these younger men Uncle Arthur is on the best and most confidential terms. Whatever else is lacking, headquarters for the first time is a happy family. . . . What seems now to be the prevailing spirit among the new governing group of the Parliamentary Labour Party is a dour determination never again to undertake the government of the country as *the caretaker of the existing order of society* . . . It is amazing, this sense of relief at having got rid of these three men, spreading right through the Labour conference of 1931. The relief has almost cancelled the bitterness. . . .

The new Coalition government called an election on 27 October. As part of a strident campaign which included a scare that Post Office savings were in danger Snowden, in a broadcast of 17 October, attacked his former colleagues for 'Bolshevism run mad'. It won a sweeping victory. The Conservatives gained 200 seats and secured a total of 472; there were also 35 Simonite Liberals, 33 Liberals and 13 National Labour victories. The Labour Party was reduced to 46 M.P.s. Clement Attlee (1883–1967) was to become leader of the Labour Party and the victor in the equally astonishing Labour landslide in 1945.

28 October. [Passfield Corner]
. . . . Ponsonby and the Marleys and we two listened to the wireless from ten to two on Tuesday the 26th. Towards the end of the tale of Labour losses we became hilarious; the unfolding situation was so absurd! MacDonald, at once author, producer and

chief actor of this amazing political drama, had shown consummate art. He had been aided and abetted with acid malignity by Philip Snowden, a malignity which could only be accounted for by the return of his recent illness. The Parliamentary Labour Party had not been defeated but annihilated, largely, we think, by the women's vote.

On the Front Opposition Bench there will be only one ex-Cabinet Minister – George Lansbury, and only two ex-Ministers of rank – Stafford Cripps and Attlee, with one or two ex-Under-Secretaries and Household officers. This Parliament will last four or five years, and the Labour Party will be out of office for at least ten years. The capitalists will remain, for this fourth decade of the twentieth century, in complete and unchallenged control of Great Britain, as they are of the U.S.A., France and Italy. They will at any rate be held responsible for all that happens at home and abroad. Meanwhile the Labour movement may discover a philosophy, a policy and a code of personal conduct, all of which we lack today. The desertion of the three leaders was not the cause of our defeat; it was the final and most violent symptom of the disease from which the party was suffering. Future historians will point out that the Labour government of 1924 was hatched prematurely; it came into office through a political episode which had no connection with the labour movement, no relation to the fitness of the Parliamentary Labour Party to become either His Majesty's Opposition or His Majesty's government. That episode was Lloyd George's smashing of the Liberal Party in 1918. The Liberal Party *did* represent, in its policy and outlook, the anti-Conservative element in the country; and if it had not been for the Great War and for Lloyd George's post-war action, it would have continued to occupy the position, with the Labour Party as a left wing. Under MacDonald's leadership, 1906–14, the forty members of the Parliamentary Labour Party had never been more than a left wing made up of trade unionists, and not very left at that! As we knew, J.R.M. was willing, in 1911, to enter the anti-Asquith Cabinet that was being engineered by Lloyd George in league with Balfour, and he actually offered Henderson an under-secretaryship, which the latter indignantly refused. The Great War and the world upheaval brought the Labour Party on to the Front Opposition Bench and transformed it into a definitely socialist party. Two spells of office and the embrace of the old governing class converted the more prominent leaders into upholders of the existing order. Gradually becoming conscious of their leaders' lack of faith, the Parliamentary Labour Party rapidly disintegrated. The dramatic desertion of the three leaders on the eve of the battle turned a certain defeat into a rout. But it revealed a solid core of seven million stalwart Labour supporters, mostly convinced socialists. Whether new leaders will spring up with sufficient faith, will-power and knowledge to break through the tough and massive defence of British profit-making capitalism . . . I cannot foresee.

Have we the material in the British labour movement from which can be evolved something of the nature of a religious order, a congregation of the faithful who will also be skilful technicians in social reconstruction? What undid the two Labour governments was not merely their lack of knowledge and the will to apply what knowledge they had, but also their acceptance, as individuals, of the way of life of men of property and men of rank. It is a hard saying and one that condemns ourselves as well as others of the Labour government. *You cannot engineer an equalitarian state if you yourself are enjoying the pomp and circumstance of the city of the rich surrounded by the city of the poor.* If we are to continue to accept the existing social order in our own habit of life, it is safer and more wholesome that these institutions should be administered by men who believe in them, and who represent those who believe in them. The Labour Party leaders have shown that they have neither the faith, the code of conduct, nor the knowledge needed for the equalitarian state. . . .

Christmas Day. [Passfield Corner]
This day forty years ago I was at Box House. Father was dying and Kate and I were at his bedside watching the flickering out of his dear life. I had been privately engaged to Sidney for some months and I was awaiting the death of the dear one to tell my family that I was bound up in the vocation of continuous enquiry into social organization. A life, it proved to be, of extraordinary happiness and some success. 'I knew my little Bee would do well for herself,' I could hear dear Father saying, with his beaming smile, if he came back to see. For he had a good opinion of my business capacity and matter-of-fact judgement. Others of his daughters had greater personal charm and good looks – 'but for sheer common sense give me my little Bee,' he would have said. And I think he was right.

'Beatrice', once said Leonard Courtney to Kate, 'has great general capacity. She is not an intellectual. She merely applies this general capacity to certain problems of the intellect.' And that is exactly what I want to do about Russia. Those who think about Russia seem to me to become hysterical – they either see red with hatred or see mythical virtues in the new social order. . . .

For the next four months Sidney and I will be turning out a textbook on Methods of Social Study – a good part of it written years ago. But our main task will be preparing our mind for seeing as much of Russia as we can afford strength and money to see. My next diary book will, I hope, tell the tale of our adventures and give our verdict on *What we can learn from Russia*, by Sidney and Beatrice Webb.

PART III

The Promised Land

January 1932–December 1937

Introduction to Part III

IT WAS a devil's decade. The 30s began with world-wide depression and ended in world war. Capitalist democracy was crumbling everywhere and there was a widespread belief that its failure was irretrievable. Even to a progressive Tory like Harold Macmillan it seemed that 'the structure of capitalist society had broken down . . . the whole system had to be reassessed . . . Something like a revolutionary situation had developed, not only at home but overseas.' Everyone was looking for a way out of disillusionment and despair. Young people particularly, idealistic and eager for invigorating panaceas, were quick to turn to the 'creed autocracies' of Communism or Fascism which were emerging as alternative ways forward. It was an atmosphere in which new kinds of social organization could flourish, particularly state-controlled dictatorships. Extreme conditions spawned extreme remedies.

The Webbs were among the first people of political and intellectual standing to make a fresh start. Within weeks of the August crisis of 1931 Beatrice had concluded that the future could and should lie with Communism, and that for all its shortcomings the Soviet Union was the exemplar. Although this appeared to be a dramatic change, it was not altogether an illogical development of the Webbs' earlier ideas. Sidney, who had always been concerned with the *machinery* of government, saw in the Soviet constitution and government a more efficient form of social engineering than the haphazard ways of western democracy. Beatrice had always longed for a faith which would satisfy both her emotional needs and her intellectual belief in equality and justice. The combination of bureaucratic centralism with fanatical zeal persuaded them that Communism was indeed the beginning of the 'new civilization' for which they had always been searching.

For all that, Beatrice had many initial doubts. In 1920 when

Leonard Krassin spoke to the Fabian summer school, she was troubled by 'the insistent demand for the subordination of each individual to the working plan' and she was plainly affected by the criticisms of Bertrand Russell and others who had seen the Soviet system for themselves. She was distinctly hostile to the repeated Communist attempts to nobble the Labour Party. In 1927, in one of her regular letters to the Labour women of Seaham, she described the Russian revolution as 'the greatest misfortune in the history of the labour movement', saying that it was likely to set back 'the achievement of economic democracy in England for half a century'. But the experience of the two Labour governments made her ask whether gradualist socialism could ever reform a decaying capitalism; and whether for all its crude and obvious faults, the Soviet Union might in the end be the harbinger of a planned, prosperous and egalitarian society. One way of resolving these doubts and uncertainties was for the Webbs to visit the Soviet Union and see for themselves how the system worked. From the frequent entries in the diary, however, it is clear that the significant change in attitude had already taken place before the Webbs left for Russia – that their journey was merely the culminating event in a process of conversion which had already largely taken place.

As soon as the fall of the Labour government released Sidney from his ministerial duties and he could retire to a quiet country life at Passfield, the Webbs settled down to finish *Methods of Social Study* and prepare themselves for their Russian trip. They read a great deal in the months before they left on their two-month tour in the summer of 1932, and they took on a Russian-speaker to abstract and translate from the Soviet newspapers. One of the weaknesses in the preparation of their vast volume on *Soviet Communism* was their readiness to rely on Soviet official statistics, reports and publications, as if these were as valid as the blue-books and White Papers they bought at the Stationery Office in London; and they seem to have been equally credulous of what they were told by Soviet officials. Beatrice wanted to be fair-minded. When a Russian-speaking student from the L.S.E. visited them at Passfield, giving a 'distinctly adverse' account of the 'hardships' of life in Moscow, Beatrice wondered whether they should take her as an interpreter: 'She would spy out defects and shortcomings which we should not see in what will necessarily be a *managed* tour – managed by the Soviet government, owing to our old age, socialist prestige and ignorance of the language.' But she was uncomfortable when she had to face more damning evidence. She noted what she was told by Rhea Clyman, a Canadian journalist living in Moscow, who also went down to Passfield. Clyman had gone to Moscow with illusions she had soon lost. 'Now she loathes Russian Communism and all its works, and spent her time trying to "disabuse us",' Beatrice wrote, dismissing her as an 'unsavoury little mortal', and expressing surprise 'that the G.P.U. has not found her out and got rid of her'. What Clyman told the Webbs, in fact, was much the same tale as they were later told by Malcolm Muggeridge, who was similarly disillusioned when he went to Moscow as correspondent for the *Manchester Guardian*: near-starvation in the towns, appalling housing conditions, famine in the Ukraine as a result of forced collectivization, and workers bound to servile employment. In both cases Beatrice tried to shrug off these disagreeable reports by impugning the character of the witnesses.

The Webbs preferred more reassuring company at Passfield. They invited the Sokolnikovs, with whom they discussed the success of the first Five Year Plan for industrialization and the prospects for the second, which was now being drafted. The Coles came, to talk about a study tour of Russia by a group from the New Fabian Research group: 'It will be an ironic development,' Beatrice noted, 'if the highly respectable Fabian Society, the upper chamber of the labour and socialist movement, becomes the protagonist of Soviet Communism in Great Britain.' Her wealthy old friend H.D. Harben, who had just financed four Communist candidates at the recent election, was there too, telling her his high opinion of the Soviet Union. So, in the next few weeks, were Dr Meyendorf, a sympathetic exile who taught at the L.S.E.; Prince Mirsky, who taught at the School of Slavonic Studies and was so well disposed towards his homeland's new rulers that he returned there – to disappear in the purges; Harold Laski, 'calmly satisfied that a modified Communism is the right way to human progress'; and Michael Farliman, a mysterious figure whom Beatrice thought had some kind of clandestine connection with the Moscow regime he eulogized, though he, too, was to be a victim of Stalin's purges. Despite the few discordant notes – R.H. Tawney, for instance, had tempered his conversion to 'the equalitarian state in practice as well as in theory' by criticizing 'the absence of personal freedom' – Beatrice was becoming convinced that the principles underlying the

Soviet state were right, and that its deficiencies were due to the backwardness of the country.

The sense that an answer to a lifelong quest might at last be in sight runs through the tentative conclusions about Russia which the Webbs jotted down on 17 May, when their departure was delayed for a week by ice in the Gulf of Finland. Like Shaw, who had visited Russia in 1931, they decided that the country was organized on more or less Webbian lines – ostensibly, at least, and with due allowance for the distortions imposed by Russian circumstances. It had political democracy, operating indirectly through the hierarchy of Soviets; vocational democracy, expressed in the analogous hierarchy of the trade unions; and consumers' democracy, exemplified by the hierarchy of co-operatives; and all three systems were bound together by the 'religious order' of the Communist Party. It had 'a creed, a discipline and a code of conduct' which permeated the whole of Soviet society, and which contrasted with 'the catastrophic failure of the motive of pecuniary self-interest' in the depression-ridden capitalist countries. In a few sentences, before the Webbs set out for Russia, they had summarized the immense book they were to write on their return.

On 21 May 1932 the Shaws and some Soviet officials went down to the Pool of London to see the Webbs sail from Hay's Wharf in the Russian steamer *Smolny*. 'The accommodation is clean and comfortable,' Beatrice wrote in the notes she and Sidney later compiled from diary entries and their joint reminiscences. 'There is little service and some of the usual furniture is missing. No chamber-pots and pans, no hot water. . . .' At the end of the voyage, in fact, she listed these and other deficiencies – pork served to Jewish passengers on Saturday, no drinking water at table, 'handles of doors hard for delicate hands' – in a three-thousand-word memorandum to the captain, who was 'very grateful'. All the same, everybody was 'jolly and friendly'; there were such diversions as a political rally for the passengers, a meeting of the ship's Soviet (on which Sidney made detailed notes), a farewell concert, and gossip with members of the Intourist package tours: Russian Jews returning from America to settle in the Siberian 'homeland of Biro-Bizhan' and 'a miscellaneous lot of cranks . . . come to see the Russian show'. When the vessel docked at Leningrad there was an impressive ceremony of welcome for the Webbs, who were always being reminded that Lenin had translated their history of trade unionism; and then they were whisked off to the Hotel Astoria before catching the night express to Moscow. 'We seem to be a new type of royalty,' Beatrice said to Sidney, as they were shown into 'two comfortable sleepers, with a lavatory between the two'.

The account of the two-month visit does not form part of Beatrice's personal diary, for the original notes on which she based her typewritten report are missing. There is a black exercise book of the usual kind, in which 'Russian Tour: 10s. reward for return if lost' is written on the inside cover, and Beatrice had pasted in sixteen headings, one to a page, as if she intended to collect appropriate information. But she left most of the book blank, except for a few jottings by Sidney. Even his entries are surprisingly scrappy, and they give the impression that the ageing Webbs (their combined age, Beatrice noted, was now 147) were finding the round of visits and interviews a strain. By the end, Beatrice was too ill to do anything but rest and chat to her guide-interpreter, Mrs Tobinson, and when they returned to Leningrad on 8 July, Sidney scratched a few weary words. 'Too exhausted for much more enquiry,' he wrote, 'or even sightseeing.'

From all the evidence, indeed, it seems that this was very much the 'managed' tour that Beatrice had anticipated. The Webbs were certainly treated more deferentially than the run of Intourist parties and foreign delegations, were housed more comfortably and welcomed by more senior officials, but they were taken on much the same round of schools, clinics, factories, farms and construction projects to the accompaniment of the same routine propaganda. Sidney's notes suggest that they tried hard to get at the facts, but even such experienced investigators as the Webbs were not accustomed to guided tours and the practised defensiveness of Communist officials. Though they seemed to have been aware that they were seeing a carefully tailored version of Soviet reality, their eager interest made them naive if not completely gullible. After they had been to a new elementary school, for instance, Beatrice remarked that it was 'evidently a show-place', and then was sufficiently carried away to tell the children 'that they must make the Russian socialist state a success so that we might imitate them, whereupon they all cheered enthusiastically'. Taken to Autostroy, the unfinished Ford-style plant at Nijni-Novgorod, which Sidney described as 'the outstanding failure' of the industrialization drive, they were perturbed by the chaos and incompetence – but cheered

273

up when they saw a newspaper report which claimed that a number of completed cars had been driven to Moscow. Sidney, touring the Ukraine on his own after Beatrice had been taken ill in Rostov-on-Don, visited the huge state farm at Verblud, where over eight thousand people lived, another agricultural complex called Gigant, and the Seattle commune founded by American enthusiasts: his only comment on the rural disaster caused by forced collectivization was a cryptic note about Stalin's policy 'incidentally liquidating the kulaks'.

After a few days in Moscow, where Beatrice thought the hygiene of the schools and clinics 'far above anything we have in Great Britain', she concluded that 'the infant, the child and the adolescent are having a fine old time, physically and mentally, and the spirit of social service and energetic activity is really stupendous.' For the first time she used the phrase that was to characterize her positive though reluctantly qualified opinion of the Soviet Union. 'A new civilization, with a new metaphysic and a new rule of conduct, is growing up. But it is a crude one, suffering from various infantile diseases.'

It was the diseases of age that were more immediately troubling. As the Webbs travelled down the Volga on the river steamer that took them to Stalingrad, making use of the stops at Kazan, Samara and Saratov to interview the municipal authorities, they both began to feel tired and rather poorly. They thought well of Stalingrad and went on to Rostov, where Beatrice collapsed with such a severe bout of what Dr Kogan called 'stomach fever' (chronic colitis) that she was shipped off to Kislovosk, a spa in the Caucasus, and spent ten convalescent days there before meeting Sidney in Moscow to begin the slow journey home. Though her account of their tour petered out at this point, Sidney filled his notebook with odds and ends of detail – about the great dam at Dnieperstroy, the cities of Kharkov and Kiev, and the farms and other institutions to which he was taken by his tour guide, W.B. Rakov, a former German prisoner-of-war who had been converted to Communism and spent a spell working for the Comintern before joining the staff of the Soviet Foreign Office. Beatrice felt sorry for Mrs Tobinson, a Polish-American who talked freely about her marital troubles, but neither she nor Sidney liked Rakov. And by mid-July they were both saturated with talk, conflicting impressions, the discomforts of travel and the erratic diet. For all the excitement of a tour which had a lasting effect on both the Webbs, and for all their enthusiasm for a society which seemed to embody so many of their own aspirations, they were glad to be returning to the domestic comforts of Passfield Corner. Once home, on 28 July, Beatrice made a long diary entry to sum up their 'conclusions about Soviet Russia and its relation to the world we live in'.

> Our first conclusion is that the Soviet government is perhaps the most firmly established government in the world and the least likely to be radically altered in the next few decades. . . . Secondly, Soviet Russia represents a new civilization and a new culture with a new outlook on life, involving a new pattern of behaviour alike in personal conduct and in the relation of the individual to the community; all of which I believe is destined to spread, owing to its superior intellectual and ethical fitness, to many other countries in the course of the next hundred years. Thirdly, Russian Communism is still immature: the plan is superior to the execution; the theory to the practice. For the raw material – the amazing mixture of races, religions and stages of social development, spread over an immense area – is very raw indeed . . . of low-grade intellect and character. Owing to this initial backwardness, some features of Soviet Russia will be and remain repulsive to more developed races. . . . I doubt whether Soviet Russia will be, for the next twenty years, a sufficiently attractive exemplar to be chosen deliberately as a model.

While she was in Moscow Beatrice had been particularly impressed by a nine-day conference of the Comsomol youth organization. She noted that there was 'singularly little spooning in the Parks of Rest and Culture', that 'European dancing is taboo', that 'promiscuity is banned by the Communist Conscience', that sports and all kinds of physical exercise were much favoured, and that alcohol, tobacco and betting were considered 'bad form'. 'The Communist discipline', she remarked, in a tone that showed her general approval for such an earnest creed, 'is in fact an almost terrifying puritanism in its subordination of man's appetites to his reason and moral purpose: a puritanism which may bring with it, among the baser sort, hypocrisy and a hiding-up of furtive vice, and which certainly leads to a lack of humour and a self-assertive priggishness. . . . But as a method of lifting the people of Russia out of the dirt, disease, apathy,

275

superstition, illiteracy, thievery and brutishness of pre-revolutionary days, the self-governing democracy of 2½ million Comsomol youth appears to be magnificently effective.'

For the rest of her life Beatrice was to watch the Soviet Union with desperate hope, as the one beacon in a darkening world of Fascism and war; and yet, at this moment of conversion, she ended with reservations. 'There is of course in our vision of Russia a dark side, which we personally had little opportunity of observing,' she noted, 'but which, according to all the available evidence, is present everywhere and at all times . . . the occasional physical terrorism; the trap-door disappearance of unwanted personalities; the harrying and back-biting, the purging out of office and power of upright but indiscreet citizens. All this breeds an atmosphere of suspicion and fear. . . . ' Her uncertainties led her to the set of questions which she and Sidney tried to answer in *Soviet Communism* – and which troubled her, on and off, whenever she let her intellect challenge what was essentially an emotional commitment.

> The question is: how far can you disentangle what is good in Russian Communism from what is bad? How far can you single out the expedients which can be usefully applied in other countries, and reject those which are either wholly evil, or which, at any rate, are only needful in Russia and among other primitive races? Can you take the economic organization of Soviet Russia and reject the 'dictatorship' of a creed or caste? Can you have the fervour of the Communist Party without its fanaticism, the free and active service of the young generation, without the repression of heresy among adult citizens?
>
> These are the sorts of problems which have to be solved by those who wish to supersede, in their own country, capitalist profit-making by the equalitarian production, distribution and exchange of the wealth of the nation.

The conversion of the Webbs to Soviet Communism was an endorsement that won members for the Communist Party and influenced a much wider circle of 'fellow travellers'. And as the trend to state control of depression-ravaged countries continued, their arguments appeared all the more telling. In January 1933 Hitler came to power with promises to restore inflation-ruined Germany. At the same time Franklin Roosevelt became President, pledged to a New Deal for America. In England, the slump which pushed unemployment to unprecedented peaks had produced a reactionary National government and increased class conflict. The Labour Party swung to the left, and social problems broke into the theatre and publishing. In 1935 Allen Lane started Penguin Books and hugely enlarged the reading public. Marxist and neo-Marxist pamphleteers flourished, especially in the astonishingly successful Left Book Club which Victor Gollancz launched in May 1936 to support the Communist-inspired Popular Front movement against war and Fascism. Within a year it had recruited 50,000 members.

Yet for all the new ideas and the alarming political events which provoked them, the Labour Party found it difficult to give any clear-cut alternative leadership. It took years to recover from the blow of MacDonald's defection and the election disaster which removed the able young men and left the leadership temporarily in the hands of the pacifist George Lansbury (though Arthur Henderson stayed on as secretary until 1934, he was preoccupied with disarmament problems at Geneva). In July 1932 the I.L.P. disaffiliated from the Labour Party; its role as a focus of left-wing rebellion was taken by the Socialist League, whose leading spirit was Beatrice's nephew, the successful lawyer Stafford Cripps. Cripps argued vigorously for a united front against Fascism as well as a more forthright socialist programme. But these policies, which had pacifist overtones, brought a new source of conflict, for they were strongly opposed by trade unionists such as Ernest Bevin and moderate Labour men like Herbert Morrison and Hugh Dalton. The Labour Party was thus in no state to make much headway when Baldwin called an election on 14 November 1935. By this time the National government was predominantly Conservative. Baldwin had taken over from MacDonald in a reshuffle in June 1935, and Neville Chamberlain at the Treasury was becoming the most powerful figure in the Cabinet.

Foreign affairs and questions of armament and disarmament dominated the election and distracted attention from intractable domestic problems. Enthusiasm for a League of Nations and disarmament jostled confusingly with the desire for collective security. Everyone wanted peace but was reluctantly having to acknowledge the likelihood of war. In April 1935 Hitler had repudiated the disarmament clauses of the Treaty of Versailles and restored conscription in Germany, and in October Mussolini invaded Abyssinia. In these anxious circumstances the British public was in no mood for a change of government, and the best the Labour Party could do was to recover much of its vote and increase its seats from 46 to 154. This election was Lloyd George's last attempt to return to power, but the Liberals had only put forward 156 candidates and their numbers fell from 26 to 17. The Conservatives, with 387 seats compared with 454 before dissolution, were still left with a majority of 247 over the Opposition. Ramsay MacDonald was among those who lost their seats but another was found for him and he remained in the government until Neville Chamberlain took over from Baldwin in May 1937. And with the new Parliament the Labour Party found a new leader, Clement Attlee, who served as a unifying force in the years ahead.

There was no honeymoon period for the government. Its tone was set from the beginning with the death of King George V on 20 January 1936. Edward VIII was now king. A new era had begun and events moved quickly. On 7 March German troops marched into the Rhineland. On 2 May Mussolini proclaimed victory in Abyssinia. In July civil war broke out in Spain. The Baldwin government, hovering between a feeling that world war was coming and a reluctance to face the political and financial consequences in domestic politics, equivocated; in any case, as the year advanced Baldwin was preoccupied with the constitutional crisis which ended in the abdication of Edward VIII in December. At the beginning of the new year Britain was at last beginning to face the coming of a second world war.

VOLUME 46

∽ 1932 ∾

4 January. [Passfield Corner]
Sidney and I have settled down to our old life of regular work . . . So far as we ourselves are concerned it is a very happy, contented life. . . . Why then does the world today seem such a gloomy place to live in? I think it is because of the strange atmosphere of fear and hopelessness; everyone apprehensive and inclined to be timid, doing without things and retiring from the fight. Every kind of social organization is on the defensive: capitalist enterprise is on the

defensive; trade unionism is still more so; political democracy is on the defensive; the British Empire is very much on the defensive; Europe is on the defensive, and the U.S.A., the big booster of prosperity only two years ago, is almost abject about its bankruptcies and deficit and empty tills, more uncertain and down-hearted about 'the American way' than even we are about the British way. Indeed the only ray of light for us, here in Great Britain, is that whereas in the last few years the rest of the world have been telling us that we are decadent and 'down-and-out' we can, today, look them all in the face and shout 'So are you!' . . .

What, of course, is satisfactory to us, as socialists, is that those who defend the present order of society, in the newspapers or over the wireless (the B.B.C. has been collared by the defenders of capitalist enterprise), are at their wits' end as to how they can explain the present world disaster – the worst collapse of profit-making enterprise the world has ever seen. There has been no failure of crops; on the contrary, nature has been over-abundant – she has mocked men with her fertility; there has been no failure in skill and knowledge, for man's intellect has been increasing his power over nature, has been decreasing the amount of necessary effort by fabulous percentages. And yet, in the midst of all this plenty, men are workless and destitute. Nor can the pundits of private enterprise tell us *what* is the cause of this mad state of things. Some say it is the stupid use of credit or currency; others, war debts and reparations; others, the denial of free trade and free exchange between countries; others, too much spending or specula-tion, whilst a few attribute it to rationalization and too little spending. . . . Not one of these clever ones, not even Keynes, dare say that the game is up for profit-making enterprise. Even the Continental socialist parties hesitate to say it. Why? Because that way lies Soviet Russia. . . . Will she become the mecca? If so, it will be the British Fabians who will show the way, not the Continental Marxists. A pilgrimage to the mecca of the equalitarian state led by a few Fabians, all well over seventy years of age, will bring about the world's salvation! Well, well; it is an exhilarating, even an amusing prospect, if only it were not so damned expensive! However, we shall get a bit back for writing for the U.S.A.

What attracts us in Soviet Russia, and it is useless to deny that we are prejudiced in its favour, is that its constitution, on the one hand, bears out our *Constitution for a Socialist Commonwealth* [published in 1920] and, on the other, supplies a soul to that conception of government which our paper constitution lacked. We don't quite like that soul; but still it seems to do the job; it seems to provide the spiritual power. Personally, being a mystic and a moralist, I always hankered after a spiritual power, always felt instinctively that there *must* be some such a force if salvation were to be found.

On the first point. The Soviet constitution, the secular side of it, almost exactly corresponds to our constitution – there is the same tripod of political democracy, vocational organization and the consumers' co-operative movement. And the vocational or trade union is placed in exactly the same position of subordination that we suggested. Also the position of the separately organized consumers' co-operative societies is similar to ours. There is no d____d nonsense about Guild Socialism! But the spotlight of intriguing difference between the live creation of Soviet Russia and the dead body of the Webb constitution is the presence, as the dominant and decisive force, of a religious order: the Communist Party, with its strict discipline, its vows of obedience and poverty. Though not requiring chastity, Communists are expected to be puritan in their personal conduct, not to waste energy, time or health on sex, food or drink, the exact opposite of the D.H. Lawrence cult of sex, which I happen to detest.

It is the invention of the religious order, as the determining factor in the life of a great nation, which is the magnet that attracts me to Russia. Practically, that religion is Comtism – the Religion of Humanity. Auguste Comte comes to his own. Whether he would recognize this strange resurrection of his idea I very much doubt. Of course the stop in my mind is: how can we reconcile this dominance of a religious order, imposing on all citizens a new orthodoxy, with the freedom of the soul of man, without which science – that sublime manifestation of the curiosity of man – would wither and decay? How can we combine religious zeal in action with freedom of thought? That is the question we want to solve by studying Russia. . . .

12 January. [Passfield Corner]
Alexanders here for week-end. . . . Alexander is a good fellow with much administrative ability, but he has the conceit and vanity of the self-made man. . . . He said, by the way, that at the

Wednesday evening Cabinet of the fateful week, at which Sidney was not present, J.R.M. had definitely talked of a National government because he said the King would not have either Baldwin or Chamberlain as P.M. but wanted *him*. They had all of them protested that this would split the Labour Party from top to bottom, and J.R.M. had accepted it and passed on. The more I listen to the gossip of the late Cabinet and watch events at home and abroad, the more content I am with the advent of an overwhelmingly strong government, made up of the propertied classes, and representing the capitalist system in all its aspects, including 'tame Labour' – Jimmy Thomas. The Labour Party has to reform, as a party pledged to the advent of an equalitarian socialist state, and remain out of office until the bulk of the people are converted. . . .

The *Listener* is a weekly journal published by the B.B.C.

23 January. 3 a.m. [Passfield Corner]
The three talks went off excellently – the last, on the capitalist system, its drawbacks and diseases, was the subject of much discussion at the B.B.C., and some perturbation. Committees sat on it: 'If it had not been Mrs Webb, it would have been censored,' I was told. Some objectionable passages were omitted from the *Listener*'s report; I had many letters from listeners. All the same, I doubt whether I shall be welcomed again – certainly not on Russia . . . And I also doubt whether I shall be able to stand the strain . . . after all, yesterday was my seventy-fourth birthday.

In the summer of 1930 Dora Russell engaged as a governess Marjorie (known as Peter) Spence, a beautiful Oxford undergraduate. Russell married her in January 1936, after a complicated divorce from Dora in 1935.

20 February. [Passfield Corner]
Graham Wallas with us. It interests me that he and we are much nearer in opinion than we have been for many a long year. . . . And though he fears the suppression of free thought in politics under Communism, the Soviet system has his sympathy in its anti-God crusade and in its subordination of the trade unions to the will of the consumer-citizen. It is strange how Graham Wallas has stuck throughout life to his leading antipathies – royalty, the priest and the trade union. But what interested me was that he had not reacted more violently against the suppression of free thought, free Press

and free speech in Soviet Russia. Poor liberalism! Even aged Liberals are reconsidering their faith out of sheer disgust at the ways of profit-making capitalists, more especially in the U.S.A. Bertrand Russell, recently in the U.S.A. and here for lunch, agreed about Soviet Russia but maintained that in spite of all the corruption and violence of the U.S.A., its oppressions and cruelties, there was more hope there for the future . . . than in Great Britain. Here the people were good-natured and tolerant, but action and thought were just petering out. He was violently indignant at the flunkeyism and treachery of J.R.M. and Snowden. Neither he nor we mentioned his wife, so apparently he accepts our refusal to associate with her.

(22 September. Alys tells me that they have separated as he has fallen desperately in love with a clever charming girl of twenty-five whom he insists must be recognized as his wife!) . . .

1 March. [Passfield Corner]
Sidney, with a little help from me, has finished the book on *Methods of Social Study*, whilst I have been reading Lenin's works and various odds and ends on Russia, trying to get 'the hang of it' before going there. The amazing intensity of Lenin's will, and certainty in his concrete aims, is revealed in the articles and letters prior to the October revolution. It is he who determined to use the Soviets of workers, soldiers and peasants as the political form, and state socialism as the economic principle of the new Russian revolutionary state. It was he who inaugurated the 'new morality' and who decided on the liquidation of religion and bourgeois civilization. What strikes me in the various novels which have been translated . . . is the emergence of the new ethic of the collectivist state, the subordination of the life of the individual to the service of the community, 'socialist emulation' replacing pecuniary self-interest. On the other hand the love of God, the sense of awe and worship towards some force beyond and above human nature, is being cast out of Communism, and with it humility and peace of mind. . . .

7 March. [Passfield Corner]
. . . . Stafford and Isobel Cripps here for the first time, for a few hours. In manners and morals, in tastes and preferences, Stafford would make an ideal leader for the Labour Party. He would be

equally at home with the trade union officials, the co-operative administrator and the socialist intellectual. He has also sufficient personality, physical and mental, for leadership; tall, good-looking, with a good voice and pleasant gestures. But he is oddly immature in intellect and unbalanced in judgement, a strange lack of discrimination and low standard of reasoning in picking up ideas, queer currency cranks or slapdash remedies. . . . I noted that Herbert Morrison, who has been intimate with him and likes him personally, threw out the doubt whether he was not being 'spoilt' by a too rapid rise to leadership. . . . Mosley's case was a caricature of this rapid inflation and deflation of a reputation. Equally sudden and complete is the present contempt, almost hatred, of MacDonald: there is not a local Labour Party in the country who would today admit him to membership! Mosley deserved this defamation on account of arrogance and loose living, MacDonald because of long continued and masked treachery. Stafford will never sin in those ways. If he does not succeed in leadership it will be from sheer lack of any intellectual standards and mature thought in public affairs, of any appreciation of his own deficiency in knowledge and judgement, which may lead him to ignore the advice of wiser men like Henderson and prefer the acquiescence of inferior intelligences like George Lansbury. . . .

19 March. [Passfield Corner]
Twelve hours' talk with the Laskis about the Labour Party and labour movement generally; his report is not encouraging! . . . . Laski is in the best of his states of mind; he has got over his slight attack of swelled-headness, but is calmly satisfied that in modified Communism he is on the right way to human progress – to use an antiquated term . . . I have ever a sneaking admiration for Mac-Donald, as perhaps the greatest and most artistic of careerists – a veritable genius – he has completely fulfilled his abiding vision of himself as a great political personage. And in so doing his career will remain the most effective danger-post to future generations of labour men and women, heading them off the suffocating embraces of Great Britain's governing class, and the devastating effects of the existing social inequality . . . MacDonald has played the part of the courtier, the man of the world, the international statesman, with a certain dignity and charm, and has attracted out of the movement the intrinsically 'classy' element . . . men and women

who were in heart against social equality and disliked and despised the rank and file of the movement. . . . MacDonald's act of treachery has, in fact, served as a drastic emetic, dangerously drastic; it has delivered the patient of poisonous substances but it has left him painfully weak. The Labour world will not easily forget the experience; over and over again it will be cited as a warning against fraternization with the enemy's forces. For the first time since Victoria's death, the Crown has been badly compromised. Moreover, the Liberal creed and the Liberal Party have been finally liquidated. Lloyd George, who dealt the final blow in 1918, is left – with son and daughter and son-in-law – 'secluded and boycotted' (to use his own words) as the only mourner at the death of the Liberal Party, born in 1832 and buried in the crowded ultra-Tory government benches of 1932. But its successor is yet to come? The Labour Party which took office under MacDonald in 1924 and in 1929 was prematurely born. Is it also dead or dying?

5 April. [Passfield Corner]
Sidney and I are immersed in Soviet literature of all types and kinds – official reports and travellers' tales, of both of which there are many, a few novels, more memoirs. At present we cannot make our way to any settled estimate of success or failure, whether success or failure be partial or on a colossal and catastrophic scale. The experiment is so stupendous, alike in area, in numbers involved, in variety, in speed, in intensity, in technological change and necessary alteration in human behaviour and human motive, that one's good mood alternates between the wildest hopes and the gloomiest fears. All I know is that I *wish* Russian Communism to succeed, a wish which tends to distort one's judgement. When one becomes aware of this distortion one has 'cold feet'. To be for or against Soviet Communism is, today, a big gamble of the intellect. Will our pilgrimage to Moscow bring enlightenment or rightly measured judgement; are events ripe for such an evaluation?

28 April. [Passfield Corner]
I attended the sectional meetings and dinner of the British Academy, of which I have been elected the first woman member. It is a funny little body of elderly and aged men, the aged predominating; broken up into sections, supposed to consist of the pundits of the several humanistic sciences as a counterpart of the Royal Society in

physical science . . . The little crowd gave a lifeless and derelict impression – very Oxford-donnish and conventional in culture and tone. It is a mystery why anyone agrees to pay £10 entrance fee and £3 3s 0d a year. I did it at Keynes's and Alexander's request, as the first woman . . . H.A.L. Fisher [the President] was very oncoming and wanted to see us when we return. . . . Our availability is slightly increased by my auntship to Stafford Cripps, who is assumed to be the future leader of the Labour Party. It is certainly a strange family episode that there should have been two 'R.P.' sons-in-law in the two Labour Cabinets and that a grandson should be the heir apparent to the Labour Party's future premiership. Dear old Father would have chuckled over it in spite of his Toryism. Mother would have been more gratified by my fellowship of the British Academy and triple doctorate. Her daughter the perfected Blue Stocking! and her own lifelong absorption in book-learning amply justified – her ambition brought to fruition in one of the ten children whom she had, at the cost of her own career as an intellectual, brought into the world. Bless her.

Frank Wells (1903–83) was the younger of the two sons of H.G. Wells. Moura Budberg (d. 1975) was a Russian aristocrat who had a mysterious life; in a posthumous memoir (1984) Wells described how she came to London as his mistress, and his distress when he discovered her dubious relationship to the Soviet authorities. He first advanced his idea of a planned society run by a special priesthood in A Modern Utopia in 1905.

4 May. [Passfield Corner]
A week-end at the Shaws. H.G. Wells with his son, Frank, and a friend, a Russian baroness, turned up to tea. The talk was fast and furious about Russia's alleged success, and capitalist civilization's alleged failure, H.G. denigrating Russian Communism as hostile to personal freedom and as having 'dropped' the notion of world government with which it started. He is still infatuated with the conception of a conspiracy of international Samurai capitalists to rule the world of common men, and he is prepared to sit down straight away and draft the requisite decrees which will bring back prosperity. . . .

The Russian 'baroness' (the widow, we afterwards heard, of a Benckendorf killed in the war; she had escaped from Leningrad in 1923 by a faked marriage with a German, afterwards dissolved, and she is now acting as Gorki's secretary in Italy), a handsome, attractive aristocrat, took a lively part in defence of Soviet Russia. So did GBS and the Webbs. H.G. did not like being on the right of the Webbs and was perturbed at our going to Russia and endorsing even a modified Communism. Today he does not know where he stands, between the terrified American capitalists and the boosting Russian Communists. . . .

The Webbs had been due to leave for Leningrad on 14 May but instead they left a week later.

14 May. 4 a.m. [Passfield Corner]
Our journey put off for one week owing to ice in Gulf of Finland, thus prolonging the worry of our elaborate preparations, alike in bodily comforts and the tutoring of our minds. Continuously revolving and discussing hypothetical conclusions about Russia and forecasting our book . . . Anyway, whether our study of Russian Communism results in anything worth publication or not, the old Webbs are finding it extraordinarily interesting, not to say exciting. 'You must not become a monomaniac about Russia,' Sidney warned me. 'What does it matter what two "over-seventies" think, say or do, so long as they do not whine about getting old and go merrily on, hand in hand, to the end of the road?', I answer back . . . In spite of old age, Sidney and I have had a delightful time since he left office, and studies and thoughts about Russian Communism have added to the zest of our honeymoon companionship. . . .

The Webbs returned to England in the last week of July.

1 August. [Passfield Corner]
Malcolm and Kitty Muggeridge here for a farewell visit before they settle down in Moscow. Kitty suddenly and unexpectedly turned up in Leningrad a few days before we sailed – she had come in the same boat as the Fabians – travelling 'hard' in a party of ninety, mostly workers of humble station. She was staying at the river-front hostel for sailors, sleeping ten in a room, and roughing it considerably in order, as she told us, to 'prospect' for work for herself and a resident's visa when she returned with Malcolm in September. Now she reports success. During her nine days in Moscow she devoted herself, apparently without any guide as she speaks a little Russian, to interviewing possible employers – and

secured a provisional engagement on the *Moscow News* and a visa for continued residence. . . . 'I was hungry, hot and tired all the time but it was tremendously exciting to get out of a dead city like Manchester into a living – intensely living – world like Moscow,' she told us . . .

These two young people are talented, adventurous and purposeful and I think will make good. Malcolm is clever, keen and unusually sympathetic and open-minded; Kitty has a stiff will and is gifted in appearance, voice and intelligence – a certain hardness diminishes her attractiveness. But if they continue to love one another – which they certainly do today – the Muggeridge pair ought to cut some ice in re-fashioning the world they live in. . . .

Edward Pease (1857–1955) was one of the founding members of the Fabian Society.

9 August. [Passfield Corner]
Graham Wallas dead; the first to go of ten persons, five men with their attendant wives all over seventy years of age, continually associated together in the last two decades of the nineteenth century in building up the Fabian Society, its doctrine and its propaganda. I name them as they figure in the founding of the Fabians. Edward Pease, in at its birth, January 1884, and for twenty-five years its general secretary; and within the following two years GBS 1884, Sidney Webb and Sydney Olivier 1885, and Graham Wallas 1886 – the last four being on the executive, and Fabian essayists when I joined the group in 1892. During the last fifty years, those five men and their wives have never quarrelled nor abused each other; formally we have remained old friends, but excepting myself the wives have taken little part in the society's work, whilst the men have drifted apart as each became absorbed in his own career. In one respect, it must be admitted, these five founders of the Fabian Society resembled each other; to a greater or lesser extent they all 'made good' according to Victorian tests of 'success'. They started poor men, without independent means or social status; they attained security and sufficiency of income in old age, from the £1,000 a year of Edward Pease's unexpected inheritance from an uncle, to the income of a millionaire earned by GBS. Four out of the five find themselves in *Who's Who*, two became peers of the realm, whilst GBS rose to be the greatest international figure in literature. . . .

Personally I enjoyed a talk with Wallas, though it was generally about old times and common friends. I read and re-read his books with pleasure, but for the life of me I have never been able to remember what they contain; they have just flowed past me – a pleasant prospect – but without altering the content of my thought one iota. It is fair to add that Wallas had 'stops in his mind' about the Webbs; we tolerated two of his devils – the monarchy and the Church – and we actually promoted the interests of the third – the trade union movement. In spite of the mutual misunderstandings, my abiding vision of Wallas was of his unflagging beneficence towards individuals, his devoted public service, his high-strung curiosity about human nature in society, his skill and industry in weaving his observations into instructive and stimulating but inconclusive social studies – in a word, his absorption in the higher values of life and his consequent happiness . . . he had lived the life he liked and done the work he wanted to do. Which can also be said of his four comrades of the 80s and 90s – Pease, Olivier, Shaw and Webb. . . .

20 August. [Passfield Corner]
Meantime I am not getting on with my task of analysing all our material and getting the Russian documents translated. Partly because I have not yet recovered from the effects of the two months in Russia and there are many persons we have to see; but also because I ponder over our conclusions about Russia, a sort of rumination which is an excuse for not writing. And alas! I lack the self-discipline which I admire so much in the Communist teaching. Old age does not increase the capacity for hygienic self-control. One is apt to indulge in another cigarette beyond the regulated number, in the cup of tea too early in the sleepless night . . . But I am not satisfied with myself and wonder whether I am at the end of my tether, physically and mentally.

Beatrice gave a B.B.C. talk on her visit to Russia on 22 September.

22 September. 9 p.m. Artillery Mansions
I delivered my talk with verve, but I felt very unequal to the strain and came back with a racing heart . . . I spent two or three weeks preparing the talk and have been dizzy ever since, so much so that it required all my courage to come up and give it. . . .

25 September. [Passfield Corner]
Too True to be Good, which we saw on Friday night, is a farce spoilt by a sermon and a sermon spoilt by a farce, the farce being far better than the sermon. The first act is pure farce and great fun; the second, because of the farcical vision of the British Army in the episode of Meek and the Colonel – Meek representing GBS's version of Lawrence of Arabia – was endurable in spite of the sermon preached by the main characters at each other; the third act, with its three sermons, was boresome, so boresome that only conventional manners kept me from shutting my eyes and ceasing to listen. The audience would also have been bored if they had not known that they were listening to GBS . . . In all his preachments there is little but a repetition of vanity, vanity, all is vanity. . . . There is not the remotest hint as to how human beings are going to improve themselves or be improved by an inner spirit or outside force. There is no redeemer.

Charlotte says that GBS wants a plot or situation provided for him as he had in *St Joan*. That he is no longer capable of inventing one. 'If he had a thread whereon to hang them,' she told us, 'he could supply endless beads of wit and wisdom. As it is he just sits in the chair, and without any clear intention, scribbles away any isolated thoughts and impressions that come into his mind. All these disjointed reflections and visions seem to him equally inspired and worth giving to the world.' Of course GBS, like all aged folk who are famous, lives in an atmosphere of affectionate tolerance from snobbish strangers which is disabling; it leads to a sort of mental flatulence in the victim. Even the old Webbs are slightly subject to it, but our output is tasteless fare, not to say indigestible, compared to GBS's sparkling and stimulating draughts. Also he has a fascinating personality to listen to and to look at. He is far more fascinating as an old man than he ever was as a young one. He *was* impish; old age has made him statuesque.

Stafford Cripps soon became leader of the Socialist League, the successor to the I.L.P. as a left-wing ginger group which had been founded by E.F. Wise, the economist and Labour politician.

3 October. 2 a.m. Labour Party conference, Leicester
A deep depression settled over the Labour Party . . . All that can be said is that though we have got rid of the rotten stuff we have not

yet produced any group of whole-hearted and strong-willed leaders capable of running an equalitarian state. The Soviet exemplar is still too uncertain, too easily and plausibly denounced as a failure to serve, as yet, as a definite stimulus, whilst the British Communist Party is a ludicrous caricature of a revolutionary movement. Altogether, viewed by an aged observer, the Labour Party of today is depressing and dreary; by its destructive criticism it may be rotting the roots of the old social order, but it is not laying the foundations of a new civilization – except possibly in the minds of a group of intellectual workers centred round Cole, Laski and Cripps, with the doubting adhesion of Morrison and a few others.

4 October. 3 a.m. [Leicester]
. . . . When I observed to Lansbury that the conference was depressed he retorted: 'You would think this conference enthusiastic if you had been at the November Trade Union Congress.' Unlike at last year's conference Stafford Cripps does not figure in the agenda, signifying that he was out of favour with the Labour Party executive as too advanced in his views. . . . Stafford would like Henderson to retire, but there is no one to take his place. When I asked Stafford whether there were any younger men coming on, he said there were some in the Oxford and Cambridge University Labour parties, but 'they are all lightweights; they are interested but they do not mean business. Perhaps the Socialist League will bind them to the Movement.' But this body does not start well, owing to the dislike of Wise, its chairman; and its inaugural meeting, which we attended, was captious and depressed. Altogether, since the rise in 1918 to the position of His Majesty's Opposition, the Labour Party has never been in such a parlous condition. . . .

5 October. [Passfield Corner]
. . . . I have come back from Leicester much exhausted and rather depressed, feeling unequal to the work before us. However, one had better wear out than rust out, and I have still some strength left in me, and Sidney has more; together we can accomplish something in the way of a bridge between the U.S.S.R. and the socialist parties who are still in the wilderness, looking towards the promised land. . . .

Muggeridge was now the *Manchester Guardian* correspondent in Moscow, replacing W.H. Chamberlin, who was on leave.

30 October. [Passfield Corner]

The Marleys are back [from two months in Russia] full of information and enthusiasm. They report that Malcolm and Kitty are reacting violently against the inefficiency, strain and stress of the Soviet regime, largely influenced by Chamberlin, who is leaving Moscow, Marley thinks for good – an enemy of the Soviet government, more especially of Stalin. . . . The plain truth is that the Russians are not yet a civilized people and won't be so for two or three decades. . . .

Inspired by Vita Sackville-West's clever wireless talk on D.H. Lawrence . . . I have been reading and pondering over his *Letters* in a vain attempt to discover what exactly his message is. On the subjects which I think I understand better than the man in the street – economics, politics, the social behaviour of the worker and the citizen – his stray observations are trivial, equivocal and inconsistent with each other, and above all, ridiculous in their arrogant self-conceit. In all these matters the dominant note is insistent anarchism, a dislike to anything that is *fixed*, to any obstacle to his doing and being anything he happens to like at one minute or another, irrespective of the right of other people to like freedom . . . His rightful sphere, in which he is a great artist – even I can appreciate his artistry, though not his intellectual understanding – is man's emotional reaction to 'Nature' in its widest sense: to the lower forms of life – flowers and crawling insects, birds, all wild young things – and to the great inanimate forces embodied in sun, moon, stars, cloudland; in stream, river, lake and encircling ocean; in mountains and plains, in deserts and forests, in all that makes up the wonder and beauty of the earth's surface. Above all, and here is the centre of his strivings after perfect expression, the physical reaction of man to woman and woman to man, and the blending of this with the same mystical appreciation of life in the universe. It is here that there seems to emerge a doctrine, bringing with it a rule of conduct which for the life of me I cannot understand. . . .

Lawrence's message to mankind seems to me a reversion to primitive religion with its, to me, repulsive mixing-up of sexual, sadist and mystical emotions, all associated with blood and abandonment to physical impulse and the dominance of the lower organs of the body over the brain. This sex relation is too divorced from conscious hygiene, personal affection or social obligation; it is wholly antagonistic both to the working of the intellect and to the development of any human or social purpose in life. Like so much else in modern art and literature, Lawrence's ideal is deliberately sub-human, a device to revert to the pre-human animal . . . And it is this forced and calculated repudiation of the heritage of man, as distinguished from that of the lower animals, that seems to me sheer blasphemy. I prefer the hard hygienic view of sex and the conscious subordination of sexuality to the task of 'building up socialism' characteristic of Soviet Russia; it may lack a sense of humour, as well as a sense of beauty, but it is more likely to lead to a healthy mind in a healthy body than Lawrence's morbid obsessions about the 'phallic consciousness' as the be-all and end-all of human life. . . .

Ivan Maisky (1884–1975), Soviet Ambassador to London 1932–43, was a Menshevik exile who became a Communist and returned to Russia in 1922 to join the diplomatic service.

24 November. [Passfield Corner]
Maisky, the new Soviet Ambassador, and his wife, whom we invited to lunch to meet some Labour men at the London School of Economics on Thursday, telephoned that he would like to consult Sidney about the negotiations for the new trade treaty, and motored down on Tuesday. He is a more accomplished diplomat and less ardent Communist than Sokolnikov – he was a Menshevik, a member of the Provisional government in 1917, but came over to the Bolsheviks after the October revolution; afterwards he was in London with Rakovsky at the time of the Arcos raid, and has since been Soviet Minister in Finland. He takes a broad view of Soviet Communism as 'in the making' – the fanatical metaphysics and repression of today are temporary, brought about by past horrors and the low level of culture out of which the revolution started. . . .

Shaw had recently published a religious fable entitled *The Adventures of the Black Girl in Search of God.*

28 November. [Passfield Corner]
GBS and Charlotte here for week-end before they start on the four months' tour round the world in a *de luxe* steamer. His lecture at Kingsway Hall was a painfully incoherent tirade about nothing in particular, except for the laudation of Oswald Mosley as the 'man of the future'! Oswald and Cynthia are among Charlotte's social

pets; their good looks, luxurious living and aristocratic ensemble appeal to her and this influences GBS. As against the Kingsway failure, there is the little brochure, beautifully illustrated, *The Black Girl*, price 2s 6d, with its epilogue on the evolution and the present state of religion, which is brilliant. If it were not for the author's prestige it would be considered blasphemous by all church-men, conventional or genuine. . . .

1 December. [Passfield Corner]
I have watched for the reviews of GBS's deadly dart – disguised as a fascinating Xmas card – and note with interest that only Gerald Gould takes our view of its potency; otherwise the reviewers have wittingly or unwittingly dismissed it as one more *jeu d'esprit* from the G.O.M. of literature; *The Times* even politely suggested that it conformed to the canon of fashionable 'modernism' in Christian exegesis. I still think, with Gould, that this 2s 6d illustrated tract for the times is perhaps the most effective single publication of GBS's wit and wisdom so far as the mass of readers, especially young readers, are concerned. . . .

Sidney was writing a series of syndicated articles on the Soviet Union.

18 December. [Passfield Corner]
As the year draws to a close, events at home and abroad get more and more gloomy. There is no sign, either in the U.S.A. or in Great Britain or on the Continent, of a definite revival of trade or of any diminution of unemployment . . . Nor is the news about the U.S.S.R. hopeful. Whilst Sidney has been writing optimistic accounts of its constitutions and activities, reports from friends as well as enemies reach us about the dearth of food and other consumable commodities; growing discontent among the peasants; fears about the next year's harvest owing to bad sowing; dissension, heresy hunts and purges within the Communist Party. . . . All of which makes thinking, reading, talking about the U.S.S.R., still more writing about it, horribly distracting. . . .

28 December. [Passfield Corner]
Sidney finished the tenth article yesterday, completing his planned output for the autumn months, yielding about £400, nearly all from the U.S.A. Considering his age, it has been a brilliant

performance. He has been in excellent health, intensely interested in his subject, enjoying his talks with friends, his comfortable home and the company of his fast-ageing wife. For aged I have felt this autumn, always tired, teased with eczema, sleeplessness and noises in the ears and head. It is partly due to an inevitable decline of vitality, partly to an almost morbid anxiety to master our immense and elusive task of understanding the why, where and how of Soviet Communism; it needs a brain in full vigour, not a mere remnant of working capacity. However, as a helpmate, I can do a little, in marking and sorting out notes, on the Webb plan. Some sort of work will emerge during the next twelve months. After that is done I shall sink back into the backwater of my reminiscences, illustrated by entries from the diaries, and Sidney can help me through, in the intervals of some new job of his own.

'Count your blessings,' is his refrain to my recurring self-pity! So ends 1932.

VOLUME 47

࿇ 1933 ࿇

4 January. [Passfield Corner]
We spent some time on New Year's Day, and after, in casting and recasting the plan of our book on Russia . . . Obviously this little book will not be a work of original research; our material will be practically second-hand — mostly American, heavily subsidized research into documents and long-term observation on the spot . . . For a year — perhaps for two years — Sidney and I will be wallowing in our material from the U.S.A. and Moscow, supplemented by help from Soviet officials in the U.K. . . . If my health holds out, we may visit the U.S.S.R. once again, say in the summer of 1934, just to put the final touches on the work. . . . But whatever may be the fate of this adventure, it will give us a daily task, a subject for mutual discussion and a reason for asking this or that person as our guests; and, last but not least, it will furnish matter for my early morning scribbling in this manuscript book, which I enjoy. It is my pet pastime, a gossip with an old friend and confidant, a sort of vent for my egotism. . . .

22 January. [Passfield Corner]

My seventy-fifth birthday. 'Mrs Webb retains to a remarkable degree her mental vigour and industry,' observed the *Evening Standard*! (Note, not her charm – 'able but not charming' – as John Morley said fifty years ago.) Telegrams and greetings, newspapers ringing me up for interviews, which I refuse. I don't feel mentally vigorous or industrious, but relatively to the senility usual at that great age, I suppose I am so. And Sidney certainly *is* so. . . .

We dined with Stafford and his family, with Tawney intervening. I had introduced the one to the other, thinking that they would like each other and that Tawney's long experience of the labour movement would be useful to Stafford. Both of these men are professing Christians, though disillusioned with the doings of the Christian Church about the Great War and the present unemployment. Tawney suggested that the Labour Party would never be effective until it was led by a compact group who would live the life. 'But where are we to get the group?' asked Stafford, 'and upon what practical code of conduct and upon what metaphysical basis is it to stand – will Christianity suffice?' 'No,' said I, 'Christianity is played out,' and then left Stafford and Tawney to talk together. Sidney did not intervene except to demur to a detailed programme of revolutionary action – the 'all or nothing' attitude for a future Labour majority. But as yet both Stafford and Tawney agreed there was no sign of a movement in favour of a Labour government, reformative or revolutionary; there is only a reaction against the present government. And the more extreme line of policy being adopted by Stafford and the Socialist League will not attract the nondescript voter, disgruntled with a Conservative government, to vote Labour, so there is little chance of a Labour Party majority, which to my mind is all to the good. Stafford and Tawney, with other stalwarts, are agreed that it would be fatal for the Labour Party to sink once more into the role of caretakers of capitalist interests. . . .

27 January. [Passfield Corner]

Kitty Muggeridge, big with child and singularly blooming and good-tempered, back from Moscow. She gives an unpleasant impression of life among the Moscow correspondents, made more depressing by Malcolm's disillusion with Soviet Communism, their bad luck in losing Kitty's promised work on the Moscow

Daily News and Malcolm's deputizing beyond next May for Chamberlin for the *Manchester Guardian*, as well as the Chamberlins' comfortable flat . . . The newspaper correspondents, of whom the majority are American . . . spend most of their time drinking at the Tourist hotels; the Press circle see few Russians . . . 'As a matter of fact,' repeated Kitty, 'we have seen very little of anyone; I was ill for the first winter, and Malcolm was hard at work on his novel.' And now comes the blow that this novel . . . is refused because the publisher's reader thinks it libellous, 'giving pain to innocent people' – the scene being a decaying city, unmistakably Manchester, and the subject being the internal life of the *Manchester Guardian* . . . through the petty personalities of the staff – the present editor of the *New Statesman*, Kingsley Martin, being among the persons caricatured.

4 February. [Passfield Corner]
Tom Jones and his wife and we listened in to a French discourse from the Moscow Central Radio giving details of the General Plan, the position of the foreign expert, the organization of the trade union movement. Rather dull and statistical, and not sufficiently subtle and insinuating to be useful for foreign consumption. More thrilling were the Kremlin bells ringing out the midnight hour, followed by the 'Internationale' – it seemed to bring us so intimately into the Soviet atmosphere. . . .

Beatrice had been treated with X-rays and doses of luminal for her insomnia and skin irritation. The beautiful Portofino peninsula is on the Italian Riviera.

14 February. [Passfield Corner]
On the eve of a holiday trip to Portofino. The X-rays proved a false hope; the luminal gave me more sleep and reduced the eczema but I felt 'drugged' – also with Soviet books and papers and secretary surrounding me, I could not refrain from trying to get on with our task. . . . So, Sidney having finished his task of turning out articles and gathered in dollars, which more than paid for the Russian trip, we thought we deserved a real rest in sun and beauty, with no revolution to distract us and no thinking to weary our aged brains. Sidney suggested that he should begin the first chapter of the book, but I scowled at him and he desisted. . . .

23 February. Portofino Villa

So here we are, some thousand feet up, overlooking a long stretch of sea and mountain to the west and to the east a wonderful view; but alas! no sun, only mere feeble glimmers through snow-storms, with a biting north wind outside and no fires inside; the central heating fails to spread adequately, a condition made just bearable by an oil-stove in our bedroom. Otherwise the hotel is comfortable: no noise, good food and a pleasant little company of eight including ourselves. . . . Sidney and I walk along the mountain paths for an hour or two in the morning and lie on sofas reading in our rooms most of the afternoon; certainly we neither of us do any work. He sleeps a good deal and I try to sleep, but my bones ache and my head whizzes, so it is not exactly a successful venture . . . Ought one ever to attempt to cure the 'natural' ailments of old age? Is it not a case of sitting still and slowly curling up, accepting inaction of body and mind? Once the book on Russia is finished (in a sense our last will and testament), I think I shall curl up into the inevitable senility, leaving Sidney to carry on. . . .

2 March. [Portofino]

Into this octet of British tourists sprang, from out of a luxurious motor car, Lion Phillimore: an exuberant, generous and witty personality with her mop of black and grey hair, tall figure, handsome features but unhealthy skin, clad in furs by day and in velvet at night, fresh from the sophisticated society of the Rome of Mussolini and of the Vatican, full of admiration for the one and of denunciation of the other, wonderfully vital and dogmatic on all subjects and persons under the sun. We openly chaffed each other and amused all the other guests with our stroke and counter-stroke of intimate criticism. When she left five days after, 'bored stiff' by the grey cold sky and not over-comfortable room, there was a chorus of 'How you must miss her!'. . . . Lion pressed us to hasten to join her at Cannes, but we thought it better to stay in the high air and quiet of this place according to plan, spending only the arranged week at Cannes before we return home on the 13th. We solace our sunless solitude in the oil-stove-heated room with reading the novels in the hotel library, among them *A Modern Comedy* by Galsworthy, a remarkable description of England after the war. . . . The two books about Soviet Communism I brought with me I handed over to Lion, as I had not the slightest desire to read them.

I wanted to be free from that obsession. Nevertheless, Sidney and I, in our walks over the hills or while drinking our early cup of tea together, discuss the coming book, and I am beginning, with improving health, to enjoy the thought of delivering it during the next twelve months or more. . . .

Odette Keun (1888–1978), a writer and journalist born in Constantinople, was an exotic figure who had been living with H.G. Wells in his *mas*, Lou Pidou, outside Grasse, for some years, but the relationship was on the point of breaking up at this time. 'Pidou' was her nickname for Wells. Somerset Maugham (1874–1965), the novelist, lived at Cap Ferrat on the French Riviera.

9 March. Cannes
A suite of two bedrooms, bathrooms and a sunny sitting-room with a wide view of the sea and mountains, together with a motor car in constant attendance, awaited us here, with Lion as hostess, dispensing her kindness with generous gestures of concern for our comfort. . . . Lion and we two went to lunch with Odette at Grasse (H.G. was away), where we met Somerset Maugham. I expected a blatant personality in our hostess. Quite the contrary; a charmer appeared, an artiste skilfully turned out, just enough rouge, powder and pencilling to add an audacious chic without vulgarity to her expression; her garments were perfect in their harmony and fitness. The only blemish in our hostess was a too continuous rapid and inconsequent chatter, fatiguing to her guests; spells of silent and attentive listening would have been welcome to the Webbs! She and Somerset Maugham behaved with alarming unconventionality; they wrangled over some story about him she wanted to tell; he angrily forbade her; she ended the wrangle by lovingly embracing him! Whereupon Lion mischievously observed, 'Lord Passfield looks jealous.'
Somerset Maugham, whose novels we have always admired for their vivid imaginative artistry and unusual characters and back-grounds, seemed to me a coarse and unsavoury personality, exuding low motive and the suspicion of low motive in others. (We heard afterwards that he has a sinister reputation here as an addict in sodomy.) German Hitlerism, Soviet Communism and the decay of capitalist democracy and Christian morals, it is needless to say, were the subject-matter of our somewhat heated discussion, but S.M. contributed little but general cynicism. I fancy that he

disliked us as much as we disliked him. 'Bought by the U.S.S.R. to propagate Communism,' was his surmise; indeed he went near to suggesting it, in an off-hand way. Odette enlarged upon H.G.'s passionate concern about the condition of the world. 'Pidou would sacrifice all things, his own health and income and myself, to carrying out his plan of a world government'. . . . The house is attractive and does credit to her taste. In a week, she goes into training as a nurse at Zurich; she intends to start a nursing home at Grasse, a philanthropic adventure I understand. Except that she has no fixed morals, she seems to me a good sort, and H.G. is fortunate in this comrade of his old age.

27 March. 2.30 a.m. [Passfield Corner]
Sidney begins the book today and I shall strain and stumble after him, picking up the bits and opening out new aspects . . . Regarded from the standpoint of research, it is an illegitimate venture − neither our equipment nor our opportunities suffice. But like a provisional examination by an experienced mechanic, or a preliminary survey of a new island by a knowledgeable geologist, it may prove useful to better-equipped observers. Anyway, it will give zest to our declining years, a subject to read and think about, to talk over in our walks, to discuss with an early morning and afternoon tea, or with our after-meal cigarette. What 'over-seventies' do is of little importance to anyone but themselves. All the same, I shall be glad to be quit of the vast and incomprehensible U.S.S.R., and back again in the easy task of selecting entries from my diaries and filling up the spaces between them with appropriate padding.

29 March. [Passfield Corner]
Malcolm [Muggeridge]'s curiously hysterical denunciations of the U.S.S.R. and all its works in a letter to me have been followed up by three articles by him in the *Manchester Guardian*, drawing a vivid and arrogantly expressed picture of the starvation and oppression of the peasants of the North Caucasus and the Ukraine. From these articles, it appears that he has had a week's tour, travelling 'hard' and talking with one or two inhabitants in a small deserted market town, and on a badly managed collective farm. I note in his letter to me the new fervour of anti-Semitism, coupling 'Jews' with 'hunchbacks, perverts, and sadists' on one page, and on the next, in his reference to the Comsomol demonstrations, using the denigrating

words, 'in the best manner of Semitic salesmanship'. . . . That there is *some* fire behind this smoke of Malcolm's queerly malicious but sincerely felt denunciation of Soviet Communism, is clear from the Soviet Press itself. Collective farming has failed to produce sufficient food for the 160 millions, assuming that some of it must be used to pay imports of machinery. In short, the U.S.S.R. has not yet solved the problem of production . . . What Malcolm asserts, without apparently any evidence except hearsay for his assertion, is that the peasant population of the U.S.S.R. is today starving, and that this starvation will become catastrophic next year. What makes me uncomfortable is that we have no evidence to the contrary, and that the violent purges of the C.P. and the passionate pleadings for greater and more sustained efforts on the agricultural front indicate a fear of catastrophe . . .

Adolf Hitler had become Chancellor of Germany on 30 January 1933.

30 March. [Passfield Corner]
Another account of famine in Russia in the *Manchester Guardian*, which certainly bears out Malcolm's reports. A melancholy atmosphere in which to write a book on Soviet Communism, especially when one of the partners is failing in strength and capacity. Sidney is not daunted. So long as I am by his side he is happy, in love with his old woman and not wanting other company, content to carry on the task day after day. The thought that there may be famine in some districts of the U.S.S.R. does not disturb his faith in the eventual triumph of the Soviet economic principle of planned production for the needs of the whole community, even with the terrible handicap of carrying out this experiment with an untrained, demoralized and in part hostile people. Fortunately for the U.S.S.R. the attention of the capitalist countries is today concentrated on the Mad Dog of Europe – Hitler's Germany. Persecution of political democrats, combined with a ferocious persecution of the Jews – financiers and scientists, teachers and doctors, as well as moneylenders, multiple shop-keepers and Communists – offends the powerful capitalist democracies of the U.S.A., United Kingdom and France. . . .

There was a diplomatic breach with the U.S.S.R. after the Russians tried a group of British engineers for espionage while they were advising on factory construction.

11 April. [Passfield Corner]

The Maiskys spent the week-end with us, an engagement made before the episode of the arrest of the British engineers, but which we hastened to endorse when the breach came. We like both husband and wife. Unlike Sokolnikov, Maisky is not a fanatical Marxist, and is inclined to apologize for the G.P.U. as an organization necessary in a time of war, but which will disappear when Soviet Communism is firmly established. Madame Maisky told me that their position was extremely unpleasant in the diplomatic circle and London society generally; that sometimes they were treated with great cordiality and then, a few days later, with positive rudeness, according to the supposed attitude of the British government. . . .

Maisky comforted us about the food shortage . . . 40,000 missionaries were being sent out by the Central Committee of the Communist Party, in some cases important commissars; these missionaries would work with and inspire the Collector and peasants. Already in the spring sowing, good results were appearing. . . .

13 April. [Passfield Corner]

We are not daunted in our effort to explain Soviet Communism to British readers. An experiment that fails is often as illuminating as one that succeeds. And when all is said and done, we still believe in its ultimate success, though we may not live to see it, or the planning of national production for consumption by the whole community. It may be a German or Italian or Scandinavian venture which will become the leading exemplar for the rest of the world to follow. . . .

'Charlotte dragged me round the world,' Shaw said: he wrote the comedy *A Village Wooing* on board ship during a world tour. The political play was *On The Rocks*.

1 May. Ayot

GBS and Charlotte in the best of health, and full of their procession round the world. GBS complains of hordes of journalists who dogged his steps as false publicity. 'The great majority of those who crowd to see me have not read a word I've written, and those who have don't understand, or disagree with my message to mankind.' All the same, he enjoys it and rides triumphant over the mob of pressmen, attracted by the force, not of his message, but of his bewitching personality and the world-wide glamour of it.

He read us a short comedy – the courtship of a man by a woman, opened on the deck of a touring steamer and continued in a village post office, clever and amusing but nothing in it. He is writing a political play – at which we tremble. 'But what else can I do but write? It is my work and my play.' And so he writes on and on, just as we do in our duller way; aged folk become either scatter-brained or obsessed: he is the one, we are the other, the greater distinction being that he has genius and we have merely industry. In our old age he and we have a new common interest, separating the four of us off from our own class – Soviet Communism.

The tension between those who accept and those who denounce the U.S.S.R. increases day by day, and I am wondering whether Charlotte will not presently feel the cold draught. We should certainly feel it if ever we went out of the narrow circle of those who wish to see us, mostly friends of Russia. It is difficult to keep off the subject; it seems to poison the air of social intercourse. 'A country of wild beasts,' Beveridge muttered under his breath when we sat with him at lunch at the London School of Economics. Charlotte's solicitor 'foamed at the mouth' and hysterically refused to obey her instructions when she asked him to invest £1,000 in the Soviet 15 per cent loan. 'Your fellow citizens in prison!' he shouted at her. . . .

Fortunately the German Nazi government, the obvious ally of the British government in its hatred of Moscow, has taken on Jewry as an enemy; otherwise there might have been a combination of capitalist democracies with Fascist autocracies against the U.S.S.R. . . . The Jews are still a power in the world. Whatever their political creed and social standing and in spite of their dispersion, the Jews are the most unified and self-defensive race. And to the children of Israel, the Soviet Union offers a warm welcome and their own autonomous republic, where not thousands but millions can find a livelihood under an all-Jewish government, so long as they are willing to accept the economic and political creed of a prophet of their own race. Moses, David, Elijah, Jesus, Paul, Spinoza, Marx and Einstein – what a glorious spiritual and intellectual heritage for one small people!

E.M. Forster was now writing a biography of Goldsworthy Lowes Dickinson

(1862–1932), humanist, historian and Hellenist, and Fellow of King's College, Cambridge.

11 May. [Passfield Corner]
Sidney and I have got really into the swim of our book-making. He writes and I study and scheme, preparing the way for him and tidying up after him. A glorious spring – the chorus of birds, the soft brilliance of leaf and bloom on earth, and the sun and cloud, sunset and sunrise. All this beauty stimulates and soothes the tired brain of old age. Friends come and go and we have always each other. Then there is the wireless music and the sometimes excellent talks, many in voices of old or new friends, as recreation when the eyes are weary and the understanding dull; altogether a good life and a pleasant one, in spite of being well on in the eighth decade and quite obviously on the downgrade in capacity. 'Speak for yourself,' I hear Sidney saying!

E.M. Forster came down to lunch and tea; a tall big-boned man with significant and attractive features and troubled expression, ultra-refined, exquisite hands (of which he is aware), interested in many things but uncertain as to ultimate values – aesthetic or social reformer, which is uppermost? Ostensibly he came to enquire about Lowes Dickinson's attachment to the London School of Economics, how and why he had occasionally lectured there almost from its very beginning in the 90s. But we talked politics and economics – U.S.S.R., Germany, U.S.A., the state of mind of the young men at the university (he is a Fellow of King's Cambridge), a state of mind just at present which he admits is definitely revolutionary to the left or the right, Communist or Fascist. I urged him to go back from the essay to the novel. *A Passage to India* was a great novel. Why not another? The present political situation in all countries had certain dramatic possibilities. With moderate means, independent of authorship, he lives with an old mother near Dorking. We disputed the relative value of tenderness and loyalty in life; he valued tenderness. I retorted that without loyalty, tenderness might easily, as with D.H. Lawrence, be transformed into conscious cruelty, and that was almost worse than mere animalism – i.e. sexual passion followed by indifference. I would rather have a relationship of *polite consideration* between individuals, and nothing more, from start to finish, than a passionate friendship ending in hatred, malice and all uncharitableness. . . .

During the last week or so I have read through and dictated notes from the seven volumes of Lenin's works, and yesterday afternoon I read Krupskaya's second volume of her autobiography. An amazing concentration and intensity of intellectual life and self-dedication under hard and dangerous conditions, in poverty and exile, spied upon by police agents, at risk of imprisonment, torture and death, surrounded by comrades in like circumstances. Comparing it with the comfort, ease, freedom, social esteem of the Shaws, Webbs, Wallases, Oliviers and other labour and socialist leaders, how soft and enervating seems our own past existence. . . .

Lady Cynthia Mosley died of acute appendicitis on 16 May 1933.

24 May. [Passfield Corner]
. . . . Bernard Shaw's personality is a work of art and grows more attractive with old age – almost mythical! But his thought is repetitive, and it seems to us today ugly and depressing, in its combination of gross farce with endless preaching his peculiar doctrines. He harps on the notion that man is not fit for freedom and demands compulsion; an unreasoning obedience to the super-man's orders is the only way of salvation. But where is this superman? GBS answers – Mussolini or Mosley, though with the advent of Hitler he is a little shy about Mosley, so we avoided discussing that political showman as the future British dictator. With the death of the charming Cynthia, he may seem less promising to GBS, as he certainly will to the rest of the political world. The British elector is too civilized to be taken in by Mosley, with his antics and his cocktails. . . .

Annie Besant (1847–1933) began her career as a Secularist speaker and author who collaborated with Charles Bradlaugh (1833–1891). She was one of the Fabian essayists and then became the head of the Theosophical movement. Mary Baker Eddy (1821–1910) was the founder of Christian Science. Aimée Semple MacPherson (1890–1940) was a Californian evangelist. Edward Aveling (1849–98) was a Secularist and the common-law husband of Eleanor Marx. Charles C. Leadbetter (1847–1934), an Anglican curate who became a Theosophist, was forced to resign from the Theosophical Society in 1906 after a scandal about his homosexual relations with young disciples. J.M. Robertson (1856–1933) was a free-thinking journalist who became a Liberal M.P. Amy Johnson (1903–1941) was the first woman to make a solo flight from London to Australia.

8 June. [Passfield Corner]

Sidney goes steadily on and I go stumbling after him. Just now I am reconstructing the chapter on Soviet trade unionism. This section of the book — the constitution of Soviet Communism — will be appallingly dull. We can give categorically the different parts of the constitution, but we have not the knowledge to give the living relations between them. We do not really know how the business works. We can't picture the daily comings and goings within the Kremlin, as we could those of the trade union world, or of Parliament and Whitehall, and municipal administration in Great Britain. But this outline of the formal constitution, as revealed in the American specialized studies and the day-to-day chronicle in the *Moscow News* of the doings of the various bodies, will be useful to future students. It will also serve as a basis of our tentative conclusion about Soviet Communism as a new civilization in rapid process of development. The longer we study the U.S.S.R. the more sure we are that it is a new civilization — crude and cruel and deplorably inefficient in some of its manifestations, but nevertheless an immense step forward in the development of a better human nature, alike in physical health and intellectual advancement, personal ethics and social relationships. But there is a long pull and a hard pull for its thinkers and organizers before it can be proven good to a hostile world.

The Passionate Pilgrim by C.M. Williams is a telling biography of [Annie Besant], the most outstanding Englishwoman between 1875 and 1925 — half a century and she is still lingering on the stage! To me the book is fascinating; we were contemporaries and on three or four occasions I ran up against her.

That strangely unsatisfactory friend and relation of mine, Margaret Harkness, introduced me to Annie Besant late in the 80s. She was a friend of hers; so was my sister Theresa, though I did not know it until after my sister's death.

I first saw and heard Annie Besant as a Fabian lecturer in about 1887, at the Chelsea Workers' Club. GBS and Sydney Olivier were in attendance. Sidney and Graham Wallas failed to get in. She was attractive, if not exactly beautiful to look at. She swept her audience away by her logical and eloquent advocacy of the collective ownership of public utilities, delivered in an exquisite voice — a voice which was neither that of a man nor that of a woman — it was the voice of a beautiful soul. The sermon or thesis — it was both —

turned me away from Fabian socialism. Why? Because in talking about the transfer of *railway administration* to the state, she used wrong technical terms and, to my pedantic mind, muddled up all her facts. To an observer of the railway policies of two continents, her argument seemed sheer nonsense.

A year or so afterwards I lunched with her in Avenue Road (J.M. Robertson was there, one of her paying guests). We had no use for each other. Our next encounter was at Benares in 1912. Sidney, who had been on the Fabian executive with her, thought it would be interesting to see the Hindu University College of which she was the principal, so we spent some hours with her, with the same result as twenty years ago – mutual dislike. We thought her disingenuous and lacking in candour about India and its problems. She was obviously bored and irritated by our visit, perfunctory in her acceptance of Sidney as a former colleague. When, ten years later, she rejoined the Fabian Society and appeared at Labour functions during 1919–20 we met again, and our mutual recognition was still colder, even hostile on her part, at any rate to the female Webb.

Annie Besant was a superlatively gifted woman – I hesitate to write a great woman. Her beauty, when she was young, and magnetic attraction, even in old age, the wonder of her voice, the skilled advocacy and the depth and breadth of the emotional appeal, together with an amazing physical endurance and capacity for long sustained brainwork, would have constituted greatness, if she had possessed an independent intellect and an honest straight character. She had neither the one nor the other, and she had no sense of humour. Secularism, birth control, the emancipation of women, Indian nationalism were all great causes, but she learnt them from other persons and she added nothing to their subject-matter either in theory or practice. Moreover, she quickly wearied of them and tossed three of them – secularism, birth control and emancipation of women – away for theosophy, her last and longest obsession, with which she was identified for forty years. In this last sphere she exhibited an intellectual shoddiness, a self-deceit and, be it added, something akin to jugglers' tricks offered as miracles, which brought her down near the level of Mrs Eddy and Aimée Mac-Pherson. Her close intimacy with the infamous Aveling and her friendship with the unsavoury Leadbetter showed low human values. Perhaps her greatest contribution, after the heroic battle for birth control with Bradlaugh, was to the self-respect of the Hindus in their struggle for political freedom, though her glorification of the ancient Hindu civilization was, so it was said by Sanskrit scholars, somewhat absurdly mythical.

All this notwithstanding, whatever may have been her sins and shortcomings, Annie Besant was the most wonderful woman of her century. Which brings me to a melancholy reflection. Looking back on half a century of contemporaries, *where oh! where are the distinguished women, relatively to men*, in art, literature, science, public affairs? I forgot. There is Amy Johnson; her record remains unbroken. But it is a record of muscle, nerve and sight, of rapid and powerful physical reactions. The few words she speaks or writes are records of the utterly commonplace. . . .

After the death of Beatrice's sister Margaret Hobhouse, her husband Henry (1854–1937) married his former secretary, Anne Grant. Hadspen was the Hobhouse family home in Somerset. The Webbs had been staying at Sidmouth to give their servants a holiday.

13 July. [Passfield Corner]
Forty-eight hours at Hadspen on our way home. The old house, beautiful garden, curving lawns bordered by flowers and overhanging trees, amid hills and villages, as a setting; our visit an unexpected pleasure. Henry, though aged and infirm, benign, courteous and intelligent, with the delightful Anne as the wife of his old age – an agreeable host. Still busies himself about country affairs, such as records and other odds and ends. These peaceful houses of the well-to-do landed gentry – old furniture, portraits and endless books, regular simple and rather stately routine, carried out by some dozen or more silent and discreet servants, half men and half women, are a pleasant environment. More than fifty years ago I first came here with Margaret on her engagement to this model 'match' for one of the Potter girls, rousing the respectful envy of all the mothers of daughters in the county of Gloucester. In a way the marriage was a happy one; they were both of them good and able. But in ideals and culture, they had little in common. Anne is exactly suited to the Hobhouse environment; Margaret was too iconoclastic in intellect and cynical in her wit. Too little refinement and good manners for the Hobhouse tradition and the 'county' status. . . .

1 August. [Passfield Corner]
After reading through what he has written on the four parts of the
U.S.S.R. constitution, with a view to draft questions to be answered
by Maisky, Sidney is much encouraged about the value of the
book. Also we are bucked up by reports of the bumper harvest in
the U.S.S.R. . . . We are of course getting a good deal of help in
our work which would not be open to other authors, either
arranged and paid for by us from non-Bolshevik Russians resident
in England or gratuitously from the U.S.S.R. authorities. What
we contribute is our long experience in scheming the investigation
and devising the scope and form of the product. . . .

Arthur Henderson was President of the Disarmament conference which
opened in Geneva in February 1932. Jean Paul-Boncour (1873–1972), French
Minister of War 1932 and Foreign Minister 1933, was the French delegate to
the League of Nations and to the Disarmament conference at Geneva. Under
MacDonald and Henderson the Labour government had some success with its
conciliatory foreign policy; there was a generally pacific mood in the country and
a reaction against the harsh terms imposed on Germany by the Versailles treaty.
On 9 February 1933 the Oxford Union passed the notorious motion that 'this
House will in no circumstances fight for its King and Country'; later in the year
a large swing enabled Labour to gain East Fulham from a Tory candidate
committed to rearmament. In September 1931 the Japanese had taken over
Manchuria and in February 1933 began their long war against China proper.
Germany had been arming secretly, even before Hitler came to power, to the
alarm of the French, who saw the apparent security of the Versailles treaty being
undermined. In the summer of 1933 Hitler made a seemingly reasonable
speech, and the British and French offered him the 'equality' he demanded by
freezing and then cutting their own armed forces. But on 14 October Germany
withdrew from the Disarmament conference and resigned from the League of
Nations. After another general election defeat, Henderson was returned at a by-
election in Clay Cross. He was still the effective leader of the Labour Party in
the country, though Lansbury, Cripps and Clement Attlee ran the rump of the
party in Parliament.

5 August. [Passfield Corner]
Dear Uncle Arthur here with his good little wife just back from 1)
his tour round European capitals, 2) a satisfactory reception in his
new constituency.

About the Disarmament conference, he is still obsessed with the
value of getting some concordat signed by the powers, however
general the terms might be. Today, after his last Paris visit and talk
with Paul Boncour, he almost despairs of success. He insists that

the French ought to accept Hitler's word and trust to the control proposed in the draft conditions, that equality in armaments must be admitted to come into force after a stated interval and that offensive weapons can be distinguished from defensive, etc. To us it seems he absurdly overrates the binding value of *signed documents*, however vague the words are, whatever the character of the individuals who sign them – a confidence which seems quite contrary to experience: first, these particular individuals pass away or are discarded by their own people, secondly they themselves have not the remotest intention of honouring their signature, *if circumstances change*, which they always do. And when the individuals are obviously half-wits and scoundrels, like the Hitler group, can you expect other parties, who have been enemies, to take their signatures at face value?

Henderson's guileless and naive dragging out of the conference over two long years has increased his reputation for dogged devotion and honesty, but diminished trust in his judgement. The great powers have found it easier to let him go on as chairman than to combine together to close the conference. The acceptance by Henderson of the safe seat of Clay Cross means, with or without the fiction of an agreement, the end of this dreary farce of the Disarmament conference. Japan in the east and Hitlerism in the west have riddled, even ridiculed, Henderson's efforts for disarmament.

About home affairs we think he is far too complacent about Transport House staff and the old programme of the Labour Party, far too certain of his own hold on the party and his capacity as Premier to carry out the necessary minimum changes under the present parliamentary constitution. Henderson is not against socialist reconstruction as were J.R.M., Snowden and Jimmy, but is he keen on it? He is a pious Christian, a good-hearted father and friend; he wishes to improve the standard of life of the working class; he is above all a good liberal . . . but does he realize that any effective personal freedom, if it is to apply to thebulk of the population, is impracticable under capitalism? . . .

I asked Henderson who, among the Liberal and Conservative leaders he had known, he had most admired and could best work with. He answered enthusiastically, 'Stanley Baldwin'. He is right. If these two men could be divorced from their respective parties and made joint dictators of Great Britain, they would reach, with the very minimum of mutual persuasion, exactly the same conclusions, alike in home and foreign affairs. Honesty, loyalty, public spirit, moderation and compromise, are their common characteristics; they neither of them understand ideas and they both dislike utopias and loathe revolutions. But the youth of today are not going that way.

I must add to this entry that Henderson is mildly concerned at the Communist obsession of the old Webbs, and he roared with laughter when I danced wildly to the strains of the 'Internationale' booming through the ether from Moscow's Red Square. 'When are you two going to tell us how to apply Communist theories to England?' 'We will leave that to the young folk,' I replied. . . .

19 August. [Passfield Corner]
Watching the milestones of declining strength. For the first two or three years of our life here – 1924–26 – the longest walk was eight miles or a little over; for the next five or six years, six to seven remained my limit. Yesterday I dared, for the first time for six months, the shorter Weavers Down round, which is five miles, and was over-tired in heart and muscle. So I doubt whether I shall do it again. Sidney could do more than I, but he claims that he is tired at five or six miles. But then he has the queer psychological habit of *sweating*, even in cold weather, so that he has to change underclothing, a habit to which I attribute his excellent health! With regard to brainwork, he goes steadily on writing and reading about the U.S.S.R. most of the working hours – he gains, relatively to past years, by having no other activity. He gives his whole mental energy to the work, which he has never been able to do before except in holiday times. We are now revising Part I, and we are fairly well content with it. We are handicapped by 1) old age, 2) ignorance of the Russian language and 3) not having visited Russia in Czarist times or being versed in her history. . . .

24 August. [Passfield Corner]
Lunched with Lloyd George, this renewal of relations arising out of his hospitality to the Fabian summer school at Frensham Heights. As an 'over-seventy' he has not changed from his former self. He has still the same easy and oncoming way, attractive personality and virile and versatile conversation; he says what he thinks (at the moment) and makes you say what you think – he is, as

he has always been, genuinely public-spirited and anxious to better the lot of humanity. But as of old he has no settled principles or values of life, personal or public; he does not know what he believes, either in respect of man's relation to the universe or men's duty to men. He professes to be a convinced Christian, but he lives and acts like any other unbeliever. There is, in his manner and outlook today, a hint of an 'inferiority complex', relatively to his great position when we met last in 1919, at Haldane's dinner-table, to discuss the composition of the Coal Commission. Then he was in the heyday of his prime ministership, one of the great figures of contemporary history; today Lloyd George is a discredited political leader with no following. But his still active brain, with its long political experience, is scanning the horizon. He is also writing his memoirs, which opens his mind to reflection on the past and leads to forecasts of the future, all of which may be interesting . . . Lloyd George is clearly at a loose end.

The Fabian school becomes every year more respectable and seedy, made up of ageing females or stray foreigners and a few younger folk who come for the bank holiday. Indeed, if it were not for Galton and the prospect of promised legacies, the jubilee year (1934) would seem an excellent date for winding up the society instead of waiting for a further stage in senility. There are, of course, a large percentage of important persons still members: not only the survivors of the historic group (GBS, Olivier and ourselves) but also younger men like Laski, Cole, Stafford Cripps, etc. But the society itself does little or nothing else but run the autumn course (which is getting stale), the summer school and a few book-boxes. So far as there is an activist group within the Labour Party it is the Socialist League, now presided over by Stafford Cripps, itself not a promising faction within the Labour Party, but at any rate a party of young people. . . .

6 September. [Passfield Corner]
I am glad I refused to review for the *Fortnightly* [*Review*] H.G.'s *Shape of Things to Come*. To 'down' that former friend or enemy would have been futile and unseemly. After all, he is on the side of the angels in his denunciation of present evils and vague yearnings after a planned civilization. But as usual he has not the remotest notion of how to get there and is ignorantly contemptuous of other people's strivings − especially so about Soviet Communism.

Throughout the book he asserts, in angry tones, that it is a stinking mess! This prejudice is still more surprising seeing that he eventually adopts Lenin's invention of the Communist Party and its role, and Stalin's Five Year Plan as the exemplar for the 'Dictatorship of the Airmen'! . . .

The Labour journalist and M.P. Mary Agnes Hamilton (d. 1966) wrote the first biographical study of the Webbs.

25 September. [Passfield Corner]
Sidney and I have been mildly interested in Mary Agnes Hamilton's biography and the reviews of it we have chanced to see. Very kindly and flattering . . . The one criticism of us, made alike by the biographer and her reviewers — that the Webbs have 'limitations', even striking and challenging limitations — is obviously true. We are specialists, and in order to extract the utmost from our joint brains, we have cut ourselves off from many pleasant pursuits and pastimes which to us, intent on getting each job finished, would have been irritating and unrestful. Also we are, as I said in my diary when we were first engaged, 'second-rate minds'; neither of us is outstandingly gifted; it is the *combinat* that is remarkable. And this brings me to a criticism of the Webbs which seems to me simply funny. We are said to lack 'humanity', to be strangely inhuman. Why? Because we have continued to be devoted to each other and have worked together ceaselessly without friction! Why should an unblemished monogamy be considered 'inhuman'?

There is one charge against us, which opens up a big controversy as to the duty of man. It is complained that we have been indifferent, even callous, to issues such as the Boer War or war in general, that we have never shown moral indignation. Well, rightly or wrongly, we don't believe in moral indignation. . . . Moral indignation is self-righteous and often perilously near hatred and is apt to take you into dangerous places — I mean dangerous from the standpoint of public welfare. It may be your duty to intervene, either with words or deeds, to prevent wrong happening, but why be indignant? . . . Moral indignation does not help — I mean the *emotion*. A kindly, and if necessary, a strong expression of disapproval — that is, public opinion against a course of conduct — may stop persons acting wrongly; but the more devoid of any anger or personal feeling the condemnation is (in a sense, the more sympathetic to the sinner), the more likely it is to be fruitful. But above all we think it is fatal and mischievous to intervene with protests when you do not know all the circumstances and have nothing to add to the controversy which is of value. Also it is doubtful whether the moral indignation of outsiders helps the cause of the oppressed. Thus we remained silent on the outbreak of the great war and, as Mary Agnes said, we seemed 'very little people'. But when you *are* of little consequence, why not hold your tongue?

The most notable over-estimation of the Webbs in the *Life* is that of our social position – a myth created by H.G. Wells in *The New Machiavelli*. Also, we have had a jolly good time of it and all the talk about 'disinterestedness' and self-sacrifice, etc. etc., is overdone. . . .

2 October. The Albany [Hastings]
Labour Party conference. I have been too unwell for the three nights we have been here to see much of the Labour Party, also the national executive have been at the Queen's Hotel whilst the Socialist League and their friends have been staying here. But it is clear that the Labour Party is in a bad state in body and mind. . . . I doubt whether the old Webbs will be seen at another Labour Party conference. With our old friendship with Henderson and our friendly relations to our gifted nephew, we are in an awkward position; we cannot help, we may hinder. Also, talking and listening tires me and I long for the quietude and small comforts of my own home. British politics seem to me to have drifted into a morass of apathy and indecision. There is *no* group of men who are at once united and single-minded; there are many public-spirited and disinterested men in politics and administration, but these good persons are wandering off on different tracks, or 'staying put' on the old highways. The net result is the *status quo* for the mass of the people, and a *status quo* that shows signs of deteriorating through old age. Existing social institutions have lost elasticity and power of self-adjustment to new conditions. Meanwhile the world outside Great Britain is changing rapidly. Whither the world? For upon that depends the fate of Great Britain. She is no longer mistress of her own destiny.

11 October. Hastings Hospital
The haemorrhage through the urine persisted and increased and my

brain began to whiz. So I called in a medical woman, who diagnosed carbuncles at the opening of the bladder and advised me to go into hospital to be explored and operated on. . . . So here I am, recovering from five hours' unconsciousness and still suffering from frequency and the debris of extensive burning, the carbuncles being more extensive than expected, but my general health a good deal better than is usual at seventy-five . . . The long sleepless nights and hours of the day between Sidney's visits in my private room hang wearily on my consciousness. Also, the thought that I may not be able to regain sufficient strength to help with the book depresses me. I try to remind my resentful soul that Sidney and I have been singularly free from pain and disability during our forty odd years of work together . . . As in all other matters we have been unusually privileged in our daily life, almost uncannily so! . . .

The first edition of *Soviet Communism* had a question mark after the sub-title *A New Civilization?* The second edition omitted it.

21 October. [Passfield Corner]
On 27 March Sidney began Part I of our book on the constitution of U.S.S.R. This morning I begin to re-sort our material for Part II. So we have spent almost exactly seven months on the six chapters. We have planned seven chapters of *Social Trends in Soviet Communism*: with my increased weakness we shall not finish them in another seven months! But if we decide not to risk a visit to Moscow at the end of May, there is no point in hurrying on with the job. If we are right in believing that the Soviet experiment will get 'better and better every day', delay in publishing our descriptive analysis will yield more conclusive proof of the rightness of our expectation and a more prepared audience for the final question, 'A new civilization?' Moreover, in some ways we can get more out of Soviet officials who come down here than from the more eminent men in Moscow. Soviet citizens are far less afraid of saying what they really think here than they are in their own country – and rightly so! Indiscretions on the part of their British friends in reporting or distorting what they say have a long way to travel, and no transport facilities from a remote country cottage in Great Britain to the Kremlin. Finally, the personalities concerned are not 'in the run' as rivals or opponents to those who are dominant in the

U.S.S.R. So we should not lose much by not going to Moscow except the excitement and satisfaction in seeing *the scene* once again.

Muggeridge began working for the International Labour Office in Geneva in the autumn of 1933. Legal difficulties long prevented publication of his novel about the *Manchester Guardian*, *Picture Palace*. His scathing account of his stay in Russia, entitled *A Winter in Moscow*, was eventually accepted by Eyre and Spottiswoode.

21 October. [Passfield Corner]
Rosy, who has been spending the summer months with the Muggeridges in Switzerland, reports that Malcolm is rabidly abusive of the U.S.S.R. and still believes that the peasants are dying in their millions. He has discarded the *Manchester Guardian* and taken on the *Daily Telegraph*. Apparently his revulsion against Communism began on the boat out, as he 'watched the expression on the faces of the crew'. Rosy had read the typescript novel about the *Manchester Guardian* which had been rejected by the publisher as libellous. It contained a scene in which Kingsley Martin's wife sat 'Buddha-like cross-legged and naked, with un-Buddha-like intent' before the hero (Malcolm). There is also a scene in which the vainglorious aged C.P. Scott, surrounded by admiring bigwigs, breaks down into senility in a public speech. It is still unpublished. His volume of sketches about the U.S.S.R. have not yet been accepted. Meanwhile he has taken a post in the International Labour Office at Geneva and is at work on Indian labour conditions, which he finds dull. 'I know I have genius, I shall succeed in the end' – which I think he will, as a *littérateur*. Rosy says he is turning to religion, under the influence of a friend who is an Anglo-Catholic priest, and is having his two boys baptized. That is good news. If you see so much of the devil and the idiot in human society, you had better believe in a god to set it right. And confession and absolution would suit poor Malcolm's complexes; he needs spiritual discipline, and he would find peace in religious rites. 'Malcolm would do well to join the Roman Catholic Church,' I suggested.

'But that would be a complete denial of all his former faith in democracy and free thought,' said Rosy, 'and Kitty is still an atheist and a rebel.' 'She might go too; she also is devil-ridden in her anger and contempt for other human beings.' That is a bearable though deteriorating state of mind during the insolence and opportunities and irresponsibility of youth, but it becomes intolerably dreary in middle life, when responsibilities and frictions increase, adventures fail and friends fall off. In old age, it is only faith in human destiny and kindly feeling towards fellow travellers that compensate for decreasing strength and decaying faculties. And the compensation and delayed benefit may be more than adequate. Old age may become the most peaceful, because the least personal part of life.

Frances Horner (1860–1940) was the wife of Sir John Horner (1842–1927) of Mells, Somerset. She was the daughter of William Graham, a Liberal M.P. and friend of Burne-Jones, Ruskin and Rossetti. Her daughter Katharine married Raymond Asquith; her son Edward was killed in 1917. Her autobiography, *Time Remembered*, was published in 1933. Lady Elcho (1864–1937) was an intimate friend of Arthur Balfour and had entertained the Webbs at her home at Stanway in Gloucestershire in the 1900s. Alfred Lyttelton (1857–1913), Colonial Secretary 1903–05, had been married to Margot Asquith's sister Laura; after her early death, he married Edith Balfour. Harry Cust (1861–1917) was the son of Lord Brownlow and editor of the *Pall Mall Gazette* 1892–96. George Wyndham (1863–1913) was Balfour's private secretary and then chief secretary for Ireland 1900–05. They were all in the late-Victorian group of clever upper-class people called 'the Souls'.

16 November. [Passfield Corner]
Frances Horner's autobiography, a naive narrative of her life, certainly bears out Mussolini's recent assertion that the last quarter of the nineteenth century, running into the first decade of the twentieth, was the period of static capitalism intervening between the dynamic period from 1800–75 and the decadence of capitalism which became obvious after the great war.

This attractive and sincere woman, the one of the female 'Souls' whom I liked best, though I knew her very slightly – I saw most of Lady Elcho – was the intimate friend of Asquith, Haldane and the other Liberal leaders, and of the intellectuals of the Conservative Party – Balfour, Lyttelton, Cust, Wyndham, Pembroke. (Incidentally, it was at her house that I first made friends with Arthur Balfour.)

The picture she presents of the inner circle of the Liberal Party is one of unbounded complacency with the existing order of society; in Haldane this was tempered by eagerness for increased education and scientific research, adult education for selected classes of the manual worker, and research and higher intellectual learning for the bourgeois specialist, who was to govern the world with the

316

benevolent overlooking of the Court, the aristocracy, the City and the capitalist Press. The only passage in the book which interested me sufficiently to quote is an intimate letter from Asquith (1892–93).

> Gradually, not at all quickly, I got on bit by bit, and in '86, in defiance of the advice of all my judicious friends, I stood for Parliament and got into the House. Helen (my wife) looked on and did not really wish it; but she was an angel and never murmured although she felt that this was the beginning of the end of our quiet unruffled uneventful companionship. I made my maiden speech (which was rather a success) and the world began to open out, and great and charming people smiled on us. . . .

A typical reaction in British public life, certainly the undoing of progressive politics, culminating in the tragedy of MacDonald, Snowden and the less advertised deterioration of the Labour Front Bench. But with Asquith it did *not* mean any desertion of the cause he had pretended to believe in; he sacrificed no principle, either in private or public conduct. What had sustained him through those years of waiting was not faith in a cause, but the intellectually disinterested desire to exercise power, to belong to the governing group, to become a Cabinet Minister before he was forty, and to do so honestly, as a good colleague and fair-minded administrator of the existing order. There was no cause in which he believed – Oxford University was, I think, his ideal institution, hence his choice of Oxford as a title – certainly no cause that entailed any sacrifice on his part; it was all plain sailing. Success in politics was no different from success at the Bar; you pleaded the causes you were paid to plead, got up the brief put before you, and compromised with the other side rather than lose the judge's or jury's verdict. It never occurred to Asquith that there was anything seriously wrong with the existing social order, or that there was any reason to bother about it out of office hours.

Asquith's brain was a fine mechanical instrument; he had a perfect style, considerable classical culture, good voice, impressive presence; perhaps his most attractive virtue was an outstanding absence of vanity and malice. He had a low scale of values. He lacked scientific curiosity and philanthropic impulse; he had not the remotest desire to make life better for the mass of humanity, and certainly no aspiration towards personal holiness. . . .

24 November. [Passfield Corner]
I have spurts of capacity in the way of scheming the book, helping to decide the scope and contents of each chapter and revising it, but I do little or nothing in its actual execution. Fortunately Sidney is thoroughly absorbed in it, either writing or reading endless material about the U.S.S.R. all day long, and he seems well and happy. If I could only get five hours' really good sleep out of twenty-four I should have nothing to complain of. . . . Still, I have my eyesight and my hearing; I can go for a three or four mile walk; sort material, read and talk, listen to the wireless; above all I have the companionship of my beloved and I realize – he makes me realize – that I am an essential background to successful work on the book. This child is our last begotten, and we are as keen on it as we were forty years ago when we were explaining British trade unionism. In *Industrial Democracy* we gave our conclusions about the factors making for progress within the capitalist system – political democracy and trade unionism, to which I had added the consumers' co-operative movement. This combination, owing to the refusal of the capitalist to play the game, has proved of no avail; a national minimum of civilized life has not been sought by successive governments; the unemployment inherent in capitalist profit-making has nullified all the advance made by increased expenditure on social services. In this work on Soviet Communism we hope to give a vision of the Communist alternative to decadent capitalism – planned production for community consumption with as much liberty and equality as is compatible with the continued progress of the human race in body and mind and social life. It is, in a sense, our last will and testament. But the sands – at any rate of my energy – are fast running out. I have a sense of working against time.

S.P. Turin (1882–1953), lecturer in Russian economics at the L.S.E. 1929–39, was employed by the Webbs to translate Soviet documents for them. His wife Lucia was private secretary to Beveridge at the L.S.E. 1928–37. They were both *émigrés* from the Soviet Union.

29 November. [Passfield Corner]
For the last week or so I have been reading up our material on the general plan and dictating notes. Turin says that we have *invented* a

constitution for the U.S.S.R. 'Are you now going to *invent* the meaning of their activities?', with a stress on the word *invent*. 'Telling the truth about things, which you cannot tell until you have discovered it, is always invention,' I retorted.

8 December. [Passfield Corner]
With the Drakes we spent three hours looking at and listening to GBS's *On the Rocks* . . . it is hardly a drama, as there is no action and scarcely an incident; it is one protracted discussion with, here and there, a monologue by the overworked hero – one long jibe and jeer at aspects of British public life, the most cutting taunts being reserved for the Labour Party. . . . Why has GBS become so persistently malicious to the Labour Party and so uncritically bitter towards the liberal belief in parliamentary democracy and personal freedom of the intellectual? Why is he always asserting that dictatorship is *good in itself* as a political system, even Hitler's medieval barbarism? . . .

The critics of future generations, if they notice *On the Rocks*, will cite it as a picture of British society in catastrophic decadence, portrayed by an aged cynic who had outlived his genius . . .

What to do with old age is a problem for the aged. We are burying ourselves in a heavily annotated volume, where failure is less spectacular than in a play. Also, we are not ourselves spectacular; we have always lived in the shadows among the dry-as-dusts, and the shadows are more suited to old age. . . .

16 December. [Passfield Corner]
Haemorrhage returned, showing that the operation was not wholly successful – consequently I am beginning to regret my decision to have it at Hastings, thinking that I might have done better to get other advice! Which is a wasted thought, because the decision seemed the best at the time and may have been so . . . Today the haemorrhage is heavier than it was before the operation, which is disturbing to one's peace of mind . . . If only I can last out the writing of the book . . . But one cannot dictate to nature the exact moment the drop of personality will fall into the ocean of impersonality.

Man, it seems to me, has no case against death; if he has been thwarted in the past and is suffering pain in the present, death comes to him as a deliverer from all his woes. If he is among the

319

fortunate ones as we have been, then he must accept the last phase, which need not be distressful if he wills to end it. . . .

Sir Arthur Steel-Maitland (1876–1935) was an economist and Conservative politician who had been chairman of the L.S.E. since 1919. The N.R.A., or National Recovery Act, was a key measure in President Roosevelt's emergency New Deal programme.

16 December. [Passfield Corner]
Beveridge here for the night; back from the U.S.A., whither he went with Steel-Maitland on behalf of the Rockefeller Trust to report on the N.R.A. He is in the depths of gloom, admits that the state of mind and state of things in the U.S.A. is far worse, from the standpoint of maintaining the capitalist state, than he had thought possible. And as he loathes Soviet Communism, alike in theory and practice, as contrary to his scale of values, he is depressed and hopeless. The callousness of public opinion about the Nazi persecution of the Jewish race, the unwillingness to save them from starvation, is also distressing him. The London School of Economics is, because of his skill and devotion, a brilliant success; he is in truth a second founder. . . .

The liberals, as a sect, are in a tragic plight; nowhere in the world do they see any respect for liberty of thought and word; everywhere political democracy of the parliamentary type is out of public favour, even falling to pieces. And of course, though Beveridge has a warm affection for us, he thinks our senile infatuation for the U.S.S.R. thoroughly mischievous. . . . He despairs; we hope. He thinks the world has gone mad in some places – Germany very mad; we think that slowly and painfully, man under Soviet Communism will become wiser and more human. . . .

26 December. [Passfield Corner]
A rather disturbing Christmas; looking forward to some weeks in a London nursing home for further exploration of my bladder trouble . . . If only I can get back sufficient physical strength and tranquillity of mind to help Sidney mould these last chapters of our last work during the next year or eighteen months. At seventy-six, one must expect to be at the end of one's tether.

'Just a few more years, Oh Mother Nature, and I will testify to your beneficence so far as I am concerned.' And the capitalist system might kindly endure until *we* are out of business! The German default has hit us badly, and what with my illness and the expenses of our Russian researches, for the first time we are overspending our income. But we can afford to be reckless in the last few years of life, alike with our strength and our fortune. The mind concentrates on the promised land for future generations of men, and about that we feel confident and content.

The last sentence of our book?

The interested and sympathetic reader will ask: 'This new civilization – will it spread to other countries?' 'Yes, it will; but how, when, where, and with what modification, are questions we cannot answer.'

VOLUME 48

↶ 1934 ↷

Although the removal of her right kidney alleviated Beatrice's bladder complaints, she continued to suffer from, and eventually died of, renal failure.

3 January. Empire Nursing Home, Vincent Square
On New Year's Day I read through, not for the first time, Sidney's chapter on 'Planned Production for Community Consumption', and I was delighted with it. It is a compelling presentation of the principle and practice of planning as conceived by Lenin and his followers, far more persuasive than any Soviet publication. Sidney is more absorbed and creative in this work than he has been in any other of our tasks, partly because the subject is so exciting, but also he has no other interest to distract him in our quiet healthy little home. Confronted with a downward trend in my own activities, with discomfort and anxiety about my wretched old body, his wellness and eagerness is most comforting and encouraging . . .

So I am here, in this ultra-comfortable and rather costly home, for a thorough testing out of my trouble, with a view to cure, if that be possible to a worn-out body. Anyway, I am not yet senile – at least I don't think I am – and for that I ought to be grateful. And in some ways it is pleasanter to be treated as an invalid and give way to illness than to try to keep up the semblance of health and regular work when feeling rotten inside, as I have been doing the last year.

So good luck to the old Webbs in 1934 and may I be alive to see it out!

6 January. [Empire Nursing Home]
. . . . A growth in the right kidney is responsible for the bleeding '— which, fortunately for the exploration, was copious, so that they could discern the source of it clearly. The only *cure* is the cutting out of the kidney — a serious matter for a woman of my age. And before doing that, the other kidney would have to be tested to see whether it will bear the burden. Death is so near at seventy-six that one wonders whether it is worth while risking immediate death in order to chance lengthening life a few months or years. I suppose I shall decide to have the preliminary test — an X-ray after injection, and then call in a second expert and abide by their joint advice. If only Sidney could be spared this time of anxiety. . . .

F.J.W. Barrington was a distinguished London urologist.

7 January. [Empire Nursing Home]
Decided to have the test today and abide by Barrington's advice whether or not to go through the serious operation of the removal of the right kidney. If one did not take this eminent surgeon's advice and went on bleeding more and more, one would be in a constant state of anxiety and regret. Also, a lingering death would be worse for Sidney and for me; it would prolong the sorrow of the parting and make it more difficult for Sidney to work whole-heartedly at the book. If I recover from the operation I shall be fit to help him, at any rate to be a source of comfort and happiness. If I drop out he is still healthy enough to go on without me and make a new life for himself. Anyway, I have done the work I intended to do and lived the life I preferred. And the problem we have been seeking to solve for the last fifty years — poverty in the midst of plenty — is today being solved, and very much as we should have solved it, if we had had our way. . . . As I lie awake during the night listening to Big Ben's chimes and the hootings of the Thames steamers I recall, one by one, all our separate researches and the writing of those unreadable books, and meditate on our happiness and interest in the work. But if Soviet Communism had not arisen, all the work we had done would have seemed to have helped on the decay of capitalist civilization, without creating a new social order

to take its place. Today we see the promised land, though not near at hand, so far as our own people are concerned. Still, there it is. . . .

12 January. 2 a.m. [Empire Nursing Home]
I spent two or three hours in the middle of last night drafting a scheme for the 'In Place of Profit' chapter, with which Sidney was delighted. It is easy to please him, poor dear, in his hour of anxiety. For me it whiled away the hours of awaiting the operation. I think I shall survive the ordeal. I have a wiry constitution, but if I don't I shall leave him with plenty of friends, a comfortable home, good health and a really exciting and creative task. We *have* been happy together and singularly at one in heart and intellect. . . .

18 January. [Empire Nursing Home]
Five days' horrid discomfort: more incidental flatulence than the wound itself, tempered by morphia. I am told, in the kindly language of a nursing home, that I am 'wonderful', 'on the road to recovery', 'an ideal patient', etc. etc., words with which the marvellously gentle and patient nurses soothe your weary hours and keep up your self-respect and optimism.

21 January. 3 a.m. [Empire Nursing Home]
At last I do feel 'on the road to recovery', after twenty-four hours solid misery in being 'purged' more than was necessary. Sidney is down at Passfield for the week-end and I see him fast asleep in his little room . . . Dancing attendance on an invalid does not suit him, though he does it with devoted dutifulness. He feels awkward and lost at it. . . .

25 January. 3 a.m. [Empire Nursing Home]
Apparently most invalids hate being in nursing homes and complain about the management. This one seems exceptionally friendly and considerate. But still it is extraordinarily trying to the temper and nerves . . . Despair enters into the soul as one looks forward to another fortnight or three weeks of the continuous discomfort. As I sleep a bare three hours in the twenty-four I sometimes wonder whether it is worth while to go on with it. Courage old lady, courage; count your blessings! . . .

29 January. 3 a.m. [Empire Nursing Home]
A fortnight and two days since the operation; kidney working well, but still suffering from flatulence, occasional pain in the wound and sleeplessness . . . In another week I shall be allowed to get up, and hope to get away a few days after, with a nurse, to Passfield. . . .

'The function of the cheque is purely therapeutic,' Shaw wrote to Sidney on 30 January. 'Nobody can resist the bucking effect of a thousand pounds in a lump. . . . The minutest push towards recovery is so priceless that thousands are as twopence in comparison.'

1 February. [Empire Nursing Home]
I get up tomorrow for the first time and if all goes well leave here on Thursday with a nurse for the week-end to see me settled in at home. . . . Meanwhile our deal old friend GBS has eased the financial situation by a generous gift of £1,000. He and Charlotte came to see me separately; they are off for a three months' tour to New Zealand and back – a way of life which offers to Charlotte pleasant distraction and to GBS the quiet and isolation of a sea voyage and the interest of seeing a new country and new people. *On the Rocks* is coming off; it soon exhausted the limited Shaw clientele for clever and perverse talk about politics among caricatured politicians . . . In Great Britain, at any rate, the Shaws neither like nor believe in the proletariat and its leaders: they live and have their being among the ennobled and enlightened plutocrats . . . But their loyalty and generosity to the old Webbs is unassailable and continuous. . . .

The United States had recently established diplomatic relations with the U.S.S.R.

4 February. [Empire Nursing Home]
Among other visitors Susan Lawrence came, full of her U.S. visit and in a great state of excitement over the 'boiling cauldron' she there witnessed, stirred this way and that by the Giant Roosevelt. She has not the remotest notion of, not even much interest in the whither of this tumultuous movement: the emotional response to Roosevelt's daily decisions on the part of the multitudes is what enchants her, the enormous growth of trade unionism – 'a new world coming into existence'. It is very much the same state of enthusiasm with which she lived in the first days of the General

Strike of 1926. . . . Meanwhile the U.S.A. broadcasting authorities are arranging for reciprocal broadcasts with Moscow. 'Everyone is speaking pleasantly about the U.S.S.R.,' reports Susan, and 'It is Wall Street and the bankers who are the *bêtes noires* today.'

The American evangelist Frank Buchman (1878–1961) founded the 'world-changing through life-changing' movement known as the Oxford Group, later renamed Moral Re-Armament.

7 February. 3 a.m. [Empire Nursing Home]
Among the books on the 'consciousness of God' drifting into my sick room is *Oxford and the Groups*. . . . That this little revivalist sect of luxuriously living youthful aspirants to direct guidance by a personal god, to be brought about by group confession of sin, should have made such a stir in English upper- and middle-class society, is a sign of the times not to be ignored. The thesis is that society cannot be regenerated without the salvation of each individual, by faith in an 'inner light' directly emanating from a personal god and witnessed to by a group of salvationists. Like other revivals of personal religion in recent times, it comes from the U.S.A., and its leader, seemingly a repulsive personality to the reserved Englishman, is a Dr Buchman. There is no suggestion of a disciplined brotherhood led by men and women who are trained, and are proving their spiritual quality by works as well as by faith. It seems to me to have all the vices and dangers of 'emotional religion' without any of the safeguards of a disciplined corps of leaders like the Roman Catholic priesthood or like the officers' corps of the Salvation Army. . . .

If I had to confess my sins, what sins should I confess: what actions, which I commit, do I feel to be wrong and regret but refuse to give up? I smoke: it is an unhealthy and expensive habit. I am aware that I often take another cigarette when it actually hurts my tongue and throat, then throw it away, which is wasteful because I smoke an expensive German brand – 'nikotine unschadlich', 8*s* 6*d* a hundred. Otherwise I think my personal habits are hygienic. I have given up alcohol; in food I try to live according to plan, guided by experience and not according to appetite. Except for smoking I have a good conscience, or rather I accept my own limitations in intellect, character and manners, and don't feel called on to regret or alter them, especially at my time of life. . . .

11 February. [Passfield Corner]
The horrid spell of pain and discomfort for me, and anxiety and unsettlement for Sidney, is ended, and we are back again in our dear little home. It will take me a month or two to recover my energy and work-worthyness and Sidney will have to give up a second visit to the U.S.S.R., a deprivation which has its advantages in hastening on the finishing of the book. As a matter of fact we have an abundance of material, and with the goodwill of the U.S.S.R. government and the help of the Turins, we do not need any more personal impressions. The book will be no more than a flashlight on Soviet Communism, but it will be a powerful flashlight and lead others to more complete and considered daylight, mapping out of the new civilization. . . .

Meanwhile I am enjoying the peace and beauty of this countryside and the songs of the birds as I lie awake in the early hours of the morning . . . I hope, when my nurse leaves me two days hence, to be able to begin sorting and taking notes from the heap of *Moscow Daily News* which lie on my table. . . .

13 February. [Passfield Corner]
With the departure of my nurse today, my illness comes officially to an end . . . The difficulty is to combine a go-easy attitude to work and exercise, as I am advised to do, while refraining from pernicious self-indulgence in cigarettes, an untimely cup of tea in the middle of the night or the use of narcotics. Meanwhile Sidney delights me with his placid satisfaction in writing the book, and his eagerness to 'listen in' to Moscow every night amuses me. In spite of being well over seventy, the study of this new civilization has kindled a sort of boyish enjoyment in an intellectual adventure, a veritable enthusiasm for his subject-matter. . . .

On 12 February civil war broke out in Austria when the Social Democrats were provoked into armed rebellion. After four days they were defeated, the party declared illegal and Chancellor Dollfuss strengthened his authoritarian control.

14 February. [Passfield Corner]
How well I remember that eight days in Vienna in the spring of 1929, and our immense admiration for the little group of Viennese socialists who had made Vienna, with its admirable housing and

other social services, the mecca of evolutionary socialism. Here at last we witnessed the Will and the Way. Those Austrian administrators had got a steady and permanent grip on the electorate of a great city; they were making all their improvements out of income – i.e. taxing the rich and thus re-distributing wealth. They had combined good art and amenity with efficient social services; they had been scrupulously honest, keeping themselves to themselves, and were acknowledged to be so by their opponents . . . Today the Viennese social democrats are being ruthlessly slaughtered in their heroic resistance to the supersession of the democratic constitution of the Austrian republic by a Fascist authoritarian state. The Social Democratic Party and the trade union movement have been swept away as completely in Vienna as they have been in Hitler's Germany. Thus the heroism and fight to the death of the Viennese socialists will serve no better than the weak-kneed submission of the German trade unions and socialist party. The Bolshevik Party and the Third International and Profintern have the laugh of the members, whether cowards or heroes, of the Second and Amsterdam Internationals. How long would the Scandinavian, French, British and Belgian labour and socialist parties be allowed to function as oppositions or as governments, *if they showed any sign of meaning business* in superseding profit-making enterprise by planned production for community consumption? . . . . Austria seems ripe for absorption by the Third Reich, with the alternative of becoming a protectorate of Fascist Italy. All the tables are turned. As for liberalism – it has been smashed to smithereens and thrown on to the dust-heap in one country after another; even in Great Britain, the home of its first beginning, it is a despised and divided minority. . . .

In a letter of 20 February, Muggeridge described the Soviet Union as 'a nasty pretentious fraud', and went on: 'The most encouraging thing I have found in the Soviet regime was its failure. If it had succeeded I think I should have committed suicide, because then I should have known that there were no limits to the extent to which human beings could be terrorized and enslaved.'

22 February. [Passfield Corner]
In a little note of regret for my illness Malcolm wrote that he was 'angry and bitter at the whole business' (Soviet Russia). In a friendly answer I asked him why he was 'angry and bitter'. He was not responsible for the U.S.S.R., nor would he be affected

materially by its success or failure. He was, in fact, in rather a pleasant position. If he was proved to be right in his prophecy of hopeless failure, moral and material, he would enjoy the consequence of being justified by the event; if he proved to be wrong, he would, at any rate, be able to rejoice that human nature even in the U.S.S.R., was not so bad as he thought it. . . .

There is a well of hatred in Malcolm's nature, and his experiences in the U.S.S.R. have released and canalized it. Barbara [Drake] reports that he seems very happy – 'in a state of exaltation'. I imagine that Hitler has released and canalized the hatred deep down in the hearts of the German youth, arising out of the humiliation of the great war, into hatred of the Jews – and they also are in a 'state of exaltation'. . . .

As far as Malcolm is concerned I am glad his hatred has been concentrated on Soviet Communism: he can neither injure the U.S.S.R. nor be injured by it. It is a safe subject for hatred and will rouse little objection in literary and journalistic circles – he will merely have to change over from the labour circles to the conservative and non-political. As an inveterate A – Artist, Anarchist and Aristocrat – by temperament, *not* by birth, he will be happier there than with our friends. But why did he *imagine* he would like Soviet Russia? All its bad features were well known. . . . That showed a lack of instinctive intelligence on Malcolm's part – he ought to have smelt the rat and, if he wanted to remain in the labour world, carefully avoided discovering its stinking body. . . .

5 March. [Passfield Corner]
If I cannot help I must not hinder. It is clear to me that Sidney ought to go to Moscow some time this year before we finish the book – alike for a change of scene from the monotony of our life down here, and also to get new light on certain issues raised by our study of the documents and the Soviet Press. . . .

The most feasible plan is for Sidney to go to Moscow in September and to take Barbara [Drake] with him, to look after him and to assist in finding out about the educational policy of the U.S.S.R. I will stay quietly here, and perhaps go for a fortnight to Bournemouth or some other seaside resort, with Annie to look after me. . . .

Current political unrest was reflected by the behaviour of students at the

L.S.E., where Communist literature circulated widely and appeals to revolt through resolutions in the Students' Union turned into an organized campaign of rebellion and vilification of the staff.

Lionel Robbins (1898–1984) was professor of economics at the L.S.E. and a strong anti-socialist.

12 March. [Passfield Corner]
Beveridge turned up yesterday as we were listening to the six o'clock news, and stayed to supper. He was full of the trouble about the misbehaviour of a knot of Marxists. . . . Beveridge has been most conciliatory. . . . This abuse of persons, accusing them of every imaginable crime and cruelty quite irrespective of facts, is a nasty characteristic, very prevalent today among the young people, but especially so among the members of the C.P. in capitalist countries. . . .

The trouble at the School is, I fear, destined to become worse during the next decade. Political and economic studies, carried on in London, one of the hubs of the political and financial world, by an assembly of some three thousand students of all races and professions – undergraduates and post-graduates, youths and maidens, and men and women in the prime of life – under the direction of a large and miscellaneous staff of professors and assistant professors, is bound to develop heated antagonism of creed and class. Beveridge cites Laski, with his Labour Party journalism and his close association with political personages, as the centre of the mischief. Laski denounces Robbins and his group of fanatical individualists for their resolute refusal to study the economic facts of today or to permit any deviation from abstract reasoning from disputed premises. And all this fanaticism will grow worse in the coming duplex struggle for power in country after country – first in the sphere of politics, between parliamentary libertarian democracy and the totalitarian state, and secondly in the sphere of economics, between capitalism and Communism. . . .

Beveridge suggested to us that all these topical issues – at any rate, any partisanship on account of them – should be ruled out, whether in the mind or conversation of the professors or of the students, as inconsistent with the scientific outlook and therefore improper subjects for discussion!

Seeing that Laski is university professor of political science and Robbins is university professor of economics, and that they each accuse the other of being unrelenting propagandists, Beveridge's naive suggestion is not likely to be accepted.

Herbert Morrison had led the Labour Party to its first and long-lasting majority on the London County Council.

14 March. [Passfield Corner]
Labour wins London: Herbert Morrison is the organizer of victory, a long pull and a hard pull lasting twenty years, the final victory doing endless credit to his doggedness, skill and masterfulness. He is a Fabian of Fabians, a direct disciple of the Sidney Webbs. His method and purpose are almost identical with that of the Sidney Webbs of 1892, applied, of course, to existing problems of 1933. . . . Forty years have passed away since the triumphant return of the Progressive Party in March 1892, largely inspired but not overtly *led* by the Fabian Society, advised by Sidney Webb. The Council returned on 12 March 1934 is completely Fabianized in personnel as well as doctrine. . . .

27 April. [Passfield Corner]
Though Sidney has finished the chapter on 'The Expansion of the Social Services' within a month, he is depressed, says that for the first time he feels himself 'to be an old man'. . . . Meanwhile I drift through the days, enjoying the beauty of springtime sight and sound, doing very little creative work but glad to be alive. Every now and again I have a bright idea; sedulously I pick out, from my reading of the spate of books and U.S.S.R. periodicals, useful extracts for Sidney's use. . . . But except for the fact that my presence comforts and encourages him, I help little with the big task. The truth is that we are about ten years too old. However, the younger British economists shirk any comprehensive examination of Soviet Communism. . . . So we *had* to do it. And learning about a new world of thought and action keeps the spirit alive. . . .

John Cripps (b. 1912), the son of Stafford Cripps, was to accompany Sidney and Barbara Drake to Moscow. Walter Layton (1884–1966), editor of *The Economist*, later became chairman of the daily *News Chronicle*. George Catlin (1896–1979) was professor of politics at Cornell University 1924–35. In 1925 he married Vera Brittain (1894–1970) who published *Testament of Youth* in August 1933.

3 May. [Passfield Corner]
Dinner at the Drakes to introduce Barbara and John Cripps to the
Maiskys: others there — Walter Laytons, Stafford Cripps, Turins
and Dick Meinertzhagen, a successful gathering lasting till twelve
o'clock. Dick Meinertzhagen — a tall, handsome, elderly colonel —
made love to Madame as he desperately wants to get a visa for a
remoter part of U.S.S.R. in search of rare birds. The Drakes like
the Maiskys far better than they did the Sokolnikovs and they, in
return, appreciated the comfort, charm and friendliness of this
typical British bourgeois family. . . .

This jaunt to London, together with entertaining Catlin and his
wife (Vera Brittain) the following day, left me a wreck so far as
work is concerned . . . Catlin, whom we did not admire when he
was last here, is much improved: the former artificiality of manner
and modish appearance diminished. But glibness and plausibility,
shallowness of thought and feeling, remain. . . . Vera is a charmer,
a competent writer and, it is said, a brilliant lecturer. F.W. Galton
was swept away by her Fabian lecture. Her lips and nails delicate
crimson, cheeks slightly and skilfully rouged; undoubtedly an
attractive little body . . . She will succeed in life; her subjects —
feminism and pacifism — are a trifle stale, but among women they
still have a vogue. Her recent autobiography sold well. Next
autumn she goes on a lecturing tour in the U.S.A., where she will
carry all before her. . . .

Felix Frankfurter (1882–1965), professor of law at Harvard University
1914–39, was a member of the U.S. Supreme Court 1939–62. Louis Brandeis
(1856–1941) was on the Court 1916–39.

20 May. [Passfield Corner]
The Laskis brought Frankfurter, an old acquaintance, down here.
This eminent professor of law, legal councillor to Woodrow
Wilson during the Versailles conference, is a warm personal friend
of Franklin Roosevelt and, together with Brandeis, he is the much
admired and admiring friend of Laski. Frankfurter certainly is a
polished and distinguished representative of American–Jewish
culture. In person and bearing he might be a European diplomat or
High Court judge, or belong to any vocation combining official
rank with intellectual distinction. He did not believe in the success
of the New Deal; it was impossible to control the great ones of

American capitalism; they would either defy or elude any attempted regulation of their conduct. He was equally convinced that Soviet Communism was beyond bounds, and refused to discuss it. But there was an alternative to big business and Soviet Communism. The ubiquitous trend towards electrification would facilitate the breaking up of the present monopoly capitalism into a number of small capitalists, and the American people would return to the health-giving competitive capitalism of the nineteenth century. . . .

As professor of law at Harvard, Frankfurter leads a sheltered life, associating with all that is distinguished in the academic and political circles of two continents. Today he is the honoured foreign lecturer at Oxford, vastly amused, almost scornful, of the 'closed minds' of the Oxford dons, surprised that such a stale atmosphere should have outlasted the troubled years of war and post-war. . . .

David Mair retired in 1933 and spent some years travelling, visiting relatives in Canada and Australia. The Mair children were now grown up – Lucy was on the staff at the L.S.E., Marjory was married and lived in Edinburgh, Philip was working in Birmingham, and Elspeth, now twenty-five, lived and worked in London. Beveridge sold his cottage – Green Street, near Avebury – to Mrs Mair in July 1932, but he was still a frequent visitor. In June 1933, after the death of his parents, Beveridge moved from Campden Hill to 3 Elm Court, in the Temple. Mrs Mair moved to 1 Brick Court in the Temple and her house in Campden Hill was sold in 1937. Beatrice wrote the following entry after a visit from the Turins. It was from Beveridge's secretary Lucia Turin, as well as from members of the academic staff, that she heard the L.S.E. gossip about Beveridge and Mrs Mair. There was considerable jealousy underlying these relationships.

25 May. [Passfield Corner]

. . . . The Beveridge–Mair entanglement has become a hot-bed of intrigue and scandal at the School. The husband has considerately left England and settled in Australia; the children refuse to live at home; Beveridge has handed over his country cottage to Mrs Mair in order to regain his freedom during the recess, and rushes off to the Continent with his motor car. He recently moved out of his next-door Campden Hill house to escape her attentions, but she followed him to a flat within sight of his new abode in the Temple, from which she spies on his movements. She also 'orders' Mrs Turin to show her Beveridge's private correspondence and his bank book. . . . But apart from the miseries of Mrs Turin, the affair is a source of demoralization at the school, an ugly feature in a co-education institution . . . What interests me as a sociologist in this unsavoury episode, is the disintegrating effect of the combination of a legalized monogamy, sanctioned by penalties for the breach of it, with a practical condonation by public opinion of illicit relations between man and woman. This contradiction makes possible emotional relationships between colleagues in one establishment. If Beveridge and Mrs Mair were married they would not be Director and Assistant Director . . . The plight of our old and loyal friend worries me – I don't see a way out for him. The woman has become a Fury and is in control of his home and his work-place. For his own and the students' sake, Beveridge would do well to move off to other work. But no one is in a position to suggest it to him. . . .

25 June. 3 a.m. [Passfield Corner]
Wasted six hours or more of excited talk with Citrine, not a wise expenditure of limited and much-needed strength. I asked him and his wife down, partly out of curiosity to see how this remarkable key man in the labour movement was developing, partly for the sake of Stafford Cripps, whose enemy he is, and partly, perhaps mainly, because we are considering a cheap edition of *Soviet Communism* to be issued to the trade unions at 5s, prior to publication. Only the first of these reasons proved justified. Citrine has become a stronger, more assured and more accomplished personage than he was three years ago. For a *personage* he is, and he knows it! . . .

Citrine is, today, the autocrat of the British trade union movement. His General Council, made up of dull-witted trade union officials, some sodden with drink, whom he at once manipulates and despises, has no policy of its own, and the Trades Union Congress seems equally subservient. 'I was forced to speak on almost all the resolutions at the last congress because the members of the Council were all too apathetic and uninterested to do more than move the resolution, which left a bad impression. This year I am insisting on their reading the report and selecting the speakers, and then I shall prepare their speeches for them and see that they understand what they are saying.' I gather that he is constantly in and out of government offices, colloguing with Ministers and officials. . . . If he has his way he will lock up the trade union movement in the *status quo* and with it, the official Labour Party for the next twenty years or more . . .

The visit, from the hostess's standpoint, was a failure, except as stock-taking. It is clear that it is useless for Stafford Cripps to cultivate his acquaintance; it is equally obvious that we shall not have his support in launching a cheap edition of our book and we had better be silent about it so far as Transport House is concerned. . . .

The Shaw play was *The Simpleton of the Unexpected Isles.*

2 July. [Passfield Corner]
GBS and Charlotte here for the week-end, as jolly as ever after their New Zealand tour. Another play of the fantastic-ethical-sociological sort – a kind of twentieth-century mystery play, or rather philosophical fantasy, tempered by the eighteenth-century *Beggars' Opera*, mystical nonsense lit up by flashes of wit and wisdom, a weird mixture ending in a 'day of judgement' and the disappearance of all those, in the play and out of it, who have no social value. The emphasis on relative value according to ethical and intellectual standards is not, at present, characteristic of GBS's own judgements of political personages! Why does GBS uphold not only Mussolini but also Hitler and Mosley as leaders to be followed? Why does he imply that their leadership is as valuable as Lenin's, that they also have a vision of a new and more desirable civilization? One would gather that the capacity to value persons is exactly what GBS not only lacks himself but ignores in other persons. . . . However, it is useless to criticize GBS. Through age and eminence he is beyond it. He is always lovable and exciting to look at and listen to. As for Charlotte, she maintains the rare quality in old age of a zest, an untiring zest, for life, i.e. for the life-companionship of the champion world *littérateur.* . . .

The following morning I told GBS what I thought about the play. . . . He agreed; he was, I think, rather discontented with his work after the three hours' reading of it. Then I asked him why exactly he admired Mussolini, Hitler and Mosley; they had no philosophy, no notion of any kind of social reorganization, except their own undisputed leadership instead of parliamentary self-government – what was the good of it all? He admitted that they had no economic principle – but they had *personality* and it was personality that was needed to save the world. (The old idea of the superman.) But Hitler's personality was a degraded one, I objected.

He was returning to old primitive values – blood-lust, racial superstition, blind obedience. As for Mosley he had not even Hitler's respectable personal character, nor Mussolini's distinction; he was dissolute and unprincipled without common sense in every sense of the word – a charlatan.

'That was said of Mussolini and is said of Hitler; but they have secured the obedience and devotion of their people. Mosley is the only striking personality in British politics; all the others are nonentities,' he replied. 'What I detest is the spinelessness of our self-complacent politicians,' he added.

He and Charlotte insisted on reading two chapters of the book – and they were very appreciative, which was comforting. . . . His main criticism was that we were *too* appreciative: 'If their methods are as effective as you suggest, why are not the results, measured in the standard of life of the mass of the people, better?' We agreed to tone down.

Beatrice Creighton (1874–?) was the daughter of Beatrice's old friends Dr Mandell and Louise Creighton.

5 July. [Passfield Corner]
Beatrice Creighton, deaconess – a sort of assistant bishop of Madras in India, a woman in holy orders – is a beautiful soul in an attractive setting: fine features and delightful expression and a musical voice, open-mindedness, kindness, will-power and a sense of humour. We had not met for ten years and the sight of her recalled to me one of the few wholly beneficent memories of past life – our friendship with the Creightons, my girlhood visits to Worcester, Cambridge, and, after marriage, to Peterborough and Fulham. She came for a night and a day with another old friend, Alys Russell. These old relationships, unchequered by dispute or friction, in the background of life, are few and far away, but very precious. In old age, memories of far-off figures surge up, as one lies awake in the night or opens the diary in the early hours of the morning – so far more vivid than the associations of yesterday and today. . . . [Creighton] would not have approved of the researches of the Webbs in their old age, and their vision of the promised land of Soviet Communism. One recalls his impression of Holy Russia, gained when he went as a great ecclesiastic to the Coronation of Nicholas II, with its magnificent ceremonies and Court splendour: that the Russian peasantry were the most pious of Christian peoples,

the most devoted and contented subjects of their 'little Father', the Czar, of all the nations in the world — when they were, in fact, illiterate, superstitious and poverty-stricken, oppressed by a brutal and corrupt governing class and seething with revolution — a rotten and distracted mass of humanity, doomed to dissolution within a couple of decades! Alas for the distortion of class bias . . . It may be added that if the Webbs had happened in those very years to meet the scruffy little Russian who was at work in the British Museum (Lenin) they would, I fear, have dismissed him as a foreign fanatic of no importance. Our contempt for the Russian revolutionaries was as perverse and short-sighted as Creighton's idealization of the Russian Court and orthodox Church. We were all of us living in a backwater — but what an agreeable backwater it was!

Eileen Power (1889–1940) was professor of economic history at the L.S.E. Beatrice (Bobo) Meinertzhagen (1885–1977) was married to Robert (Robin) John Grote Mayor (1869–1947), an assistant secretary at the Board of Education. She was the daughter of Beatrice's sister Georgina and wrote plays. On 30 June 1934, in 'the Night of the Long Knives', Hitler had brutally purged the storm troop militia (S.A.) of his own party. In all some 1,200 people were killed.

13 July. [Passfield Corner]
The Coles here: turning out continuously books, treatises, relieved by detective stories — devoted to each other, an unblemished monogamy, somewhat aloof from active participation in the labour movement. Cole thinks that there is 'nothing doing' at official headquarters. 'Stafford Cripps is the best man in the movement, but he will not be chosen as leader. Transport House, both Labour Party and trade union, will see to that. Cripps is immature politically, he does not realize that economic and political policy cannot be mastered like a lawyer's brief — that these questions need prolonged study and experience,' is Cole's conclusion. Cole's general attitude to capitalism and Soviet Communism is very similar to our own. . . .

Eileen Power for the week-end; the Laskis, Robin and Bobo Mayor and their three children, and Kingsley Martin kept me walking and talking all Sunday from nine o'clock in the morning to nine o'clock at night, with no rest in the afternoon. The Laskis are in a state of exhilaration about the hope and adventure, the social equality and universal activity in the land of the Soviets, [and are] ready to sacrifice themselves on the altar of freedom, so long as Laski may argue in favour of Communism, or against it, in London or Moscow . . . The three weeks' visit seems to have been mainly spent in being entertained and talking until two o'clock at night with different groups of the Moscow intellectuals. . . .

Kingsley Martin, who stayed for supper, thought that Beveridge intended to get rid of Laski, and that whilst the British government would be more polite to the Soviet government, the opposition to Soviet Communism would grow. 'You must be prepared for a bad Press for your book,' he said. 'Our career is behind us: we shall enjoy our last shot whatever the upshot,' I answered. K.M. professes anxiety about the upgrowth of Fascism of the Continental kind. To which we answered that Hitler had destroyed Mosley. But even without the Nazis' last disreputable display of medieval brutality, the British people will always prefer a dignified passive resistance to social reform and to public expenditure, and the continuance of an unobtrusive tightening of the grip of the minority of the well-to-do class over the masses of the poor to melodramatic appeals of highly strung and masterful counter-revolutionaries. Hitler is a great asset to anti-Fascists throughout the world and the U.S.S.R. in particular.

The course of lectures which Laski had been invited to give in Moscow provoked a storm of criticism. There were questions in the House and letters in the Press suggesting that Laski should not have been given a passport and that the grant of public money to the L.S.E. should be cut.

23 July. [Passfield Corner]
. . . The row in Parliament and in the Press over Laski daring to discuss the relative advantages of parliamentary democracy and Soviet Communism in Moscow (no one would have noticed exactly the same lecture if it had been delivered at Oxford or Harvard) is a sign of the depths of mingled fear and contempt of otherwise educated and sensible people for the Union of Socialist Soviet Republics. This hatred will grow as the success of planned production for community consumption, involving the liquidation of the land-lord and capitalist, becomes more difficult to ignore and impossible to disprove, in so far as the mass of the workers are concerned.

28 July. [Passfield Corner]
. . . I am getting anxious about Sidney's health: he has an inter-

mittent pulse and quick breathing, but he won't see a doctor — anyway, I think he had better go on this trip as he is 'fed up' with continuous writing, and badly needs a change and a rest. His exhaustion may be neurotic. The ten days on the steamer going and coming will be a complete rest from the daily grind. The truth is, this book is too big and exciting a task for 'over-seventies'! . . .

On 1 September Sidney sailed for a five-week visit to the U.S.S.R., where Soviet officials were to review and revise the draft chapters of *Soviet Communism*. All through the tour, Barbara Drake later said, 'Sidney would whisper to me, with the relish of a scientist whose theoretical proposition has stood the test of practical experiment: "See, see, it works, it works."'

22 August. [Passfield Corner]
About the book we are in good spirits; everyone who reads chapters of it seems interested and surprised at its contents. Henderson, who happened to take up my little 1891 volume on *The Co-operative Movement*, declared that the Soviet constitution as described by us was in the last chapter of that book (which, I observe in the preface to the 1930 edition, was the first result of our putting our heads together). 'Ah! but we forgot the Communist Party,' said I. 'We discovered the body but left out the soul of the constitution of a Socialist Commonwealth: and we repeated the omission in our 1922 publication. It is this religious order that's done the trick: an absurdity in the twentieth century, all liberals will say'. . . .

27 August. 3 a.m. [Passfield Corner]
As the time flies before the fateful September 1st I get into a worse panic about Sidney's state of health — I think it must be a subconscious desire to stop his going which clothes itself in concrete fears, which I tell myself are unreasonable and without foundation. However, he stands firm and refuses to see a medical man. It will by a joyful day when I see him back in good spirits with new zest to finish the book — our last will and testament. And then we can saunter down the last lap of our partnership, being wise after the event, over entries in my diary and other contemporary accounts of what has happened in the past forty years of English political history.

2 September. Parmoor
Two nights at the Drakes' dispelled my fears. Sidney is well and in

good spirits; and poor Bernard's obvious depression at Barbara's departure diverted my self-pity to another's distress. As a matter of fact, it is absurd for either of us to feel anxious about our beloveds; they will be waited on hand and foot. . . .

7 September. [Passfield Corner]
I devour books about Germany: one wants to understand how it is that that gifted race has drifted into disaster . . . For after all, the Weimar Republican Germany was a full-blown political democracy (it had even proportional representation) supplemented by highly organized trade union and co-operative movements and a powerful socialist party. And yet the whole structure was swept away in a few days without the pretence of a struggle, without even a murmur of dissent – and replaced not by a shrewd personal dictator like Mussolini, working under an established constitution, but by a group of gangsters, led by a neurotic genius of an orator. This dictator has, in two short years, antagonized all the great international powers of the world: Jewry, the Roman Catholic Church, the working-class movements in all countries, and international finance, not to mention the four great powers – France, Great Britain, the U.S.A. and Italy. Incidentally, Hitler has raised the U.S.S.R. from being an outcast state into a leading guarantor of the peace of the world, courted by France, supported by Great Britain, accepted by the U.S.A. and finally offered a permanent seat on the Council of the League of Nations. And this is the regime which Hitler asserts will last a thousand years. . . .

15 September. [Passfield Corner]
'We are all in the best of health, the weather continues sunny in a cloudless sky,' writes Sidney, which comforts me. Today I start on my fortnight's holiday among nephews and nieces, ending with a stay with Molly Holt with her motor car at Bournemouth. It has been a melancholy time: clearing up the debris of our eighteen months' work on the book; looking at Sidney's chair in the study and wandering alone with Sandy over the moors in the afternoon; anxious about his health. He also has felt the separation, in spite of the excitement of being again in Moscow. But one must not become 'maudlin' in old age. There remains the solid fact that all through our married life we have never before been separated for five weeks, and this separation is aggravated by the five-day post on

both sides. However, there is the flashed message to and fro to fall back upon in case of disaster. Silence means continued safety. . . . But I doubt whether either of us would consent to be parted again. 'And then,' he writes, 'I shall be within a week of rejoining my Bee, not again to leave her until the end.'

19 September. Hadspen
The Stafford Cripps and Arthur Hobhouse households are singularly unalike, remembering they both belong to what may be called the aristocratic bourgeoisie. Hadspen, the 160-year-old family seat, with lovely gardens broadening out into avenues and parkland, fields; and Goodfellows, a much smaller Cotswold manor house, the country place of the successful barrister and Front Bench politician, laid out with classical taste – waterways, terraces, yew hedges and brilliant herbaceous borders. But these sumptuous surroundings lap round mutually hostile spirits – Stafford Cripps fanatically revolutionary and Arthur Hobhouse conventionally conservative. They barely know each other, and certainly regard each other as persons of no importance. Isobel and Konradin are both singularly pleasant hostesses, excellent mothers to attractive children, kindly neighbours: but Isobel, attractive but workaday, follows Stafford in opinion, works hard, associates with Labour women, dresses simply, whilst Konradin is almost a professional beauty, the last word of class-conscious Toryism, ignoring the poverty of the poor, contemptuous of socialists, loathing Communism, consorting with the wealthy and fastidious, and generally disporting herself in the diplomatic circles of London and the Continent. Naturally enough, the old aunt finds herself more at home in the house of the fanatic, and was certainly disconcerted when Konradin told her that John (the boy of eleven) observed that 'having Aunt Bo to stay with you is like entertaining a Victorian princess(!)' A most inept remark! . . .

W.T. Stead (1849–1912) wrote to Beatrice on 13 February 1886 offering to print a letter she had written on public works as a signed article.

27 September. Royal Bath Hotel, Bournemouth
I posted last night, to catch today's air mail, my last letter to Sidney, while he is staying in the new land of hope and glory! His batch of letters give their daily doings – and it all seems worth while. Meanwhile I have been living a half-life without him,

dragging my uneasy body and dulled brain through pleasant scenes and comfortable circumstances, but suffering acute emotional starvation, and now and again panic fear that some ill may befall him. Here at Bournemouth, in near neighbourhood of Kildare, the house Father and I occupied for four winters, I recall those days of painful endeavour and wonder at my good fortune. I am listening early in the morning to the breaking of the waves on the sand. . . . I remember one early morning in February 86 when exactly the same waves of movement and sound and rhythm seemed to express despair, the despair of suppressed passion and a hopeless outlook, an utter failure to believe that I had the faculty to do the work I wanted to do. A few days later came the letter from Stead, the editor of the *Pall Mall Gazette*, asking whether he might print a letter I had sent him, with little hope of acceptance, as an article, with my name attached! And this minute encouragement became the signpost which told me that I was on the right road to the end I had in view. After that I never looked back or to the right or to the left. And here I am at seventy-five, with the beloved companion of the past forty years, marching together to the end of the road. What amazing good fortune. . . .

4 October. [Bournemouth]
. . . . Yesterday Betty Balfour came for lunch and the afternoon. As a woman verging on seventy she seems as charming to me as she was as a young one thirty years ago: she retains the gift of intimacy, of affectionate interest in your concerns, of intellectuality and wit, of wide experience of men and affairs, set forth through a most musical voice. She used to be good to look at – so she is at present, as a somewhat withered flower: if the form is crippled and the movements are infirm, there is the same charm of expression in those large grey eyes. So we embraced each other, and set out at once on a five hours' talk about old times at Whittingehame, the changing scene in British politics and finally about Soviet Communism, about which she is gently shocked but keenly interested. The background of her life – the Balfour clan – has lost its former ease and splendour and political importance. Arthur Balfour, when I first knew him, as Premier, was reputed to have £20,000 a year, with Whittingehame and Carlton House Terrace as his homes. Today Whittingehame is shut up, Carlton House Terrace with all its furniture sold, and what was left of his property was valued at

£40,000. So the son of Gerald lives in a small house on the estate and provides a home for old Miss Balfour and farms for his maintenance; whilst Gerald and Betty keep a modest house at Fishers Hill, with aged Mrs Sidgwick as a helpless invalid and an old gentleman as a friendly lodger. Of the five daughters, only the eldest made a good marriage from the worldly point of view – and as Betty said, somewhat wistfully, 'Gerald (now over eighty) has to earn our living by attending board meetings two or three times a week'. . . . He is apparently a serene old man, but dominated by the old economics and politics of capitalist civilization. He thinks that the London School of Economics is a nest of revolutionaries. I tried to reassure her by describing the economics faculty dominated by Professor Robbins and Sir William Beveridge. I emerged out of this interview with a dear old friend somewhat exhausted but pleased with the reminder, if not the renewal, of an old tie of friendship. We are both of us too old and too occupied to see much of each other.

5 October. [Oxford]
I motored to Oxford and spent the night with another old friend – a very old and faithful one, Louise Creighton, now eighty-four. The visit saddened me. . . . Louise is hopelessly crippled and creeps about the house. Her mind is clear, and old age and helplessness have softened her outlook on the world: she has lost the censoriousness of her vigorous and public-spirited youth and prime of life. But she is desperately lonely and bored with existence, hurt that the young people no longer care to come and see her. The plain truth is that the aged feel what their children and many of their friends are thinking about them, and sometimes even hinting at in conversation – 'If you are not enjoying life why don't you die and be done with it.' And the old person may feel that there is no answer, except that he does not want to die, or does not see any comfortable way of doing it. . . .

Ada Wallas died unexpectedly a few days after this entry was written.

7 October. [London]
Three days with Lion at the Carlton Hotel awaiting Sidney: lunched with the Shaws, distracted conversation with Desmond McCarthy, Beveridge, Lion. 'Why was Beatrice Webb so snappy?'

Desmond asked Lion (I was desperately tired, and disappointed at the delay in the arrival of the Soviet steamer). I spent the time seeing old friends — Audrey and May Wallas, Alys Russell and finally Susan Lawrence, with whom I had a heart-to-heart talk about the condition of the Labour Party. She is wringing her hands over the Labour Party conference: the old gang had triumphed, Stafford had muddled things and had been deliberately put on the executive to muzzle him, as they were trying to muzzle her . . .

10 October. [Passfield Corner]
Barbara's voice from Hay's Wharf came through my bedroom phone, just as I had finished my coffee — 'Sidney is coming direct to the Carlton Hotel.' What a joyful moment, and then the meeting, Lion laughing at our glee. Once at Passfield that afternoon I collapsed in happy passivity — a whole day in bed. He is well and certain that the journey and separation was worth while, completely reassured as to the eventual success of the new social order. There is one dark spot — the lack of free expression among those intellectuals who are against the Communist creed and the practice thereof, and would like to be an acknowledged opposition. But this freedom for adverse propaganda can hardly be accorded, or rather would not be permitted by the government of any country so long as they do not feel secure against active revolt and deliberate sabotage, so long as there is open or underground civil war. What has not yet been attained under Soviet Communism is the fullest measure of intellectual freedom and the absence of fear and hypocrisy arising from enforced conformity.

17 October. [Passfield Corner]
Rosy Dobbs here for a week — strong in body and mind and happier than I have ever known her. Nearly seventy years of age, she has become a globe-trotter with a purpose — the enjoyment and picturing of nature and architecture . . . Her husband and children are more or less dependent on her for subsidies and she certainly is generous with her limited income — travelling third-class or cheap tourist, staying at cheap lodgings and generally denying herself in order to provide extra income for the four married children and an allowance to her husband, now retired from business.

The secret of her happiness is her art, her freedom to go and do what she likes and make casual friends by the way, and, be it added, her control of the family purse. In her old age, Rosy has a sense of fruition, of creativeness, and of power over others. Perhaps, as a consequence, she is more vigorous than she has ever been before and less subject to neurotic manias. . . .

Wells called his book *An Experiment in Autobiography.*

25 October. [Passfield Corner]
H.G. sent us his autobiography. I have been browsing through its pages, an agreeable pastime for a tired brain. As an observer of H.G.'s conduct and philosophy during the prime of life and advancing old age, this frank self-exposure interests me. The account of his mental and social environment during childhood and youth explain his shortcomings. The servant's hall and housekeeper's room, on the one hand, and a series of unsuccessful apprenticeships to local drapers' shops and one chemist's shop on the other, was a servile and sordid surrounding for the youthful genius . . . Except for his admiration for Huxley, Wells grew up with a contempt for his fellow human beings, notably for the existing governing class on the one hand, and for the multitude of manual workers on the other. His swift rise, through his rare gift for imaginative journalism, to wealth and social position increased his self-conceit and stabilized his bad manners. Hence his incapacity for working with his equals in public affairs, and his total unawareness of the mental toil involved in any scientific research into man in society. . . .

H.G.'s autobiography may not be a great book; but it is fascinating reading, alike in its self-revelation and in its casual portraiture. The portrait of Arthur Balfour is perfect; the caricature of Haldane witty and apt. Towards the Fabian group he is friendly, if contemptuous; Graham Wallas was the one he liked best and learnt most from, perhaps because they shared common hatreds: the monarchy, the Church and the manual workers' trade unions. H.G. was jealous of G.B.S.'s prestige and fame; he envied his attractive figure and personality; he was intuitively hostile to the Webbs' long-winded investigation of social institutions; he did not want to examine the origin, growth, disease and death of social institutions; he wanted to judge them. To sum up: H.G. Wells emerges from his autobiography a splendidly vital man: an explorer of man's mind, a critic, artist, derider and visionary all in one. In spite of deplorable literary manners and mean sexual morals, H.G.

is to me a likeable and valuable man. He has been on the side of the angels; he has wanted to make life better for the masses of men and he has subordinated his art to that purpose. . . .

The Shaws tell us that H.G. is today ill and worried; has parted with Odette, having endowed her with the Grasse villa and a small annuity. He has fallen to the charm of 'Moura', the aristocratic Russian widow of Nicolas Benckendorf, vividly described by the infatuated Bruce Lockhart in his *British Agent in Moscow*. 'She will stay with me, eat with me, sleep with me,' whined the lovesick H.G. to GBS, 'but she will not marry me.' H.G., aware of old age, wants to buy a 'sexual annuity' by marriage. 'Moura', looking back at his past adventures, refuses to give her independence and her title away. And no wonder!

Sir John Simon (1873–1954), a Liberal lawyer, was Foreign Secretary in the National government 1931–35.

27 November. [Passfield Corner]
The Maiskys spent Sunday with us: he wanted to hear Sidney's report of the visit to the U.S.S.R. and also to report an interview he had had with Simon. It appears that Litvinov had instructed him to suggest to the British Foreign Secretary a more friendly attitude towards the Soviet government – some gesture that the aloofness between these two great powers was at an end. Simon had intimated that he could not make such a gesture without 'consulting the Cabinet' and Maisky was awaiting some sort of response – would he get it?

Sidney told him that he doubted whether Simon would bring the matter before the Cabinet, or whether, if he did, any step would be taken in that direction – for instance, the visit to Moscow of the Prince of Wales. Apparently some months ago the latter personage had gone out of his way to talk to Maisky about the extraordinary interest of the vast experiment being carried out in the U.S.S.R. and had intimated that he would like to go there! . . . What is more apparent than genuine friendliness to the U.S.S.R. is fear of the mad dog – Hitler's Germany. That fear is becoming a veritable obsession in the west, as fear of Japan is in the east. The great capitalist powers are far too frightened of each other to trouble about the apparently pacific, preoccupied and unwieldly U.S.S.R. . . . This trend in foreign affairs makes the Third International calling from Moscow for proletarian risings throughout the world all the more futile and insincere. Stalin and the C.P. may not dare to call off the old Bolshevik stunt of world revolution but they will let it peter out by starving it of brains and funds.

29 December. [Passfield Corner]
To me it seems that one of the problems before humanity is to acquire a reasonable outlook on death. Hitherto mankind has found an escape from the fear of death in some sort of faith in immortality. Yet this very faith has brought with it fear of Hell, or of another martyrdom, on 'the wheel of life', possibly a more painful experience than the life already lived. Hence Buddhism envisages Nirvana as the final escape, to be won by a good life, or a series of good lives; that is the cessation of thought, feeling and action, through the absorption of personality into the impersonality of the Universe – which is exactly what seems to happen in the death of the individual, observed and verified by science. So why wish to escape from the fact of death as we watch it happen, in the leaves of the trees themselves, in animals and in man? What stands between us and this simple and realistic outlook on death is the intolerable egotism of the human being . . . Our social aim should be to organize society so as to bring about a joyous and creative existence for all men, through serving their fellows and being served by them, with leisure to develop individual tastes and new faculties. When decay of bodily and mental health makes this no longer possible, why not a painless dissolution, leaving happy memories in the minds of those whom you have loved, and who have loved you?

VOLUME 49

∽ 1935 ∾

1 January. 4 a.m. [Passfield Corner]
I have had the forbidden cigarette to celebrate the New Year. Except for eczema and sleeplessness, I am much better than I expected to be this time last year. I can use my brain on the book and walk three or four miles. The first volume is in print; we are at work preparing the first three chapters of Volume II for the printer by the light of new material of Sidney's journey to the U.S.S.R. . . . .

12 January. [Passfield Corner]
We went to London to see the Shaws, both of whom have had alarming attacks – GBS, a collapse after producing one of his plays for the Vic before Christmas and Charlotte, a few days ago, blood-poisoning from a blow when packing up for their trip. They were glad to see us – Charlotte, who was still in bed, told Sidney that when GBS fainted in her arms she felt that if anything happened to Shaw she had only him to rely on. The two old couples are each other's oldest friends and we all dread the death of anyone of the quartet, and would feel responsible for the remaining partner. But they are both recovering and off they will go, in ten days' time, on their long ocean trip, in spite of our demurrer. . . .

29 January. 2.30 a.m. Ventnor
We came here for a long week-end. I was fed up with day after day on the book . . . I longed for the sea and a change of thought and feeling. Sidney was acquiescent . . . Cold blast of wind and snow for these last days throughout Great Britain, but here we have had sun and shelter from the north-easter: two mornings mild walking along the coast, two mornings motoring round the island and one evening at the cinema. It has been a refreshing change of scene, but alas, my worn-out body does not respond to unaccustomed circumstances, and the dizziness has come on again. My one abiding comfort is Sidney's wellness and happiness and self-confidence about finishing the book in good style. . . .

Martin's book *The Magic of Monarchy* was published in 1937. The *New Statesman*, under his editorship, was at last moving towards a good circulation and solvency.

22 February. [Passfield Corner]
Kingsley Martin down here for a talk. He is an emotional and somewhat neurotic type; the son of a distinguished Nonconformist minister, pious modernist – a serene old man whom we have met. K.M. passed through Cambridge under the not very wholesome influence of Keynes, Lowes Dickinson and E.M. Forster; married another neurotic with whom he has unstable relations . . . Kingsley Martin is a good sort, a careful liver, very intelligent, a clever journalist and a not unsuccessful editor, as the *New Statesman*'s rise in circulation proves. But his mind is a pendulum and moves from side to side over all issues in a rather tiresome fashion. He can't

make up his mind, for instance, whether or not Soviet Communism is a pretentious façade doomed to ultimate failure or the salvation of the world! He questioned us and listened to our confident replies uneasily, first seizing on some points for future use, and then obviously doubting the validity of our argumentative tirades.

His colleagues on the paper complain that he lacks any permanent scale of values or estimates about men and affairs. 'If I could only find my place in British politics,' he said to me. 'What do you think ought to be the course taken by the Labour Party?' 'I don't trouble to think about it,' I replied. 'We are old people sitting on the bank; we can't influence the Labour Party and we don't want to. On the whole I am on Stafford's side but I don't attach any importance to my opinion.' Which was not very helpful to poor Kingsley Martin. I think he is on the side of Morrison. He does not believe in universal suffrage; he particularly dislikes monarchy, and is planning a book on the status of the monarchy in Great Britain; he fears Fascism; he is sceptical about the eventual success of the U.S.S.R. But he wants to be advanced . . .

K.M. is a typical specimen of a new type of mugwump; in economics he vacillates between Keynes and the Webbs, in ethics between his puritan father and the Lowes Dickinson–E.M. Forster Greek ideal of 'free personal relationships' as the main source of cultured happiness. 'You ignore persons as individuals, they are each and all members of a category or class to be appropriately dealt with,' he complained. But he means well . . .

As Germany armed and became more bellicose, there were signs of a change in foreign affairs. The U.S.S.R. had joined the League of Nations in September 1934, and even before the Cabinet reshuffle on 7 June (when Baldwin took over from MacDonald and Samuel Hoare (1880–1959) replaced Simon as Foreign Secretary) the French had signed a treaty of friendship with Russia and the visit of Anthony Eden (1897–1977), Minister without Portfolio responsible for League of Nations affairs, to Moscow was seen as another sign of this new mood. Robert Vansittart (1881–1957), who was a notable opponent of appeasement of Nazi Germany, was chief diplomatic adviser to the government 1931–41.

16 March. [Passfield Corner]
Maisky down here, very triumphant, glad that it is Eden and not Simon who he is chaperoning to Moscow on the 27th. He dislikes Simon intensely, mainly because he feels that, in this slippery lawyer, the U.S.S.R. has an enemy. Also, Eden represents the

Conservative Party and is an 'English gentleman' — qualifications which Simon lacks, according to the Soviet diplomat. He is also pleased with the increasing friendliness of Japan; the Japanese Ambassador had intimated that a non-aggression pact with Japan would presently be offered. This change of tone was due to the enormously increased defences of the U.S.S.R. on the Manchukuo frontier. . . .

About our book he is very complimentary. He wanted an historical introduction emphasizing the value of the hundred years' revolutionary training — the self-denying and self-sacrificing atmosphere in which the old guard had been brought up: it was this new code of revolutionary tradition and personal suffering for the cause that had made the Bolshevik Party and enabled them to carry out and maintain the seizure of power from 1917 onwards. . . . Maisky, by the way, likes Vansittart and says the British Foreign Office, unlike Simon, is now genuinely friendly to the U.S.S.R. and hostile to Hitler's Germany. We warned him that the more successful the U.S.S.R. becomes in producing equality in the midst of plenty, the more alarmed, and therefore the more hostile, the wide-awake capitalists and economists will become . . . He and we spent most of our time over our proofs, he giving us corrections and additions to our statements or criticizing our conclusions. . . .

11 April. [Passfield Corner]
Exhausted with entertaining, on successive days and nights, the E.D. Simons, C.P. Trevelyan and Henry Hobhouse and his wife.

In the prime of life, able, public-spirited, wealthy, generous and personally attractive, the Simon couple are the pleasantest of guests, especially as he is a very old admirer and supporter of the Webbs, she dutifully following suit — though she is even more of an orthodox Liberal than he is. . . .

C.P. Trevelyan had asked to have our proofs as he was going with his wife and daughter to Moscow; he was so enthusiastic about the excellence of our output that he insisted on coming to spend the day with us. 'You state, you do not argue,' was his summary and impression. He and I went for a walk before lunch and he and Sidney for another after lunch. C.P. is past the prime of life. In politics for thirty years or more, first Under-Secretary in the pre-war Liberal government, then Cabinet Minister in the two Labour governments, he has been for a long spell on the Labour Party executive. He has now definitely retired in order to manage his big estate – land and capital investments. He is decidedly left in politics, dislikes Morrison and accepts Cripps but thinks that the task of the next few years must be to build up a convinced socialist movement with a group of leaders who will be wisely revolutionary when they come into power. Unfortunately, though he is very wealthy he is a miser; cannot bring himself to contribute any substantial amount to the cause he has, I think quite genuinely, at heart. Hence though he is respected, he is not liked in the labour movement; and his wife is equally if not more unpopular. Trevelyan is a singular case of a man who has had every endowment – social position, wealth, intelligence, an independent outlook, good looks and good manners, and no vices except an overwhelming meanness in spending of his large income so far as other people's needs or his own 'causes' are concerned. Whether he is as mean towards his children as his father was to him and his brothers (all three to become millionaires, or nearly so), I do not know. It may be added that George Trevelyan the historian, now a convinced Conservative, is the only one of the three brothers who has given handsomely to the public causes in which he believes. Robert, the poet, is as unproductive a citizen as is the Labour politician, though it is said that Clifford Allen extracted a livelihood out of his friendship. However, C.P.T. was lavish in his admiration of the book, which was comforting – and perhaps deserves a more flattering entry in the diary than here given of an old acquaintance (I hesitate to say friend), political associate and fellow traveller of fifty years standing. . . .

The aged Henry Hobhouse, with the devoted Anne, were our other guests – and he and I talked together of the discomforts of old age and our changing outlook. He said that he no longer thought of the future; I said that I no longer thought of the present; when I thought of myself it was past scenes that I recalled, when I thought of the race it was the distant future that I dreamt of. To which he replied: 'You have a faith in a new social order.'

Mainly in order to let their two maids have a holiday in Scotland, the Webbs had planned a tour of relatives and friends up and down the country. When Beatrice became ill they decided to go to Hastings instead.

21 April. Easter Sunday. [Passfield Corner]
A nervous breakdown has compelled – or shall I say enabled – me

to cancel all the visits arranged for the four weeks out of our home . . . Sidney himself is considerably exhausted and looks a deal older; every day he slogs at the book all the long morning from 7.30 coffee to one o'clock lunch, and is reading and thinking about it the rest of the day. The task has been too big and too exciting for our strength – let us hope not for our reputation! We have arranged for a 5s edition through the Workers' Educational Association – to be bought prior to the publication at 35s – and it is selling twenty a day. If we sell 5,000 we shall get some £800 before we have to pay our printer and, what is more important, the pure word of desirable doctrine will have gone forth to the scouts of the proletarian party of Great Britain . . .

9 May. [Albany Hotel] *Hastings*
Five days here finds me still in a state of collapse and great discomfort . . . The aged cannot be cured; a few months more or less of life is of little account. So here I must stay and cultivate a passive and peaceful mind, and just await events without fussing myself or anyone else . . .

16 May. [Hastings]
The X-ray examination which the clever young doctor insisted on my undergoing was cheerful news. There is no obstruction and no growth in the lower bowel; the trouble is weakness of the muscle of the colon and slight bulge out on the wrong side, which I suggested was due to the absence of the right kidney. The remaining kidney is O.K. . . . So that all that is needful for continued life for yet a while is strict diet and a quiet life, sufficient and not too much exercise. But my dependence on the right food etc. will make our vision of future journeys, to Scandinavia and the U.S.S.R., not to be fulfilled. It may well be that the attack means a lower level of energy, mental and physical.

The Silver Jubilee of King George V's accession was celebrated on 6 May with street parties and pageantry. Though the government denied Churchill's claim that the German airforce now equalled and would soon outnumber the R.A.F., it now proposed substantially to increase the number of front-line planes by 1937. Labour voted against this and other arms programmes while demanding collective security against such threats to peace as the expected Italian invasion of Abyssinia, which actually began on 3 October. At the same time a national canvass of opinion, called the Peace Ballot and published on 27 June,

351

gave strong and subsequently misrepresented support for disarmament under the auspices of the League of Nations; it was not in fact pacifist, for it also endorsed military measures to support collective security.

23 May. 12.15 a.m. [Hastings]
Suffering continual pain in my intestines – I walked about one mile this morning and have suffered ever since. Dr Daunt [local physician] told me to take 'moderate exercise'. Though I enjoy looking at the sea by day and night from our pleasant rooms and fill up my time reading Tolstoy and Dostoyevsky and listening to the wireless, I long to get back to Passfield, but have to wait until the girls are back from their holidays on Sunday. Also I want to improve the last chapter on 'Science the Salvation of Mankind' before submitting it to critics or sending it to the printer. Shall I have strength? If only science would tell me what exactly I ought to do! Or whether it is useless to do anything for the worn-out body. I tried two days' starvation and made the pain worse. We motor back to Passfield on Sunday morning. Shall I hold out during the next three days? Sidney had to go to Manchester . . . for the lecture on the constitution of the U.S.S.R.

While I have been suffering this setback, the National government has been driving ahead, by the amazingly popular Jubilee celebrations, the self-confident propaganda of 'returning prosperity' and the plans for aerial rearmament, to meet the menace of Hitler's Germany. The international situation gets steadily more hopelessly warlike – Italy v. Abyssinia, the France–Soviet pact, the refusal of Hitler to have any dealings with the U.S.S.R. and his menacing attitude towards Lithuania and Austria. There is a certainty of immediate reconstruction of the National government, with Baldwin as P.M. and an election within the next six months. Labour seems to be losing heavily in the constituencies owing to its ambiguous attitude about the monarchy, rearmament and revolutionary social-ism, and its poor and divided leadership. According to present signs, if a general election has to come within the next three months, the Labour Party would not reach its 1929 high mark. The only hopeful note in the present position is the rising prestige of the U.S.S.R. . . .

30 May. 2.30 a.m. Passfield Corner
Back again and feeling much better . . . Sidney came back pleased with the obvious success of his Ludwig Mond lecture to Manchester

University . . . while I struggle to recast the order of the section on Communist ethics. So we are at work again . . . If only I could get four hours' solid sleep in the twenty-four, or make up my mind to do without it. However, there is the chorus of birds to delight me in the early morning and the memory of the waves of the sea in the moonlight. And our blessed comradeship even in the last days of life.

4 June. [Passfield Corner]
. . . . We need to enlarge the paragraphs on the scientific enquiry into human behaviour by adding the question: does the process of instilling hatred and libelling your opponents achieve the purpose of attaining your ends? The hatred of and libelling of the Germans during the great war, and during the election campaign after the armistice, did not pay the British Cabinet . . . Has it paid the Soviet government to instil *hatred* and publish libels about capitalist countries, and also – in respect of their own kulaks and intellectuals – into the minds of the workers and peasants of the U.S.S.R.? Have they not been hampered by this mentality among members of the C.P. and the Comsomols in getting Soviet Communism accepted as a desirable new social order? It has certainly hampered their foreign policy. . . .

If those who give up traditional moral codes would only try to work out a science of human behaviour we should have more kindliness and truthfulness in the world, for the simple reason that it might – and I believe it would – discover that by telling the truth and being kind, the humanitarian is more likely to attain his end, i.e. the progress of the human race in happiness and knowledge.

Whit Monday, 10 June. 2.30 a.m.
Yesterday Sidney made the first draft of the final paragraph of our book: it will need redrafting, but it is 'The End'. A thrilling moment when he read it to me! Our last will and testament. We have lived the life we liked to live and we have done the work we intended to do, in blessed partnership. What more can mortal want?

1 July. [Passfield Corner]
. . . . GBS and Charlotte down here for a long week-end, she exuberant with the enjoyment of the African trip and he somewhat

353

seedy with another play finished: *The Millionairess*. He told us the gist of it. It is another bag of tricks – the conflict of unpleasant and caricatured personalities one with the other, representing his queer philosophy of life, an admiration for what is *forceful*, however ugly and silly may be the use of the power of the personality described. This strange admiration for the person who *imposes* his will on others, however ignorant and ugly and even cruel that will may be, is an obsession which has been growing on GBS for the last years of his life. And yet he himself is so kindly and tolerant towards others, so attractive and refined in his manner of life, in his relations towards other men and women, in his sensitiveness to music and other forms of beauty. From whence does it arise? As a young social reformer, he hated cruelty and oppression and pleaded for freedom. He idealized the rebel. Today he idealizes the dictator, whether he be a Mussolini, a Hitler or a Stalin, or even a faked-up pretence of a dictator like Mosley. He refuses to discriminate between one dictator and another. Has the possession of wealth, of easily acquired and irresponsible wealth, had something to do with this queer transformation? . . . . And yet GBS publicly proclaims that he is a Communist and warmly approves of our 'writing up' the U.S.S.R. as the hope of the world. What he really admires in Soviet Communism is the *forceful* activities of the Communist Party. He feels that this party has a powerful collective personality that imposes itself willy-nilly on the multitude of nonentities, thereby lifting the whole body of the people to a higher level of health and happiness. He has no faith in science and very little in a 'peaceful penetration' of goodwill and science. It is the *will to power* over other mortals that is the creative element in human society. He is essentially – or has he become? – an aristocrat: we are essentially democrats, tempered by faith in the peaceful penetration of the knowledgeable man in the management of the common interest of mankind . . .

Edward Pease, born in 1857, survived until 1955; his wife, Marjorie, died in 1950. William Sanders (1871–1941) succeeded Pease as secretary of the Fabians in 1914.

16 July. [Passfield Corner]
. . . . The aged Peases, one of the five, or rather four surviving couples – the Wallases having recently dropped out – who made the Fabian Society, visited us yesterday and we welcomed them warmly.

Physically they are the toughest of the lot. Pease is a month older than I, and Mrs Pease four years younger. A romantic memory of her presence at the first meeting of Sidney and Beatrice binds us to her. Did not Sidney write to her that first evening to ask for my address? 'I still see the reply postcard: Miss Potter, Box Cottage, Minchinhampton, Gloucestershire,' recalls Sidney. Pease was the honest, steadfast but somewhat unimaginative secretary of the Fabian Society for twenty-five years until he came into an income of £1,000 a year from an uncle, and Sidney told him he must go and make room for the younger, more energetic but equally unimaginative Sanders. He is still on the Fabian executive, resisting any change from the old policy of 'going slow'! But today the tough old lady who drives her own motor car three hundred miles in one day, wants to go to the U.S.S.R. on a cheap holiday and is decidedly going 'left', while Pease busies himself for thirteen hours out of the twenty-four in working in his garden. They and the old Oliviers remain intimate, but the Peases have dropped out of any acquaintance with the aged Shaws, as we have with the aged Oliviers.

Have there ever been five more respectable, cultivated and mutually devoted, and be it added, successful couples – the ultra-essence of British bourgeois morality, comfort and enlightenment – than the Peases, Shaws, Wallases, Oliviers and Webbs, who founded and carried on the Fabian Society during the half-century from 1883 onwards? And it must be added that they all made the best of both worlds. Two became Cabinet Ministers and peers, one the most famous and largest income-earning *littérateur* of his generation, and another a revered philosophic writer and lecturer in the U.K. and the U.S.A. Only Pease remained comparatively unknown, but it was he who was the axle of the Fabian Society and is still most intimately connected with it. The Fabian Society is the oldest and the most continuous and effective British centre of socialist thought and propaganda. Today it is from among its members that Soviet Communism finds its most effective exponents and defenders: Shaw and Webb, Laski and Cole. We have all been very comfortable and even honoured in the old civilization of profit-making capitalism: we welcome and are welcomed to the new civilization of revolutionary Communism. How different from the fate of the typical revolutionary of the past, and of the millions of *émigrés* from Russia, Germany, Austria and Italy who wander disconsolate over the earth today! The ten of us have had one characteristic in common; an almost comical *self-complacency*.

The Countess of Wemyss, one of the leading 'Souls', had been an intimate friend of Arthur Balfour. In the Edwardian years the Webbs had several times visited her at Stanway Court in Gloucestershire. Gosford was the Wemyss family estate in East Lothian, Scotland. Stanway was at this time rented by the playwright Sir James Barrie (1860–1937), who retained Lady Wemyss as his hostess and employed her daughter Cynthia Asquith (1887–1960) as his secretary. The great-grandson of Lady Wemyss now occupies the house.

22 July. [Passfield Corner]
. . . . On Saturday a gentle, fragile and somewhat decrepit little old lady, a ghost from our past, who for the last year has been asking to see us – Lady Wemyss, the beautiful and charming Mary Elcho of thirty years ago – motored down and spent the afternoon here. Like the Balfour clan, she and her family have been impoverished, have sunk from their political importance, since the great war. The great mansion, fifteen miles from Whittingehame, has been turned into a hotel, the London house has been given up, and she leads a secluded life at Stanway . . . She talked about old times, about A.J.B. and his political career, about the strange people she met at Grosvenor Road, about our visits to Stanway, about the survivors of the one-time famous 'Souls'. It was all very pathetic, left a scent of the decay and dissolution of a governing class. She was comforted when we told her that though we believed that Soviet Communism had come to stay and would spread to other countries, there would be no revolution in Great Britain during the lifetime of her children – her descendants might still be living in Stanway fifty years hence. I wonder.

24 August. [Passfield Corner]
I asked Olivier, who was staying with us before lecturing to the Fabian summer school at Frensham, which part of his varied career – clerk in the Colonial Office and youthful propagandist of Fabian socialism, governor of Jamaica, permanent head of the Board of Agriculture or Secretary of State of India and peer in the first Labour government, he had enjoyed most. 'Governor of Jamaica,' he answered unhesitatingly. 'It was like managing your own estate' – to which he ought to have added, 'with the prestige of being "Your Excellency" to all concerned'. What sanctimonious nonsense was that Victorian slogan 'the white man's burden', whether measured

in profits, prestige or irresponsible power. To share that 'burden' is today the ambition of Mussolini, Hitler and and the military castes of Japan: an ambition which will, sooner or later, lead to another world war, for the good reason that the burden is precious, beyond its yield in gold, to those who 'bear it'. . . . .

2 September. [Passfield Corner]
Susan Lawrence, the hardened old warrior of the Labour Party, obsessed with getting back into Parliament at the next general election, spent two days with us on her way to the Trades Union Congress and the meeting of the Labour Party executive at Margate. She and we are very good friends – we have quite forgotten the little friction of our joint occupation for six years of 41 Grosvenor Road, and we can gossip intimately about the personalities of the Labour Party: the rivalries of Morrison and Cripps for the leadership of the party, her bugbear Dalton, dear old Uncle Arthur, the betrayer MacDonald and the contemptible Ethel Snowden. 'I have lost all my illusions about people and retained all my hatreds,' she observed . . .

She had been staying at Goodfellows with Maisky, and the Soviet Ambassador had been trying to persuade Stafford Cripps to support the coalition between the U.S.S.R. and the political democracies of France and Great Britain against the Fascist powers of Germany, Japan and Italy, collective security under the auspices of the League of Nations. Stafford Cripps had intimated that he would not advocate any joint action between 'capitalist powers', which is rather amusing! Susan was not in the least interested in the U.S.S.R. – she resolutely turns her eyes away from it. She had spent three weeks in Palestine and thought the Jewish communes on Tolstoyan principles a far more attractive and important experiment . . .

She belongs to the old order of irreproachable female celibates, which used to be an important caste in Victorian days, and which has no votaries among the young generation – a fact, by the way, which she denies . . .

The Socialist League, which had held its annual conference at Bristol earlier in the summer, was opposing the Popular Front policy adopted by the recent 7th World Congress of the Comintern in Moscow; it objected to the collaboration with 'capitalist states' against Fascism.

28 September. [Passfield Corner]
Stafford and John here for twenty-four hours on the way to the Brighton conference. Stafford has grown in stature and charm as a political leader, but he is in a somewhat embittered and rebellious state of mind; thinks that the outcome of the present demoralized state of the labour movement will lead to a Fascist government in Great Britain and probably in the U.S.A. and France – in Great Britain of a well-bred type. Stafford is, in fact, more pessimistic than we are. . . . Stafford intimates, and we gather rightly, that he himself is the only leader who raises enthusiasm among the rank and file and can attract crowded meetings. Dalton and Morrison have, as public speakers, no success, nor has Attlee who, though gifted with intellect and character and also with goodwill has, alas!, no *personality*! He is neither feared, disliked nor admired; he is merely respected by Labour men and approved by the government bench. . . .

Muggeridge had spent a year in Calcutta as assistant editor of the *Calcutta Statesman*. While he was there he wrote a book about Butler, which had been commissioned by Jonathan Cape.

10 October. [Passfield Corner]
. . . Rosy here for a week, between her voyage to the Arctic regions round about Spitzbergen, and returning to Majorca for the winter. Reports that Malcolm 'hated India'; he threw up his position as assistant editor of the *Statesman* at £1,500 a year and is now one of the sub-editors and contributors to the Londoner's Diary in the *Evening Standard* at £1,000 a year . . . His *Life of Samuel Butler*, which had been commissioned, has been rejected by the publishers on the ground of its laying bare the great man's homosexual relation to the lifelong friend who deceived him, etc. etc. . . . To watch the tangled skein of life in our nephews and nieces is in itself an occupation for our old age, though a somewhat depressing one – it is difficult to be helpful. . . . At seventy, Rosy is happier and healthier than I have ever known her during her youth or prime of life, and bids fare to excel her eight sisters in length of life, if in nothing else. She is a rolling stone in all aspects of life – physical, intellectual and ethical – and will, seemingly, roll on until she dies: somewhere on the road.

23 October. [Passfield Corner]

. . . . Arthur Henderson dead: Sidney's oldest and most continuous friendship and colleague in the labour movement of the last twenty years. He was the exact opposite number to GBS. He had no intellectual distinction; no subtlety, wit or personal charm. Nevertheless he was an outstanding personality, because of his essential goodness, absence of vanity and egotism, faithfulness to causes and comrades, and a certain bigness, alike of soul and person, which made him continuously impressive in all the circles he frequented. There is no one in the labour movement of today who is his equal in character and judgement; there are many who excel him in intellect, eloquence and good manners. He was immensely respected by the party in the country, more so than any other leader. He was disliked by the Court, the City, and London Society, which stands to his credit. Non-smoker, teetotaller, chapel-goer, estimable husband, father and friend, he was scrupulously honest, hard-working and incorruptible, and yet widely tolerant of other people's lapses and laxities. Henderson was a model puritan, dutiful without being censorious. . . .

Baldwin fought a quiet election, playing down the question of rearmament. On polling day, 14 November, the Conservatives won 387 seats, the Liberal National group came back with 33 and National Labour with 8. The Labour Party made a modest recovery from 46 to 154 M.P.s. The Liberals, led by Herbert Samuel, were reduced to 17 seats. Ramsay MacDonald was defeated in Seaham Harbour.

15 November. [Passfield Corner]

'I shall want plenty of whisky tonight,' observed Ponsonby as he joined us after dinner to listen to the election results. 'I am beginning to fear that we may get a majority.' We agreed. But as the meagre victories came through – not a hundred seats in all, as it proved after the next day's results were given over the wireless last night – they were a trifle depressing even to our cautious minds. . . . The Conservative Party have been left, with a 250 majority, securely in command of the British people for the next four years. Over the larger part of Great Britain there is not the remotest sign of any widespread discontent with the existing social order. The leadership of the Labour Party during the election was ineffectual and divided. Morrison stands out as the one and only successful leader, and he is absorbed in directing the L.C.C.

Meanwhile I am back at work on *Our Partnership*, an easy and comforting task . . . In the course of the next few days we shall be sending out some eighty copies of the book to friends who have helped us or deserve a copy. Longman will be despatching some hundred copies to the Press for publication on 25 November. . . . We have already sold 6,000 copies of the cheap edition to W.E.A. lecturers and students, and we shall probably issue another edition to the trade union movement after Christmas. . . . We are feeling very jolly over having finished the d____d thing and are always laughing over it and congratulating one another on the birth of our last and biggest baby.

27 November. [Passfield Corner]
The irreproachable and colourless Attlee elected chairman of the Parliamentary Labour Party and Leader of His Majesty's Opposition. Of the four men offered nomination, the gentle-natured and ageing Clynes refused the honour. In the first ballot Attlee had 58, Morrison 44, Greenwood 33; in the second Greenwood's supporters went over to Attlee rather than to Morrison. The decision is, on balance, a wise one, as during the next four years Morrison is far more important as London County Council administrator than as leader in the House of Commons. Also in the disunited state of the Labour Party . . . Attlee, the neutral and least disliked member of the Front Bench, may be better than Morrison, the dictator of policy . . . All the same, Attlee is a somewhat diminutive and meaningless figure to represent the British labour movement in the House of Commons!

8 December. [Passfield Corner]
A scholar, a saint and a social reformer, R.H. Tawney is loved and respected by all who know him. His wife, who was here with him, asked me to dissuade him from sacrificing his health and his livelihood by accepting a seat in the House of Commons from the miners or other proletarian admirers . . . An Oxford fellowship or professorship (which he had been offered some years ago) is what she wanted for him, so that he might have more time and greater quietude for thought and authorship on present-day problems. This was not possible at the London School of Economics. 'There is far more freedom of expression at Oxford today than at the L.S.E.,' he observed to me as we discussed his future walking across Ludshott

Common. Apparently there is turmoil at the London School of Economics. The Director, harried by Mrs Mair and worried by the growth of Marxism among the students and the vehement objection to it on the part of the City governors, is getting more and more autocratic in his manner and bearing towards the professoriate; he is shackling the newcomers among the staff with restrictions and prohibitions and is bitterly resentful of Laski's continuous propagandist articles in the *Daily Herald* and elsewhere (Baldwin, in a recent speech, quoted Laski and Cole as mischievous incendiaries).

Tawney is critical about the state of the Labour Party; chaos of opinion and professional jealousy on the one hand and steam-rolling of all opposition to the official propaganda by Transport House on the other. He is scornful of the British C.P., with its drawing-room cult of violence. But what troubles him is his conscience. Is he pulling his weight to make things better during his lifetime? Ought he to give up his agreeable life of ease and freedom for the turmoil of politics? I assured him that his influence would be hopelessly wasted in the House of Commons – that he would find life in the House of Commons as a private member intolerable, that his gift for thought and expression ought to be used to think out the broad lines of Labour policy during the next decade, in principle and in detail. . . .

Louis Fischer (b. 1896), for many years an American correspondent in Moscow, also wrote biographies of Lenin and Gandhi. The Liberal journalist J.A. Spender (1862–1942), was the biographer of H.H. Asquith. Noting that the cheap edition and early sales covered all the costs of publishing *Soviet Communism*, Beatrice remarked: 'All the same, we could not have done the job without an independent income (one up to the capitalist system!), to which must be added that no such glorification of "the other way" would have been permitted in the U.S.S.R.'

15 December. [Passfield Corner]
Our book has had a good Press. *The Times* gave it a column on the day of publication, flattering to the authors and hostile to the subject, and a sympathetic review in the *Literary Supplement*. Other papers followed suit . . . Louis Fischer gave us a good review in the *New Statesman* which, because it contained some criticism and a few corrections on minor matters, led to an outburst of admiration from E.D. Simon. . . . Citrine spitted at us in the *Daily Herald*. The most hostile review was that in the *Observer* by our old

acquaintance J.A. Spender, which opened with: 'It is impossible to read this book with patience and composure,' and went on to a two-column tirade against the U.S.S.R. as an inhuman society of robots, whilst treating us with the respect due to the misguided skill and industry of the aged Webbs. . . .

Lancelot Hogben (1895–1975) was professor of social biology at London University 1930–37. Patrick Blackett (1897–1974), a distinguished physicist, and Hyman Levy (1889–1975), a professor of mathematics, both had strongly pro-Soviet opinions. Theresa Clay (b. 1911), was a grand-daughter of Margaret Hobhouse. Lord Strabolgi (1886–1953), was a former Liberal, then a Labour M.P. The publisher Victor Gollancz (1893–1967), was soon to found the Left Book Club. David Low (1891–1963) was the outstanding cartoonist of the period.

20 December. [Passfield Corner]
Two most agreeable gatherings – one at which we were hosts, the other, the honoured guests – celebrated the publication of our book. Our lunch at the London School of Economics (Maiskys, Hogbens, Shaws, Laskis, Lloyds, Turins, Beveridge, Professor Blackett and Levy – Horrabin was ill and couldn't come) represented those who had read and corrected the proofs. It was a lively affair but there were no speeches. At the Soviet Embassy the Maiskys entertained at dinner some forty admirers of the Webbs' work – half our own family and friends, the others mostly Soviet officials, diplomatic and trade, with their wives. It was equally informal and homely, with no ceremony or glamour – a sort of family gathering of brainworking men and women inspired by a common purpose. Stafford, John, the Drakes and Dick Meinertzhagen, attended by Theresa Clay (Dick has become, in spite of his reactionary opinions, a personal friend of the Maiskys), represented our relations; C.P. Trevelyan and daughter, the Shaws, Marleys, Alexanders, Herbert Morrison, Strabolgi, Kingsley Martin were there as our political associates, whilst Gollancz and David Low and wives and some others were Soviet sympathizers. Maisky, in proposing our health, and the wide circulation of our book, described how as an undergraduate at St Petersburg, he had bought the Webbs' *History of the English Working Class* (Lenin's translation of the *History of Trade Unionism*) and forthwith became a political revolutionary. GBS, Morrison and Alexander, C.P.T. and others followed suit – all words of affectionate appreciation, somewhat too reverential of the old Webbs, but very pleasant for us to experience in our old age.

Who would have foreseen this proletarian gathering – in sympathy, not in class – at the Russian Embassy, with eminent Fabians as the central figures, in those pre-war days when the Czarist diplomats were the wealthiest, the most sophisticated and the most accomplished aristocrats in London society. . . .

The League of Nations had condemned Italy's invasion of Abyssinia and called for effective sanctions. The Labour Party supported this policy, but the Baldwin government was reluctant to risk a military confrontation in the Mediterranean. Early in September the British Foreign Secretary, Sir Samuel Hoare (1880–1959), began to concoct a peace plan with Pierre Laval (1883–1945), his opposite number in France. The scheme would have given Italy two-thirds of a country which had not yet been overrun. When the proposals were published on 9 December, there was an outcry which led to Hoare's resignation on 18 December – this betrayal was generally thought to have been the death-knell of the League. Anthony Eden became Foreign Secretary.

25 December. [Passfield Corner]
The year ends with the Cabinet's mad muddle – the sudden and wholly unexpected presentation to Italy, Abyssinia and the League of the disgraceful peace terms hastily devised by Laval and Hoare, dismembering the victim of the war for the benefit of the violator of world peace; the immediate and wide public condemnation at home and abroad of this bewildering collapse of British calm and British courage, followed by the abject apology of Baldwin, the tearful resignation of Hoare and the triumphant emergence of the popular Anthony Eden as Foreign Secretary, pledged to carry out the sanctions even at the cost of war with the mad Mussolini. How and why all this happened no one knows and no one seems to care. . . .

VOLUME 50

⇜ 1936 ⇝

2 January. 4 a.m. [Passfield Corner]
Howling gales and continuous rain outside the house and dizziness and discomfort inside the brain have been my lot this Christmastide – relieved, it is true, by the comforting thought that the book is out and an undoubted success and that one partner is still able-bodied

and active-minded and needs the other, however feeble she may be, to complete the age-old picture of the indivisible Webbs at work by their own fireside. We are even planning a holiday the end of February – five weeks of sun and beauty at Majorca. For the last two years I have risked continuous work; having weathered that risk successfully, I might as well risk a pleasurable change of scene before settling down to another continuous task – if I ever do – very big *if*, worse luck! This day next year I shall know (or other people will) the answer to that melancholy and haunting query of an aged author: how long before the scribble ends for good and all. . . .

George V died on 20 January at Sandringham and was succeeded by his son Edward VIII (1894–1972).

21 January. [Passfield Corner]
About nine o'clock last night Sidney was rung up from Moscow and became entangled in a conversation with two Soviet officials who asked for a message from him glorifying Lenin on the twelfth anniversary of his death; the upshot, I gathered, was not satisfactory, as his many-syllabled words were not understood at the other end, so he agreed to telegraph the message. At five o'clock this morning the girls were awakened by the continuous ringing of the front doorbell; the constable at Liphook brought a telephone call from London announcing the King's death and summoning Sidney to the Privy Council today to receive the new Sovereign. Old age and the absence of correct uniform is a sufficient excuse for staying at home.

Will Great Britain under the new King or the U.S.S.R. under the testament of Lenin prevail during this century? Maybe they will approximate peacefully in their social order; if not, one or the other will go under as a great power. . . .

22 January. 4 a.m. [Passfield Corner]
My seventy-eighth birthday – two years off eighty! I reflect. As a brainworker I feel a wreck: I can read and I can walk two or three miles, but I can't think with sufficient clearness to write – if I try to do so I go still dizzier. *Our Partnership* must lie in its pamphlet box until we return from our holiday in Majorca and Sidney is clear of the publication business arrangements for new editions of the book. He is very happy in the success of the book, and, in spite of my

consciousness that I am running down too rapidly, I also am content, grateful for our good fortune.

The new civilization that we have described is ugly in its manners; cruelties and narrow-mindedness still cast their shadows. But the leaders, through planned production for community consumption, have solved, once and for all, the tragic problem of poverty in the midst of potential plenty presented by capitalist civilization; they have succeeded, under unheard-of difficulties, in providing for all men alike within their own territory, continuously increasing opportunities of health and happiness, vigorous work and gayful leisure – above all, the vision of universal brotherhood, if other countries follow their example. This is a happy thought to soothe the discomforts of old age.

Hugh Gaitskell (1906–63) became Chancellor of the Exchequer in 1950 and succeeded Attlee as leader of the Labour Party. Evan Durbin (1906–48) was an economist and moderate Labour politician who was drowned in a swimming accident. Arthur Salter (1881–1975) was a distinguished economist and civil servant.

15 February. [Passfield Corner]
E.D. Simon and Robson motored down here yesterday morning for two hours' talk about their prospective visit to the U.S.S.R. in September to investigate and report on the municipal government of Moscow. . . .

In the afternoon Eileen Power and Gaitskell came for the night – she is always charming, and he is said to be one of the rising young men in the socialist movement. Like Durbin he is fat and self-complacent: clever, no doubt, but not attractive. Like Durbin he is contemptuous of Cripps and a follower of Morrison and Dalton, and, I think, he is anti-Communist. But as he had not read our book, it was heavy-going to discuss with him the pros and cons. I suggested that he should describe the economics of Soviet Communism as he had done, with remarkable lucidity, the economics of capitalism, from the standpoint of social reformers. Eileen Power is unhappy about the School – Beveridge, she says, is breaking down in health and his influence over the staff, largely owing to the Mair entanglement, is nil. *Mrs Mair must go* is the solution of the difficulty (the poor lady is nearing sixty), and the governors must refuse all extensions of her term. Eileen would like Beveridge to go too and, like everyone else, she wants Arthur Salter as the next

Director. What with the Mair entanglement and the feud between Robbins and his die-hard group of economic individualists on the one hand, and Laski supported by the social reformists on the other (the Marxists are apparently lying low and behaving themselves), there is unrest and cynicism among the students. Gaitskell altogether demurs to our view that the young generation are going definitely Communist. 'They pass through a stage of Communism; but they find that the working class are unaffected by Communist propaganda and they drift back to the Labour Party, unless they drift out altogether from the progressive movement to become conventional Tories or, what is more likely, uninterested in politics'. . . .

Political action of a reformist character, including municipal administration, was the one and only way, according to Gaitskell: he was in fact an orthodox Fabian of the old pre-war school. What is wrong about this group of clever and well-meaning intellectuals, politicians, professors of economics and philosophy or economists, is the comfort and freedom of their own lives; they have everything to gain and nothing to lose by the peaceful continuance of capitalist civilization. . . .

The Webbs arrived in Majorca after a stormy five days' sail during which Sidney was dazed by a bump on the head after a fall. The Dobbses were staying nearby and Beveridge was also in the party. They planned to leave on 31 March.

13 March. [Majorca Hotel, Palma]
A bad night of intolerable dizziness convinced us that we must get home earlier: so we get to Marseilles on the 25th, travel through France and reach Passfield (the fates permitting) on 27 March, twelve days before we intended. Now for a struggle for patience and composure in an aged woman. Meanwhile I have been shocked by the sudden death of a very old friend, Bice Ross, Mary Playne's devoted companion for over forty years. A merciful event. She had no preliminary illness: a stroke directly after a hot bath and never recovered consciousness. . . .

17 March. [Majorca]
Recovering tone and enjoying the complete change of scene, with the prospect of being in our comfortable home in ten days' time . . . Our visit has been enlivened by Beveridge's companionship and made homely by the near neighbourhood of the Dobbses.

The little group of British residents are wholly unconcerned with the life of the 'natives'; none of them can tell Sidney what is the constitution and working of the local government. . . . The main interest is gossip about the antecedents, quarrels, means or lack of means of the foreigners living here. The Dobbses, with their strangely scatterbrained life in their ramshackle but picturesque flat, are thoroughly at home here and they all three – father, mother and son – seem to enjoy the life, taking tea with the other foreign residents every day or entertaining them in their flat. Bridge and mountaineering are the relaxations, sharing each others' books and newspapers the cultural equipment. . . .

2 April. [Passfield Corner]
The three days' and two nights' journey from Palma through France completely exhausted me, and we shall certainly not go far abroad again. . . .

10 April. [Passfield Corner]
Foreign affairs, whether over the air or in the printed word, are like a bad dream: frustration of the peace-makers, success for the war-makers. Japan and Italy carry on their conquests by land, sea and air without hindrance. Germany breaks her bonds and rearms; all three aggressive powers openly glorify war as an instrument – as *the* instrument to settle the relation of one state to another. They even declare the conquest of other races, with the incidental killing of these human beings, the most essential and holy of all human activities! The satiated and therefore pacific powers, hugging their possessions, go on arguing and protesting at Geneva and in their respective Foreign Offices, but nothing comes of it . . . Meanwhile the U.S.S.R. has notified Japan that if they invade Outer Mongolia it means war. The Bolshevik leaders at any rate mean business and know their own mind!

22 April. [Passfield Corner]
Nearly three weeks since we returned and I am still suffering from continual whizziness of ear and muzziness of brain, complicated during the first week by painful piles . . . So I am experimenting in a course of massage by an osteopath who calls himself a nature-pathist . . . I doubt whether my aged muscles and nerves are susceptible of betterment, but the risk of worsening through

massage seems negligible, and the probability of better circulation and consequent improvement encourages the adventure. . . .

29 April. [Passfield Corner]
After three trials of massage, decided against continuance of the experiment. No improvement of ear and head troubles and exhaustion with racing heart followed the last sitting. I am glad I tried it; I should have worried if I had not. . . . There is no cure for old age; all that one can do is to live simply and endure cheerfully until the way is opened by death the deliverer from the ills of life. One trouble is swept away: the fear of death! . . .

In the perfect Communist society there will rise up 'Temples of Death' where, in an environment of peaceful charm and beauty of sight and sound, any human being who is weary of life could fade out of existence without pain or distressing circumstances and without discredit to surviving relatives. . . . if there were complete security under pleasant conditions for all who are sick or disabled, which there will be under Communism, and if there were not inheritable wealth, everyone would be benefited by these voluntary withdrawals from life. Indeed it might bring about a kinder and more sympathetic attitude to the old and the sick. . . .

Maisky's remark about British faint-heartedness and his reference to the Nazi take-over of Austria and the possible cession of the German-speaking districts of Czechoslovakia are among the earliest hints that the Soviet Union might abandon its support for collective security and make its own settlement with Nazi Germany.

11 May. [Passfield Corner]
The Ernest Simons here for the week-end to consult about their U.S.S.R. tour to investigate Moscow municipal government. . . . The Maiskys came down Sunday morning to meet them; he has been helpful in making all arrangements. But naturally Maisky was anxious to talk about the humiliating collapse of British–Franco policy and the triumph of Mussolini over the League and collective security. He intimated that the Soviet government, though convinced that only by an enforced collective security against aggression could peace be secured, were beginning to doubt whether it was worth while binding themselves up with such half-hearted partners as the British government. It might be wiser for them to withdraw and mind their own business. That would mean

that Germany would absorb Austria and the German districts of Czecho-Slovakia.

After an unguarded remark which led to anticipation of the Budget and Stock Exchange speculation, J.H. Thomas resigned his seat in Parliament. Bertrand Russell divorced his second wife, Dora, early in 1935 and married Peter Spence in January 1936. They returned to Telegraph House in Sussex, which had been vacated by Dora after the divorce. She had moved Beacon Hill School to Brentford, Essex.

23 May. [Passfield Corner]
So J.H. Thomas passes out of political life, a discredited and disreputable character! If his rise to Cabinet rank is to the discredit of the Labour Party his continuance, as Cabinet Minister, in two Conservative Cabinets, is a disgrace to the gentleman's government of the British Empire. He was the quintessence of gross vulgarity in appearance and speech, in his liking for low company, in his appalling sycophancy to royalty and to high life, in his boozing and gambling, in his ignorance of all that made for wisdom in home administration and consistency in foreign policy. The only qualities he showed in his career were shrewdness in trade union negotiation, successful demagogy, a capacity for good fellowship and coarse wit, above all a hard-grained insistence in pushing his way upward through the mazes of parliamentary democracy. That such a personality should come to the top proves the need for a vocation of leadership, to enter which some sort of standards of conduct and understanding, of culture and professional competence, are required and enforced. How can we get this selection of those entitled to become candidates for the suffrages of the people? We have got it for civil servants and for the recognized professions. It is absurd not to require it for those whose special business is to direct and supervise the policy of all other professions. . . .

The annual visit of the Shaws. This winter's three months' cruising has left them the worse for it; like ourselves they are on the downward journey of old age. He brought a new play – the very title of it, *Geneva*, made us apprehensive. We listened to it for well over an hour yesterday morning. It is another and worse example of the *Beggars' Opera* type of production: fantastic farce, whether in its characters or in its situations, but alas! without the *Beggars' Opera* lightness and wit, every character depraved in morals and manners and futile in intellect, with here and there dull dissertation on public affairs. . . .

The one success of the visit was an expedition to Telegraph House, with its attractive vision of the elderly philosopher's charming young wife 'Peter Spence', who captured the hearts of GBS and Charlotte. Will this coupling of elderly genius (sixty-five) with youthful charm (twenty-five) endure to the end of the road? It is to be hoped that Bertie will die suddenly, while still a brilliant talker and a successful writer and lecturer, otherwise I should fear a solitary end for this ageing adventurer in matrimony. Amber Blanco White tells me that Peter worked her way up, from a poverty-stricken home and board-school education, through scholarships, to Oxford – where she met Bertie as lecturer. For four years she has been his companion and literary assistant; she suffers from the inferiority complex, alike in social origin and conventional ethics, but is wholly devoted to her great man. Amber has, I gather, helped her to get back her self-respect and self-confidence. Amber, a good wife and mother and clever thinker, lecturer and writer, with her own past experience, is the best of counsellors. . . .

19 June. [Passfield Corner]
Two nights and three mornings in London: lunch with Susan one day, with the Keyneses the next; the afternoons and evenings at Barbara's, Laski to dine, saw ten nephews and nieces, had a talk with the Maiskys in the morning at the Embassy . . .

But it was my lunch with the Keyneses that interested me most – for Keynes had, in his attractive way, boomed our book in his recent broadcast talk and had incidentally said that 'abstract economics were no longer in the news' for the intelligentsia, as the recognized economists could not agree on anything, whether definitions, data or conclusions. For 1¼ hours he and I argued, with Lopokova listening with her charming tact. He still refuses to regard the U.S.S.R. as anything more than an interesting experiment which has neither failed nor succeeded in providing a decent livelihood for its people. 'It is not more bread that people want, it is poetry, it is "mental equilibrium", it is "faith"; it is not a contented common people, but an aristocracy of intellect and emotions that has to be created.' I could get nothing more concrete than that; he even admitted that he himself had no faith and was still looking for one. For some reason he was always citing Baldwin as a model statesman who could bring about a modified socialism if his party would let him. Keynes has an unmitigated contempt for the official Labour Party (especially Morrison), also for the Communist undergraduates. The younger generation, he says, are suffering from neurosis, due to the absence of any creed or code of conduct. . . .

Keynes is not serious about economic problems; he plays a game of chess with it in his leisure hours. The only serious cult with him is aesthetics: the Chinese conception of the art of a pleasurable or happy life for the man with a secured and sufficient livelihood, however obtained. . . .

25 June. [Passfield Corner]
A sad drive to the Haslemere dogs' home so that Sandy might be 'put to sleep', never to wake again. What with the coming of old age, aggravated by the hot weather, he had been unusually subject to gusts of passion; he had to be tied up whenever postmen or tradesmen came to the house; Annie dare no longer wash or even brush him; and on Saturday, when I touched his back inadvertently, he flew at me and mauled my leg badly. He has been a source of interest and companionship, especially when Sidney was away; he had a striking personality, extremely intelligent, but a rebel to all authority and with a violent temper alike with dogs and men. But for all that he was a lovable little brute owing to his high spirits and bright intelligence, and his affection, when he was not thwarted and ordered about. I doubt whether I shall get another dog. They add to the duties and risks of life, and neither the two old Webbs nor the two girls have any surplus energy to dispose of. And with dogs, if they live to become infirm, the parting from them is a real sorrow.

3 July. [Passfield Corner]
A pleasant four days at Hadspen with Henry and Anne; Arthur and Konradin and their charming children intervening. My aged brother-in-law has improved with old age, owing to his marriage with the sensible, intelligent and kindly Anne; he is far more tolerant, has lost all his pomposity and censoriousness and accepts his physical disability with patience and composure; he keeps his interest in public affairs in a surprising way. . . .

Sir Josiah Stamp, later Lord Stamp (1880–1941), an economist and businessman, was chairman of the L.S.E. Sir John Clapham (1873–1946) was a distinguished professor of economic history at Cambridge.

12 July. [Passfield Corner]
Josiah Stamp and his wife spent the week-end with us; we had not had them here for six years. The immediate reason for the meeting was the crisis at the London School of Economics. According to Stamp, who is chairman of the governors, there is a violent upheaval led by the representative committee of the professors on the Committee of governors against the Beveridge–Mair director-ship or, as they style it, dictatorship. Mrs Mair will be sixty this year, the age of retirement, unless the governors extend it for four years or less. Beveridge insists that her term must be extended for the five years and threatens to resign if it is not. Robbins and his group – Laski and Eileen Power backed by their friends – in spite of their divergent views on politics and economics, unite to denounce such an extension, and threaten a scandal and wholesale resignation if Mrs Mair is retained. But this is not all. Outside authorities – the university inspectors (he showed us a letter from Clapham) and the U.S.A. donors of funds – object to Mrs Mair. Sidney and I, in spite of our warm liking for Beveridge and desire not to break with him, agree that the crisis must be ended and *Mrs Mair must go.* . . .

The distinguished physicist J.D. Bernal (1901–1971) remained a senior member of the Communist Party until his death.

18 July. [Passfield Corner]
John Strachey, today one of the leading Communist publicists, came here to hear our criticism of his latest typescript book explaining Soviet Communism [*The Theory and Practice of Social-ism*] which he had sent us for suggestions. Tall and stout is he, with his oddly Jewish face and lisp, inherited from his grandfather Nassau Senior. He is an outwardly pleasant and accomplished person, with a somewhat dubious personal and political record, a quondam associate of the talented political adventurer Mosley, with whom he broke when this disreputable leader repudiated socialism in the summer of 1931, to become the organizer of Fascism in Great Britain. Whether or not Strachey has been admitted to the Communist Party we do not know. Anyway, he is an ardent adherent of the Third International and tells us that the cause is making rapid progress among the young intellectuals in Great Britain and the U.S.A. . . . He told us that the scientist Bernal of

Cambridge was the ablest of the younger Communists; he had listened to a hot dispute between Robbins and Bernal about the validity of the *laissez-faire* solution to the troubles of capitalist civilization. If the unchecked and uncontrolled economic calculus were the correct way of solving these problems, why had *laissez-faire* been repudiated by the British Conservative and Liberal governments of the twentieth century; why had the cost of social services grown from fifty millions to a hundred in the last few decades? Bernal asked. After a short silence, Robbins answered 'The Webbs', which pleases our vanity. . . .

20 July. [Passfield Corner]
Our old friends the Coles came for the night; middle-aged and thoroughly stabilized in all their relationships, endlessly productive of books, whether economic and historical treatises or detective stories, mutually devoted partners and admirable parents of their promising children, they lead their little troop of admiring disciples along the middle way of politics, rather to the right of the aged Webbs – a curious commentary on the would-be revolutionary Guild Socialist movements of the second decade of the twentieth century. . . .

In the evening Bertrand Russell and his attractive young wife joined us. 'If I had to live my life over again I should devote it to physics or bio-chemistry. I have largely wasted it on philosophy' (dabbling in economic and political problems, he ought to have added), confessed the ageing aristocrat, roué, scholar and brilliant lecturer. 'Wasted gifts' is writ large over Bertrand Russell's life.

The military revolt against the liberal government in Spain, led by General Francisco Franco (1892–1976), began on 19 July. Despite massive support for Franco from Italy and Germany, and the failure of other democracies to give aid to the legitimate government, the ensuing civil war ran on until 30 March 1939. It became the outstanding 'cause' of the 1930s and the harbinger of the greater war against Fascism which followed. France at this time had a Popular Front government headed by the socialist Léon Blum (1872–1950).

24 July. [Passfield Corner]
The forty-fourth anniversary of our marriage was spent at Parmoor with our aged brother-in-law and his invalid wife. Alfred, despairing of the League of Nations, is an isolationist, and wants Great Britain to retire from world affairs in so far as taking sides for or

against Germany, which means siding with Germany in her
extensionist policy on her eastern frontier. Meanwhile we listen
with excited interest to the news about the Spanish revolution,
broadcast from governmental and rebel stations. The civil war is
developing into a definite class war; soldiers and sailors revolting
against the rebel officers; the government arming the workers and
peasants against the Fascist leaders and actively inciting the common soldier and sailor to depose their officers. Much depends in
foreign affairs on what side wins in Spain; if the duly elected left
government succeeds in its proletarian aims, the example of Spain
will lead to similar results in other countries: perhaps France,
under the United Front government, will follow suit. If the rebels
become the government, Spain joins the Fascist league against
political democracy. . . .

Zinoviev had already been imprisoned for a year when Kamenev and thirteen
other old Bolsheviks were tried and executed for conspiracy. It was the first of
the show trials accompanying the large-scale purges which decimated the party
organization, the officer corps and the Soviet intellectual élite. Beatrice was
hesitant about the trials but she allowed herself to be persuaded by Soviet
apologists and by analogy with British repression in Ireland and India. She also
felt that the Spanish government might have saved itself by draconian measures
against the military plotters.

28 August. [Passfield Corner]
For the defenders of Soviet Communism in foreign parts the
sensational trial in Moscow, denounced by Trotsky as a monstrous
lie, is a nasty shock. To re-open a criminal indictment concerning a
particular episode when the principal individuals accused have
already been tried, convicted and are in confinement, is repugnant
to the British conception of jurisprudence. For the defendants to
plead guilty, to refuse the aid of counsel, to vie with each other in
abject confession of their crime and an accusation of other persons –
in the case of Zinoviev and Kamenev, a revolting exhibition of
treachery to the government and to former comrades, of cringing
cowardice and repetitive lying – lends a suspicion of torture behind
the scenes, or of promises of pardon not fulfilled by the G.P.U.,
capped by the immediate execution of the whole sixteen of them
after the verdict. Even if you desire to destroy your enemies, the
violence of the prosecution, indictment and denunciation, and the
savage demands for death sentences by workers all over the country,

repeated night after night in Moscow broadcasts, is offensive to British calm and good manners. We blew our rebels from the cannon's mouth after the Indian Mutiny; we massacred crawling men, women and children at Amritsar not so long ago; we hung poor old Casement, shot the romantic Erskine Childers, slaughtered innocents by the Black and Tans in the Irish rebellion in the 20s, with an easy conscience; but we did not talk about it, or revel in reviling our victims.

Why the Stalin governing group decided on this melodramatic staging of their revenge on enemies who had already been punished and were in confinement, and therefore not participating in the conspiracy of today . . . is impossible to understand and justify. One has just to shrug one's shoulders and mutter 'After all, the Soviet government has only just emerged from the middle ages,' which is not quite consistent with welcoming Soviet Communism as a new *civilization*! My own explanation is that all the leading men in the U.S.S.R. have been brought up in the atmosphere of violent revolution, of underground conspiracies and ruthless killings, and they cannot get out of this pattern of behaviour. Those who have the power suspect all those who disagree with their policy of being counter-revolutionists, ready to murder and conspire against their former comrades, whilst some of those who dissent do actually revert to revolutionary practices – certainly Trotsky did, and the evidence is that Kamenev and Zinoviev were also conspiring against Stalin. But whether or not these dissenters were guilty of conspiracy to murder they were bound to be thought so, and treated according to the revolutionary principle of kill your enemies, otherwise you will not survive yourself. . . .

The labour organizer and Liberal politician John Burns (1858–1943) had been President of the Local Government Board and the target of Beatrice's criticism when she was a member of the Royal Commission on the Poor Law in 1906. Burns noted in his diary on 14 December 1917, after meeting Beatrice again, that she was 'grey, old, faint, yet pursuing her ideals of numbering us all . . . deindividualizing us all, and taking emotion out of character, soul out of body, joy out of work, and delight that springs from variety out of existence.'

3 September. [Passfield Corner]
Decided, with Sidney's approval, not to write for publication in composing the chapters of *Our Partnership*. It is clear that even these chapters I have already finished could not be published so

long as persons described therein are still alive: John Burns, for instance, is a melancholy instance. His career was cut short when still in his prime through a maniac personal vanity which negatived all his considerable gifts — mental vigour, physical health, good looks, oratorical powers, sense of humour, conscientious industry and personal asceticism in food, drink and, so far as I know, scrupulous honesty in money matters — all brought to a standstill because he was always thinking about himself and his career. He absurdly overrated his own capacity for leadership; and was at the same time ludicrously sensitive to other people's opinion of him. Hence he withdrew from the battlefield of political life on the outbreak of the great war, and lived in day-dreams of coming back as a conqueror. But it would be cruel to imply this, as it is implied in the entries of my diary, for him to read in his last days. He has no descendants — his wife and son are dead. So no one will be hurt or injured if the truth — or what most people think the truth — is told when he is gone. It may even be a useful warning to other people . . . So I shall just jog on with the daily task, without any hurry or expectation of publication. . . .

The Webbs founded the London School of Economics in 1895 and the *New Statesman* in 1913.

14 September. [Passfield Corner]
In old age it is one of the minor satisfactions of life to watch the success of your children, literal children or symbolic. The London School of Economics is undoubtedly our most famous one; but the *New Statesman* is also creditable — it is the most successful of the general weeklies, actually making a profit on its 25,000 readers, and it has absorbed two of its rivals, the *Nation* and the *Week-end Review*. Kingsley Martin, with his queer, shifting, alive intelligence, his careless hygiene, his miscellaneous ethical code (he is not a whisky addict which apparently the majority of journalists are, especially the Americans; but he has got rid of his wife) and loose views about his neighbour's morals, has turned out a successful editor. He vacillates between Communism and mere capitalist reformism, between John Strachey and Keynes, Bertrand Russell and the Soviet Embassy; between complete isolationism in foreign affairs and helping the Spanish government and thus risking war . . . He has no philosophy of life; he flits from one viewpoint

to another. He delights in gossip. That gives the *New Statesman* its variety of outlook – perhaps makes it popular in this dissolving world.

George Jeffreys (1645–89) tried the Popish plot conspirators and put down the Monmouth uprising in 1685 by hanging two hundred rebels and transporting another eight hundred.

15 September. [Passfield Corner]
. . . . When I am asked 'What do you think about the Moscow trials?' I point to our own revolutionary period of the seventeenth century and early eighteenth centuries, when we were changing over from a Catholic and divine right monarchy to the Protestant and statutory monarchy. What about all the beheadings of great personages and shootings down of the common people – e.g. Judge Jeffreys, etc. – or our century-long holding down of the Irish race that went on in our tiny state of Great Britain? We do not condemn our own revolution or regret that it happened. Revolutions are nasty episodes, especially when they don't succeed or drag on indefinitely as they have done in Spain. How much bloody revolution will be needed to convert the world to a step forward from capitalist profit-making to Soviet Communism? That is the question before the human race. At present the preparation for mutual massacre looks ominous. . . .

21 September. [Passfield Corner]
Lion Phillimore, generous, dogmatic and excessively tiresome in the most literal sense of the word, here for the week-end . . . She argued and laid down the law on all matters secular and divine, scientific and philosophical, political and economic . . . Bless her! She is a real good sort in personal conduct but wearisome as a companion for tired minds.

29 September. [Passfield Corner]
A two days' visit to Goodfellows: Stafford and Isobel were in excellent spirits and health . . .
Two nights with the Shaws: GBS failing, Charlotte still going strong. Sidney well and I ailing. Shall we four meet again here or at Passfield? I have my doubts . . .
After a morning at the London School of Economics . . . we

partook of a lively lunch with Laski and other lecturers in the restaurant of the School. I finished up at Barbara's for dinner and the night, talking to nephews and nieces of the Meinertzhagen clan. . . .

The Hogbens and Bertrand Russell spent the evening here – Russell is very admiring of Hogben's latest publication *Mathematics for the Million* . . . They both agreed that nearly all the clever and public-spirited young men were Communist – only a few were Fascist, but liberalism was dead.

At the Brighton conference in October 1935, the Labour left and the pacifists had been heavily defeated in a vote which committed the party to support the League of Nations, but left the question of rearmament unsettled. At Edinburgh in 1936, the party supported the policy of non-intervention in Spain and rejected yet another motion for a united front with the Communists and the rump of the I.L.P.

20 October. [Passfield Corner]
The reports of the Labour Party conference in the Press are hopelessly discouraging. What should have been its main objective – the transformation of this country into a socialist society – hardly appears in the proceedings. The rearmament question, the Spanish revolution and foreign policy generally, all matters about which the leaders are in disagreement, seem to have been the only questions in which they were interested – except, by the way, a perfunctory and cut-down debate, ending in a block-vote refusal to admit the Communist Party to membership, and a peremptory dissolution of the League of Youth, which has gone Communist. The dark shade of the Spanish civil war, its hideous cruelties, the miserable failure of the non-intervention policy of Great Britain and France, the chance of this creed war spreading to France and leading to a world war, revealed the Labour Party without a decisive policy, not knowing, as in the case of Abyssinia last year, whether they were prepared to risk war in order to prevent gross injustice in the international sphere, and whether or not they would trust the National government with increased armaments. As it is the Fascist states are carrying all before them and look like continuing to do so, owing to the fact that the capitalist democracies cannot make up their minds . . . What seems inevitable is a world war.

'I don't complain of being frustrated personally. I've had a wonderful time,'

378

H.G. Wells wrote to Beatrice on 29 October. 'But Man is being most damnably frustrated and I've tried to diagnose why.' He was displeased with 'the mess of a film' that Alexander Korda had made from his book *The Shape of Things to Come*. Raymond Massey played the part of the airman-scientist in the post-catastrophe utopia.

2 November. [Passfield Corner]
. . . H.G.'s semi-autobiographical *Anatomy of Frustration* (though he denies that it is autobiographical) displays his self-conceit. As is usual with his later philosophical essays, he asserts that he knows the way out of the tragic world situation, that he could save the world from the coming disasters if he were dictator. But his vision of the future turns out to be a series of bombastic sentences, big emotional phrases without intellectual content.

Out of friendly curiosity Sidney and I went to see his film at Farnham. The first part – the destruction of civilization by world war – is vividly impressive; without H.G.'s expansive imagination and artistic talent it could not have been conceived and produced. The second part, visualizing the new social order, is the epitome of meaningless mechanization. The human home of future ages is to be without an outlook on the beauties of nature; with artificial sunlight and conditioned air, there is no need for windows. Within masses of moving machinery, multitudes of men and women and children scurrying about like ants in a broken-open ant-hill; they seemed moved by hero impulse, not by individual minds. Restless, intolerably restless, is this new society of men, ugly and depressing in its sum total. The world in ruins as depicted in Part I, open to visions of land and sea, plain and mountain, sun and cloud and the universe of the sky, is more invigorating. The only feature in the new social order which is attractive is the face and attitude of the hero. The women, by the way, are nonentities and rather graceless nonentities: the children are little prigs. The voices are raw and rasping: that side of film technique is a failure. As an attempt to depict *a new civilization* the film is a disastrous failure.

25 November. [Passfield Corner]
The birthday of our biggest and most self-important child – *Soviet Communism* – certainly the best-seller of all our works. 20,000 in Great Britain, 5,000 in the first six months in the U.S.A.; penetrating into Japan, Australia, South Africa, New Zealand and India – so enthusiastic readers in those parts inform us . . .

What do we think of our child today? So far as the material and constitutional progress of the U.S.S.R. is concerned our presentation has been more than justified . . . But there remains as the big blot on the picture the terror, suspicions, suppression of free opinion, the arrests, prosecutions, death penalties, characteristic of an unfinished revolution. Those amazing confessions, which would not be considered as evidence in an English court, how are they obtained? . . .

The bad manners, the vilification of Trotsky, of accused persons generally, the florid denunciation of condemned criminals in newspapers and broadcasts, are revolting to British calm! And the sycophantic adulation of Stalin – also unpleasant to British ears . . . The U.S.S.R. is still medieval in its savage pursuit of the heretic.

Edward VIII had been very popular as Prince of Wales, but Court officials had long been nervous about his erratic behaviour. His relationship with Mrs Ernest Simpson, a twice-married American, was reported in foreign newspapers and was generally known in London society. But after Mrs Simpson's divorce on 27 October there was a long and discreet tussle between the King and Baldwin. The matter became public on 2 December, when it was in its first stages. The King privately told Baldwin on 5 December that he proposed to abdicate, but there was much agitation before this was announced as settled on 10 December. The King left the country the next night and his brother the Duke of York (1895–1952) became King George VI.

5 December. [Passfield Corner]
If the Queen Bee in a densely packed hive crawled out of her cell and wended her way towards the outer world, there could hardly be a bigger buzzing in the company of bees than there has been among the humans of the British Empire about King Edward's proposal to marry Mrs Simpson. In Labour circles there are two strains of thought and feeling. The most spontaneous reaction is 'Why should not the King marry the woman he loves, even though she be a commoner, a foreigner and a divorcee?', reinforced by the openly expressed suspicion that the whole episode is a conspiracy against the King – the outcome of the reactionary government and the offended Church's hatred of a monarch who busies himself, not with Church and Court functions, but with the miseries of the common people and the way to end them at the cost of the rich. . . .

What comes out of the whole business is that neither the Church nor the Court circle would have objected to a King's mistress –

Edward VII had a succession of these, openly accepted by all concerned; what they do refuse to endure is a Queen who does not conform to Court usage, still more to a King who dislikes conforming to Church rites and is on the side of the common people. If the King refuses to relinquish the proposed marriage, or to step down from the throne, the Cabinet will resign. The Opposition will refuse to take office, the scratch government he will get together (Winston Churchill, Lloyd George?) will have to dissolve, and the electorate will be divided according to distorted class bias. No one knows what will happen, except a vitiated and muddled public opinion expressed by a scratch majority. If he abdicates and York is proclaimed King, reaction will have won. If he withdraws the question of marriage and just 'carries on', he might win through. No Conservative government would risk a general election on the Cabinet's right *to compel a King to promise not to marry*, if he had the common people on his side. No one knows what are Edward VIII's opinions, except that he loathes the Anglican Church, associates with a bad-mannered lot, and cares for the comfort of the unemployed men. Whether he is atheist or tends to the Roman Catholic Church, Communist or Fascist is unknown. He may not know himself. Some say he is intimate with the German Embassy and is a reactionary: Rothermere and Mosley support him. He is neurotically excitable, obstinate, hates show and has a warm heart for the underdog; but he is not an intellectual. It is said that he is, in conversation and conduct, coarse and common. *'What do you really believe, Mrs Webb?'* in an earnest tone and with a nervous gesture, is the only sentence in his talk with me that I remember! What struck me as most certain is that he is an unhappy man who has not found as a royal personage a comfortable private life. Which is to his credit . . .

The King made a broadcast from Windsor Castle on the evening of 11 December, before leaving for France.

12 December. [Passfield Corner]
The events of the last week are the most superb manifestation of good manners on the part of the British governing class. To engineer the abdication of one King and the enthronement of another in six days, without a ripple of mutual abuse within the royal family or between it and the government, or between the

government and the opposition, or between the governing classes and the workers, was a splendid achievement, accepted by the Dominions and watched by the entire world of foreign states with amazed admiration. An exquisite example of British calm, British solidarity, British kindliness and British common sense. What could be more convincing and disarming than Baldwin's homely and sympathetic account of his friendly remonstrances to the King about his disreputable appearance with his acknowledged mistress at home and abroad? A month later, the King asks, 'What about a morganatic marriage?' 'Impossible', answers Baldwin, after consulting the Cabinet. '*I intend to marry Mrs Simpson,*' answers Edward, 'and go', he adds. So he announces his abdication. The Cabinet begs him respectfully, even affectionately, to reconsider, etc., etc. He refuses. Hence the swift passage, in a single day, of the necessary Bill through both Houses of Parliament and, within a few hours, the proclamation of the new King and Queen; and then, that very evening, the touching farewell of Edward to his people over the air.

What behaviour could have been more suited to unite the House of Commons, to pacify the mob, to damp down, once for all, the upgrowth of a King's party? 'Manners maketh man,' is the old adage. 'Good manners hideth a multitude of sins,' is more to the point in British politics.

As a compromise, Mrs Mair's term of office was extended until 1938. In April 1937 Beveridge accepted the headship of University College, Oxford. Mrs Mair accompanied him and, after the death of her husband in 1942, became Lady Beveridge. 'The only fly in the ointment,' Beatrice wrote, 'is that Beveridge seems sore about the Webbs' intervention, and especially about my part in demurring to his relations to Mrs Mair.'

31 December. [Passfield Corner]
The last day of the year we had a painful visit from Beveridge. There had been a meeting of some of the governors at Stamp's office, which Sidney attended, when the Director came to plead for the continuance of Mrs Mair in office for another five years after she had attained the sixty-year-old limit. Owing to the universal strike of the professorial staff against her interferences in academic affairs, coupled with the scandal of the relationship, Stamp and his inner circle of governors had decided that she must go, and Sidney supported them. Beveridge was indignant and suggested that if

they were guilty of 'breaking the heart' of this admirable woman he could no longer associate with them! He came down here to talk it over. He and Sidney had a long interview during which Sidney spoke of the 'impossible situation' at the School. Beveridge said he had never heard of the 'scandal'!!! But he looked tragic after the interview; and though there was no further discussion and I was not involved, the rest of the visit was painful. We parted with affectionate words, but we are anxious about the effect of the visit on his and Mrs Mair's intentions. . . .

VOLUME 51

∽ 1937 ∾

7 January. [Passfield Corner]
Here we are, once again, at the opening of another year of the mad century.

So far as we are personally concerned, we are rather more comfortable than we were this time last year; for I am slightly more able-bodied and workable. But Europe and Asia are in the same cruel turmoil, killing and being killed, as they were in 1935–36. The Fascist powers are rather more outrageous in their acts, words and intentions, the capitalist democracies no less divided in their loyalties. Which do they fear most – the Fascist powers, intent on more territory acquired by war, or the U.S.S.R., pacific in its foreign policy but propagandist, through its successful building up, on a huge scale, of a new socialist and equalitarian civilization? . . .

Our Partnership is growing steadily; four chapters are finished – so far as I can see at present, about half the first volume. But work on it is painfully tiring. But muddling through a couple of hours every morning, thinking about it and reading endless biographies and reminiscences the rest of the day, gives meaning to my life and interest to our talks together. . . .

Muggeridge had now given up his job on the *Evening Standard* to be a freelance writer. He and his family had moved from London to Whatlington, near Battle and Hastings.

30 January. [Passfield Corner]
Five days at Hastings to rest ourselves and our two girls, and see a few friends and relatives. Among these Malcolm Muggeridge, whom we had not seen for five years, not since he was here in June 1932, as an enthusiastic denigrator of the capitalist system and would-be admirer of the Soviets . . . The queer thin little figure, colourless face and hair, neurotically active eyes and continuously moving mouth, with his ingratiating manner (continual repetition of 'Aunt Bo'), his pleasant and clever talk, half repelled, half attracted me. Is he a bit mad, I wondered? He told us that he had become a 'mystic' and I can well believe it; he would need some escape from the reality of other people's human nature *as he visualizes it*. It is this obsession for searching out all that is detestable in persons and institutions that is so odd and repulsive in Malcolm . . . However, we parted friends.

What new ugliness of body and mind he will have discovered in the aged Webbs, I do not know; some fresh reason for denouncing us will have become apparent. Poor Malcolm; I doubt whether he will succeed in making a comfortable income: debunking is today at a discount. Times are too tragic. . . .

Among the convicted in the 1937 Moscow trials was Grigory Sokolnikov, whom Beatrice had known well as Soviet Ambassador in London. Though her Communist acquaintances energetically justified the trials, she was not wholly convinced: 'It is impossible to believe that all this is being invented by the witnesses to confirm an invention by the prosecution,' she remarked on 17 February. After she had read the official Soviet transcript, she vacillated between reluctant conviction and equally reluctant scepticism, with an overall disposition to believe that the accused really were conspirators. Both Sokolnikov and Karl Radek (1885–1939), the well-known journalist, died in prison.

20 February. [Passfield Corner]
Certainly the more one studies the verbatim report of the Moscow trials the greater is the puzzledom as to the psychology involved. Why did those intelligent and strong-willed men get involved in that crazy conspiracy at a fearful risk of death? The fact that the first lot – Kamenev, Zinoviev and Co. – helped to start the second centre, because of the probability that they would be arrested, showed that they knew the risk and therefore foresaw their own execution. That looks like heroism? And yet the rest of their conduct was despicable, in their snivelling confession, time after

time, of their own and each others' sins? Then the extraordinary casualness with which Sokolnikov, Radek and others connected up with each other, at home and abroad, carried on criminal correspondence with Trotsky and foreign diplomats, and yet never attempted to escape over the frontier, when discovery seemed imminent. The matter-of-fact details of the evidence, and the self-possession of the witnesses and apparent unconcern about their lives and their reputations, are also amazing to a foreigner. Again, why, if it is a 'frame-up', the Soviet government should wish to publish to the world such a damaging libel on Soviet Communism and its strength, is utterly bewildering. *Unless the facts are true* the whole business is absolutely incomprehensible, whether on the part of the government or on the part of the accused but innocent victims. . . .

Shaw's play *Candida*, first performed in London in 1904, was revived at the Globe Theatre on 10 February.

27 February. [Passfield Corner]
Two nights at Barbara's, where we met fourteen nephews and nieces, lunched with the Maiskys and the Shaws, saw *Candida*, besides Sidney attending a dinner and various meetings. . . .

Maisky thought that after the experience of Spain and the shilly-shallying of the British and French governments, the U.S.S.R. might virtually withdraw from any further collaboration with western powers and devote itself to the building up of socialism and the further development of defence; quite recently the Soviet government has decided to construct a powerful navy in the next five years: five battleships are on the way. Germany will attack Czechoslovakia if Franco succeeds in Spain, Maisky maintains.

We and the Drakes were delighted with the arrival of *Candida*, which is having crowded houses. Partly this return to the little domestic problem of home life was a welcome relief from the sensational and dangerous battlefields of international affairs, where murder and arson and famine seem part of everyday life . . .

As for the fourteen nephews and nieces and their friends, we have found them as charming as usual – well-mannered, refined, cultivated and even public-spirited in a mild way – but not promising material for a revolution!

My impression grows that the British governing class, with its conventional good morals and manners, will hold the fort of capitalism, and there will ensue a polite and painless decline of Great Britain and her Empire.

Russell gave up his house on the Downs near Harting in 1937.

15 March. [Passfield Corner]
We motored over to Telegraph House, through its dishevelled grounds of chalk pits and undergrowth, unkempt high beech hedges, all alike infested with rabbits, grey squirrels and rats and other vermin, to the odd dwelling-place of two successive Earl Russells, distinguished for their gifts, heresies and unsuccessful matings and consequent poverty: both of whom have been our intimate friends. Poor Bertrand, today sixty-five, with a young wife and a coming child, with little or no income beyond what he earns, looked physically worn out and mentally worried. And well he may be. He would like a professorship, but he is past the age at which any British university could appoint him. His only hope is the U.S.A. But his particular subject, the philosophy of mathematics, is off the modern curriculum: physical science and sociological investigation are in the ascendant. Russell's wit and subtlety, his literary skill and personal charm, his particular obsessions in favour of freedom for the intellectual coupled with non-resistance, are all demoded in favour of factual (not philosophical) studies of how we can climb out of the terrible tragedy of international hostilities and decadent capitalism.

Sidney and I have been revolving in our minds how we can help him. We owe him a debt of gratitude for his generosity in giving the London School of Economics five years' fellowship income in the early days of the School's career. Impulsive generosity, like his temporary sexual infatuations, have dissipated the small inherited income with which he started out on his disinterested but disjointed adventure in brilliant thinking and promiscuous intercourse. He ought to have a Civil List pension, but what government would reward so distinguished a rebel against authority, human or divine?

19 March. [Passfield Corner]
What troubles me, in the task of building up successive chapters of *Our Partnership* from diary entries and contemporary writings and present-day reflections, is twofold. How big is the work to be? As one long chapter after another unrolls itself in masses of typescript I

386

wonder whether any reader will or could get through it all; also many reflections about manners and morals, and more especially about religion, are not my present way of thinking: am I there and then to say say so and give my present point of view? Finally there are the critical, sometimes the defamatory character of the notes about people, friends, acquaintances and enemies, observations which are often hasty and unwarranted, contradicted or modified by later impressions. Of course, I console myself with the thought that I can always leave out (or my literary executor can leave out) what is not desirable to print, when the day of publication comes along. But if that be so, why trouble to select? Why not leave the diaries intact and not bother myself to make a book out of them? This question I think suggests the answer . . . one could find a skilled editor to cut down the book to what was a desirable length and content according to the circumstances of the time. . . .

Norman Thomas (1884–1968) was leader of the American Socialist Party.

16 April. [Passfield Corner]
Five nights and six days away from home. . . . The most exhausting but entertaining episode was my stay at Goodfellows . . . the central figure was the imposing leader of socialism in the U.S.A. – Norman Thomas, three times presidential candidate. He looks it and behaves like it. Tall, clean-shaven with an agreeable loud voice, compelling gestures of mouth and hands – it is impossible not to *look* at him. He is obviously a kindly man and public-spirited citizen with a clear but commonplace mind, dominated by the American assumption that individual liberty equals absence of restraint in act, thought and speech, to which he adds the shibboleth of nationalization of the means of production, distribution and exchange. In attendance was a pleasant and intelligent little wife. To this company was added on Sunday afternoon some twenty other guests – mostly Oxford dons from the university. After tea we sat in the large sitting-room and the presidential candidate addressed us on American politics. . . . He reminds me in some ways of Bryan, except that he is far more reasonable and matter-of-fact – and though a good speaker he is not an orator and lacks the burning faith of the former democratic leader . . . At present he is a figure-head without a following. . . .

18 April. [Passfield Corner]

To return to our round of visits. Our stay at Longfords . . . and the expedition to Standish, our old home, seemed like visiting a family graveyard . . . Longfords is today sold to be cut up into lots; the neighbouring woods and fields have been increasingly supplanted by little villas, each with its patch of garden and outbuildings. The enlarged mill has eaten up most of the beautiful garden and woods; what is left has fallen into disorderly decay. The whole neighbourhood has become urbanized: the nine-mile drive to Standish House is today through streets of little shops and rows of small houses, interspersed with new mills and little villas.

When we reached the old home, the house and its spacious gardens was the habitation, not of a family, but of 260 tuberculosis patients with a complete staff of medicals, nurses, mechanics and gardeners. When we introduced ourselves as the Webbs, 'a remnant of the Potter family', we were welcomed as honoured guests and allowed to wander about at our own sweet will – I, with queer memories associated with this room or that, this corner of the garden or that view of the valley of the Severn or the Standish woods. To outlive one's own generation, to realize that even the memory of these men and women has passed away – well, it all adds to the melancholy of old age, to which is added, in our case, the consciousness of decay in our own civilization, our own race, our own class, of the beloved and oneself! . . . .

Beatrice, approaching eighty, arranged a reunion party for what she called 'the R.P. clan'.

5 May. [Passfield Corner]

. . . We are looking forward to the family party on 12 June, to which I have asked the 150 or more nephews and nieces. Then our proposed stay in Switzerland, from about 18 June to 8 July, to let the two girls have three week-ends in Scotland. After that I hope to get back to my own job . . . The spring has come at last and as I write these words, 4.30 a.m., the chorus of birds I love so well begins. So I shut the book and listen in. . . .

14 May. [Passfield Corner]

We listened in to the magnificent medieval pageant of the Coronation of George VI. How strangely Jewish, alike in the words (nearly all from the Old Testament), in the rites-of-human-sacrifice doctrine of the atonement, the priestly anointing, and above all in the dominating ideology of a divinely appointed King, of a chosen people, to rule by the sword, over the rest of mankind. So much for the Abbey service. The Alice in Wonderland of the procession, the gorgeousness of the scene, centred round two little robots in the glass coach, preceded and followed by the armed forces from all parts of the Empire – one long orgy of glorification of the imperial mission of Great Britain, manifested in five continents . . .

To me the revolting role in the massive spectacle served to the multitude is that of the Anglican bishops. Is it conceivable that these highly selected scholars and would-be philanthropists honestly believe in these rites and ceremonies, in this strange mixture of magic with the deification of force, pure and simple, as a way of organizing mankind for the glory of God? What about the pacifists, the secularists, the old evangelical Quaker element – why have they not protested? Why this ironic silence on the part of the intellectual élite, the total absence of moral indignation on the part of the followers of Jesus of Nazareth at this adoration of power and riches? . . .

30 May. [Passfield Corner]
H.D. Harben, our old friend, spent five hours here. After years of waiting he has come into his aged aunt's £1¾ million fortune: the three-quarters goes in death duties, and the rest he is transferring into a family trust for himself, his wife, his sons and daughters and their children. He lives a leisurely and luxurious life in Paris, his wife lives in London, and they exchange visits in a friendly sort of way. Their children are all convinced conservatives, he is extreme left, a devoted admirer of the U.S.S.R. and incidentally of our book. As of old he is an agreeable cultivated man, talks loudly and well; reads all the newest books in three or four languages and travels extensively, picking up on the way the news of the world with avidity. . . .

5 June. [Passfield Corner]
Our dear old friends – GBS and Charlotte – spending a few days here, he visibly frail and in decline, distressed that he can no longer write his plays . . . He cannot visualize complicated social institutions and their reactions on individuals: his detail is all wrong and

389

his philosophy not thought out. And he knows it! . . . They consulted Sidney about what to do with their respective fortunes; they want to endow (Charlotte brought a draft will endowment for the Irish Free State) 'culture' or, as GBS puts it, 'knowing *how to behave* in public administration, or in any other career' . . . What kind of testament he will sign, seal and deliver, heaven only knows. Sidney spent an hour or two drafting some description of what he thought GBS really wanted to do, in language which might be understood by an intelligent trustee, and another hour or so discussing with Charlotte her draft. In return GBS will go through the proof of the postscript to our chapters [for the revised edition of *Soviet Communism*]. So continues the old unbroken comradeship in work, started forty-five years ago, between GBS and the Webbs. . . .

13 June. 4 a.m. [Passfield Corner]
The family party . . . was a decided success. Over one hundred of the descendants of Richard and Lawrencina Potter assembled in our garden, with a few old friend outsiders – the Bernard Shaws, Ponsonby, Snell, Beveridge, five former secretaries, casual cousins like the Meinertzhagens and Ritchies – Mrs Richard Potter and daughter, and one or two Heyworths. But it was my sisters' children, grandchildren and great-grandchildren that interested me most. It pleased me to think how the seven sisters would have loved to be there and watch their descendants eagerly talking and laughing together. Dear old Father, how delighted he would have been at the thought of the successful careers of many of his descendants and their spouses. Three peers, four privy councillors, two Cabinet Ministers, two baronets and two Fellows of the Royal Society – a typical nineteenth- and twentieth-century upper-middle-class family, rising in the government of the country . . .

But it was an exhausting episode for the aged Webbs and their two girls, with the Mileses and my old servant Jessie and my secretary Gabrielle Irwin to help. I doubt whether this experiment of a large garden party will be repeated. The garden looked lovely, the three sitting-rooms were enlarged by a pavilion, the weather was perfect and there was a due consumption of tea and cakes and sherry and cigarettes. So all went well . . .

I wrote that the R.P.s had during the last fifty years risen in the world. But this is only true of half a dozen individuals who stand out from the others as undoubted successes in the world's estimation. As a group, the R.P.s have become poorer. At the end of the nineteenth century the combined business and professional incomes of R.D. Holt, Daniel Meinertzhagen and the Crippses must have hovered somewhere near £100,000, whilst Henry Hobhouse, Arthur Playne and even Leonard Courtney (after he had been endowed by his wealthy brother-in-law Richard Oliver) reckoned their income in thousands, rising in the case of Henry Hobhouse and Arthur Playne to £5 or £6,000 a year. Only Rosy and I were at the £1,500 level and were considered by the other members of the clan to be 'poor', if we had children, which I had not. . . .

The Webbs spent a holiday at the Kurhaus at Beatenburg near Interlaken.

12 July. [Passfield Corner]
We enjoyed our first flight in the air to Basle and back again, an ideal way of travelling for an aged couple. Instead of the tiresome journey by rail and steamer — with all the trouble of transferring from one crowded London station to another, the hurried transfer from rail to steamer and steamer to rail through customs and the night journey, arriving at Basle at 6 a.m. — we motored to the Croydon aerodrome, where we lunched, entered the plane at 1.45 and arrived at Basle 4.15, owing to a north-west wind which shortened the official time-table by one hour! The journey back was rather more exhausting, since we added the journey down from Beatenburg to Basle and did not begin our flight till 3.30, arriving Croydon 7.15 — from where we motored back here, arriving 9.30, somewhat exhausted . . .

The three weeks at Beatenburg at the Kurhaus was delightfully restful. George and Rosy Dobbs were with us for the first ten days and Rosy, as our guest, stayed on . . . Rosy, with her obsession — the search after beauty and the attempt to portray it — was a pleasant companion. So was George in his more conventional way. Sidney and I wandered about in a honeymoon spirit. . . I returned home feeling much stronger for the three weeks' isolation from talks with clever guests, reading with a purpose and listening to the wireless, all of which one does at home. . . .

While we were away, my aged brother-in-law Henry Hobhouse died. Throughout our lengthy relationship, from his marriage to Margaret in 1879 and her death in 1921 he and we, though respecting each other, were not friends or associates. I think he disliked me: in the main because of my old intimacy with Margaret before her marriage, which he thought had influenced her – and would continue to influence her – to be unconventional in manners and risky and queer in thought and behaviour . . . But after her death and his remarriage he became very much attached to me – a sort of remorse, I think, for his detachment from his wife during the last days of painful illness. I grieve today that I did not go to see him last spring, when he begged me to come.

Henry Hobhouse came of a good vintage and in old age became kinder and kinder, more tolerant of other people's ideas and defects, humbler and broader-minded. He always had high principles and courtly manners: he was reputed one of the ablest of the unpaid county administrators. His second wife, Anne Grant, for twenty years his secretary and Margaret's housekeeper, proved a treasure as a wife, as stepmother and 'in-law' to his wife's relations. Our visits to Hadspen and their visits here have been happy episodes alike for the aged Henry Hobhouse and the old Webbs. Bless him.

10 August. [Passfield Corner]
When I read through the diaries, year after year, I wonder whether all our personal work (coupled with intrigue) to get this reform or that carried into law, to convert this group or that of men and women to our way of thinking, was worth while from the standpoint of the community? From our own standpoint of happiness and continual interest and mutual love, it was supremely worth while. But judged by the state of Great Britain today, with its low level of health and culture and with its stationary and probably declining population, its permanent unemployment, its disintegrating morals and lack of faith, it looks as if we socialist reformers failed to stop the rot, as if our self-complacency was unwarranted. Sidney maintains his faith and contradicts my pessimism. . . .

Sir Alexander Carr-Saunders (1886–1966) was a demographer who remained Director of the L.S.E. until 1956.

27 August. [Passfield Corner]
Carr-Saunders, the new Director of the School of Economics, here with his wife alone. Sidney and he together the whole evening up till 12.30, Sidney telling him the story of the School and all its

many difficulties with the four successive Directors, whilst I entertained the pleasant little lady for a suitable spell, both of us going early to bed. So far as we can see, Carr-Saunders is the right man for the job. He is attractive in person and sane in outlook; came to be a sociologist from zoology, an expert on the population question with no particular political or economic creed that can be discerned, an essentially open-minded, pleasant-mannered man, discreet and somewhat reserved. I doubt whether he is as able, either intellectually or administratively, as Beveridge; far less power of initiative and fulfilment, but he has more judgement and far better manners – 'the manners that maketh man'. To be the head of the London School of Economics with its 120 professors and lecturers and its 3,000 students in these tumultuous times of mutually hostile political and economic creeds, held with religious fervour, is a difficult business. . . .

The Carr-Saunders' are well off and it is unlikely that he will care to remain in office for more than ten years, which is all to the good. The directorship of the School is a post in which the holder gets quickly 'worn out'. The last time Sidney lunched at the School, Beveridge was sitting absolutely alone at the Director's table, whilst the two others were crowded. He had in fact been boycotted. There were unpleasant incidents during his farewell address too, a marked coldness in the audience. . . .

7 September. [Passfield Corner]
The world event which every day animates our evening listening to the news is the Sino–Japanese war. We have always been admirers of Japan, alike before and after our visit in 1911. But since the great war she has been an evil influence in the world, intensely imperialist, militarist, insincere in her religious faith, reactionary in her political and economic doctrine. Japan has, in fact, 'lost her head' and, I think, her soul. China, meanwhile, has been finding herself – a new self, patriotic and with an understanding of science and a growing appreciation of the new civilization of the U.S.S.R. Japan has, by her insolent aggression, thrown China into the arms of the Soviet government; the Chinese C.P. have enthusiastically joined Chiang Kai-shek in his defence of the homeland. . . .

1 October. [Passfield Corner]
A charming note from Beveridge saying farewell to the old Webbs

as Director of the London School of Economics. Sidney attended the last meeting of the executive of the School at which Carr-Saunders took over the directorship from Beveridge. All was promising: accounts satisfactory, building progressing, students increased and peace reigning. Even Mrs Mair showed herself as highly efficient and gracious in manner. So all is well with the child we brought into the world over forty years ago. . . .

If I live and keep any kind of strength of body and mind I may complete *Our Partnership* up to 1932, with an epilogue on the U.S.S.R., by 1942 – the year of our Golden Wedding. It is assuredly a pleasure to us that *Soviet Communism* in its first edition sold 20,000 and that we have sold Gollancz, for immediate distribution to the Left Book Club, 15,000 of the second edition, with its postscript, before publication this month. We are now disposing of 3,000 to trade unionists, leaving 200 for Longman to sell to those who will pay 35*s* to possess the book that poorer persons are acquiring for 5*s*! To each according to his need and from each according to his capacity. Quite a paying principle, which we began to apply to bookselling early in the twentieth century, and which the Left Book Club has developed on a huge scale. Apparently you can have two prices in one market if you can restrict the cheaper article to a particular class within that market.

In January 1937 the Labour Party executive expelled the Socialist League and it was dissolved in March, leaving the weekly *Tribune* as its legacy. The party conference in Bournemouth registered a large majority against any form of collaboration with the Communists, though three unity campaign supporters – Cripps, Laski and the lawyer D.N. Pritt, were elected to the newly created constituency party section of the national executive. Lola Holt was Beatrice's great-niece, who earned a living chauffeuring her own car. Benjamin Jones (1847–1941), for many years a senior member of the Co-operative movement, had helped Beatrice with her first work.

11 October. [Parmoor]
Four nights and six days spent, three at Bournemouth Highcliff Hotel among the Labour leaders and two at Parmoor, all in the company of Lola Holt, who acted as chauffeur and supplied the car. She is a pleasant and capable girl and a good companion.

The conference revolved round the left revolt from the policy and discipline of Transport House: Dalton was chairman, Morrison leading speaker, Cripps, followed by Laski, the principal rebels.

The outcome, a characteristic British compromise between the assertion and acceptance of executive authority and the passing of the desired reform of the constitution of the Labour Party, with Cripps and his three principal associates safely installed on the new executive. . . .

One of the pleasantest episodes of our stay at Bournemouth was a visit from my old friend Benjamin Jones, today ninety years of age, living in a comfortable little home with a kindly housekeeper and companion near Christchurch. . . . He has become in his old age a gentle, wise old man, refined in body and soul, but with the same frank and ultra-realistic outlook on life, but of course failing in the faculty to give and take in intercourse. It was a real pleasure to me that he had recovered from that strange coarsening of his manner of life which overtook him after his remarkable wife's death, and led to his departure, while still in the prime of his energies, out of a movement which he had done so much to develop. . . .

The American journalist Edgar Snow (1905–1975) made a long visit to Yenan, a remote region of China where the Communists had set up their own regime under Mao Tse-Tung (1893–1976). Lord Nuffield (1877–1963) made a fortune from the manufacture of Morris cars.

18 October. [Passfield Corner]
Red Star Over China by Edgar Snow is a dynamic work. The subject-matter, Soviet China, hitherto hidden from the world, may prove to be an all-important factor in altering the balance of power between the old civilization and the new. Owing to the courage and capacity of the author, Soviet China has not only been discovered, but described and explained with vigour and discernment. What interests me most is not the skill and determination of the Red Army, but the new philosophy of life and code of conduct that has transformed the Chinese from passive to active agents of human progress. To us it seems confirmatory of our analysis of the new synthesis in Soviet Communism of economic plenty combined with self-subordinating ethics. Mao and his comrades are not interested in their own personality, nor even in their own prowess and success; they are impersonal in their outlook, absorbed in the welfare of the Chinese race and humanity as a whole. What is ethically wrong with western civilization is that it is based on pecuniary self-interest and personal advancement, that men are valued and praised for their inherited position (kings and great

personages) or their success in amassing personal wealth and personal power (Lord Nuffield and the Press Lords). The Red Army of China, its officers and men, have been ready to sacrifice themselves to their cause. If they succeed in throwing back the Japanese invaders, if they are able to convert their fellow citizens to planned production for community consumption, with the object of raising the Chinese people to a higher level of well-being, good conduct, intellectual curiosity and artistic culture, they will have accomplished a great step towards the triumph of the new civilization among oppressed races. . . .

GBS was still working on *Geneva*. J.B. Priestley wrote three plays which were based on the theory of time advanced by the writer J.W. Dunne (d. 1949).

27 October. [Passfield Corner]
A week-end away, first two nights at the Shaws', then a night and day in London with Barbara Drake. A happy affectionate meeting with our dear old friends – Charlotte in good health but growing deaf, GBS looking frail, with uncertainty in his glance and gait, as if he did not know his way about in thought or expression. 'If he would only give up working at that play about the League of Nations,' murmurs Charlotte. 'He can't get it right'. . . .

In the evening of Monday Barbara and we went to Priestley's play *I Have Been Here Before* – based on Dunne's hypothesis that you can, if you have the gift, see forward as well as backward in time and (this seems self-contradictory) *by knowledge alter the happening*. The metaphysics of the play, as expounded by the German philosopher, were absurd, but he and four of the other characters were cleverly conceived and admirably acted . . . altogether the play excited and never bored us. . . .

MacDonald had resigned from the government at the end of May and on 5 November he set off for an extended holiday to South America. He died of heart failure during the journey on 9 November, and his body was taken back to England when the ship reached Bermuda on 15 November.

11 November. [Passfield Corner]
Sidney was rung up by various Press agencies and newspapers for appreciation of Ramsay MacDonald on his death at sea. Sidney 'begged to be excused'. Allen of Hurtwood gave a sanctimonious broadcast calling for honour and pity for the *lonely* soul of his past

leader. J.R.M. *was* lonely, because he had no genuine feeling for causes or comrades. He had been born in the wrong class, and he had started out in the wrong political group. He had no sympathy with the poor of today; he had a vision of a utopia, perhaps, but this vanished early in his career and he became a simple careerist, singularly mean in his methods. When successful, he began to hate his proletarian and lower-middle-class associates and found his rest and recreation among those who . . . lived in great houses and conversed in cultured tones about the unessentials of life. From reports and the unkind snapshots appearing in the Press, MacDonald became in his last years a miserable man, suffering in body and mind, in search of rest and not finding it. His best friend must rejoice that he 'passed peacefully away'. History will not be kind to his memory. Arthur Henderson will stand out as the wisest and most disinterested of the labour leaders of 1906–36.

29 November. [Passfield Corner]
Sidney was slightly ailing. So I seized the opportunity to pick out a future medical attendant for the aged Webbs, Lynn Allen having retired and left the neighbourhood. I chose Ronald Gray, a youngish and reputed clever man, physician and surgeon. He overhauled both of us, reported us in first-rate condition considering our age: no blood pressure, good kidneys, healthy heart and lungs. . . .

6 December. [Passfield Corner]
Had to call in Gray again, as Sidney developed severe pain in the leg whenever he walked more than a few yards. Diagnosed an intermittent claudication – which means lack of elasticity in the artery, when subject to the increased call for blood produced by exercise: an infirmity characteristic of old age. However, Gray thinks it will yield to treatment, plus warmer weather. But for the time I have to take solitary walks – without even a dog to solace my loneliness. All the same, we two aged ones *are* fortunate. . . . The one drawback to happiness is the nightmare abroad and at home of war and the fear of war; the ghastly thought of what is happening in Spain and in the vast continent of China. There is also uneasiness as to the internal condition of the U.S.S.R., the continuance of conspiracy trials and executions, which we explain so plausibly to others but do not altogether accept as *inevitable* ourselves! There is

always the lurking suspicion that Stalin and his clique *may* have lost their heads! . . .

Walter Elliott (1888–1958) was Secretary of State for Scotland; Leslie Hore-Belisha (1893–1957) was Secretary of State for War; Cliveden was the Thames-side house of Waldorf and Nancy Astor. Sir Thomas Inskip (1876–1947) became Lord Chief Justice in 1940. Lord Halifax (1881–1959), a leading exponent of appeasement of Hitler, became Foreign Secretary in 1938 and then Ambassador in Washington. Geoffrey Dawson (1874–1944) was editor of *The Times* between 1912 and 1941. In November, on a nominally unofficial visit as master of the Middleton Hunt, Halifax went to Germany and had a long discussion with Hitler at Berchtesgaden: an ambivalent visit which convinced Hitler that Britain would offer no check to his territorial ambitions, and persuaded Chamberlain, who had replaced Baldwin as Prime Minister in 1937, that Hitler wanted a peaceful settlement in Europe. A few weeks later Anthony Eden, dismayed at Chamberlain's quiescent attitude to the dictators, resigned as Foreign Secretary.

13 December. [Passfield Corner]
The Maiskys here for a day and a night: he in good spirits, frank and talkative; she tired, and I think, depressed. Of course he is reserved about the arrests and rumours of arrests; justifies some, denies the fact of others . . .

Maisky talked mostly about foreign affairs: why could not the British government be sensible and come in wholeheartedly to a pact against the aggressors? . . . The British government can't protect their far-eastern possessions and doubtfully the Mediterranean. Why will they not join the Soviet government in providing arms to the Chinese government? They could do so through French or even British territory. Many of the younger members of the government, headed by Eden, Walter Elliott, Hore-Belisha and others, want to do it. But the 'Cliveden coterie' – Lady Astor, Samuel Hoare, Simon, Inskip, Halifax, with Garvin and Geoffrey Dawson in attendance – are die-hard pro-German and, in their hearts, desire Germany to extend her territory and her influence in the near east, to the detriment of the Soviet Union. They would like to see the new social order disappear by foreign invasion and renewed civil war, even at the cost of imperilling the British Empire. It was this set that sent Halifax to Germany; it was Eden who countered this movement by the visit of the French Minister to London. The P.M. holds the balance: he is a hard-headed businessman with no imagination; he is equally hostile to the

U.S.S.R. and Germany. Above all, he wants to keep out of war. But unless some steps are taken by the British government to show a stern front against the aggressive nations, war there will be, and against the British Empire. . . .

14 December. [Passfield Corner]
I went up to London for Xmas shopping and lunched with Susan. Our old house reeked with escaping gas: gas cookers, gas fires, gas heaters, from the basement to the attic. Susan looked alarmingly changed: swollen figure and sallow face: Emily told me she had been seriously ill with swellings and sores, poor dear. . . .

To me, the old home with the roaring traffic, facing the Thames river with its barges and bridges, the old servant and the old friends and the old old gossip about the Labour world, was like ghost-land, the old Mrs Webb of eighty being the oldest ghost of the lot. I was glad to get back to our silent and comfortable cottage home with my old man. We too are ghosts of our former selves haunting this mad century with its tragic happenings; but we are happy ghosts, loving each other and always with a job in hand, like two aged craftsmen . . .

PART IV

Fallen on the Way

January 1938–April 1943

Introduction to Part IV

By the beginning of 1938 the Webbs were feeling their age. Their walks were shorter, they rested more, they had less energy for writing. Yet their life at Passfield Corner was comfortable and far from secluded. They listened a good deal to the wireless and read a great many books. Beatrice especially kept up with new books on politics and she was in the habit of recording her comments and impressions in her diary. From 1938 until her death she mentioned well over one hundred books. Her interest ranged from autobiographies by writers such as Somerset Maugham, Huxley and Priestley, biographies of Halifax, Churchill, John Morley and Arnold Bennett to current political journalism, books such as *What Are We to Do?* by John Strachey, *Insanity Fair* by Douglas Reid, *American Testament* by Joseph Freeman, *The Culture of Cities* by Lewis Mumford, *Guns or Butter?* by R. Bruce Lockhart, *My Country and My People* by Lin Yu-tang, *Guide to Modern Wickedness* by C.E.M. Joad, *Mein Kampf* by Adolf Hitler, *Inside Asia* by John Gunther, *The Scum of the Earth* by Arthur Koestler, *Scorched Earth* by Edgar Snow and *Conditions of Peace* by E.H. Carr. In 1938 Penguin Books, which had first appeared three years before, published Beatrice's *My Apprenticeship*, and she liked to give away signed copies to family and friends.

Although Beatrice was no longer directly in touch with political events her interest never flagged. And she always had a taste for political gossip, which was fed by such L.S.E. professors as Laski, Tawney and Robson, by energetic Fabians like the Coles and by journalists who had been to Russia. The Russian Ambassador Ivan Maisky and his wife were frequent visitors at Passfield Corner — they were in the habit of going down there every two months for tea and supper. In 1940 Beatrice records ten visits by them and they sometimes met for lunch in London. In these last years Beatrice

403

drew closer to her only surviving sister, Rosy Dobbs, becoming more affectionate towards her and more tolerant of her eccentricities. Rosy sometimes stayed for a week at a time but when this became too difficult during the war she would stay at the Passfield Oak Hotel nearby as Beatrice's guest. There were now a considerable number of nephews and nieces who liked to keep in touch with their aged and famous aunt. Barbara Drake, Beatrice's favourite niece, was a frequent visitor and Beatrice always stayed with her on her visits to London. And neighbours such as the Ponsonbys and Lord Arnold also kept in touch.

The visitors who went down to Liphook continued to find the Webbs bracing company. Kingsley Martin recalled how demanding they were as hosts: 'their immense fund of argument and conversation was bottled up inside them' and 'the long, meaty conversation' went on into the evening, over breakfast and during the required stroll across the common. Eventually, Martin added, 'a taxi arrived to take one home, so full of mental food that even the strongest digestion was somewhat exhausted.' As Beatrice's health failed and she suffered more and more from sleepless nights, some of this intellectual energy spilled over into her diary and she would fill in the long night hours with her thoughts on her visitors and the rapidly deteriorating political situation. Her diary during this period is longer than it had ever been since the lonely days of her childhood and youth; she herself confessed that she suffered from logorrhea. But, for all her despondency and fits of depression, her vitality and interest in people and society never left her.

The dominant theme of the diary in this period was the collapse into war. Hitler's threatening speeches and the arrival of Jewish refugees from Germany, like the newspaper pictures of bomb damage in Spain and the first obvious defence preparations in Britain, gave a vivid immediacy to the diplomatic and military disasters which preceded the outbreak of war in 1939 – the annexation of Austria in 1938 and the step-by-step dismemberment of Czechoslovakia, the drawn-out agony of the Spanish civil war that began in 1936, Mussolini's invasion of Albania at Easter 1939, and the continuing Japanese advance into China. They were all the opening and demoralizing phases of a war which was eventually to spread across the world.

Beatrice was as critical as others on the left of Chamberlain's self-deluding belief that he could mollify Hitler into reasonable behaviour; she supported Litvinov's efforts to rouse the League of Nations for a policy of collective security; and she favoured the campaign to convert the Labour Party to the policy of the Popular Front. But these were all losing battles, and the worse the situation became the more she began to feel that the only hope for the future lay in the survival and success of the U.S.S.R. That feeling had coloured her attitude to the Stalin purges. It led her, reluctantly, to accept the Soviet occupation of eastern Poland and the Baltic states as well as the Russian attack on Finland. And it became the abiding concern of her last two years, after Hitler had invaded Russia in June 1941. She put aside her faltering attempts to complete *Our Partnership* so as to write articles, give interviews and produce a final pamphlet on Soviet Communism. In the pro-Soviet climate of public opinion which followed Russian resistance to the Nazi attack, she seemed and felt like a vindicated prophet. And before she died she had seen the tide of war turn at El Alamein and Stalingrad in the autumn of 1942.

A few days after Beatrice's eightieth birthday Sidney had a stroke, which broke the satisfying tenor of this busy retirement; even then Beatrice did her best to maintain its familiar rhythms. Sidney made a good recovery and although he could no longer work he could read and follow a conversation. The Webbs took on Mrs Grant as a full-time nurse-companion and although they managed to retain four servants right into the war years – the two Smith sisters and Miles the gardener as well as Mrs Grant – Sidney's illness added to the difficulty of maintaining a fairly isolated household under wartime conditions.

Sidney's stroke gave Beatrice an added stimulus to keep going and checked those moments of despair when she considered taking her own life – 'V.W.L.' (voluntary withdrawal from life), she called it. She felt that he needed her almost more than he had ever done and she could not bear the idea of deserting him. The long years of loving companionship, uninterrupted since their marriage fifty years before, was one of the most remarkable things about this remarkable partnership. 'What really impressed me most about the Sidney Webbs,' wrote Cynthia Asquith, daughter of Beatrice's old friend Lady Elcho, 'even more than their amazing industry, was their mutual devotion. There can be no doubt that theirs was a deep and lasting love affair.'

VOLUME 52

∽ 1938 ∾

4 January. [Passfield Corner]
. . . . The New Year finds me in good health and Sidney in good
spirits and able to get through a good deal of indiscriminate work —
articles, etc. But he is suffering from the claudication of the artery
of the left leg and I have to take lonely walks while he walks and sits
down for short spells of exercise, which distresses both of us. All
the same we *are* fortunate and no mistake about it! . . .

5 January. [Passfield Corner]
Laski's hostile review of our second edition of *Soviet Communism*
and its postscript in the *Political Quarterly* for January is only one
more sign of the swing over from the Soviet Union on the part of
the left intellectuals who claim to lead the rising generation. . . .

   The old Webbs are distinctly out of favour with the intellectuals,
whether right or left; but owing to their old age they are treated
with kindly respect. We shall end as we began, in a small group of
dissentients from the existing social order, the difference being that
in the nineteenth century that order seemed stabilized, today it is in
dissolution and everyone not only knows but proclaims it. . . .

23 January. [Passfield Corner]
Yesterday's eightieth birthday was entertained and distracted by the
greetings of friends and relations. The *Spectator* had a two-column
article by GBS, the *New Statesman* a short one from H.G. Wells
and two long letters from Laski and Margaret Cole — all delightfully
appreciative; even the *Evening Standard* and the *Observer* gave me a
paragraph. There were three bouquets from the London School of
Economics, from the students, teachers and staff, and an imposing
one from the National Council of Labour; altogether a grand
display from the left of kindly remembrance of the Webbs'
services. We finished up the day by an afternoon concert at the
Ponsonbys from the Booth quartet; and another bouquet and
another testimony to the Webbs. What amused me most was the

singling out by H.G. Wells and some other friends of my capacity as a *manager*, or as H.G. called it, as a Great Lady – 'the greatest lady I have ever met', which seemed to me rather absurd, seeing my intensely bourgeois simplicity of life, and preoccupation with what most people consider dreary drudgery of an ant-like type. What strikes the Webbs about their own career is that we have had a precious good time of it – perhaps too good a time of it. But as our conception of a 'good time' has included a regular and planned working day we have got more credit than we deserve, most people disliking this sort of life, especially the young people of today. Anyway it is very pleasant, even in old age, to be admired and flattered. And no one is the worse for it. Perhaps that is why this testimony to the aged so often happens. It serves as a sort of religious rite to reverence those who will soon be gone. Bless them!

25 January. [Passfield Corner]
The end of our partnership?

The inevitable has come, one of the partners has fallen on the way, the youngest and the strongest. He may lie there for a while, but we shall never march together again in work and recreation. I cannot march alone.

On Monday Ronald Gray saw and examined him: his leg was sufficiently cured to walk two miles and all seemed well, though I had been startled sometimes by his tired and woebegone look. Yesterday morning, when I knocked at his door at 6.30, his voice sounded queerly grim; when I returned from refilling my hot water bottle, he was standing by the bed seemingly puzzled how to get in – and then after he had gulped down his tea there was silence, with a twitching of the hand. He insisted on getting up for his breakfast downstairs, but when I joined him he was again silent and when he tried to answer me his answers were difficult to understand. But he seemed in no pain and did not complain. Ronald Gray gave the verdict: it was a stroke, a clot in the arteries on one side of the brain. It might pass away – but . . . So there he is lying in the bed of the south-west room with a day and night nurse in attendance. He will have care and love so long as I am strong enough to give it. Loneliness will not last long for the one that is left, and I would rather bear it than that he should. If only we could talk together. He tries over and over again and occasionally there will be a word, 'yes' or 'no', or some slight indication of a word, but then silence and a pained expression of frustration. But he smiles and nods his head when I kiss his hand and hold it in my mine. Anyway I can spend hours petting him, telling him the news or talking about past times, or saying 'We have written the book,' which always makes him smile.

Beatrice had cared for her father after a stroke until his death in January 1892 released her to marry Sidney.

3 February. [Passfield Corner]
'I have been there before.' Over fifty years ago, one morning in the autumn of 1885, I began a life of waiting on a loved one: the routine of watching helplessness of body and mind, of dealing with affairs left unfinished by an active brain, of reorganizing the domestic doings to the best advantage of a permanent invalid, without knowing what would happen in the future to him or to oneself. Today I am in the same plight. But this time the problems are easy ones: instead of large establishments in London and the country, countless business commitments of an international capitalist to settle up, eight sisters and their seven husbands all equally affected (one sister indeed living at home in a state of neurotic collapse), and my own career, intellectual and emotional, in the melting-pot, I live today in comfort in a small house with sufficient income for our needs and little financial responsibility, with no one to consider but the loved one. . . . If only he can recover his speech so that we can commune together, our daily existence will not be an unhappy one. A gentle melancholy at leaving life, redeemed by gratitude for the good time we have enjoyed together and perhaps enlightened by sympathetic intercourse with others interested in the destiny of man.

11 February. [Passfield Corner]
It is clear that the only time I shall have for thought and its expression will be the early hours of the mornings; the remainder of my waking hours will be taken up with waiting on the beloved one, transacting business and dictating letters, intervals of outdoor exercise, and resting in the sitting-room over a book with, now and again, a bit of a cigarette. Aged and infirm, my thought is of doubtful value; I no longer have his mind to submit it to; and there will be the perpetual strain of watching helplessly his gallant struggle to make good. He is the best of the stricken, gentle and

uncomplaining, with a pathetic resolute intention to get back his speech and handwriting in order to carry on. If only he could express himself fully: all he can do is to mutter words which are more often than not the wrong words, from which I try to gather his meaning. If I fail we sometimes laugh and kiss each other and I beg him 'wait till you are stronger'. Dr Gray assures me that unless he gets worse he will undoubtedly get better and might even return to normality, but on a low level of achievement. But for both of us it will be intellectually, though not emotionally, a lonely life. At present, I am isolated from friends and relations. The only person I have seen since he was struck down twenty days ago, outside my own servants, nurse and medical man, is Barbara Drake, who spent one night here and as always was affectionate, interesting and helpful. When Father collapsed at York House in November 1885 I had a period of utter loneliness, though with a far larger circle of relations and paid servants and far more business that had to be transacted. I had more intellectual energy, but no self-assurance that I had any kind of capacity for a career of my own in the realm of creative intellect. Today, though my capacity is shrinking, what I write will be accepted. . . .

As a young woman of twenty-eight I heard around me a whispering, occasionally openly said: 'What a failure she has made of her life.' As an aged woman of eighty there is a tuneful chorus, even in the Press, singing of the successful achievement of the Webbs. When one is about to quit the stage of life, it is consoling to hear the applause of a great audience. Alas! for human vanity in its most harmless form of delight in flattery. Is it wrong or is it right? At least it adds to the happiness of the human race; and no one suffers from the undue appreciation of the aged, seeing that they are about to depart.

12 February. [Passfield Corner]
Sidney is making a good recovery; his speech is coming back and he is practising his writing, but it will be a long time, if ever, before he can live a normal life without a constant attendant. And this necessity of adding another member to the household will be a source of worry to me. . . .

17 February. [Passfield Corner]
In the intervals of watching over my dear old man, I ponder over

the all-important question: how long will it take to stabilize Soviet Communism in the U.S.S.R.? At present there is hardly a day passes but we hear of conspiracies, trials and executions, or of the sudden disappearance from foreign capitals of the Soviet Ambassadors or chargé d'affaires, in flight from the danger of indictment and execution by the Moscow authorities. That, to say the least of it, is a disreputable state of affairs and so long as it continues will be the cause of scandal and condemnation of the U.S.S.R. . . . .

22 February. [Passfield Corner]
It is exactly a month this morning since Sidney showed signs of a stroke . . . He is undoubtedly better, but he is disabled and downcast – he broods over his condition, wondering whether he will recover. Would Dr Gray tell him, he asked me, what exactly he is suffering from? I told him that it was an affection of the arteries – I thought it better to be quietly frank – that it had affected his speech but that Gray thought he would get back ninety per cent of his strength, but would have to lead a quiet life . . . He is the best of invalids, spends most of his waking hours in reading, never complains and is kindly and considerate to his nurse. . . . During the three or four hours we spend together we take little turns on the landing and the other bedrooms; I read to him or talk, or we listen to music over the wireless in his bedroom. We are very very happy together, those hours are my anchorage, my home – the rest of my life is lonely, especially the walks over commons or through woods where we have wandered together in the past fourteen years . . .

Eden resigned on 20 February in protest against Chamberlain's conciliatory attitude towards Mussolini: 'The dark walls of despair overwhelmed me,' Churchill wrote of that night.

23 February. [Passfield Corner]
The general impression of the Eden–Chamberlain crisis is that the hard-grained commonplace narrow-minded capitalist Prime Minister is intent on keeping out of war, preserving what he can of the British Empire and virtually joining, without saying so, the anti-Comintern pact so as to effectively isolate and discredit the U.S.S.R. and stop the spread of Communism in Europe and Asia. Franco is to win in Spain, and Japan in China, Italy in the more barren districts of Africa. Meanwhile the three Fascist powers will have exhausted themselves – bitten off more than they can chew –

and Great Britain, with her piled-up armaments and submissive working class, will be impregnable. But don't talk about it —stick to the slogans: be strong, but keep out of war, extend your trade and isolate the U.S.S.R. I think Chamberlain will succeed in keeping public opinion on his side, in spite of the fact that all the talents and idealists are against him: Lloyd George, Churchill, Cecil; intellectuals like Harold Nicolson, Boothby, as well as the Labour and Liberal parties . . . When I saw Galton and GBS on a flying visit to London they were both on the side of Chamberlain: GBS because of his admiration for Mussolini and Galton because he wants to keep out of war and instinctively dislikes contact with the U.S.S.R. . . . .

Yet another purge trial had begun in Moscow.

9 March. [Passfield Corner]
Every now and again I relapse into gloom: continued physical discomfort leading to a distaste for life. When I am with him, I am relatively happy in giving care and love; it is when I wander alone in my morning walk, or sit by the fire in the evening, listening to the news of war and of fear of war, and latterly to the turbid revelations of the Moscow trials, wondering what is the true meaning of all these horrors. It is then that my poor old brain begins to whizz and ache and I feel worn out, too old to live. Indeed one of the puzzles is: how far are my aches and pains produced by thoughts, gloomy and disturbing? How far are these unpleasant sensations the direct effect of my loneliness, fear of losing my life companion and, last but not least, deep distrust of what is happening in the U.S.S.R.? It is clear that this trial is not a frame-up: it is a genuine revelation of a widespread plot, but so many of the old leaders are involved and involved in such a fulsome way, that it darkens that great continent with its 170 millions and gives it more the features of hell than of heaven. . . . The sickening vilification of all who differ from the policy of the government clique, the perpetual fear of innocent citizens of being wrongly accused and convicted, is a terrible social disease . . . The poor Maiskys, what a life they must be leading!

Joachim von Ribbentrop (1893–1946), later Foreign Minister of Nazi Germany, was executed as a war criminal: at this time he was Ambassador in London.

12 March. [Passfield Corner]

Sitting alone in an armchair by the fire, I listened last night to the French news at eight o'clock, the English at nine o'clock and then turned to Moscow. Tense and agitated was the French voice, tense but coldly composed was the English. Hitler had annexed Austria was the fact if not the form of this amazing recorded happening. After that, the droned-out last act of the Moscow trial was an insignificant item of scandalous news. What did the so-called 'witch trials' of the far-off Eurasian continent matter compared to the triumphant march of Hitler's Third Reich to a German domination of central Europe – the very disaster that the great war was waged to prevent! A comic anti-climax was the statement in the 'rest of the news' that von Ribbentrop had been received by the King and lunched with Chamberlain that very morning . . .

Strachey's new book, arguing for a Popular Front, sold 48,000 copies in the Left Book Club edition. It also favourably described the Communist Party as a 'new model' capable of disciplined resistance if a progressive government was threatened by counter-revolution, as in Spain.

20 March. [Passfield Corner]

What Are We To Do? by John Strachey is an accomplished debunking of the Webbs and their Fabianism – in a sense complimentary, as it makes us the centre of the picture! How far is he right and how far is he wrong? He contrasts our Fabian collectivism with its slogan of the 'inevitability of gradualness', meaning the peaceful transformation of the capitalist system by consent of a political democracy, with the Marxist 'scientific socialism' and the inevitability of class war and the seizure of power by the manual working class, involving the subsequent 'dictatorship of the wage-earner' replacing the dictatorship of the capitalist. . . .

To me it seems that where we went wrong was in ignoring Marx's demonstration of the eventual breakdown of profit-making capitalism. The profit-making motive, Marx held, would defeat its own aim by restricting production when it ceased to be profitable and influencing it unduly when and where speculation was monetarily profitable. Indirectly the exploitation of new countries led to wars between the exploiting countries, for the waste spaces of the world, and for those parts inhabited by lower races who could be even more easily exploited than their own people. Our failure to realize the eventual breakdown of capitalism, as a way of producing plenty, led to a virtual acceptance of the system as the dominant form of enterprise qualified by a policy of a national minimum of civilized existence, obtained by public regulation and social services. We did not realize that the capitalist system *could not produce the plenty* required to give this national minimum of civilized existence. Where we were *right* was in refusing to accept Marx's theory of value, which led to a vision of workers' control, with no determination by expert brains in the interests of the community of the desirable character and equitable distribution of the product. . . . .

1 April. [Passfield Corner]
Sidney is apparently happy and hopeful – he suffers no pain or discomfort, always excepting getting very tired towards the end of the day; he goes to bed directly after seven o'clock supper, wakes up in the night and reads for an hour or so and then sleeps again. When I come in at 6.30 a.m. he greets me with smiles and kisses and wants to have the last news or about any talk I have listened in to. The weather has been glorious and the chorus of birds in the morning consoling. The one tiny snag are the roaring army aeroplanes, many by day and some by night, reminding us of the coming war. . . .

9 May. Eastbourne
For the first three weeks of our stay I made no entry in the diary. The days pass here automatically without distinguishing one day from another. My dear man is enjoying the change of scene and diet; the drives every other morning in Lion Phillimore's car, the walks on the charming esplanade towards Beachy Head, which we know so well, the wireless, the browsing over the score or more books which we brought with us. He is, I think, a little stronger on his feet; but his powers of expression and speech are still too defective for him to enjoy the give and take of conversation with anyone but me and his nurse, who have learnt to understand him. Occasionally he wonders whether he will ever be back at his desk. His deep-down unselfishness and humility and kindly consideration of others are even more striking as an invalid than they were in active life. . . .

19 May. [Passfield Corner]
Our four weeks at Eastbourne was ended by Lola Holt motoring

Sidney and nurse home whilst I travelled up to the lunch at the London School of Economics in honour of my eightieth birthday – an exciting and exhausting episode for the aged Beatrice Webb. Over eighty of the lecturers and one or two governors attended. . . . Eileen Power in a witty and charming speech and Carr-Saunders in a serious and kindly one, proposed my health and I responded, I was told 'brilliantly' (but how the aged are flattered!). Anyway I made two points, one of which may bear fruit, but I doubt it. I described how the little Fabian group who started the School had benefited by the fact that the Fabians were not concerned with the great controversies which raged in the 90s and the first decade of the twentieth century: Irish Home Rule, Free Trade v. Protection, Imperialism v. Pro-Boer; Religious Education v. Secularism, Temperance v. Drink; and therefore were on friendly terms with the leaders of both parties. Hence we had secured as the three first presidents of the School such very established public personages as Creighton, Rosebery and Rothschild. The two first Directors had been Tories and the two next Liberals of unquestioned orthodoxy. Today the situation was completely changed. Intellectually we are all at each other's throats. But the School had fortunately maintained its reputation for being the middle way. My practical suggestion was: in the interest of future historians would it not be desirable for the members of the Senior Common Room to set down and write out, in a dogmatic form, without attempting to argue about it, each his or her *living philosophy*, describing frankly their conclusions as to man's relation to man, and man's relation to the universe? I livened up this ponderous suggestion by chaffing the opposite numbers as well as the compromisers in political and economic and religious opinion about their multitudinous and contrary interpretations of what is happening in the world today. Altogether it was an amusing but exhausting affair for a woman of eighty. . . .

Muggeridge wrote about his mystical experiences in his book *In the Valley of the Restless Mind* but it was, he said, a 'total failure'.

31 May. [Passfield Corner]
A month ago when we visited from Eastbourne the Malcolm Muggeridges, I was puzzled by Malcolm's coldness and his refusal *to look at us*: he is usually so oncoming and personally affectionate. His latest book *In the Valley of the Restless Mind* gives the explanation.

One chapter is an obvious caricature of the Webbs as Mr and Mrs Daniel Bret with their 'blueprint of the good life'. To me these pages are one amusing and quite harmless episode. Why, by the way, do people object to literary caricature when they don't to pictorial? The public personage is hurt if he is *not* cartooned.

What distresses me about this strange autobiographical work is the horrid mixture of religious strivings and continuous amatory adventure: also the obsession with dirt in body and mind might be a pathological record except that it is without scientific content or purpose. In essence it is pornography, glossed over by a certain literary charm and cleverness. . . . Malcolm is always dwelling on sadistic senility. *Lust* (a word he delights in) and cruelty are in the background of Malcolm's mind. One wonders where exactly he will end? Could he have been cured by psychoanalysis and early treatment in the nursery and the school? Kitty has outgrown the hysteria of her youth; she is a handsome woman and devoted wife and mother. They seem a happy couple in their mutual relations, which is to Malcolm's credit. . . .

Mary Booth's daughter Antonia (or 'Dodo') was married to the High Court judge Sir Malcolm Macnaghten (1869–1955).

30 June. [Passfield Corner]
Thirty-six hours away from Sidney, wandering in luxurious surroundings, chiefly seeing 'the Sacred Aged' (as the Chinese call all mortals who have survived the three score and ten). Actually I embraced three over eighty and one over ninety. (Actually embraced, and for the first time I kissed GBS!) First with Lola to Parmoor where, in the big house with its enormous rooms, lives the aged and somewhat senile brother-in-law, once a brilliant lawyer, attended by the devoted Marion, she, poor dear, a martyr to her devotion, suffering from arthritis largely brought about by being kept in closed-up rooms and denied physical exercise. I chatted with Alfred and took Marion for a walk, which she said did her good. Then on to London, where I visited the aged Shaws in their luxurious flat and found GBS lying on the sofa with Charlotte bending over him with motherly affection, having persuaded him to be injected with insulin for the pernicious anaemia which had reduced him to a white-skinned shadow. He was full of wit and delighted to see his old friend. Then on to the L.C.C. palace on the river . . .

From the L.C.C. offices Barbara [Drake] motored me to the Macnaghtens, where I met and embraced warmly the ninety-year-old Mary Booth, my oldest living friend. We were genuinely glad to see each other once again, and recall those decades of warm friendship, ignoring the chill period of the Booths' avoidance of the Webbs as undesirable intimates, the partial reconciliation early in the twentieth century, followed by Charles Booth's anger at my activities on the Royal Commission of the Poor Law which he thought, quite wrongly, had been directed to nullifying his rightful influence over the chairman and the majority of the members. He is dead and gone, more than twenty years ago. His widow lives on, a veritable miracle, at the age of ninety, of good health and eager interest in life. Dodo welcomed me most affectionately and Mr Justice Macnaghten was pleasantly hospitable to his aged cousin.

Sidney met me at Haslemere. I told him that of all the aged mortals I had seen he was the least egotistical, and the best to live with for his attendant relative . . .

Jawaharlal Nehru (1889–1964) a leader of the Indian National Congress, became the first Prime Minister of India. His daughter Indira Gandhi (1917–1984) also became Prime Minister.

3 July. [Passfield Corner]
Nehru, the leader of the Indian Congress, and his lovely daughter spent some hours here on Saturday with Ponsonby to meet them. I had read and admired his autobiography and welcomed him warmly. He is the last word of aristocratic refinement and culture dedicated to the salvation of the underdog whether in race or class, but I doubt whether he has the hard stuff of a revolutionary leader. He is in theory a Communist; but doubts the possibility of the complicated Soviet organization among the mixed races of the Indian continent. 'Between two worlds, one dead and one powerless to be born' is a quotation which he recognized but did not agree with. He believes with fervour that a united India can be born; is, in fact, being born, largely owing to the teaching of Gandhi, whose power as a saint and a missionary he realizes and admires, but whose economic proposals he dismisses as romantic remnants of the past. Nehru is convinced that the freedom of the individual, as manifested in the presence of opportunity to live the good life, cannot be secured without the organization of principal services and main industries deliberately for communal consumption and with-

out the profit-making motive. Today the Indian people are too primitive for Soviet Communism. But they have been roused, not only by internal conditions of India but by the horrors of the invasion of China by Japan and their sympathy with other oppressed races. . . .

Beatrice was now reviewing her diary entries for the years 1908–10 when she and Sidney ran the campaign for the policies set out in the Minority Report on the reform of the Poor Law.

1 August. [Passfield Corner]
Hard at work and on the whole successfully on Chapter IX – 'The Plunge into Propaganda'. This entails reading up the history of the last thirty years in respect to the Insurance Act of 1911–13 – especially insurance for sickness and unemployment, which was the government alternative to the Minority Report proposals for public health, salaried medical services under municipal control for sickness, and a national authority for organizing the labour market and maintenance with training for the unemployed. Our health proposals, though not completely adopted, have been justified; our unemployment proposals have not been justified. We are now convinced that unemployment cannot be prevented or the unemployed wisely provided for, under profit-making capitalism. I have got to make that clear . . . The able-bodied *have* been taken out of the Poor Law; they have been dealt with by a national authority under a Ministry of Labour as the Minority Report suggested they should be. But it is a damned failure. It is clear to me that it would not have been less of a failure if the other proposals of the Minority Report had been carried out – in so far as we had any proposals. We were wrong in thinking that the problem could be solved under capitalism. It is impossible to treat the unemployed and their dependents in the way they ought to be treated without making their conditions more attractive than that of the ordinary wage-earner under capitalism. . . . From the standpoint of capitalism and its continuance, the Royal Commission for the Poor Law and Unemployment was a disaster of the first magnitude. The Minority reporters were the white ants of the capitalist system! No wonder there was a reaction against the Webbs on the part of the Conservative and Liberal political leaders. We were 'traitors to our own class', as young Rockefeller said of President Roosevelt, and far more successful traitors, because at the back of our minds we had a vision of a socialist society which Roosevelt had not.

10 August. [Passfield Corner]
Beveridge here in high spirits, thoroughly enjoying his new life as Master of University College, Oxford: an easy job, within a cultured and well-mannered group; dignity and prestige without any particular responsibility or hard work; able to concentrate on his statistical investigation of prices and trade cycles. Also feels himself 'King of Unemployment Insurance' as chairman of the Unemployment Insurance Statutory Committee, telling Parliament what it ought to do about the insurance fund; the combined salaries of two posts add up to a good income. What a change from the turbulent atmosphere and continuous work and friction of the London School of Economics.

He reminded me that it is just thirty years ago (it is thirty-one) since he came to stay with us at Ayot to discuss his first findings on unemployment, its cause and its cure. Ever since that time we have been loyal friends to each other; and certainly his attitude to the old Webbs has been extraordinarily kind and appreciative, ideal good manners which in other relationships he has lacked. We had two three-mile walks together, discussing mainly unemployment and its remedies. His conclusion is that the major, if not the only remedy for chronic unemployment is lower wages, according to the old argument that if this does not happen the capitalist will take his money and his brains to other countries where labour is cheap . . . He, however, expressed the desire to see family allowances introduced which would enable wages to be lowered without endangering the birth-rate or the health of the rising generation . . . Beveridge asserted that the Oxford dons interested in economics were superior to the London School of Economics staff . . . Anyway the under-graduates were more cultured and better mannered than the students of the London School of Economics. Those of his own college welcomed him as a father and adviser; when he came into their meetings they all rose and greeted him respectfully and affectionately. Elspeth Mair is his housekeeper and Mrs Mair a constant visitor; she is also hostess of Avebury, his country home. So all is well with Beveridge.

13 August. [Passfield Corner]
. . . . Here is E.M. Forster's view of *personal relationships*, which he regards as the main ingredient of an enjoyable life:

All history, all our experience, teaches us that no human

relationship is constant, it is unstable, as the living beings who compose it, and they must balance like jugglers if it is to remain; *if it is constant it no longer is human relationship but a social habit, the emphasis in it has passed from love to marriage.* (The italics are mine.)

Clearly Sidney and I prefer a *social habit* to a *personal relationship*: a preference which has made our mutual relations perfect and enduring. In old age and infirmity we love each other more tenderly than we did in the prime of life. It is only fair to add that neither Sidney nor I, in our contacts with other people, have had those absorbing personal relationships of which Forster speaks; we are both of us impersonal, though, I think, not unkind or disloyal to fellow workers. Sidney tends to ignore personalities and I study them as specimens. Our main end and preoccupation has been to discover how to change society in order to increase the well-being, energy and dignity of the human race. Lowes Dickinson and E.M. Forster would say that this outlook on life – the perfecting of social habits – makes the Webbs' work dry dull stuff without beauty or charm. The tenderness which two aged mortals have for each other, just because they have been comrades in work and faith for near fifty years, would seem to these devotees to emotional and necessarily transient relationships simply queer, even laughable. They would say this constancy may be ethical but it is not aesthetic. It is the presence of beauty of soul and body they desire, not a comfortable code of conduct or desirable social habits. That may be so. The individual human being is very limited: one virtue or gift may exclude others. Perhaps man cannot be at once aesthetic and ethical? It is worth observing that neither Lowes Dickinson nor E.M. Forster have married and both the one and the other are believed to have been homosexuals. They are both violently anti-Christian; upholders of individual liberty, by which they always mean the absence of restraint for the elect, not the presence of opportunity for the multitude. . . .

1 September. [Passfield Corner]
Harold Laski here for five hours' talk before he goes for nine months' sojourn in the U.S.A. lecturing at universities, interviewing notables and ending with a visit to Roosevelt in Washington – so he says. His usual clever gossip and philosophic reflections. He is today completely convinced that the Soviet trials and executions

were at once justified in fact and necessary to save the revolution from counter-revolutions, a change-over from his critical review of our postscript to the second edition. He reports the conversion of eminent outsiders — scientists and military experts — to the soundness of the U.S.S.R. government in theory and practice. In fact we found ourselves in complete agreement; he was even less doubtful than I am about the one-party system and the difficulties and dangers of a planned mental environment. All would be right when the new civilization was stabilized. . . .

After Austria was annexed Hitler began to put pressure on Czechoslovakia, his first objective being the take-over of the German-speaking borderlands by October 1938. Chamberlain attempted to act as intermediary between the Germans and the Czechs in an effort to avert the war. On 12 September at Nuremburg, Hitler made a menacing speech to the chanting of 'Sieg Heil' by his audience; next day the appeasers in the French Cabinet decided against mobilization and in favour of Chamberlain's offer to visit Hitler. Neither France nor her ally Russia had land frontiers with Czechoslovakia, and both political prejudice and a belief that the Russian army was weak led the Western powers to ignore the Soviet Union. Chamberlain flew to Berchtesgaden on 15 September and found Hitler unwilling to bargain unless the Czechs surrendered the Sudetenland. When Chamberlain returned to London, where the French leaders joined him, it was agreed that the Czechs must be sacrificed to preserve peace — if they could be persuaded to accept the disruption of their state. On 22 September, when Chamberlain returned to meet Hitler at Bad Gödesberg, he was faced by a demand for an immediate cession of the Sudeten districts. Chamberlain returned to find opinion in Britain and France was hardening against such a humiliating capitulation to threats of force, but he persisted while war preparations continued. By 27 September war seemed imminent, but when Chamberlain spoke to a recalled House of Commons next day he said that Hitler had invited him, Mussolini and the French Premier, Edouard Daladier (1884–1970), to Munich. There, on 30 September, the four leaders agreed on the dismemberment of Czechoslovakia. When Chamberlain returned next day he claimed he had brought back 'peace with honour . . . peace in our time'. The immediate relief that war had been avoided for the present was soon followed by the widespread conviction that before long it was inevitable, though the French had been demobilized, the Czech defences ruined, the Poles exposed to invasion and the Russians left isolated.

13 September. 4 a.m. [Passfield Corner]
We listened last night to Hitler's passionate oration and the thunderous applause. His voice, its amazing volume and range of intonation, accounts for some of his potency in exciting mob devotion. So far as we could understand an unfamiliar language, he denounced western civilization: its capitalism, its political democ-

racy, its religion and code of conduct, with almost equal passion as he did Bolshevism, with its 'Jewish commissars'. The fury and inconsequence of his words, without any definite commitment, left a strange impression of madness. Why should he denounce *capitalism*, which exists and is his ally in Germany, not to mention political democracy, which is certainly not Bolshevism? Why add to his enemies? Hitler and his followers have shown such a mania for persecution at home and aggression abroad that one wonders whether there is not an internal explosion coming and whether this craze for violence is not an attempt to divert the explosion away from revolution to patriotic aggression? It is inconceivable that the British government should not take up the challenge and defend the *status quo* in central Europe. On the merits of the case – the inclusion of three million Germans in the new-fangled Czechoslovakia created by the Versailles treaty – I have my doubts. Can that state of things be defended, except that the present-day alternative – allowing Hitler with his barbaric cult and cruel regime to annex the German Sudetenland and thus dominate and practically annex Czechoslovakia – would be letting the devil have his own way. . . .

20 September. [Passfield Corner]
For the last three days and nights, indeed ever since Hitler's excited oration, heightened by the sinister impression of Chamberlain's flight to sit at Hitler's feet, we have been living through a nightmare of foreign news. I try to take my own little mind off the horror and humiliation of the situation with the reflection, 'After all *we* are not responsible and never have been; why should we not continue to be mere lookers-on, just as one looks back on the horrors of history?' But. . . . Czechoslovakia, the darling child, the creation of the British and French governments at Versailles in 1919, petted and praised for the last twenty years as the one sane political democracy in central Europe, neither pacifist nor Communist, and eminently well-behaved. And now handed over, in the course of three days, without any consultation with its government, by the British and French governments to Hitler with his pack of German Hun wolves. . . .

Well, well, need we think about it? And I try to get on with the book and Sidney, almost equally perturbed, turns to his old-fashioned novels. But the nightmare persists, kept alive by the French and English broadcasts: 8.30 a.m., 12.45 a.m., 6 p.m.,

7 p.m., 9.40 p.m. – all shamefaced, a queer tone in the announcer's voice – 'a horrid business, don't think *I* approve'; they all seem to mutter beneath the words they send over the air. . . .

21 September. 3 a.m. [Passfield Corner]
A sleepless night after listening to the 9.40 news. . . . It is strange that no Minister or government supporter has been heard over the wireless? The inner circle, which we are told in every broadcast is always meeting – Chamberlain, Simon, Halifax and Samuel Hoare, plus four officials (among them that odious Horace Wilson, my old enemy) – refusing all information to the public. The foreign policy of Great Britain is completely out of democratic control. We shall be at war or at an agreed peace in a few days or perhaps hours, according to the prejudice, temper and tactics of a tiny group of mediocre men – a shameful peace or a world war . . .

1 October. 3.30 a.m. [Passfield Corner]
At 8.30 yesterday morning I heard over Paris radio that peace had been signed at Munich by Hitler, Mussolini, Chamberlain and Halifax. A sense of profound relief, or a consciousness of disgust for one's own outlook on life – which was the greatest? I think the sense of relief. Not in our time, O Lord! The wild enthusiasm of the reception of the two Prime Ministers in London and Paris proved that it was so with the man and the woman in the street. Chamberlain showed courage and will-power in taking the decisive step towards a Four Power pact with Hitler and Mussolini, excluding the U.S.S.R. in defiance of socialist political democracy and old-fashioned liberalism, with its pathetic faith in a League of Nations and collective security, not to mention the little group of British imperialists who see disaster in this one-sided alliance with the aggressive powers in search of new lands to conquer. Chamberlain deserves the gratitude of the Crown, the City and the Archbishops for his anti-Communism; he will get it from the bulk of the middle class of Great Britain because he has saved them from war . . . All the same, the victory of sheer force brutally expressed, and the abject repudiation by the French government of their oft-repeated guarantee of Czechoslovakia and their retreat from the Franco–Soviet pact, a terrible sign of weakness in the two European political democracies. It means the dominance of Germany in

Europe through the threat of brute force. Taken with the acquiescence of the two great democratic powers, in Italy's conquest
of Abyssinia and avowed help to Franco in Spain and Japan's
barbaric invasion of China, it kills the League of Nations with its
strivings for a reign of new international affairs.

22 October. [Passfield Corner]
Home from Hastings, Sidney the better, I the worse for the
change; the hotel food did not suit my sensitive intestines. I
sometimes wonder whether I shall hold out, as a domestic attendant
on another 'aged and infirm' – I hope so.

Saw much of Rosy and her children . . . At present her main
anxiety are the Muggeridges with their four children; Malcolm
failing to make a decent livelihood. They both came to see us. They
dislike us; they say 'they hate rich or successful people'. He writes
reviews – quite competent ones – for the *Daily Telegraph* and
articles for *Time and Tide*, but they are desperately hard-up. In the
crisis Malcolm has become a war-like anti-Fascist and was eager to
join in a defensive war – to save Czechoslovakia. . . .

31 October. [Passfield Corner]
The Maiskys here for five hours on Sunday afternoon and in good
spirits. He and I talked incessantly, Madame and Sidney intervening. . . . Maisky was convinced that Germany was immensely
powerful in the air, 7,000 warplanes and another 3,000 in reserve
with a capacity of manufacturing 700(?) a month, England's being
100 a month. Her bluff could have been called by Great Britain,
France and the U.S.S.R.: she could not have fought a long war.
But today she is far more powerful, and without the U.S.S.R.
Great Britain and France could not protect themselves. He declared
that Germany is going to demand back some if not all of her
colonies within the next year and that Chamberlain and Halifax
(and the Cabinet generally) intend to meet her wishes. Will the
people of Great Britain stand it? . . . So long as Hitler has
bloodless victories there will be no revolution in Germany. If there
had been actual war, there would have been. . . . He thought the
British Empire doomed; and wonders when the British people
would wake up and realize it. He had been amazed at the
shortsightedness of Chamberlain, Halifax and Co. . . .

1 November. [Passfield Corner]
Annie exploded in a most unseemly way against Mrs Grant. As on other occasions she presented me with an ultimatum and lost her temper and her good sense. . . . Unless she mends her manners I am afraid she and Jean must go and I must get two Austrian or Czech servants. British women are no longer suited to domestic service in private houses, especially in the country . . . The plain truth is that the old standard upper- and middle-class home is no longer practicable. . . . Unfortunately at eighty years of age one cannot change one's social habits, and I have to see Sidney comfortably out of life and then disappear myself, leaving *Our Partnership* unfinished. Shall I succeed in doing so? If I drop out who will take care of my beloved? That is the question that worries me.

Walter Adams (1906–77) was secretary of the L.S.E. 1938–46 and its Director 1967–74.

10 November. [Passfield Corner]
A week of worry, enjoyment and work, with on the whole a comfortable conclusion. On 2 November, the day after the domestic upset, I was due in London to lunch with Carr-Saunders and his wife at the London School of Economics to fix up which room should be named after Sidney and Beatrice Webb, and to meet the new secretary, Adams, a remarkably able, pleasant and attractive young university man, exactly the sort for that key position. Then on to Barbara's for the family party on the next day: eighty R.P.'s turned up, all most kind to their aged aunt, and I talked incessantly that afternoon and also on the two evenings with one or other of them. . . .

13 November. [Passfield Corner]
The sinister madness of the Nazi persecution of the Jews, on a scale and with a publicity unprecedented in world history, has roused the U.S.A. from its isolation and also magnified the objection on the part of the British governing class to ceding colonies to Hitler's Germany. The Pope too is up in arms, some Nazi authorities declaring that when Judaism has been disposed of, the Roman Church will become the next victim of their insensate hate. There seems today something indecent in Chamberlain's friendliness to Hitler at Munich. And the P.M.'s refusal to tell the House of

Commons whether or not he is prepared to discuss with Hitler the transference of mandated territories back to Germany is rousing Conservative M.P.s out of their complacency. . . .

24 December. [Passfield Corner]
A white but gloomy Christmas: the one bright spot in the world situation is the outspoken contempt of American statesmen and the American Press for Hitler's Germany and their helpfulness towards the Spanish Republican government on the one hand, the Chinese resistance to Japan on the other. Altogether Chamberlain's policy of 'appeasement' is proving a tragic absurdity − the aggressor states, far from being satisfied, are every day more outrageous in their demands, and war seems inevitable. It looks as if the governments of Germany, Italy and Japan *dare not stand still*: they must conquer or dissolve. Hitherto they have conquered, but at a terrible cost to their own people. How weak is the spirit of resistance to evil in the relatively rich capitalist political democracies of Great Britain and France and above all the U.S.A. . . . .

New Year's Eve. [Passfield Corner]
. . . . Looking back on 1938, in spite of Sidney's breakdown early in the year, my dominant feeling is one of gratitude that Our Partnership has survived, though on a lower level of activity. He is no longer an active partner, but he is still the beloved companion − in body and mind. He is happy and suffers no pain. He no longer reads anything but novels: he is interested in current works and reads reports and scholarly histories and biographies. Meanwhile I potter on with odd jobs. . . .

VOLUME 53

✍ 1939 ✎

6 January. [Passfield Corner]
We listened on Wednesday afternoon to that world performer President Roosevelt, addressing all the nations as to what is right and what is wrong in public affairs at home and abroad. Religion, democracy, the acceptance of international law are the three funda-

mental principles of the good life. In voice and manner he is a great orator; he is self-convinced of the rightness of his cause and the essential superiority of the American civilization over all other civilizations. He has the added charm of belonging obviously to the aristocracy of that civilization. His foreign policy was accepted with enthusiastic applause by Congress at Washington – an applause which has no doubt been echoed by the millions of listeners in the British and French Empires, the U.S.S.R. and in little European democratic states.

11 January. [Passfield Corner]
Two nights and three days away – mostly with the Shaws. GBS active-minded but frail, Charlotte continuously anxious about him . . . GBS, in spite of old age and recent breakdown in health, is enjoying success in theatre and film. More unexpectedly he is writing a new play, which promises well: *In Good King Charles's Golden Days*. I read the first scene – brilliant dialogue: Isaac Newton, George Fox, Charles and his ladies and James. If he can bring in some sort of striking incident into the play and not limit himself to sparkling talk, it may turn out A.1. . . .

GBS made me envious with his present success and future promise – at eighty-three years of age. How long shall we four old friends linger on the stage? Of the four I think I am the most willing to sink into nothingness and GBS least so: he still feels inspired to tell the world what to be or not to be, mostly not to be. He delights in letters and the answering of letters, so Charlotte tells me – the bigger the pile the better he is pleased. So long as the medicals can inject red corpuscles his intellect will go on glittering. What he seems to have lost is any definite scale of values. . . .

The Webbs had shown little interest in the Fabians since their attention had turned towards the U.S.S.R., and the Society itself was little more than a means of organizing the summer school and autumn lectures. But the New Fabian Research Bureau, founded in 1933, had worked steadily and usefully. When F.W. Galton was about to retire as secretary of the Fabian Society, negotiations began for a merger, and agreement was reached on 26 September 1938, at the height of the Munich crisis.

20 January. [Passfield Corner]
A tiresome job for a tired brain! Elected President of the newly constituted Fabian Society merged with the New Fabian Research Bureau, under the direction of the Coles. I have to explain in an

article in the February *Fabian News* the reasons for this amalgamation and the consequent change in the rules, and in the future work of the reorganized society. . . .

On 26 January Stafford Cripps was expelled from the Labour Party. Beatrice was convinced that expulsions 'will disrupt the Labour Party for years to come', and on 27 February she compared the party's heresy-hunting with the tolerance of the Liberals in 1895–1905, when the party was deeply split over the Boer War.

21 January. [Passfield Corner]
. . . . R.H. Tawney, always delightful to talk to, with his moral judgements and warm-hearted culture. Just off to Chicago University, drawing £1,200 for a three months' course of lectures. These high fees are useful at paying off debts, he declares. He takes the same view as we do of Stafford Cripps's brilliancy and charm – but inability to take counsel with fellow workers, and instability in ends and means. 'It was only yesterday that Stafford was insisting on uniting in the Socialist League the extreme left – C.P., I.L.P. – with the Labour Party against the two other parties, in favour of thoroughgoing socialism with no compromise. Today he argues for joining hands with Liberals and dissentient Conservatives with a moderate programme in another sort of National government, dominated by the Labour Party. 'It is difficult to accept a heretic into your command who is always changing his creed,' says Tawney.

Sir John Anderson (1882–1952), a civil servant who had become a Tory politician, was Home Secretary 1939–40 and gave the name to a back-yard air-raid shelter. He was a wartime Chancellor of the Exchequer.

25 January. [Passfield Corner]
Exactly one year this night Sidney was struck down and out of active life. Today we are living on a low level, not of mutual love and companionship, but of outside interests and usefulness. I can dawdle over one tiny job after another, and take a year in writing another chapter of *Our Partnership*, but I cannot hope to get much out of myself. Poor Sidney has to accept, as he sometimes sadly says, a 'do-nothing life'. One day passes after another, lived without pain, peacefully and in comfort. The worst aspect is the horrible world outlook – every morning in the newspaper, every evening in the broadcast news. Last night we listened to John

Anderson broadcasting from the Albert Hall, in a singularly pleasant and polished voice, the imminence of war and a call to personal service. To which I replied by meditating what I should do with my one spare room . . . How long shall we linger on the stage and watch horror we cannot prevent? One of the painful thoughts of old age is that one is a parasite, no longer worth keeping alive . . .

In *The Holy Terror*, a novel about an authoritarian leader in Britain published early in 1939, Wells gave an astonishing prediction of the circumstances surrounding the death of Stalin fifteen years later.

11 February. [Passfield Corner]
Wells's *Holy Terror* is a splendid sample of senile genius. There are brilliant patches describing states of mind in individuals and crowds. But for the most part it is one long screed of abuse of existing men and women and of all present-day manners, customs and creeds – with a fatuous glow over a world state brought about by a dictator and his group of followers. The hero is a caricature of Hitler. . . . But the most striking feature of this romance is the absence of any code of ethics: H.G. has apparently no use for loyalty, honesty, truthfulness or loving kindness in forecasting the new social order. The dictator is a queer type of mental defective with a mystical strain of self-deification and a superb energy and cunning in the attainment of his end: becoming the world dictator. Why have Wells and GBS, Somerset Maugham and so many other intellectuals become brilliant cynics, gloating over the ridiculous vileness of man, without hope of betterment? . . .

13 February. [Passfield Corner]
The Maiskys here for four or five hours: in good spirits about the U.S.S.R. The Ambassador is convinced that Great Britain and France will be faced, during the next months, with war if they refuse to surrender territory to German and Italy. Hitler and Mussolini cannot afford to wait another year – with their own people over-worked and discontented, whilst the Western democracies are financially prosperous and busy with rearmament on a grand scale. For Hitler and Mussolini it is now or never . . . I asked whether the U.S.S.R. would come in but he refused to express an opinion. . . .

428

Hesketh Pearson (1887–1964) published his biography of Shaw with the title *GBS*. Sir Francis Galton (1822–1911) was a remarkable statistician and pioneer of the theory of eugenics. Henry Labouchere (1831–1912) – 'Labby' – was a Liberal journalist and politician. Beatrice had put *Our Partnership* aside to attempt a short and popular book (to be called *Our Pilgrimage*) made up of three parts – one on Fabian socialism, one on the decay of capitalism, and the third on the new civilization. She hoped to finish it within two years but it was never done.

9 March. [Passfield Corner]
Malcolm Muggeridge brought down here, for four hours' talk, Hesketh Pearson, an elderly *littérateur* – biographer of 'Labby' and others – on the plea that he was writing GBS's life. As he had also an introduction from GBS I felt free to tell him of the fine qualities of the Hero and his devoted wife. Also Pearson is the great-nephew of Francis Galton, for whom as a girl I had an unbounded liking and admiration – as the typical scientific mind without qualification, no personal vanity nor ambition, no prejudice that I could detect. This biography is, I think, another instance of GBS's kindness. Pearson is not in the first rank among present writers (not in *Who's Who*) but he is an old acquaintance of GBS's of the Frederic Harrison group, hard-up and has been offered a big sum in advance from the publishers. It meant an exhausting talk. Malcolm was as agreeable as usual, but sniffing for something unworthy or ugly *re* GBS or the Webbs. I chaffed him about his perpetual denigration of men and institutions, told him that he was an inverted idolizer and ought to have been psychoanalysed as a child, to rid his mind of the *search after the Devil* instead of a search after God. . . . Poor Malcolm, he is not helped in his literary career by the strange mania for libelling individuals and institutions: it is too unmeasured and all-pervading; no light or shade, no wit or kindly pleasantry (like GBS) shows when he describes what he does not like in men, manners or institutions.

But alas! with all this talking and dictating letters, I don't get on with the book. I feel tireder and tireder! I want to write those last pages before I depart, not merely to bring in some needed income from books but also to express our final view of the world we have lived in. I doubt whether I shall do it.

On 10 March Chamberlain said that Europe 'was settling down to a period of tranquillity' and Samuel Hoare denounced 'jitterbugs' who were predicting war. On 15 March, in a few hours, German troops occupied the rump of Czechoslovakia and declared it a protectorate. In Birmingham on 17 March Chamberlain peevishly denounced Hitler for a personal affront and began the slow turn of foreign policy towards resistance to the Fascist powers. President Roosevelt announced a revision of the U.S. Neutrality Act to permit the sale of arms to countries resisting aggression.

16 March. [Passfield Corner]
The news last night of Hitler's crash into Czechoslovakia and the Halifax–Chamberlain shamefaced admission of it, in Lords and Commons, roused in me horror at the cruelty to Czechoslovakia, and a sort of grin – a contemptuous grin – at the imbecility a bare six months ago of the Munich episode. Also there was satisfaction that all notions of a Four Power pact with Germany and Italy were killed for good and all; that the U.S.S.R. has become our inevitable ally in its resistance to the aggressive states in the near future, and that the U.S.A. would be Hitler's Public Enemy No. 1, ready to help in supplying arms even if not ready to use them.

18 March. [Passfield Corner]
Chamberlain's unexpected oration over the air from the Birmingham Town Hall last night, with the thunderous applause of the ancestral audience in the city of his birth and of the life of his great father, will certainly impress the world of listeners that, at long last, he and his government mean to resist Hitler's lawless use of force – at least against France and Great Britain. An honest man of limited intelligence and intense class consciousness, ugly in voice and manner, intent on pursuing peace for his own country at almost any cost except loss of territories by France and Great Britain. To preserve these Empires he would be ready to risk war. He looks across the Atlantic for the support of the great power in the West; he cannot bring himself even to glance at the other great power in the East.

20 March. [Passfield Corner]
Addressed after lunch seventy wives of university professors and a few women lecturers on the need for the study of social institutions. It is a sort of 'Half-Circle Club': except no men are admitted to their entertainments. A kindly intelligent group, one or two Communists among them, but mostly conventional and politely open-minded to a distinguished guest of undoubted standing. Then on for a chat, first with Galton, secondly with Susan Lawrence.

Galton reluctantly came round to co-operating with the U.S.S.R. but still maintains that we could not have risked war in September – we were hopelessly unprepared. Susan, he said, had been again appointed Fabian delegate to the Southport conference but, because she voted for Stafford's expulsion, been denied her Fabian mandate to serve on the executive. So I found Susan in a state of defiance. She argued against it and proposed a compromise. But Stafford was insolent and stuck out his lower lip and chin in contemptuous defiance. 'He wanted to be a martyr'. . . . The Labour Party executive was a hopeless body of which Dalton was the devil! Greenwood a confirmed drunkard and Attlee of no account. . . .

On 21 March the Germans made a score of demands on Poland, including the recovery of the 'free city' of Danzig and part of the corridor dividing Germany from East Prussia. Poland appealed for help and on 31 March, with French support, Chamberlain gave Poland a military guarantee – an offer followed by a formal agreement on 6 April. This offer was made, however, without any attempt to involve the U.S.S.R., Poland's near (but disliked) neighbour.

31 March. [Passfield Corner]
. . . . I lunched with H.G. Wells yesterday in his attractive and luxuriously fitted house in Hanover Terrace, Regent's Park. He has sent me his latest book, *The Holy Terror*, and begged me to come and see him – he wanted to know whether *we* had invented the term *industrial democracy* and what we meant by it. He was at work summing up the human race – as a species of animal, living on this planet . . . I found him a physical wreck. He had flown to Australia and back by Rangoon and had picked up some poison. He was obsessed with his own vague vision of a world order, with his search for a 'competent receiver' of the power to organize mankind. The mass electorate and its representatives were totally unfit for the job. But he utterly failed to make me understand what sort of social institution he had in mind. . . . Poor old Wells. I was sorry for him. I doubt whether we shall meet again – we are too old and tired. He is contemptuous, even angry, with the Soviet Union. I asked him about his elder son, the scientist. 'He has gone "left" like so many of the younger scientists,' he observed. 'But he will recover from this intellectual adolescence,' he added. GBS told me that 'Moura' has her own 'Russian house' but visits him daily. . . .

The following morning I called on the Maiskys: Madame

Maisky was upset by the putting off, day after day, of the proposed interview of Maisky with Halifax about the threat to Poland. Were the British and French governments arranging a pact with Poland omitting the U.S.S.R. and even antagonistic to its interests? Then the Ambassador came in: he had been interviewing Lloyd George's private secretary and others in search of information. We went into the little dining-room for coffee. Presently a message was brought in from Halifax asking Maisky to call at the Foreign Office at one o'clock: upon which I departed, after wishing them well. The Shaws, where I lunched, were in good spirits: GBS looking his best and obviously enjoying the success of *Pygmalion* on the films, and *Geneva* and *The Doctor's Dilemma* on the stage. There is a marked Shaw revival: his witty and unconventional cynicism, with its queer freedom from apparent bias for or against any of the current ideologies, is evidently refreshing to the public mind. Fundamentally the Shaws are pro-Soviet, but GBS refuses to accept the self-righteous indictment by British liberals and labour leaders of the totalitarian states. Also he despises *little peoples* like the Czechoslovaks or Abyssinia – he admires the full-blooded dictator who splashes about and asserts his right and his people's right to rule over others, especially if he defies conventional morality, which GBS considers hypocrisy. . . .

On Good Friday (7 April) Mussolini attacked and annexed Albania – a move which provoked the British and French governments to offer guarantees to Rumania and Greece. On 26 April the British government introduced military conscription for the first time in peace. Hitler, it was later revealed, had already decided to invade Poland, and his Reichstag tirade of 28 April began the six-month build-up to war.

8 April. [Passfield Corner]
The Maiskys called here yesterday – they had driven out into the country to get some rest from the turmoil. Just before they left the Embassy the Ambassador had been called up by a friendly American journalist and informed of the Italian invasion of Albania (I had heard it over the wireless at 12.25). He shrugged his shoulders when I asked him what he thought of it, as if to say: 'What else can Chamberlain expect?' 'How do your people put up with him?' he asked me presently. He has been proved to be disastrously wrong; why does the Conservative Party continue to trust him? He intimated that Moscow did *not* trust him and it was doubtful

whether they would join a pact if he remained Premier. The British and French governments seemed to him to be sliding down the slope into a war with Germany, Italy and Japan under the worst possible terms. He dismissed the Labour Party as negligible: they would have to support the government when war came and would get nothing out of it for the workers. . . .

8 April. [Passfield Corner]
Meanwhile I have broken down in health. I can no longer walk because of sores on my shins, which compel me to keep my legs up. I can no longer sleep except by taking alonal, both of which treatments are laid down by Orr, our medical attendant. Also Sidney has been laid up, but is now getting back to normal. The book is laid on one side, and will not be resumed until we return, I hope rested, from our holiday in North Cornwall. Which is depressing. Have I not reached senile incapacity for further clear thought, I ask myself? Anyway, I am tired of living. I should welcome a painless death if I could take my beloved with me. He would think it hysterical, certainly unreasonable, to desire it, but I doubt whether he would resent it. He feels, as I do, that our living life is finished: we are merely waiting for the end.

Ella Pycroft (1855–?), a social worker, had been Beatrice's colleague in 1885, when they managed the 'model' tenement Katherine Buildings, near Tower Bridge. Canon Samuel Barnett (1844–1913) and his wife Henrietta (1851–1936) had been notable reformers in late Victorian London.

5 May. Polzeath, Cornwall
A long and expensive journey here, with a night at Exeter . . . The one redeeming feature was Ella Pycroft's evening with us at Exeter. An aged and fragile but dear old lady, with her outstanding honesty, sympathetic intelligence and all-pervading kindliness still strong, in spite of loss of memory and tottering steps. She and I talked of old times, my work as rent-collector of East End dwellings, and her naive response when I suggested that I might marry Sidney Webb: 'Oh! Beatrice, you couldn't.' And then her ten years' service as woman inspector of technical education under Sidney at the T.E.B. I never met a more dutiful and broad-minded woman than Ella. She has, however, one obsession – anti-God: she could not get on with clerics; she even disliked and distrusted Canon Barnett, still more his well-intentioned, clever but tactless

433

wife. This intolerance arose from her doubts whether these highly intelligent professional Christians did really believe in the Christian mythology which they sponsored. Even this prejudice seems to have passed away with old age, owing to the modesty and tolerance which old age brings to the best type of human beings. I gathered that she enjoys life, in spite of her infirmity and narrow means; she reads, and gardens her little plot. . . .

22 May. [Cornwall]
Our stay here has been restful, the loneliness, the beauty – the strange beauty – of the Cornish coast has been a real relaxation for a troubled mind and tired and worn-out body. Whether I shall be able to continue my book I do not know. But what does it matter? . . . So back home tomorrow; a ten hours' journey.

Charlotte endowed the Shaw Library at the L.S.E.

18 June. [Passfield Corner]
Two nights at Barbara's, first to introduce the Carr-Saunders and Adamses to the Shaws at lunch, with a view of help from Charlotte for the new cultural library and lecturers to carry out GBS's variation of the principle 'manners maketh man'; secondly to attend a meeting of the newly constituted Fabian Society and, incidentally, to lunch with the Maiskys to meet Harold Nicolson, with family gatherings thrown in. . . . The lunch with the Maiskys and Harold Nicolson entertained me. I had been interested by Nicolson's trilogy – the biography of his father and of Curzon, culminating in his description of the Peace conference; in his broadcasts and his queer career, as a diplomat, a writer, as follower of Mosley for a few weeks, and then as National Labour M.P. He certainly is a political personality – but without influence. . . . He and Maisky like each other: I think I liked him more than he liked me! . . .

Meanwhile the news from the Far East looks like Japan joining the Axis in war with Great Britain – for which we are all preparing. Maisky still believes that there will be a pact with Moscow which will paralyse Hitler's will to war. Nicolson suggested that Japan, conscious of failure to conquer China, is today ready to seize all the ports of the continent, including Hong Kong, so as to oust Great Britain from the Far East. He actually suggested that we should be compelled to evacuate Hong Kong and concentrate our defence on Singapore, boycotting Japanese trade with Europe. . . .

King George VI and Queen Elizabeth had just made the first visit by reigning British monarchs to the United States.

24 June. [Passfield Corner]
How amazingly personal the world has become: the mob idolizing particular individuals instead of claiming, as they did in the nineteenth century, the right of groups to govern themselves through mechanically ascertained majorities, without distinguishing one individual from another. And this idolization of persons on account of their assumed and exceptional goodness and infallible wisdom is not confined to the so-called totalitarian states. The British people, with their genius for compromise, have lit on the device for a robot King and his wife – who have no power but are treated with extreme deference and arouse in the mob worshipful emotion. The efficiency of the device has been shown by the enormous success of the British King and Queen not only in Great Britain but in Canada and the U.S.A. They are ideal robots: the King kindly, sensible, without pretension and with considerable open-mindedness, and the Queen good-looking and gracious and beautifully attired, who blows kisses to admiring Yankees in New York but looks the perfect dignified aristocrat in London. Is this turn towards idolizing particular human beings characteristic of the last two decades, the reaction from a loss of faith in a supernatural god or gods? This mania for a *leader* seems a similar instinct to that shown by wolves – and even by dogs, when the dogs have lost contact with the idolized man. It is clearly a dangerous human instinct when manifested towards men who exercise personal power over multitudes of their fellow men, as do Hitler and Mussolini. . . .

28 June. [Passfield Corner]
Alike in France and Great Britain, the governments and the inner circle, war is expected to break out in July, August or September . . . The only excuse for Munich put forward by those in authority is that Great Britain and France had shamefully neglected to arm themselves for the inevitable struggle with the Fascist states. That, obviously, was the fault of the Conservative governments who have ruled Great Britain for the last twenty years, except for the short interlude of the two minority Labour governments – one of nine months and the other two years – neither the one nor the other controlling Parliament. The root of this disaster lies in the hatred

and fear of Soviet Communism on the part of the all-powerful capitalist and landlord class, reinforced by the dislike of public expenditure. And dearly will they pay for it!

Sir William Ramsay (1852–1916) was a Nobel Prize-winner and professor of chemistry at University College, London. Stafford Cripps returned to politics in the wartime Coalition, and then in the post-war Labour government.

9 July. [Passfield Corner]
Stafford and Isobel paid us their annual visit of a couple of hours. . . . He despaired of the Labour Party: they were losing ground in the country: no one was interested in their worn-out programme. . . . About the future of world affairs, Stafford foresees a dark world of disasters. Unless our policy is drastically altered, there will be world war and revolution. The British governing class is played out: they have no settled policy except to resist any change in the control and distribution of the wealth of the nation. There is no creed of right and wrong. . . . Chaos everywhere was his summing-up of life at home and abroad.

For leadership in the labour movement Stafford had a most unfit upbringing. Born and bred in a luxurious Tory household, brilliantly successful as a Winchester scholar, winning a New College scholarship which he refused in order to study science under Professor Ramsay at University College, he married, at a little over twenty years old, a wealthy girl with a millionaire mother. Hence he was able to settle in a charming country home of his own as a well-to-do squire. It is to his credit that he became a successful barrister, the youngest K.C. at the Bar, earning a big income by his wits. Then he was suddenly selected by MacDonald as Solicitor-General in the spring of 1930 and thus entered Parliament, at the age of forty-two, not as a private member who had to make his reputation, but as a Front Bencher. He knew nothing whatsoever about the internal life of the labour movement and though our nephew, so far as I can remember he had never been in our house. . . . From the first he had a subconscious contempt for his colleagues, old and young alike. For a few months after the MacDonald–Snowden–Thomas betrayal of the Labour Party . . . Stafford stood out as the Good Boy of the Labour Party led by Henderson. But as years went by, whilst contributing handsomely to party funds and entertaining Labour men and their wives lavishly at Goodfellows, he failed to consider their views of any importance. He organized first the Socialist League, then the Popular Front, practically in direct opposition to the Labour Party executive. How could he expect that his rivals for leadership, Hugh Dalton more especially, should not succeed in getting rid of him? I doubt whether he will reappear in the inner counsels of the Labour Party . . . More likely he will find himself eventually on the Front Bench of a National government composed mainly of the old governing class, converted by the course of events, to a compromise with the new social order.

13 July. [Passfield Corner]
Sidney's eightieth birthday. . . . Testimonies of affection and respect drifted in during the day. Sidney happy and peaceful, pleased with his past life of successful adventure in public administration and the writing of books, content with the comfort and friendly consideration which envelops his old age, above all the continuous comradeship with his aged but loving wife. So all is well with the Webbs. If only I could get on with the book! . . .

23 July. [Passfield Corner]
Forty-seven years today we were married in the shabby little office of the Registrar of St Pancras Workhouse – a fitting spot for the opening of our recognized partnership, dedicated to the abolition of poverty in the midst of riches. Since that date we have been one and indivisible, in work and in rest, at home and abroad, in our private life and our public career. Looking back on those forty-seven years of companionship in thought and action, I remember no single note of discord. In stating our conclusions we have sometimes disagreed, but it has ended either in a compromise or in the dismissal of the problem from our thoughts in order to hasten on with the job and take on yet another task. Perhaps during the nine years Sidney was in Parliament, especially for the three years as a Cabinet Minister, we were most separated in thought and feeling and even in residence. So far as I was concerned, this episode was wearisome and dispiriting, owing to disillusionment with the British social system and hopelessness about the future of western civilization. Watching from inside, our powerful governing class embracing the Labour leaders and their wives, our Court with its flunkey Anglican Church pandering to the landlord and the financier, was not an inspiring spectacle! Then there was the renewal of hope

through the U.S.S.R.; and, in spite of my illness, owing to Sidney's continued strength the authorship of *Soviet Communism: A New Civilization*, the crowning effort of Our Partnership. Today Sidney and I have ceased to work together. But we love each other more and more, and when one dies, I think, the other will die too. . . .

British and French negotiations with the U.S.S.R. had continued all summer, with distrust on both sides making them both dilatory and inconclusive. On 27 July it was agreed to send a joint but not top-rank military mission to Moscow. It did not arrive until 11 August, and while the talks stalled on the Russian demand for rights of military transit across Rumania and Poland, the Soviet government had secretly responded to Hitler's approaches. Suspecting that the Western powers might be seeking to embroil him in war if Hitler attacked Poland – and to give Hitler covert encouragement in his anti-Communist crusade – Stalin decided to turn the tables on them. On 19 August he signed a commercial agreement with Germany and agreed to receive von Ribbentrop in Moscow on 26 August. Poised to attack Poland on 1 September, counting on a feeble response from London and Paris, Hitler sent Ribbentrop on 23 August to sign a hurriedly drafted treaty of non-aggression, which bought Russian neutrality in exchange for the three Baltic states, Bessarabia and a large part of a newly partitioned Poland. On the previous day – 22 August – Hitler had given orders for the invasion of Poland, using provocative incidents in Danzig as the excuse. Maxim Litvinov, the public advocate of collective security, had been dismissed as Commissar for Foreign Affairs on 3 May. He was replaced by V.M. Molotov (b. 1890).

23 August. 4 a.m. [Passfield Corner]
'A day of holy horror' – for me at any rate. Sidney remained calm, awaiting events. . . . Yesterday morning the front page in *The Times* and *Daily Herald* gave the sinister news that an anti-aggression pact between the U.S.S.R. and Germany had been negotiated and that Ribbentrop was flying to Moscow to sign it. A horrible thought for the friends of the Soviet Union: it looks a complete reversal of the foreign policy of the U.S.S.R. – all the more discreditable because of its secrecy and obvious inconsistency with the anti-aggression protestations of the Soviet government at Geneva and elsewhere on behalf of Spain, Czechoslovakia and China. What was the cause of this sudden and hidden change in Soviet statecraft? And does it explain the resignation of Litvinov?

25 August. 4 a.m. [Passfield Corner]
The German–Soviet pact seems a great disaster to all that the

Webbs have stood for. Even Sidney is dazed and I am, for a time at least, knocked almost senseless! The manner of its making is even worse than its meaning. If the Soviet statesmen had, after the breakdown of collective security (professed to be the policy of Great Britain and France), retired from European politics, and then entered into non-aggression pacts with other countries, even with Germany, or insisted that they would remain neutral (like the Scandinavian government), they would have retained the respect of the world. But to become fervent supporters of collective security, to be missionaries of resistance against aggression and all attempts to extend territories by force, to be leaders all over the world of anti-Fascist and anti-Nazi movements, and then to conclude suddenly and secretly an alliance with Hitler's Germany, is a terrible collapse of good faith and integrity. Further, if Stalin and his colleagues were, during the last four months, turning towards Hitler and actually secretly discussing this alliance, they ought not to have been discussing with British and French diplomats, openly and apparently sincerely, an alliance against Germany in her march towards European domination. The military discussion, involving intimate exchange of military information, was especially dishonourable. To continue these discussions to the very night of the signature of the Soviet–German Pact was a disgraceful proceeding. . . . I console myself with the thought of how rapidly currents of thought and feeling throughout the world change their course. Meanwhile I am in a state of collapse. Courage, aged mortal, and get back to your own task of being devoted to your mate, kindly to others and finishing *Our Pilgrimage*. . . .

27 August. 3 a.m. [Passfield Corner]
The Turins here for a night. She is hard at work as Carr-Saunders' secretary, packing up at Houghton Street so as to move to Peterhouse College, Cambridge, if war breaks out: the Foreign Office taking over the London School of Economics' building. . . . We and they listened over the wireless to the final stages of the fateful decision of the British Cabinet on Sunday and today. Shall it be peace or war?

I am in a state of utter exhaustion . . . haunted by the agony of the world we live in, this terrifying vision of herds of human beings being prepared for mutual slaughter in their millions. No wonder that Stalin prefers to keep his 170 million out of the battlefield, whether in Europe or in Asia, whilst the anti-Comintern Axis and the Western capitalist democracies – both ostensibly hostile to the new civilization – destroy each other in Europe, and Japan gets bogged in China. In a disreputable way, Stalin's foreign policy is a miracle of successful statesmanship. Surely the aged and decrepit Webbs, having proclaimed Soviet Communism as a *new civilization* and the hope of the human race, can sink out of life with a smile? A consoling thought. . . .

1 September. [Passfield Corner]
Owing to Annie's skill and industry, with Jean's help, we have solved the blacking-out of our little abode successfully. I am in a state of utter exhaustion, with the 'frequency' worse. I try to get on with the book. So I must limit my entries in the diary to other people's thoughts, and not waste my minute energy in expressing my views. . . .

Despite last-minute attempts to avert war, the Germans invaded Poland early in the morning of 1 September. There were some hours of delay, while Chamberlain seemed still to hesitate, but after Parliament and the House of Commons had met on the evening of Saturday 2 September, Chamberlain said that everything he had hoped and wished for in his public life had 'crashed in ruins'.

3 September. [Passfield Corner]
Listened at eleven this morning to Chamberlain's admirably expressed declaration to the House of Commons of war with Germany. His voice, amplified by the wireless, was strikingly like his father's. In his sorrowful admission of the failure of his policy of appeasement and sombre but self-controlled denunciation of Hitler and his monstrous ways, he was at once appealing and impressive. Now that we are at war -- a war during which we personally can take no part – I feel detached and calm; the strain has ceased . . .

7 September. [Passfield Corner]
Our first air raid, which turned out to be a false alarm; the enemy aeroplanes never got beyond the east coast. A banging at the front door and a grim voice calling 'Air raid'. I had just come from my bath and looked out of my window. There stood a man with a bicycle, his gas mask slung over his shoulder, who explained that a warning had been given from Portsmouth that German aeroplanes

were in the neighbourhood. A few minutes later, I went into Sidney's room and saw him sitting up with his gas mask on! I suggested that he should take it off, which he promptly did. Mrs Grant had been in and was angry. '*You have no right* to tell Mr Webb to take his off,' she said in a menacing voice. 'Pardon me,' I laughed. 'I am his wife and the mistress of this house. Keep yours on if you like. It is damned nonsense putting on gas masks out in the countryside. The Germans won't waste their gas on us. Our only danger – if there is one – is an explosive bomb. Even a quarter of a mile off I am told it might bring our house down!' Annie and Jean were slightly excited and interested, but went on with their work. In two hours' time the all-clear was sounded. We who live round about the camps – there is a firing-range for tanks a quarter of a mile away – are fortunate in being in a *neutral* area – neither so dangerous for our own children to be evacuated nor sufficiently safe for strange children to come. We are free from lodgers and yet, for sensible folk, not subject to panic. So all is well. . . .

18 September. [Passfield Corner]
Satan has won hands down: Stalin and Molotov have become the villains of the piece. Molotov's broadcast to the peoples of the U.S.S.R. justifying the march of the Red Army into Poland is a monument of international immorality, cloaked in cynical sophistry. At twelve o'clock we listened in to the news over the wireless: at three o'clock a telephone message from the Soviet Embassy that the Ambassador was detained in London – Madame Maisky hoped they might be able to come later on. Poor Maiskys, we shall never see them again: if we did we should not know what to say to them, nor they to us. With their friend Litvinov they will disappear, let us hope safely, somewhere in the background of that enormous and enigmatic territory. The aged Webbs will fade out presently: but the horror of a raging war, which can neither be lost nor won, will destroy the old without bringing the new civilization within sight of this generation. Owing to the lust for the old territories of Czarist Russia to be won by force, the statesmen of the U.S.S.R. have lost not merely moral prestige, but also the freedom to develop the new civilization, whilst the old western civilization was being weakened and perhaps destroyed by war. To me it seems the blackest tragedy in human history. Sidney observes that, within a century, it may be 'a forgotten episode'. He refuses to be downcast.

441

24 September. [Passfield Corner]
A flurried visit from the Maiskys yesterday. On Friday they phoned they would come to tea on Saturday; on Saturday morning that they must either come to lunch or not at all. At two o'clock the motor car drove up. . . .

Maisky no longer 'chuckled': he was grim and somewhat defiant; she was excited, carried away by the thought that the world revolution towards Communism was in progress. Maisky began cross-examining me. What was the intention of our present government; did they really mean to beat their way through into Germany, or were they *staying put*, relying on the blockade and a revolution in Germany? Unless the British people would dismiss Chamberlain, there would be no helpful relation with the Soviet government, and unless they came to terms with the Red Army (today in possession of more than one half of Poland), they could not destroy Hitlerism, leave alone reconstitute the old Poland. . . .

Maisky's parting words were: 'Power politics, pure and simple, are now at work in all the foreign offices of the world. All idealism has vanished.' And he signified, though he did not actually say it: the Soviet government has the power to spread Communism through alliance with Germany, and she will do it. The British and French armies cannot arrest it by reconstituting the Poland of the Versailles treaty. . . .

2 October. 4 a.m. [Passfield Corner]
Winston Churchill (as First Lord of the Admiralty)'s broadcast on 'The First Month of the War' is a notable event. His reference to the U.S.S.R. ought to revive the spirit of downcast friends of the Soviet Union. If only our old acquaintance were the Prime Minister in the place of the reactionary and mechanical-minded Chamberlain, the prospect of a right and rapid ending of this murder and waste of the war would be more hopeful. Anyway, he becomes the leader of the progressive forces in Great Britain, and the leaders of the Labour Party will have to follow suit or lose their influence on public opinion, owing to their attitude to the Soviet Union . . . Maisky, by the way, implied that Winston Churchill would be trusted by the Kremlin in a way which Chamberlain would not . . .

5 October. [Passfield Corner]
. . . Everyone I speak to seems utterly bewildered and downcast –

far more so than in the early days of the great war. There is no war enthusiasm – at best, a dull acquiescence. The imminence of air raids, the black-out at nights, the evacuees and their parents, the heavy taxation and drastic rationing of light, heat and food already enforced, and a hundred other grievances, irritate and depress the spirit of the nation.

8 October. [Passfield Corner]
An hour with the Booths at Funtingdon Lodge. George and Margy looked tired and strained. The old nurse who lived with them had died a few weeks ago; and now my old friend Mary Booth, and much-loved mother of a devoted family, has passed away in her ninety-second year. . . .

Leonard Woolf had written the first of an intended series of books on nineteenth-century politics. Virginia Woolf began to write *The Years* in the autumn of 1932. She had much trouble with the novel before she completed it in March 1936. She felt that it was an artistic failure, though it was well reviewed and sold satisfactorily.

27 October. [Passfield Corner]
I journeyed up to London in a train crowded with officers in uniform and youths looking sad and distraught, saying farewell to mothers and sweethearts, and a few older men to wives and children at the stations – to lunch with Barbara and meet the Leonard Woolfs. They had expressed a desire to meet me again. Leonard was looking terribly ill with his trembling hands, but was as gently wise as ever. I told him how interested I had been in his last volume of *After the Deluge.* But I hoped in his next, dealing with the period 1832–92, he would bring in the *Housekeeping State* provided by the Municipal Corporation Act of 1835 – which changed local government from being manorial or chartered trade guilds with law enforced by magistrates in town and country, into *associations of consumers* with compulsory powers to regulate and to provide public services for the whole community. He demurred: the local authority of Lewes, their neighbouring town, was corrupt and incompetent. I retorted that the corruption and ill will of many municipal corporations had not prevented the upgrowth of beneficial public services, health and education, housing and lighting, drainage and water, parks and libraries, and the prevention of nuisances. These services to the community could not have been achieved by

voluntary associations of consumers. In fact, it was the proved incapacity of voluntary associations of householders in cities to do the job that led them to apply for local acts giving the compulsory power of levying rates and regulating conduct. . . .

Virginia seemed troubled by an absence of any creed as to what was right and what was wrong. I asked her whether she was going to write a second volume of *Years*. I longed to hear how the family she described so vividly would respond to this new war. Would they be as unconcerned as they were during the great war of 1914–18? She gave me no answer except that she did not know her own mind about what was happening – so how could she describe the mind of others! . . . This gifted and charming lady, with her classic features, subtle observation and symphonic style, badly needs a living philosophy. Brought up in the innermost circle of the late Victorian intellectuals, in revolt against the Christian religion with its superstitions and its hypocritical conventions, they were between *laissez-faire* and *laissez-aller* in all the circumstances of life. *Absence of restraint* was to them the one and only meaning of liberty, for they personally enjoyed the presence of opportunity to lead the life they liked, or thought they liked. Virginia Woolf realizes that this creed has broken down; but she sees no way out . . . We all aim at maximizing human happiness, health, loving kindness, scientific certainty and the spirit of adventure together with the appreciation of beauty in sight and sound, in word and thought. Where we differ is how to bring about this ideal here and now. . . .

Finland resisted the Soviet attack until March. The British and French governments seriously considered sending military aid to the Finns; and the war had an aggravating effect on western relations with the U.S.S.R. The Finns supported Hitler's invasion of the Soviet Union in 1941.

1 December. [Passfield Corner]
Another shock for the friends of the Soviet Union! the march of the Red Army into Finland and the bombing of the towns by a Red Air fleet. As before it is the *manner of doing it* – the working-up of hard hatred and parrot-like repetition of false – glaringly false – accusations against poor little Finland, which is so depressing. From the standpoint of power politics, the recovery of territory taken from Russia during her revolutionary helplessness can hardly be criticized if power politics is accepted; Great Britain has done many

worse deeds in building up her huge Empire by force, but she has done them silently, sometimes without her people knowing it. *Manners maketh man* fit for evil deeds as well as good. As yet, the revolutionary leaders of the U.S.S.R. have not learnt good manners; they will have to suffer for it. . . .

Christmas Day. [Passfield Corner]
On Friday the Maiskys telephoned that they would like to come down to tea and supper on Sunday. As we had heard. . . . that the Allies were going to break off diplomatic relations with the U.S.S.R. we assumed that it was a farewell visit. . . .

What Maisky did not realize, or at any rate would not admit, is that the war in Finland is the main issue; the Finnish people and their constitution are idealized by British liberal and conservative intellectuals; an idealization which has been strengthened by their successful resistance to the mass attack by the colossal Red Army owing to its poor equipment . . .

I console myself with the thought that the defeat of the Red Army by the Finnish, whether temporary or permanent, may teach Stalin and his associates that in spite of their success in reorganizing the 170 million of mixed races, mostly uncivilized, on Communist principles, they have still to learn the way of the good life in manners and methods, in times and seasons, if the new civilization is to prevail. If they fail to mend their manners and improve their methods, anything may happen, even a temporary collapse of the new social order within the U.S.S.R. All the same, owing to its intrinsic rightness I believe that the new civilization will eventually replace western civilization.

We parted with the Maiskys affectionately. We like both of them; she is charming, he is not personally attractive but he is honest, shrewd and courageous . . . They both declared that the happiest times of their presence in Great Britain have been their visits at the home of Sidney and Beatrice Webb. . . .

VOLUME 54

✎ 1940 ✎

8 January. [Passfield Corner]
H.G. Wells has sent me his latest work – *The New Moral World*, a continuation and repetition of *The Fate of Homo Sapiens*, published a year ago. He has become a revivalist preacher, warning men that they are rushing headlong to extermination and showing them the narrow way of salvation. His God is Science, served by countless public-spirited scientists; his Devil is Religion, or more precisely the Roman Catholic Church with its infallible Pope (Protestantism he dismisses as the halfway house to Secularism) . . . .

Today he is advocating that men of science should draw up a *Declaration of the Rights of Man* (he gives his own blueprint) which every one would be compelled to accept. He is scornful and angry because the reading public will not accept these suggestions and act on them. All the same Wells's description of human society as it exists today is devastatingly brilliant and serves to destroy faith in western civilization – that discordant triplet of the Christian faith, capitalist profit-making and political democracy! According to H.G. the first is a pernicious falsehood; the second a worn-out and poisonous practice; and the last – one of the fundamental features of the new civilization but taken alone, failing to afford comfort or shelter for the human race even for breeding purposes, let alone for the progress to a higher form of life. . . . For forty years, since he published *Anticipations* to the present day, he has been preaching the gospel of human progress – a fine record, in spite of all lapses in good manners and his invidious personal relationships with women.

The cold first winter of war kept the Webbs relatively isolated. Beatrice was suffering from insomnia and eczema and the loss of her able secretary Gabrielle Irwin made life and work more difficult.

22 January. [Passfield Corner]
My eighty-second birthday: two years since Sidney was on the eve of the stroke which withdrew him from a working life. Two years

more and we shall be in our Jubilee year, when I want to publish my last literary work, *The Three Stages of our Pilgrimage*. In the last year I have only accomplished three chapters out of five of *First Stage: Fabian Socialism*. If I could finish the other three this coming year I could do it: assuming that I cut down the last stage to one chapter on Soviet Communism. Of course there is a possibility that the U.S.S.R. may collapse and the *New Civilization* appear as a dream dreamt by the aged Webbs. . . .

Beatrice was on a brief visit to London, staying with the Drakes. The legislative programme Attlee introduced after Labour's election victory in 1945 was essentially set out in his 1937 book *The Labour Party in Perspective*.

29 February. [London]

. . . . Barbara and I went to hear Attlee lecture on War Aims at Canterbury Hall, Cartwright Gardens – the London centre of the London School of Economics. He was rather unfriendly to me at the reception before the lecture. His hour's lecture was pitiable: he looked and spoke like an insignificant elderly clerk, without distinction in the voice, manner or substance of his discourse. His address was in fact *meaningless*; there were neither statements or arguments that you could take hold of, whether to accept or to deny; it was a string of vague assertions about an international authority, peace *not dictated* but agreed to by a new Germany without Hitler or his party, economic reform of some undefined type controlled by the International Labour Office which should fix eventual rates of wages for all countries! No mention of the supersession of a profit-making motive – only abuse of all totalitarian governments, whether Fascist, Nazi or Communist, as inconsistent with 'political democracy'. Altogether a hopeless failure. I doubt whether anyone in the audience – they were mostly middle-aged men – had any notion of what he actually advocated, either about the desirable peace or about the internal social organization after the war. To realize that this little nonentity is the Parliamentary Leader of the Labour Party, the representative of His Majesty's Opposition at £2,000 a year, and presumably the future P.M., is humiliating. There is no one on the Front Opposition Bench who approaches in distinction J.R. MacDonald, Philip Snowden, Arthur Henderson; Alexander, who *has* a personality but an unpleasant one, is not a socialist – he is the paid representative of the Consumer's Co-operative Movement; Clynes is decrepit. Morrison is able and

447

incisive but reactionary; Dalton an *arriviste* and untrustworthy at that. Alas! for the Labour Party; the young and able men of left views will not join it even if permitted to.

The Maiskys looked in about 6.30 in excellent spirits, confident that the Red Army is going to win in Finland. He believes that the Conservative government does *not* want to go to war with the U.S.S.R. but may find it difficult to resist pressure from the Labour Party in that direction.

The psychologist Havelock Ellis (1859–1939) was one of the first Fabians. The South African novelist and feminist Olive Schreiner (1855–1920) was best known for *The Story of an African Farm*.

11 March. [Passfield Corner]
. . . . *The Thirties* by Malcolm Muggeridge – chosen as 'the book of the month' and well reviewed by the *New Statesman* and *Times Literary Supplement* – is a clever bit of work and may bring in some much-needed income. It is harmless, as the witty caricatures of J.R. MacDonald and other politicians are not unduly libellous, except about the dead one, who does not matter. He comes to no conclusion, except that Homo Sapiens is incurably contemptible; he suggests that only in 'communion with God' can the restless spirit find consolation. Whether he believes in the existence of God I do not know. Anyway the phrase provides an ethical refuge for ugly cynicism, as does the mysticism of Aldous Huxley. He mentions the Webbs, but in a harmless way. A strange scrap-book, light reading for these troublous times.

My Life by Havelock Ellis is a sickly book, mostly self-exhibition in his love affairs, which I failed to read through. I knew Olive Schreiner, both as an attractive girl author and as an embittered old woman after the war, and did not like her.

The German defences in the West were known as the Siegfried Line.

14 March. [Passfield Corner]
It is with relief I listened to the doleful admission by the British and French wireless that Moscow had made a triumphant peace with Finland. Sidney admitted that he also welcomed the news. After the systematic abuse of the Soviet government and the repeated assertion of the utter failure of the Red Army and amazing success of the Finnish resistance, the peace terms sounded like a big defeat for

Great Britain and France. The neutral world, however prejudiced against Soviet Communism, observes that the Red Army has done its job, whilst the French and British armies are still peacefully contemplating the Siegfried Line. . . .

20 March. [Passfield Corner]
Now that the U.S.S.R. with its 'new civilization' is out of the war, I can turn to and concentrate on Chapter III of *Our Pilgrimage.* . . .
The Minority Report of the Poor Law Commission (1906–09) will be the final chapter of Part I of *Our Pilgrimage.* The leading feature of the Minority Report of the Poor Law Commission – our last contribution to Fabian Socialism – was that it accepted capitalist profit-making, for the time at any rate, as the dominant method of organizing the production, distribution and exchange of commodities and services. One outstanding fact will appear in the final stage of *Our Pilgrimage*: all the institutions described in Part I – the Consumers Co-operative Movement, the Trade Union Movement, the Housekeeping State with its social services and even the legislative regulations – were taken over by Lenin and his followers and adapted to the promotion of the Communist ideal of from each according to his faculty and to each according to his need. The one new institution – at once the most powerful for good and the most doubtful in its direct effect – is the Vocation of Leadership. It has so far led in fact to a dictatorship. But need it do so? What is increasingly clear is that government by the counting of the votes of the common man as he appears in the western democracies does *not* lead to an efficient and progressive community. In one way or another it is the exceptional man in character and intellect who must be singled out for the leadership of the multitude. How can you get him? There must also be some sort of accepted creed as to the ultimate values in human society that you want to bring about. At present there is no such faith, whether about means or ends. The British and the French are distracted and disheartened peoples and the wage earners of the U.S.A. are becoming so.

27 March. [Passfield Corner]
Easter week and seeing relatives. The assembled Booth family at Funtingdon Lodge, including the Drakes . . . Then the next day arrived for lunch my old friend and secretary Molly Bolton and her devoted husband – two first-rate citizens and public servants,

Molly in close collaboration with Barbara on the L.C.C. . . . .
Today Charles Webb came to see Sidney. And so my little world
goes on with us, the stalemate war, darker and darker background
of world events making individual effort seem meaningless. . . .

Miss Burr, a former secretary, now came one half day a week.

3 April. [Passfield Corner]
. . . . Meanwhile I creep along with my work, tired by day and
sleepless by night, looking after my dear one except when I go with
Peter [her new dog] for a walk of two or three miles (I exhausted
myself yesterday with a four-mile walk) whilst Sidney goes with
Mrs Grant for a one or two miles, sitting down on the camp-stool
which she carries. One day passes into another night rapidly; the
week seems ended unexpectedly; the only time that drags are the
hours in the night – that is why I scribble in this diary with which I
deaden my dislike of living, a dislike which becomes acute in the
early hours of the morning before my cup of tea brings back a
common sense resignation to the decrepitude of old age. If I
succeed in writing a thousand well-chosen words to add to my
Chapter I am satisfied – even if I have to re-write it the next day!
And so I creep on until Saturday when Miss Burr comes and I
dictate the net result and deal with the week's correspondence. . . .

On 4 April Chamberlain declared that Hitler, by not attacking Britain and
France, had 'missed the bus'. On 9 April Germany occupied Denmark and
began an invasion of Norway that, despite British intervention, conquered most
of the country in a matter of days and overran the last pockets of resistance in
early June.

10 April. [Passfield Corner]
Denmark conquered; then parts of Norway seized, Sweden threatened unless she accepts the protection of Germany. Such are the
activities, within a few hours, of Nazi Germany – nominally in
answer to our laying of mines in Norwegian territorial waters, but
actually prepared and even begun before that event. The lightning
speed of German aggression and its ruthless efficiency is amazing.
Even I must admit that Hitler's Germany *must be conquered* if life is
to be bearable for the rest of Europe. If Hitler succeeds in bringing
the whole of Scandinavia under his domination, I shall be surprised
if the U.S.S.R. does not become more friendly to the Allies and

colder towards Germany. Pro-German Finland might hope to regain her lost territory and prefer the 'protection' of Hitler to that of Stalin. If the Allies are wise they will drop their anti-Soviet propaganda in the Press or over the air. The Anglo–French–Soviet pact may again appear in the background as a dimly perceived alternative policy in London, Paris and Moscow? It took the Red Army six months and hundreds of thousands dead and wounded to grab a small part of Finland. *In six hours, with no loss of life,* Germany has annexed the whole of Denmark and is in control of the capital and southern ports of Norway. A sinister warning for Moscow, and a dramatic challenge to the Allies' blockade and their confidence in ultimate victory.

A parliamentary debate on the loss of Norway held on 7–8 May ended in a vote in which eighty Conservatives abstained and fifty actually voted against the government. Chamberlain at once asked the Labour leaders to join a coalition. The national executive refused to negotiate if Chamberlain remained Prime Minister. On Friday 10 May the Germans invaded Holland and Belgium. At six in the evening Churchill agreed to form a government including Labour and Liberal leaders. Attlee went to Bournemouth where the Labour delegates were assembling for its annual conference and got his party's agreement to enter the Churchill coalition. Chamberlain remained in the Cabinet until 30 September, when he resigned for reasons of ill health. He died on 9 November.

11 May. [Passfield Corner]
At long last we are actively at war. There will be no more French communiqués – All quiet on the Western front. We have the invaded Holland and Belgium on our side, not yet defeated, fully prepared to resist, with the defeated Czechs, Poles, Norwegians and I assume Danes as our allies; which means the navies and shipping of six European naval powers under our command. There are signs that the U.S.S.R. will not be against us – the Kremlin offered a mutual defensive pact (against German aggression) to Sweden and Finland! His Holiness the Pope has denounced this new wickedness on the part of pagan Germany; the American President will doubtless do likewise. . . . Chamberlain is no longer Premier; Churchill is our Champion, and the Labour Party have accepted office. All of which we heard over the wireless yesterday . . . I felt converted to fighting Hitler to the bitter end. His mad aggression has become irredeemable: *'Il faut en finir'* the French are reported to be saying. And the Soviet Union is left standing more or less on one side. . . .

451

The French government led by Paul Reynaud (1878–1966) left Paris for Bordeaux, refused Churchill's dramatic offer of an Anglo-French union, and then capitulated. General Weygand (1867–1965) became the French commander-in-chief on 19 May. Marshal Pétain (1856–1951) became the head of the collaborationist Vichy regime, which sued for peace on 17 June and ceased fighting on 25 June.

22 May. 2 a.m. [Passfield Corner]
The literally and unmistakably *awful* news last night, which we listened to over the French wireless at 7.30, may mean disaster to France and perhaps to Great Britain. Reynaud's speech to the French Senate came over the air in a tragically excited voice. The French army had failed to destroy the bridges over the Meuse, whether because of latent treachery or by cowardly flight was not told; but someone 'would be punished'. Gamelin, the French generalissimo, was not mentioned; but he was suddenly superseded by General Weygand and eighty-year-old Marshal Pétain, the hero of Verdun, was to be deputy premier to Reynaud! . . . But will there be time to save France with Italy coming in in the Mediterranean tomorrow! And if France is overrun, what will happen to Great Britain: will the British Expeditionary Force get back across the Channel before they are mopped up by the victorious Germans? . . .

This is the last meeting with the Shaws that Beatrice records in the diary. Charlotte became increasingly immobilized with lumbago; she died on 12 September 1943, aged eighty-six. Shaw lived on until 1950.

24 May. [Passfield Corner]
Yesterday we drove up to lunch with the Shaws at Whitehall Court. Sidney insisted on doing so: he had not seen them for two and a half years and wanted badly to see them 'once again' and to speak to Charlotte about endowing the London School of Economics, which he did and was comforted to hear that she had sent £1,000 to Carr-Saunders for the teaching of 'good manners and general culture' to the students. They were delightfully affectionate. . . .

Stafford Cripps had made an extended visit to India and China. The new government now dispatched him to Russia to negotiate a trade treaty. He remained there as Ambassador until the German invasion in 1941 led to a full and formal alliance.

28 May. [Passfield Corner]

. . . . Yesterday's news. Stafford departed by air for Moscow; leading article in *The Times* approving of his visit. 'Increasing gravity of the situation' reported with the usual spate of stories of the marvellous heroism and skill of our air crews. Concentration on home defence and evacuation of eastern ports. *The invasion of Great Britain* threatened from France, Belgium and the Dutch ports. And our intellectuals have been spending their time in discussing what exactly should be the terms of a *dictated* peace imposed on Germany! While the French and British armies sat confidently behind the Maginot line, leaving the neutral frontiers wholly undefended; and yet threatening to send an expeditionary force to beat back the Red Army in far-off Finland and add the U.S.S.R. to our enemies. There is a sinister comedy in the doings of the Chamberlain Cabinet during the last five years. For comfort we fall back on historical precedent. Great Britain has always begun her great wars with defeat and ended in victory.

29 May. [Passfield Corner]

Reynaud's dramatic broadcast following the 8 a.m. British news, reporting capitulation of the Belgian army, was a dead stop to the morning's mite of work. It means, I assume, the evacuation of the B.E.F., under German fire, either back to an English port or to a French port in Western France?

On 20 May German units reached the Channel coast, cutting off all the British and part of the French army. On 29 May an improvised ferry service from the Dunkirk beaches began to bring out the remains of the B.E.F. and the cut-off French troops. By 1 June four-fifths of the British army had been saved. Churchill's speech in the House of Commons on 4 June ended with the words: 'We shall fight on the beaches, we shall fight on the landing grounds, we shall fight in the fields and in the streets, we shall fight in the hills; we shall never surrender. . . .'

5 June. 1 a.m. [Passfield Corner]

Churchill's remarkably frank and rhetorically eloquent speech summing up the events of the last five days will echo round the world. Over three hundred thousand Allied troops have been brought over the Channel from Dunkirk to English ports under perpetual German bombing and gun-fire, by some thousand ships and boats of all sorts and kinds escorted by the navy and air force.

The B.E.F. leaves behind them thirty thousand dead, wounded and missing. We have lost the whole of our armaments – guns, transport, tanks. Our small air force has proved itself, man for man, machine for machine, far superior to the Germans, who have lost four to one in the battle in the air. In a sense it is a glorious adventure; but from a realistic standpoint, Winston admits it, it is the greatest military disaster which has ever overtaken the British army. Today we have to defend our own island from invasion; he thinks that in this homely task we are invincible. But the French army – can it stand up against the German hordes, possibly reinforced by the Italians? That is left in doubt. . . .

How can a decrepit and sleepless brain work at a given task with this tragic world we live in? The most I can do is to keep the dear one happy and remain calm and helpful in my little group of relatives and friends. . . .

Roosevelt's promise to make the United States 'the arsenal of democracy' was followed up by the immediate transfer of much-needed destroyers, by accelerated shipments of arms and, in 1941, the helpful financial provision of the Lend-Lease agreement.

11 June. 4 a.m. [Passfield Corner]
Six o'clock news: Mussolini declares war on France and Great Britain and denounces the senile pluto-democracies who are keeping down the young and virile races seeking living room in the world. . . . Awake and restless I slipped down at twelve o'clock to hear Roosevelt's promised oration at 12.15 a.m. He is a great personality over wireless – far surpassing in decision, dignity and eloquence any other leader of today. The audience were the college students of the University of Virginia. The subject was the future of America and the outlook for her youthful citizens. This war was a crisis – perhaps the greatest in history of a freedom-loving democratic self-governing country confronted with a mortal enemy, i.e. dictators aiming at world dominion through brutal force. . . . The American government, backed up by all the other governments of the great American continent, could have but two aims: help to the Allies through supplying materials for winning the war, and increased speed in rearmament so as to secure the safety of America from this Evil One. Applause of a wild character echoed across the aerial waves of the Atlantic. Short of declaring war on Germany and Italy the oration could not have been more helpful to the Allies.

Paris had been occupied on 14 June. The undefeated but outflanked French armies on the Maginot line surrendered on 17 June.

18 June. 15 Sheffield Terrace
I travelled up to London to attend the annual meeting of the Fabian Society. Over the wireless had come the news that the French government had asked for an armistice. The train was crowded with soldiers and officers and civilians on government business: all were silent as if they were going to a funeral. Opposite me the handsome young private, travelling first class, looked tragically wretched; two ugly businessmen were talking about some war business in a morose murmur. Bardie [Barbara Drake] received me with her usual affectionate greetings and abuse of our ruling class. There were about fifty persons present at the little reception at the Fabian office, among them the ever-present Coles, Ellen Wilkinson, Susan Lawrence, Leonard Woolf and some younger men who seemed pleased to be introduced to me. I made my little speech as President in a nearby hall, extolling the Society and its combination of intellectual tolerance and research, and pointing out the problem to be solved if we survived as an independent country. No one I spoke to saw hope; the general feeling was anger at the government, humiliation and fear — sometimes one, sometimes another uppermost. Bernard [Drake] looked desperately unhappy, but he still asserts we shall hold out, even if the French army and fleet surrendered. I wondered whether I would go straight home today. Then I thought of poor old Parmoor, whom I am not likely to see again. Better carry on as planned; it will be long before I shall leave my dear one again. The slogan is 'stay as you are put'.

19 June. Parmoor
Came down to Parmoor exhausted for two nights. The large, luxurious house, set in its spacious grounds, beautiful trees and lovely view, brings back the memory of the dignified and charming setting of our old governing class. Poor old Parmoor is feeble in body and mind; he can't read continuously, he dislikes the wireless and only listens to the news, which distresses him, for he hates the war and Marion is tied to his side by night and day, almost as a slave. The remnants of a dead world of power, enjoyment and security for all those who had made good with the landlord capitalist civilization of the nineteenth century.

In a broadcast on 18 June Churchill warned that a German attack was imminent. 'Let us therefore brace ourselves to our duties, and so bear ourselves that, if the British Empire and its Commonwealth last for a thousand years, men will still say: "This was their finest hour."'

25 June. [Passfield Corner]
. . . . Winston's message to the peoples of Great Britain and France yesterday was admirably conceived and perfectly expressed: he is wise and eloquent, a great wielder of words. The behaviour of the Bordeaux government proves the internal rottenness of France; and the panic fear of the inner set of financiers and landed proprietors of ruin and revolution – the preference for the Nazi domination to the loss and suffering of defeat without surrender accepted by the Dutch and Norwegians. . . .

27 June. [Passfield Corner]
The first night of what will be continuous air raids over this neighbourhood of camps, aerodromes and searchlights: they began about 11 p.m. and stopped about 4 a.m. Sombre humming of the planes overhead . . . an occasional booming of guns. I looked out at the sky, and watched the searchlights playing up and down the clouds – sometimes to the west, sometimes the east – or north – and felt comforted that they were not shining overhead. I suppose as the weeks go on we shall cease to be interested, unless the noise becomes thunderous and we take refuge at the back of the dining-room. Mrs Grant wanted Sidney to go downstairs the first night, but he refused. The danger of another stroke through over-excitement and fatigue is far greater than the house being bombed or even the windows shattered. 'If *you* like to sit downstairs, by all means do.' And that settled it.

2 July. [Passfield Corner]
The amazing beauty of this spring and summer, the sheer delight of the morning walks in the woods and on the moorland, is a strange background to the ever-present prospect of invasion from the air and the probable entry of armed men on the roads. We have dug-outs and trenches at our gates and have bombs dropping and guns booming almost every night; we are warned over the wireless that these isolated flights are merely the forerunners of more formations of enemy bombers later on; as Hitler must win now or never. . . .

A series of defiant broadcasts by Churchill did much to rally opinion during the air campaign known as the Battle of Britain, which began on 10 July. He made a world broadcast on 14 July. The novelist J.B. Priestley (1894–1984) began a series of talks after the nine o'clock radio news on Sundays which combined patriotic nostalgia and aspiration for social change. The talks were curtailed after conservative critics – including, it was said, Churchill himself – had complained.

15 July. [Passfield Corner]
Assuredly personality has an enormous opportunity owing to wireless: Churchill's broadcast on Sunday night was a model of wisdom, courage and decisive leadership, a perfect manner and impressive voice. J.B. Priestley's postscript, describing Margate in brilliant sunshine – intact but deserted, noiseless and empty, a mysterious and beautiful vision, with a background of memories of the crowded beaches, hotels and cinemas, shops and stalls, of laughter and shouting, swimming and scrambling in the sea and on the sand, of men, women and children in the mass – was a fitting contrast and emotional relief from Churchill's sincere appeal to statesmen, thinkers and citizens of all countries, to have a faith in the British will and capacity to beat the evil power of Hitler's barbarous Germany. The one drawback to the B.B.C.'s daily emissions is its romantic optimism about British exploits on the sea and in the air, an optimism which has hitherto been contradicted by the event. Defeat has been our destiny, not victory. Germany rules Continental Europe and threatens Great Britain as she has never been threatened before. We have dramatically and conclusively failed Norway, Holland, Belgium and France; in the Far East we have been thrown back by Japan. Invasion by armed forces may be impracticable; but a smashing blow on London and other crowded areas from thousands of aeroplanes may be more fatal if these be shot down, than if they merely drop bombs and fly away.

Franklin Roosevelt was the first American President to run for three terms of office – and, in 1944, for a fourth term broken by his death in the following spring.

20 July. [Passfield Corner]
Roosevelt accepts nomination for a third term; and asserts the American detestation of the brutal aggression of godless Germany against the independence of Christian democracies. Hitler's address to the Reichstag gives the oft-told story of the humiliation of the

German people by the Versailles treaty and their emancipation by his leadership, and ends by offering the immediate negotiation of peace with Great Britain. Meanwhile, as a minor incident, Stafford has a friendly talk with Stalin which *The Times* reports with approval. Hitler's peace overture is indignantly refused in the Press of Great Britain and contemptuously rejected in the U.S.A. So we may expect a 'blitzkrieg' within a few days or weeks. To keep up his almost super-human reputation with his own countrymen and his allies he has to smash Great Britain's resistance. . . . I am so unutterably tired of living that I am free of all fear of being destroyed. There seems very little panic among the inhabitants: the vast majority will stay put; and those who are fit will fight to the end. . . .

11 August. [Passfield Corner]

. . . . Poor Beveridge was in a state of collapse. I have never seen him so despondent about public affairs, so depressed about his own part in bettering them. The collapse of France and the obvious incompetence of our own government and governing class to foresee the catastrophe of Hitler's march to power to counter it, has overthrown his old confidence that the Allies would win the war and dictate the peace. What is even more personally depressing is that he has been ignored; his services as an administrator have not been requisitioned – all that has happened is that Bevin (I think at Cole's suggestion) has appointed him as *adviser* (not as administrator) in respect of the organization of manpower for the supply of munitions and carrying on the war. . . . He agrees that there must be a revolution in the economic structure of society; but it must be guided by persons with training and knowledge – i.e. by himself and those he chooses as his colleagues. . . .

On 13 August the Germans began a full-scale attack on the airfields and radar stations in South-East England.

14 August. [Passfield Corner]

Yesterday morning, as I was enjoying my hot bath, there opened a roar of aeroplanes overhead, then machine guns and rapid explosions, shaking the walls and the roof. 'I must not be found naked,' I thought, and hurriedly put on my underclothing. Mrs Grant, white and trembling, was downstairs and stationed herself in the back kitchen with white face and her hands folded: whilst Annie went about her business preparing our breakfast. Apparently there was a battle in the air between seventy German aeroplanes and the Longmoor and Bordon air defences. The roar overhead raged for half an hour and then slowly died away. At one o'clock the B.B.C. mentioned the Hampshire camps as one of the targets for the four hundred German invading aeroplanes. The usual disproportionate German losses were announced during the day. . . . The best we can hope for is that *we* shall not be conquered, that Germany will become more hopelessly paralysed by the battles in the air than we shall be. . . . Anyway there is a growing anger against Germany — not only within the armed forces but among ordinary men and women carrying on the civil life of the nation. Disillusioned but determined to best the invader sums up my impression of the national consciousness. Those who desire to make peace with Hitler before we have beaten his dream of conquest decisively are a tiny minority of the governing class and they judge it better to be silent. They are mainly haters of the Soviet Union or merely fanatical supporters of the capitalist profit-making system, which they think will be endangered by a long war, in which conclusion I think they are right.

20 August. [Passfield Corner]
Another night of bomb explosions, but not the furious roar of German planes and attacking British planes overhead we experienced on Friday. But sleep is impossible and poor Mrs Grant is crouching in the back of the kitchen, comforted by Annie, whilst Sidney and I keep to our beds; and I try to get on with my chapter, without having the strength to do so. I note that my neighbours, rich and poor, are not suffering from panic — everybody staying put during the raids and gossiping about what has actually happened in the longer intervals of peace on earth and in the sky. The countryside is beautiful in the continuous sunshine and I go my two-hour walk every morning. Sidney remains philosophical in mind and physically comfortable, reading incessantly newspapers, official documents, propagandist literature, and his bevy of books from the London Library and *The Times* Book Club. . . .

Leon Trotsky was assassinated by a Spaniard, Roman Mercader — an agent of Stalin — in Mexico, where he had been living in exile since 1936.

25 August. [Passfield Corner]

Trotsky murdered. . . . That tiny event compared with the war raging over Europe and Asia ends the most disastrous episode in the history of the counter-revolutionary upheavals in the U.S.S.R. of the 20s and 30s – so damaging to the reputation of the 'New Civilization' within the labour and socialist movements of the western democracies. How will the Soviet Press report it? If they are wise they will report it accurately, without abuse of Trotsky, as an event of no importance to the present government of the country. Our Press, including the *New Statesman*, suggests that in spite of the evidence to the contrary, the murderer was an agent of Stalin! How the educated public opinion in Great Britain hates the increasing prestige of the Soviet Union. . . .

9 September. 4 a.m. [Passfield Corner]

Every night the battle over the air begins about nine o'clock and ends in the early morning. I thought I heard the 'all clear' half an hour ago; but now the war has started again, judged by the roar of the aeroplanes overhead and the searchlights playing about the sky when I put the light off and look out of the window. Sidney and I are little disturbed by it; but Mrs Grant and the girls are up most of the night, which means fatigue and irritated tempers throughout the day, and I have to live in a state of uncertainty as to whether my little group will hold together by being mutually friendly and helpful. Certainly other citizens are suffering far more than the few inhabitants of Passfield Corner!

On 7 September the Germans turned their attack on to London and away from the fighter bases in Kent – a disastrous tactical error. A last great effort was made on 15 September.

15 September. 3 a.m. [Passfield Corner]

Since the sustained attack in London opened, we here have had a relatively quiet time – air warnings and all-clear notices happening during day and night, but few and distant bombs or gunfire. Letters from Barbara [Drake] and Alys Russell and B.B.C. and newspaper reports describing the noise and danger, destruction of homes, hospitals and churches, of deaths and woundings of men, women and children, illustrated by pictures, lend a background of continuous tragedy, which even the good-tempered heroism of the cockney and his perpetual sense of humour does not cancel out. J.B.

Priestley's broadcasts on Sunday evenings stand out as superlative expressions of all that is good and helpful. Meanwhile the crisis in my household has petered out; and our triplet staff is at peace. Mrs Grant has got over her panic, and realizes how fortunate she is to evade ill-paid service in a hospital and enjoy well-paid service and an easy life in a comfortable home. Annie and Jean are reconciled and behave to me with due kindness and respect . . . I crawl on with my chapter. . . .

2 October. [Passfield Corner]
The Dobbses here for a week together – Rosy staying with us and George at the Passfield Oak Hotel, and then Rosy at the Passfield Oak Hotel for another week – have stopped me from doing my daily inch of work on the book. Walking and talking with them have exhausted what little strength I have left . . . She and I, the last of the Potter sisters, have common memories of a world which is no more. Her *will to live* is far greater than mine, but we have one common characteristic: we both delight in expressing ourselves, I in words and she in sketches, and are both aged – I several years more decrepit than she is and far more conscious of it. Rosy, though seventy-four, is physically energetic. She does most of the work in her cottage home. She walks six or seven miles a day and talks incessantly, and when not writing, walking or talking, reads new books and pamphlets. George is a kindly, active-minded and accomplished tourists' agent; able to get on with any individual, of any class or rank. Nominally a Conservative and a Christian, he is really indifferent to all philosophic questions, and loves gossip and bridge . . .

9 October. [Passfield Corner]
Churchill's eloquent but sombre speech to the House of Commons yesterday dismisses pessimistic defeatism and foolish optimism with equal force. He emphasizes our success in the air and over the sea; he admits our deplorable failure to prevent the French cruisers and destroyers from passing through the Straits of Gibraltar and reinforcing Dakar. All that is clear is that we are in for a long war; and that while we have resisted successfully German invasion there is as yet no decisive turn of the tide in Europe, Africa or Asia. . . .

London was bombed every night from 7 September to 2 November. The City of London, and particularly the East End, was devastated.

13 October. [Passfield Corner]
A desperately tired body and mind struggling to be active in three ways: looking after my dear one and my little staff and being helpful to a few friends and relations, getting on with my literary jobs, and lastly taking in, by reading papers, pamphlets and books and listening to wireless, the tragic happenings of today, wondering about the future of the human race. . . . Carrying on my personal vocation in life and trying to sum up what is happening to the world of man today seems the only way to make my own life worth living. Otherwise I should sink into despondency, which would actually prevent me from being a 'good companion' to the Other One. So cheer up, old lady, accept the inevitable, like the unfortunate bombed inhabitants of the East End are doing, with courage and good humour. . . .

Churchill broadcast in French and English on 21 October, to rally the French nation. The Italians had now attacked Greece from their base in Albania.

22 October. [Passfield Corner]
Churchill's address to the French people was admirable in its attitude towards the French people themselves, but brutally abusive of Hitler and contemptuous of Mussolini. But what is the meaning of the last words: 'Long live the forward march of the common people in all lands towards their just and true inheritance'? Is it mere rhetoric on the part of the recently elected chief of the Conservative Party? Or is it a realization, deliberately expressed, that the old order is doomed and a new social order must be created? . . .

9 November. 4 a.m. [Passfield Corner]
The victory of Roosevelt and the gallant resistance of Greece are two signs of the turning of the tide; also the failure of the Italian air force, army and navy to fight effectively – if the reports are true – is the third necessary condition of victory. Meanwhile my decrepitude increases: sleeplessness, whizzing of the brain and the worsening of the frequency due to chronic cystitis, above all the incapacity even to crawl on with the book, makes me long for release from life, especially during the night. . . The one redeeming feature is watching the heroism and common sense of the ordinary British citizen, together with the growing conviction that the social order

462

within our own country will be fundamentally changed after the war, and the Webbs believe much as according to their faith or social pattern . . .

In mid-November Beatrice was asked to write an article for a Communist publication to refute allegations that the U.S.S.R. was a dictatorship.

9 December. [Passfield Corner]
I am hard at work, with my decrepit intellect, writing that d____d article for the *Anglo-Soviet Journal* to be published in its January number. I have finished the first part – Is Stalin a legalized dictator as Hitler and Mussolini are? – and I am now wrestling with the second question. Is the Soviet Union a political democracy? . . . How can I combine an admiration for the constitution and activities of Soviet Communism with a frank admission of its defects, summed up in the suppression of free thought and free expression, and the obvious cruelty of many of its methods of implementing its policy of planned production for community consumption? What is happening, for instance, in the Soviet part of former Poland? According to a pamphlet issued by *Free Europe*, the occupation of the Red Army and the establishment of the Soviet regime has not only been brutal to the old governing class, but wholly unsuccessful in giving the means of subsistence to the people, leave alone culture and the consciousness of self-government. According to the *Moscow Weekly News*, the people of the new provinces are revelling in the better conditions of life and the sense of emancipation. Where lies the truth? Between the heaven of the Moscow vision and the hell described by the Polish refugees in Great Britain?

VOLUME 55

ᴄᴑ 1941 ᴑᴅ

5 January. [Passfield Corner]
Trouble again in my little household – fortunately it broke out after I had sent off that d____d article! Miles down with influenza; Annie suffering from headache and sickness; Mrs Grant intent on getting a meat ration for Peter, the dog, her one obsession; and

everyone in a state of nervous tension, blaming each other, with the aged head of the household trying to keep the peace, so that the daily needs, measured in keeping the hot water going and the food for all concerned, are daily supplied. I try to remind them all, including myself, that our little inconveniences are trifling compared to the tragedy of the war, death and destruction of property, for millions of our people, leave alone the unfortunate inhabitants of the conquered countries. Cheerfulness and kindness with a sense of humour are the only way out of our petty troubles. Then, perhaps, I can keep the pot boiling and get back to my book, as my own recreation.

The Webbs were in fact able to issue a wartime edition of *Soviet Communism*, using Beatrice's article for the *Soviet Journal* as the basis of a new introduction, by binding up copies of the cheap edition which were in stock at the Edinburgh printers R.R. Clark.

15 January. [Passfield Corner]
We have had a shock. In the devastating German raid on London on 29 December all our books, bound and unbound – seven thousand volumes – were destroyed. At first I was downcast, but Sidney was more philosophical: he reckoned that our present income from books was only £200 to £300 a year and would dwindle year by year, and that had to be cut by 9s in the pound taxation – also it might lead to the surtax on surplus income. When in the six o'clock B.B.C. news we are told that five million books had been swept away, I was consoled by the feeling that 'we are all in it', and had no reason to feel specially injured. What is regrettable is that our books will not be obtainable until after the war. Then we shall only be able to print the best-sellers; the two on trade unionism, and the two volumes of *Soviet Communism*. We must leave it to our executors, who will have the means to bring out a complete edition of the Webbs' works – for those students who desire to study them as relics of the past research into contemporary events of the end of the nineteenth and first half of the twentieth centuries.

21 January. [Passfield Corner]
I often wonder whether I shall survive this year? Tomorrow I shall be in the eighty-fourth year of my too long life. I feel desperately ill – my little household, owing to Miles's illness, and Annie's

nervous breakdown, which means constant upsets – she won't do this, she won't do that – adds to my mental worry. What is clear is that *if* I drop out of the scene, Barbara will have to arrange for Sidney to go, with his maid-valet, to a residential hotel; and either shut this house up or let it to someone connected with the L.S.E. Indeed I may have to do that myself – whether to save expense, or, more likely, to save my own peace of mind and therefore prevent a breakdown. However, sufficient for the day is the evil thereof – we may be bombed out, or we may lose the war, or all be ruined in winning it. Meanwhile I had better grin and bear it, which so many others are doing, and doing it bravely, and with far less peace and comfort than the eight inhabitants of Passfield Corner and its bungalow enjoy, day in and day out – a fact they would, each one of them, discover if they had to find another home during the war.

Priestley had recently joined with the Liberal M.P. Sir Richard Acland (b. 1906) in forming a political group which became the Commonwealth Party and won some notable by-elections in the later years of the war.

11 March. [Passfield Corner]
J.B. Priestley is the dominant literary personality of the England of today; he has out-distanced the aged H.G. Wells and GBS, owing to his superlative gift for broadcasting. He is revolutionary left and exhorts the Labour leaders to leave off kowtowing to the reactionary groups of big capitalists, aristocratic landlords, led by Winston Churchill and the puppet King and Queen. He comes out boldly for complete socialism. He never mentions the U.S.S.R. or Soviet Communism – I doubt whether he has any notion of what should be the manifold structure of a socialist state. His one great gift is that of broadcasting, owing to his voice, manner and imaginative yet homely treatment of his thesis. Like H.G. he has gone out of his way to form a *group* – it is a pity he does not join the Fabian Society or at any rate the Labour Party. . . .

19 March. 4 a.m. [Passfield Corner]
A terrific battle is going on to the south; the roar of the aeroplanes, widespread gun-fire, searchlights and bursting shells in the moon and starlit sky – perfect weather for the invasion about which Herbert Morrison warned us over the wireless last night, as if it were imminent. Our bored troops would welcome it; also it would prove that Hitler was desperately intent, at the risk of the destruc-

tion of his army, to strike before the advent of America's over-whelming strength. But we shall have a nasty but exciting time – to relieve the boredom of the whizzing head. . . .

Leslie Stephen (1832–1904), man of letters, was the founder and editor of the *Dictionary of National Biography*. Alice Stopford Green (1847–1929), the widow of the historian J.R. Green, had been a friend of Beatrice's in her youth.

7 April. [Passfield Corner]
In the morning news: 'Mrs Virginia Woolf, missing from her home since Friday 28th . . . assumed drowned in the river Ouse.' During the day and for some days afterwards, ghosts from the past haunted me – that tall, talented woman with her classic features, her father Leslie Stephen, also tall, good-looking, highly cultured, with whom in the 80s I used to discuss English history in the house of Alice Green in Kensington Square. An old man, seemingly kind and courteous to a young writer but pictured as a supreme egotist towards his family by his daughter with a bitter pen in *To the Lighthouse*, perhaps her most successful novel.

Virginia was a beautiful woman and a writer of great charm and finesse – in her *uniqueness* the most outstanding of our women novelists. The Woolfs stayed with the Webbs, and the Webbs with the Woolfs, and Leonard was one of Sidney's most intimate colleagues in international propaganda during the great war; but we never became sympathetic friends. I think we liked them better than they liked us. In a way which I never understood, I offended Virginia. I had none of her sensitiveness, her understanding of the inner life of the subjective man, expressed in the birth, life and death of social institutions. Also we clashed with Leonard Woolf in our conception of what constitutes human freedom: the absence of restraint for the intellectual or the presence of opportunity for the ordinary man – which element was to be the foremost object of the social reformer? In particular, he abhorred Soviet Communism. But in spite of this mental aloofness from the Woolfs I am pained by the thought of that beautiful and brilliant Virginia yielding to the passion for death rather than endure the misery of continued life. Twenty years ago her devoted husband had nursed her through a period of mental derangement and suicidal mania. In middle age she became a vigorous and a seemingly self-assured woman, an eminently successful author and a devoted companion to her distinguished husband. What led to the tragedy? And what is happening to the ultra-refined, public-spirited and gifted Leonard Woolf? The last time I saw them both was at a luncheon at Barbara's about eighteen months ago. Her last words to me, as she and Leonard met, were 'I have no living philosophy' – which may probably account for her voluntary withdrawal from life. Can man continue happy without some assured faith as to what should be the right relation of man to man, also of man's relation to the universe? On the first I have a clearly defined conclusion; on the other I am a religious agnostic. I do not know, I only have an emotional feeling that there *is* a spirit of love at work in the universe, and I pray from time to time that it may help me to act rightly to my fellow men. But if I were not supremely fortunate in my circumstances, would that vague and intermittent faith save me from despair during these days of death and destruction, by day and by night? . . . .

20 April. 3 a.m. [Passfield Corner]
These two last nights have been the most fearful of the war. The Battle of Britain is raging round us. Tonight continuous bombing and gunfire has shaken the house. A huge fire has lit up Aldershot and Farnham to the east; whilst gunfire and flares light up Bordon and the south coast. Mrs Grant is cowering downstairs in the kitchen; I find Sidney reading, but glad to have a cup of tea. Neither he nor I are perturbed; Annie wanders up and downstairs, looking out for fire bombs. I tell her that the Germans won't waste any on us in a non-built-up area; and anyway if a fire bomb falls on the house and gets through the roof, we should hear it. Meanwhile, last night, London has had a terrific attack. . . . Can we and the Americans keep the Allied shipping safe across the Atlantic? That is the question. If we repel invasion and safeguard our supplies across the Atlantic, Great Britain will survive, but we shall owe our survival not to our own strength but to help from the U.S.A. We may save Egypt and retain control of the Suez Canal and Gibraltar. But we are a long way off recovering the freedom of Europe from the rule of Hitler's Germany. What blind fools our governing class of aristocratic and wealthy men have been in their foreign policy since 1931. First appeasing Japan, Italy and Germany by refusing to condemn their military aggression in Manchuria, Spain, Abyssinia and Central Europe; then declaring war on account of the invasion of Poland with its two million German inhabitants and guaranteeing other small states we could not reach, like Norway,

with our armed forces. Lastly increasing the hostility of the U.S.S.R. by threatening to send an army to Finland – all through fear of the spread of Soviet Communism. . . .

So I return to my task of finishing the Introduction before Sidney and I drop out of existence. The nights of battle and days of peace are the strangest sort of life the British people have ever experienced. Just as I feel that we and our generation are, through old age, on the verge of non-existence, so do I envisage that the present-day Great Britain and her ruling class are doomed to disappear within the next few years. Our little island will become subordinate – either to the U.S.A. and the Dominions or to Germany, or to the U.S.S.R. and its new civilization, creeping over the world. As we happen to believe in the *rightness* and eventual success of Soviet Communism, we are not despondent about the future of mankind. . . .

After a series of visits and letters the officials of the Society for Cultural Relations with the U.S.S.R. tried to persuade Beatrice to remove critical statements from the article they had invited her to write. She refused, and withdrew the article.

18 May. [Passfield Corner]
A correct little note from Beatrice King closes the episode of writing an article for the *Anglo-Soviet Journal*: the Russian representative of *Voks* could not tolerate the suggestion that Soviet Communism had *any* 'infantile diseases', refused to admit that Lenin and Stalin had been 'idolized' or that there was any restriction on free criticism of Stalin's policy by word or by script. So the printers first sent off the proofs with my signature *without* the final paragraph of criticism, and when I telegraphed that I must have that part printed before passing it for publication, the editorial committee sent the editors down here to persuade me to omit it. . . .

C.E.M. Joad (1891–1953), who taught philosophy at Birkbeck College, London, made a wartime reputation as a member of the radio 'Brains Trust'. Dorothy Woodman (1902–1970), a member of the I.L.P. and secretary of the Union of Democratic Control 1927–47, had been living with Martin since 1935.

31 May. [Passfield Corner]
Kingsley Martin, with his life companion Dorothy Woodman, a

well-known left-wing and former Quaker journalist and organizer, here for a couple of hours. Our old friend was exactly the same genial, intellectually scatter-brained clever editor of the *New Statesman* whom we knew so well in the 20s, but whom we had not seen for five or six years. He told us about the new intellectuals – the extraordinary vogue, through their success as broadcasters, of Priestley and Joad, who find themselves leaders of the young generation, bombarded with letters and able to attract large audiences wherever they go, but both alike with no clear vision of what they want to happen in Great Britain or in the world after the war. . . . He is pessimistic over Great Britain after the war, and agrees that even if we win the war (he thinks official public opinion is unduly optimistic, or at any rate pretends to be so), Great Britain will become a fortified outpost of the American Confederation of English-speaking Republics. He is not hostile to the U.S.S.R. and is friendly with the Maiskys, but is not an admirer of its present internal organization. Stalin is a dictator. . . . The U.S.S.R. is no longer honestly Communist in the distribution of the wealth of the nation. There are all sorts of evils – poverty, scarcity, corruption, intolerance are rife here, there, and everywhere. . . . Dorothy Woodman is a tall bulky woman with an attractive but not especially good-looking face. She has been in the U.S.S.R. and is more of an admirer than Kingsley, but is also disturbed by the lack of idealistic Communism, the absence of free criticism of Stalin and his policy and the tortuous propaganda of the Third International. . . .

Kingsley Martin agreed that there was no unity within the ranks of those who wanted, or said they wanted, a 'New Social Order'. He felt that he himself changed his opinion from day to day as to which policy was 'the lesser or the greater evil' and was at a 'loose end' as to what constituted the good, the beautiful and the true in social organization. . . .

Stafford and Isobel Cripps had returned to London from Moscow. He had already passed on to the Russians the warning, derived from intelligence sources, that Hitler was about to attack the U.S.S.R.

14 June. 2 a.m. [Passfield Corner]
A year ago, I journeyed up to London on the day of the collapse of France, 14 June 1940, to stay with Barbara and attend the annual meeting of the Fabian Society. I witnessed the horrified silence of

my fellow travellers as to what was the meaning of the terrific fact of a beaten France. Yesterday, 13 June 1941, I was again at Barbara's a little after noon. She greeted me with, 'Stafford thinks the crisis will come this Sunday; we shall know whether it is war between Germany and Russia or peaceful surrender of Stalin to Hitler.' I had come up to meet Stafford and Isobel Cripps who were staying with the Drakes. First Isobel appeared and gave me an account of their year in Moscow. . . . Stafford joined us just as we were finishing lunch. He was serious: if war broke out the German army would take Baku; without the oil of Baku the highly mechanized Red Army and Air Force could not survive. If Stalin gave way to Hitler, the recently acquired prestige of the Soviet Union would be lost and the Bolshevik government might collapse through internal treachery and intrigue. . . .

Stafford had had long and confidential talks with Churchill, who was in first-rate form; a splendid leader for the purpose. The sensational and much advertised meeting of the day before, of 'the Allies' – Great Britain and the representatives of the conquered countries – when Churchill made his oration damning 'that bad man Hitler with his ragged lackey, Mussolini' and vowed war 'to destroy Hitlerism', was staged in order to encourage Stalin to resist, to satisfy him that the U.S.S.R. would not be betrayed by the Allies, through a negotiated peace with Hitler. . . .

The Germans invaded Russia on 22 June. Despite repeated warnings from the British government and Soviet intelligence agents, Stalin had suspected a trap and failed to deploy his forces properly; they were surprised and heavily defeated in the early battles.

23 June. [Passfield Corner]
Yesterday, Sunday morning, over the nine o'clock news, came the momentous – or shall I write *monstrous* – proclamation by Hitler of a state of war with the U.S.S.R. – as usual with a vilification of his victim, not only for acts hostile to Germany, but guilty of the sin of Communism, the devil at work in the world today. This ultimatum had been handed to the Soviet Ambassador in Berlin at 5 a.m. after the German air force had bombed Kiev and other Russian cities. Finland and Rumania were announced as Hitler's allies and were also on the march into the Soviet Union. Molotov's matter-of-fact broadcast to the Russian people at twelve o'clock added little to the scene. Then at nine o'clock that evening, we had Churchill's

sensational oration to the world, especially designed for the U.S.A. with its anti-Communist prejudice. . . . It is the full co-operation of the U.S.A. which is the crucial event of today and tomorrow if we are to beat Hitler and the German people to their knees, as Churchill says we must. On balance, in spite of the danger of a routed Russian army, Sidney and I welcome this declaration of war on the U.S.S.R.: it saves Great Britain from defeat or a stalemate peace. . . .

25 June. 2 a.m. [Passfield Corner]
The House of Commons debate with Foreign Secretary Eden announcing, in the most friendly words, a whole-hearted alliance with the Soviet government, as one more victim of Hitler's barbarous aggression, was yet another avowal of the staggering world event — this time wholly in the right tone from the standpoint of the Webbs. He explains in the most courteous phrases that the British people had a different creed from that current in the U.S.S.R.; but that was equally true of several of their old allies, and need not interfere with a loyal co-operation in foreign affairs. . . .

3 July. [Passfield Corner]
Over midday wireless we heard of Alfred's death [Lord Parmoor] . . . Among my brothers-in-law when I was a young woman, he was the one I liked best, and he was undoubtedly Father's favourite son-in-law, by whom he was entitled 'the little jewel of an advocate'. Also he and Sidney collaborated in the early years of the twentieth century in getting the Anglican and Roman Catholic schools on to the rates; and they were closely connected in the last Labour Cabinet as members of the House of Lords. In the last years of decrepitude he was somewhat of an egotist, and poor devoted Marion had a hard life of it. But in spite of a strong strain of personal egotism, Alfred was essentially a good man, a genial and pious Christian, a public-spirited citizen, hating war and social injustice and strictly correct in his family relationships in all their characteristics — a striking contrast to his clever unscrupulous brother, also my brother-in-law, the distinguished surgeon Harrison Cripps, of evil repute as husband of my tragic sister Blanche. . . . His death is another 'passing over' of the world I have lived in, and adds to my ghost-like consciousness during these terrible days of world war. . . .

The B.B.C., which played all the anthems of the Allies on Sunday evenings, had so far failed to include the 'Internationale' – it was rumoured that the Foreign Office had objected until all the formalities of alliance were complete.

14 July. [Passfield Corner]
Yesterday on the one o'clock news, the announcer stated solemnly that at two o'clock an important statement on foreign affairs would be made. 'That will be an whole-hearted alliance with the U.S.S.R.,' said I to Sidney. 'I don't think so, it will be about America,' he answered. At two o'clock came the terms signed by Molotov and Stafford. 'That means that we shall have the Internationale tonight.' 'Wait and see,' he observed, and he was right.

30 July. [Passfield Corner]
Isobel sent me a batch of letters from Stafford, a day-to-day account of his doings, intensely interesting, culminating in the big achievement of the Anglo–Soviet pact, which he and Stalin negotiated and he and Molotov signed. He likes Stalin, with whom he is now on intimate and confidential terms. From his picture, he seems a singularly direct and honest-minded man, with no pretentiousness, no sign of wishing to be a personage; not too optimistic – in short, a *business man*, completely absorbed in carrying out scientific humanism in his own country with the largest measure of health and happiness for all the people and getting a durable world peace. . . .

8 August. [Passfield Corner]
In the last ten days I have had a nightmare of a life of physical and mental exhaustion. . . . What is significant is the suddenness and magnitude of the change in public opinion; from refusal, even on the part of the left wing, to see anything that is good in Soviet Communism, to the equally sudden waking up of the ordinary conservative-minded man to a lively interest in the surprising courage, initiative and magnificent equipment of the Red armed forces – the one and only sovereign state that has been able to stand up to the almost mythical might of Hitler's Germany. . . .

A new edition of *Soviet Communism* brought a lot of publicity for the Webbs.

11 September. [Passfield Corner]
I am being drugged by Orr, to secure rest for my exhausted brain, whilst the Press and periodicals are advertising the Introduction.

Picture Post, the *Tablet*, *Reynolds News* and the *News Chronicle* and the *Journal of the National Association of Local Government Officers* are publishing pictures and accounts of the aged Webbs — *Picture Post* with letterpress by GBS. I was somewhat shocked but also amused by the caricature in a close-up photograph of the aged woman in *Picture Post*, for it represented my present plight of utter exhaustion. How far will this pre-publication and gratuitous advertisement of the book help its immediate sale? is the question we ask each other. And when shall I be fit and free to get back to the book? Am I at the end of my wits, except for writing in my diary — an old habit which I can't cure, any more than Rosy can her passion for sketching. . . .

The writer Stephen Potter (1900–1969) became known after the war for his book *Lifemanship*. Madame Chiang Kai-shek (b. 1898), married to the Chinese leader, herself played an active part in public life, especially in organizing American support for her husband in his struggles with the Communists. Marie Curie (1867–1934) was, with her husband, one of the discoverers of radium. She won two Nobel prizes and was professor of physics at the Sorbonne. Alexandra Kollontay (1872–1952) was an old Bolshevik and campaigner for women's rights.

27 September. [Passfield Corner]
Stephen Potter, a friend of Barbara's, tall, good-looking and a clever talker, a B.B.C. official of three years' standing, came down to interview me. He is proposing a series of biographic broadcasts on eminent men of today who represent the happenings in Great Britain of the last fifty years — artists, scientists and literary men. Not statesmen, I gather. The B.B.C. wanted a woman so they picked me out as old, distinguished and writing — also to our being the leading exponents of Soviet Communism 'in the news'.

It is odd how few distinguished women there are today in Great Britain and elsewhere. I suggested to my interviewer that Madame Kai-shek was the only outstanding woman: why not get the Chinese Ambassador to get a record from her flown from Chungking? Madame Curie is dead, Virginia Woolf — who was, at any rate, *unique* in literary gift, though her particular type was not impressive — is also dead. How few women have been or are distinguished except in their personal relation to men — how few have influenced public opinion and public activities, independently to their sexual relationship to men? There have been and are today distinguished

473

actresses and dancers, singers and other types of musicians, but no musical composers, painters or architects. In the art of writing there have been two great novelists, George Eliot and George Sand − today there is no woman who is the equal of H.G. Wells as a novelist, or GBS as a playwright. No scientist or philosopher; there has never been a great poet, except in mythical Greece, or dramatist. What about the two great women who have been the acknowledged heads of Sovereign States − Elizabeth of Great Britain, Catherine the Great of Russia? No one would suggest that Queen Victoria was a distinguished personality − she was utterly commonplace in intellect and conventional in conduct.

And so the B.B.C. has to fall back on the aged Beatrice Webb for a contemporary notable woman, just as the British Academy had to a few years ago. But even here it was a personal element that gained me the prestige − it was *My Apprenticeship* that has singled me out today just as it was *The Diary of a Working Girl* in the first years of authorship. The most striking case of the absence of distinguished women has been in politics and administration. There is no outstanding woman M.P. either in Great Britain or elsewhere. In the U.S.S.R., where women are admitted to all vocations, even to command in the army, navy and air force, no woman stands out as influential except perhaps Kollantay, the Soviet Ambassadress in Sweden. But she owes this celebrity largely to having been an intimate friend of Lenin, and through this friendship becoming the first woman to be an Ambassadress to a foreign power. . . .

6 October. 2 a.m. [Passfield Corner]
I worried all yesterday afternoon at 15*s* loss in my cash; my legs ached with fetching the eggs, my brain whizzed with making the last arrangements about the book, answering telegrams and letters asking me to contribute articles or speak at meetings − all of which made me wonder: what would happen to Sidney if I collapsed? He could not carry on here alone, or earn the extra income made necessary by increased taxation and the loss of our books . . .

But what are all these petty troubles compared to the tragedy of the world war? Can the Soviet Union repel the all-out attack of the whole might of the greatest armed force that the world has yet seen − the almost mythical efficiency and savage cruelty of Hitler's Germany, with all the resources in men and material of conquered

Europe? That is the dark background of my daily struggle to keep the pot boiling for my little group, in spite of dwindling strength of body and mind. A longing for the eternal sleep of death dominating my consciousness by day and by night. Yesterday afternoon, when he and I were sitting in the garden, I asked Sidney: 'Do you wish to go on living?' He sat silent, surprised at the question, then slowly said '*No*'. He is physically comfortable, he is always reading and not actually bored; he loves and is loved, he is mildly interested in other people and keen to hear the news. But he resents not being able to think and express his thoughts, and thus help the world he lives in. . . .

The German armies had now surrounded Leningrad and were driving on towards Moscow. Russian losses of men and material had been immense.

26 October. [Passfield Corner]
The Maiskys came to tea and talk yesterday afternoon. Outwardly they were exactly the same cheerful friendly couple: he with his mocking smile and talkative and inquisitive friendliness towards his old friends the Webbs; she with her usual charm, both alike appreciative of our support of the Soviet cause. But from the tenor of his talk, telling us of his contact with members of the government and the British public and from his insistent question as to what I thought about working-class and middle-class opinion as to help for Soviet Russia, I gathered they were pessimistic about the successful resistance of the allied forces if the Germans penetrate into the U.S.S.R. They were disappointed by the inadequacy and delay in military help from Great Britain and the U.S.A. Though they (especially Madame Maisky) were certain that Stalin and the Soviet Union would fight on, and, come what may, that the German hordes would be beaten back, it would be after an amount of destruction of the lives and property of the Soviet people unparalleled in the history of the human race. . . .

20 November. [Passfield Corner]
Longman writes that they have already disposed of seven hundred copies of the book, which is heartening to my satisfaction and will enable us to live within our income in the coming years . . .

24 November. [Passfield Corner]
Another distracting row in my little household with the Smiths and

Mrs Grant on food for Peter, about whose treatment I found Mrs Grant weeping, and Annie in a state of angry denunciation of Mrs Grant's unjustified activities and demands. I am suffering badly from cystitis and long to disappear from the scene, if I could only take the beloved one with me. . . .

Early on the morning of 7 December Japanese aircraft launched a surprise attack on the U.S. base at Pearl Harbor in Hawaii, causing heavy damage and casualties. The United States now declared war on Japan, Germany and Italy.

9 December. 3 a.m. [Passfield Corner]
Roosevelt's authoritative and admirably delivered address to Congress – broadcast at 6.30 p.m. – and the long continued and deafening applause by the Congress announcing the treacherous and pre-arranged attack on American islands in the Pacific, involving serious military and naval losses, is a landmark in world history. . . . All the Great Powers will be at war: the three great Democracies – the U.S.A., the U.K. and the U.S.S.R. – and China, with an overwhelming preponderance of the inhabitants of our planet and control over its territory, will be fighting the military might of Germany and Japan, with their satellite states of Italy, Spain and Vichy's France, and the three little states of Finland, Rumania and Hungary – the only neutrals are Switzerland and Sweden, and possibly some South American peoples. What a world war! Does it mean the temporary debasement of the human race, or its rise with the next generation into a New Civilization, intent on realizing the good, the beautiful and the true – human ethics, art and science? That is the issue to be decided in 1942–43. Meanwhile we are all in for a hard time of it. . . .

14 December. [Passfield Corner]
Bernard Drake dead. He and Barbara were the central figures of the Meinertzhagen–Potter families and their charming house in London has become the family meeting-place. He was also the family solicitor, upon whose advice most of us depended so far as wills, trusts and all other contracts with the law of the land. . . . Bernard Drake had a painless death. He had been in bad health for years and his daily devotion to hard work in London, for the last two years, meant mental depression and physical discomfort. So one cannot regret his retirement from life. But his loss opens another gap in the community life of the descendants and their

mates of Richard and Lawrencina Potter, now numbering well over a hundred and fifty individuals. . . .

Churchill went to Washington to co-ordinate plans with Roosevelt and addressed Congress on 26 December.

26 December. [Passfield Corner]
Sidney, Barbara and I listened yesterday at 6.30 p.m. with an all-out admiration to Churchill's oration to the Congress of the United States at Washington. The applause before and after the speech was deafening. His opening allusion to his American mother was perfect in its tact; the summary of past events, of present difficulties, of future prospects, of the supreme dominion, in deciding the fate of the world, of the U.S.A. and the British Empire, was all exactly suited to the occasion. . . . The speech was, in fact, wise, eloquent, perfectly phrased and admirably delivered in its tone and timing of one sentence after another. . . . Its one weak point, not from the standpoint of expediency, but from that of a forecast of future events, was the tacit refusal to recognize the Soviet Union as the equal to the U.K. and the U.S.A. in determining the terms of the eventual peace and practically the paramount power in deciding what shall be the new international order imposed, by force of arms, on Germany and Japan – and acceptable to Europe and America, Asia and Africa. . . .

VOLUME 56

∽ 1942 ∾

7 January. [Passfield Corner]
During the next weeks I have to decide whether to reprint the Introduction, GBS's Preface and the Constitution of 1936 as a booklet on what paper is available. . . . But with a whizzing brain, a failing memory and above all painful intestines and sleeplessness, it is unlikely that I shall be fit to do it. This year will decide whether the aged Beatrice Webb is worn out as an author. . . .

22 January. 3 a.m. [Passfield Corner]
My eighty-fourth birthday. . . . The weather is depressing, bitterly

cold, snow piled up on the lawns and roads which makes walking difficult. The news from the Far East front is alarming and public opinion is indignant at the lack of preparedness and the foolish underrating of Japan's strength, which has meant humiliating defeat for the U.K. and the U.S.A. in the first stages of the war. The striking success of the Soviet armed force in beating back the hitherto invincible Germany army over the immense frontier of the U.S.S.R. is producing a sudden change of opinion about Soviet Communism among the workers and the younger intellectuals, which may change the political situation. . . .

9 February. 2 a.m. [Passfield Corner]
Sleepy by day and sleepless by night, paralysed by bitter cold weather, my senile brain can barely tackle my correspondence, asking for articles, messages or advice. Hence though I knew that Stafford would broadcast the postscript after yesterday evening's, Sunday, 9 p.m. news, I failed to hear, through sleeping, the first words of his appeal for greater effort to help heroic Russia. Though he has a good voice he is not an effective broadcaster; he is dull and monotonous in tone, and conventional in wording. . . . His postscript was more like the appeal of a Christian gentleman for 'a good cause' than the pronouncement on world policy by the future leader of an insurgent political party – which we are hoping he will turn out to be before the next general election.

Cripps had returned from his post as Ambassador to Russia and, still excluded from the Labour Party, was a hero of the discontented left. Churchill appointed him leader of the House of Commons as a gesture to left-wing opinion, now calling for a 'Second Front' in Europe – an immediate invasion of the Continent.

22 February. [Passfield Corner]
Yesterday I journeyed up to London, in bitter cold weather, to meet the Cripps' at a Lunch in St Ermin's Hotel given us by Barbara.

On Thursday evening we had heard over the wireless that Stafford had had an audience with the King and had stayed to lunch; on Friday the papers announced that Churchill had reorganized his War Cabinet and appointed Stafford as 'Leader of the House of Commons' – virtually second in command. . . . Time will show whether he will succeed or fail in becoming the leader of the British people and future Prime Minister of Great Britain. We have never been intimate with Stafford as we were with Haldane and Balfour or Arthur Henderson and many other politicians and civil servants. He has been affectionate and respectful to his aged uncle and aunt: that is all. We have never had any *personal influence* over him – at least I think not. The most significant and unusual fact about him is that he belongs to *no political party* and shows no sign of joining one that already exists or of creating a new one. . . .

24 February. [Passfield Corner]
Confronted with a domestic dilemma. The heroic Annie is suffering from influenza and her gall-bladder is affected – Jean in bed with a similar attack. Mrs Grant maintains her egotistic aloofness and I am at once ignorant of all domestic service and somewhat unsafe in the use of my hands and feet through old age. If only I had been brought up to know how to cook and clean. Rosy can do it, but I can't and I am too feeble to learn; nor could any of my older sisters. Music and painting, languages and literature, the four rules of arithmetic and a smattering of mathematics and philosophy were imparted to us by resident governesses, and visiting minor Canons of the nearby Cathedral town. But we were not even taught to mend our clothes, leave alone to make them. Today, even the daughters of noblemen and wealthy businessmen are taught and practise the domestic arts – cooking, cleaning, the use of electric, gas and Aga stoves, washing and mending the clothes – because of the difficulty of getting servants or because they no longer can afford them.

28 February. [Passfield Corner]
Took Sidney and Lady Whitley and Mrs Grant to see a film of Bernard Shaw's *Major Barbara*. When the play was first performed early in the 1900s the character of Undershaft, the glorification of the Maker of Munitions, the triumph of his philosophy of life, the dismissing of the Christian faith, the ultra-cynicism, sounded out of keeping with the progressive thought of the time and the optimistic vision of the future. Today it is dramatically topical. War has come on a world-wide scale, with a reckless brutality which no one in the early days of this century imagined possible, leave alone probable. . . .

30 March. [Passfield Corner]
The Times yesterday announced the death of the Countess of Balfour

after a short illness. She was the only woman, outside the family group, I loved and cared to see and write to. Witty and wise, she was charming in person and conversation, without egotism or vanity, devoted to her husband and children, and an adorer of Arthur Balfour, who spent the last years of his life and died in her home at Woking. She and I saw little of each other after the outbreak of the 1914–18 war. Indeed during those years she shunned seeing me, for reasons I have never understood. They were, I think, political and not personal, and had to do with Arthur Balfour's attitude to the Webbs as political personalities. In the late 20s we resumed our friendship and, after the great man's death and Sidney's retreat from the political scene, we became again intimate and began to write letters to and visit each other. To me a light has gone out of the world I live in. Poor old Gerald! an ailing decrepit man. I always liked and respected him. . . .

17 April. 2.30–3.30 a.m. [Passfield Corner]
The raids begun again: the wailing of the siren, the bombs dropping nearby, which gives me an extra excuse for this cup of tea and writing in the diary. Rosy here for a week's holiday from nursing George, cooking and cleaning, looking after grand-children. . . . A wonderfully active old lady, but a rather trouble-some guest to the household she visits, scattering papers and prints, clothes and books, ideas and requests, and using other people's belongings wherever she stays or goes. But as the two last of the Potter sisters we have a certain permanent relationship in affections and remembrances which I respect, and my household accepts if it is limited to a week's visit here twice a year. . . .

Churchill sent Cripps to India on 22 March to try to win over Indian opinion in view of the increasing threat from Japan, but by 10 April the talks had broken down and Nehru joined Gandhi in passive disobedience. Leopold Amery, a one-time Fabian, had become a vigorously imperialist Secretary of State for India. A series of setbacks – the loss of Malaya and Burma, Singapore, no progress in the Middle East – had political repercussions. Between February and November the Coalition government lost four by-elections to Independents. This spirit of revolt found expression in the emergence of a new party – the Commonwealth Party, whose scattering of victories were a harbinger of the Labour landslide in 1945. Beatrice had just completed her pamphlet *The Truth About Russia*, which was to be published by Longmans.

1 May. [Passfield Corner]
. . . . It is noticeable that while Stafford's speech in the House of Commons about his mission to India was received by Conservatives and Liberals with complete agreement, the Labour Ministers were markedly silent and the two Labour M.P.s who spoke were critical: 'Sir Stafford Cripps has been tied down to the reactionary policy of Churchill and Amery,' they declared. Meanwhile two independent left-wing candidates, opposed by the official Labour Party, have won two seats formerly held by reactionary Tory Ministers . . . It is clear that there is growing up a left-wing socialist party – alike among the civilian workers and also within the couple of million standing army in Great Britain bored by their inactive and badly paid daily life. Meanwhile all aged and infirm householders are threatened with rationed light and heat, which will make a cold winter almost unbearable! 'Ought the aged and infirm to go on living?' I sometimes wonder. If it were not for Sidney I should long for painless extinction – I am deadly tired in body and mind. . . .

11 May. [Passfield Corner]
Churchill returns to the limelight. On the second anniversary of his premiership he broadcast an eloquent and shrewd address to the British people. His voice came over well and he was in first-rate form. He contrasted the situation in 1940, when Britain stood alone, with today, when they had as allies the two most powerful peoples of the world – the U.S.A. and the U.S.S.R., not to mention China and the refugee governments of Norway, Holland, Belgium and Greece. The Allies were confident of victory but it would mean the utmost work, courage, initiative and self-sacrifice. . . .

13 June. [Passfield Corner]
Lloyd George . . . paid us a surprise visit yesterday afternoon. We had not seen him since we lunched with him eleven years ago on the eve of the election of 1931. . . .
Today the great statesman of 1914–22 is a picturesque aged elder with flowing white hair, excited gestures and vehement opinions, hating Churchill's government. . . . gloomy about the future of the British Empire. The war would go on for another year or more. Assuming that the Allies beat the Axis powers it

481

would be the Soviet armed forces who had done it. The U.S.S.R. would be the paramount power in Europe, only she could hold Germany down . . . We parted the best of friends. Poor old man. The Wizard of Wales, who ruled the Great Britain that won the war of 1914–18 and lost the peace in 1918–21 seemed to me to be, like the aged Webbs, a ghost from the past wandering about the ruins of his old home – the British Empire of the nineteenth century. . . .

27 June. [Passfield Corner]
The Maiskys drove down for a couple of hours. Being in the news and among the leading personalities in the world of today has not altered Maisky; it has not made him more self-important, nor less whimsically critical of the British governing class . . .

The Maiskys are confident of the final victory of the U.S.S.R. over Germany even if they lose Sebastopol; both armies are digging themselves in; the German army is no longer capable of any advance that would win the war. Will the victory be won this year, as it might be, if the British and American forces created a Second Front in Europe? Or will it be after the Russian winter has rendered the German army incapable to resist the offensive by the Red forces? He told us that Roosevelt desired a Second Front and the American generals who have come over with the American forces are trying to persuade the British High Command to carry it out; Churchill would prefer to give precedence to reinforcing the Libyan front so as to save British prestige. . . .

Tobruk had fallen to Rommel's forces on 20 June, provoking a vote of no confidence in the government.

2 July. [Passfield Corner]
Listened yesterday evening to an almost verbatim account of Churchill's frank and eloquent speech in his own defence as to supreme authority in the waging of the war – on the motion of no confidence, owing to the fall of Tobruk. He did not attempt to deny the extent of the disaster, or the fact that it was the result of military incapacity on the part of the British army. What he did prove was that any disunity on the part of the British people – any change of government, or even any lessening of the prestige of the Prime Minister – would be an even greater disaster. So he got a vote of 476 to 25, with some 50 abstentions, which was sufficient for

achieving his purpose . . . The opposition to Churchill's leadership is made up of hard-grained Tories . . . clever but inexperienced left-wing Labour men – Shinwell and Aneurin Bevin, one or two Liberals and newly elected 'independents' of no importance. There is no one in the official Conservative or Labour parties who has the qualifications for supreme leadership as Lloyd George had in the great war of 1914–18. . . . Our defeat in Libya, coming after the conquest by Germany of the European countries and by Japan of Hong Kong, Singapore and Burma, leaves the Red Army as the Hero on the battlefield, and the U.S.A. as our superior in supplying the instruments of war. . . .

14 July. [Passfield Corner]
Again I am feeling desperately ill, troubled with my intestines, which keeps me awake at night and in discomfort all day – doubtful whether I ought to eat or not and what I ought to eat – made more difficult by rationing. Also trouble in my little staff: Annie and Jean continually quarrelling with Mrs Grant and vice versa. Friends and relations turning up to tea which compels me to walk and talk more than I am equal to. As everyone seems to be suffering a similar if not worse strain than I am, with mass murder going on over the whole world, I try to compel myself to be indifferent to my own troubles. . . .

25 July. [Passfield Corner]
Yesterday our golden wedding. I had not notified it to my relatives and friends. But the Press discovered it. The *Daily Herald* and *News Chronicle* phoned the day before to ask whether the editor or his representative could come down to interview us, a proposal which I politely refused. The *Daily Telegraph* rang me up on the day: they wanted me to answer the question, 'How does the state of the world war today differ from that of the day of your silver wedding twenty-five years ago (1917)?', a question to which I tried to give an impromptu answer. A few telegrams and letters trickled through . . . But my own family were not aware of it, and as they do not read the *Daily Herald*, the one paper to publish it, they did not trouble me with telegrams or letters to answer. I was desperately tired, suffering from intestinal troubles, sleeplessness and general weariness of living in this tragic world. . . .

Can I be sufficiently useful to make life worth living? Our

booklet is selling out rapidly . . . The British Embassy at Kuibishev has applied . . . for an article by the veteran Webbs for their new weekly *Our British Ally* . . . which will keep me busy for the next few mornings. So it looks as if I am still useful. Certainly we have a debt to pay back to our country. We have had an exceptionally prosperous and pleasant life these last fifty years – in personal comfort, in interest and influence in the world we have lived in and had our being. What more can mortals want? So carry on, old lady, and don't grumble about the pain and penalties of old age. Even here you are fortunate – you can hear and see, you can walk and you can talk and you can work.

Early in August Churchill flew to Cairo, a visit which resulted in the appointment of General Alexander (1891–1969) and General Montgomery (1887–1976) in North Africa. He went on to Moscow to tell Stalin of the proposed landing in French North Africa. After widespread demonstrations, Nehru was detained in October until Japan was defeated. He was not a Communist, though sympathetic to the Soviet Union.

11 August. [Passfield Corner]
India has become the black spot in the news about Great Britain. There is a rumour that Churchill is in Moscow to discuss with Stalin about the Second Front and also about India. . . . Gandhi stands out as one of the great personalities in world affairs . . . To me his saintly egotism and clever contortionist policy, his absurd economic dreams of a return to hand-work in the work-shop and the field, makes him a repulsive figure. But he has built up a revolutionary movement in India, which means, sooner or later, the withdrawal of the British supremacy, over the portions of India which are governed by the British . . .

The India conquered by Great Britain is an impossible unit for a sovereign state, with its powerful eighty million Mohammedan population, its princely provinces, its discordant religious sects and castes. Even within the Congress itself there is no common living philosophy – Nehru is a Communist, Gandhi is a visionary of a fantastic type, the majority being just ordinary profit-making businessmen, or rent-receiving landlords, with a medley of inexperienced reformers of the democratic brand, and a smattering of orthodox and pious Hindus belonging to different sects who would be dead against democratic government, political and industrial, liberal or socialist.

A three-volume edition of the Webb correspondence was published in 1978.

26 August. [Passfield Corner]
As writing another chapter of *The Three Stages of Our Pilgrimage* seems impossible during these exciting and depressing days of total war, with victory or defeat just around the corner, I am using up my dwindling faculties in sorting out our correspondence for the last years . . . Also our correspondence is distinctly valuable for future histories of the last fifty years . . . At times I think that I am no longer fit for continued authorship for publication and that it would be wiser to give it up and merely go on reporting events in the diary. . . . Authorship seems to be a profession from which you cannot retire – you long to carry on, however unfit you may be to do so. GBS and H.G. Wells cannot stop writing; they will die with an unfinished book on their desk. And I shall die with my diary, pen and ink in a drawer by the side of my bed.

28 August. 2 a.m. [Passfield Corner]
Twenty-five Fabians from the summer school at Frensham Heights visited us yesterday morning and afternoon – mostly young people on leave from army work of one sort or another. They reported universal unrest and the growth of 'revolutionary feeling', but neither unity nor leadership about the new world they wanted to create nor the way to get it. . . .

Dr Hodgkinson now replaced Dr Orr as the Webbs' doctor. Beatrice was treated with nitrate of mercury.

13 September. 2 a.m. [Passfield Corner]
I have been feeling desperately ill for the last week or so, longing for an escape from life and yet fearing its effect on Sidney. I have just discovered blood in my urine – which is, I think, the sign of my remaining kidney going rotten, with death round the corner. So I shall call up Hodgkinson and ask him to come and tell me what lies before me . . . What haunted me during the night was not the prospect of death but the presence of pain.

13 September. 11 a.m.
Hodgkinson gives me hope that it is only an inflamed bladder that is troubling me and that if I drink liquid – whether china tea or

citrine-tempered water − and stay in bed and keep warm, the chances are that I shall recover . . .

17 September. [Passfield Corner]
Hodgkinson came to see me yesterday. He had consulted Orr, our late medical man, who has been called up for service in India. They advised me to spend a night in the Haslemere Nursing Home in order that they may examine my bladder, to find whether or not it is the source of the bleeding. If there be a growth there it can be removed, and Orr is an accomplished surgeon. The operation will not be dangerous and will need only a slight anaesthetic and I can return here in the afternoon. If the bladder is clear there is nothing that can be done. . . .

22 September. [Passfield Corner]
Hodgkinson reported today that Orr was leaving for service abroad on Friday and would not be able to carry out the operation on Thursday morning. Hence it would involve my getting up to London. Also the operation would have to be more extended and injurious to my strength than a mere examination of the bladder; it would involve investigating the condition of the kidney before it could be settled whether or not I was likely to live or die in the near future. So we decided against it on the ground that you cannot cure old age, and a lengthy period of increased disability would be worse than a peaceful death.

John Parker (b. 1906) was elected as Labour M.P. in 1935, and was the longest surviving member of the House of Commons when he retired at the 1983 general election.

25 September. [Passfield Corner]
On hearing that I am seriously ill Barbara Drake came down for the night, and I and she discussed the disposal of the Webb property, as Sidney and I were adding a codicil to our will, appointing two trustees in place of two who were no longer desirable. The trustees under the present will are Barbara Drake, Carr-Saunders, Laski, C.M. Lloyd and Herbert Morrison. Lloyd is dying of cancer; and Herbert Morrison has become reactionary and anti-Soviet. So we are appointing, at her suggestion, John Parker, M.P. (general secretary of the Fabian Society) and

Margaret Cole, who will represent G.D.H. Cole and herself, who practically share our views as to the future organization of society, national and international . . . The only question we did not discuss was what should be done about our own books and the various pamphlets we have written; and how my diaries and my unfinished *Our Partnership* and *The Three Stages of Our Pilgrimage* are to be dealt with. It is clear that I shall not be able to finish either the one or the other for publication before or after my disappearance from the scene. . . .

30 September. [Passfield Corner]
Hodgkinson and I had a final talk about my state of health and he will not come again unless I send for him. He tells me to eat more, lead as normal a life as I have strength to carry out. There is no *cure* for old age – the only alleviation is courage to go on helping other people to live a peaceful and happy life . . .

15 October. [Passfield Corner]
The Maiskys down here for two hours, depressed by the absence of settled determination to open a Second Front in Europe; and the undercurrent among the British generals and governing class, anxious that the German and Russian armies should exterminate each other and thus enable capitalist Great Britain and the U.S.A. to dominate the peace-making. He even thinks that they might come to terms, not with Hitler and his Nazi party, but with the German capitalists glad to resume control of Germany. . . .

Muggeridge had been recruited into the Intelligence Corps after a brief time at the Ministry of Information. He had left Lisbon in May for Laurenco Marques. His job was to stop the enemy getting information about convoys to Africa.

25 October. [Passfield Corner]
Kitty Muggeridge turned up yesterday as my guest at the Passfield Oak Hotel in succession to her mother, who left yesterday morning. I should not have recognized her. She is a tall and attractive young person, with a crop of dark and carefully curled chocolate-coloured hair, dark grey eyes and appropriately tempered complexion and lips. She had affectionate and pleasant manners towards her aged uncle and aunt. She reported that Malcolm Muggeridge, a captain in the army . . . . was depressed about the world situation

but 'enjoying his life', first in Portugal, now in Portuguese South Africa . . . She said he was attracted to the Roman Catholic Church, but hesitated to join that powerful organization because he had no faith in a 'force that makes for righteousness' and doubts its existence – it is the Devil not God who is dominating this unhappy place and its human inhabitants. . . . Altogether my niece struck me as an unexpectedly attractive young woman and devoted mother, who represented the cynicism of this generation that grew up during the first great war. . . .

Beveridge had been appointed chairman of the Inter-Departmental Committee on Social Insurance and Allied Services, and had drafted a comprehensive set of proposals for providing social security from the cradle to the grave. There was strong opposition to the Beveridge Report from Conservative members of the Cabinet. The attempts to limit the report – and its circulation in the army – merely enhanced its popularity as the first earnest of post-war reconstruction.

26 October. [Passfield Corner]
Stafford lunched here . . . On balance his visit depressed us . . . I tried to extract from him what was his outlook on future recon- struction of our social order. He intimated that he wished the Church to be disestablished and disendowed in order that it should adopt Christian Socialism. He believed in the projects of Keynes and Beveridge, both of whom were going 'left'. . . . He seemed too self-centred and self-confident, and did not share our own outlook and hopes for the future. Perhaps I am too tired mentally and physically to be otherwise than bewildered by Stafford's aloofness and self-estimation . . . Sidney agrees and thinks Churchill will offer him the viceroyship of India in order to be rid of him as a successor to the premiership . . .

On 4 November the British 8th Army won the decisive battle of El Alamein and began to drive west towards the Anglo–American force which had landed in Morocco. The Soviet Union was about to launch the massive offensive which led to a German disaster at Stalingrad. The tide of war was beginning at last to turn.

9 November. [Passfield Corner]
The amazing victory of the British armed forces in Egypt and the successful invasion of North Africa by the American army, re- inforced by British air and naval units, have been the outstanding news of the last few days. . . .

11 November. [Passfield Corner]

Carr-Saunders spent three hours here on Friday afternoon to be informed about our will as one of the five trustees, and to look over our house and grounds and furniture and books, all of which are to go to the L.S.E. when we are dead. . . . He is a conscientious and kindly man, quite oddly *neutral* towards other people's opinions, habits and manners; he seems never to quarrel with anyone, while maintaining his own authority. Exactly what is his living philosophy no one knows: his wife is a Roman Catholic and I think his children are being brought up in that faith. So far as I can judge he is mildly conservative in politics and agnostic in religion . . .

Stafford Cripps resigned as Leader of the House and took over the Ministry of Aircraft Production. Sir William Jowitt had followed MacDonald into the National Government and then rejoined the Labour Party. He was a prominent lawyer and became Lord Chancellor in 1945. The four freedoms – of speech and worship, from want and fear – were the core of Roosevelt's speech to the U.S. Congress on 6 January 1941; and they were incorporated in the Atlantic Charter which Roosevelt and Churchill signed at sea on 14 August 1941.

6 December. [Passfield Corner]

The publication of the Beveridge Report, the endorsement of it by Sir William Jowitt and the House of Commons, the extraordinarily favourable reception of it by public opinion, by *The Times* and other papers, and by the B.B.C. in its news bulletins, is a striking testimony to Beveridge's outstanding capacity for invention and argument. . . . Beveridge himself calls it a revolution, though a peaceful one. But it is based on what seems to me a radically false hypothesis: that it is consistent with the continued existence of the capitalist and landlord as the ruling class . . . He states emphatically that this lifelong security to every man can be obtained under the present system of capitalist profit-making. . . .

The unemployment insurance, the sufficient livelihood for the unemployed man or woman, would increase the number of unemployed persons living without earning, through the failure of the capitalist to offer work with adequate livelihood to the unemployed person if they could live without earning their livelihood. In short, if Beveridge's scheme is adopted as the law of the land, we shall have a catastrophic increase in the number of unemployed persons together with a collapse of the means of maintaining them. The more carefully the scheme is examined, the more it will be condemned both by the capitalists, who will be keeping low profits, and by whole-hearted believers in the four freedoms of the Atlantic Charter. Hence it is destined to fail. It will either be rejected, which I think is the most probable result, or if accepted and applied will be catastrophic in its results – and in both cases it will divide the country into two political parties, those who insist on maintaining our present capitalist civilization and those who would substitute the new civilization of Soviet Communism.

9 December. [Passfield Corner]
Beveridge's crowded meeting at Oxford yesterday, with the extraordinary applause of the audience of some two thousand and of crowds outside, has added to his reputation as an agitator for his scheme . . . The increasing prestige of Beveridge's Report . . . resulted in a request to me from the *Cooperative News* to review it, which I shall try to do, in spite of being incapacitated by an attack of intestinal trouble, swollen feet and tingling legs, which has kept me in bed for ten days under the orders of my kind and clever medical adviser, Dr Hodgkinson. I am still in a state of mental depression, a feeling that I am too ill to live, let alone to give interviews and write articles for the Press. However, we live in the most comfortable home, and owing to Annie's kindness and care, I can just carry on! . . .

Mrs Mair's husband had died on 21 July and she was at last free to marry Beveridge. He had been knighted and became a peer in 1946. Beatrice had 'the most friendly letter' inviting her to the wedding.

15 December. [Passfield Corner]
Today Beveridge married Mrs Mair. He wrote some time ago to tell me of the coming event and I sent him our warm greetings on his marriage to his lifelong companion and long continued colleague in research and administration in the public interest . . . It is to be hoped that the past will be forgotten and that Lady Beveridge will be accepted by the world they live in in London and Oxford.

19 December. [Passfield Corner]
The Times gave a list of peers and peeresses, Ambassadors and their wives and eminent politicians who attended the Beveridge–Mair marriage luncheon . . . It is rumoured that Churchill favours the Report; the Liberal Party has endorsed it enthusiastically, and the

Labour Party has accepted it with qualifications, and demanded that it should be passed into law at once . . . Beveridge has had a great personal triumph . . . It is a queer result of this strange and horrible war that Beveridge, whose career as a civil servant and as Director of the School of Economics was more or less a failure, should have risen suddenly into the limelight as an accepted designer of a New World Order. I wonder whether he will see my criticism of the Report – if so, whether we shall see the Beveridges again. I doubt it!

Xmas Day. [Passfield Corner]
Over the wireless comes, day after day, the cheering news of continuous victories on the Soviet front of a thousand miles; the collapse of the German armies, the taking of huge quantities of munitions, and above all the surrender of thousands of German soldiers to the Red Army. As this coincides with the retreat of the Germans in North Africa and the air supremacy of the Americans and British in the Mediterranean, it looks as if victory were bound to come. Meanwhile the Japanese are on the defensive everywhere in the Far East . . .

29 December. [Passfield Corner]
Barbara Drake, the nearest of my nephews and nieces to us in affection and creed, spent the last days of 1942 with us; elderly and well-off, she is the centre of the family of the descendants of Richard and Lawrencina Potter . . .

During her visit I was suffering acutely from piles and my swollen feet and she was most sympathetic. We gossiped about the family, past and present, and about old friends, and enjoyed each other's company.

So ends the year of 1942.

VOLUME 59

ᢙ 1943 ᢛ

4 January. 4 a.m. [Passfield Corner]
The worst night of unremitting abdominal pain compelled me to
call up Annie to help me to bear it. I had some soup for supper,
made of vegetable boiled with a mutton-bone, in which I had
soaked a piece of toasted bread. When she was with me I belched up
wind and was sick – the soup had evidently not agreed with me. She
stayed with me, sleeping on the sofa until near five o'clock. I had
done a morning's work, answering letters and keeping others to
dictate to Miss Burr on Thursday. The pain of living, with rotten
intestines, swollen feet and a tired and sleepless brain, is qualified
by the fear for Sidney if I am not there to look after his daily life
and be his loving companion of fifty years standing. . . .

4 January. 12 p.m.
Hodgkinson came and told me that gastric dysentery was everywhere, and all his own household had been suffering from attacks
of sickness – which comforted me. . . .

22 January. 5.30 a.m. [Passfield Corner]
My eighty-fifth birthday! I have a swollen foot, painful intestines,
but an active brain. The two aged Webbs are still in request – we
have a stream of visitors and I have a big correspondence with
people who want to know about Russia or our opinion of the
Beveridge Report, which interests numberless people here and in the
U.S.A. So I carry on. Sidney is well and happy, and I am, in spite
of my rather painful existence, interested in the world we live
in . . .

The amazing success of the Soviet people in beating back
Hitler's powerful army is delightful news over the radio and in the
newspapers, and makes life worth living to those who believe in the
living philosophy of scientific humanism and its application to
national and international well-being. I sometimes wonder whether
I shall be alive this day twelve months hence. I should be glad to be

spared the pain of living, but so long as my dear one lives on, I wish to be here to look after him.

The critic Raymond Mortimer (1895–1980) was for some years the Literary Editor of the *New Statesman*.

12 February. [Passfield Corner]
Kingsley Martin and Raymond Mortimer here for tea and talk. K.M. was most affectionate to the aged Webbs . . . Raymond Mortimer is an attractive and successful literary journalist – cultivated, has travelled widely and is today working in the foreign department of the B.B.C. and Ministry of Information. He has come down with K.M. because he was a great admirer of *My Apprenticeship* – he and Kingsley Martin wanted me to contribute extracts from my diary about Bernard Shaw. I told them that would be undesirable. Our relations with GBS had been those of warm friendship and courteous co-operation, but nearly all the entries in the diaries were about our brilliant friend's troublesome antics, his queer dealing with current events and contemporary personalities, and were, in a sense, mainly critical. Sidney and he had co-operated and he had always been most generous in his appreciation of our work. He was a great dramatist, but whimsical in his dealings with other men. I preferred to abstain from any quotation from the diaries until both the Shaws and the Webbs were no longer living personalities . . .

20 February. [Passfield Corner]
Over the wireless came the news of Sydney Olivier's death at Bognor Regis, not far from here. He was Sidney's oldest intimate friend and colleague of more than fifty years' standing. First in the early 80s, when they became the two resident clerks at the Colonial Office; then as one of the group of five intellectuals who founded the Fabian Society as the main political centre of socialist propaganda at home and in the colonies; and finally as fellow members of the first MacDonald Cabinet in 1922–23. A year older than Sidney and a few months younger than I am, he had become an aged but rather worn-out figure, still intent on furthering the cause of racial equality within the British Empire, but not a very comfortable companion for his wife.

493

24 February. [Passfield Corner]
Hodgkinson turned up on Monday morning to see how I was after being dosed with the liquid narcotic. I complained that though I slept a little longer in the night, I was comatose all the day and too tired to go for my usual walk. So he ordered me to return to the taking of two alonal and two veganin at ten o'clock at night. After three days I am much better. So I get four or five hours' sleep at nights and can work and walk better during the day. Which is hopeful. . . .

9 March. 6 a.m. [Passfield Corner]
I was awake when at 2 a.m. there sounded the loudest alarm we have had – from Bramshott I think – followed by gun-fire, which shook the door. I looked behind the curtain, there were searchlights and the shining of flickering lights in the skies over to the South-East. Presently there appeared eight brilliant stars from which dropped endless streams of incendiary bombs over one particular spot which remained stationary . . . The raid lasted for two hours, concentrated on the camps and munition works on the way from the south coast to Woking and London. That made me feel slightly ashamed of myself. It had interested me, and in that spirit of exhilaration I forgot that it might mean hundreds of dead and wounded, while we, being a mile or two off the target, might be exempt from the danger of being involved. With my continuous discomfort – or even pain – it is a queer distraction from physical pain and mental depression!

10 March. 10 p.m. [Passfield Corner]
This morning's papers report that . . . three enemy bombers were brought down and the crew of two killed, with one wounded pilot who became a prisoner of war. What *did* happen, bringing an interesting souvenir to the Webb household, was the fall of a German balloon [a parachute] and the acquisition of enough white silk to furnish all the household with silk night-gowns. The balloon – with its yards of silk and its long cords of white rope, at the end of which were the empty containers of the flares – I had noticed in the sky. . . . Unless the government claims them we shall keep them as a record of the second great war . . .

11 March. [Passfield Corner]
The return to a bleeding bladder – the pain by day and night

bringing a depressing mental state – has raised the question whether in the future there will not be established a Temple of Anaesthesia, providing a recognized way for a voluntary retirement, as honourable as the retirement of a professional man or woman from the practice of their profession. . . .

25 March. [Passfield Corner]
Dead tired with dictating some dozen letters and settling with Longmans about the telegrams I have had to answer from rival New York publishers for permission to publish *The Truth About Russia*, one offering us a 2,000 dollar advanced royalty, another wanting to publish it for the South American states. . . . It is satisfactory to our pride, but with other demands on my exhausted brain and a painful intestine, it has made my desire to leave life still more dominant. We have lived the life we liked and done the work we intended to do; and we have been proved to be right about Soviet Communism: a new civilization. What more can we want but a peaceful and painless ending of personal consciousness? But I can't desert Sidney, who is still content to live.

2 April. [Passfield Corner]
Another trouble in my household. The devoted Annie exploded with Jean yesterday afternoon and shouted abuse at me! All because I asked them for some information for Miss Burr, but really because they dislike Mrs Grant and think she has too easy a time of it! I begged them not to go on shouting abuse, but in spite of my dizzy head and the smarting state of my feet and hands they shouted while I was making tea for Sidney and myself. It is partly due to the strain of being at war – a war which the news over the B.B.C. and in the papers tell us will be long, and perhaps last until 1944–45 . . . I suggested that if they went, Sidney and I, with Mrs Grant and Peter, would go to a hotel – which neither Sidney nor I would like but which would exactly suit Mrs Grant. I think that impressed them and they became good and devoted servants again!

9 April. 1 a.m. [Passfield Corner]
Last night I was desperately tired – I wondered whether my brain was going and I was likely to become insane tonight. So I went to bed at 8.30 and took one alonal. What tired my bewildered brain was going up and downstairs for the nine o'clock news, which is

generally a repetition of the six o'clock. So I think I shall go to bed earlier. What suits me is to spend more time in bed in my room, and less downstairs. If I leave Sidney down in the library alone, of course it gives Annie and Jean more to do and Mrs Grant more to do as they have to see to his comforts. But Annie and Jean want me to do it and it is Mrs Grant's job to look after Sidney, which she does not object to doing except on Thursdays. But I feel very tired.

19 April. 7 a.m. [Passfield Corner]
My present state of body and mind is a combination of physical discomfort and mental satisfaction. I find living a painful experience. Severe cystitis and a paralysed colon means physical pain by day and by night. But it is clear that so long as Sidney is alive I could not leave him. When he is dead I shall at once disappear gladly and by my own act. It will suit the public interest; as it would be easier for our trustees . . . to wind up our affairs. This house, with its comfort inside and beauty and usefulness in its twenty-one acres, will be able to be returned to the public advantage.

This is Beatrice's last entry in her diary.

19 April. 7 p.m. [Passfield Corner]
The most amazing fact is that the history of mankind is happening as I write these words. Tonight when we were listening to wireless the B.B.C. broadcast and the electric fire suddenly ceased. Sidney and Mrs Grant and Annie all asserted that it was accidental. But presently (as I write these words) the B.B.C. ceased its activity and my cup of tea went cold – so did Sidney's glass of sherry. Annie came to tell me that two British air-machines had passed low over our house and they had suddenly disappeared. At the same time I felt that I must go to the water closet and I had an action which seemed to clear away all unnecessary excreta, and I couldn't for the next few hours get my feet warm and comfortable. But suddenly I ceased to exist. So did Annie and Jean and Mrs Grant and Sidney. So we are having a painless death as I had longed for. For if my reasoning is right we shall all disappear, including the *Germans themselves from the territory which they have conquered.* There will be no Jews, no conquered peoples, no refugees. The garden will disappear and all our furniture, the earth and the sun and the moon. God wills the destruction of all living things, man, woman and child. We shall not be frozen or hurt. We should merely – not

exist (never even have existed). It all seems incredible and therefore is worth noting. Even Churchill and Roosevelt, states and king-doms, would disappear! No one would fear, it will be sudden and complete, so no one need worry, and we can go on as long as we are conscious that we do exist. It is as ridiculous as it is terrifying. Annie as she left me said she would bring me my breakfast, and even offered to stay with me during the night so that I should not be lonely. So I kissed her and said good-night. I thought it kinder not to tell Sidney and Mrs Grant. We shall none of us suffer pain and discomfort; it will be sudden, complete, as the wireless set was in its broadcast, and the fire and the electric light, the chairs and the cushions, and the kitchen, the dining-room, the study and the sitting-room. What an amazing happening, well worth recording in my diary, but that also will suddenly disappear even if I went on with this endless writing. As I turn out the light and heat up my tea kettle and hot water bottle, so my stomach may no longer pain me, I feel that this is *inconceivable — and therefore that it will not happen.*

Beatrice Webb died eleven days later, on 30 April 1943. She was cremated. On 13 October 1947, Sidney died. On his death Shaw wrote to *The Times* suggesting that 'to commemorate an unparalleled partnership' the remains of the Webbs should not lie in the garden at Passfield (as they had directed), but in Westminster Abbey. On 12 December 1947, in the presence of a Labour Cabinet which contained a majority of Fabians, they were interred together in the Abbey, the first wife and husband to be so honoured.

A memorial stone with the name 'Beatrice' stands in the wood at Passfield Corner.

Chronology

1924 January First Labour government appointed after a general election in December 1923. Sidney Webb appointed President of the Board of Trade
April British Empire exhibition at Wembley. Publication of the Dawes plan
July Inter-allied conference in London. Beatrice receives honorary degree at Edinburgh
August Breakdown of Russian trade negotiations. Editor of *Worker's Weekly*, J.R. Campbell, arrested on charge of incitement to riot
September MacDonald scandal over McVitie & Price shares. Tory motion of censure on Campbell case and vote of no-confidence in government
October General election. Zinoviev letter
November Tory government with Stanley Baldwin as Prime Minister
December Webbs decide to share 41 Grosvenor Road with Susan Lawrence

1925 April Britain returns to the gold standard. Beatrice at Freshwater with Kate
June Coal-owners cancel existing wage agreements
September Royal Commission on mining industry appointed
October Locarno Pact

1926 January Webbs holiday in Sicily
February Publication of *My Apprenticeship*
March Publication of Royal Commission report on mining industry
April Deadlock over negotiations between miners and mine-owners

May General Strike
August Labour party Garden Party at Passfield
September Webbs at T.U.C. Bournemouth
December B.B.C. charter as public corporation

1927 *May* Trades Disputes Act. End of trade agreement with Russia
October Death of Jane Wells

1928 *January* Beatrice's seventieth birthday. Floods at Grosvenor Road
February Death of Asquith
July Webbs on holiday at Val d'Isère
August Death of R.B. Haldane. Kellogg–Briand pact. Beatrice tours mining districts of South Wales
December Webbs' poor law history concluded. Vote given to all women over twenty-one

1929 *January* Webb portrait presented to the L.S.E.
March Death of Kate Courtney. Beatrice makes her first broadcast
April Webbs on holiday in Greece and Turkey
May Webbs receive honorary degree in Munich. General election
June Second Labour government. Sidney becomes Secretary of State for the Dominions and Colonies and goes to the House of Lords
August Webbs take first flight
September Webbs give up Grosvenor Road and move to Whitehall Court. MacDonald in America to discuss naval disarmament
October Wall Street crash

1930 *January* Mosley's economic proposals rejected by the government
April Gandhi arrested for civil disobedience. Webbs move to Artillery Mansions
May Mosley resigns
June Thomas takes over the Dominions. Webbs holiday in the Channel Isles
July Webbs dine with Prince of Wales
October Imperial conference. Crash of R101

1931 February Beatrice starts *Our Partnership*. Mosley resigns from the Labour Party
April May Committee set up
May Failure of the Kredit-anstalt bank
July Report of May Committee. GBS visits Russia
August Crisis in Labour Cabinet and fall of Labour government
September Japan invades Manchuria – the first violation of peace since the war
October General election and formation of the National government

1932 February Disarmament conference opens at Geneva
April Beatrice elected to the British Academy
May Webbs visit Russia
July Webbs return from Russia. I.L.P. disaffiliates from Labour Party
August Death of Graham Wallas

1933 January Hitler becomes Chancellor in Germany
February Webbs on holiday in Italy. Japan invades China. Oxford Union motion on whether to fight for 'King and Country'
October Germany resigns from League of Nations and withdraws from Disarmament conference. Webbs attend Labour Party conference in Hastings. Beatrice undergoes operation on her bladder at Hastings

1934 January Beatrice undergoes second operation for removal of kidney
February Civil war in Austria
June Baldwin takes over from MacDonald. The 'night of the long knives' in Germany
September U.S.S.R. joins the League of Nations. Sidney Webb visits Russia
October Sidney returns from Russia. Death of Ada Wallas

1935 January Webbs in Isle of Wight
April Webbs in Hastings
May George V's silver jubilee
June The Peace Ballot
October Italy invades Abyssinia

November General election resulting in Conservative government under Baldwin. Attlee elected leader of the Labour Party
December The Hoare–Laval Pact

1936 *January* Death of George V
March Hitler invades Rhineland. Webbs on holiday in Majorca
July Spanish civil war begins. Purge trials in Russia
December Abdication of Edward VIII

1937 *January* Labour Party expels Socialist League
April Beveridge appointed head of University College, Oxford
May Chamberlain becomes Prime Minister
July Webbs in Switzerland. Death of Henry Hobhouse
October Carr-Saunders becomes the new Director of the L.S.E.
November Death of Ramsay MacDonald

1938 *January* Beatrice's eightieth birthday. Sidney has a stroke
February Eden resigns as Foreign Secretary. Ribbentrop becomes Foreign Minister in Germany
September Hitler's speech at Nuremburg. Chamberlain makes peace agreement with Hitler at Munich
October Hitler takes over Sudetenland

1939 *March* Hitler occupies Czechoslovakia. British give guarantee to Poland
April Mussolini attacks Albania. Britain introduces conscription
August Soviet–German pact
September Germany invades Poland. Britain declares war
December Russia invades Finland

1940 *April* Germany occupies Denmark and Norway
May Germany invades Holland and Belgium. Churchill replaces Chamberlain as Prime Minister and forms a Coalition government
June Paris occupied. French army surrender. Vichy government sues for peace. British Expeditionary Force evacuates at Dunkirk

August Trotsky assassinated
September Climax of the Battle of Britain
November Death of Chamberlain

1941 April Death of Virginia Woolf
June Hitler invades Russia
July Death of Lord Parmoor
December Japanese attack Pearl Harbor. America declares war

1942 March Death of Betty Balfour
June Fall of Tobruk
July Webbs' golden wedding
November Victory at El Alamein
December Publication of Beveridge Report

1943 April Death of Beatrice

A Short Bibliography

Autobiography

L.S. Amery, *My Political Life* (II and III) (London, 1953 and 1955).
Anne Olivier Bell (ed.), *The Diary of Virginia Woolf* (III and IV) (London, 1980 and 1982).
W.H. Beveridge, *Power and Influence* (London, 1938).
Fenner Brockway, *Inside the Left* (London, 1942).
Walter Citrine, *Men and Work* (London, 1964).
J.R. Clynes, *Memoirs* (London, 1937).
Margaret Cole, *Growing Up Into Revolution* (London, 1949).
Duff Cooper, *Old Men Forget* (London, 1953).
Hugh Dalton, *Call Back Yesterday* (London, 1953).
Hugh Dalton, *The Fateful Years* (London, 1957).
R.B. Haldane, *An Autobiography* (London, 1929).
Mary Agnes Hamilton, *Remembering My Good Friends* (London, 1944).
Patrick Hastings, *Autobiography* (London, 1952).
Thomas Johnston, *Memories* (London, 1952).
Thomas Jones, *Diary with Letters* (II and III) (Oxford, 1952).
Kingsley Martin, *Editor* (London, 1968).
Herbert Morrison, *An Autobiography* (London, 1960).
Oswald Mosley, *My Life* (London, 1968).
Harold Nicolson, *Diary with Letters* (I) (London, 1969).
Lord Parmoor, *Retrospect* (London, 1936).
John Paton, *Left Turn!* (London, 1936).
D.N. Pritt, *Right to Left* (London, 1965).
J.A. Salter, *Personality in Politics* (London, 1947).
Emmanuel Shinwell, *Conflict without Malice* (London, 1955).
Philip Snowden, *Autobiography* (II) (London, 1934).

Stephen Spender, *World within World* (London, 1951).
John Strachey, *The Strangled Cry* (London, 1966).
J.H. Thomas, *My Story* (London, 1937).
H.G. Wells, *An Experiment in Autobiography* (I and II) (London, 1934). (III) (London, 1984).
Leonard Woolf, *Beginning Again* (London, 1962).
Leonard Woolf, *Downhill All The Way* (London, 1967).

Biography

Quentin Bell, *Virginia Woolf* (II) (London, 1972).
Eric Bentley, *Bernard Shaw* (London, 1957).
Alan Bullock, *Life and Times of Ernest Bevin* (London, 1960).
Russell Clark, *Bertrand Russell* (London, 1975).
Margaret Cole, *Beatrice Webb* (London, 1945).
Margaret Cole, *The Life of G.D.H. Cole* (London, 1971).
Margaret Cole (ed.), *The Webbs and their Work* (London, rep. 1974).
C.A. Cooke, *Richard Stafford Cripps* (London, 1957).
Bernard Donoughue and G.W. Jones, *Herbert Morrison* (London, 1973).
Keith Feiling, *Neville Chamberlain* (London, 1946).
Michael Foot, *Aneurin Bevan 1897–1945* (London, 1962).
T.N. Graham, *Willie Graham* (London, 1947).
Mary Agnes Hamilton, *Arthur Henderson* (London, 1938).
Kenneth Harris, *Earl Attlee* (London, 1982).
Norman and Jeanne MacKenzie, *The Time Traveller: The Biography of H.G. Wells* (London, 1973).
David Marquand, *Ramsay MacDonald* (London, 1977).
Kingsley Martin, *Harold Laski* (London, 1953).
Alan Marwick, *Clifford Allen* (London, 1969).
F.B. Maurice, *Viscount Haldane of Cloan* (II) (London, 1939).
Harold Nicolson, *King George V* (London, 1952).
Raymond Postgate, *George Lansbury* (London, 1951).
C.H. Rolph, *The Life, Letters and Diaries of Kingsley Martin* (London, 1973).
Kenneth Rose, *George V* (London, 1983).
Robert Skidelsky, *Oswald Mosley* (London, 1975).
Hugh Thomas, *John Strachey* (London, 1973).
Duncan Wilson, *Leonard Woolf* (London, 1978).

Communism and the Soviet Union

Max Beloff, *The Foreign Policy of Soviet Russia 1929–1941* (Oxford, 1949).
Walter Citrine, *I Search for Truth in Russia* (London, 1936).
W.P. and Zelda Coates, *A History of Anglo–Soviet Relations* (London, 1945).
John Lewis, *The Left Book Club* (London, 1970).
L.J. Macfarlane, *The British Communist Party* (London, 1966).
Kenneth Newton, *The Sociology of British Communism* (London, 1969).
Henry Pelling, *The British Communist Party: An Historical Profile* (London, 1958).
John Strachey, *The Coming Struggle for Power* (London, 1932).
John Strachey, *The Theory and Practice of Socialism* (London, 1936).
Nigel Wood, *Communism and the British Intellectuals* (London, 1959).

Foreign Policy

J.M. Brown, *Gandhi and Civil Disobedience* (Cambridge, 1977).
Winston Churchill, *The Gathering Storm* (London, 1948).
Winston Churchill, *Their Finest Hour* (London, 1949).
Maurice Cowling, *The Impact of Hitler: British Politics and British Policy 1933–40* (Cambridge, 1975).
Martin Gilbert, *The Roots of Appeasement* (London, 1966).
S.R. Graubard, *British Labour and the Russian Revolution 1917–1924* (Cambridge, Mass., 1956).
J.F. Naylor, *Labour's International Policy: the Labour Party in the 1930s* (London, 1969).
William Ray Rock, *British Appeasement in the 1930s* (London, 1957).
Anil Seal, *The Emergence of Indian Nationalism* (Cambridge, 1957).
A.J.P. Taylor, *Origins of the Second World War* (Oxford, 1961).
Hugh Thomas, *The Spanish Civil War* (London, 1961).
Neville Thompson, *The Anti-Appeasers: Conservative Opposition to Appeasement in the 1930s* (Oxford, 1971).
K.W. Watkins, *Britain Divided: The Effect of the Spanish Civil War on British Public Opinion* (London, 1963).

J. Wheeler-Bennett, *The World of Reparations* (London, 1933).
J. Wheeler-Bennett, *The Disarmament Disaster* (London, 1934).
J. Wheeler-Bennett, *Munich: Prologue to Tragedy* (London, 1948).
E. Windrich, *British Labour's Foreign Policy* (Stanford, 1952).

Labour Politics

Paul Addison, *The Road to 1945* (London, 1975).
R.P. Arnot, *The Miners: Years of Struggle* (London, 1953).
Clement Attlee, *The Labour Party in Perspective* (London, 1939).
Reginald Bassett, *1931: Political Crisis* (London, 1958).
C.A. Cline, *Recruits to Labour: the British Labour Party 1914–31* (Syracuse, 1963).
David Coates, *The Labour Party and the Struggle for Socialism* (Cambridge, 1975).
G.D.H. Cole, *A History of the Labour Party from 1914* (London, 1948).
R.E. Dowse, *Left in the Centre: the Independent Labour Party 1893–1946* (London, 1966).
R.W. Lyman, *The First Labour Government 1924* (London, 1957).
Keith Middlemas, *The Clydesiders* (London, 1965).
Ralph Miliband, *Parliamentary Socialism* (London, 1961).
Henry Pelling, *A Short History of the Labour Party* (London, 1961).
Henry Pelling, *A History of British Trade Unions* (London, 1963).
Gordon Ashton Phillips, *The General Strike* (London, 1957).
Ben Pimlott, *Labour and the Left in the 1930s* (Cambridge, 1977).
John Scanlon, *The Decline and Fall of the Labour Party* (London, 1932).
Julian Symons, *The General Strike* (London, 1957).
Egon Wertheimer, *Portrait of the Labour Party* (London, 1930).

Miscellaneous

Lewis Chester (*et al.*), *The Zinoviev Letter* (London, 1967).
Cyril Connolly, *The Enemies of Promise* (London, 1938).
Colin Cross, *The Fascists in Britain* (London, 1961).
Leon Edel, *A House of Lions* (London, 1979).
José Harris, *Unemployment* (Oxford, 1972).

Edward Hyams, *The New Statesman* (London, 1963).

Samuel Hynes, *The Auden Generation: Literature and Politics in England in the 1930s* (London, 1976).

George Orwell, *The Road to Wigan Pier* (London, 1937).

J.B. Priestley, *English Journey* (London, 1934).

Peter Quennell (ed.), *Life in Britain between the Wars* (London, 1970).

W.A. Robson (ed.), *The Political Quarterly in the 1930s* (London, 1971).

B. Seebohm Rowntree, *Poverty and Progress* (London, 1938).

Politics and History

Mark Abrams, *Condition of the British People 1911–1945* (London, 1945).

Samuel Beer, *Modern British Politics* (London, 1965).

Ronald Blythe, *The Age of Illusion* (London, 1963).

David Butler, *The Electoral System in Great Britain 1918–1951* (Oxford, 1953).

David Butler and John Freeman, *British Political Facts 1900–67* (Oxford, 1968).

G.D.H. Cole and Raymond Postgate, *The Common People* (London, rev. 1946).

Robert Graves and Alan Hodge, *The Long Weekend* (London, 1940).

Sean Glynn and John Oxborrow, *Inter-War Britain: A Social and Economic History* (London, 1976).

A.F. Havighurst, *Twentieth Century Britain* (New York, 1962).

H.J. Laski, *Democracy in Crisis* (London, 1933).

H.J. Laski, *The State in Theory and Practice* (London, 1935).

Alan Marwick, *The Explosion of British Society 1914–62* (London, 1963).

Alan Marwick, *Britain in the Century of Total War* (London, 1968).

R.T. McKenzie, *British Political Parties* (London, 1955).

W.N. Medlicott, *Contemporary England 1914–1964* (London, 1967).

C.L. Mowat, *Britain Between the Wars 1918–40* (London, 1955).

Malcolm Muggeridge, *The Thirties* (London, 1940).

W.G. Runciman, *Relative Deprivation and Social Justice* (London, 1966).

L.C.B. Seaman, *Post-Victorian Britain 1902–51* (London, 1966).
K.B. Smellie, *A Hundred Years of English Government* (London, 1937).
Julian Symons, *The Thirties* (London, 1960).
A.J.P. Taylor, *English History 1914–45* (Oxford, 1965).
Trevor Wilson, *The Downfall of the Liberal Party 1914–35* (London, 1966).

Index

The italic numeral *I*, *II* or *III* indicates that previous references may be found in these volumes of the diary.

Dec 29. 1934

"If a man has learned to think, no matter
what he may think about, he is always thinking
of his own death. ... And what truth can there
be, if there is death?" [Tolstoy quoted by Gorki
Reminiscences of Tolstoy Chekhov & Andreev. L. 57]

[Tolstoy felt he was]
"Asked of it some time "jeering at Death, with his
own "wolf's eyes": What will it seem like? What follows
the hereafter? Will there destroy me altogether,
or will something in me go on living?" [Rev 53]

[Gorki reflection ["this disproportionately "...
overgrown individuality is a monstrous phenomenon,
almost ugly, & there is in him something of Svyatogor
the bogatyr, whom earth cannot hold." [Rev 49]

[To me it seems that one of the problems before
humanity is again a reasoned outlook on death.
Hitherto mankind has formed an escape in some
sort of faith in immortality. Yet this very faith has
brought with it, fears of Hell, or of another
Martyrdom, in "wheel of life" — perhaps
a more painful existence than this life already
lived. Hence Buddhism envisages as final escape,